For Reference

Not to be taken from this room

Novels
for Students

National Advisory Board

Novels for Students

Presenting Analysis, Context, and Criticism on Commonly Studied Novels

Volume 13

Elizabeth Thomason, Editor

Foreword by Anne Devereaux Jordan

GALE GROUP

★

™

THOMSON LEARNING

*Detroit • New York • San Diego • San Francisco
Boston • New Haven, Conn. • Waterville, Maine
London • Munich*

Novels for Students

Staff

Editor: Elizabeth Thomason.

Contributing Editors: Anne Marie Hacht, Michael L. LaBlanc, Ira Mark Milne, Jennifer Smith, Carol Ullmann.

Managing Editor, Content: Dwayne D. Hayes.

Managing Editor, Product: David Galens.

Publisher, Literature Product: Mark Scott.

Literature Content Capture: Joyce Nakamura, *Managing Editor*. Sara Constantakis, *Editor*.

Research: Victoria B. Cariappa, *Research Manager*. Sarah Genik, Ron Morelli, Tamara Nott, Tracie A. Richardson, *Research Associates*. Nicodemus Ford, *Research Assistant*.

Permissions: Maria Franklin, *Permissions Manager*. Kim Davis, *Permissions Associate*.

Manufacturing: Mary Beth Trimper, *Manager, Composition and Electronic Prepress*. Evi Seoud, *Assistant Manager, Composition Purchasing and Electronic Prepress*. Stacy Melson, *Buyer*.

Imaging and Multimedia Content Team: Barbara Yarrow, *Manager*. Randy Bassett, *Imaging Supervisor*. Robert Duncan, Dan Newell, Luke Rademacher, *Imaging Specialists*. Pamela A. Reed, *Imaging Coordinator*. Leitha Etheridge-Sims, Mary Grimes, David G. Oblender, *Image Catalogers*. Robyn V. Young, *Project Manager*. Dean Dauphinais, *Senior Image Editor*. Kelly A. Quin, *Image Editor*.

Product Design Team: Pamela A. E. Galbreath, *Senior Art Director*. Michael Logusz, *Graphic Artist*.

Copyright Notice

Since this page cannot legibly accommodate all copyright notices, the acknowledgments constitute an extension of the copyright notice.

While every effort has been made to secure permission to reprint material and to ensure the reliability of the information presented in this publication, Gale Research neither guarantees the accuracy of the data contained herein nor assumes any responsibility for errors, omissions, or discrepancies. Gale accepts no payment for listing; and inclusion in the publication of any organization, agency, institution, publication, service, or individual does not imply endorsement of the editors or publisher. Errors brought to the attention of the publisher and verified to the satisfaction of the publisher will be corrected in future editions.

This publication is a creative work fully protected by all applicable copyright laws, as well as by misappropriation, trade secret, unfair competition, and other applicable laws. The authors and editors of this work have added value to the underlying factual material herein through one or more of the following: unique and original selection, coordination, expression, arrangement, and classification of the information. All rights to this publication will be vigorously defended.

ISBN 0-7876-4896-5
ISSN 1094-3552

Printed in the United States of America.

10 9 8 7 6 5 4 3 2 1

Table of Contents

The Informed Dialogue: Interacting with Literature

When we pick up a book, we usually do so with the anticipation of pleasure. We hope that by entering the time and place of the novel and sharing the thoughts and actions of the characters, we will find enjoyment. Unfortunately, this is often not the case; we are disappointed. But we should ask, has the author failed us, or have we failed the author?

We establish a dialogue with the author, the book, and with ourselves when we read. Consciously and unconsciously, we ask questions: "Why did the author write this book?" "Why did the author choose that time, place, or character?" "How did the author achieve that effect?" "Why did the character act that way?" "Would I act in the same way?" The answers we receive depend upon how much information about literature in general and about that book specifically we ourselves bring to our reading.

Young children have limited life and literary experiences. Being young, children frequently do not know how to go about exploring a book, nor sometimes, even know the questions to ask of a book. The books they read help them answer questions, the author often coming right out and *telling* young readers the things they are learning or are expected to learn. The perennial classic, *The Little Engine That Could, tells* its readers that, among other things, it is good to help others and brings happiness:

"Hurray, hurray," cried the funny little clown and all the dolls and toys. "The good little boys and girls in the city will be happy because you helped us, kind, Little Blue Engine."

In picture books, messages are often blatant and simple, the dialogue between the author and reader one-sided. Young children are concerned with the end result of a book—the enjoyment gained, the lesson learned—rather than with how that result was obtained. As we grow older and read further, however, we question more. We come to expect that the world within the book will closely mirror the concerns of our world, and that the author will *show* these through the events, descriptions, and conversations within the story, rather than *telling* of them. We are now expected to do the interpreting, carry on our share of the dialogue with the book and author, and glean not only the author's message, but comprehend how that message and the overall affect of the book were achieved. Sometimes, however, we need help to do these things. *Novels for Students* provides that help.

A novel is made up of many parts interacting to create a coherent whole. In reading a novel, the more obvious features can be easily spotted—theme, characters, plot—but we may overlook the more subtle elements that greatly influence how the novel is perceived by the reader: viewpoint, mood and tone, symbolism, or the use of humor. By focusing on both the obvious and more subtle literary elements within a novel, *Novels for Students* aids readers in both analyzing for message and in determining how and why that message is communicated. In the discussion on Harper Lee's *To Kill a Mockingbird* (Vol. 2), for example, the mockingbird as a symbol of innocence is dealt with, among other things, as is the importance of Lee's use of humor which "enlivens a serious plot, adds depth to the characterization, and creates a sense of familiarity and universality." The reader comes to understand the internal elements of each novel discussed—as well as the external influences that help shape it.

"The desire to write greatly," Harold Bloom of Yale University says, "is the desire to be elsewhere, in a time and place of one's own, in an originality that must compound with inheritance, with an anxiety of influence." A writer seeks to create a unique world within a story, but although it is unique, it is not disconnected from our own world. It speaks to us *because* of what the writer brings to the writing from our world: how he or she was raised and educated; his or her likes and dislikes; the events occurring in the real world at the time of the writing, and while the author was growing up. When we know what an author has brought to his or her work, we gain a greater insight into both the "originality" (the world of the book), and the things that "compound" it. This insight enables us to question that created world and find answers more readily. By informing ourselves, we are able to establish a more effective dialogue with both book and author.

Novels for Students, in addition to providing a plot summary and descriptive list of characters—to remind readers of what they have read—also explores the external influences that shaped each book. Each entry includes a discussion of the author's background, and the historical context in which the novel was written. It is vital to know, for instance, that when Ray Bradbury was writing *Fahrenheit 451* (Vol. 1), the threat of Nazi domination had recently ended in Europe, and the McCarthy hearings were taking place in Washington, D.C. This information goes far in answering the question, "Why did he write a story of oppressive government control and book burning?" Similarly,

it is important to know that Harper Lee, author of *To Kill a Mockingbird,* was born and raised in Monroeville, Alabama, and that her father was a lawyer. Readers can now see why she chose the south as a setting for her novel—it is the place with which she was most familiar—and start to comprehend her characters and their actions.

Novels for Students helps readers find the answers they seek when they establish a dialogue with a particular novel. It also aids in the posing of questions by providing the opinions and interpretations of various critics and reviewers, broadening that dialogue. Some reviewers of *To Kill A Mockingbird,* for example, "faulted the novel's climax as melodramatic." This statement leads readers to ask, "Is it, indeed, melodramatic?" "If not, why did some reviewers see it as such?" "If it is, why did Lee choose to make it melodramatic?" "Is melodrama ever justified?" By being spurred to ask these questions, readers not only learn more about the book and its writer, but about the nature of writing itself.

The literature included for discussion in *Novels for Students* has been chosen because it has something vital to say to us. *Of Mice and Men, Catch-22, The Joy Luck Club, My Antonia, A Separate Peace* and the other novels here speak of life and modern sensibility. In addition to their individual, specific messages of prejudice, power, love or hate, living and dying, however, they and all great literature also share a common intent. They force us to *think*—about life, literature, and about others, not just about ourselves. They pry us from the narrow confines of our minds and thrust us outward to confront the world of books and the larger, real world we all share. *Novels for Students* helps us in this confrontation by providing the means of enriching our conversation with literature and the world, by creating an *informed* dialogue, one that brings true pleasure to the personal act of reading.

Sources

Harold Bloom, *The Western Canon, The Books and School of the Ages,* Riverhead Books, 1994.

Watty Piper, *The Little Engine That Could,* Platt & Munk, 1930.

Anne Devereaux Jordan
Senior Editor, TALL
(Teaching and Learning Literature)

Introduction

Purpose of the Book

The purpose of *Novels for Students* (*NfS*) is to provide readers with a guide to understanding, enjoying, and studying novels by giving them easy access to information about the work. Part of Gale's "For Students" Literature line, *NfS* is specifically designed to meet the curricular needs of high school and undergraduate college students and their teachers, as well as the interests of general readers and researchers considering specific novels. While each volume contains entries on "classic" novels frequently studied in classrooms, there are also entries containing hard-to-find information on contemporary novels, including works by multicultural, international, and women novelists.

The information covered in each entry includes an introduction to the novel and the novel's author; a plot summary, to help readers unravel and understand the events in a novel; descriptions of important characters, including explanation of a given character's role in the novel as well as discussion about that character's relationship to other characters in the novel; analysis of important themes in the novel; and an explanation of important literary techniques and movements as they are demonstrated in the novel.

In addition to this material, which helps the readers analyze the novel itself, students are also provided with important information on the literary and historical background informing each work. This includes a historical context essay, a box comparing the time or place the novel was written to modern Western culture, a critical overview essay, and excerpts from critical essays on the novel. A unique feature of *NfS* is a specially commissioned critical essay on each novel, targeted toward the student reader.

To further aid the student in studying and enjoying each novel, information on media adaptations is provided (if available), as well as reading suggestions for works of fiction and nonfiction on similar themes and topics. Classroom aids include ideas for research papers and lists of critical sources that provide additional material on the novel.

Selection Criteria

The titles for each volume of *NfS* were selected by surveying numerous sources on teaching literature and analyzing course curricula for various school districts. Some of the sources surveyed included: literature anthologies; *Reading Lists for College-Bound Students: The Books Most Recommended by America's Top Colleges*; textbooks on teaching the novel; a College Board survey of novels commonly studied in high schools; a National Council of Teachers of English (NCTE) survey of novels commonly studied in high schools; the NCTE's *Teaching Literature in High School: The Novel*; and the Young Adult Library Services Association (YALSA) list of best books for young adults of the past twenty-five years.

Input was also solicited from our advisory board, as well as educators from various areas.

From these discussions, it was determined that each volume should have a mix of "classic" novels (those works commonly taught in literature classes) and contemporary novels for which information is often hard to find. Because of the interest in expanding the canon of literature, an emphasis was also placed on including works by international, multicultural, and women novelists. Our advisory board members—educational professionals—helped pare down the list for each volume. If a work was not selected for the present volume, it was often noted as a possibility for a future volume. As always, the editor welcomes suggestions for titles to be included in future volumes.

How Each Entry Is Organized

Each entry, or chapter, in *NfS* focuses on one novel. Each entry heading lists the full name of the novel, the author's name, and the date of the novel's publication. The following elements are contained in each entry:

- **Introduction:** a brief overview of the novel which provides information about its first appearance, its literary standing, any controversies surrounding the work, and major conflicts or themes within the work.

- **Author Biography:** this section includes basic facts about the author's life, and focuses on events and times in the author's life that inspired the novel in question.

- **Plot Summary:** a factual description of the major events in the novel. Lengthy summaries are broken down with subheads.

- **Characters:** an alphabetical listing of major characters in the novel. Each character name is followed by a brief to an extensive description of the character's role in the novel, as well as discussion of the character's actions, relationships, and possible motivation.

  Characters are listed alphabetically by last name. If a character is unnamed—for instance, the narrator in *Invisible Man*—the character is listed as "The Narrator" and alphabetized as "Narrator." If a character's first name is the only one given, the name will appear alphabetically by that name.

  Variant names are also included for each character. Thus, the full name "Jean Louise Finch" would head the listing for the narrator of *To Kill a Mockingbird*, but listed in a separate cross-reference would be the nickname "Scout Finch."

- **Themes:** a thorough overview of how the major topics, themes, and issues are addressed within the novel. Each theme discussed appears in a separate subhead, and is easily accessed through the boldface entries in the Subject/Theme Index.

- **Style:** this section addresses important style elements of the novel, such as setting, point of view, and narration; important literary devices used, such as imagery, foreshadowing, symbolism; and, if applicable, genres to which the work might have belonged, such as Gothicism or Romanticism. Literary terms are explained within the entry, but can also be found in the Glossary.

- **Historical Context:** this section outlines the social, political, and cultural climate *in which the author lived and the novel was created.* This section may include descriptions of related historical events, pertinent aspects of daily life in the culture, and the artistic and literary sensibilities of the time in which the work was written. If the novel is a historical work, information regarding the time in which the novel is set is also included. Each section is broken down with helpful subheads.

- **Critical Overview:** this section provides background on the critical reputation of the novel, including bannings or any other public controversies surrounding the work. For older works, this section includes a history of how the novel was first received and how perceptions of it may have changed over the years; for more recent novels, direct quotes from early reviews may also be included.

- **Criticism:** an essay commissioned by *NfS* which specifically deals with the novel and is written specifically for the student audience, as well as excerpts from previously published criticism on the work (if available).

- **Sources:** an alphabetical list of critical material used in compiling the entry, with full bibliographical information.

- **Further Reading:** an alphabetical list of other critical sources which may prove useful for the student. It includes full bibliographical information and a brief annotation.

In addition, each entry contains the following highlighted sections, set apart from the main text as sidebars:

- **Media Adaptations:** if available, a list of important film and television adaptations of the novel, including source information. The list also includes stage adaptations, audio recordings, musical adaptations, etc.

- **Topics for Further Study:** a list of potential study questions or research topics dealing with the novel. This section includes questions related to other disciplines the student may be studying, such as American history, world history, science, math, government, business, geography, economics, psychology, etc.

- **Compare and Contrast:** an "at-a-glance" comparison of the cultural and historical differences between the author's time and culture and late twentieth century or early twenty-first century Western culture. This box includes pertinent parallels between the major scientific, political, and cultural movements of the time or place the novel was written, the time or place the novel was set (if a historical work), and modern Western culture. Works written after the mid-1970s may not have this box.

- **What Do I Read Next?:** a list of works that might complement the featured novel or serve as a contrast to it. This includes works by the same author and others, works of fiction and nonfiction, and works from various genres, cultures, and eras.

Other Features

NfS includes "The Informed Dialogue: Interacting with Literature," a foreword by Anne Devereaux Jordan, Senior Editor for *Teaching and Learning Literature* (*TALL*), and a founder of the Children's Literature Association. This essay provides an enlightening look at how readers interact with literature and how *Novels for Students* can help teachers show students how to enrich their own reading experiences.

A Cumulative Author/Title Index lists the authors and titles covered in each volume of the *NfS* series.

A Cumulative Nationality/Ethnicity Index breaks down the authors and titles covered in each volume of the *NfS* series by nationality and ethnicity.

A Subject/Theme Index, specific to each volume, provides easy reference for users who may be studying a particular subject or theme rather than a single work. Significant subjects from events to broad themes are included, and the entries pointing to the specific theme discussions in each entry are indicated in **boldface**.

Each entry may include illustrations, including photo of the author, stills from film adaptations (if available), maps, and/or photos of key historical events.

Citing Novels for Students

When writing papers, students who quote directly from any volume of *Novels for Students* may use the following general forms. These examples are based on MLA style; teachers may request that students adhere to a different style, so the following examples may be adapted as needed.

When citing text from *NfS* that is not attributed to a particular author (i.e., the Themes, Style, Historical Context sections, etc.), the following format should be used in the bibliography section:

"Night." Novels for Students. Ed. Marie Rose Napierkowski. Vol. 4. Detroit: Gale, 1998. 234–35.

When quoting the specially commissioned essay from *NfS* (usually the first piece under the "Criticism" subhead), the following format should be used:

Miller, Tyrus. Critical Essay on *Winesburg, Ohio. Novels for Students.* Ed. Marie Rose Napierkowski. Vol. 4. Detroit: Gale, 1998. 335–39.

When quoting a journal or newspaper essay that is reprinted in a volume of *NfS,* the following form may be used:

Malak, Amin. "Margaret Atwood's *The Handmaid's Tale* and the Dystopian Tradition." *Canadian Literature* No. 112 (Spring, 1987), 9–16; excerpted and reprinted in *Novels for Students*, Vol. 4, ed. Marie Rose Napierkowski (Detroit: Gale, 1998), pp. 133–36.

When quoting material reprinted from a book that appears in a volume of *NfS,* the following form may be used:

Adams, Timothy Dow. "Richard Wright: 'Wearing the Mask,'" in *Telling Lies in Modern American Autobiography*. University of North Carolina Press, 1990. 69–83; excerpted and reprinted in *Novels for Students,* Vol. 1, ed. Diane Telgen (Detroit: Gale, 1997), pp. 59–61.

We Welcome Your Suggestions

The editor of *Novels for Students* welcomes your comments and ideas. Readers who wish to suggest novels to appear in future volumes, or who have other suggestions, are cordially invited to contact the editor. You may contact the editor via e-mail at: **ForStudentsEditors@galegroup.com.** Or write to the editor at:

Editor, *Novels for Students*
Gale Group
27500 Drake Road
Farmington Hills, MI 48331–3535

Literary Chronology

1660: Daniel Defoe is born in London, England.

1722: Daniel Defoe's *Moll Flanders* is published.

1731: Daniel Defoe dies in London, England, on April 24.

1811: William Thackeray is born in London on July 18.

1847–1848: William Thackeray's *Vanity Fair* is published.

1856: L(yman) Frank Baum is born in Chittenango, New York, on May 15.

1863: William Thackeray dies in London on December 24.

1897: William Faulkner is born on September 25.

1899: Elizabeth Bowen is born in Dublin, Ireland, on June 7.

1900: Baum's *The Wonderful Wizard of Oz* is published.

1903: Evelyn Waugh is born in the London suburb of Hampstead, England, on October 28.

1905: Robert Penn Warren is born in Guthrie, Kentucky, April 24.

1909: Eudora Welty is born in Jackson, Mississippi, on April 13.

1917: (Lula) Carson (Smith) McCullers is born in Columbus, Georgia, on Februray 19.

1919: L(yman) Frank Baum dies in Hollywood, California, on May 16 after gall bladder surgery complications.

1924: Kamala (Purnaiya) Taylor, who writes under the pseudonym of Kamala Markandaya, is born in India.

1936: William Faulkner's *Absalom, Absalom!* is published.

1938: Elizabeth Bowen's *The Death of the Heart* is published.

1939: Margaret Atwood is born in Ottawa, Ontario, Canada, on November 18.

1940: Russell Banks is born in Newton, Massachusetts, on March 28.

1945: Evelyn Waugh's *Brideshead Revisited: The Sacred and Profane Memories of Captain Charles Ryder* is published.

1946: Robert Penn Warren's *All the King's Men* is published.

1946: Carson McCullers's *The Member of the Wedding* is published.

1947: Robert Penn Warren wins the Pulitzer Prize for Fiction for *All the King's Men*.

1952: Amy Tan is born.

1954: Kamala Taylor's (Kamala Markandaya's) *Nectar in a Sieve* is published.

1954: Kazuo Ishiguro is born in Nagasaki, Japan, on November 8.

1956: David Guterson is born on May 4.

1962: William Faulkner dies in Byhalia, Mississippi, on July 6.

1966: Evelyn Waugh dies in Combe Florey, Somerset, England, of natural causes.

1967: Carson McCullers dies on August 15 after a massive brain hemorrhage. She is buried in Nyack, New York.

1968: L(yman) Frank Baum wins the Lewis Carroll Shelf Award.

1972: Eudora Welty's *The Optimist's Daughter* is published.

1972: Margaret Atwood's *Surfacing* is published.

1973: Elizabeth Bowen dies in London, England, on February 22 from lung cancer.

1973: Eudora Welty wins the Pulitzer Prize for Fiction for *The Optimist's Daughter*.

1988: Kazuo Ishiguro's *The Remains of the Day* is published.

1989: Robert Penn Warren dies in Stratton, Vermont, on September 15 of cancer.

1991: Amy Tan's *The Kitchen God's Wife* is published.

1991: Russell Banks's *The Sweet Hereafter* is published.

1994: David Guterson's *Snow Falling on Cedars* is published.

1998: Evelyn Waugh earns a citation from the the editorial board of the Modern Library, citing the novel *Brideshead Revisited* as one of the 100 best English language novels of the twentieth century.

1998: Elizabeth Bowen earns a citation from the the editorial board of the Modern Library, citing the novel *The Death of the Heart* as one of the 100 best English language novels of the twentieth century.

2001: Eudora Welty dies of pneumonia on July 23 in Jackson, Mississippi, at the age of 92.

Acknowledgments

The editors wish to thank the copyright holders of the excerpted criticism included in this volume and the permissions managers of many book and magazine publishing companies for assisting us in securing reproduction rights. We are also grateful to the staffs of the Detroit Public Library, the Library of Congress, the University of Detroit Mercy Library, Wayne State University Purdy/Kresge Library Complex, and the University of Michigan Libraries for making their resources available to us. Following is a list of the copyright holders who have granted us permission to reproduce material in this volume of *Novels for Students* (*NfS*). Every effort has been made to trace copyright, but if omissions have been made, please let us know.

COPYRIGHTED MATERIALS IN *NfS*, VOLUME 13, WERE REPRODUCED FROM THE FOLLOWING PERIODICALS:

American Literature, v. 62, December, 1990. Copyright ©1990 by Duke University Press, Durham, NC. Reproduced by permission.—*Belles Lettres*, v. 7, Fall, 1991. Reproduced by permission.—*BookPage* for "A Wonderful Irony: The Quietest of Books Makes the Splashiest Debut," by Ellen Kanner. (c) 1996, ProMotion, Inc. Retrieved January 25, 2001 from http://www.bookpage.com. Reproduced by permission.—*English: The Journal of the English Association*, v. 43, Spring, 1994. Reproduced by permission.—*Mosaic*, v. 29, March, 1996. © Mosaic 1996. Acknowledgment of previous publication is herewith made.—*The Nation*, New York, v. 253, December, 1991. © 1991

The Nation magazine/The Nation Company, Inc. Reproduced by permission.—*North Dakota Quarterly*, v. 62, Fall, 1994–95. Copyright 1994–95 by The University of North Dakota. Reproduced by permission.—*Papers on Language and Literature*, v. 25, Fall, 1989. Copyright © 1989 by The Board of Trustees, Southern Illinois University at Edwardsville. Reproduced by permission.—*The San Francisco Chronicle*, January 1, 1995 for "A Friendship Shattered by War," by Stan Yogi. Reproduced by permission of the author.—*Studies in the Novel*, v. 25, Fall, 1993. Copyright 1993 by North Texas State University. Reproduced by permission.—*The Times Literary Supplement*, no. 4646, April 17, 1992 for "A Town Divided," by Donna Rifkind. © The Times Supplements Limited 1992. Reproduced from *The Times Literary Supplement* by permission.

COPYRIGHTED MATERIALS IN *NfS*, VOLUME 13, WERE REPRODUCED FROM THE FOLLOWING BOOKS:

Austin, Allan E. From *Elizabeth Bowen*. Twayne Publishers, Inc., 1971. Copyright © 1971 by Twayne Publishers, Inc. All rights reserved. The Gale Group.—Brooks, Cleanth. From "History and the Sense of the Tragic: Absalom, Absalom!" in *William Faulkner: The Yoknapatawpha Country*. Copyright © 1963 by Cleanth Brooks. Reproduced by permission of Louisiana State University Press.—Justus, James H. From *The Achievement of Robert Penn Warren*. Louisiana State University Press, 1981. Copyright © 1981 by Louisiana State University Press. All rights reserved. Reproduced by permission.—Pathania, Usha. From *Human Bonds and Bondages: The Fiction of Anita Desai and Kamala Markandaya*. Kanishka Publishing House, 1992. © Usha Pathania. Reproduced by permission.—Richetti, John J. From *Twayne's English Author's Series Online*. G. K. Hall & Company, 1999. Retrieved from http://www.galenet .com. The Gale Group.—White, Barbara A. From "Loss of Self in 'The Member of the Wedding,'" in *Modern Critical Views: Carson McCullers*. Edited by Harold Bloom. Chelsea House Publishers, 1986. © 1986 by Chelsea House Publishers, a division of Chelsea House Educational Communications, Inc. All rights reserved. Reproduced by permission.

PHOTOGRAPHS AND ILLUSTRATIONS APPEARING IN *NfS*, VOLUME 13, WERE RECEIVED FROM THE FOLLOWING SOURCES:

Allied officials drafting the Versailles Treaty, December 2, 1918, photograph. © Bettmann/Corbis. Reproduced by permission.—Andrews, Anthony (left) as Sebastian Flyte, Diana Quick as Julia and Jeremy Irons as Charles Ryder, in a vintage automobile in front of Brideshead Castle in the serialized television drama *Brideshead Revisited*, based on Evelyn Waugh's novel, photograph. © Virgin Vision.—Atwood, Margaret, photograph. The Library of Congress.—Banks, Russell, photograph by Horst Tappe. Hulton/Archive. Reproduced by permission.—Baum, L. Frank, photograph. The Library of Congress.—Beller, Kathleen as Kate in the 1980 film version of Margaret Atwood's novel *Surfacing*, photograph. Kobal Collection/Surfacing Film. Reproduced by permission.—Boddie, Jane, curator at Evergreen Plantation, Edgard, Louisiana, January 15, 2000, photograph by Judi Bottoni. AP/Wide World Photos. Reproduced by permission.—Bowen, Elizabeth, photograph. The Library of Congress.—Crawford, Broderick (right to left), John Ireland and John Derek, photograph. The Kobal Collection. Reproduced by permission.—Defoe, Daniel, drawing. The Library of Congress.—Denslow, W. W., illustrator. From an illustration in *The Wonderful Wizard of Oz*, by L. Frank Baum. George M. Hill Company, 1900.—Faulkner, William, photograph. Archive Photos. Reproduced by permission.—Hawke, Ethan, and Kudoh Youki, in the 1999 film version of the novel *Snow Falling on Cedars*, written by David Guterson, photograph. The Kobal Collection. Reproduced by permission.—Ishiguro, Kazuo, photograph. © Jerry Bauer. Reproduced by permission.—Lahr, Bert, with Jack Haley, Judy Garland, and Ray Bolger, in the movie *The Wizard of Oz*, 1939, photograph. The Kobal Collection. Re- produced by permission.—Lakeside house surrounded by forest on a spit of land, aerial view, located between Quebec and Mont Sainte Anne Park, Quebec, Canada, c. 1970–1998, photograph. © Yann Arthus–Bertrand/Corbis. Reproduced by permission.—Long, Huey P., drawing. The Library of Congress.—Manzanar War Relocation Center, photograph by Ansel Adams. The Library of Congress.—McCullers, Carson, photograph. AP/Wide World Photos. Reproduced by permission.—Polley, Sarah (looking at Holm), and Ian Holm in the film *The Sweet Hereafter*, 1996, photograph by Johnnie Eisen. The Kobal Collection. Reproduced by permission.—Prisoner sitting in cell at Newgate Prison, photograph. Corbis Corporation. Reproduced by permission.—Racket Court, in the interior of the Fleet Prison which was used for debtors mainly, 1774, engraving by Fleming. Archive Photos, Inc. Reproduced by permission.— Rural Indian village (huts and mosque), 1848, Sheebpore, India, lithograph by Philip DeBay. Historical Picture Archive/Corbis. Reproduced by permission.—A seated Indian man works a large piece of wooden equipment in a leather tannery in Kampur, India, c. 1985–1995, photograph by David Cumming. © Eye Ubiquitous/Corbis. Reproduced by permission.—The spire of Exeter College Chapel rises beyond the c. 16th century buildings of Brasenose College, Oxford, England, c. 1985–1995, photograph by Brian Harding. © Eye Ubiquitous/Corbis. Reproduced by permission.—Tan, Amy (left), and her mother "Daisy" sitting on a sofa, smiling and reading a letter from family in China, photograph. *People Weekly* © 1989 Jim McHugh. Reproduced by permission.—Tan, Amy, 1993, photograph. AP/Wide World Photos. Reproduced by permission.—Thackeray, William Makepeace, engraving. The Library of Congress.—Thackeray, W. M., illustrator. From a cover of *Vanity Fair*, by W. M. Thackeray. W. W. Norton & Company, 1847.— Vaughn, Peter (left), and Anthony Hopkins in a scene from the 1993 film version of *The Remains of the Day* from a novel by Kazuo Ishiguro, photograph. The Kobal Collection/Derrick Santini/Columbia /Merchant Ivory. Reproduced by permission.—Warren, Robert Penn, photograph. The Library of Congress.—Waters, Ethel, posing with two unidentified actors in the film *The Member of the Wedding*, photograph. AP/Wide World Photos. Reproduced by permission.—Waugh, Evelyn, photograph. The Library of Congress.—Welty, Eudora, 1962, photograph. NYWTS/The Library of Congress.—Wright, Robin, as Moll Flanders, in the film *Moll Flanders*. The Kobal Collection. Reproduced by permission.—Zedong, Mao (Mao Tse-tung), with Lin Biao (clapping hands), photograph.

Contributors

Jennifer Bussey: Bussey holds a master's degree in interdisciplinary studies and a bachelor's degree in English literature. She is an independent writer specializing in literature. Entries on *Absalom, Absalom!*, *The Kitchen God's Wife*, *The Member of the Wedding*, *Nectar in a Sieve*, *The Optimist's Daughter*, *The Remains of the Day*, *Snow Falling on Cedars*, *The Sweet Hereafter*, and *The Wonderful Wizard of Oz*. Original essays on *Absalom, Absalom!*, *The Kitchen God's Wife*, *The Member of the Wedding*, *Nectar in a Sieve*, *The Optimist's Daughter*, *The Remains of the Day*, *Snow Falling on Cedars*, *The Sweet Hereafter*, and *The Wonderful Wizard of Oz*.

Candyce Norvell: Norvell is an independent educational writer who specializes in literature. She holds degrees in linguistics and journalism. Entry on *Vanity Fair*. Original essay on *Vanity Fair*.

Wendy Perkins: Perkins is an associate professor of English at Prince George's Community College in Maryland and has published several articles on British and American authors. Entry on *Surfacing*. Original essay on *Surfacing*.

Susan Sanderson: Sanderson holds a master of fine arts degree in fiction writing and is an independent writer. Entries on *All the King's Men*, *Brideshead Revisited*, *The Death of the Heart*, and *Moll Flanders*. Original essays on *All the King's Men*, *Brideshead Revisited*, *The Death of the Heart*, and *Moll Flanders*.

Absalom, Absalom!

William Faulkner

1936

Published in 1936, *Absalom, Absalom!* is considered by many to be William Faulkner's masterpiece. Although the novel's complex and fragmented structure poses considerable difficulty to readers, the book's literary merits place it squarely in the ranks of America's finest novels. The story concerns Thomas Sutpen, a poor man who finds wealth and then marries into a respectable family. His ambition and extreme need for control bring about his ruin and the ruin of his family. Sutpen's story is told by several narrators, allowing the reader to observe variations in the saga as it is recounted by different speakers. This unusual technique spotlights one of the novel's central questions: To what extent can people know the truth about the past?

Faulkner's novels and short stories often relate to one another. *Absalom, Absalom!* draws characters from *The Sound and the Fury,* and it anticipates the action and themes of *Intruder in the Dust.* Further, *Absalom, Absalom!* is one of Faulkner's fifteen novels set in fictional Yoknapatawpha County. This is the first of Faulkner's novels in which he includes a chronology and a map of the fictitious setting to better enable the reader to understand the context for the novel's events. The map includes captions noting areas where certain events take place. The map shows events that happen in *Sartoris, The Sound and the Fury, As I Lay Dying, Sanctuary,* and *Light in August,* as well as those that occur in *Absalom, Absalom!*

William Faulkner

Despite Faulkner's roots in the South, he readily condemns many aspects of its history and heritage in *Absalom, Absalom!*. He reveals the unsavory side of southern morals and ethics, including slavery. The novel explores the relationship between modern humanity and the past, examining how past events affect modern decisions and to what extent modern people are responsible for the past.

Author Biography

William Faulkner was born on September 25, 1897, to a genteel southern family that had lost most of its money during the Civil War. Faulkner grew up in Oxford, Mississippi, which is recast as the fictional town of Jefferson in many of his stories. Jefferson is placed in fictional Yoknapatawpha County, the setting for fifteen of Faulkner's novels and many of his short stories.

As a child, Faulkner was a capable but uninterested student. He left school in 1915, prior to graduating, and went to work in his grandfather's bank as a clerk. A friend of Faulkner's, Phil Stone, went to Yale after graduation. Stone recognized Faulkner's literary ability, and when Faulkner

briefly attended Yale Law School, the two enjoyed discussing literary theory and literary movements. With the outbreak of World War I, Faulkner decided to enlist but was turned away. (He was short and slightly built.) With Stone's help, he falsified papers in 1918 so he could join the Canadian Air Force. The war ended, however, before Faulkner completed his training.

Upon returning to Oxford with his uniform and fictitious war stories, Faulkner briefly attended classes at the University of Mississippi in 1919 before taking a job as the university postmaster. He read students' magazines before distributing them, and he was often so immersed in his writing that he ignored his responsibilities. In 1924, Faulkner resigned before he could be terminated. He then went to New Orleans to visit his friend Elizabeth Prall, who was married to author Sherwood Anderson. Despite Faulkner's desire to be a poet, he had come to realize that his talent was for prose, and Anderson encouraged him to pursue this craft. The following year, Faulkner and a friend traveled around Europe, returning home in 1926.

Over the next four years, Faulkner wrote a number of novels but garnered little commercial success. When he decided to stop writing for the public and focus on writing for himself, the result was *The Sound and the Fury*. From this point through the end of his career, his work became particularly complex and challenging to his readers, as he employed complicated structure, characterization, and fictional techniques.

Faulkner is considered one of the great American authors as well as one of the world's finest contemporary writers. In his fiction, Faulkner depicts people facing the problems of living in modern society. He believed that human beings possess the ability to overcome overwhelming challenges by drawing on qualities that are distinctly human, including virtue, love, loyalty, and humor. In 1949, he won the Nobel Prize for literature. A controversial choice for the Prize (his work was criticized as being both too innovative and too regional), Faulkner delivered a speech in which he proclaimed that the crux of his fiction is "the human heart in conflict with itself." The speech was so moving that many of his critics changed their minds about him. Faulkner also won the Pulitzer Prize for fiction twice: in 1955 for *A Fable* (which also won the National Book Award) and in 1963 for *The Reivers*.

Faulkner died on July 6, 1962, in Byhalia, Mississippi.

Plot Summary

The Main Story

The story of Thomas Sutpen is told by four different narrators during the course of *Absalom, Absalom!* First, Rosa Coldfield tells the story, then subsequent versions reveal added elements of Sutpen's story.

Thomas Sutpen arrives in Jefferson, Mississippi, in 1833. An enigmatic figure, he never reveals much about his past or his reasons for choosing Jefferson as the site for his home. He comes with a group of "wild" slaves (presumably from Haiti), a French architect, and construction tools. Rumors abound about the mysterious Sutpen, and two years later, his plantation home is complete but empty. Sutpen's relationship with the community becomes friendlier when he begins inviting the men to come stay and hunt on his land. Nestled on one hundred square miles of land that he cheated out of a Native American, the estate is named Sutpen's Hundred.

Sutpen enjoys violent wrestling with his slaves. This sport, like his ambition to execute his great design for a plantation, indicates his drive to control and tame that which he perceives as wild. To everyone's surprise, he asks for Ellen Coldfield's hand in marriage. The Coldfields are a respectable family in Jefferson but have little money and are known for being righteous. Sutpen makes an arrangement (the details of which are never revealed to the reader) with Mr. Coldfield, and Sutpen and Ellen are married. They have two children, Henry and Judith.

Once married, Sutpen makes no effort to gain the community's approval. He does not attend church and continues to wrestle with his slaves. On one occasion, Ellen discovers, to her horror, that Sutpen has brought Henry to the stable to watch the wrestling, which the boy finds frightening and sickening. In contrast, Judith secretly watches the wrestling and is unfazed by the violence.

As a young man, Henry attends law school at the University of Mississippi where he becomes great friends with Charles Bon. Henry brings Charles home with him for a visit, and Charles and Judith fall in love. Despite Sutpen's objections to the union, the couple plans to marry. Their plans are interrupted by the Civil War because Charles, Sutpen, and Henry must all go and fight.

The men in Sutpen's unit lose faith in their commander and choose Sutpen as their new leader. Meanwhile, Henry and Charles fight together, ce-

menting their bond. Henry and Charles discover that they are half-brothers. Before coming to Jefferson, Sutpen had lived in Haiti, where he married a woman and had a son. When Sutpen learned that his wife had black ancestry, he disowned her and his son and left Haiti. Years later, the son, Charles, enrolled as a student at the University of Mississippi. With this information, Henry insists that Charles tell him what he plans to do about his engagement to Judith. Charles will not say, and when the war is over, Charles and Henry return to Sutpen's Hundred. As they come in sight of the house, Henry tells Charles that he cannot marry Judith. When Charles responds nastily that he will marry her, Henry kills him on the spot and then flees.

Sutpen returns from the war to an overgrown estate where his buildings are in shambles, his slaves are all gone, and his wife is dead. Although he plans to marry Ellen's much younger sister, Rosa, when she realizes that he expects her to produce a son before the marriage, she refuses. Sutpen then seduces Milly, the teenaged granddaughter of Wash Jones, a poor man living on his land. She becomes pregnant, but when she has a girl instead of a boy (which Sutpen needs to create a dynasty), he becomes cruel toward Milly. Even though Wash has always admired Sutpen, he kills him for mistreating his granddaughter.

When Henry returns to Sutpen's Hundred years later, he stays in the abandoned estate with his sister and Clytie, the illegitimate daughter of Sutpen and one of his slaves. When Clytie thinks that the law is coming to capture Henry for murdering Charles, she sets fire to the house, destroying it and killing Henry and herself.

Characteristics of Rosa's Version

Rosa is the only narrator who lived during the events of the story. Still, her recollection is filtered through forty years of bitterness and hatred toward Sutpen. She refers to Sutpen as a demon, a *djinn* (similar to a genie), and a fiend. Her version of the story has an accusatory tone, and she blames Sutpen for all the miseries of the Coldfields. Further, she interprets the fall of the South as being the result of the influence of men like Sutpen.

In chapter five, the reader comes to understand why Rosa accepted Sutpen's marriage proposal. As a young woman, she was optimistic and perhaps romantic. Not knowing Sutpen very well, she thought of him as a mysterious, dashing, and intriguing man. When he crudely proposed to her and then abandoned her, she lost her innocence and optimism in the heartbreak. The reader may assume either that it was after this point that she began to hate him or that she disliked him all along but had no other marriage prospects.

Because Rosa hardly knew Sutpen, she speculates on his motivations. When Sutpen opposes the marriage plans between Judith and Charles, for example, Rosa believes he does so on a cruel whim. Faulkner never gives any indication that Rosa knows anything of Charles' background or lineage. It is, therefore, ironic when she refers to Henry's murder of Charles as being almost fratricide (because they were almost brothers-in-law), when in fact, it was fratricide.

Characteristics of Mr. Compson's Version

Mr. Compson's father was one of the first men in Jefferson to accept Sutpen, so this version is sympathetic toward Sutpen. Compson describes Sutpen as brave, strong, determined, and individualistic. Compson finds it difficult, therefore, to understand why Rosa is so harsh in her denouncement of Sutpen.

Compson's version of the story introduces speculation regarding Henry's relationships with his sister and with Charles. Compson's account suggests that Henry had feelings for his sister that were beyond normal sibling affection. Although he does not say that Henry had incestuous desires, he implies it. Compson also seems to suggest that Henry had an unusual attraction to Charles. According to Compson, while Henry initially supported the marriage of Judith and Charles as a way to resolve his yearnings, his realization that Charles was partly black and his half-brother prevented Henry from allowing the union to take place.

Characteristics of Quentin's Version

Quentin is preoccupied with the Sutpen story as he attempts to make sense of his own past and better understand his role in the present. He has heard the story so many times that he feels like "a barracks filled with stubborn back-looking ghosts." Quentin's version contains some details of the story missing from the other versions. The reader later learns that Quentin's grandfather told Quentin things about the story that he had not told his own son (Mr. Compson).

When Quentin's roommate Shreve asks about the South, Quentin begins telling the Sutpen story. Although the story took place before Quentin's time in Jefferson, he feels a strong connection to

the story and is compelled to uncover its meaning for his own life.

Characteristics of Shreve's Version

Shreve is introduced in chapter six and asks to hear about the South. As the chapter progresses, it becomes clear that Quentin has told Shreve the Sutpen story before. Shreve knows many of the events of the story but serves as sort of a spokesperson for the reader, asking questions the reader would like to ask. Because he is the furthest removed from the story, Shreve brings an objective view of the story to the novel and is in a position to question certain aspects of the narrative.

Characters

Charles Bon

Charles is Thomas Sutpen's son by his Haitian wife. Although Sutpen abandons Charles and his mother, Charles' path later crosses Sutpen's when he attends law school with Sutpen's son Henry, and the two become great friends. Charles falls in love with Henry's sister, Judith, and they plan to marry, but their plans are interrupted by the Civil War. As Henry and Charles fight together, they learn more about each other. When Henry realizes that he and Charles are half-brothers, Charles refuses to tell his friend what he plans to do about his engagement to Judith. After the war, Charles tells Henry, quite nastily, that he is going to marry Judith, and Henry kills him immediately.

Charles wants only the slightest acknowledgement from Sutpen that he is his son but never gets it. Charles knows that his plan to marry Judith means that Sutpen will either have to accept him as a son-in-law or admit that he is his son to stop him from marrying his daughter. Although in life, Charles never receives the acknowledgement he wants from Sutpen, he is buried in the family plot.

Charles Etienne Saint Valery Bon

This character is Charles Bon's son by a one-eighth black woman.

Jim Bond

Jim is the mentally-handicapped son of Charles Etienne Saint Valery Bon (who is Charles Bon's son) and his black wife. Jim is, in the end, the only survivor of Thomas Sutpen's family.

Clytie

Clytie (Clytemnestra) is the illegitimate daughter of Thomas Sutpen and a slave woman. She stays in the Sutpen house during and after the Civil War. When Henry returns, she thinks the law is chasing him for killing Charles, so she sets the house on fire, killing herself and Henry.

Ellen Coldfield

Ellen is Sutpen's wife in Jefferson, Mississippi. She is proper and innocent with a disposition in stark contrast to her husband's wild nature. She has two children with Sutpen, Henry and Judith. During the Civil War, she dies, and in her last moments, she asks her sister Rosa to protect Judith.

Goodhue Coldfield

Goodhue is Ellen's father. Thomas Sutpen chooses him as a father-in-law (perhaps more than he chooses Ellen as a wife) because of his righteousness and respectable standing in the community. There is some arrangement between Mr. Coldfield and Sutpen, the details of which are never revealed, but Mr. Coldfield apparently comes to regret it.

Rosa Coldfield

One of the novel's narrators, Rosa is Ellen Coldfield's sister. Rosa is twenty-seven years younger than Ellen, so she is closer in age to her niece Judith than to Ellen. When Mr. Coldfield dies, Rosa goes to live at Sutpen's Hundred. After Ellen's death, Sutpen asks Rosa to marry him. She agrees but is abandoned by Sutpen before they can marry. She lives the rest of her life bitter and alone and, in the end, she calls for Quentin so she can tell him Sutpen's story.

Rosa starts out a typical, optimistic young woman, but the Civil War and the ruin of her family turn her into a resentful and lonely woman. In her youth, she was the town's poetess laureate. Her mother, because of her age at the time of Rosa's birth, died in childbirth, and Rosa resents her father for her mother's death. Throughout her life, her focus is on her family, and as each member is taken away, she is forced further into solitude.

General Compson

Quentin's grandfather, General Compson was one of the first men in Jefferson to accept Thomas Sutpen into the community. Because he personally knew Sutpen, he tells his son Jason and his grandson Quentin much about him.

Mr. Jason Compson III

One of the novel's narrators, Mr. Compson is Quentin's father. His telling of the story reveals his deterministic and cynical views of the world. He admires Sutpen greatly and is struck by his failure. Compson imagines that if a courageous and hardworking man like Sutpen could fail so thoroughly, his pessimistic view of the world must be correct. Compson believes that fate and destiny rule the course of people's lives and that there is little they can do to change the course set for them.

Quentin Compson

One of the novel's narrators, Quentin is a student at Harvard who comes from the small town of Jefferson. Faulkner describes Quentin as a young man torn between two selves: an educated Harvard man full of promise and potential and a native of the South who has much in common with people like Rosa. He struggles to make sense of his southern heritage, and when asked by his roommate to tell about the South, Quentin tells Sutpen's story. Because the Sutpen story is so integral to the town of Jefferson and, in Quentin's mind, to the South, he searches the saga for answers to life's questions.

Faulkner's chronology at the end of the novel reveals that Quentin commits suicide just after the events of the novel.

Major de Spain

Major de Spain is the sheriff who investigates Sutpen's murder. When he discovers that Wash Jones is responsible, the sheriff kills him.

Milly Jones

Milly is Wash Jones' fifteen-year-old granddaughter. Sutpen, who desperately wants a son, seduces her. When Milly has a girl, Sutpen insults her, and Wash kills Sutpen, Milly, and the child.

Wash Jones

Wash is a poor man who is a squatter on Sutpen's land during the Civil War. He is a great admirer of Sutpen, yet he kills Sutpen, Milly, and their child when Sutpen abuses Milly.

Shreve McCannon

Quentin's roommate at Harvard, Shreve (Shrevlin) not only listens to Quentin's account of

Media Adaptations

- Audio adaptations of *Absalom, Absalom!* have been made by Everett/Edwards in 1977 and Books on Tape in 1993.

Sutpen but also tries to help Quentin fill in the blanks in the story. Because Shreve is Canadian, he has few preconceptions about the South and its history.

Eulalia Bon Sutpen

Eulalia is Thomas Sutpen's wife in Haiti. She bears him a son, Charles, but when Thomas discovers that a small portion of her heritage is black, he leaves her and Charles in Haiti.

Henry Sutpen

Henry is the son of Thomas Sutpen and Ellen Coldfield. When Henry attends law school, he befriends Charles Bon, who then falls in love with Henry's sister Judith. Charles and Judith plan to marry, but the men are called to fight in the Civil War. Henry fights alongside Charles and discovers that he is the son Thomas Sutpen left behind in Haiti. This means that Charles is the half-brother of Henry and Judith. Despite Henry's insistence on knowing how Charles plans to handle his engagement to Judith, Charles will not tell.

After the war, Henry returns to Sutpen's Hundred with Charles, and as they approach the house, Charles reveals that he intends to marry Judith. Henry responds by immediately killing Charles and then running away. Many years later, Henry reappears at Sutpen's Hundred, where he is taken in by his sister and Clytie. He later dies there.

Judith Sutpen

Judith is the daughter of Thomas Sutpen and Ellen Coldfield. Judith has her father's hardy nature and does not flinch at witnessing violence. When she meets her brother's college friend Charles Bon, the two fall in love and plan to marry. Henry later kills Charles in front of the house, and Judith never marries.

Thomas Sutpen

Thomas Sutpen is the main figure in the story that is retold throughout the novel. Many critics note that Sutpen represents the work ethic of the South, along with its decline and failures. Sutpen comes from a poor family and is unconcerned with wealth until one day when he takes a message to a large estate. The uniformed servant informs him that he should go to the back entrance on future visits. After this incident, Sutpen decides that, some day, he will own a large estate and be in a position to tell people to go to the back. Part of his master plan is to have sons, a preoccupation that leads to ruin. (One son kills another, and the killer later dies in Sutpen's mansion; Sutpen's anger at not having a son by Milly brings about Sutpen's own death.)

As a young man, Sutpen travels to Haiti, where he marries a plantation owner's daughter, and they have a son. When he learns that his wife has remote black ancestry, he disowns her and their son. He returns to the United States, where he chooses Jefferson, Mississippi, as the site for his mansion in the wilderness. With the help of a French architect and a group of "wild" slaves (presumably from Haiti), Sutpen clears land and builds an estate that he names Sutpen's Hundred. Next, he marries into a respectable family and has two children, Henry and Judith.

Sutpen is a power-hungry man who seeks to create and control his environment. When he leaves to fight in the Civil War, he soon becomes his unit's leader. Upon returning to Sutpen's Hundred after the war, he finds his estate in ruins and his slaves gone. Further, his wife has died, and his son has run away after killing Charles Bon. Although he crudely asks his wife's sister to marry him, he abandons her and seduces the teenaged granddaughter of a poor man living on his land. She bears him a child, but not the son Sutpen wants. His cruelty to the girl provokes her father to kill him.

Themes

The American South

In *Absalom, Absalom!,* Faulkner openly criticizes the ethical and moral practices of the American South. The story of Sutpen is analogous to the story of the South, and Faulkner suggests that they ultimately fail for the same reasons. By building its success and comfort on the enslavement of another

Topics For Further Study

- Think of a story that is told in your family, especially by the older members. Write three versions of the story as told by three very different members of your family.

- Faulkner died in 1962, just as the civil rights movement was gaining momentum. Evaluate the modern-day South and prepare a speech or essay containing what you believe would be Faulkner's views on the results of the civil rights movement.

- Create a multimedia character study of either Thomas Sutpen or Rosa Coldfield from a psychological perspective. To complete this project, you will need to conduct basic research on psychological theories of personality and behavior.

- Research the Irish poet William Butler Yeats. Prepare a comparison of his relationship to Ireland and Faulkner's relationship to the South. Be sure to explore how these relationships are expressed in the men's writing and to pay particular attention to each writer's attempts to create a mythology for his land.

- Examine the various mythic elements of the Sutpen story. In what ways does Faulkner create a mythical setting and characters? Look for allusions, themes, techniques, and other connections to myth. Present your findings in an essay.

- Faulkner originally planned to entitle the book *Dark House.* Why would this have been a good title, and how would it have altered your reading of the novel? Also consider why *Absalom, Absalom!* is a good title. Review the biblical story of Absalom's death in Samuel 18:2 and how it affects David. Which of the two titles do you think is the better choice?

- Some readers believe that Henry kills Charles because he cannot allow his sister to marry her own half-brother. Others maintain that he kills Charles because he cannot allow his sister to marry a man who has black ancestry. Hold a debate in which one side argues for the first motivation, and the other side argues for the second motivation. The strongest arguments will come from the action of the novel, the character of Henry, and the cultural context of the story.

---

race, the South is doomed to fail because an immoral design is not sustainable. Both Sutpen and the South believe that it is possible to set aside morality at times to pursue a larger social goal. Rosa comments to Quentin that the South was doomed to lose the war because it was led by men like Sutpen, whom she perceives as dishonest, cruel, and manipulative. She remarks in chapter one:

> Oh he was brave. I have never gainsaid that. But that our cause, our very life and future hopes and past pride, would have been thrown into the balance with men like that to buttress it—men with valor and strength but without pity or honor. Is it any wonder that Heaven saw fit to let us lose?

The novel contains references to the Civil War and the destruction of the South in the war's aftermath. Rosa tells Quentin that she suspects that af-

ter he graduates from Harvard, he will practice law somewhere besides in his hometown of Jefferson because "Northern people have already seen to it that there is little left in the South for a young man." Mr. Compson explains to Quentin that he should listen politely to Rosa's story because long ago the South made its women into ladies, and then the war made the ladies into ghosts. He adds, "So what else can we do, being gentlemen, but listen to them being ghosts?"

Truth

Each version of Sutpen's story is different because it is told through the memories and perceptions of each narrator. When the reader reaches the end of the novel, the basic facts are in order, but there is uncertainty regarding many aspects of the story. None of the narrators is completely reliable, which poses a problem to the reader accustomed to depending on at least one trustworthy narrator.

Faulkner shows his reader that there are limits to how fully people can know the truth about the past. Truth seems to be in the eye of the beholder, as is evident with each telling of Sutpen's story. The challenge is for the reader, then, to make decisions about which narrators are reliable in which instances. Then, the reader must speculate about other aspects of the story. Because no two narrators tell the exact same story, and different readers can interpret the story in different ways, knowing the truth about Sutpen's story becomes impossible. Add to that the exceedingly complex narrative structure, and the events told in the novel become even more uncertain and difficult to manage. Thus, Faulkner uses both form and content to demonstrate the limited capacity people have to know the truth of past events.

The Past

In his character portrayals, Faulkner expresses his belief that people should be aware of the past and learn what they can from it, but they should not allow it to shape their lives. Each narrator has a different relationship with the past. Rosa finds the past to be a source of bitterness and disappointment, yet she is unable to live in the present. Mr. Compson finds in the past evidence that his fatalistic view of the world is correct. He also believes that past generations were greater than the present generation, so while he may draw inspiration from the past, he must live in the present, which is discouraging for him. Quentin feels deeply connected to his heritage, and because Sutpen's tale is legendary in his hometown of Jefferson, he becomes obsessed with making sense of the story. At the beginning of chapter two, the narrator comments that in Jefferson, Quentin breathes the same air and hears the same church bells as Sutpen did in the past. Because Quentin feels so connected to the South, he has difficulty coming to terms with his love for his region and the shame of its past. He is burdened by his responsibility for events of long ago and struggles to understand his role as a modern-day man of the South.

Characters within the story are also affected by their pasts. Sutpen is driven by his need to distance himself from the poverty of his past. He seeks to reinvent himself so that his past will have no hold on him. When he leaves Haiti, he is certain that he is leaving another segment of his past behind, but he later realizes that his past has found him in the person of Charles. Charles is also mo-

tivated by events from his past. He is wounded by his father's sudden departure in his childhood, and he seeks to be validated. When he encounters his father in America, he longs to heal his past by reconnecting with him. His determination to be accepted by Sutpen, however, leads to his death. Charles insists that he will marry Judith, even though she is his half-sister. Although it is not clear, the reader assumes that he hopes that either he will be accepted as a son-in-law (if not a son) by Sutpen or Sutpen will be forced to tell the real reason he objects to the marriage, thus claiming Charles as his son. Charles does not take into account the possibility that Henry will kill him rather than allow him to marry Judith.

Style

Narrative Structure

Absalom, Absalom! is considered to be one of Faulkner's most difficult novels because of its complex narrative structure. In a sense, the story becomes part of an oral tradition among the residents of Jefferson and, as Shreve becomes involved, people living beyond Jefferson. Many of Faulkner's characteristic structural innovations are employed in *Absalom, Absalom!,* such as long sentences, flashbacks, and multiple points-of-view describing the same events. Because the narrative structure is so unusual, the reader is kept off balance from the opening pages to the end of the novel and must learn how to read it as the book unfolds.

There are four characters narrating the story, and a fifth omniscient narrator also occasionally speaks to the reader. The challenge is often determining who is speaking at any given time because Faulkner switches from narrator to narrator without always signifying the change. The reader must be particularly adept in chapter five when the narration switches between Quentin and Shreve and then back to Quentin as he tries imagining how Shreve would tell the story. Further, the novel's overall design is not clear until the end of the book. There is no introductory paragraph to provide a framework for the reader. Instead, the book begins with Rosa talking to Quentin with Quentin wondering why she called for him. This lack of context is very perplexing to readers, and navigating the headwaters of the novel requires a great deal of effort. Additionally, readers expect a novel to start at the beginning of a story and move through a series of events toward a satisfying end. In *Absalom, Absalom!*, however, there is no true beginning or end, so the reader must submit to hearing each narrator's version of the same story and come to understand what the story means on individual and social levels.

Of the four characters who narrate the story, none of them is completely reliable. Each has his or her own bias, and it is up to the reader to determine what the biases are and how they affect the telling of the story. In her old age, Rosa experiences the memory of the events differently than she experienced the events when they happened. For this reason, she is an unreliable narrator. Mr. Compson knows the story from his father, who admired and respected Sutpen. This, coupled with the fact that Mr. Compson did not witness the events of the story himself, makes him an unreliable narrator. Quentin is even further removed from the story than his father is, and he seeks answers to some of life's big questions, so he is also unreliable. Shreve is not invested in the story at all and hears the story after it has come through various people's biases (General Compson's, Mr. Compson's, Rosa's, and Quentin's), so he is also unreliable. Many critics note that because of the burden on the reader, he or she essentially becomes a narrator, hearing the story numerous times and being forced to make assumptions about missing or conflicting information.

Faulkner also tends to mention new characters in passing, as if the reader knows who they are. Not until later does the reader learn how they fit into the overall story and structure. Then, the reader struggles to recall what was said earlier in the novel about the various members of the growing cast of characters.

Regionalism

Absalom, Absalom! is regional in scope although its themes extend well beyond the South. Except for the room that Quentin and Shreve share at Harvard (where they sit and tell the story of Sutpen), all the action of the novel takes place in the South; the concerns of the characters are confined to the small southern town of Jefferson, Mississippi. Although there are no dialects, the novel portrays the manners, habits, and lore of the South. As with any truly regional novel, *Absalom, Absalom!* would not work in any other setting. Its characters would not be believable in another geographic area, and its depiction of the consequences of slavery is unique to the South.

Literary Devices

Faulkner employs a variety of literary techniques throughout *Absalom, Absalom!*, notably several significant instances of irony. He uses irony when Rosa speaks of Henry's murder of Charles as being almost fratricide. (She is not aware that the two men were half-brothers.) Another instance of irony is when, after all his failed efforts to be accepted by Sutpen as his son, Charles is buried in the family graveyard. Another even more disturbing example of irony is the fact that Charles, who has black ancestry, fights as an officer for the Confederacy.

A simile appears near the beginning of the novel where Faulkner writes that Sutpen came upon "a scene peaceful and decorous as a schoolprize water color." And, describing Quentin, Faulkner employs a metaphor, noting that

> his very body was an empty hall echoing with sonorous defeated names; he was not a being, an entity, he was a commonwealth. He was a barracks filled with stubborn back-looking ghosts still recovering.

Through various literary techniques, Faulkner creates a mythic atmosphere for Sutpen's saga. The reiteration of the story is reminiscent of the legends and folktales kept alive by oral tradition. Rosa describes Sutpen in supernatural terms including ogre, *djinn,* fiend, and demon. In fact, she believes that his evil is so intense that he brings curses on those with whom he comes in contact. In this way, Sutpen becomes almost a supernatural figure. Further, the grand scale and headstrong ambition of Sutpen's plans align him with mythical and heroic figures.

Biblical and classical allusions appear throughout the novel. Ellen is likened to Niobe, a character in Greek mythology who is turned to stone while weeping for her children. Rosa is compared to Cassandra, the daughter of the King of Troy who possessed prophetic powers, according to Greek mythology. The book's title is a biblical reference to David's mournful cry at the death of his son Absalom.

Historical Context

The Civil War Aftermath

Almost one-third of the southern men who went to fight in the Civil War (1861–1865) died, and almost as many suffered serious injuries. Because slaves were available to perform work, nearly

Compare
&
Contrast

- **1800s:** Heroes are drawn from legends and from stories of people (usually men) demonstrating great bravery and wisdom.

  1900s: Heroes are often men who figured prominently in the Civil War, such as Robert E. Lee and Ulysses S. Grant. Often, soldiers, returning to their hometowns after the war, become local heroes.

  Today: Heroes are more often celebrities than historical figures, and hero status is more a product of success than of bravery. Professional athletes, captains of industry, and entertainers are most often named as heroes. A person who commits an act of courage is often a hero for a short while, usually because of press coverage. The effect of the media on hero status is profound; few people who remain out of the public eye are idolized as heroes.

- **1800s:** Social status is primarily the product of lineage. In early America, social status often dictates marriage choices, occupational decisions, and political affiliation.

  1900s: Social status is the product of lineage and wealth. In the South, where many "respectable"

families fall on hard economic times, the ability to build wealth brings more social influence.

  Today: Social status is primarily the product of wealth. While there are privileged "dynasties" in some major cities, anyone who can acquire enough wealth can move up in society. Social status, however, is less a determining factor in people's lives than it was in the past.

- **1800s:** Slavery provides the backbone of economics in the South. Slaves are the source of labor for everything from farming to domestic duties.

  1900s: With the 1863 Emancipation Proclamation, slavery is outlawed. Slaves are given their freedom, but their struggles are far from over as they seek to support themselves and their families in a culture that fears and despises them. Racism is harsh and overpowering.

  Today: African Americans continue to grapple with the pain, injustice, and indignity of their history in America. Although the civil rights movement of the 1960s made great strides for minorities in terms of rights and liberties, racism is still a divisive force that serves as a grim reminder of the past.

---

eighty percent of eligible (by age and health status) white southern men were able to fight in the Civil War. They all brought home emotional, if not physical, scars. During the war, thousands of refugees in the South, black and white, lost everything they owned and faced uncertainty and terror about the future. Many families were forced to seek ways to get by without their fathers, husbands, and brothers to support them. Children who grew up without men in their families felt incomplete, and they often grew up thinking that they could never achieve the bravery and nobility of their fallen relatives.

To make matters worse, the South was in financial ruin at the end of the war. Railroads, manufacturing equipment, farm machinery, and livestock were destroyed. The destruction was so severe that industry in the South was set back a full generation. During Reconstruction (1865–1877), the North and South struggled to come to terms with the new legal and social parameters of the nation. The central concerns of the Reconstruction Period were: defining the relationship between the former North and the former South; determining who was responsible for the Confederate rebellion and whether punishment was in order; deciding which rights would be granted to former slaves; and conceiving a recovery plan for the southern economy. The transition was tense and arduous because Southerners were angry and uncooperative in the wake of their defeat. Memorials to the war in the South were slow coming, but, in time, Southerners renewed their sense of regional pride.

Southern Social Life

In the South, gender roles were specific and were taught at an early age. According to *Encyclopedia of American Social History,* a young man in the North entered adulthood by undertaking religious training or an apprenticeship and by reading works by English moralists, while young men in the South read traditional courtly works and planned their futures with a focus on the land. Young southern men demonstrated their manhood to their families by working hard to show that they would be good providers for their future families. Social structure and habits in the South were rooted in chivalry and hierarchy, and the prevailing code of honor sometimes included the aristocratic tradition of dueling. In contrast, the ideology of the North was based on ethics and conscience. The courtly foundation of many southern traditions extended to its treatment of women. Women were regarded as delicate creatures to be admired for their beauty and grace. They were expected to avoid competition and to prepare for romantic, submissive love relationships with their future husbands. Young people were taught to respect their elders, a characteristic exhibited by Quentin when he insists that Shreve refer to Rosa as "Miss Rosa," not as "Aunt Rosa" or as an "old dame."

During the Civil War, women were given an opportunity to be more independent and to adopt formerly masculine roles as nurses, factory workers, farmers, and clerks. At the end of the war, however, women returned to their positions as domestic figures, except that their status was reduced because of the absence of slaves. Now, women were expected to do more work in their homes and to occupy the most submissive position in the house.

Although their duties were concentrated on domestic affairs and their power was non-existent, southern women symbolized the virtue and goodness of the South. When men returned from the war, they depended on their women to provide reassurance and comfort. The southern patriarchy quickly reestablished itself, and the women were integral in helping men recover from the horrors of war and the humility of defeat.

Naturalistic and Symbolistic Period in American Literature

The Naturalistic and Symbolistic Period in American Literature extended between 1900 and 1930. Early in the century, the country witnessed a rise in journalistic exposés, and a movement toward unflinching realism in literature was seen in the works of Henry James, Theodore Dreiser, and Jack London. After World War I came the emergence of the Lost Generation, a group of writers disillusioned by American idealism. These writers longed for something new and innovative and found it in French symbolists like James Joyce and Marcel Proust. They rejected many aspects of American culture, in some cases creating a new polished style of writing, in other cases writing satire, and in still other cases recalling simpler times in American history when society was more structured and had a sense of tradition. In this last group were many prominent southern writers, including Faulkner.

Critical Overview

At the time of its publication, *Absalom, Absalom!* encountered mixed responses to its unorthodox narrative structure. Some critics regarded the novel's structure as overly confusing and involved, deeming it ineffective. Over time, however, scholars have come to universally commend Faulkner as a genius who was able to fuse content and form perfectly in this novel. The existing body of criticism covers virtually every aspect of the novel, from obvious themes and techniques to subtle relationships between characters and the psychological motivations behind the action of the story.

The structural complexity of the novel presents a unique set of challenges to the reader although critics regard time spent unraveling the novel well spent. David Minter of *American Writers* observed that Faulkner specialized in fragmented narratives that demonstrate little interest in traditional, continuous forms. "As a result," Minter added, "the role of the reader would necessarily be enlarged and made more creative as well as more challenging." The writer Cleanth Brooks commented in *William Faulkner: The Yoknapatawpha Country* that *Absalom, Absalom!* is Faulkner's greatest work, but it is also the least understood because of the challenges in reading it. For this reason, Brooks maintained that the novel is highly subject to in-

The Evergreen Plantation in Edgard, LA, one of the largest and most intact plantation complexes in the South and much like the house Thomas Sutpen builds as part of his "great design"

terpretation and thus can be meaningful to a wide audience. He noted:

> The property of a great work, as T. S. Eliot remarked long ago, is to communicate before it is understood; and *Absalom, Absalom!* passes this test triumphantly. It has meant something very powerful and important to all sorts of people, and who is to say that, under the circumstances, this something was not the thing to be said to that particular reader?. . .Yet the book has its own rights, as it were, and in proportion as we admire it, we shall want to see not merely what we can make of it but what it makes of itself.

Scholars consider the regional elements of *Absalom, Absalom!* to be realistic and vibrant. In *The Achievement of William Faulkner,* Michael Millgate commented that the novel's tragic power

> derives both from this profoundly localized sense of social reality and from a poignant awareness of the proud and shameful history of the courageous, careless, gallant, and oppressive South. At the same time, to concentrate too exclusively on this aspect of his work is to be in danger of mistaking means for ends and of seeing Faulkner as a lesser figure than he really is.

Faulkner's novel is not simply about the South, and critics readily praise the author's ability to portray universal themes and experiences in the southern context he knew so well. In fact, some critics

have marveled at Faulkner's ability to portray such profound and universal ideas, given his isolated, regional background. Many critics admire the way Faulkner seamlessly wove his various themes together into a cohesive whole and made them relevant to modern life. Faulkner's idea that history's truths are not completely knowable was addressed by Brooks, who remarked:

> Most important of all, however, *Absalom, Absalom!* is a persuasive commentary upon the thesis that much of 'history' is really a kind of imaginative construction. The past always remains at some level a mystery, but if we are to hope to understand it in any way, we must enter into it and project ourselves imaginatively into the attitudes and emotions of the historical figures.

The characters in *Absalom, Absalom!* are also the subjects of much critical attention. Rosa is considered by some to be a typical southern woman who is quiet and easily dismissed. After all, the argument goes, she lacks social influence in the small town of Jefferson and never moves into the accepted female roles of wife and mother. On the other hand, some feminist critics point to evidence in the novel of her importance in preserving Sutpen's story, adding that her account is so valuable that it is offered first and provides the basis for the discussion between Quentin and Shreve. Brooks called the introduction of Shreve into the novel a stroke of brilliance, as it acknowledges the modern-day reader's cynicism and rationalism regarding localized tales. Brooks also described Judith as "one of the most moving [characters] that Faulkner has ever written" because of the endurance of her basic humanity in the face of misfortune.

Absalom, Absalom! is revered by numerous scholars as Faulkner's best work or, at the very least, one of his top three novels. Brooks found it to be Faulkner's most memorable novel, writing:

> *Absalom, Absalom!* is in many respects the most brilliantly written of all Faulkner's novels, whether one considers its writing line by line and paragraph by paragraph, or its structure, in which we are moved up from one suspended note to a higher suspended note and on up further still to an almost intolerable climax. The intensity of the book is a function of its structure.... There are actually few instances in modern fiction of a more perfect adaptation of form to matter and of an intricacy that justifies itself at every point through the significance and intensity which makes it possible.

Criticism

Jennifer Bussey

Bussey holds a master's degree in interdisciplinary studies and a bachelor's degree in English literature. She is an independent writer specializing in literature. In the following essay, she examines Rosa's, Mr. Compson's, and Quentin's versions of the Sutpen story, determining what each narrator brings to the telling of the story. She also considers what is at stake for each narrator that may account for the differences in their perceptions of the story.

The complex narrative structure of *Absalom, Absalom!* presents a major challenge for William Faulkner's readers. The story does not unfold in a familiar way; the reader must learn how to read it as the story is told and retold, piecing together elements of the Sutpen story and then trying to understand Faulkner's underlying design. Because the novel consists of different narrators telling the same story (a story that occurred in the past and is, therefore, more subject to interpretation than a story happening in the present), variations arise that provide insights into the characters who serve as narrators. To better understand the novel, a close examination of these variations is extremely useful. Each narrator has something at stake in the story,

> " Despite his admiring account of Sutpen's life, Mr. Compson is deeply cynical and fatalistic. Sutpen's story is, for Mr. Compson, proof that his worldview is correct; even a great man like Sutpen was unable to escape his fated doom."

and each, therefore, perceives the characters and events differently. Each narrator also belongs to a different generation, and this, too, affects each one's view of the story.

Rosa is the first narrator to tell the story of Thomas Sutpen, a mysterious stranger who arrives in Jefferson, Mississippi, one day and forever changes the lives of many of its residents. Rosa is the oldest of the narrators and was living at the time the events took place. Over forty years have elapsed, however, and her longstanding hatred for Sutpen is a major influence in how she remembers the events. She recalls simpler, happier days in her family and believes that its downfall began when Sutpen married Rosa's older sister, Ellen. Rosa tells the story in a bitter and accusatory tone that places all blame for her family's demise on Sutpen, whom she describes as a demon, an ogre, a *djinn* (similar to a genie), and a fiend. Over the years, she has convinced herself that he was so evil that he brought curses upon those with whom he came in contact. By imagining that Sutpen possessed an almost supernatural evil, Rosa is able to color her memories in sharp black and white, with no shades of gray and nothing open to alternative interpretations.

After Rosa's sister died, Sutpen crudely proposed to Rosa but then suggested that they have a son before marrying. It was clear that Sutpen had no intention of going through with the marriage unless Rosa was able to produce a male heir. Rosa's dignity and optimism were shattered, and Sutpen moved on to find someone who would go along with his plans. Consequently, Rosa lived out the rest of her life alone and bitter, watching each member of her family die over the years. Readers are often surprised that Rosa would accept the proposal of a man she deems so reprehensible, but there is reason to believe that she began to feel this way after he abandoned her to spinsterhood. In fact, Rosa seems to have been an optimistic and romantic young woman; she wrote poetry and was active in her community. Even after her sister married Sutpen, Rosa saw little of him and may have seen him as a heroic and exciting man. Thus his bad treatment of her would have come as a shock and crushed her hopes for a happy ending, leaving her cynical about life's opportunities. Forty years later, Rosa has nothing to look forward to and little to enjoy in the present, so she is stuck in the past. The way her life has turned out—what she has become and has not become—is a result of Sutpen's story. She must find in the story a way to understand and interpret her life. She has allowed her life and personality to be determined by events that happened over forty years ago, so when she is described as a ghost, it is a fitting metaphor.

The second narrator is Mr. Compson, the son of General Compson. General Compson was among the first members of Jefferson to accept Sutpen, so the version of the story he told his son was undoubtedly complimentary rather than reproachful. As a result, Mr. Compson's descriptions contrast with Rosa's, as he portrays Sutpen as a strong, brave individual with an ironclad work ethic. It becomes clear to the reader that Mr. Compson, from having heard the story so many times and from the laudatory accounts of his father, is carried away with the legend. He sees Sutpen not as a demon, but as a heroic and mythic figure who breathed life and adventure into the small town of Jefferson. Mr. Compson tells how Sutpen cleared a large tract of land and built a stunning mansion in the wilderness. He also emphasizes that when Sutpen went to fight in the Civil War, he was bold, and his men looked to him for leadership.

Mr. Compson overlooks the less admirable aspects of Sutpen's story, such as the fact that he cheated a Native American out of the land on which he built his estate. He interprets Sutpen's unbending determination as an admirable quality rather than as the driving force behind his mistreatment of people around him. There is a reason that Mr. Compson is compelled to find in Sutpen's story the saga of a great man who ultimately fails. Mr. Compson believes in a world dictated by destiny in which men and women have no control over their fates. Despite his admiring account of Sutpen's life, Mr. Compson is deeply cynical and fatalistic. Sutpen's story is, for Mr. Compson, proof that his worldview is correct; even a great man like Sutpen

was unable to escape his fated doom. Perhaps Mr. Compson feels that he has not achieved much in his own life and seeks reasons to believe that he is right to not take risks or to not try to do great things. He believes that past generations were greater and more impressive than his own (a view that certainly is supported by the mythology of Sutpen's story), so he feels inferior to Sutpen. For Mr. Compson, his way of seeing and interpreting the world is at stake in the Sutpen story. He emphasizes those elements of Sutpen's story that confirm his beliefs and glosses over elements that would challenge them.

Except for Shreve, Quentin is the narrator furthest removed from Sutpen's story, yet he feels a deep connection to it. When Shreve asks Quentin about the South, Quentin chooses to tell him about Sutpen. This indicates that Quentin equates this story with the story of the South. All of Quentin's information comes from primary sources, but Quentin himself can never be more than a secondary source. Unlike his father, however, Quentin receives information from a variety of sources. Besides having heard the story from his father and Rosa, Quentin has also heard details of the story from his grandfather, who shared information with Quentin that he did not share with his own son. In a sense, Quentin becomes an archivist for the Sutpen story although his personal investment in the story is profound.

For Quentin, the story potentially contains the answers to his questions about how he should live his life in the modern world. He grew up in Jefferson, hearing about Sutpen throughout his childhood and youth, and his connection to the town and its folklore is a defining element of his personality. This may be difficult for some modern readers to understand, but at the beginning of the book, Quentin is preparing to leave his comfortable hometown to go to Harvard. Additionally, the year is 1909, a time when young people felt more involved in their communities and often formed their identities around their hometowns. This need to understand his past is intensified by the fact that he comes from the South, a region where people are deeply aware of and still closely connected to a tragic and shameful history. Quentin feels a degree of responsibility for the past, which affects how he carries himself in his present-day world. Making sense of the Sutpen story becomes critical to his understanding of himself and his role in the world; he searches for answers and lessons that he can apply in his own life. This aspect differentiates Quentin from the other two narrators because they are recalling events as they know them while Quentin becomes obsessed with the story and seeks details and information from all possible sources.

Quentin is at times impatient when he feels that he is hearing information he has already heard many times. He is searching for new insights, which is why he agrees to visit Henry, who is dying. After he sees Henry, who is frail and torn down by life, Quentin rides away like he is being chased. Rosa's grim account of the story and the tragedy that befell everyone involved seems to be accurate. This creates an emotional and urgent reaction in Quentin, who desperately seeks something hopeful and logical in the story because he sees it as the story of his own past and as a key to his present and future. Although Rosa sees Sutpen as an evil force and Mr. Compson sees him as a victim of fate, Quentin sees him as a representative of all that was good and bad in the Old South. Quentin admires Sutpen, but with reservations; he sees the admirable qualities in the man, but he also sees the immorality of his decisions. Quentin alone sees Sutpen as a human being who was complicated and fallible. For Quentin, his view of himself in the world is at stake in Sutpen's story. If he cannot find guidance in the story, he has nowhere else to turn. The chronology at the end of the book indicates that Quentin commited suicide just after the events of *Absalom, Absalom!,* which suggests that he either did not find the answers he was seeking or found answers that left him hopeless.

The story of Thomas Sutpen looms large in the life of each of these residents of Jefferson—Rosa, Mr. Compson, and Quentin. They seek understanding of their past, present, and future lives in the narrative, so it is not surprising that they interpret the story in unique ways. The dramatic tale takes on new dimensions with each generation of storytellers, yet the true meaning of the story remains elusive.

One of Faulkner's themes in the novel is the ultimate incapacity to know the truth about historical events, and the narrators' variations of the story support that theme. At the same time, Faulkner demonstrates the importance of trying to understand the past and the validity of personalizing stories in the pursuit of personal and social insight. Such insight can never be perfect, but it can, nevertheless, be instructive.

Source: Jennifer Bussey, Critical Essay on *Absalom, Absalom!,* in *Novels for Students,* The Gale Group, 2002.

Cleanth Brooks

In the following essay, Brooks examines "the quality of Sutpen's innocence" to "understand the meaning of his tragedy."

Absalom, Absalom!, in my opinion the greatest of Faulkner's novels, is probably the least well understood of all his books. The property of a great work, as T. S. Eliot remarked long ago, is to communicate before it is understood, and *Absalom, Absalom!* passes this test triumphantly. It has meant something very powerful and important to all sorts of people, and who is to say that, under the circumstances, this something was not the thing to be said to that particular reader?. . .

Harvey Breit's sympathetic introduction to the Modern Library edition provides a useful—because it is not an extreme—instance of the typical misreading that I have in mind. Mr. Breit writes:

> It is a terrible Gothic sequence of events, a brooding tragic fable. . . Was it the "design" that had devoured Sutpen and prevented him from avowing the very thing that would have saved the design? Was it something in the South itself, in its social, political, moral, economic origins that was responsible for Sutpen and for all the subsequent tragedy? Quentin can make no judgment: Sutpen himself had possessed courage and innocence, and the same land had nourished men and women who had delicacy of feeling and capacity for love and gifts for life.

These are questions which the typical reader asks. Shreve, the outsider, implies them. But it is significant that Quentin does not ask them. The questions are begged by the very way in which they are asked, for, put in this way, the questions undercut the problem of tragedy (which is the problem that obsesses Quentin). They imply that there is a social "solution." And they misread Sutpen's character in relation to his society and in relation to himself.

It is the quality of Sutpen's innocence that we must understand if we are to understand the meaning of his tragedy, and if we confuse it with innocence as we ordinarily use the term or with even the typical American "innocence" possessed by, say, one of Henry James's young heiresses as she goes to confront the corruption of Europe, we shall remain in the dark. Sutpen will be for us, as he was for Miss Rosa, simply the "demon"—or, since we lack the justification of Miss Rosa's experience of personal horror, we shall simply appropriate the term from her as Shreve, in his half-awed, half-amused fashion, does.

Faulkner has been very careful to define Sutpen's innocence for us. "Sutpen's trouble," as Quentin's grandfather observed, "was innocence." And some pages later, Mr. Compson elaborates the point: "He believed that all that was necessary was courage and shrewdness and the one he knew he had and the other he believed he could learn if it were to be taught." It is this innocence about the nature of reality that persists, for Sutpen "believed that the ingredients of morality were like the ingredients of pie or cake and once you had measured them and balanced them and mixed them and put them into the oven it was all finished and nothing but pie or cake could come out." That is why Sutpen can ask Quentin's grandfather, in his innocence, not "Where did I do wrong" but "Where did I make the mistake. . . what did I do or misdo. . . whom or what injure by it to the extent which this would indicate? I had a design. To accomplish it I should require money, a house, a plantation, slaves, a family—incidentally of course, a wife. I set out to acquire these, asking no favor of any man."

This is an "innocence" with which most of us today ought to be acquainted. It is par excellence the innocence of modern man, though it has not, to be sure, been confined to modern times. One can find more than a trace of it in Sophocles' Oedipus, and it has its analogies with the rather brittle rationalism of Macbeth, though Macbeth tried to learn this innocence by an act of the will and proved to be a less than satisfactory pupil. But innocence of this sort can properly be claimed as a special characteristic of modern man, and one can claim further that it flourishes particularly in a secularized society.

The society into which Sutpen rides in 1833 is not a secularized society. That is not to say that the people are necessarily "good." They have their selfishness and cruelty and their snobbery, as men have always had them. Once Sutpen has acquired

enough wealth and displayed enough force, the people of the community are willing to accept him. But they do not live by his code, nor do they share his innocent disregard of accepted values. Indeed, from the beginning they regard him with deep suspicion and some consternation. These suspicions are gradually mollified; there is a kind of acceptance; but as Quentin tells Shreve, Sutpen had only one friend, Quentin's grandfather, General Compson, and this in spite of the fact that the society of the lower South in the nineteenth century was rather fluid and that class lines were flexible. Men did rise in one generation from log cabins to great landed estates. But the past was important, blood was important, and Southern society thought of itself as traditional.

That Sutpen does remain outside the community comes out in all sorts of little ways. Mr. Compson describes his "florid, swaggering gesture" with the parenthetical remark: "yes, he was underbred. It showed like this always, your grandfather said, in all his formal contacts with people.". . . Yet though Sutpen's manners have been learned painfully, Sutpen has complete confidence in them. "He may have believed that your grandfather or Judge Benbow might have done it a little more effortlessly than he, but he would not have believed that anyone could have beat him in knowing when to do it and how."

Mr. Compson is not overrating the possession of mere manners. More is involved than Miss Rosa's opinion that Sutpen was no gentleman, for Sutpen's manners indicate his abstract approach to the whole matter of living. Sutpen would seize upon "the traditional" as a pure abstraction—which, of course, is to deny its very meaning. For him the tradition is not a way of life "handed down" or "transmitted" from the community, past and present, to the individual nurtured by it. It is an assortment of things to be possessed, not a manner of living that embodies certain values and determines men's conduct. The fetish objects are to be gained by sheer ruthless efficiency. (Sutpen even refers to "my schedule.") Thorstein Veblen would have understood Sutpen's relation to traditional culture. . . The New York robber baron's acquiring a box at the opera did not usually spring from a love of music, and one is tempted to say that Sutpen's unwillingness to acknowledge Charles Bon as his son does not spring from any particular racial feeling. Indeed, Sutpen's whole attitude toward the Negro has to be reinspected if we are to understand his relation to the Southern community into which he comes.

It would seem that the prevailing relation between the races in Jefferson is simply one more of the culture traits which Sutpen takes from the plantation community into which he has come as a boy out of the mountains of western Virginia. Sutpen takes over the color bar almost without personal feeling. His attitude toward the Negro is further clarified by his attitude toward his other part-Negro child, Clytie. Mr. Compson once casually lets fall the remark that Sutpen's other children "Henry and Judith had grown up with a negro half sister of their own." The context of Mr. Compson's remarks makes it perfectly plain that Henry and Judith were well aware that Clytie was indeed their half-sister, and that Clytie was allowed to grow up in the house with them. This fact in itself suggests a lack of the usual Southern feeling about Negroes. . .

After Sutpen has returned from the war, Clytie sits in the same room with Judith and Rosa and Sutpen and listens each evening to the sound of Sutpen's voice. When Sutpen proposes to Rosa, he begins, " 'Judith, you and Clytie—' and ceased, still entering, then said, 'No, never mind. Rosa will not mind if you both hear it too, since we are short for time.' " Clytie is accepted naturally as part of the "we." She can be so accepted because acceptance on this level does not imperil Sutpen's "design." But acceptance of Charles Bon, in Sutpen's opinion, would. For Sutpen the matter is really as simple as that. He does not hate his first wife or feel repugnance for her child. He does not hate just as he does not love. His passion is totally committed to the design. . .

As for slavery, Sutpen does not confine himself to black chattel slavery. He ruthlessly bends anyone that he can to his will. The white French architect whom he brings into Yoknapatawpha County to build his house is as much a slave as any of his black servants: Sutpen hunts him down with dogs when he tries to escape.

The trait that most decisively sets Sutpen apart from his neighbors in this matter of race is his fighting with his slaves. Sutpen is accustomed to stripping to the waist and fighting it out with one of his slaves, not with rancor, one supposes, and not at all to punish the slave, but simply to keep fit—to prove to himself and incidentally to his slaves that he is the better man. Some of Sutpen's white neighbors come to watch the fights as they might come to watch a cockfight. But it is significant that they come as to something extraordinary, a show, an odd spectacle; they would not think of fighting with

their own slaves. To Miss Rosa, Sutpen's sister-in-law, the ultimate horror is that Sutpen not only arranges the show but that he enters the ring himself and fights with no holds barred—not even eye-gouging.

Sutpen is not without morality or a certain code of honor. He is, according to his own lights, a just man. As he told Quentin's grandfather with reference to his rejection of his first wife:

suffice that I. . . accepted [my wife] in good faith, with no reservations about myself, and I expected as much from [her parents]. I did not [demand credentials] as one of my obscure origin might have been expected to do. . . I accepted them at their own valuation while insisting on my part upon explaining fully about myself and my progenitors: yet they de-

What Do I Read Next?

- Faulkner's *The Sound and the Fury* (1929) is tangentially related to *Absalom, Absalom!* because it shares several characters. Besides being one of Faulkner's most widely read books, *The Sound and the Fury* is one of his many Yoknapatawpha novels, all of which are interrelated to varying degrees.

- *Roots,* Alex Haley's 1976 masterpiece, tells the story of the author's ancestors, beginning with the African slave Kunta Kinte. Haley recounts his family's history in an effort to bring them to life for the reader and to understand his own identity.

- *The Complete Stories of Flannery O'Connor* (1971) provides a collection of short fiction that continues to reach readers through its universal themes and depictions of black and white relations in the South.

- *The Collected Stories of Eudora Welty* (1980) contains the short fiction of Eudora Welty, one of Mississippi's most respected authors. Welty is known for her distinctly southern storytelling style, and her work is a must for students of southern literature.

liberately withheld from me one fact which I have reason to know they were aware would have caused me to decline the entire matter.

But Sutpen, as he tells General Compson, "made no attempt to keep. . . that [property] which I might consider myself to have earned at the risk of my life. . . but on the contrary I declined and resigned all right and claim to this in order that I might repair whatever injustice I might be considered to have done [in abandoning my wife and child] by so providing for" them.

Moreover, Sutpen is careful to say nothing in disparagement of his first wife. Quentin's grandfather comments upon "that morality which would not permit him to malign or traduce the memory of his first wife, or at least the memory of the marriage even though he felt that he had been tricked by it." It is Sutpen's innocence to think that justice is enough—that there is no claim that cannot be satisfied by sufficient money payment. Quentin imagines his grandfather exclaiming to Sutpen: "What kind of abysmal and purblind innocence would that have been which someone told you to call virginity? what conscience to trade with which would have warranted you in the belief that you could have bought immunity from her for no other coin but justice?"

Sutpen thinks of himself as strictly just and he submits all of his faculties almost selflessly to the achievement of his design. His attitude toward his second wife conforms perfectly to this. Why does he choose her? For choose he does: he is not chosen—that is, involved with her through passion. The choice is calculated quite coldbloodedly (if, to our minds, naïvely and innocently). Ellen Coldfield is not the daughter of a planter. She does not possess great social prestige or beauty and she does not inherit wealth. But as the daughter of a steward in the Methodist church, she possesses in high degree the thing that Sutpen most obviously lacks—respectability. Mr. Compson sees the point very clearly. He describes Mr. Coldfield as "a man with a name for absolute and undeviating and even Puritan uprightness in a country and time of lawless opportunity, who neither drank nor gambled nor even hunted." For Sutpen, respectability is an abstraction like morality: you measure out so many cups of concentrated respectability to sweeten so many measures of disrespectability—"like the ingredients of pie or cake."

The choice of a father-in-law is, in fact, just as symbolically right: the two men resemble each other for all the appearance of antithetical differences. Mr. Coldfield is as definitely set off from the community as is Sutpen. With the coming of the Civil War, this rift widens to an absolute break. Mr. Coldfield denounces secession, closes his store, and finally nails himself up in the attic of his house, where he spends the last three years of his life. No more than Sutpen is he a coward; like Sutpen, too, his scheme of human conduct is abstract and mechanical. "Doubtless the only pleasure which he had ever had. . . was in [his money's] representation of a balance in whatever spiritual counting-house he believed would some day pay his sight drafts on self-denial and fortitude."

This last is Mr. Compson's surmise; but I see no reason to question it or to quarrel with the motive that Mr. Compson assigns for Coldfield's objection to the Civil War: "not so much to the idea of pouring out human blood and life, but at the idea of waste: of wearing out and eating up and shooting away material in any cause whatever." Mr. Coldfield is glad when he sees the country that he hates obviously drifting into a fatal war, for he regards the inevitable defeat of the South as the price it will pay for having erected its economic edifice "not on the rock of stern morality but on the shifting sands of opportunism and moral brigandage."

Some critics have been so unwary as to assume that this view of the Civil War is one that the author would enjoin upon the reader, but William Faulkner is neither so much of a Puritan nor so much of a materialist as is Mr. Coldfield. The truth of the matter is that Mr. Coldfield's morality is simply Sutpen's turned inside out. Faulkner may or may not have read Tawney's *Religion and the Rise of Capitalism;* but on the evidence of *Absalom, Absalom!* he would certainly have understood it.

Sutpen is further defined by his son, Charles Bon. Bon is a mirror image, a reversed shadow of his father. Like his father, he suddenly appears out of nowhere as a man of mystery: "a personage who in the remote Mississippi of that time must have appeared almost phoenix-like, fullsprung from no childhood, born of no woman and impervious to time." Like his father, Bon has an octoroon "wife," whom he is prepared to repudiate along with his child by her. Like his father, he stands beyond good and evil. But Bon is Byronic, rather than the go-getter, spent, rather than full of pushing vitality, sophisticated, rather than confidently naïve.

Sutpen is the secularized Puritan; Bon is the lapsed Roman Catholic. Whereas Sutpen is filled with a fresh and powerful energy, Bon is world-weary and tired. Bon is a fatalist, but Sutpen believes in sheer will: "anyone could look at him and say, *Given the occasion and the need, this man can and will do anything.*" Bon possesses too much knowledge; Sutpen on the other hand is "innocent." The one has gone beyond the distinction between good and evil; the other has scarcely arrived at that distinction. The father and the son define the extremes of the human world: one aberration corresponds to—and eventually destroys—the other. The reader is inclined to view Bon with sympathy as a person gravely wronged, and he probably agrees with Quentin's interpretation of Bon's character: that Bon finally put aside all ideas of revenge and asked for nothing more than a single hint of recognition of his sonship. Faulkner has certainly treated Bon with full dramatic sympathy—as he has Sutpen, for that matter. But our sympathy ought not to obscure for us Bon's resemblances to his father, or the complexity of his character. Unless we care to go beyond Quentin and Shreve in speculation, Charles Bon displays toward his octoroon mistress and their son something of the cool aloofness that his father displays toward him. If he is the instrument by which Sutpen's design is wrecked, his own irresponsibility (or at the least, his lack of concern for his own child) wrecks his child's life. We shall have to look to Judith to find responsible action and a real counter to Sutpen's ruthlessness.

These other children of Sutpen—Judith and Henry—reflect further light upon the character of Sutpen—upon his virtues and upon his prime defect. They represent a mixture of the qualities of Sutpen and Coldfield. Judith, it is made plain, has more of the confidence and boldness of her father; Henry, more of the conventionality and the scruples of his maternal grandfather. It is the boy Henry who vomits at the sight of his father, stripped to the waist in the ring with the black slave. Judith watches calmly. And it is Judith who urges the coachman to race the coach on the way to church.

Henry is, of the two, the more vulnerable. After Sutpen has forbidden marriage between Bon and Judith and during the long period in which Henry remains self-exiled with his friend Bon, he is the one tested to the limit by his father's puzzling silence and by his friend's fatalistic passivity. But he has some of his father's courage, and he has what his father does not have: love. At the last moment he kills, though he kills what he loves and apparently for love. It is the truly tragic dilemma. Faulkner has not chosen to put Henry's story in the forefront of the novel, but he has not needed to do so. For the sensitive reader the various baffles through which that act of decision reaches us do not muffle but, through their resonance, magnify the decisive act.

Henry's later course is, again, only implied. We know that in the end—his last four years—he reverted to the course of action of his grandfather Coldfield, and shut himself up in the house. But there is a difference. This is no act of abstract defiance and hate. Henry has assumed responsibility, has acted, has been willing to abide the consequences of that action, and now, forty years later, has come home to die.

If it is too much to call Henry's course of action renunciation and expiation, there is full justification for calling Judith's action just that. Judith has much of her father in her, but she is a woman, and she also has love. As Mr. Compson conjectures:

> And Judith: how else to explain her but this way? Surely Bon could not have corrupted her to fatalism in twelve days. . . No: anything but a fatalist, who was the Sutpen with the ruthless Sutpen code of taking what it wanted provided it were strong enough. . . [Judith said] *I love, I will accept no substitute; something has happened between him and my father; if my father was right, I will never see him again, if wrong he will come or send for me; if happy I can be I will, if suffer I must I can.*

It is Judith who invites Charles Bon's octoroon mistress to visit Bon's grave. It is Judith who, on his mother's death, sends to New Orleans for Bon's son and tries to rear him. Some years later she also tries to free him (as Quentin conjectures) by promising to take care of his Negro wife and child if he will go to the North to pass as white, and Quentin imagines her saying to him: "Call me Aunt Judith, Charles." But Quentin's conjectures aside, we know that Judith did take him into the house when he was stricken with yellow fever, and that she died nursing him. The acknowledgment of blood kinship is made; Sutpen's design is repudiated; the boy, even though he has the "taint" of Negro blood, is not turned away from the door.

Both Henry's action, the violent turning away from the door with a bullet, and Judith's, the holding open the door not merely to Bon, her fiancé, but literally to his part-Negro son, are human actions, as Sutpen's actions are not. Both involve renunciation, and both are motivated by love. The suffering of Henry and Judith is not meaningless, and their very capacity for suffering marks them as having transcended their father's radical and disabling defect. . .

One must not alter the focus of the novel by making wisdom won through suffering the issue.

But the consequences entailed upon Judith and Henry have to be mentioned if only to discourage a glib Gothicizing of the novel or forcing its meaning into an overshallow sociological interpretation.

Miss Rosa feels that the Coldfields are all cursed; and certainly the impact of Sutpen upon her personally is damning: she remains rigid with horror and hate for forty-three years. But it is Miss Rosa only who is damned. Judith is not damned; nor am I sure that Henry is. Judith and Henry are not caught in an uncomprehending stasis. There is development: they grow and learn at however terrible a price. . .

Sutpen, as has been pointed out, never learns anything; he remains innocent to the end. As Quentin sees the character: when Charles Bon first comes to his door, Sutpen does not call it "retribution, no sins of the father come home to roost; not even calling it bad luck, but just a mistake. . . just an old mistake in fact which a man of courage and shrewdness. . . could still combat if he could only find out what the mistake had been." I have remarked that Sutpen's innocence is peculiarly the innocence of modern man. For like modern man, Sutpen does not believe in Jehovah. He does not believe in the goddess Tyche. He is not the victim of bad luck. He has simply made a "mistake." He "had been too successful," Mr. Compson tells Quentin; his "was that solitude of contempt and distrust which success brings to him who gained it because he was strong instead of merely lucky.". . . Sutpen resembles the modern American, whose character, as Arthur M. Schlesinger has put it, "is bottomed on the profound conviction that nothing in the world is beyond [his] power to accomplish." Sutpen is a "planner" who works by blue-print and on a schedule. He is rationalistic and scientific, not traditional, not religious, not even superstitious.

We must be prepared to take such traits into account if we attempt to read the story of Sutpen's fall as a myth of the fall of the Old South. Unless we are content with some rather rough and ready analogies, the story of the fall of the house of Sutpen may prove less than parallel. The fall of the house of Compson as depicted in *The Sound and the Fury* is also sometimes regarded as a kind of exemplum of the fall of the old aristocratic order in the South, and perhaps in some sense it is. But the breakup of these two families comes from very different causes, and if we wish to use them to point a moral or illustrate a bit of social history, surely they point to different morals and illustrate different histories. Mr. Compson, whose father, General

Compson, regarded Sutpen as a "little underbred," has failed through a kind of overrefinement. He has lost his grip on himself; he has ceased finally to believe in the values of the inherited tradition. He is a fatalist and something of an easy cynic. His vices are diametrically opposed to those of Thomas Sutpen, and so are his virtues. . . Indeed, Sutpen is at some points more nearly allied to Flem than he is to the Compsons and the Sartorises. Like Flem, he is a new man with no concern for the past and has a boundless energy with which to carry out his aggressive plans.

Yet to couple Sutpen with Flem calls for an immediate qualification. Granting that both men subsist outside the community and in one way or another prey upon the community, Sutpen is by contrast a heroic and tragic figure. He achieves a kind of grandeur. Even the obsessed Miss Rosa sees him as great, not as petty and sordid. His innocence resembles that of Oedipus (who, like him, had been corrupted by success and who put his confidence in his own shrewdness). His courage resembles that of Macbeth, and like Macbeth he is "resolute to try the last.". . .

Up to this point we have been concerned with the character of Thomas Sutpen, especially in his relation to the claims of the family and the community. We have treated him as if he were a historical figure, but of course he is not. More than most characters in literature, Thomas Sutpen is an imaginative construct, a set of inferences—an hypothesis put forward to account for several peculiar events. For the novel *Absalom, Absalom!* does not merely tell the story of Thomas Sutpen, but dramatizes the process by which two young men of the twentieth century construct the character Thomas Sutpen. Fascinated by the few known events of his life and death, they try, through inference and conjecture and guesswork, to ascertain what manner of man he was. The novel, then, has to do not merely with the meaning of Sutpen's career but with the nature of historical truth and with the problem of how we can "know" the past. The importance of this latter theme determines the very special way in which the story of Sutpen is mediated to us through a series of partial disclosures, informed guesses, and constantly revised deductions and hypotheses.

Young Quentin Compson, just on the eve of leaving Mississippi for his first year at Harvard, is summoned by Miss Rosa Coldfield and made to listen to the story of her wicked brother-in-law, Thomas Sutpen. Sutpen had been a friend of

Quentin's grandfather, General Compson, and as Quentin waits to drive Miss Rosa out to Sutpen's Hundred after dark, as she has requested, Quentin's father tells him what he knows about the Sutpen story.

Nobody had really understood the strange events that had occurred at Sutpen's Hundred—the quarrel between Thomas Sutpen and Henry, the disappearance of Henry with his friend Charles Bon, the forbidding of the marriage between Judith and Bon, and later, and most sensational of all, Henry's shooting of his friend Charles Bon at the very gates of Sutpen's Hundred in 1865. Mr. Compson makes a valiant effort to account for what happened. What evidently sticks in his mind is the fact that Charles Bon had an octoroon mistress in New Orleans. Presumably Judith had told General Compson or his wife about finding the octoroon's picture on Charles Bon's dead body. But in any case the visit, at Judith's invitation, of the woman to Charles Bon's grave would have impressed the whole relationship upon General Compson and upon his son, Mr. Compson. Mr. Compson thinks that it was the fact of the mistress that made Thomas Sutpen oppose Bon's marriage to his daughter, but that Henry was so deeply committed to his friend that he refused to believe what his father told him about Bon's mistress, chose to go away with Charles, and only at the very end, when Charles Bon was actually standing before his father's house, used the gun to prevent the match.

It is not a very plausible theory. For, though it could account for Sutpen's opposition to Bon, it hardly explains Henry's violent action, taken so late in the day. Mr. Compson does the best that he can with this aspect of the story and says: "[Henry] loved grieved and killed, still grieving and, I believe, still loving Bon, the man to whom he gave four years of probation, four years in which to renounce and dissolve the other marriage, knowing that the four years of hoping and waiting would be in vain." But Mr. Compson has to concede that, after all, "it's just incredible. It just does not explain. . . Something is missing."

Quentin's other informant about the Sutpens is Miss Rosa Coldfield, Sutpen's sister-in-law. Miss Rosa clearly does not understand what happened. She exclaims that "Judith's marriage [was] forbidden without rhyme or reason," and her only theory for accounting for the murder is that Sutpen was a demon, and as a demon, dowered his children with a curse which made them destroy themselves. Even Judith evidently did not know why her marriage

was forbidden nor did she know why her brother killed Charles Bon. After the murder and Henry's flight, Judith tells Mrs. Compson, the General's wife, that the war will soon be over now because "they [the Confederate soldiers] have begun to shoot one another." The remark indicates her bafflement as well as her despair.

By the time we have reached the end of section 5—that is, halfway through the book—we have been given most of the basic facts of the Sutpen story but no satisfactory interpretation of it. We know the story of Sutpen's life in the Mississippi community pretty much as the community itself knew it, but the events do not make sense. The second half of the book may be called an attempt at interpretation. When section 6 opens, we are in Quentin's room at Harvard and Quentin is reading a letter from his father telling about the death of Miss Rosa Coldfield. From this time on until past midnight, Quentin and Shreve discuss the story of Sutpen and make their own conjectures as to what actually happened. In this second half of the book there are, to be sure, further disclosures about Sutpen, especially with reference to his early life before he came to Mississippi. Sutpen, it turns out, had once told the story of his early life to General Compson, and his information had been passed on to Quentin through Mr. Compson. As Shreve and Quentin talk, Quentin feeds into the conversation from time to time more material from his father's and grandfather's memory of events, and one very brilliant scene which he himself remembers: how, hunting quail on a gray autumn day, he and his father came upon the graves in the Sutpen family graveyard and his father told him the touching story of Judith's later life. But as the last four sections of the book make plain, we are dealing with an intricate imaginative reconstruction of events leading up to the murder of Charles Bon—a plausible account of what may have happened, not what necessarily did happen.

If the reader reminds himself how little hard fact there is to go on—how much of the most important information about the motivation of the central characters comes late and is, at best, vague and ambiguous—he will appreciate how much of the story of Sutpen and especially of Sutpen's children has been spun out of the imaginations of Quentin and Shreve.

Absalom, Absalom! is, indeed, from one point of view a wonderful detective story—by far the best of Faulkner's several flirtations with this particular genre. It may also be considered to yield a nice instance of how the novelist works, for Shreve and Quentin both show a good deal of the insights of the novelist and his imaginative capacity for constructing plausible motivations around a few given facts. . . Most important of all, however, *Absalom, Absalom!* is a persuasive commentary upon the thesis that much of "history" is really a kind of imaginative construction. The past always remains at some level a mystery, but if we are to hope to understand it in any wise, we must enter into it and project ourselves imaginatively into the attitudes and emotions of the historical figures. . .

To note that the account of the Sutpens which Shreve and Quentin concoct is largely an imaginative construct is not to maintain that it is necessarily untrue. Their version of events is plausible, and the author himself—for whatever that may be worth—suggests that some of the scenes which they palpably invented were probably true: e.g., "the slight dowdy woman. . . whom Shreve and Quentin had. . . invented" and who was probably "true enough." But it is worth remarking that we do not "know," apart from the Quentin-Shreve semifictional process, many events which a casual reader assumes actually happened.

To provide some illustrations: Charles Bon's telling Henry "So it's the miscegenation, not the incest, which you cant bear" is a remark that rests upon no known fact. It is a conjecture, though a plausible one. Again, Bon's agonized waiting for his father to give him the merest hint of a father's recognition and Bon's comment that this was all that Sutpen needed to do to stop his courtship of Judith are both surmises made by Quentin and Shreve. So too is the scene in which the boys imagine the visit of Bon and Henry to New Orleans and hear Bon's mother's bitter question, "So she [Judith] has fallen in love with him," and listen to her harsh laughter as she looks at Henry. The wonderfully touching scene in which Judith asks Charles Bon's son to call her "Aunt Judith" is presumably an imaginative construction made by Quentin.

One ought to observe in passing that in allowing the boys to make their guesses about what went on, Faulkner plays perfectly fair. Some of their guesses have the clear ring of truth. They are obviously right. On the other hand, some are justified by the flimsiest possible reasoning. For example, notice Shreve's argument that it was Henry, not Bon, who was wounded at the battle of Shiloh.

One of the most important devices used in the novel is the placing of Shreve in it as a kind of sounding board and mouthpiece. By doing so,

Faulkner has in effect acknowledged the attitude of the modern "liberal," twentieth century reader, who is basically rational, skeptical, without any special concern for history, and pretty well emancipated from the ties of family, race, or section. . .

Shreve teases Quentin playfully and even affectionately, but it is not mere teasing. When Shreve strikes a pose and in his best theatrical manner assigns a dramatic speech to Wash, Faulkner, in one of his few intrusions as author, observes: "This was not flippancy. . . It too was just that protective coloring of levity behind which the youthful shame of being moved hid itself.". . .

The last sections of the novel tell us a great deal about Shreve's and Quentin's differing attitudes toward history and of their own relation to history. Shreve has been genuinely moved by the story of Sutpen. For all of his teasing, he is concerned to understand, and late in the evening he says to Quentin: "Listen. I'm not trying to be funny, smart. I just want to understand it if I can and I dont know how to say it better. Because it's something my people haven't got." And though he cannot suppress his bantering tone in alluding to the Southern heritage—it is "a kind of entailed birthright. . . of never forgiving General Sherman, so that forevermore as long as your children's children produce children you wont be anything but a descendant of a long line of colonels killed in Pickett's charge"—Shreve's question is seriously put. What is it that Quentin as a Southerner has that Shreve does not have? It is a sense of the presence of the past, and with it, and through it, a personal access to a tragic vision. For the South has experienced defeat and guilt, and has an ingrained sense of the stubbornness of human error and of the complexity of history. The matter has been recently put very well in C. Vann Woodward's *The Burden of Southern History:* "The experience of evil and the experience of tragedy," he writes, "are parts of the Southern heritage that are as difficult to reconcile with the American legend of innocence and social felicity as the experience of poverty and defeat are to reconcile with the legends of abundance and success."

In remarking on how little of hard fact one has to go on, we should bear in mind particularly the question of Bon's Negro blood and of his kinship to Henry. Quentin says flatly that "nobody ever did know if Bon ever knew Sutpen was his father or not." Did anyone ever know whether Bon knew that he was part Negro? In their reconstruction of the story, Shreve and Quentin assume that Bon was aware that he was Henry's part-Negro half-brother (though a few pages earlier Quentin and Shreve assume that Bon did not know that he had Negro blood). If in fact Bon did have Negro blood, how did Shreve and Quentin come by that knowledge? As we have seen, neither Judith nor Miss Rosa had any inkling of it. Nor did Mr. Compson. Early in the novel he refers to Bon's "sixteenth part negro son." Since Bon's mistress was an octoroon, his son could be one-sixteenth Negro only on the assumption that Charles Bon was of pure white blood—and this is evidently what Mr. Compson does assume. Mr. Compson, furthermore, knows nothing about Bon's kinship to Henry.

The conjectures made by Shreve and Quentin—even if taken merely as conjectures—render the story of Sutpen plausible. They make much more convincing sense of the story than Mr. Compson's notions were able to make. And that very fact suggests their probable truth. But are they more than plausible theories? Is there any real evidence to support the view that Bon was Sutpen's son by a part-Negro wife? There is, and the way in which this evidence is discovered constitutes another, and the most decisive, justification for regarding *Absalom, Absalom!* as a magnificent detective story. Precisely what was revealed and how it was revealed are worth a rather careful review.

In the course of his conversation with Quentin, Shreve objects that Mr. Compson "seems to have got an awful lot of delayed information awful quick, after having waited forty-five years." Quentin confirms the fact that his father *had* got delayed information—had got it from Quentin himself—had got it, indeed, the day after "we" (that is, Quentin and Miss Rosa) had gone out to Sutpen's Hundred. A little later, when Quentin tells Shreve of Sutpen's long conversation with General Compson about his "design" and about the "mistake" that Sutpen had made in trying to carry it out, Shreve asks Quentin whether General Compson had then really known what Sutpen was talking about. Quentin answers that General Compson had not known; and Shreve, pressing the point, makes Quentin admit that he himself "wouldn't have known what anybody was talking about" if he "hadn't been out there and seen Clytie." The secret of Bon's birth, then, was revealed to Quentin on that particular visit. Shreve's way of phrasing it implies that it was from Clytie that Quentin had got his information, but, as we shall see, it is unlikely that Clytie was Quentin's informant. In any case, when Shreve puts his question about seeing Clytie,

he did not know that another person besides Clytie and her nephew was living at Sutpen's Hundred.

Miss Rosa has sensed that "something"—she does not say *someone*—was "living hidden in that house." When she and Quentin visit Sutpen's Hundred, her intuition is confirmed. The hidden something turns out to be Henry Sutpen, now come home to die. Presumably, it was from Henry Sutpen that Quentin learned the crucial facts. Or did he? Here again Faulkner may seem to the reader either teasingly reticent or, upon reflection, brilliantly skillful.

We know from the last section of the book that after Miss Rosa had come down from the upstairs room with her "eyes wide and unseeing like a sleepwalker's," Quentin felt compelled to go up to that room and see what was there. He does go, though Faulkner does not take us with him into the room. He descends the stairs, walks out of the house, overtakes Miss Rosa, and drives her home. Later that night, however, after he has returned to his own home and is lying sleepless, he cannot—even by clenching his eyelids—shut out his vision of the bed with its yellowed sheets and its yellowed pillow and the wasted yellow face lying upon it, a face with closed, "almost transparent eyelids." As Quentin tosses, unable to erase the picture from his eyes, we are vouchsafed one tiny scrap of his conversation with Henry, a conversation that amounts to no more than Quentin's question "And you are—?" and Henry's answer that he is indeed Henry Sutpen, that he has been there four years, and that he has come home to die. How extended was the conversation? How long did it last? Would Henry Sutpen have volunteered to a stranger his reason for having killed Charles Bon? Or would Quentin Compson, awed and aghast at what he saw, put such questions as these to the wasted figure upon the bed? We do not know and Faulkner—probably wisely—has not undertaken to reconstruct this interview for us. (It is possible, of course, that Henry did tell Miss Rosa why he had killed Bon and that Miss Rosa told Quentin in the course of their long ride back to Jefferson.)

At all events, the whole logic of *Absalom, Absalom!* argues that *only* through the presence of Henry in the house was it possible for Quentin—and through Quentin his father and Shreve and those of us who read the book—to be made privy to the dark secret that underlay the Sutpen tragedy.

At the end of the novel Shreve is able to shrug off the tragic implications and resume the tone of easy banter. His last comment abounds with the usual semi-sociological clichés: the Negroes "will bleach out again like the rabbits and the birds. . . In a few thousand years, I who regard you will also have sprung from the loins of African kings." Though the spell of the story has been powerful enough to fire his imagination and involve all his sympathies, he is not personally committed, and we can see him drawing back from the tragic problem and becoming again the cheery, cynical, commonsense man of the present day. In the long perspective of history, how few issues really matter! The long perspective is antihistorical: make it long enough and any "sense of history" evaporates. Lengthen it further still and the human dimension itself evaporates.

From his stance of detachment, Shreve suddenly, and apropos of nothing, puts to Quentin the question "Why do you hate the South?" And Quentin's passionate denial that he hates it tells its own story of personal involvement and distress. The more naïve reader may insist on having an answer: "Well, does he hate it?" And the response would have to be, I suppose, another question: "Does Stephen Daedalus hate Dublin?" Or, addressing the question to Stephen's creator, "Did James Joyce hate Ireland?" The answer here would surely have to be yes and no. In any case, Joyce was so obsessed with Ireland and so deeply involved in it that he spent his life writing about it.

At this point, however, it may be more profitable to put a different question. What did the story of Sutpen mean to Quentin? Did it mean to him what it has apparently meant to most of the critics who have written on this novel—the story of the curse of slavery and how it involved Sutpen and his children in ruin? Surely this is to fit the story to a neat and oversimple formula. Slavery was an evil. But other slaveholders avoided Sutpen's kind of defeat and were exempt from his special kind of moral blindness.

What ought to be plain, in any event, is that it is Henry's part in the tragic tale that affects Quentin the most. Quentin had seen Henry with his own eyes and Henry's involvement in slavery was only indirect. Even Henry's dread of miscegenation was fearfully complicated with other issues, including the problem of incest. In view of what we learn of Quentin in *The Sound and the Fury,* the problem of incest would have fascinated him and made him peculiarly sensitive to Henry's torment. Aside from his personal problem, however, Sutpen's story had for Quentin a special meaning that it did not have for Shreve.

The story embodied the problem of evil and of the irrational: Henry was beset by conflicting claims; he was forced to make intolerably hard choices—between opposed goods or between conflicting evils. Had Henry cared much less for Bon, or else much less for Judith, he might have promoted the happiness of one without feeling that he was sacrificing that of the other. Or had he cared much less for either and much more for himself, he might have won a cool and rational detachment, a coign of vantage from which even objections to miscegenation and incest would appear to be irrational prejudices, and honor itself a quaint affectation whose saving was never worth the price of a bullet. Had Henry been not necessarily wiser, but simply more cynical or more gross or more selfish, there would have been no tragedy. . . But Shreve is measurably closer to the skepticism and detachment that allow modern man to dismiss the irrational claims from which Quentin cannot free himself and which he honors to his own cost.

The reader of *Absalom, Absalom!* might well follow Quentin's example. If he must find in the story of the House of Sutpen something that has special pertinence to the tragic dilemmas of the South, the aspect of the story to stress is not the downfall of Thomas Sutpen, a man who is finally optimistic, rationalistic, and afflicted with elephantiasis of the will. Instead, he ought to attend to the story of Sutpen's children.

The story of Judith, though muted and played down in terms of the whole novel, is one of the most moving that Faulkner has ever written. She has in her the best of her father's traits. She is the stout-hearted little girl who witnesses without flinching scenes which force poor Henry to grow sick and vomit. She is the young woman who falls in love with a fascinating stranger, the friend of her brother, who means to marry him in spite of her father's silent opposition, and who matches her father's strength of will with a quiet strength of her own. She endures the horror of her fiancé's murder and buries his body. She refuses to commit suicide; she keeps the place going for her father's return. Years later it is Judith who sees to it that Bon's mistress has an opportunity to visit his grave, who brings Bon's child to live with her after his mother's death and, at least in Quentin's reconstruction of events, tries to get the little boy to recognize her as his aunt and to set him free, pushing him on past the barriers of color. When she fails to do so, she still tries to protect him. She nurses him when he sickens of yellow fever, and she dies with him in the epidemic. She is one of Faulkner's finest characters of endurance—and not merely through numb, bleak stoicism but also through compassion and love. Judith is doomed by misfortunes not of her making, but she is not warped and twisted by them. Her humanity survives them.

Because Henry knew what presumably Judith did not know, the secret of Bon's birth, his struggle—granted the circumstances of his breeding, education, and environment—was more difficult than Judith's. He had not merely to endure but to act, and yet any action that he could take would be cruelly painful. He was compelled to an agonizing decision. One element that rendered tragic any choice he might make is revealed in Henry's last action, his coming home to die. One might have thought that after some forty years, Henry would have stayed in Mexico or California or New York or wherever he was, but the claims of locality and family are too strong and he returns to Sutpen's Hundred.

Absalom, Absalom! is the most memorable of Faulkner's novels—and memorable in a very special way. Though even the intelligent reader may feel at times some frustration with the powerful but darkly involved story, with its patches of murkiness and its almost willful complications of plot, he will find himself haunted by individual scenes and episodes, rendered with almost compulsive force. He will probably remember vividly such a scene as Henry's confrontation of his sister Judith after four years of absence at war—the boy in his "patched and faded gray tunic," crashing into the room in which his sister stands clutching against her partially clothed nakedness the yellowed wedding dress, and shouting to her: "Now you cant marry him. . . because he's dead. . . I killed him." Or there is Miss Rosa's recollection of the burial of Charles Bon. As she talks to Quentin she relives the scene: the "slow, maddening rasp, rasp, rasp, of the saw" and "the flat deliberate hammer blows" as Wash and another white man work at the coffin through the "slow and sunny afternoon," with Judith in her faded dress and "faded gingham sunbonnet. . . giving them directions about making it." Miss Rosa, who has never seen Bon alive and for whom he is therefore a fabulous creature, a mere dream, recalls that she "tried to take the full weight of the coffin" as they carried it down the stairs in order "to prove to myself that he was really in it."

There is the wonderful scene of Thomas Sutpen's return to Sutpen's Hundred, the iron man dismounting from his "gaunt and jaded horse," saying to Judith, "Well, daughter," and touching his bearded lips to her forehead. There follows an exchange that is as laconically resonant as any in

Greek tragedy: "'Henry's not—?' 'No. He's not here.'—'Ah. And—?' 'Yes. Henry killed him.'" With the last sentence Judith bursts into tears, but it is the only outburst of which Judith is ever guilty.

The reader will remember also the scenes of Sutpen's boyhood and young manhood—perhaps most vivid of all of them, that in which the puzzled boy is turned away from the plantation door by the liveried servant. Sometimes the haunting passage is one of mere physical description: the desolate Sutpen burial ground with the "flat slabs. . . cracked across the middle by their own weight (and vanishing into the hole where the brick coping of one vault had fallen in was a smooth faint path worn by some small animal—possum probably—by generations of some small animal since there could have been nothing to eat in the grave for a long time) though the lettering was quite legible: *Ellen Coldfield Sutpen. Born October 9, 1817. Died January 23, 1863.*" One remembers also the account of something that had taken place earlier in this same graveyard, when Bon's octoroon mistress, a "magnolia-faced woman a little plumper now, a woman created of by and for darkness whom the artist Beardsley might have dressed, in a soft flowing gown designed not to infer bereavement or widowhood. . . knelt beside the grave and arranged her skirts and wept," while beside her stood her "thin delicate child" with its "smooth ivory sexless face."

There is, too, the ride out to Sutpen's Hundred in the "furnacebreathed" Mississippi night in which Quentin shares his buggy with the frail and fanatical Miss Rosa, and smells her "fusty camphor-reeking shawl" and even her "airless black cotton umbrella." On this journey, as Miss Rosa clutches to her a flashlight and a hatchet, the implements of her search, it seems to Quentin that he can hear "the single profound suspiration of the parched earth's agony rising toward the imponderable and aloof stars." Most vivid of all is the great concluding scene in which Clytie, seeing the ambulance approaching to bear Henry away, fires "the monstrous tinder-dry rotten shell" of a house, and from an upper window defies the intruders, her "tragic gnome's face beneath the clean headrag, against a red background of fire, seen for a moment between two swirls of smoke, looking down at them, perhaps not even now with triumph and no more of despair than it had ever worn, possibly even serene above the melting clapboards."

These brilliantly realized scenes reward the reader and sustain him as he struggles with the novel; but it ought to be remembered that they are given their power by the way in which the novel is structured and thus constitute a justification of that peculiar structure. . .

Absalom, Absalom! is in many respects the most brilliantly written of all Faulkner's novels, whether one considers its writing line by line and paragraph by paragraph, or its structure, in which we are moved up from one suspended note to a higher suspended note and on up further still to an almost intolerable climax. The intensity of the book is a function of the structure. The deferred and suspended resolutions are necessary if the great scenes are to have their full vigor and significance. Admittedly, the novel is a difficult one, but the difficulty is not forced and factitious. It is the price that has to be paid by the reader for the novel's power and significance. There are actually few instances in modern fiction of a more perfect adaptation of form to matter and of an intricacy that justifies itself at every point through the significance and intensity which it makes possible.

Source: Cleanth Brooks, "History and the Sense of the Tragic: *Absalom, Absalom!*," in *Faulkner: A Collection of Critical Essays,* edited by Robert Penn Warren, Prentice-Hall, Inc., 1996, pp. 186–203.

Sources

Brooks, Cleanth, *William Faulkner: The Yoknapatawpha Country,* Yale University Press, 1963.

Caesar, Judith, "Patriarchy, Imperialism, and Knowledge," in *North Dakota Quarterly,* Vol. 62, No. 4, Fall 1994–1995, pp. 164–74.

"Manners and Etiquette," in *Encyclopedia of American Social History,* Charles Scribner's Sons, 1993.

Millgate, Michael, *The Achievement of William Faulkner,* Constable, 1966.

Minter, David, *American Writers, Retrospective Supplement,* Charles Scribner's Sons, 1998.

Further Reading

Backman, Melvin, *Faulkner, The Major Years: A Critical Study,* Indiana University Press, 1966.

Backman reviews Faulkner's major writing, both novels and short stories, and provides a critical overview of the author's development and contribution to American letters.

Brooks, Cleanth, *William Faulkner: Toward Yoknapatawpha and Beyond,* Yale University Press, 1978.

Respected literary critic Cleanth Brooks focuses on Faulkner's Yoknapatawpha stories, exploring why they are important to Faulkner's writing as a whole and what importance they have in the American literary tradition. Brooks evaluates early influences and innovations made by Faulkner over the course of his writing career.

Cowley, Malcolm, ed., *The Portable Faulkner,* Viking, 1946.

When Cowley, a literary historian and poet, collected Faulkner's writing in this volume, he renewed interest in Faulkner at a time when Faulkner's work was being neglected and narrowly categorized as regional writing. Critics often note that many of Faulkner's novels had gone out of print prior to the publication of Cowley's collection.

Edenfield, Olivia Carr, " 'Endure and Then Endure': Rosa Coldfield's Search for a Role in William Faulkner's *Absalom, Absalom!*," in *Southern Literary Journal,* Vol. 32, No. 1, Fall 1999, pp. 59–70.

Edenfield examines Rosa Coldfield's quest for a feminine role in Faulkner's novel.

Faulkner, William, *Collected Stories,* Random House, 1950.

This volume collects Faulkner's short stories. It has been reprinted over the years for its value to students of Faulkner.

———, *A Fable,* Random House, 1954.

This is the novel for which Faulkner was awarded the Pulitzer Prize in 1955.

———, *The Reivers,* Random House, 1962.

This is the novel for which Faulkner won the 1963 Pulitzer Prize.

———, *William Faulkner's Speech of Acceptance Upon the Award of the Nobel Prize for Literature: Delivered in Stockholm, 10th December 1950,* Chatto and Windus, 1951.

This booklet contains Faulkner's memorable and moving acceptance speech upon winning the Nobel Prize for literature.

Meriwether, James B., and Michael Millgate, eds., *Lion in the Garden: Interviews with William Faulkner, 1926–1962,* Random House, 1968.

This collection of interviews contains the reclusive author's views on literature and a variety of other subjects.

All the King's Men

Robert Penn Warren

1946

Critics greeted the August 1946 publication of *All the King's Men* with immediate high praise. Diana Trilling in the *Nation* proclaimed it "a very remarkable piece of novel-writing," adding, "I doubt indeed whether it can be matched in American fiction." Two years later, Walter Allen, reviewing the novel's British release in *The New Statesman & Nation* called it "a very formidable attempt at a novel on the grand scale."

On a very basic level, Robert Penn Warren's *All the King's Men* can be identified as a *roman à clef,* a novel in which real persons appear as fictional characters. Readers recognized the novel's demagogic southern governor, Willie Stark, as similar to Huey P. Long, "the Kingfish," former governor of Louisiana and that state's U. S. senator in the mid-1930s. Jack Burden, right-hand man to Governor Stark, narrates the novel, recounting the rise and fall of his boss. Willie starts as an idealistic young lawyer, committed to helping the "little guy," but evolves into a politician whose power hinges on the numerous shady deals he makes to carry out his vision of what government should be doing.

But multiple generations of readers can testify that *All the King's Men* is much more than merely a political or historical novel. Jack's story parallels Willie's; he is a young man struggling to understand who he is and what he believes in. His and Willie's personal transformations rise above the mere retelling of a political tragedy.

If there was any doubt as to the novel's ongoing influence, in 1996, Joe Klein, under the name

Robert Penn Warren

Anonymous, published *Primary Colors,* a novel based on Bill Clinton's political rise and machinations. The novel was deeply influenced by Warren's *All the King's Men.*

Author Biography

Robert Penn Warren is best known for his 1946 Pulitzer Prize-winning novel *All the King's Men,* chronicling the rise and fall of Willie Stark, the powerful governor of a southern state. Although Warren continually denied the connection, most critics agree that the novel is a thinly disguised telling of the life story of Huey P. Long, the populist governor of Louisiana during the 1930s. Like Stark, Long was assassinated in 1935 by a physician although the real-life assassin had fuzzier motives than the fictional Dr. Adam Stanton has when he murders Stark in the state capital.

Born in Guthrie, Kentucky, on April 24, 1905, Warren grew up in the southern agricultural tradition and was nurtured in oral history and poetry by his maternal grandfather. Warren planned to become a naval officer and was accepted into the United States Naval Academy, but an injury to his eye kept him from attending. Instead, he went to

Vanderbilt University in 1921 to study chemical engineering. Within a matter of weeks he realized he was much more interested in literature and history. His freshman English teacher, fellow southerner John Crowe Ransom, invited him to join the Fugitives, a group that met to discuss American social issues and literature—quite an honor for someone so young. Even though he received a degree from Vanderbilt in 1925 and went on to attend other prestigious educational institutions, Warren reported that he always considered this experience with the Fugitives to be a critical part of his education, fueling his interest in poetry, critical theory, and the struggle of southern agrarian traditions against the cultural clout of the industrial North.

Warren received a master's degree from the University of California at Berkeley in 1927 and attended Yale and Oxford as a Rhodes scholar. In 1929, he published his first book, the nonfiction *John Brown: The Making of a Martyr.* He began teaching English at the Louisiana State University in 1934. While teaching in Baton Rouge, Warren had a front-row view of the political machinations of Governor Long. During this time, he also co-founded the literary journal *Southern Review* with Cleanth Brooks and Charles Pipkin. The journal espoused the New Criticism, which argues for an analytic reading of a text and for appreciating the text on its own, independent of external information.

In the late 1930s and early 1940s, Warren and Brooks collaborated on a series of influential books on the New Criticism, including *An Approach to Literature* and *Understanding Poetry.* Warren went on to teach at the University of Minnesota and Yale University.

As a poet, playwright, critic, teacher, and novelist, Warren probably won more prizes and honors than any other American writer. He is the only person to have won a Pulitzer Prize for both fiction and poetry and enjoyed a large amount of both critical and commercial success. In 1986, the Library of Congress named Warren the first Poet Laureate of the United States. Warren died of cancer on September 15, 1989, in Stratton, Vermont.

Plot Summary

Chapter One

When *All the King's Men* opens, it is the summer of 1936, but Jack Burden is telling the story of himself and Willie Stark from the vantage point of 1939. Sugar-Boy is driving Governor Willie Stark, his son and his wife, and his assistants Jack Burden, Sadie Burke, and Tiny Duffy to Stark's father's farm outside Mason City, a medium-sized town in the southern United States. They stop in Mason City, where Willie and the others go into a drugstore for a soft drink. From the behavior of the customers and those who work in the store, and from the fact that there is a huge picture of Governor Stark there, he clearly is very well known and well liked among these people.

Willie and the group continue to Willie's widowed father's farm. Willie and the group have come here primarily to take some poignant photographs of Willie at his boyhood home. Sadie, the governor's secretary, alerts Willie and Jack that Judge Irwin has reneged on a promise to support Willie's preferred candidate for the U. S. Senate. After dinner, Willie and Jack drive to Burden's Landing, Judge Irwin's home, as well as Jack's childhood home, to pay a call on the judge. The judge is an old friend of Jack's family, and Jack cautions his boss that the judge does not scare easily.

Willie demands to know why the judge has changed his backing to Callahan, the man running against Willie's candidate, Masters. After Willie vaguely threatens Judge Irwin, the judge tells Willie and Jack to leave. Willie demands that Jack find some dirt on the judge, however long it takes.

The chapter ends with Jack, in 1939, reflecting on what has happened since the summer of 1936. Masters won the Senate race, but he is now dead. Jack's friend, Adam, is also dead, and Jack indicates that he did get some dirt on the judge.

Chapter Two

It is 1922, and Jack is writing for the *Chronicle* and travels to Mason City to find out about a school construction scandal. Willie is the county treasurer, and he is trying to get the people of the county to see that the county commissioners are scheming to give the construction contract to J. H. Moore, a company that has come in with the highest bid but has ties to one of the county commissioners. Willie has reasons to believe that the bricks J. H. Moore will use are substandard. The commissioners argue that the company with the low bid is unacceptable because it will bring in blacks to do the work at low pay, taking jobs away from whites. Lucy, Willie's wife, loses her teaching job, and Willie loses the next election for county treasurer. He goes back to helping his father on their farm and studying for the bar exam.

Two years later, three children die and a number are crippled when the fire escape pulls away from the brick siding of the school house. Willie's earlier warnings are remembered, and he becomes a hero in the county. Willie is drafted to run in the Democratic gubernatorial primary but doesn't realize that he is part of Joe Harrison's campaign plot to siphon rural votes from a third candidate, Sam MacMurfee. Jack is assigned by his newspaper to cover Willie's campaign.

Willie is a terrible campaigner because his speeches are about the technical details of his ideas for a new tax code. Sadie Burke, who has been secretly assigned to monitor Willie's campaign for Harrison, finally can't stand that Willie is so naïve, so she tells him all about the scheme. Willie is angry and gets drunk for the first time. Jack helps him make a campaign barbecue the next day, at which he tells the voters how he has been duped. The crowd loves his "I am a hick, just like you" speech. He drops out of the campaign, backs MacMurfee, and swears that he will be back.

In 1930, Willie runs in the Democratic primary again and goes on to win the governorship. Jack resigns from the newspaper because he doesn't feel good about using his column to support the other candidate, which the paper's management has been pressuring him to do. Willie calls him and offers him a job.

Chapter Three

The year is 1933. Jack shares more about his childhood and family. He takes some time off and returns to Burden's Landing to visit his mother. They go to Judge Irwin's house for dinner, where a conversation about Governor Stark begins among the guests. The guests complain that he has "taxed this state half to death," but Judge Irwin responds that government must provide more services now than in the past. When Jack speaks about his boss, the guests are stunned because they see that he actually believes in Stark.

Back at work, Jack walks in on the governor berating Byram White, the state's auditor, for attempting to scam the state out of some money. Willie has agreed to fix it for Byram so that he is not impeached, but this means he will be beholden to Willie for the rest of his life. Willie blackmails the legislators who want to prosecute White (and take Willie down with him). Hugh Miller, Willie's attorney general, resigns over this matter. Lucy becomes even more estranged from Willie and eventually moves out of the governor's mansion. In

1934, Willie runs again and wins by a huge majority.

Chapter Four

Jack remembers the visit he and the governor paid to Judge Irwin in the middle of the night and the demand Willie made, concerning Jack digging up some dirt on Irwin. This particular effort to uncover a man's past is Jack's second such historical excursion. The first took place when Jack was in graduate school when he took a year or more to read and write about the journal of his Great Uncle Cass Mastern, who died in the Civil War. Jack receives the journal from another relative and ends up using it as the basis for his doctoral dissertation in history. Jack never finishes the dissertation but falls into one of his depressive states, which he calls the Great Sleep. The weight of his ancestor's history weighs heavily on Jack's mind, and he still feels the evil and shame of slavery.

Chapter Five

Jack, after months and months of research and travel and talking to many people, does find the skeleton in Judge Irwin's closet. He starts by figuring out when the judge was in need of money and follows the trail to when the judge was the state attorney general under Governor Stanton (Anne and Adam's father). He discovers that the American Electric Power Company bribed the judge with a high paying position after he left public service, to dismiss a case against another energy company associated with American Electric. When American Electric gave Irwin the position and the salary, it fired the current employee in that job, Mortimer Littlepaugh. Littlepaugh went to Governor Stanton to tell him about the scheme, but the governor would not listen to him. Soon after, Mortimer fell from a hotel window and died. But, his sister still has the suicide letter Mortimer wrote her, outlining the entire episode. In March of 1937, Jack finds the sister and the letter.

Chapter Six

While Jack is researching the skeletons in Judge Irwin's closet, between the summer of 1936 and the spring of 1937, a number of things happen. One is that Tiny Duffy is annoying Willie by suggesting that the construction contract for the new Willie Stark Hospital go to Gummy Larson, a contractor in MacMurfee's district. The hospital, in fact, is occupying a majority of Willie's time and energy, and he intends for it to be the biggest and best free hospital in the world. Willie asks Jack to get Adam Stanton to serve as the hospital's director. Jack asks Adam, but Adam refuses. Anne tells Jack that she really wants Adam to accept the governor's offer. Jack is surprised because, after all, the Stanton family has never been particularly fond of Governor Stark. Jack decides to tell Anne that Judge Irwin took a bribe and that her father was mixed up in it.

A few days later, Anne calls Jack and demands to see the papers that connect her father to the bribery incident. He gives them to her, and she returns them after about a week, noting that she has shown them to Adam and that he has agreed to take the job as director of the Willie Stark Hospital. Later, Jack begins to wonder how Anne knew about the hospital director's job being offered to Adam. He finds out from Sadie that Anne is Willie's mistress. Jack is stunned and goes to see Anne, who admits to the affair.

Chapter Seven

The shock of imagining Anne as Willie's mistress provokes Jack to leave town for about eight days, to drive west to Long Beach, California. He imagines that the West is "the end of History" and where you go "when you get the letter saying: *Flee, all is discovered.*" Along the drive, he sees a "home movie" in his mind of his life, mostly featuring Anne. He remembers most the summer that he came home from college and realized that he was in love with the seventeen-year-old Anne. Eventually, in Jack's memories, they drift apart. Jack leaves graduate school, gets a job at the newspaper, and marries Lois. Anne goes to college for a couple of years, returns to Burden's Landing, and becomes engaged a number of times. The relationships never result in marriage. Lois and Jack's marriage ends in divorce. After sleeping in a Long Beach hotel for a few days, Jack drives back home.

Chapter Eight

After his drive to the West Coast, Jack returns home refreshed, seemingly a changed man. A man hired by MacMurfee comes to Adam's apartment to pressure him to give the hospital construction contract to Larson. This enrages him, and he writes a letter to Willie resigning his position but does not mail it. Anne asks Jack to get Adam to remain the director. Through some fast talking, Jack is successful, and Adam tears up the resignation letter. Anne also mentions to Jack that she loves Willie, and that he intends to marry her after he runs for the U. S. Senate the following year.

Another crisis ensues when Tom apparently gets a girl, Sibyl Frey, pregnant. The girl's father lives in MacMurfee's district. MacMurfee says that he will help Tom get out of the problem if Willie supports him for the Senate race the following year; but Willie is planning to run himself. Willie asks Jack if he was able to get any dirt on Judge Irwin because he thinks he can force the judge to put some pressure on his friend MacMurfee about this incident. Jack replies that before he tells Willie any of what he's found, he needs to speak with the judge.

Jack goes to Burden's Landing to talk to the judge about the bribery, but the judge acts as though he isn't worried and sends Jack away. Later that day, Jack and his mother get a phone call that the judge has shot himself. This is when Jack discovers that the judge was his real father.

Chapter Nine

Willie decides that the only way to deal with MacMurfee is to give the hospital construction contract to Larson—in effect, buying out Larson so that MacMurfee will help him appease Sibyl's father.

Tom is quarterbacking an important game and is injured. At the hospital, the doctors realize that his injuries are severe, and he may be paralyzed for life. Adam, with Willie's consent, operates on Tom in hopes of repairing the damage to his spine. But Tom's spinal cord has been crushed, and the prognosis is complete paralysis.

When Willie gets back to the office a couple of days later, there are indications that the injury to his son has made him see things in a different light. To begin with, he takes the hospital contract away from Larson and demands that Tiny tell Larson this news.

Anne is frantic because Adam has found out about her and Willie; she believes that her relationship with the governor is why he is the new hospital director. She pleads with Jack to search the town for him. She also tells Jack that Willie is breaking it off with her and going back to Lucy.

Jack eventually finds Adam, looking ragged and tired, at the Capital. Adam, feeling that his sister has been debased by being the governor's mistress, quickly shoots Willie, and Sugar-Boy responds by shooting and killing Adam. Willie lives for a few days in the hospital, then dies. Thousands of people from the country and the city throng the funeral.

Chapter Ten

Jack asks Anne if she knows who called Adam and told him about Anne and Willie's relationship. She says no. Jack returns to town to look for Sadie, one of the few people who knew about Anne and Willie. He discovers that she has checked herself into a sanatorium.

Sadie admits that she told Tiny Duffy to call Adam because she was jealous of Willie's affair with Adam's sister, Anne. She now regrets setting the entire tragedy in motion. But, she remembers that Duffy wasn't so horrified by the result because Willie's death advanced him from lieutenant governor to governor. It is implied that Duffy knew his actions might lead to Willie's death. Jack and Sadie hatch a plan to go after Duffy. Duffy offers Jack a job in his administration, but Jack refuses it.

The next time Jack sees Sugar-Boy, he considers telling him of Duffy's role in Willie's death, hoping that Sugar-Boy will kill Duffy. He decides not to do this. As well, he decides not to go after Duffy because that would mean that Anne and Willie's affair would be made public.

Tom eventually dies of pneumonia associated with his paralysis. Jack goes to see Lucy and discovers that she has adopted Sibyl's child, believing it to be Tom's child, too. Jack eventually moves back to Burden's Landing, to Judge Irwin's house, which he has inherited, and marries Anne.

Characters

Ellis Burden

Ellis is Jack's father. He was formerly a well-respected and wealthy attorney from Burden's Landing but left his family to become a missionary in the slums. He spouts religious rhetoric, and the few times Jack visits him, Jack does not understand anything about his father or why he left the family.

Jack Burden

Jack is the first-person narrator of the novel. He is the only son of a well-to-do family in Burden's Landing, named for his relatives. Jack begins his career as a journalist working for the *Chronicle* but quits after he refuses to write a column in support of Sam MacMurfee's gubernatorial campaign. Eventually, he works as Willie Stark's hatchet man.

Media Adaptations

- In 1949, Columbia Pictures released a film based on *All the King's Men* and having the same title. It stars Broderick Crawford, John Ireland, and Mercedes McCambridge. It won the 1950 Oscar for Best Picture and garnered other Oscar awards and nominations. The movie is available on videotape.

- The novel was adapted for television as an opera by Carlisle Floyd and entitled *Willie Stark.*

- Adrian Hall adapted the novel for his play *All the King's Men*, presented by the Trinity Repertory Company of Providence, Rhode Island, in April 1987.

Jack's mother is astounded that Jack works for Willie, and on numerous occasions she tells Jack that any one of their well-placed friends would be happy to find him another job. Jack always refuses because he takes some pride in having made his own way throughout his adult life. When his mother expresses disappointment that he wants to attend the local state university instead of an East Coast college, he becomes angry and sarcastic toward her, finally telling her that he doesn't need her money.

Jack has a very subdued personality and has periods of depression. He refers to these as "Great Sleeps"; he sleeps a lot and doesn't leave the house much. He falls into one of these episodes in school when he is about to finish his doctoral degree and again after he leaves the newspaper.

Jack is not a very companionable man and appears to have little social life. His closest friends as an adult are still his former childhood playmates, Anne and Adam Stanton, the children of one of the state's past governors. Jack and Anne fell in love when he was twenty-one and she was seventeen, but for most of his adult life Anne has not returned Jack's interest in her.

Although he doesn't see him often, Jack has a special relationship with the family friend, Judge Irwin. When Jack was a child, he and the judge worked together on building military models. Jack is very aware of the judge's exemplary military service and respects him greatly for this. Jack could not get into the army because of bad feet.

Lois Burden

Lois Burden (her maiden name is Seager) is Jack's ex-wife. He leaves her because of her intellectual dullness, despite the fact that they are physically attracted to each other.

Sadie Burke

Sadie is Willie's secretary and occasionally his lover. She begins the story as an assistant to Joe Harrison when he is running for governor but is the one who breaks it to Willie that he has been taken for a sucker, having been encouraged to run in the primary to siphon off votes from Harrison's main opponent.

Sadie is not a beautiful woman but is very sharp. The indication is that she has pulled herself up from very impoverished beginnings and has made something of her life by her smarts and her willingness to work hard. Jack finds her moderately attractive and is impressed by her political savvy and her toughness.

Count Covelli

Count Covelli is Jack's mother's second husband. She meets him in Europe on one of her trips. He is handsome and rides horses well, but apparently abuses Jack's mother. She eventually divorces him.

Tiny Duffy

Tiny is first seen as a campaign aide to Joe Harrison and is involved in tricking Willie into running in the Democratic primary to siphon votes off Harrison's opponent, MacMurfee. Despite this history, Tiny later works as an assistant to Willie and serves as his lieutenant governor. When Jack asks him why he keeps Tiny around, Willie answers, "'When they come to you talking sweet, you better not listen to anything they say. I don't aim to forget that.'"

Sibyl Frey

Sibyl gets pregnant and claims that Tom Stark is the father. She and her father live in the fourth district, MacMurfee's power base, and this event sets off another struggle between Willie and Mac-Murfee.

Joe Harrison

Joe Harrison is a candidate in the Democratic gubernatorial primary. His aides execute a scheme that encourages Willie to run in the primary. His political bases are the urban areas of the state.

Judge Montague Irwin

Judge Irwin is a long-time family friend of the Burdens and lives near Jack's family home in Burden's Landing. He is well educated, a decorated World War I hero, and a political enemy of Willie Stark. Willie is angered when the judge switches his backing from Willie's preferred senate candidate to another candidate, and when the judge doesn't back down, Willie tells Jack to find any dirt he can on the judge. The judge cannot understand why Jack works for Willie.

Jack has a special relationship with the judge and has childhood memories of the two of them playing with models of military equipment and plotting the movements of ancient battles. When Jack finds out about a bribe the judge took twenty-five years previously, he holds onto the information until he can show it to the judge.

Gummy Larson

Tiny wants Gummy Larson to receive the construction contract for the new Willie Stark Hospital, but Willie will hear none of it. Larson is a powerful businessman in the fourth district, which is run by Willie's enemy, MacMurfee.

Mortimer Littlepaugh

Mortimer Littlepaugh is the vice president and counsel for the American Electric Power Company until he is asked to leave to make room for Judge Irwin. He kills himself and leaves a suicide letter incriminating Judge Irwin and ex-governor Stanton.

Sam MacMurfee

MacMurfee is a candidate in the Democratic gubernatorial primary. His political base is in the rural areas of the state, and Willie is unwittingly brought in by Joe Harrison's campaign to siphon off votes from MacMurfee. Willie discovers this and steps out of the primary, swinging his support to MacMurfee. MacMurfee wins the primary and the election. He is governor until Willie wins the next election but remains a constant thorn in Willie's side.

Hugh Miller

Hugh Miller is attorney general under Governor Willie Stark. He was chosen early in Willie's career as a good person to have around because he is a war hero, was educated at Harvard, and has "clean hands and a pure heart." Eventually he resigns over Stark's unethical behavior in the Byram White incident.

Mrs. Murrell

Mrs. Murrell is Jack Burden's mother. She is an attractive woman in her mid-fifties and is now married to Theodore Murrell, her third husband. She comes from a modest background in rural Arkansas, where Ellis Burden met her and brought her back to Burden's Landing to make her his wife. Mrs. Murrell appears to want only the best for her son and is puzzled by his lack of interest in money and social position. His job with Willie Stark is beyond her, and she continues to suggest that various family friends could help him find other work.

Theodore Murrell

Theodore Murrell is Jack's mother's current husband. He is younger than she is, blond, and handsome. Jack refers to him as the "Young Executive."

Sugar-Boy O'Sheean

Sugar-Boy is Willie's driver while he is governor. He is a reckless driver, taking huge risks with the lives of his passengers by driving well over the speed limit and by passing slow-moving vehicles in the face of oncoming vehicles on the highway. Sugar-Boy carries a .38 special and stutters. Even though he does not appear to be very bright, Willie trusts him to be around when Willie is involved in private conversations. Sugar-Boy received this name because of his fondness for eating sugar cubes.

Dolph Pillsbury

Dolph is the Mason County Commission chairman who helps Willie get into his first political position as county treasurer. He and Willie are at odds, though, when Willie gets wind of a crooked scheme in which Pillsbury is involved.

Sen-Sen Puckett

Sen-Sen is an aide to Joe Harrison's gubernatorial campaign and is credited with probably being the one who thought up the scheme that had Willie running in the primary. He and Sadie date,

but not seriously. He gets his name from chewing Sen-Sen mints to keep his breath fresh.

Adam Stanton

Adam is a childhood friend of Jack, the brother of Anne Stanton, and the son of ex-governor Stanton. He is a surgeon and does much of his work for free. He lives in a small apartment where the only valuable piece of furniture is a piano, and he has never married. Jack is able to convince Adam to accept Willie's offer to become the director of the new Willie Stark Hospital, even though Adam does not like the way Willie does business. In the end, Adam murders Willie and is in turn shot to death by Willie's driver, Sugar-Boy.

Anne Stanton

Anne is a childhood friend of Jack, the sister of Adam Stanton, and the daughter of ex-governor Stanton. She is tall and slender. She has never married. Jack was once in love with her and has attempted to date her but is always rebuffed. Anne becomes Willie's mistress. She hides this from Adam and Jack, but they eventually discover it. She does charity work with the underprivileged and sick and seeks to open a children's home.

Lucy Stark

Lucy Stark is Willie's wife. She believes deeply in Willie when he begins in politics but wishes that he would stay in Mason County, practicing law and helping on his father's farm.

Warren draws Lucy as a conservative character who does not drink and behaves very properly. She and Willie have one child, Tom. Willie worries that Lucy is turning Tom into a "momma's boy" because he studies a lot and makes good grades.

Lucy stands by Willie throughout much of the turmoil of his political career and through his womanizing, but eventually she leaves him. Lucy travels to Florida for her "health." When she returns, she moves to her sister's place in the country. Even after that, Lucy occasionally comes to town to attend special events at Willie's side, to keep up appearances for Willie's political career.

Old Man Stark

Old Man Stark ("Pappy") is Willie Stark's father. He is a widower living on the family farm, a very modest property that Willie is improving in small ways, such as by adding a water pump.

Tom Stark

Tom is Lucy and Willie's only child. He is a well-behaved and studious child, but Warren indicates that he has some underlying anger and sullenness. He is a star football player for his high school team. Tom seems to be aware of the increasing tension between his mother and father as Willie's career progresses. When Willie runs home to tell his wife about a rally in his support, Tom appears in front of Lucy's locked bedroom door and tells his father that she does not wish to be disturbed. As he gets to be a teenager, he becomes surly and argumentative and also realizes that he is blessed with great athletic ability.

Willie Stark

Willie Stark ("Boss") is the state governor, elected in 1930. He began his political career in the early 1920s as the county treasurer for Mason County. Willie was raised on a farm, and his political style is grassroots.

Willie's introduction to politics exposed both his sincere desire to help the "little guy" and his naiveté. Willie unsuccessfully tried to warn Mason County voters about their corrupt county commissioners' scheme to buy defective bricks for a schoolhouse project. The schoolhouse was built, but two years later, the school's fire escape collapsed, resulting in the deaths of three children. After that, Willie became a hero in the county.

Willie practices law in Mason City until a group asks him to run in the Democratic gubernatorial primary. Unbeknownst to Willie, Joe Harrison's campaign is using him to draw rural votes from Sam MacMurfee, another candidate in the Democratic primary. Eventually, Sadie and Jack tell Willie of this scheme. He angrily exposes the entire ruse to the voters, drops out of the race to support MacMurfee, and successfully captures the governor's mansion in the next election.

Willie is a brilliant politician and knows how to manage both his friends and his enemies to his advantage. He is ruthless but desperately wants to do good and have the love of the voters. Willie ends up making some sneaky deals, offering bribes, and threatening his enemies with exposure but believes that the good coming from all of this bad is the price he and others must pay for a government that helps the "little guy."

Byram White

Byram White is the state auditor while Willie is governor. Willie catches him trying to set up an illegal scheme to get rich and, instead of allowing him to be impeached, creates a situation where Byram's job is saved, but he owes Willie his career and his life. To do this, Willie digs up dirt on the group in the state legislature that is going after White and blackmails them. Willie's attorney general quits over this affair, and his wife becomes even more alienated from him.

Themes

History

An overarching theme in All the King's Men is history and how it affects the present. Structurally, the entire novel can be viewed as the history of Willie Stark's political rise and fall, mimicking in many ways the rise and fall of the real-life southern governor Huey P. Long. Willie uses his associates' personal histories to get them to do his bidding. He believes that all people have something in their past that they do not want known.

Warren places the history of Jack Burden's search for identity and maturity alongside Willie's history. Burden studied history in college and wrote about an ancestor's journal in his abandoned doctoral dissertation; the excerpts of Cass Mastern's journal add yet another layer of history to the novel. In fact, Jack is a repository for histories. Some are secret histories, such as Anne's information about her affair with Willie, and some are not-so-secret histories, such as Cass Mastern's journal.

When Jack has had enough of political machinations, he leaves town and drives to the West, where, he imagines, there is no history—or at least history does not matter and a person can start again without a past.

Finally, when Jack comes to terms with his life and his own past at the end of the novel, he states that he and Anne will "go out of the house and into the convulsion of the world, out of history and into history and the awful responsibility of Time."

Political Power and Corruption

The novel tracks the career of Willie Stark, an absolute expert on wielding political power and achieving what he wants done. Willie receives his baptism by fire into the brotherhood of politicians as an unwitting part of Joe Harrison's scheme to cheat Sam MacMurfee out of the rural vote in a gubernatorial primary. Before he is told of the scheme, Willie is an earnest, if naïve, public servant, traveling throughout the state giving dry but factual campaign speeches. He is motivated by the desire to do good for the little people in the state. The knowledge that he has been duped lights a fire under him, and he gives a speech that makes people realize he has potential as a politician.

When Willie becomes governor, he does not lose the desire to help the voters, but he has acquired the savvy about how that must be done. He now believes that in the world of politics the ends justify the means, and he does everything possible to make sure that his vision succeeds, no matter the cost. Willie believes that sometimes bad things must be done before good can be accomplished and that "goodness" is made out of "badness" because there isn't anything else to make it out of. During a rally in chapter six, Willie tells the supportive crowd, "Your will is my strength," and "Your need is my Justice."

While Willie will swing a contract a certain way to get something accomplished, he feels less comfortable buying out an adversary and more comfortable having that person indebted to him. When he is forced to give the new Willie Stark Hospital construction contract to Larson because his son has most likely made a girl pregnant, Willie gets drunk and shouts, "They made me do it." Says Tiny Duffy in chapter five, "He'd rather bust a man than buy him." There is little illicit exchange of money in Willie Stark's administration and much exchange of secret information. As Jack says in chapter eight, "knowledge is power."

Alienation

Even though he is the son of a prominent family, Jack Burden suffers from a lack of bonds; he feels no strong connection with anything or anyone. He wants nothing to do with his supposed father, the attorney-turned-missionary, and he feels no warmth for his mother. He has no network of friends outside of work. Anne and Adam are his only social contacts, and they are friends from childhood. His attempt to consummate his relationship with Anne fails until the very end of the novel, and he cannot finish his dissertation, primarily because to complete these things would be to make a commitment or shoulder an obligation.

Jack's living arrangements are spartan and noncommittal; he lives in a residential hotel with very few personal items. When Jack finds the real world, as he has constructed it, too much, he retreats into one of his Great Sleeps.

Topics for Further Study

- *All the King's Men* was made into a movie in 1949. If you were making a new movie of the novel, what actors would star in your version? Would you change anything about the place or time of the novel in your movie? What theme song would you use and who would perform it? Write a "pitch" for your movie that answers these questions and urges a studio to finance your film.

- Would you like to have a job like the job Jack Burden does for Governor Willie Stark? Write an opinion essay that answers this question and gives reasons for your opinion.

- Politics in *All the King's Men* is filled with bribery and schemes and secret deals. Do you think that politics today is similar or different? Explain your answer in an essay.

- Do research to learn about Huey P. Long. Compare and contrast Long and Willie Stark, presenting your findings in a graphic organizer, such as a Venn diagram or a two-column table with the headings Same and Different.

- Jack observes a frontal lobe surgery late in the novel. Learn about these surgeries and why they were used for treating mental illnesses. Are they still being done today? Present your findings in a research report.

When Jack begins to work for Governor Stark, he is someone who views the passing world from cars and trains. He wonders about the men and women he sees from his position on the road but never wades into the fray. Even before he is on the governor's staff, Jack almost effortlessly performs the duties of a newspaper reporter, researching and investigating but never becoming emotionally involved in a story. When he goes to Mason City for the first time to investigate the story about the school house contract, his technique for getting information out of the old men who hang out on the bench in front of the harness shop is to slide in and out of their conversation, nearly undetected.

Jack's ability to conduct research on Willie's enemies and think about how the information might be used makes him invaluable. Even when investigating the background of his close family friend, Judge Irwin, he pursues his goal with a kind of relentless and cold fervor, never imagining the impact of the fruits of his labors.

Duty and Responsibility

Jack's search for who he is and what he believes occupies a large portion of the novel. While he is telling the story of how Willie Stark became the governor, he is also telling the story of how he changed from a man with no connections with the world around him into someone who can begin to take some responsibility for his actions.

Jack begins to understand how his choices affect those around him after Judge Irwin's suicide. The shock of the judge's death as well as the discovery that the man was his biological father force him to see that the choices he makes have results; he also comes to understand that he must learn to deal with those results. As he watches the effects of his actions, he also sees the effects of others' actions for the first time; in chapter nine, Jack reminds Willie that his son Tom's indiscretions have forced Willie to have to deal with Larson. Further, Jack sees Tiny and Sadie's personal resentments against Willie snowball into a scheme that results in Willie's death. But after all the blood and violence of the novel's final pages, Jack rejects the easy opportunity to set in motion yet another killing, realizing the responsibility that would be on his hands if he said but a few simple words to Sugar-Boy.

By the end of the story, Jack has begun to understand that he is an undeniable part of history and that he must take responsibility for who he is and what he does. Toward this end, Jack takes in Ellis Burden, marries Anne, and tries to honorably dispose of the money he inherits from Judge Irwin's estate.

Style

Point-of-View

The character of Jack Burden tells the story of *All the King's Men* from his point of view. While most of Jack's narration is first person, Warren occasionally switches Jack's narration to third person. In those few cases, the narrator is put at a greater distance from the story and the action, as if Jack is speaking about someone other than himself.

Chapter four includes an instance of Jack speaking of himself in the third person. Jack is telling about a time when his mother came to the university to visit him in his apartment, a filthy, rundown flat he shared with two other students. Upon leaving the apartment, Jack's mother asked him why he lived in such a place, to which he responded: " 'It's what I'm built for, I reckon.' " Another incidence appears at the end of chapter one, when Jack alters his name slightly, creating even more distance between the action and the narrator. When Willie, the "Boss," asks Jack to find dirt in Judge Irwin's past, and to make it stick, Jack says, almost to himself, "Little Jackie made it stick, all right."

Repetition of Words and Phrases

When an author repeats particular words or phrases, he or she is usually alerting the reader to pay attention to these passages. Warren does this on several occasions, including when Jack suggests to Willie that the judge might not have any skeletons in his closet. Willie responds in chapters one, four, and five each time with: "Man is conceived in sin and born in corruption and he passeth from the stink of the didie to the stench of the shroud. There is always something."

Sometimes, an author may repeat a phrase simply because of the way it sounds. In chapter seven, when Jack remembers Anne as a seventeen-year-old, he remembers her with a "tight-muscled, soft-fleshed, golden-shouldered body." The words and the beat they produce are repeated again in the paragraph following this sentence.

Foreshadowing

When a story is told through a single first-person narrator, that narrator has the power to tell facts and events in any order he or she chooses. In *All the King's Men,* Jack tells the story of Willie Stark from the vantage point of 1939 so he has had time to think about how the story should be told, what information he wants to release, and when he will release that information for the maximum effect. This provides Jack with an almost omniscient view, and allows him to foreshadow certain events. In chapter one, Jack provides a list of people who will be dead three years later, including Willie and Adam, but doesn't give any information about how or why. And when Willie offers Jack a job that he can't quite define, Willie says, "Something will

turn up." Jack remembers from his vantage point of 1939, almost with a wink, "He was right about that."

Simile

Warren spent much of his writing life as a poet, and his rich use of imagery is apparent in the prose of *All the King's Men.* One tool he uses frequently is the simile, comparing one thing with another using words such as *like* or *as.* Throughout Jack's narration, similes give a broader understanding of an event or moment. In chapter two, Jack is watching Tiny Duffy fall off a stage and describes Tiny as having "a face which was like a surprised custard pie with a hole scooped out of the middle of the meringue." Many of Warren's similes compare a human feature, such as a face or a voice, to an inanimate thing. Some are brief, but many cover several lines, such as the one comparing a house to a middle-aged woman in chapter eight. As well, Warren uses similes when expressing difficult concepts. Describing how Cass Mastern sees interconnectedness of events, Warren explains:

> He learned that the world is like an enormous spider web and if you touch it, however lightly, at any point, the vibration ripples to the remotest perimeter and the drowsy spider feels the tingle.

Sarcasm

Jack often uses sarcasm when he feels threatened or has been taken off his guard and wants to appear in control. When Anne tells Jack that she has had lunch with Willie, he hides his shock by responding, "Your frock, my dear—what frock did you wear? And flowers? Did you drink champagne cocktails?" Jack also is sarcastic with Ellis Burden, and with some of Willie's assistants. He is even sarcastic about his own situation as Willie's hatchet man. When Jack is searching for information on Judge Irwin for Willie, he goes to Anne. She wants to know who is interested in Judge Irwin, and Jack answers, belittling himself and his position, "It is a pal wants to know. He is my best pal. He hands it to me on the first of the month."

Historical Context

Louisiana Politics and Huey P. Long

The Populist Movement, which espoused increased powers for the farmer and the working man, swept through a large part of the post-Civil War South but failed to find a foothold in

Compare & Contrast

- **1930s:** A huge dust storm, described by some as a "Black Blizzard," strikes Kansas in 1934. For the next six years, farmers in the Midwest and Southwest struggle to grow crops and raise livestock in a terrain that is nearly stripped of topsoil and suffers from high temperatures and little rain. Hundreds of thousands of Midwesterners move to California, hoping for a better life.

  Today: Some experts worry that the increasing temperatures and reduced rainfall in parts of the United States have increased the risk of severe drought. The U.S. Department of Agriculture maintains numerous assistance programs to help victims of drought, and the federal government's National Oceanic and Atmospheric Administration maintains a Drought Information Center.

- **1930s:** The American Hospital Association creates the Blue Cross plan for hospital costs in 1933, which leads to the Blue Shield program in 1939. In 1938, a national health conference emphasizes the need for a national health program. In 1939, supporters introduce a bill in Congress incorporating the report's recommendations, but it fails to pass the House. Willie Stark's opinion that access to health care is a basic right is still considered radical.

  Today: More than forty-two million Americans are without health insurance, and the issue continues to be one of the most hotly debated topics in the public arena.

- **1930s:** The glamorous world depicted by Hollywood is cited as an important morale-booster during the Great Depression. A groundbreaking film starring Judy Garland, *The Wizard of Oz,* opens in 1939. In the novel, Jack Burden goes to the movies to escape his psychological depressions.

  Today: The movie industry still provides an escape from personal and societal problems. Some organizations and individuals, however, voice concerns that movies are increasingly brutal and have spurred violence at schools and other public places.

Louisiana, thanks to the entrenched wealthy interests that had historically governed Louisiana: Standard Oil, the banks, the railroads, and rich landowners. Average citizens struggled along, sending their children to poorly supported schools over unpaved, pot-holed roads. Many were sharecroppers, who didn't own their own land and who barely made enough money to buy seeds for the next year's crop.

Huey P. Long, the widely acknowledged model for Willie Stark, began his life in politics by winning a position on the state railroad commission. He promptly set up that position as a bully pulpit from which he attacked Standard Oil. He accused the corporate giant of influencing the state government in its favor, making him a hero of the "little people," who felt left out of the prosperity many in Louisiana enjoyed. In 1923, he ran an unsuccessful campaign for the governorship, lacking the usual big-money support a candidate would attract in that state. In 1928, he came back to win, supported by a huge majority. Long's impassioned speeches and vibrantly written pamphlets attracted those who felt it was time for a change.

The tension between the group of wealthy landowners who had ruled Louisiana for a hundred or more years and Long's supporters forms the backdrop for the relationship between Willie Stark and Anne Stanton in the novel. Anne's family was a part of the elite ruling class, and her father had served as governor. Willie stood for clearing out the ruling elite and spreading their wealth through increased taxes. Their affair would have been a scandal not only because Willie was a married man but because of the taboo associated with members of these two classes associating with each other.

As governor, Long instituted a series of programs to benefit what he saw as the majority of Louisiana citizens, who had never enjoyed any representation in their state government. These included public works programs (for bridges, roads, schools, airports, and municipal buildings) that expressed the optimism of a new period. To pay for all of this, he increased the taxes on the smaller and wealthier portion of Louisianans who did not vote for him. His attempt to impose a tax on Standard Oil resulted in an effort to impeach him. This failed, and he emerged from the fight stronger and more popular than ever.

In 1930, Long was elected to the United States Senate, but he still firmly held the reins of power in Louisiana for some time to come. In fact, the Long family controlled state politics in Louisiana until 1960. Long's heavy-handed tactics to achieve his goals and visions were legendary, but apparently Long felt that he had to employ such means to accomplish his goals.

The Dust Bowl

On April 14, 1934, after months of intense drought, extremely high temperatures, and non-stop winds, huge dark dust clouds blotted out the sun in western Kansas. Over the next few days, the clouds of dust sped south and west toward Texas, western Oklahoma, eastern Colorado, and New Mexico, eventually covering more than three hundred thousand square miles. But the dust storms affected more than just these central and western states; between May 10 and 12, 1934, about twelve million tons of soil fell on Chicago, and a dust cloud covered the entire East Coast.

In the areas referred to as the Dust Bowl, agriculture slowed significantly or stopped completely. Temperatures remained above one hundred degrees for weeks on end. The winds from additional dust storms cut down stalks of wheat and covered crops still in the fields waiting to be harvested. As farmers lost their crops, loans became due, and banks foreclosed on many properties and families. More than 350,000 people, often referred to as Okies, left the Dust Bowl for California and what they hoped was a better life.

Unfortunately, California was not the land of milk and honey as so many had hoped. Images from Hollywood films had given the migrants the impression of a golden land where they could make a new start. As in the novel, many who fled to California eventually returned to their homes in the Midwest.

By 1939, heavy rains and efforts by President Roosevelt's administration had reduced the Dust Bowl area from a high of more than eight million acres to a bit over one million acres.

The Great Depression

Within two years of the stock market crash of 1929, economic depression was worldwide. In the United States, unemployment soared from a pre-crash rate of just over three percent to more than twenty-five percent in 1933. The drop in the gross national product (the amount of goods and services produced in a year) by 1933 sent that index to levels not seen in twenty years. Why this happened was a mystery, as there were plenty of men lined up to work while factories stayed shuttered and dark. There had been no war or natural disaster, and yet there were stories of men in the Pacific Northwest setting forest fires just to be hired to extinguish them. Young men wandered the country searching for any kind of work, and families lived in small shantytowns called Hoovervilles (after Herbert Hoover, the president at the time of the crash) on the outskirts of the cities. The suicide rate rose thirty percent between 1928 and 1930. Farmers began dumping or holding back their products to protest the low prices they were receiving. The dust storms in the Midwest also contributed to the depression.

Eventually, through various government efforts, signs of a recovery began to appear in 1937. Huey P. Long, the model for Willie Stark, led a movement that pushed for a dramatic redistribution of wealth through taxes and other programs. But the economy showed mixed signals until after 1939, when the United States began increasing its military spending in anticipation of World War II.

African Americans in the 1930s

The language used in the novel to describe African Americans—specifically the use of the word "nigger"—reflected common practice in the 1930s southern United States. Blacks in the South found movie theaters, water fountains, hotels, restaurants, and swimming pools either off limits or restricted in their use by blacks. In many states, African Americans were kept from voting through a number of techniques including poll taxes and literacy tests. Jim Crow laws (legislation separating the races) in many southern states relegated blacks legally to second-class status. Lynchings of innocent blacks were not uncommon.

But there were signs that the times were changing. Roosevelt appointed blacks to positions in the

John Derek (left) as Tom Stark, John Ireland as Jack Burden, and Broderick Crawford as Willie Stark in the Academy Award-winning 1949 film version of the novel

administration of the New Deal programs and nominated the first African-American federal judge, William Hastie. In 1939, African-American author James Baldwin published *Native Son,* and the book became an immediate hit. African Americans suffered disproportionately from the depression but took steps to help their communities through the economic downturn. For example, in New York, Harlem residents led the "Don't Shop Where You Can't Work" campaign.

Critical Overview

By the time *All the King's Men* was published in 1946, Robert Penn Warren was a highly respected writer, probably better known for his poetry and criticism than for fiction. But this novel firmly placed him on the fiction map, especially with laudatory reviews such as the one written by Diana Trilling in the *Nation:*

> For sheer virtuosity, for the sustained drive of its prose, for the speed and the evenness of its pacing, for its precision of language, its genius of colloqui-

alism, I doubt indeed whether it can be matched in American fiction.

And while critics and readers received the novel with generally high praise, Richard Luckett in *The Spectator* notes that the book caused a fuss upon its release because Willie Stark bore a great resemblance to the audacious and powerful Louisiana governor Huey P. Long, assassinated eleven years prior. Long evoked either adoration or abhorrence, and Warren's attempt to write about him in "a fairly sympathetic manner caused him to be branded a fascist" by some, according to Luckett. Critic R. Gray, in the *Journal of American Studies,* notes that these commentators attacked Warren for squelching some of Long's less pleasant activities for the sake of his tale, asking "how can this ever be defended?" Trilling, too, questions whether Warren properly exposed the evil behind a powerful and corrupt politician, noting, "it is in fact difficult *not* to infer from Mr. Warren's novel that Willie Stark's absolute power is justified by such public benefactions as the fine hospital he builds."

According to Gray, most critics have approached the novel either by taking issue with Warren's accuracy in recounting the story behind Huey Long or by analyzing the book's symbols and images. As well, Gray notes that many critics have attempted to study the novel outside of its obvious historical references, focusing entirely on the author's fictional skills and thereby paying tribute to the school of New Criticism, or formalism, to which Warren ascribed early in his career. This school of criticism argues for an analytic reading of a text and for appreciating the text on its own, independent of external information.

But the very fact that the novel has remained on bookshelves for more than a half century makes any analysis or criticism based on history a moot point, according to Joseph Blotner in the foreword to the book's fiftieth anniversary edition:

> Its early classification as just another violent *roman à clef* has faded as the years have distanced it from Huey Long, and the private and public—the global— violence of this century has shown it to be realistic rather than melodramatic.

According to Blotner, the novel "has a firm moral basis and philosophical implications" and goes well beyond merely being one more historical or political novel.

One interesting anomaly appears when looking over the differences between the American and English reviews of the novel before the 1970s. English publishers originally released the book without its fourth chapter, the one that covers Jack Burden's telling of Cass Mastern's journal and the part it played in his incomplete doctoral dissertation. Not until the mid-1970s did the book appear in England with the deleted chapter restored. Luckett explains this bit of surgery as a symptom of the times, when publishers (on both sides of the Atlantic, he argues) "had strong views on what national audiences would or would not take." Jonathan S. Cullick, in *Studies in American Fiction,* argues, however, "We might question whether the narrative of Stark would even exist had Burden not read Mastern's journal, because it is from that journal that Burden learns to place himself in history." So, this editing of the English edition might explain Walter Allen's review in 1948 in *The New Statesman & Nation.* While generally positive, Allen does comment that Jack Burden's character "will probably be something of a problem for the English reader," unable to reconcile the tough talk of Burden the newspaperman and the historical awareness of Burden the scholar. But the American educator Leslie Fiedler, in *The Collected Essays of Leslie Fiedler,* makes a similar complaint about Burden's language, commenting that one of the problems of the novel lies in the fact that "its hysterical rhetoric had to be disguised as the tough-guy patter of Jack Burden."

As well, much has been made of how Jack Burden deals with history. Cullick writes, "As Burden discovers his connection to history, he becomes less detached as a narrator, surrendering his pose of objectivity." The younger Burden feels alienated from his family and world, but this defense mechanism falls away as he learns more about how his actions have an effect on his surroundings. And the more Burden learns about history, according to Cullick, through both Cass Mastern's journal and the historical work he does for Willie Stark, the more he must "correct his false assumption that he can remain neutral." Philip Dubuisson Castille, in *The Southern Literary Journal,* also notes that only by acknowledging his past, especially his supposed father, Ellis Burden, can Burden come to terms with being an adult and throw off feelings of inadequacy and failure spawned by his sexual underperformance with Anne. "After half a lifetime of feeling inadequate and seething in shame and spite, Jack can at last claim an adult identity as a committed husband and perhaps, in time, a father."

Ultimately, *All the King's Men* has survived the half century since its original publication because it is a book that tackles issues well beyond

the purely historic. According to Blotner, the novel's lessons that "means can contaminate ends, no matter how idealistically inspired, and evasion of responsibility can prove fatal" are messages that exceed the limits of literature fixed in time.

Criticism

Susan Sanderson

Sanderson holds a master of fine arts degree in fiction writing and is an independent writer. In this essay, she examines how Warren's novel can be viewed as a story of Jack Burden overcoming three father figures in his life to emerge from the story closer to being an adult and less detached from the world.

Jack Burden's value as a character in *All the King's Men* goes well beyond his usefulness as narrator and recorder of Willie Stark's political rise and fall. Woven through Jack's description of Willie's machinations is his own chronicle of interior thoughts and dreams. The novel serves as a record not only of a politician's downfall but also of the emotional and ethical maturation of a man who has been unable to complete the steps toward adulthood despite being close to forty years old. Jack's success in coming to grips with his three father figures—Willie Stark, Judge Irwin, and Ellis Burden—opens the way for him to become more involved in the world.

When Jack begins telling the story, he views the world from a safe distance. This distance allows him to feel superior and detached from humanity, protects him from messy commitments, and, as well, puts him in a position to display the sarcasm he so often does. When he and Willie and the others drive to Mason City that summer day in 1936, Jack is literally along for the ride, squished in the back seat like a child. As the car gets closer to Old Man Stark's farm, Jack looks out the car window and imagines the people inside the houses he is passing in the car. "She listens to the flies cruising around the room, and then she listens to your motor getting big out on the road, then it shrinks off into the distance," he thinks, painting an image of his coming and going without much of an impact.

This image is repeated throughout the early part of the novel. One evening before Willie is elected governor, Jack's connection with the world

> " In the scheme of Jack's maturation, Willie must die. With Willie alive, Jack might have continued as Willie's errand boy, avoiding responsibility and watching life from the sidelines."

is through the thick glass of a train window. He sees a woman standing in her backyard, and as the train pulls away he thinks, "She'll stay there. And all at once, you think that you are the one who is running away." Moments later he sees a cow through the window and becomes sad. "And all at once you feel like crying. But the train is going fast and almost immediately whatever you feel is taken away from you, too." Jack's shaky relationship with the world is as fragile as a young child's, whose emotions can be fleeting.

When Jack is faced with a real, live human being, even one he knows well, his response is hardly that of someone who has emerged from adolescence. While leaning against a fence in chapter one, he hears someone walk toward him but does not turn around to see who it is:

> If I didn't look around it would not be true that some-one had opened the gate. . . . I had got hold of that principle out of a book when I was in college, and I had hung onto it for grim death. . . . It does not matter what you do or what goes on around you because it isn't real anyway.

Jack's response here is similar to that of a child who hides his head or closes his eyes and believes that if he can't see something, it doesn't exist. And such philosophies serve him well as Willie's chief investigator and hatchet man. Jack views his job simply as being Willie's errand boy and doesn't believe that his actions have any impact on the world around him. His choices and actions mean nothing, and that is how he would have it. He doesn't see any complicity on his part in finding out about Judge Irwin's bribe-taking twenty-five years in the past, even though he accepted Willie's assignment to find the dirt and pursued it with some relish. When Anne is upset at learning about the bribe and her father's part in it, Jack's response has all the sensitivity expected in someone who hasn't reached

maturity: "I only told her the truth . . . and she can't blame me for the truth!"

Jack's relationships with women are like those of a teenage boy, and he hasn't a clue about how to act around women. He feels absolutely no warmth for his mother, and while he thinks she is an attractive woman, he considers her unearthly, "something which was so precious that it couldn't be tied down to God's green globe." He condemns his father for walking out on his mother but, at the same time, speaks of her as if she always has something up her sleeve. His and Anne's relationship is stagnant, stalled out nearly twenty years previous when Jack couldn't make love to her. After his love for Anne fails to progress, Jack marries Lois, a rich girl whose only attraction seemed to be that they were great in bed together. In chapter seven, he thinks of her, remembering that "as long as I hadn't begun to notice that the sounds she made were words, there was no harm in her and no harm in the really extraordinary pleasure she could provide." The distance he feels from people and from women especially is revealed in his frustrated comment that Anne and Lois are exactly alike and, in fact, there are no differences among any women.

As well, Jack's behavior when making decisions about school and a career is positively Peter Pan-like; he doesn't want to grow up. Annoyed when Anne asks him what he might do after college, he blurts out "law school," even though he has absolutely no interest in it. After attending law school briefly, he takes great glee in getting kicked out. He re-enrolls at the university as a history graduate student, works at that for quite some time, but then one day begins one of the three periods he calls the Great Sleep. Not wanting to make any decision or take any action, Jack sleeps for twelve or more hours a day, days on end, not doing much of anything else. While these Great Sleep periods are no doubt extreme bouts of depression, Jack's tendency to revert into a womb-like place when life demands action or choice reaffirms his pre-adult stage throughout more than half of the novel.

Yet, by the end of the novel, Jack has married Anne, accepted responsibility for Judge Irwin's death, come to terms with his mother, and taken in his sick father—a man whom he long avoided and despised for being weak and foolish. What happens to bring about this change?

Before Jack can put himself on the road to becoming an adult, he must come to terms with the three father figures in his life: Willie Stark, Judge Irwin, and Ellis Burden. Willie is a man of action, something Jack always condemned Ellis Burden, whom he thought was his father, for not being. Jack believes that Ellis left his mother because he couldn't give her what she wanted or needed. Judge Irwin was always around when Jack was a child, both before and after Ellis left the family, and Jack has fond memories of spending time playing with the judge. Jack discovers after the judge's suicide that he is his biological father.

Like many tragic heroes of myth and literature, Jack must overcome each of his "fathers" before he can consider himself a full-fledged adult and member of the community. And it is an incident involving Willie that helps Jack see where he stands. Jack's discovery of Anne and Willie's affair begins to make him aware that even his inactions have consequences. While on a sudden car trip to the West Coast prompted by the shock of the affair, Jack remembers the events and choices nearly twenty years prior that ended his relationship with Anne. Even though he drives to the West, into a land "at the end of History," the trip forces him to come to grips with the fact that his lack of decisive actions has handed Anne over to Willie.

Jack sees a change in Willie in the few days between Tom's injury and Willie's assassination, and learns from it. Willie's last words to Jack, whom he no doubt loved, are, "It might have been all different, Jack," referring to possibilities of choice. In the scheme of Jack's maturation, Willie must die. With Willie alive, Jack might have continued as Willie's errand boy, avoiding responsibility and watching life from the sidelines. But soon after Willie dies, Jack gets a chance to make a decision and to understand the ramifications of that choice when he decides not to tell Sugar-Boy about Tiny's part in Willie's death. Thinking back on that incident, Jack says to himself, "But there was a difference now, in my own mind if not the circumstances of my life."

And as it was necessary for Willie to die so that Jack could grow, Judge Irwin's death fulfills a similar role. Even though Jack's story does not completely mesh with the ancient tale of Oedipus (he does not mistakenly marry his mother), enough similarities exist to warrant some mention. In fact, as with Oedipus' discovery about the identity of his father, Jack does not discover that Judge Irwin is his father until after the man's death, when Jack's mother begins to scream, "Your father and oh! you, killed him." But the result is the same; the father moves out of the way so that the son may fulfill his own role in the world. As well, the judge's death

allows Jack to see the relationship between act and consequence; Jack's information about the bribery sets the wheels in motion that culminate in the judge's suicide. Jack's epiphany about these consequences comes at the end of chapter eight when, after laughing at the irony that he is the sole heir to Judge Irwin's estate, he discovers that he is really weeping "and saying over and over again, 'The poor old bugger, the poor old bugger.' It was like the ice breaking up after a long winter. And the winter had been long." A change is taking place in Jack.

After Willie's assassination and Judge Irwin's suicide, Jack is well on his way to seeing that living his life as a child has consequences he does not want. Acceptance of Ellis Burden, the man he believed to be his father for nearly forty years, is one of Jack's last acts signifying his exit from childhood. Jack's mother, with whom he comes to some resolution, precipitates Jack's acknowledgment and forgiveness of Ellis. "My mother gave me back the past. I could now accept the past which I had before felt was tainted and horrible," says Jack.

When Jack accepts Ellis into his house, his transformation into adulthood is complete. He realizes that the story all along has not only been Willie's but his own:

> It is the story of a man who lived in the world and to him the world looked one way for a long time and then it looked another and very different way. The change did not happen all at once. . . . There was, in fact, a time when he came to believe that nobody had any responsibility for anything.

But now, Jack Burden knows that to be untrue. He and Anne will leave Burden's Landing, the home of two of his fathers. They will return but not to either father's house, he swears. With that step, Jack, who at the beginning of the novel surveyed the world through car and train windows, embraces the world.

Source: Susan Sanderson, Critical Essay on *All the King's Men,* in *Novels for Students,* The Gale Group, 2002.

James H. Justus

In the following essay, Justus examines Warren's inspiration and intent in All the King's Men, *calling it "in the most explicit way a fictional ordering of events and motifs crucial to Warren's maturity."*

1.

Warren reports that he "stumbled" into the writing of fiction when he was at Oxford, where he

> Into this study of a southern demagogue. . . went not only the example of Huey Long but also Warren's wide reading in Dante, Machiavelli, Elizabethan tragedy, American history, William James, and his observation of the very real day-to-day melodrama of depression in America and fascism in Italy."

sought to put down on paper some of the "tales" he had once talked about with his friend Paul Rosenfeld. "Fiction was for me," he remembers, "a way of reliving life that I was separate from—3,000 miles away from." Those oral tales became "Prime Leaf," and this early version of *Night Rider* reflected the imaginative "reliving," not of narrative lines (whose literal events occurred about the time Warren was born), but of the human circumstances of the action readily available to the amalgamating memory of a young Rhodes Scholar: people whose characteristic principles and behavior were recognizably human because they were first true to the place that nurtured them. If poetry is what Warren calls "a more direct way of trying to know the self, to make sense of experience—freer from *place*" than fiction, both modes are imaginatively generated from "an observed fact of life," which then invites an "ethical issue" that will invest the fact with significance. From "Prime Leaf" onward, Warren's fiction reveals the double predilection of a writer who imposes ethical patterns on the felt life of a place he is separate from.

By the time *All the King's Men* appeared in 1946, Warren had already explored the hardy theme of the conflict between the public and private self, the actual and the ideal, commitment and disengagement—primarily by concentrating on the uses of political power. In both *Night Rider* and *At Heaven's Gate* he had tried to transform relatively abstract embodiments of power (the tobacco growers' association in one, Bogan Murdock in the

other) into particularized, sensuously immediate politicians whose motives and acts are set in a context of rich circumstantiality.

That brand of circumstantiality is most decisively apparent in his third novel, in which Warren was able to give credible life to a political organization, as he was not able to do in *Night Rider,* and to a flesh-and-blood political boss, which he was not able to do in *At Heaven's Gate.* Warren's tenure at Louisiana State University (1934–1942) encompassed both the kinetic atmosphere of Huey Long's awesome and sometimes comic domination of state politics and the corrupting aftermath of the Kingfish's assassination. There is no doubt that Warren's residence in Long's Louisiana constitutes the generative base of his most popular novel, and *All The King's Men* is not merely an extension of the compositional pattern of the "observed fact" and the "ethical issue" which is evident in the first two novels; it is also an intensification of this pattern. *Night Rider* is the re-creation of events of his father's generational—a collocation of regional history and family legend centering upon the Black Patch Wars; *At Heaven's Gate* has at its center a fictionalized version of Luke Lea, a Tennessee financier the peak of whose shady career coincided with Warren's undergraduate years at Vanderbilt. *All the King's Men,* despite its publication date, is in the most explicit way a fictional ordering of events and motifs crucial to Warren's maturity—events transpiring in his day-to-day activities at "Huey Long's university" and motifs of profound relevance to a Great Depression society of which he was still a part. For the first time in his career, that relevance in the actual world of the 1930s—politically, psychologically, philosophically, and culturally—intersects with Warren's most significant aesthetic and moral concerns.

Just as Huey Long was not merely another in the familiar class of southern demagogue, so Willie Stark is given the insight, procedural skill, and innovative intelligence lacking in such real-life demagogues as Theodore Bilbo of Mississippi or "Pitchfork" Ben Tillman of South Carolina. The career of Warren's politician generally follows that of Huey Long, not some conflated history of the southern demagogue. *All the King's Men* is of course more than this, and it is unsurprising that, faced with so many literalist sensibilities, Warren has always been prompted to deemphasize the convergence of his fiction and modern Louisiana history. His explanation, however, that Long provided him merely with atmosphere or "myth" should not obscure the nature of that convergence.

In addition to the literal pattern of similarity, there is the pragmatic base of end over means in Long which becomes a central philosophic issue in Warren's novel. "You sometimes fight fire with fire," Long is quoted as saying. "The end justifies the means. I would do it some other way if there was time or if it wasn't necessary to do it this way." As recounted in T. Harry Williams' superb biography, certain details about Long's career are also reflected in Warren's account of Stark—Long's practice, for example, of requiring political appointees to sign undated resignations, or the aristocratic conservatives' opposition to most of Long's measures partly because a boor was proposing them. Warren's Sugar-Boy bears a striking resemblance to Joe Messina, Long's devoted but unintelligent bodyguard. Long's matter-of-fact assumption that every man had something in his past worthy of concealing is dramatized in Stark's pungent doctrine of man, and Jack Burden as Stark's chief investigator of opponents' secrets dramatizes Long's well-known practice of keeping a lockbox stuffed with damaging records of and affidavits on potential enemies that could be used when the governor thought it necessary. Warren's fictive economy shows up in the case of Tiny Duffy, a conflated and concentrated example of many figures in Long's retinue. "He liked to break people, especially the strong, and then build them up again," intimates reported of Long; "then they knew their place."

That Willie Stark strongly resembles Louisiana's potlikker *tyrannos* would be, finally, a contention of little moment were it not for the fact that it simultaneously seems so obvious to so many and so critically disreputable to so many others. Most of the early reviewers made much of the resemblance and waxed moralistically because of it; later critics of *All the King's Men* have tended to see Huey Long almost as an accidental ingredient in the novel's genesis. Neither position should be ignored, though Warren's entire career, from which perspective we can see a persistent personal engagement with his own past, suggests that the author's Baton Rouge years—coming at the end of the era of Long's hegemony—should not be underestimated in their contribution to what Warren has called "the coiling, interfused forces" that go into literary decisions.

Warren tells us that worrying his politician into shape began in the winter and summer of 1938 in Louisiana and Italy (in a verse drama called *Proud Flesh*), resumed in the summer of 1940 and in the spring of 1943, and only gradually emerged as the

Former Louisiana Governor and U. S. Senator Huey P. Long

protagonist of *All the King's Men.* Into this study of a southern demagogue, whose name was changed from Talos to Stark, went not only the example of Huey Long but also Warren's wide reading in Dante, Machiavelli, Elizabethan tragedy, American history, William James, and his observation of the very real day-to-day melodrama of depression in America and fascism in Italy. Like so many American works written in the shadow of World War II, *All the King's Men* is infused with the theme of power, its distribution, ethics, and consequences.

The urge to dramatize the Willie Stark story was not lessened by the enormous critical and popular response to the novel nor by its author's winning of the Pulitzer Prize. Warren was not yet done with his politician. The tinkering and reshaping of the by now multiversioned drama resulted in numerous theatrical performances, most of them short-lived, from 1946 to 1959. Finally the text of *All the King's Men: A Play* appeared, presumably in the dramatic form that satisfied Warren. The weaknesses of these versions are apparent: stilted dialogue, old-fashioned artiness in the Eliot manner, abstract moralisms imposed upon the action,

What Do I Read Next?

- *The Collected Poems of Robert Penn Warren* (1998), edited by John Burt, Warren's literary executor, gathers together every poem Warren ever published, with the exception of "Brother to Dragons."

- Robert Penn Warren's *All the King's Men: Three Stage Versions,* published in 2000, includes two previously unpublished stage plays that were precursors to the novel, *Proud Flesh* and *Willie Stark: His Rise and Fall,* and a dramatic version of the novel that was later published as *All the King's Men.*

- *Making History: The Biographical Narratives of Robert Penn Warren* (2000), by Jonathan S. Cullick, surveys the entire biographical work of Robert Penn Warren.

- *Primary Colors* (1996), by Anonymous, is Joe Klein's fictionalized account of Bill Clinton's campaign for the presidency in 1992. The story is told through the eyes of Henry Burton, campaign aide to Jack Stanton, a fictional southern governor running for president of the United States.

- *The Grapes of Wrath,* written by John Steinbeck and originally published in 1939, tells the story of the Joad family as they flee the Dust Bowl for California, only to find that hunger, discrimination, and death await them there.

belabored polarities too categorically parceled out. But the most obvious reason for the dramatic failures was the generic necessity to deemphasize Jack Burden, the narrator of the novel. This diminishment looms over all, changing all. Burden's transformation from a nearly undifferentiated bystander to chief among the king's men, from mere observer of the spectacle to narrator of and participator in the Willie Stark story, is, as most critics now agree, the peculiar strength of *All the King's Men* as a novel.

2.

The fleshing out of Burden was from the start, as Warren himself has pointed out, a technical choice. The novel fairly cried out for a more sensitive consciousness than that of the politician whose story had to be told. Call him Ishmael or Carraway, Burden is another in a long line of American narrators who by dint of their special positions in the stories they tell end by telling their own stories as well. The case of Willie Stark readily invited naturalistic treatment, but the "impingement of that material. . . upon a special temperament" allowed Warren "another perspective than the reportorial one," and it also provided the basis for "some range of style." Both author and narrator finally agree that the story of Willie Stark is also the story of Jack Burden.

Almost alone among the earliest critics, however, Norton Girault was able to see the focus of the novel in the character and sensibility of Burden, in his language of rebirth, in his halting, stumbling movements from ignorance to knowledge. Though the progress from Cousin Willie to Governor Stark may be the tale told in the book, it is Burden's revelation of that progress that is the experience of the book. And *revelation* in two ways: first, his discovery of the meaning of Stark's rise and fall and of his own identity through these events, and second, his articulation of those meanings in a long I-narration. Perhaps no other modern novel so clearly demonstrates the fact that a happy technical choice alters the very meaning of materials that it must shape.

Nothing is more naturally dramatic or susceptible of significance than Willie Stark's story, the hard narrative facts isolated and untouched by a consciousness other than the author's. But both the drama and the meaning of that story are significantly redirected and heightened by having those facts experienced and related by an intervening consciousness. As a man of imagination and intelligence, Burden's own drama is, as James observed of Lambert Strether's, "under stress, the drama of discrimination," the shucking off of first one, then another, alternative to meaning until he *sees* and in the seeing allows the reader to follow the painful progress to moral awareness. From the desire to remain innocent, to resist the costly maturity of rebirth, Burden moves through even more costly immersions into experience, which he misinterprets and revises until he is forced to acknowledge his portion of evil.

Burden is a most unlikely learner when we meet him. Smug, astute, world-weary, he could almost pass for a New South variety of Conrad's Decoud in *Nostromo*. But the empty *boulevardier*, who scribbles his self-regenerative letter in the focus of battle, has pushed a habit of vision to its limits; Burden's memoir is itself the symbol of regeneration, a product of, not an ingredient in, his moral education. Such a memoir is *All the King's Men*, produced by a man who, after having arrived at a certain stage of self-knowledge, reenacts the costly process. We are constantly aware of growth as something both achieved and being achieved. But however insistent the interweaving of product and process—the necessary impingement of present attitudes on past beliefs and acts—the shaping perspective is that of the educated Jack Burden, the "legal, biological, and perhaps even metaphysical continuator" of the earlier king's man.

Burden's change has sometimes been thought phony or self-deceiving. It is true that Jack Burden is no Cass Mastern; neither is he a Scholarly Attorney. He has nothing of the humility of the first nor the radical spirituality of the latter. But in his learning Burden does achieve a measure of both humility and spirituality. If we are tempted to think of Burden as unchanging because he does not become either a Cass Mastern or a Scholarly Attorney, we might well speculate on the novelistic failure of *All the King's Men* had Burden's conversion taken on the obsessive coloration of those two figures. One of the thematic constants in Warren's fiction is that single-mindedness of whatever sort destroys human balance; it leads to a warping of man's need for community as well as for personal identity. Hence, the narrator's slower progress. If with his customary brio Burden calls Trollope "Anthony," it is only good craftsmanship to make the new Burden in certain tangible ways consistent with the old. Even the disasters tumbling in profusion about him cannot rout the tendencies of a lifetime—the easy cynicism of the newspaperman grafted onto the floating romanticism of the graduate student.

It is also true that the narrator seems callous in episodes that, upon proper assessment, require sensitivity; and he turns unduly sensitive at times when we would prefer the Hurt Young Man to be less touchy in his garrulity. But we are offended, and properly so, by his on-again, off-again, hardboiled detective moods interspersed with debilitatingly romantic fancies. Hemingway demonstrated long ago that the modern stoic tough guy hides a sentimental idealist. Warren suggests such a func-

tional split in Burden by vacillations between pretentious philosophizing and wise-guy witticisms. The split in his narrator serves in fact as a trope, compacted and made interior, for the entire novel. If a study of its theme and structure shows anything, it is that *All the King's Men* is one writer's concern about "the terrible division of [our] age," explored not only through explicit antitheses (man of idea/man of fact, means/ends, science/nature) but also through the subtle and pervasive doubling of characters: Stark/Burden, Burden/Duffy, Irwin/Mastern, Stark/Irwin, Stark/Stanton. Burden, with his problems of spiritual integration, is the front-and-center figure within the play of larger, if not more meaningful, antitheses; furthermore, we know him only through a narration that reveals qualities which in actual people we could just as well do without. Tough guys and ersatz philosophers in our own time can be just as tiresome as the efficient housekeepers and virtuous companions of Victorian fiction.

As the twentieth-century wise guy who has put his learning to work for him, Burden must take shape, more imperatively even than Stark, literally through his own words. As public figure, he is in-the-know; as private figure, he seeks to know. His rhetoric, both as narrator and as character, reflects this split, appropriately embodying the strain between Burden as Sam Spade and Burden as Stephen Dedalus. He is alternately garrulous and noncommittal; he is cynically efficient, always prepared to "deliver" or to "make it stick." Privately, he belittles his efficiency, and we become increasingly aware of his real distaste for the particular person he has become. He chides himself frequently, referring to himself in the third person. With cocksure stridency he announces "the curse" of Jack Burden: "he was invulnerable." But even as he talks, he shows how vulnerable he is—to nostalgia, sentimentality, and those tangential events that nudge him into newer versions of himself and reality.

The Burden who remains after the fall of the king is a different person from the king's man; indeed, after those ambivalent and tentative loyalties, he takes a stand similar to Cass Mastern's. Partially responsible for at least three deaths and several lesser disasters, he comes to accept them fully in the "awful responsibility of time." He ends with a healthier respect for flawed humanity, extending to both Judge Irwin and Willie Stark, and with discomfort even sees his connection, spiritual as well as physical, with such a hack as Tiny Duffy. As acting son and stenographer, he cares for the Scholarly Attorney in his last days; and instead of condescending toward his marriage-prone mother he shows an admirable if low-keyed compassion. He devotes himself to the long-delayed editorial task of publishing the diary of Cass Mastern. He refuses to say the word to Sugar-Boy that would destroy not only Duffy but Sugar-Boy as well. In marrying Anne Stanton he wins a belated victory over the paralyzing image of purity that he holds of her throughout much of the novel. Perhaps most important, he even hints of his return to active politics in some future administration.

Burden is a conscious artist, scrupulously constructing his story from an open position, manipulating the early versions of himself from his newer one of control, growth, and moral self-evaluation. Although he perceives more at the end than at the beginning of the novel, he is careful in his verbal reconstruction to permit his earlier self full rein to maneuver within those limited terms. If he occasionally sounds hysterical or even absurd, that impression is one that the narrator who reconstructs himself is the first to recognize. Such is the risk that the educated Burden willingly takes to present honestly the learning Burden. Certainly the final position at which he arrives is neither absurd nor hysterical. It is, in fact, a measure of his integrity that he can submit an imperfect image of himself with only such sporadic glossing as "that was the way I argued the case back then."

Burden's rhetoric throughout maintains certain characteristics: wisecracks, fancy metaphors, self-irony, the mingling of the elegant and the colloquial. His general diction and syntax do not change substantially, since the entire story is a memoir of events from 1922 (and occasionally earlier) to 1939, told in the language of the latest stage of his growth. Just as there is no dramatic physical alteration in Burden—he presumably looks much the same in the late 1930s as he did in the early 1920s—so there is no obvious change in the physical shape of his words. The changes in Burden are philosophical and psychological, and the changes in his language are largely tonal. The mature Burden still clings to the wise-guy idiom of his Great Twitch days, but more important is the fact that the tone of that idiom shifts perceptibly. Here is the typical early Burden style:

> In a town like Mason City the bench in front of the harness shop is—or was twenty years ago before the concrete slab got laid down—the place where Time gets tangled in its own feet and lies down like an old hound and gives up the struggle. It is a place where you sit down and wait for night to come and arte-

riosclerosis. It is the place the local undertaker looks at with confidence and thinks he is not going to starve as long as that much work is cut out for him. . . You sit there among the elder gods, disturbed by no sound except the slight *râle* of the one who has asthma, and wait for them to lean from the Olympian and sunlit detachment and comment, with their unenvious and foreknowing irony, on the goings-on of the folks who are still snared in the toils of mortal compulsions.

The subject, courthouse characters, is not an unusual one for the narrator at any time; neither is the feeling of bemused superiority which seeps out of his own Olympian syntax and the brash imagery. But if the subject and the observer's clear-eyed view of it do not vary greatly during Burden's education, the tone does. Here is a similar passage from the last chapter: "And I sat for hours in the newspaper room of the public library, the place which like railway stations and missions and public latrines is where the catarrhal old men and bums go and where they sit to thumb the papers which tell about the world in which they live for a certain number of years or to sit and wheeze and stare while the gray rain slides down the big windowpanes above them." In his final phase the narrator's wisecracks become muted, the tough line relaxes, the naturalistic observations become a trifle lame, the superiority itself undergoes chastening: all these changes reflect the sadness and near-inertia of an exhausted man.

Warren has said that the key device for making his narrator work satisfactorily was finding his "lingo", and certainly Burden's striking shifts from pretentious philosopher to streetwise pol attest to both his literal position in the narrative and the symbolic self-division of a character whose moral drama claims its own share of our attraction. But there is also a quieter, less intrusive verbal pattern in *All the King's Men* that is shaped more directly by the author himself than by his narrator. There is, for example, the steady accretion of the contrasting images of ice and water, corresponding to emotional states of, on the one hand, rigidity, stasis, and purity, and on the other, immersion, flowing, drowning. Fixity—psychological and ideological—means protection from the contingence of actuality. Both Adam Stanton and Sugar-Boy are significantly linked by the image of ice: the bodyguard stares at Jack in the library "through the last preserving glaze of ice," and Adam's smile is described as "the stab of an icicle through the heart." Primitive purity and lethal innocence find common spiritual ground. Burden's dominant image of Anne is that of "some clean bright and gold leaf" buried in the clear ice of a frozen stream; later that image "breaks up" as in a spring thaw, which then threatens to sweep him under, to engulf him in "the moving stream of time." The thaw of Chapter 6 continues in later chapters as "the full dark stream of the world," "the flow," "the flux," "the current," and "drowning in West."

Such informing images verbally reinforce the narrator's efforts to close his emotional and intellectual gaps. Burden's struggle for spiritual unity is in fact reinforced by every aspect of the larger scheme of the novel. Consider, for example, the title of *All the King's Men* and its Dantean epigraph. With these juxtaposed elements Warren establishes, anterior to the novel itself, two apparently contradictory positions that suggest the basis of the conflict in Burden's difficult progress to self-knowledge. The title, with its nursery-rhyme allusion, connotes a pattern of thought and behavior dominated by acquiescence to the phenomenal, the factual, the way things are. The factual motif is posited by Stark's own proverb: "Man is conceived in sin and born in corruption and he passeth from the stink of the didie to the stench of the shroud." Like older tragic protagonists, Willie Stark falls from the clash of opposing motives. His doubleness cannot be erased; he is now tyrant, now hero, alternately damned and praised. As Burden finally and reluctantly discovers in his Case of the Upright Judge: "There is always the clue, the canceled check, the smear of lipstick, the footprint in the canna bed, the condom on the park path, the twitch in the old wound, the baby shoes dipped in bronze, the taint in the bloodstream." And that discovery brings Burden around once again to his kinsman's final vision of "the common guilt of man." These conclusions are further reinforced by the Scholarly Attorney's tract statement that "the only way for God to create, truly create, man was to make him separate from God Himself, and to be separate from God is to be sinful." This pattern, in short, asserts the natural depravity of man, the way—whether he likes it or not—man is.

Against the shattered world of Humpty-Dumpty, Burden comes to juxtapose his own experience in that tragedy and to conclude from it that he has not only been affected by the tragedy but that he has also affected it. As a Student of History, he must accept Cass Mastern's insistence upon personal involvement in the guilt of others; as a student of human nature he must share the blame in an affair that takes the lives of his two best friends and almost wrecks the life of the woman he loves. The deterministic resonance of the title, however, is counterpointed by the fragmentary epigraph from the *Purgatorio—Mentre che la speranza ha fior del verde*. The hope that survives the Stark story may appear more gray than green, but it is hope nevertheless.

Acceptance of the way things are, without hope, may be merely sentimental complacency. As a graduate student Burden had flippantly visualized his future in some junior college "long on Jesus and short on funds" where he would have watched "the slow withering of the green wisp of dream," but later he can find a green wisp in the most basic fact of all: "there were some of us left." Since he halts further bloodshed by a willed silence in his last meeting with Sugar-Boy, survival is earned. He and Anne read Trollope together, uncurious about how equilibriums are changing; caught in a "massive and bemusing tide," they accept that tide's own "pace and time." Acceptance is earned. Seeing the grandson of Stark, Burden agrees with Lucy that she must believe that the Boss had been a great man even though the "greatness and ungreatness" had been so mixed he could not tell them apart. History is neutral, but man, working through history, is not. For all the ruck of irresistible fact that conditions him, man must still exercise his will. There is fact and there is hope. Certain theological and psychological benefits may be gained from accepting the way things are; but whatever his nature man still lives in a defective world with other defective men, and mutual responsibility involves more of his energies than a posture of weary resignation. Picking up the pieces may not put together another king, but the reminder of human fragility may stimulate the survivors to cherish what virtues remain.

These opposing attitudes associated with the factual and the hopeful are established, then, before the novel begins, in its title and epigraph. Within the novel they are developed through the metaphorical possibilities of *rest* and *motion*. The way things are, man's depravity, the familiar pattern of failure after great effort: all these suggest rest, the state of certainty, the problem solved, the contest won (or lost). The possibility of hope even in these terms, the perpetual testing of values, the willingness to risk becoming reconciled after grandly repudiating: all these suggest motion, the trying-out of grace, direction if not destination. The confident Burden is the cocky newspaperman who pursues the embarrassing deed out of the past to "make it stick," the cynical observer of the political animals at play, the Student of History who exchanges without undue upheaval his brass-bound Idealism for the positivism of the Great Twitch (and is perfectly certain that in each case he has arrived at Truth, or at least truth). In one of his definitive acts—his flight West—he says, "meaning is never in the event but in the motion through event." This assertion that, for man, "direction is all" is confirmed in his theological parries with the Scholarly Attorney. "Life is motion," Burden repeats several times; "if the object which a man looks at changes constantly so that knowledge of it is constantly untrue and is therefore Non-Knowledge, then Eternal Motion is possible." But these statements of self-assurance come from the king's man; in the end Burden affirms the truth of both rest and motion.

The famous final paragraph of *All the King's Men* is a capping rhetorical union of these two patterns. With its emphasis on depleted energies, memory, and nostalgia, the emotional associations are with rest; but the syntax and diction suggest motion: *to walk down the Row, walk down the beach, diving floats life gently, footfall, we shall move, we shall go out, and go into.* The substance of the final paragraph is that even nostalgia will have no easy time of it; even that indulgence "will be a long time from now." The price of seeing things as they are has been high. Burden has seen his two friends, Stark and Stanton, "doomed," but they have also been men of individual will. Thus the burden of Jack Burden is what he learns to bear: man, though he accepts inscrutable providence, cannot luxuriate in inaction because of that surety. The tone of the later Burden cannot be called optimistic. He no longer rests his case in the firmly bound, well-labeled file folders of the private eye. Except for his acknowledgment of man's situation "in the world in which we live from birth to death," he comes to see all other judgments as tentative, judgments that therefore require retesting to be continually relevant.

Our pervasive sense of this work's political context in its largest sense, the great world in which personal values are ratified, extended, distorted, or extinguished, accounts for the special poignancy of the final chapter of *All the King's Men,* particularly its sliding weariness of nuance that reminds us of the frightful toll that the public life extracts from the individual. The shattering of private lives is the most obvious sign of that toll: in the inner narrative, that of Cass Mastern, his adulterous partner, and the slave Phebe, a physical and moral collapse which images forth the great public issues of slavery, secession, and war; and in the central narrative, the lives of most of Jack Burden's friends who are caught up in the swirling issues of demagoguery, dictatorship, and the political testing of personal loyalties. The sad waste dramatized by the deaths of the governor and the doctor is not completed in that violent moment but is extended through days of anticlimax. Sadie Burke vegetating in the sanitarium, a purposeless Sugar-Boy idling his time away in the public library, Tiny Duffy eagerly assuming the stained mantle of Willie Stark: all become visible analogues for Jack Burden of his potential fate. What is notable about Warren's ethical denouement is that, despite the treacherous impact of public life on private identity, *All the King's Men* is finally not a preachment against the bruising and corrupting world of politics and the mixed rewards of social reform.

Jack Burden is a most battered man at the end of the novel, yet the most poisonous influence has not been Willie Stark's pragmatic political programs or the sour rankling between the partisans of Mason City and Burden's Landing. Jack Burden suffers most from a sense of self-betrayal. He himself pictures for us how easy it was for him to live with a fuzzy self-definition before there was a public context to his life: his lazy tennis-and-swimming summers with Anne Stanton, his professional drift, his self-indulgent marriage to Lois. Subliminal discontent, however, like a faint toothache, can be tolerated without substantial disruption of the psyche; not so the blatant daily barrage of conflicting principles and loyalties. Burden's victory in coming through the Willie Stark years with self-respect is obviously limited. Salvaging honor in purely personal ways is an understandable resolution to this protagonist's dilemmas, and the most engaging of his acts after the deaths of Stark and Stanton are acts of reclamation in personal relationships: becoming a husband to Anne, serving as stenographer and nurse to Ellis Burden, understanding his mother. Important as they are, however, two other decisions suggest that for Jack Burden the merely personal is not enough for the satisfactory definition of the self: leaving Irwin's house and selling the family property that is now legally his, and his tentative interest in reentering politics, this time under the aegis of the honest Hugh Miller. Both decisions imply that there is no *achieved* self-definition possible, that it is only *process,* and that such a process necessarily requires the continued testing of the self in the great world. Thus, like Warren's view of Conrad, the lesson of Jack Burden is the human necessity to go "naked into the pit, again and again, to make the same old struggle for his truth." Like *Nostromo, All the King's Men* dramatizes "the cost of awareness and the difficulty of virtue. . ."

If Burden achieves a victory, it is in recognizing that the self must be submitted to motion, that it must act upon the slender green hope in the face of defeat. One of the achievements of Burden's memoir is that it can reveal the victory while simultaneously celebrating the often debilitating movements toward it. While in the tentative rest of the final period the tone of the narrator is less patronizing, less dogmatic, the basic thrust of his rhetoric is the same. Burden as narrator never allows even his guilt, rooted in the magnitude of recent events, to paralyze his ability to tell his own story effectively; and although he reconstructs his own past with as much detachment as he does the whole Stark era, he still bears the personal marks of that ordeal. His name, we can see now, suggests his vital centrality in that general reconstruction. Thematically he bears his past with difficulty, heavy obligation, and great expense. And even the future must be borne. Structurally, and here the musical signification of *burden* is pertinent, his story carries the "ground" for the more obvious pattern of Stark's story—those obligatory measures in the novel. When Burden permits the learning character to catch up with the narrator who has learned, he admits how tempting it has been to try to shoulder the least painful parts of his burden. He is denied, for instance, the "inexpensive satisfaction in virtue" when, upon trying to give what is left of Irwin's estate to Miss Littlepaugh, he finds she has died.

At the end of *All the King's Men,* Burden is both his own judge and his own accused who, deprived of many of the intellectual and emotional conditions that he formerly demanded, must now accept his own burden of being man. He is like Bunyan's Christian at the beginning of the journey. But for Jack Burden that journey lies beyond the confines of the novel, beyond 1939, in the "convulsion of the world" where, we may assume, his own travail will be convulsive before his burden can be rolled away.

3.

When *All the King's Men* appeared in 1946, most readers saw it as a political novel, and most of them were not overly concerned that the fictive testing of its philosophical assumptions resembled spiritual autobiography more than it did fiction by Upton Sinclair (who was still writing his Lanny Budd novels) of John Dos Passos. More serious readers, however, directed us properly and acutely to the moral import of the novel. So successful were they that most of us now tend to regard *All the*

King's Men almost solely as a moral fiction. But its original reception was not wholly misinterpreted; the political base of the novel is firm. I have already suggested that for those readers who do not remember the Huey Long years, T. Harry Williams' definitive biography suggests the revealing parallels of Warren's novel and this historical moment as well as some equally revealing divergences. Despite Warren's own exasperations with having such links pointed out, logic will have its say.

But there is another logic at work, too, one that is both farther reaching in the political implications of the novel and more narrowly relevant to the story of Jack Burden's struggle for moral identity. This logic is located within the novel itself, both what is put in and what is left out. If Jack Burden can at one point muse on the curious and unsettling feeling that he is like God brooding on history (during the impeachment proceedings), it is also true that overall, at all points, Warren is like the historian, another surrogate God, brooding on history.

When Jack writes on the last page, "So by the summer of this year, 1939, we shall have left Burden's Landing," we are suddenly jolted by the specificity of the date (more than a year has passed since Stark's assassination in late 1937). The narrative sequence in the last fourth of the novel requires no such specificity: only the sequence of deaths and their causes are required. After the profusion of losses, Jack and Anne slowly regain their "perilous equilibrium" in the lemon-pale sun of late autumn, reading Trollope, and submitting themselves to the "enormous drift" of events that knows "its own pace and time." But then the pace and time pick up. Jack's final meeting with Sugar-Boy in the public library occurs in February. In May, Jack goes to see Lucy Stark in the country. In "early summer" he returns to Burden's Landing for a final visit with his mother. When she remarks vaguely that she had originally intended to go to Europe, Jack responds with "You better stay out of Europe. . . All hell is going to break loose over there and not long either." This seemingly is Warren's only direct allusion to the events that were to crowd and jostle each other until their eruption on September 1, 1939.

Despite the rhetorical dying fall of the last several pages of the novel, despite the exhaustion and weariness that hound Jack Burden in his fragile task of picking up the pieces of at least two shattered lives, the moral note suggested by these pages is a curious compound of wary hope and nostalgia: that is, the *text* of the novel looks both forward and backward. And in the interstices of the text we can read the larger implications of a regional story of morality and politics.

Although the composition of *All the King's Men* stretches from at least 1940 to 1945, the action of the novel ends during the year before the first stage of composition. Thus, what is omitted from the story is the convulsion of the world *beginning* with 1939. Jack Burden stands at the threshold of World War II, but his creator stands at its conclusion. Warren's strategy is a rhetorical one, incorporating within the experience of the novel, as one critic has put it, "the knowledge of a reader who has lived through what it anticipates."

The confused moral principles working themselves out in such violent ways in a southern state in the 1930s, especially as they are registered on a tortured sensibility, have their louder political resonance in the ideological debates in Europe. In fact the story of Jack Burden, the divided man who after spiritual drift and moral paralysis finally comes to do the right thing, reads like a conflation, a miniaturized history, of the larger political and moral story of the late 1930s. Warren, no less than his contemporary W. H. Auden, knew the truth of what 1939 was like:

> In the nightmare of the dark
> All the dogs of Europe bark,
> And the living nations wait,
> Each sequestered in its hate;

a similar registering can be found in some of Warren's poems contemporaneous with the early composition of the novel and preserved in *Selected Poems: 1923–1943*. One of the recurring themes in these is echoed in Warren's theory that the man of power is powerful only because he responds to the blank needs of people around him. What is missing in these poems is the explicit man of power (though Fascist leaders lurk in the shadows); what we see instead are the confused and compensatory acts of those cursed with "blanknesses and needs": Harry L., whose "heart bled speed" in a plane; some "whose passionate emptiness and tidal/Lust swayed toward the debris of Madrid"; and still others awash in Europe's greater tidal lust who continue to "sink/To rest in lobbies, or pace gardens where/The slow god crumbles and the fountains prink..." Both the flight to surrogate commitments and the heedless pursuit of transient pleasures are seen as postponements of an inevitable reckoning. For the personae in these early poems, self-confrontation cannot be denied:

> Till you sit alone—which is the beginning of
>   error—
> Behind you the music and lights of the great hotel:
> Solution, perhaps, is public, despair personal,
> But history held to your breath clouds like a
>   mirror.

On the battlefield or on the beaches of fashionable watering places, the spiritual state is the same.

For the narrator of *All the King's Men,* the Great Sleep and the Great Twitch are psychologically definitive gestures of a man who cherishes his innocence and his spiritual stasis all the more urgently as events nudge him into facing truths about himself and his involvement in those events. Jack Burden's political experiences, no less than his personal ones, turn out to exemplify the truths he would shun. Evasions, feints, and flanking actions are not necessarily easier maneuvers than headlong confrontations; but they are partial, inadequate, and finally dishonest.

Self-confrontation means holding history to your breath; the personae in these early poems and Jack Burden in *All the King's Men* must admit their participation in history—and thus their responsibility to it. If, as Warren knew, betrayal stained so many lives and careers in a political machine in the South, betrayal on a grander scale, as he knew equally well, was to become the name of diplomacy in all the Mason Cities of western Europe. Behind Warren's sonorous abstractions—"into the convulsion of the world, out of history into history and the awful responsibility of Time"—are those specific public convulsions that give resonance to and that perhaps are the literal referents of these abstractions: Spain, Poland, Czechoslovakia, France; the Channel War, Dresden, Belsen, Stalingrad. These public eruptions, varied as they were militarily, demonstrate a common fact, the inescapable entanglement of the moral and the political—which is also the inescapable lesson that Jack Burden learns. History is neutral, but man is not. Breathing the very air of depletion, Jack Burden muses on his own lately recognized responsibility; in the retrospection of recent history, Robert Penn Warren suggests that the bouts of European Great Sleeps and European Great Twitches merely postponed the reckoning.

Source: James H. Justus, "All the Burdens of *All the King's Men,*" in *The Achievement of Robert Penn Warren,* Louisiana State University Press, 1981, pp. 191–206.

Sources

Allen, Walter, Review in *New Statesman & Nation,* Vol. 25, No. 900, June 5, 1948, p. 464.

Blotner, Joseph, Preface to *All the King's Men,* by Robert Penn Warren, Harcourt, Brace & Company, 1996, pp. vii–x.

Castille, Philip Duboisson, "Spiritual and Sexual Healing in Robert Penn Warren's *All the King's Men,*" in *The Southern Literary Journal,* Vol. 31, No. 2, Spring 1999, p. 80.

Cullick, Jonathan S., "From 'Jack Burden' to 'I': The Narrator's Transformation in *All the King's Men,*" in *Studies in American Fiction,* Vol. 25, No. 2, pp. 197–211.

Fiedler, Leslie, "Three Notes on Robert Penn Warren," in *The Collected Essays of Leslie Fiedler, Volume I,* Stein and Day, 1971, pp. 33–53.

Gray, R., "The American Novelist and American History: A Revaluation of *All the King's Men,*" in *Journal of American Studies,* Vol. 6, No. 3, December 1972, pp. 297–307.

Luckett, Richard, "Richard Luckett on a Novelist of Fact," in *Spectator,* Vol. 232, No. 7596, January 26, 1974, p. 106.

Trilling, Diana, "All the King's Men," in *Nation,* Vol. 163, No. 8, August 1946, p. 220.

Further Reading

Blotner, Joseph L., *Robert Penn Warren: A Biography,* Random House, 1997.
This work is the first full-scale biography of Robert Penn Warren. The author began this book with Warren's approval and help.

Long, Huey P., *Every Man a King: The Autobiography of Huey P. Long,* De Capo Press, 1996.
This text is the Louisiana governor's autobiography, originally published in 1933, some say as a piece of campaign material for his hoped-for run at the United States presidency.

Williams, Thomas Harry, *Huey Long,* Vintage Books, 1981.
This extensive biography won a Pulitzer Prize when it was published.

Brideshead Revisited

Evelyn Waugh

1945

Evelyn Waugh's novels written before 1945 are typically satiric and filled with dry humor and sarcasm, and many critics view *Brideshead Revisited* as heralding a change in Waugh's writing style. *Brideshead Revisited* presents a more nostalgic story based on the main character's memories of a wealthy English Catholic family he befriended before World War II. In an England where most people are Protestant, being Catholic makes the family—despite their land ownership and high social status—a minority, subject to a degree of prejudice. Many of the characters and events in the novel reflect Waugh's life when he was in school and later as an adult.

Brideshead Revisited was the first of Waugh's novels to come to the attention of the American public. In fact, soon after the publication of *Brideshead Revisited, Life* magazine printed an interview with Waugh. But critics were split over the quality of the novel, and some have criticized it for being too romantic and lacking the brilliance of Waugh's other novels. James Carens in *The Satiric Art of Evelyn Waugh* notes that even though the critic and author Edmund Wilson was an admirer of Waugh's earlier works, he condemned *Brideshead Revisited* as a "disastrous" novel. In contrast, Carens notes that the review in *Catholic World* magazine praised the novel, calling it "a work of art."

Author Biography

The religious issues appearing in *Brideshead Revisited* concerned Evelyn Waugh from a relatively young age. Born Evelyn Arthur St. John Waugh on October 28, 1903, in the comfortable London suburb of Hampstead, England, Evelyn was the youngest son of Arthur Waugh, a devout member of the Anglican Church. He was educated at Lancing, a preparatory school that specialized in educating the sons of Anglican clergy. Like all students at Lancing, Evelyn was required to attend chapel every morning and evening and three times on Sundays. According to Waugh in his unfinished autobiography, *A Little Learning: The Early Years*, he does not remember thinking that these requirements were unreasonable.

Arthur Waugh worked as a publisher, critic, author, and editor, which provided Evelyn with daily exposure to books and writing. In addition, Evelyn's father, together with his mother, Catherine Charlotte Raban Waugh, regularly read aloud to both their sons. At age seven, Evelyn had already written a short story, and by age nine, with a group of friends, he had produced a magazine. Eventually, his older brother, Alec, went on to write best-selling novels and travel books.

Waugh's years as an adult were remarkably similar to the experiences of Charles Ryder, the protagonist in *Brideshead Revisited.* By the time Waugh left Lancing for Oxford, he reported that he was no longer a Christian, thanks in part to an instructor who encouraged him to think skeptically about religion, as well as to his extensive reading of philosophers of the Enlightenment (a movement in the eighteenth century that advocated the use of reason in the reappraisal of accepted ideas and social institutions). While at Oxford, Waugh studied some and drank and socialized a great deal with an artistic and literary crowd. He left Oxford before receiving a degree to attend art school.

The next few years saw Waugh drinking too much. He was unhappy and unsure as to his life's calling. He left art school to become a teacher but was fired from three schools in less than two years. Finally, in 1927, he began to write on a regular basis and a year later published his first novel, *Decline and Fall.* The book, a humorous and satiric look at a young man's efforts to find his way in a world where evil is rewarded and good is punished, was a controversial success. That same year he married, but the marriage soon broke up because of his wife's infidelity.

Evelyn Waugh

In 1930, Waugh became a Roman Catholic, his conversion brought about by his wife's unfaithfulness and by his disenchantment with modern society. In 1936, he received an annulment of his marriage and the next year married Laura Herbert, a member of a prominent Catholic family. They had six children. Just as his character Ryder does, Waugh traveled extensively to exotic places during the 1930s and 1940s, including Africa and Central America. His travels provided fuel for many of his books.

By the time Europe was preparing for the second world war, Waugh was a well-respected author. But his patriotism, along with a sense that his life had become too comfortable, prompted him to pull some strings to receive a post with the Royal Marines in 1939—not an easy accomplishment at the age of thirty-six. According to Paul S. Burdett, Jr., in *World War II,* Waugh's health was suspect, his eyesight was limited, and "his physique tended toward the pudgy," but he showed himself to be an eager soldier. His wartime experiences informed his later novels, including *Brideshead Revisited.*

When he died in Somerset, England, in 1966, Waugh had published more than thirty books, fourteen of which were novels. He also published travel books, biographies, short stories, and essays, securing his position as one of the most respected English authors of the twentieth century. His reputation as a man with a bitingly sharp wit gave many people the impression that he was an uncaring person; but those who knew him tell of a man who was exceedingly generous with his money and time, especially to those in financial need and to aspiring writers.

Plot Summary

Prologue

In *Brideshead Revisited,* Charles Ryder is a middle-aged captain in the British Army during World War II, stationed in the Scottish countryside in 1942. He organizes his troops to move them to another location via train overnight. When the sun comes up, he realizes that the new encampment is in England near a mansion whose owners he once knew.

Book One

Chapters One–Four

In 1923, Charles is at Oxford studying history, and in his third term he meets fellow student Sebastian Flyte, the son of a wealthy Catholic family, who carries around a stuffed bear named Al. Sebastian asks Charles to lunch with his friends (including Anthony Blanche), who are witty and worldly. Sebastian later takes Charles on a day trip to the countryside, where they have a picnic. On this excursion, Sebastian brings Charles to his family's home, a mansion named Brideshead. Charles is very impressed with Sebastian.

The following year, after Charles has been associating with Sebastian and his friends for a while, Charles' cousin Jasper scolds him for hanging around with a bad set of people. Charles is not swayed. Anthony Blanche invites Charles to dinner, where Anthony discusses in great detail the members of Sebastian's family and their peculiarities.

Charles travels to London to spend the summer vacation with his father. Their time together is uncomfortable, and Charles refers to it as a "war." Sebastian sends Charles a telegram stating that he is gravely injured, and that Charles must come to his aid at once. When Charles arrives at Brideshead, he discovers that Sebastian has merely cracked a small bone in his foot. Charles meets Julia, Sebastian's sister.

Charles spends the rest of summer break with Sebastian, and he later recalls having a wonderful time, "very near heaven during those languid days." They stay at the Brideshead mansion, where Charles begins to paint a mural in one of the rooms. He meets Cordelia, Sebastian's youngest sister, and his brother, Brideshead. The issue of the family's Catholicism comes up in conversations a number of times. The two friends also travel to Venice, Italy, to visit Sebastian's father, Lord Marchmain, and his mistress, Cara.

Chapters Five–Eight

Charles and Sebastian return to Oxford in the fall, where they discover that Anthony Blanche has failed his classes and has moved to Munich. The two friends begin to feel older and less like pursuing their frivolous lifestyle of the previous year, and Sebastian puts away his stuffed bear. Charles begins to take art classes. Rex Mottram, Julia's boyfriend, invites them to a party in London, and they end up at a whorehouse. Later that evening, the police stop Sebastian while he is driving drunk, and everyone, including Charles, is sent to the jail. Rex bails them out. Charles goes to Brideshead mansion for the Christmas holidays, and Lady Marchmain talks to him about becoming a Catholic. Sebastian is drinking even more heavily and is worried that Charles is watching his behavior at his mother's request.

There is an ugly scene at Brideshead mansion during the Easter break in which Sebastian is drunk and then leaves. There is another drunken scene at school later. Sebastian fails his classes at Oxford, and Lady Marchmain warns him that she will send him to live with an old priest if he does not straighten up. Sebastian goes to Venice to be with his father, instead, and Lady Marchmain plans to have Mr. Samgrass, a history don (tutor), watch over him and take him on a vacation to the Middle East when he returns from Italy. Charles tells his father that he wants to leave Oxford to attend art school.

Charles does, in fact, go to Paris to attend art school. Sebastian and Mr. Samgrass return from their trip. Charles comes to Brideshead mansion for Christmas and sees that Sebastian is drinking even more and looks ill. Everyone discovers that Sebastian left Mr. Samgrass during the trip and wandered about on his own for a time. Sebastian was found only after he couldn't pay his hotel bill, and the hotel management called his family. The whole family is on edge about Sebastian's depression and drinking, but he agrees to go on a hunt, which encourages Lady Marchmain. They make sure he has no money so he cannot stop and get a drink at a pub, but Charles gives him money in secret. Sebastian is found later that day, at a pub, drunk. Lady Marchmain finds out and is very angry with Charles. Rex attempts to take Sebastian to a doctor he knows in Zurich who can help him with his alcoholism, but Sebastian gives him the slip and disappears. Rex visits Charles, looking for Sebastian. Charles and Rex go out to dinner, where Rex tells Charles of Lady Marchmain's illness and the Flyte family's money troubles. Rex and Julia get married in a small ceremony. Sebastian is not present.

Charles recalls the story of Rex and Julia: when Julia was a debutante, how she and Rex met, their courtship, and the problems with their engagement and marriage ceremony. Lady Marchmain believes that Rex is beneath Julia and demands that their engagement remain a secret although their news gets out. Rex wants a very fancy wedding, with important guests and at an important cathedral, but because he is not Catholic, this is not possible. He takes classes with a priest to become a Catholic, but he is not terribly bright. The Catholic wedding is eventually called off because Julia's brother, Brideshead, discovers that Rex has been divorced. The wedding finally takes place at a Protestant church known for marrying couples in Rex and Julia's situation.

The spring of 1926 sees Charles leaving Paris for London because he feels he must be in his country of birth during its difficult economic times. The General Strike occurs, and Charles signs up to help distribute food. One evening he goes to a jazz bar and runs into Anthony Blanche, who reports having allowed Sebastian to stay with him in Marseilles. He says that Sebastian was still drinking heavily and was stealing things from him to sell and pawn. Julia asks Charles to come to see Lady Marchmain at the family's London house, as she is dying. Charles does so, then goes to Morocco to find Sebastian, as Lady Marchmain has asked to see him one last time before she dies. He finds Sebastian in a hospital in Fez, very ill from his drinking. He is with a German named Kurt, who is also ill. Sebastian cannot travel to England because of his poor health, so Charles stays for a week and helps him settle his financial affairs. Charles returns to England and agrees to paint four oils of the soon-to-be torn down Marchmain house in London, as requested by Brideshead. Lady Marchmain dies. Cordelia later tells Charles that Lady Marchmain's funeral mass was the last event at the family chapel at Brideshead before it was closed up.

Book Two
Chapters One–Five

The story now moves to the late 1930s, when Charles is a painter of some repute, primarily of buildings about to be razed. He is married to Celia, the sister of a fellow Oxford student, and they have two young children. He is returning from a two-year trip to Mexico and Central America, where he was drawing ruins. He meets Celia in New York City, and they leave for London on a ship. They seem to have a cool relationship although Celia is a very friendly woman who loves to entertain. They give a cocktail party on board the ship the first night and also discover that Julia is on board. A storm hits the ship, and Celia retires, seasick, to her room throughout the storm's duration, about three days. Charles and Julia get reacquainted during this time, and they eventually make love in Julia's stateroom. Charles recalls that Celia once had an affair, and Julia tells Charles of her failed marriage with Rex and of her stillborn daughter. Charles sends Celia to their home while he stays in London to set up his next art show and to see Julia.

Charles and Julia continue their affair in London, and his art show is a success. There is talk of war at the show. Anthony Blanche appears at the show's opening, and he and Charles go to a bar to talk about old times. He knows about Julia and Charles's affair, having heard people speak of it at a luncheon that day.

Charles and Julia have been together for two years but haven't sought divorces from their spouses. They are now at Brideshead, as is Rex. One evening, Brideshead arrives from London with the sudden news that he is getting married to Beryl Muspratt, a widow with three children. He also mentions that his fiancée probably will not come to Brideshead to see Charles and Julia, as she is a very proper Catholic woman and would disapprove of their living arrangements. He also expects that Julia and Rex and Charles will leave the mansion to make room for his new family. This greatly upsets Julia, and she begins to question whether she is a sinner in the eyes of her God. Rex arrives with his political friends and there is more talk of war.

Both Charles and Julia begin the process of divorcing their spouses. Rex gives patriotic speeches in the House of Commons, and the country is full of the talk of avoiding war with the Germans. Cordelia shows up at Brideshead after years as a nurse and aid worker in Spain. She has seen Sebastian; he is living in Tunis, still drinking heavily and ill but living at a monastery.

Brideshead marries Beryl. Given the increasing political tensions in Europe, Lord Marchmain decides to return to England and the Brideshead mansion with his mistress in the winter. He arrives seriously ill. Julia and Charles, who had moved out of Brideshead, move back to the mansion to be with Lord Marchmain. He tells Julia and Charles that he dislikes Brideshead's new wife, Beryl, and cannot imagine her as the lady of the manor after he dies. He says he is seriously considering leaving the estate to Julia and Charles, which stuns them.

By Easter, Lord Marchmain is getting sicker and closer to death, and Brideshead demands that a priest be sent for. The priest comes, but Lord Marchmain sends him away because he is a nonpracticing Catholic. Charles is very disdainful of Brideshead's bringing in the priest. In June, Charles and Celia's divorce is final, and she marries again. In July, Lord Marchmain is unconscious, and Julia brings back the priest. Charles disagrees with this but is not surprised at her actions—he has seen her becoming more religious during the summer. The priest arrives, gives Lord Marchmain the final blessing, and he responds when the priest asks him if he is sorry for his sins. This apparent sign that Lord Marchmain has accepted Catholicism again overwhelms Charles, who kneels and says a short prayer. Julia decides that she can no longer be with Charles, in what she now sees as a sinful relationship.

Epilogue

The story ends where it began, with Charles as a captain in the British Army, encamped near the Brideshead mansion during World War II. Julia, who is overseas with Cordelia helping with the war effort, now owns the mansion. Brideshead is serving with the British cavalry in Palestine. Charles wanders around the old place, reminiscing, and bumps into a few of the staff still there. The family chapel is open, with a light burning upon the altar. Charles says a short prayer and leaves.

Characters

Mrs. Abel

Mrs. Abel is Edward Ryder's cook. According to Charles, her cooking skills are not very good.

Alfred

Alfred is one of Charles's cousins. Alfred gave advice to Charles's father about how to dress at school, which he steadfastly followed.

Aloysius

Aloysius is the teddy bear that Sebastian carries with him nearly everywhere he goes during his first year at Oxford, contributing to Sebastian's colorful reputation. Sebastian even goes so far as to refer to Aloysius as if he were a living creature, with likes and dislikes and moods. As Sebastian's drinking gets worse, he leaves Aloysius in a dresser drawer.

Antoine

See Anthony Blanche

Monsignor Bell

Lady Marchmain asks Monsignor Bell to give Sebastian a number of firm lectures about his failures at school and his heavy drinking. Sebastian's family later threatens to make him live with the monsignor if he does not straighten up, but Sebastian escapes this fate.

Anthony Blanche

Anthony is a student at Oxford and Sebastian's friend. He is a boisterous character, interested in food, wine, and having a good time. Charles refers to him as an "aesthete par excellence." There are indications that he is homosexual.

Everyone at school is in awe of Anthony. Charles remarks that even though he was barely older, Anthony seemed more mature and knowledgeable about the world than any of his other friends and acquaintances at Oxford. His background and experiences are somewhat romantic and mysterious. His mother lives in Argentina with his Italian stepfather, and Anthony has spent time with them traveling to exotic places. Anthony is always dropping names of famous people and places in his conversations with Sebastian and Charles.

Lady Brideshead

See Beryl Muspratt

Bridey

See Lord Brideshead Flyte

Cara

Cara is Lord Marchmain's mistress. She is a middle-aged, "well-preserved" woman, who speaks very plainly and honestly about her lover and his family.

Caroline

Caroline is Celia and Charles' infant daughter. She is born while Charles is overseas, and he takes very little interest in seeing her when he returns.

Collins

Collins is one of Charles's earliest friends at Oxford. Charles and Sebastian refer to him a number of times as someone who is studious and a solid person.

Earl of Brideshead

See Lord Brideshead Flyte

Effie

Effie is a prostitute at Ma Mayfield's, a whorehouse. She is with Sebastian, Charles, and Boy Mulcaster when they are stopped by the police for drunken driving.

There is also an "Effie" who works for Nanny when Brideshead is nearly empty and part of an army camp during World War II in the novel's epilogue.

Lord Brideshead Flyte

Brideshead is Sebastian's brother and the eldest son of Lord and Lady Marchmain. He gives the impression of someone who is more mature than his years, even though he is only three years older than Sebastian and Charles. He is very serious and does not have many friends. He is a devout Catholic.

Brideshead is unmarried throughout most of the novel and is searching for a vocation, having thought briefly about becoming a Jesuit priest or a politician. When Charles visits the family about ten years after the novel opens, Brideshead has become a prominent collector of matchbooks and spends most of his time on that hobby.

One day he suddenly announces that he has found a bride, Beryl Muspratt. She is the widow of another prominent matchbook collector and a devout Catholic with children.

Lady Cordelia Flyte

Cordelia is Sebastian's sister, Lord and Lady Marchmain's youngest daughter. When the book opens she is a precocious pre-teen and a serious Catholic. Catholicism is a common topic of her conversation.

Later in the novel, just before the outbreak of World War II, Cordelia works as a nurse in Spain, taking care of soldiers fighting in the Spanish Civil

Media Adaptations

- *Brideshead Revisited* was adapted as a television mini-series in 1982, starring Anthony Andrews, Jeremy Irons, Diana Quick, and Laurence Olivier, and produced by Granada Television. A six-volume VHS tape set of the series is available from Anchor Bay Entertainment.

- Harper Audio has produced a cassette recording of *Brideshead Revisited,* and Chivers Audio Books has produced a compact disc recording of the unabridged novel. Jeremy Irons narrates both versions, which were released in 2000.

- In 1994, Roger Parsley adapted the novel into a play entitled *Brideshead Revisited: A Play.*

War. When Charles finds himself at Brideshead during World War II, she is reported to be in Palestine with Julia, working in some medical capacity. She never marries.

Lady Julia Flyte

Lady Julia is Sebastian's younger sister by a couple of years and the eldest daughter of Lord and Lady Marchmain. At the beginning of the novel, she is eighteen years old and involved in her debut to English society at parties in London. She is a classic beauty and is charming like her brother Sebastian, and her name appears in the newspapers frequently. She is a non-practicing Catholic, like Sebastian.

She eventually marries Rex Mottram, an aspiring politician, but the marriage is not a solid one. She tries to provide Rex with a child, but the daughter is stillborn. Julia runs into Charles and Celia on a cruise ship crossing the Atlantic from New York, where she has been pursuing a love affair. She and Charles fall in love by the time the ship docks in London. She and Charles seek separations and divorces from their respective spouses, but never marry each other.

Julia, through the death of her father, acquires a stronger sense of her Catholicism. When Charles returns to Brideshead during World War II, he discovers that she is with Cordelia in Palestine, working for the war effort. She never remarries.

Lord Sebastian Flyte

Sebastian is the charming youngest son of Lord and Lady Marchmain and Charles's closest friend at Oxford. They meet when Sebastian is drunk and vomits through Charles's window one night. The next day, Sebastian apologizes and asks Charles to lunch; they and others talk and drink until late in the afternoon.

Sebastian is not only charming; he is, in Charles's words, "magically beautiful." Charles becomes quite taken with Sebastian and even seems to fall in love with him although they do not appear to be lovers in the novel. Charles, while recounting his lonely and serious childhood, credits Sebastian with giving him a second, happier childhood through their joint escapades, even though those escapades include drinking heavily and spending lavish amounts of money on clothes and cigars.

The novel chronicles Sebastian's descent into an alcoholic haze, beginning with a drunk driving incident and ending with him very ill, nearly destitute (despite the money his family sends him), and living with monks in Tunis. Through Cordelia's report, the Brideshead family and Charles learn that Sebastian has become religious.

Hardcastle

A friend of Sebastian's at Oxford, Hardcastle regularly loaned him his convertible, two-seater Morris-Cowley car.

Mrs. Hawkins

Mrs. Hawkins is the childhood nanny to Sebastian, his older brother, and two sisters. She still lives at Brideshead in an out-of-the-way room. Nanny Hawkins is much loved by the four Brideshead children, so much so that Sebastian makes a special trip out to his home to have Charles meet her. She is a devout Catholic.

Mr. Hooper

Mr. Hooper is Charles Ryder's new platoon commander as the novel opens. Charles does not particularly trust Mr. Hooper to accomplish a task but claims to have affection for him because he tolerated being the focus of an embarrassing incident. Charles views Hooper as a symbol of "Young England," with his relaxed dress and attitude.

Jasper

Jasper is Charles's older cousin. He has been at Oxford for a few years and is very fond of giving Charles advice on how he should live his life and spend his money, what classes to take, what clubs to belong to, how to wear his clothes, and whom to associate with. Charles does not follow any of his suggestions. Jasper visits Charles toward the end of his first year at Oxford and scolds him for hanging out with a "bad set" and getting drunk frequently.

Kurt

Kurt is a young German who lives with Sebastian in Algeria and then follows him to Greece. He left Germany to join the French Foreign Legion but ended up in Fez, sick and apparently living off Sebastian. There is some indication that they may be lovers.

Lunt

Lunt is Charles's valet at Oxford, also referred to as his "scout." He is very patient with Charles concerning his carousing and drinking.

Father MacKay

Father MacKay is the priest brought in by Brideshead to give Lord Marchmain his last rites. Lord Marchmain sends him away, very politely, the first time he shows up. Father MacKay is very eager to give Lord Marchmain his last rites, so he makes a second, successful attempt when Lord Marchmain is semi-conscious.

Lord Alex Marchmain

Lord Marchmain is Sebastian's father. He left the family at the time of World War I, when he went to Italy, and never returned. He lives in Venice with his mistress, Cara.

He and Lady Marchmain have never divorced because of her strong Catholic beliefs, of which he is openly disdainful. Lord Marchmain will agree to nearly anything his children ask of him if he thinks it will upset Lady Marchmain. Cara believes that he truly hates his wife.

Lord Marchmain returns to Brideshead after Lady Marchmain's death when he knows that he himself is near death. His death and his apparent acceptance of last rites have a profound effect on Charles and Julia's feelings about Catholicism and religion.

Lady Teresa Marchmain

Lady Marchmain is Sebastian's mother. She is separated from Lord Marchmain and has a companion, the poet Sir Adrian Porson. She is devoutly Roman Catholic and even has tried to convert Charles. She is very fond of Charles and tries to recruit him to help Sebastian stop drinking. She dies just before World War II.

Marquis of Marchmain

See Lord Alex Marchmain

Marquise of Marchmain

See Lady Teresa Marchmain

Julia Mottram

See Lady Julia Flyte

Rex Mottram

Rex is Lady Julia's boyfriend and eventually her fiancé and husband. He is originally from Canada, which prompts many to see him as an inferior match for Julia. He is presented as somewhat stupid and dull when he takes lessons in Catholicism before marrying Julia. He is handsome and seems very open with information about himself and his business dealings. Ironically, his past catches up with him when he tries to marry Julia in the Catholic Church, and Brideshead discovers that he has been married before.

Rex is a member of Parliament and a businessman who knows all the right people and is always offering to connect friends and colleagues with one another. He bails out Charles, Sebastian, and Boy Mulcaster when they are thrown in jail and suggests a physician he knows for Lady Marchmain and a place where Sebastian can get treatment for alcoholism.

Eventually, Julia separates from Rex, and after two years she secures a divorce. His political power increases during World War II.

Boy Mulcaster

Boy Mulcaster is Sebastian and Anthony's friend who seems to always be in trouble. Charles does not like him although he becomes his brother-in-law when Charles marries Celia, Boy's sister.

Celia Mulcaster

Celia is Boy Mulcaster's sister and, eventually, Charles' wife. She has two children with Charles before they agree to a separation and eventual divorce.

Celia is charming, loves to give parties, and easily makes friends. She is unfaithful to Charles just before he leaves for Mexico and Central America for a two-year working trip. They separate when Charles returns, and he falls in love with Julia; they eventually divorce. Celia then marries Robin, a man who is seven years her junior.

Viscount Mulcaster

See Boy Mulcaster

Beryl Muspratt

Beryl Muspratt is Brideshead's fiancée and eventually his wife toward the end of the novel. She is the widow of Admiral Muspratt, a collector of matchboxes, and has three children. Beryl is a devout Catholic, and Brideshead is worried that she will be offended if she is asked to come to Brideshead Castle while Julia and Charles are there, living together outside of marriage.

Father Phipps

Father Phipps is a priest brought to Brideshead to conduct mass. He appears to be somewhat a fool because he believes that Sebastian and Charles are interested in cricket even when they keep telling him that they know nothing about the sport.

Charles Ryder

Charles Ryder is the novel's narrator: everything the reader sees and knows is told through his eyes. He first appears as a captain in the English army during World War II, stationed in the Scottish countryside. He is a man who is filled with memories, a bit nostalgic for an earlier time in his life.

Later in the novel, Charles is in his first year at Oxford, studying history. He is very eager to do the right things in this new environment. When he meets Sebastian, he is swept off his feet by his charm and immediately becomes deeply and exclusively involved with his new friend. He feels that, as child who had a grim, rather serious childhood, he is finally being given a chance to have fun. He and Sebastian spend time together drinking, attending parties, and avoiding their studies.

Charles is a budding artist and painter and occasionally works on a mural at Brideshead Castle, Sebastian's home. Eventually he leaves Oxford, sensing that he is not accomplishing much, and attends art school in Paris. He becomes a relatively well-known painter of buildings and architectural subjects.

Charles at one point declares himself an agnostic, but he is curious about what it means to be a Catholic. Lady Marchmain has many talks with him in her attempt to convert him to Roman Catholicism, but Charles steadfastly believes religion to be useless. At the end of the novel, at Lord Marchmain's death, he seems to have a sort of religious epiphany when he kneels and prays for the dying man.

His marriage to Celia ends in divorce when he meets Julia, after not seeing her for a number of years, and falls in love with her.

Edward Ryder

Edward Ryder is Charles's father, who lives with his household staff in London. He is in his late fifties, but Charles says that he could be mistaken for a man in his seventies or even eighties.

Edward and Charles have a distant relationship. Charles seems to rely on his father for money and not much else. He mentions that his father gave him no advice on being at Oxford. Edward has an odd sense of humor, and people around him often find it difficult to know if he is making an obscure joke or simply behaving strangely.

Mr. Sammy Samgrass

Mr. Samgrass is an Oxford don originally hired by Lady Marchmain to pull together a memoir of her three dead brothers. He is asked to keep an eye on Sebastian when he returns to school for his second year. He appears to be a man who wants only to help the family set their drunken son straight but is ultimately revealed to have taken advantage of their generosity and faith in him. On a foreign trip with Sebastian he is asked to keep track of Sebastian but loses him and tries to hide this fact from Lady Marchmain.

Themes

Religion and Catholicism

Brideshead Revisited is filled with references to its characters' views on religion. Charles Ryder is an agnostic, having received little or no religious training as a child, and each member of the Flyte family presents a different image of a Catholic. Charles' cousin Jasper advises him in book one, chapter one, "Beware of the Anglo-Catholics—they're all sodomites with unpleasant accents. In fact, steer clear of all the religious groups; they do nothing but harm." Throughout the novel, Charles

questions members of the Flyte family about their beliefs and even makes light of religion until his epiphany at the end of the book.

Sebastian is a believer but has trouble staying within the rules and strictures of Catholicism. "Oh dear, it's very difficult being a Catholic," he notes in book one, chapter four. In that same chapter, he and Charles have their first discussion, of many, about Catholicism, and Charles expresses great amazement that Sebastian believes the "awful lot of nonsense" that Catholics ascribe to, such as the story of Christ's birth. "Is it nonsense? I wish it were. It sometimes sounds terribly sensible to me," answers Sebastian. His life is a struggle between what he wants to do and what he believes his church requires him to do. After years of drunkenness and wandering around the world, Sebastian ends up as an aide at a monastery in Tunis, in a sense returning to his religion while still being very much a worldly man.

Lord Marchmain is openly disdainful of Catholicism, having rejected the Church when he left Lady Marchmain. Like Sebastian, he appears to come back to his religion in book two, chapter five when, on his deathbed, he mutely signals that he is sorry for his sins in response to a priest's questions. Charles's response upon witnessing this, despite his previous dismissal of religion and Catholicism, is to say a brief prayer under his breath. Lady Marchmain is adamantly Catholic and in book one, chapter five announces that the Flyte family "must make a Catholic of Charles." The fact that she will not give Lord Marchmain a divorce is attributed to her being a devout Catholic.

When Cordelia is young, she attends a convent, and she tells Charles that because he is an agnostic she will pray for him. Her love of religion at that age takes typically childlike forms, such as saying a novena (a series of prayers recited for nine days) for a dead pet, but as an adult, her love of God is manifested in pursuing good works as a nurse during wartime. She is the only Catholic character who truly seems to enjoy her religion and her relationship with God. Brideshead is a Catholic strictly because he was born one—he has no real interest in or passion for the subject. Most of his utterances about religion are legalistic, such as when he discovers that Rex cannot marry Julia in the Catholic Church because he is divorced.

Julia appears throughout most of the book to be uninterested in her Catholicism, except as it is a barrier to marrying her social equal. Only toward the end of the novel, after she has started her affair with

Topics For Further Study

- Research the Spanish Civil War and how the numerous volunteers from all over the world played a part. Where did they come from, and why did they volunteer for what was often dangerous duty?

- How does Charles's college life compare to your school experiences? Write an essay in which you consider the similarities and differences.

- Think about how Sebastian's drinking is described and dealt with in the novel. Are attitudes about drinking different today? How do the Flytes handle Sebastian's drinking problem, and how does this compare to the way similar problems are handled today?

- If possible, find someone who lived through the Great Depression in the United States or elsewhere. Interview the person to learn what life was like then, and how it was different from life today. If you are unable to interview someone, read first-hand accounts of depression-era people and write an essay describing their way of life during that period.

- When Sebastian wants to escape his family, he travels to the Middle East and North Africa. When Charles Ryder leaves his wife to paint and draw for two years, he goes to Mexico and Central America. Why do you think each chose the place he did? Where would you go to if you wanted to get away for a while?

- Think about the transatlantic cruise Charles and Celia take from New York to London. Imagine what it would be like to travel with a group of strangers on a ship that takes days to get to Europe. Write a series of diary entries as if you were Charles or Celia describing the trip and your feelings and experiences. You may want to do some historical research to help you make your entries accurate and detailed.

Charles and divorces Rex, does she begin to think about being a Catholic. Even though she loves Charles, she expresses concern that her behavior—her "waywardness and wilfulness, a less disciplined habit than most of her contemporaries" when she was a young girl, as well as her illicit affair with Charles—has filled her with sin. When she tells Charles after her father's death that she can no longer see him, she admits, "I've always been bad. Probably I shall be bad again, punished again. But the worse I am, the more I need God." The Epilogue finds Charles saying a small prayer in the chapel at Brideshead, and he is pleased that the chapel is open years after he has last seen the family.

Alcoholism

The novel provides an overview of how Sebastian's family and friends react to his increasingly destructive reliance on alcohol. At first, Sebastian seems to be a typical college student, drinking frequently, but always with friends and never suffering an unhappy consequence. Charles notices that the amount of Sebastian's drinking, as well as his generally happy demeanor, changes when they return to Oxford after their blissful summer at Brideshead mansion.

A number of incidents follow that mark the beginning of the end of the close friendship between Charles and Sebastian. After a party in London, Sebastian drives drunk with other people in the car, including Charles, and is stopped by the police. They are all taken to jail. During Easter at Brideshead, Sebastian is drinking heavily, missing meals, and treating Charles badly. He accuses Charles of spying on him for the family and eventually leaves for London.

The family's response to Sebastian's drinking is a classic case of denial. At Easter, no one in the family is willing to face what is happening to Sebastian, instead seeking out Charles to fix it for them. Lady Marchmain asks Charles about Sebastian's behavior. Charles covers for his friend, saying that Sebastian is getting a cold. Julia acknowledges to Charles that she knows of her brother's drinking but tells Charles that he must take care of Sebastian. "Well, you must deal with him. It's no business of mine," she says. Brideshead also asks Charles to help Sebastian stop drinking, and Lady Marchmain expects Charles to keep an eye on Sebastian. "You've got to help him. I can't," she pleads.

Eventually, a dean finds Sebastian wandering around the university drunk. The school agrees to allow him to stay if he moves in with a monsignor (a member of the Roman Catholic clergy), something that Sebastian absolutely refuses to do. Sebastian leaves Oxford and sets out on a trip to the Middle East with Mr. Samgrass as his guardian, as arranged by his mother. This trip, rather than helping Sebastian, launches him on a lifetime of drinking and wandering around the Middle East and North Africa. Charles and Sebastian see each other only briefly after Sebastian leaves Oxford.

Male Friendship

Sebastian and Charles's friendship is an intense one. In fact, while their relationship appears to be platonic, the words Charles uses to describe their relationship border on the romantic. The picnic they take together in book one, chapter one is portrayed in dreamy and romantic terms:

> We lay on our backs, Sebastian's eyes on the leaves above him, mine on his profile... and the sweet scent of the tobacco merged with the sweet summer scents around us and the fumes of the sweet, golden wine seemed to lift us a finger's breadth above the turf and hold us suspended.

Cara, Lord Marchmain's mistress, notes the closeness between the two friends and surprises Charles by asking him about it in book one, chapter four. She approves of relationships between young men, "if they do not go on too long," and adds that at their young age it is better "to have that kind of love for another boy than for a girl."

The intensity of Charles and Sebastian's friendship transforms Charles. He changes his group of friends at Oxford after meeting Sebastian, and he even alters how his room is decorated and the books he reads based on what Sebastian and his friends like. Charles also becomes deeply involved with Sebastian's family, and they come to think of him almost as one of their own. When Charles is later involved in his love affair with Julia, Sebastian's sister, he indicates that Sebastian was the "forerunner," the first person in the Flyte family with whom he fell in love. This all-encompassing

friendship makes Sebastian's eventual drunkenness and depression especially painful for Charles.

Memories and Reminiscences

The entire novel is drawn as a series of Charles's memories; indeed, the novel's subtitle, *The Sacred and Profane Memories of Captain Charles Ryder,* makes this clear. The book opens in the present with Charles surprised to discover that he is encamped near Brideshead mansion, which sets off the memories that make up the body of the book. The novel closes with him in the present again and briefly walking through the house, running into Nanny Hawkins and savoring a few more memories about his friendship with the Flyte family.

As well, Charles is a man who values the past, whether imagined or real. Book one is entitled "Et In Arcadia Ego," which is Latin for "I, too, lived in Arcadia," referring to a pastoral and mountainous region of ancient Greece used extensively in painting and literature to denote a sort of Utopia, or a place where life is wonderful and well lived. Book one tells the story of meeting Sebastian, and the blissful time they spent together.

Throughout the novel, Charles believes that what *was* is preferable to what *is;* in the Prologue he complains about the current behavior of "Young England." He bemoans young people's lack of an education, their dress, and their manner of speech. Even as a student at Oxford, he complains, as book one opens, when women arrive for a week of dances and parties. The change in atmosphere at his school upsets him.

All of Charles' memories of Sebastian during their first year as friends are romanticized. In book one, chapter four, for example, Charles fondly remembers a summer, spent almost always alone with Sebastian, when, "I, at any rate, believed myself to be very near heaven, during those languid days at Brideshead." And Sebastian, as well, realizes that this summer of their youth will be something they always look back on: "If it could only be like this always—always summer, always alone, the fruit always ripe."

Style

Point of View

Brideshead Revisited is written completely from the first person point-of-view; that is, solely through the eyes of Charles Ryder. Charles is the only one telling the story, so the reader must decide whether he is a reliable or an unreliable narrator. Are his impressions of the events and characters in the story to be believed?

In general, Charles is a trustworthy narrator. He does not obviously exaggerate or provide unbelievable information. But, when only one person is telling a story, that person's background and experiences color the telling of the tale. In Charles' case, his childhood was a serious one, with very little happiness. His mother died when he was young and his father pays little attention to him. The absence of his own family may have made it easy for him to become intimately involved with the Flyte family, and because of this closeness he may be blind to some of their faults. A number of times other characters refer to the less-than-wonderful characteristics of the Flytes, including Sebastian, and this either confuses or upsets Charles.

Charles tells the story of his relationship with the Flytes and Sebastian with the benefit of hindsight. He has had time during the intervening fifteen to twenty years to reconsider events. The story is framed by the present, with a Prologue and an Epilogue, but takes place primarily in the past.

Satire

Waugh is well-known for his satirical novels, books that make fun of social customs and the people who participate in them. While *Brideshead Revisited* is not truly a satirical work and marks a change in Waugh's writing style, he does not completely abandon this favored technique. Satire is found in the book, particularly where religion is concerned. Depictions of priests are not always complementary. For example, the priest who visits Brideshead during Charles and Sebastian's summer vacation can't seem to understand that the two friends know nothing about cricket, even though they tell him this repeatedly. In addition to making subtle fun of Rex Mottram and his eagerness to be an important political player, Rex is made to look dim-witted when he takes classes to convert to Catholicism. And when issues of Catholic doctrine are discussed, such as how the final rites should be given to Lord Marchmain, everyone in the Flyte family seems to have a different and confused impression as to the correct way.

Romance

Romantic settings and events are prevalent in *Brideshead Revisited*. Romantic technique in a work of fiction refers to the use of language that is flowery or characters and events that are idealized. Waugh employs what critic James F. Carens calls "purple" language and draws almost fantasy images of a number of characters.

Charles's two most serious relationships, with Sebastian and his sister Julia, are pursued in the countryside, in idealized pastoral settings. Charles and Sebastian have a picnic early in their relationship, and at Brideshead they spend a summer that is described as "near heaven." He and Julia move to Brideshead to continue their love affair in the country. In book two, chapter three, for example, one evening at Brideshead is remembered as "tranquil, lime-scented," and Julia is pictured "in a tight little gold tunic and a white gown, one hand in the water idly turning an emerald ring to catch the fire of the sunset." Waugh's language here is almost dreamlike.

Setting in Time

The novel's main action takes place in England between World War I and World War II. While international events barely impact the story line, Waugh drops numerous hints in the narrative to help the reader know what is happening outside of the characters' immediate surroundings.

The Prologue and the Epilogue take place in a wartime encampment in the English countryside. When women are part of an event at Oxford early in the novel, Charles's servant comments that such a thing would not have happened before World War I. Numerous hints are given that war with Germany and Italy is on the horizon. When Rex returns to Brideshead with his political friends, the conversation is filled with references to running into fake tanks in the Black Forest and to leaders such as Franco and Chamberlain. One of the reasons Lord Marchmain gives for moving back to England is the "international situation."

Simile

Augmenting the relatively rich language in *Brideshead Revisited*, Waugh occasionally uses similes. These are phrases that compare two seemingly unlike things. For example, in book one, chapter five, Charles compares Sebastian to "a Polynesian," happy when left alone but threatened when "the big ship dropped anchor beyond the coral reef." In book two, chapter one, Charles remarks that bats in a cave "hung in the dome like dry seed-pods." These images contribute to the nostalgic and lush tone of the novel's language.

Historical Context

The Pre-War Years and World War II

The book's events take place between 1922 and World War II. Charles Ryder's generation at Oxford was one that found itself too young to fight in the first war but well into its thirties by the time the Second World War erupted. Throughout the body of *Brideshead Revisited,* Waugh indicates that something is brewing outside the walls of the stately mansions and colleges where most of the novel's actions take place. Europe between World War I and World War II was a place of both great prosperity and dismal poverty, of social innovations and political disarray.

As an adult, Cordelia serves as a nurse during the Spanish Civil War, which lasted from 1936 to 1939. This war was fought between the Nationalists, who were fascists supported by the Italian and German governments, and the Loyalists, who were supported by many thousands of volunteers from other nations. When it was all over, hundreds of thousands were dead, and a fascist regime held power in Spain. The Nazis in Germany took note that other European governments were reluctant to step into the fray; this isolationism indicated that Europe might not interfere in the Nazis' own plans for world domination.

Germany suffered great losses during the First World War and was in political and economic disarray after the war. By the early 1930s, Germany's military and economic might began to recover under Adolf Hitler. By the middle of the 1930s, Hitler's political party, the Nazi Party, was firmly in command. Germany began to make territorial claims on other parts of Europe in the late 1930s. European leaders, including those of England, desperately wanted to avoid another world war, so they capitulated to Germany's demands. British Prime Minister Neville Chamberlain signed the Munich Pact, hoping that Germany would hold to its promise that the Sudetenland, a part of Czechoslovakia, would be its last aggressive territorial claim. The effort at appeasing the Nazi government did not work, and Germany continued to invade other countries. In September 1939, Germany invaded Poland, and Great Britain and France jointly declared war on Germany. The war spread to nearly every corner of the globe, including Africa and Asia, and ultimately involved the United States, Russia, Japan, Italy, and others. By the time the war ended in 1945, a year after Waugh finished writing *Brideshead Revisited,* the United Kingdom alone had sustained more than nine hundred thousand military and civilian casualties.

Economic Depression

After World War I, England suffered serious economic decline, yet the privileged classes continued to consume at a fever pitch. The Flytes are a fabulously wealthy family, although by the late 1920s Rex reports that the family is having some money difficulties.

England's coal, steel, cotton, and shipping industries were in serious financial trouble by the mid-1920s. Coal miners initiated incidences of labor unrest and struck for improvements in their working situations in 1925. The following year, England's General Strike involved some six million union workers. This event prompts Charles and several fellow English art students to leave Paris for their homeland, to see how they can be of help. However, the strike lasted only six days. The economic bad news continued, however, and 1929 brought a stock market crash. The crash and the resulting Great Depression had global effects, and the misery spawned by the worldwide economic downturn contributed to the rise of the Nazi Party in Germany.

Literature

English and American literature from World War I to 1944, when Waugh finished writing *Brideshead Revisited,* was very diverse. Authors experimented with a variety of forms and styles and dealt with subjects formerly considered risqué, such as sex; D. H. Lawrence's novel *Lady Chatterley's Lover* is one example. The horrors of the First World War and the Great Depression prompted writers to consider a world where the old rules had failed, and many traditional religious, political, and social institutions no longer held the authority they once did. Ernest Hemingway and John Steinbeck were two American writers who captured these feelings of disillusionment, and in 1932 British author Aldous Huxley published his futuristic novel, *Brave New World,* in which he expresses a deep-seated suspicion of totalitarian government and societal uniformity.

In *Brideshead Revisited,* Anthony Blanche, as a student at Oxford, recites a passage from T. S. Eliot's poem *The Waste Land.* This work, published in 1922, focused on loss of faith and on the destruction of civilization as previously understood. It was a huge hit with the post-World War I generation that had witnessed how far human nature could degenerate. The poem questions the

Compare & Contrast

- **1920s and 1930s:** The African-American singer and dancer Josephine Baker creates a sensation in Paris with her risqué nightclub show in which she wears an outfit made primarily of feathers. When Anthony and Charles go to a jazz club in London, Charles alludes to having gone to such clubs in Paris, where this kind of entertainment is more accepted than it is in London.

  Today: African American Queen Latifah is one of the most prominent performers in the world. She has starred in a television series, hosted her own talk show, been featured in television commercials, and produced top-selling albums.

- **1920s and 1930s:** Art Deco is the primary artistic style. The name is derived from a 1925 exhibition of decorative and industrial arts in Paris. Art Deco style incorporates straight lines and symmetry using manufactured rather than naturally occurring materials. Charles's art is not influenced by this modern style; he prefers more traditional subjects and styles.

  Today: Art Deco is considered a "retro" style but is still widely appreciated and collected.

Web sites devoted to preserving and studying Art Deco buildings and decorative objects number in the hundreds and are based around the world, from New Zealand to Washington, D.C., to Miami.

- **1920s and 1930s:** The period between World War I and World War II is marked by both prosperity and economic crisis worldwide. European nations are working to rebuild after the First World War. After the stock market crash of 1929, much of the industrialized world suffers through record high unemployment and inflation. Wealthy families like the Flytes are somewhat insulated from the devastation by their inherited land and capital.

  Today: Most of the industrialized world has enjoyed at least four years of unparalleled economic prosperity. Among the wealthiest individuals in the world are those who started innovative companies in the high-technology industry, which is fueling economies worldwide.

---

premise that civilization is progressing. So ingrained did this work become in that generation's consciousness that college students everywhere, like Anthony Blanche, memorized its lines.

Critical Overview

The reviews of *Brideshead Revisited* ranged from adoring to condemning when the book was first published in 1945. James F. Carens in *The Satiric Art of Evelyn Waugh* notes that while the magazine *Catholic World* raved about the novel and called it "a work of art," critic Edmund Wilson (as quoted by Carens) was less positive. Even though Wilson was an admirer of Waugh's earlier, more satirical works, he called *Brideshead Revisited* "disastrous" and declared that the author "no longer knows his way." John K. Hutchens, reviewing the novel in

1945 for the *New York Times,* wrote that the novel "has the depth and weight that are found in a writer working in his prime."

Carens encourages readers to weigh the book carefully, advising, "A novel that has provoked such diverse views deserves consideration. It may be an imperfect work; it can scarcely be a vapid one." Indeed, despite many critics' disappointment with the book's lack of satirical sharpness, *Brideshead Revisited* is the book that introduced American audiences to Waugh.

Much of the negative criticism of *Brideshead Revisited* has charged that in this book, Waugh leaves his earlier empire of hard-bitten satire and wades into the gentler world of romance. Some critics, such as Paul Fussell in the *New Republic,* appear to suggest that Waugh has become soft in his middle age. Comparing *Brideshead Revisited* with

Anthony Andrews (left) as Sebastian Flyte, Diana Quick as Julia, and Jeremy Irons as Charles Ryder in front of Castle Howard in Yorkshire, England, the setting for the 1981 television adaptation of the novel

Waugh's short stories written in the 1930s, Fussell argues:

> If in that overripe fantasy, manufactured in the grim 1940s, he seems at pains to register his worshipful intimacy with the aristocracy, in these stories of the 1930s he exhibits for the unearned-income set an intellectual and moral disdain hard to distinguish from that of a contemporary Marxist-Leninist. If he'd conceived Sebastian Flyte in 1935, he'd have little trouble discerning from the start the selfishness, cruelty, and fatuity behind those expensive good looks.

For many critics, *Brideshead Revisited* marks a change in Waugh's style that continues for the rest of his writing life. Richard P. Lynch, in *Papers on Language and Literature,* remarks that Waugh's later novels, except for *The Loved One,* "are more reassuring to readers of conventional romance." The fact that the novel is completely created from the mist of Charles Ryder's memories gives it a certain wistful quality that his earlier novels lack. In fact, Lynch says in his criticism that it is "atypical among Waugh's novels in its triumph of sentiment over satire."

But others argue that *Brideshead Revisited* still has some of the satire and sharpness of the earlier novels, but it is done in a more mature and learned way. Hutchens argues in his *New York Times* review that the story of Charles and the Flyte family contains much of the "deadly use of detail, the scorn of vulgarity, the light summary touch with minor characters," such as Anthony Blanche and Charles's father. But in this new novel there is now "one sentence and one paragraph after another of reflection and description, [which] could have found no place in the staccato atmosphere of his other works." In Hutchens's eyes, *Brideshead Revisited* is a more fully-grown novel, benefiting from the narrator's years of distance from the story's events and characters and from the author's own maturity.

This assertion of maturity does not sit well, though, with some critics. Barry Ulanov, in *The Vision Obscured: Perceptions of Some Twentieth-Century Catholic Novelists,* cites *Brideshead Revisited* as evidence of Waugh's mid-career decline. Echoing Lynch, Ulanov argues that most of Waugh's books after 1945 "are blighted by the disease of Brideshead, an egregious inclination to take religion seriously, accompanied by a marked distaste for the world that does not share that inclination—the modern world."

In fact, Waugh's own worldview can be seen in such novels as *Brideshead Revisited,* in which there is a sense that the past is preferable to the present and that the current generation has lost touch with the values and graciousness of its history. According to Ulanov, Waugh, in his own life, "became a furious partisan, fighting for the survival of ancient values, ancient worlds, ancient rituals." As a Catholic, he worked against the reforms of the Second Vatican Council, which promoted such changes as translating the Latin of the Mass into English.

Waugh's Catholicism and how it is reflected and used in his novels is a continuing subject for critics. Most agree that the author's conservative and traditional outlook is revealed in his work, but while Carens notes that *Brideshead Revisited* is the first of Waugh's books where his interest in Roman Catholicism is so broadly exhibited, he declares that the novel is not an apology for Catholicism. "It is not a preachy book," he asserts. As Carens points out, readers can see evidence of Waugh's past satiric craftsmanship; satire is blended with religion in the book, specifically where the confused Flyte family is discussing whether the dying Lord Marchmain should receive last rites from a priest. "Over this entire scene Waugh has cast his satirical irony; the scene exists for novelistic purposes rather than dogmatic reasons," writes Carens. And the difficulty of Catholicism in Britain, as portrayed in the novel, might well erase any critic's concerns that the book slips into romance, according to Frank Kermode in *Encounter.* To the Flytes, their religion is a burden to shoulder, for "only in misery, it seems, will the Faith be restored in the great families of England."

Whether *Brideshead Revisited* is a book without any teeth or evidence of a writer's development is a topic that critics will continue to debate. But the novel has withstood the test of time, as it was recently cited by the editorial board of the Modern Library as one of the 100 best English language books of the twentieth century.

Criticism

Susan Sanderson

Sanderson holds a master of fine arts degree in fiction writing and is an independent writer. In this essay, she examines how Waugh's novel can be read as the author's own fictionalized memories

> Charles, the middle-aged, wifeless, and childless child of a grim and unloving family, who once admitted that very few things gave him as much happiness as being with Sebastian, finally seems to have found a constant source of love in his life. Real life, however, rarely produces such neat endings."

of his steps toward Catholicism and a relationship with God.

Evelyn Waugh was widely known to be a conservative man, a man who felt more comfortable with the warm burnish of tradition than with the bright shine of the modern. Most of his novels written before 1942 are considered masterworks of satire. So the critics' nearly unanimous howl in 1945 upon the publication of *Brideshead Revisited*—a collective complaint that Waugh had lost his spark and had gone soft—should not come as a surprise. The novel was condemned as a romance, even a fantasy, and the knock against Waugh became that he had done his best work before World War II.

But after getting over the expectation that every scene should poke fun at something or someone (while still experiencing the occasional pleasure of Waugh's wit in *Brideshead Revisited*), readers familiar with Waugh's earlier satires need only look to Waugh's life for an explanation of the change in his writing. Even a brief examination of Waugh's background makes clear that many of the elements in *Brideshead Revisited* are taken from his own experiences. Waugh's partiality to traditional institutions and patterns shines through the novel's protagonist, Charles Ryder. Charles is a lover of old buildings, ancient cemeteries, and old wine; he dislikes new styles, be they displayed in a piece of jewelry or through the interior designs of a ship, and he feels that young people are not as attached to their history as they should be. From that common ground, Charles's story can be read as a version of Waugh's story. Each is a story of a young man searching for stability in a world that seems turned upside down by war and the dissolution of established social institutions.

Literature and myth are filled with tales of young men finding their way in the world via circuitous routes, each man descending into a dark wilderness before emerging into the light of his destiny. While this book is certainly not an autobiography, it can be read as Waugh's reflection on how his search for love and constancy brought him through a rambunctious youth, an unhappy marriage, and ultimately to the Catholic Church.

Like Charles, Waugh attended a private English boys' school, then moved on to Oxford to study unsuccessfully for his undergraduate degree. Waugh fell in with a group that was much more interested in drinking and carousing than in studying—not unlike Charles' group of friends at Oxford, which included the charming Sebastian Flyte and the always clever Anthony Blanche. And both the author and his fictional protagonist dabbled in the decorative arts while at the university, eventually quitting to attend art school.

But unlike Waugh, who expressed interest in religion at an early age and found it to be one of the primary themes of his life, Charles is baffled by the Flytes' Catholicism. Early in the novel he asks Sebastian, who is no pillar of Catholic doctrinal behavior, about his religion. Sebastian tells him that he thinks about it all the time, even though it doesn't show on the outside. Charles is amazed and simply can't believe that his friend actually believes in what he perceives as myths and trickery. In fact, Charles comes from a family that has paid almost no attention to religion, except to warn him of associating with religious groups, especially Catholics.

Waugh uses a present-day, middle-aged Charles, serving as a captain in the British Army during World War II, to frame the story with a prologue and epilogue. Interestingly enough, when Waugh wrote *Brideshead Revisited,* he was on extended leave from the British military, in which he saw quite a bit of action, especially for a man in his late thirties and early forties. Waugh was of the right age and situation to be thinking back on his life, much as Charles does as he narrates the novel. And even though Waugh succeeded in completing a number of hazardous missions for the war effort, his early wartime encounters were remarkably sim-

ilar to Charles'—waiting around the local countryside, cleaning up military encampments, always thinking the next move would bring him closer to the real action.

Sparked by his troop's new encampment near Brideshead Castle, Charles remembers his friendship with the Flyte family, a wealthy Catholic household whose wayward son, Sebastian, becomes the first real love of his life. Life before Sebastian was passionless and grim for Charles, and Sebastian's appearance offers him a more spontaneous and colorful life. Critics differ on whether their relationship is sexual or not, but the flowery language Waugh uses when the two are together during their first year of friendship (one of the novel's features that drives critics to distraction) leaves no doubt that Charles is smitten; and Sebastian's letters to Charles on vacation indicate that his affections are returned. But Sebastian, for all his magic, is still a fallible human and disappoints Charles with his destructive drinking and lifestyle.

Charles continues to seek out love and stability, but with little success. After Sebastian, to whom he refers as the "forerunner," he tries marriage to a woman too busy with her huge circle of friends and with improving Charles's art career to be a true love interest. In book two, chapter one, when Celia asks Charles if he has fallen in love with anyone during his two-year absence, he assures her flatly, "No. I'm not in love." Like Waugh's first wife, Celia is unfaithful to her marriage vows, and this contributes to Charles's two-year excursion into the wilds of Mexico and Central America to draw ruins. While Charles sought the wilderness, however, Waugh sought the comfort and discipline of the Catholic Church. Waugh's biographers point to his wife's infidelity as pushing him toward a conversion to Catholicism.

Charles's two years in the "jungle" are a turning point in his understanding of himself. Middle-aged boredom, dissatisfaction with his marriage, and a fear that life is slipping away propel him into the dark "wild lands" of another continent. In chapter one of the second book, Charles admits that before the trip his apparent success masked a hidden withering of his soul. "For nearly ten years I was thus borne along a road, outwardly full of change and incident, but never during that time, except sometimes in my painting—and that at longer and longer intervals—did I come alive as I had been during the time of my friendship with Sebastian." He seems to believe that if he leaves his usual haunts and goes out into the wilderness to live a simple life among ancient ruins, away from the talk of war and the crush of modernity, he will return a changed man—alive again.

But the trip does not fulfill him in the way he needs. Even though the new paintings he exhibits after returning to England are hailed as dramatically different and more vibrant and passionate than his earlier work, Charles feels as though the wilderness experience has not changed and healed him sufficiently. "There is still a small part of me pretending to be whole," he says. To fill the emptiness, Charles begins a passionate affair with Julia, Sebastian's sister. They both leave their spouses and for two years live together at Brideshead Castle, the scene of Charles's first and only other love, Sebastian. They plan to secure divorces and marry each other.

While Charles's love for Julia is true, it eventually changes and ends, being simply the next step toward a final love. In the last chapter of book two, Lord Marchmain returns to Brideshead and everyone except Sebastian (who is living, ill and nearly destitute, at a monastery in Tunis) has gathered at the ancestral homestead for his impending death. When Julia's brother, Brideshead, asks that a priest be brought for his father's final sacraments, Charles finds the whole effort ridiculous, saying, "It's such a lot of witchcraft and hypocrisy." But Lord Marchmain has not been a practicing Catholic for almost twenty-five years and sends the priest away. Charles's hostility about the priest creates tension between him and Julia and prompts Julia to say, "Oh Charles, don't rant. I shall begin to think you're getting doubts yourself."

Finally, a number of weeks later, when Lord Marchmain is nearly unconscious, Julia brings the priest back for her father's final sacraments. What happens next is so dramatic that it might seem more fit for a scene in an earlier Waugh satire, yet here the intent is not satiric. The priest asks Lord Marchmain if he will give a sign that he is sorry for his sins. Charles suddenly drops to his knees and says a small prayer to "God, if there is a God," longing for such a sign. He cannot decide if he desires this for Julia's sake or for other reasons, but in an instant he gets that prayer answered—Lord Marchmain makes the sign of the cross, and Charles recognizes that this "was not a little thing, not a passing nod of recognition."

After Julia witnesses her father's signal, she decides she cannot go against her religion's doctrines and marry Charles. Her divorce and subse-

England's Oxford University

quent marriage to Charles would make her an adulteress in the eyes of the Roman Catholic Church; she must live a life that is pleasing to her God. "But the worse I am, the more I need God. I can't shut myself out from His mercy," as she tells Charles.

Given Charles's usual disparaging response to a member of the Flyte family explaining Catholicism to him, his telling Julia that he understands her actions signals a huge step toward his embracing religion and God. And when Charles appears again in the Epilogue, a few years later, he has obviously begun to accept the traditional tenets of religion, if not the Catholic Church. He makes a special trip to Brideshead Castle's chapel, closed after Lady Marchmain's death many years previously. Much to his pleasure, the chapel is open and in respectable shape, with a small lamp burning at the altar. God is still present and accounted for, unwavering and forever. He kneels and says a prayer, "an ancient, newly learned form of words."

Charles has made a journey similar to the one Waugh made in the first half of his life: from a declared agnostic, educated to believe that religion is all smoke and mirrors, to a middle-aged man believing in the power of God's grace. This is not an easy journey for either man, beset by pains and temptations. Unlike Charles, though, Waugh was

> The text represents the experience of modernity as the force of history invading a tradition of memory protected within the Catholic enclave at Brideshead."

able to have his first marriage annulled, making his marriage the very next year to a devout Catholic woman sanctified in the eyes of the church.

When Charles returns from praying at the old Brideshead chapel, his second-in-command comments, "You're looking unusually cheerful today." Charles, the middle-aged, wifeless, and childless child of a grim and unloving family, who once admitted that very few things gave him as much happiness as being with Sebastian, finally seems to have found a constant source of love in his life. Real life, however, rarely produces such neat endings. While Waugh was, by all accounts, very satisfied with his second marriage, stories have emerged that in his later years, well after the writing of *Brideshead Revisited,* he was depressed and drank heavily.

Source: Susan Sanderson, Critical Essay on *Brideshead Revisited,* in *Novels for Students,* The Gale Group, 2002.

David Rothstein

In the following essay, Rothstein examines "the ways in which Brideshead Revisited *is preoccupied with the issue of preserving Catholic identity and Catholic memory."*

In a 1969 article "The Uses of History in Fiction," based on a panel discussion at a meeting of the Southern Historical Association, C. Van Woodward notes that "Over the last two centuries novels have become increasingly saturated with history, and novelists have been becoming ever more deeply historically conscious. In a sense, all novels are historical novels. They all seek to understand, to describe, to recapture the past, however remote, however recent." Woodward and the other participants in this discussion go on to talk about the relations between storytelling and historiography, examining how both reflect a growing histor-

ical consciousness in western society, and how they serve to satisfy a desire for historical understanding. Evelyn Waugh's *Brideshead Revisited* offers an example of this mutual interrelation between fiction and history, demonstrating how both support each other in accomplishing a very specific and, as critics have seen it, politically charged task, namely the preservation and fictional reconstitution of an aristocratic Catholic heritage in England.

Though purely religious and spiritual considerations tend to elide this implicit purpose behind the novel, the task of this essay will be to explicate the ways in which *Brideshead* is preoccupied with the issue of preserving Catholic identity and Catholic memory. More specifically, it will discuss how the novel is about the decline of a family tradition of memory and the emergence of an historical subjectivity that prompts individual characters to recapture their past by "revisiting" or remembering those "sites of memory" containing a family history and identity. Sebastian's wish to "bury something precious in every place where I've been happy" is a perfect example of how sites of memory function within the text.

The term "sites of memory" is borrowed from an article by Pierre Nora, "Between Memory and History: *Les Lieux de Memoire.*" In this article, Nora develops a philosophical interpretation of what contemporary western society experiences as an increasingly historicized world. Nora states that within modern historical societies, individuals keenly sense their growing distance from traditional societies of the past, with their gradually evolving, self-contained modes of identity realization, resulting in the need to consecrate sites of memory that provide some sense of connection to a collective heritage of the past:

> Our interest in *lieux de memoire* where memory crystallizes and secretes itself has occurred at a particular historical moment, a turning point where consciousness of a break with the past is bound up with the sense that memory has been torn—but torn in such a way as to pose the problem of the embodiment of memory in certain sites where a sense of historical continuity persists. There are *lieux de moire,* sites of memory, because there are no longer *milieux de memoire,* real environments of memory. . . The "acceleration of history," then, confronts us with the brutal realization of the difference between real memory—social and unviolated, exemplified in but also retained as the secret of so called primitive or archaic societies—and history, which is how our hopelessly forgetful modern societies, propelled by change, organize the past.

Nora goes on to outline this key distinction between a "real" or social memory and the modern transformation of memory into an historicized memory:

> Memory is a perpetually actual phenomenon, a bond tying us to the present: history is a representation of the past. . . it is an intellectual and secular production [that] calls for analysis and criticism. Memory installs remembrance within the sacred; history, always prosaic, releases it again. Memory is blind to all but the group it binds—which is to say, as Maurice Halbwachs has said, that there are as many memories as there are groups. . . Memory takes root in the concrete, in spaces, gestures, images, and objects; history binds itself strictly to temporal continuities, to progressions and to relations between things. Memory is absolute, while history can only conceive the relative.

The ideas that Nora articulates here offer a philosophical groundwork for the study of the intimate link between historical and literary modes of memory representation. *Brideshead Revisited* uniquely contains this intimate link within its thematic structure and character development; it represents historically conscious characters (especially Charles the narrator) who are acutely aware of their break with the past and seek to anchor themselves through their active relation to sites of memory.

In many ways, therefore, the novel is about tracing one's history by studying the traces and sites of memory that provide one with a sense of historical identity. This historical identity is uniquely modern and as portrayed in the novel results from an awareness of the distance between a coherent, meaningful past identity, enclosed and enshrined in memory, and a present experience of dislocation, of having been severed from an ancient bond of identity. On one side of this gulf, as we see in the novel, is an intimate link to a tradition of memory, namely the Catholic culture that once gave ground and direction to members of the Marchmain family. On the other side are characters drawn away from this enclosed culture, either willingly or unwillingly, by other relationships, by political forces, and by the broad possibilities for alternate modes of existence in a modern mass culture. Both Sebastian and Lord Marchmain seem desperate to escape the heavy responsibility attendant on maintaining membership in their family's isolated Catholic culture, and so seek other identities in other relationships: Sebastian, shutting out the world to become the "subject of charity" with Kurt; and Lord Marchmain, the Byronic exile with Cara in Italy. Julia's relationship with Rex offers her a way out of the confinement of family tradi-

What Do I Read Next?

- *Brideshead Benighted* is a collection of politically incorrect satire authored by Evelyn Waugh's son, Auberon. The 1986 book was originally published in England with the title *Another Voice: An Alternative Anatomy of Britain.*

- In Evelyn Waugh's *A Handful of Dust,* Tony Last's wife grows bored with their country aristocrat lifestyle and takes a lover and a flat in London. Waugh wrote this satiric depiction of life among the English upper crust in 1934.

- Anthony Blanche recites from memory part of T. S. Eliot's *The Waste Land* (1922). This is the quintessential poem capturing post-World War I despair.

- Graham Greene's 1951 novel *The End of the Affair* uses flashback and memories to return to the events that take place between a married woman and her lover during the German bombardments of World War II London. Greene and Evelyn Waugh are of the same English generation, and Greene is also sometimes considered a "Catholic novelist."

tion into a world of international, Gatsbyesque play. The Second World War and the strike of 1926 represent the broader political forces that surround and threaten the insular aristocratic paradise at Brideshead. Even Cordelia, who chooses social service over the stability of aristocratic Catholic culture, is drawn away from Brideshead where she experiences a violent modern world and the devastation of war in Spain.

The text represents the experience of modernity as the force of history invading a tradition of memory protected within the Catholic enclave at Brideshead. Pierre Nora describes this living tradition of memory, which we see fading at Brideshead, as "an integrated, dictatorial memory—unselfconscious, commanding, all-powerful, spontaneously actualizing, a memory without a past that ceaselessly reinvents tradition, linking the history of its ancestors to the undifferentiated time of heroes, origins, and myth." On his deathbed, Lord Marchmain nostalgically retraces this link to an ancestral memory, a link that barely survives and that he himself has all but broken: "Those were our roots in the waste hollows of Castle Hill, in the brier and nettle; among the tombs in the old church and the chantrey where no clerk sings. . . We were knights then, barons since Agincourt." In the novel's epilogue, as Charles reflects on the chapel's beaten-copper lamp, he also draws this connection between the house at Brideshead and the ancestral memory contained there: "Something quite remote from anything the builders intended has come out of their work. . . the flame which the old knights saw from their tombs, which they saw put out; that flame burns again for other soldiers, far from home, farther, in heart, than Acre or Jerusalem. It could not have been lit but for the builders and tragedians, and there I found it this morning, burning anew among the old stones."

Though the burning lamp is often read as the religious focal point of the novel, signifying a rekindling of faith in each of the characters, it is crucial to note that Waugh places this image of faith within a context of a faith tradition stretching back through Marchmain family history to the time of the crusades. Only in this context of tradition, legend, and memory does faith achieve any significance, the text seems to tell us. Through Charles's comprehension and articulation of this vital context, Waugh urges the point that faith needs to be linked simultaneously to the preservation of a Catholic identity, a sense of historical continuity, threatened with extinction by the forces of modern culture.

Waugh demonstrates this point primarily through Charles, who finds a means to understand and redeem his personal history of dislocation ("I'm homeless, childless, middle-aged, loveless") through his newly formed link to an ancient tradition and memory barely surviving among their historical remnants, the sites of memory at Brideshead—the old stones, the chapel, the lamp. Yet despite his intimate bond with this tradition of memory, Charles does not experience it from inside, since it no longer exists either for himself or the other characters as a social, collective, and all-encompassing form of subjectivity. Rather, he experiences his bond with Catholic memory indirectly, as a psychological, individual, and subjective phenomenon. What Charles experiences is an historicized memory, which Pierre Nora defines as "voluntary and deliberate, experienced as a duty, no longer spontaneous." Since he himself was neither born into the Catholic tradition nor sustained within

an environment of memory such as Lady Marchmain and her ancestors once were, Charles can only look longingly in on this rapidly disintegrating Catholic society as a double outsider; that is, through his own memory of those whose memories and lives provided him with a record of a more noble and meaningful existence, a grandeur that is lost.

Though a lonely individual believer at the story's end, Charles has interiorized the Catholic memory enshrined at Brideshead and now recognizes his allegiance to this fading Catholic heritage by dutifully maintaining his "ancient, newly learned form of words" (though his conversion to Catholicism is, perhaps necessarily, only hinted at in the epilogue). Moreover, the novel shows us that in being severed from a collective experience of lived memory all of the characters, not only Charles, become in their own degree "memory individuals." No longer on the inside of a tradition of memory, but longing to be there, the characters can only experience it through its outward signs, through rituals, symbols, modes of behavior. The characters become obliged to defend and preserve these markers of identity against the disintegrating power of the modern world.

Waugh portrays his characters in *Brideshead* as modern outsiders, modern misfits, always trying to get inside of a more meaningful existence, always experiencing life on the fringes. Throughout his fictional existence, Charles has always been the outsider lacking an experience of being inside. His childhood has left him without any knowledge of what it means to be *in* a family. Later, we see him as the outsider trying successively in different ways to get inside of Brideshead. At first, his love for Sebastian offers him one level of entry into the world of Brideshead. At Oxford he follows Sebastian through "that low door in the wall. . . which opened on an enclosed and enchanted garden," an experience leading into other gardens, orchards, and parlors during their languid summer at Brideshead. This first extended stay at Brideshead offers Charles a chance to relive a more meaningful childhood. Brideshead becomes a kind of nursery where he is given an "aesthetic education" simply by living in its environs with Sebastian. Moreover, Charles develops a powerful, art historian's attraction toward all he sees at Brideshead, and he carefully records each detail of landscape, architecture, art work, and interior design. Yet despite his appreciation of the physical environment, Charles's entry into Brideshead at this point goes nowhere beyond a comprehension of its historical and aesthetic significance.

Later still, Charles's expected marriage to Julia renews the promise of entering and possessing Brideshead. However, just as he feels he's about to get inside, the vision eludes him. Through this final disappointment, Waugh tells us that Charles has misunderstood what it means to get inside of Brideshead. For an outsider (or a reader of the novel), getting inside of Brideshead requires more than an understanding of Brideshead as an historical monument dedicated to aristocratic and aesthetic values. Getting inside requires that one understand Brideshead above all as a shrine dedicated to an ancient religious tradition, and more specifically as a refuge or sanctuary where one finds the living heart of a Catholic family memory. As Charles learns later in life, to truly enter Brideshead would be to merge into this living tradition of memory, like Nanny Hawkins does. But since he arrives at this understanding too late, it seems the low door in the wall is closed to him for good. The closest he can come is to interiorize the memory that Brideshead evokes and preserve it through a personal acceptance of Catholic faith.

One finds this ending somewhat illogical, however, when considering that by becoming a Catholic, Charles eventually could have been reunited with Julia; the two of them could then have returned to inherit Brideshead and there revitalize a Catholic family and tradition. But to go this route, Waugh would have had to make Charles's conversion more obvious, and thus make his theme too exclusive, his appeal too limited. Waugh was obviously writing something more than a simple *Fr. Brown* story of conversion. As it actually stands, the plan of the novel enables Charles to become a broader type of character, a representative modern Western individual. Charles's experience represents the modern experience of human subjectivity in its almost constant state of flux. Early on in Book 2 he expresses this sense of modern existence after having been expelled from the Edenic garden of Book 1: "we are seldom single or unique; we keep company in this world with a hoard of abstractions and reflections and counterfeits of ourselves—the sensual man, the economic man, the man of reason, the beast, the machine and the sleepwalker, and heaven knows what besides, all in our own image, indistinguishable from ourselves to the outward eye."

Sebastian is a more tragic type of modern misfit, torn more radically than Charles between the pull of competing impulses. The spell of memory continually pulls him back toward a primal identity associated with family, ritual, and a specific place: Brideshead. Yet memory more than anything is what Sebastian resists through drink: "I was determined to have a happy Christmas," said Sebastian. "Did you?" asked Charles. "I think so," he replied. "I don't remember it much, and that's always a good sign, isn't it?" Sebastian's life becomes a pattern of weaving in and out of memory, of moving back toward his origins and obliterating the memory of these origins. Cordelia sums up his pattern of existence at the monastery in Morocco in a line that perfectly comprehends his struggle: "He'll live on, half in, half out of the community." Perhaps the main difficulty for Sebastian is mirrored in the situation of the monastery to which he half-attaches himself—it is another ancient community of memory, like the Marchmain family, that is inwardly compelled by the need to remember what it is, and must struggle to maintain its own unique values and identity at the fringes of a modern mass culture. Troubled by similar tensions, Sebastian represents the almost totally fragmented modern subject, torn between the restless search for a meaningful identity and the need for a stable existence, torn between desire and commitment.

Cordelia is a less extreme case; but even she recognizes her own split subjectivity, her misfit nature, which is similar to Sebastian's: "people who can't quite fit in either to the world or the monastic rule. I suppose I'm something of the sort myself." Julia, too, after her own long and restless search, arrives at a sense of split subjectivity which she anticipates will be her continued mode of existence: "I've always been bad. Probably I shall be bad again, punished again. But the worse I am, the more I need God. I can't shut myself out from His mercy."

There is also, however, another critical angle to consider in analyzing these modern misfits, and that involves Waugh's insistence on closing down almost every possible future for his characters which does not smack of a nearly monastic adherence to a traditional Catholic lifestyle, or at least an ambivalent magnetic pull toward such a lifestyle. According to Stephen Spender, this insistence on the part of Waugh indicates his "puzzling ethics" and "lack of sense of moral proportion." Characters like Sebastian, Cordelia, and even Julia "can't quite fit in either to the world or the monastic rule"; no balanced form of life incorporating human desire, love, and religious practice is open to them. Moreover, God's plan regarding Julia and Charles seems to involve separating those who truly love each other on the grounds of religious doctrine.

Critics of *Brideshead* have often sounded similar complaints against Waugh's Catholic self-assuredness and snobbery. Sean O'Faolin argues that "A religious theme given institutional treatment is always liable to get lost in the embroidered folds of ecclesiasticism; and so is the author. The old detachment is sold to loyalty, and while one admires loyalty there is no place for it in art." He goes on to accuse Waugh of lowering his art to the level of a snarling argument about "the superiority of the Catholic squires of England to the non-Catholic salesmen of England." However, aside from the elitist tendencies one finds in the novel, Waugh also chose to portray, in a consistent and fairly accurate manner, the power of Catholic conscience over members of the Catholic faith living in a pre-Vatican II world. Contemporary Catholics and non-Catholics may find the novel's portrayal of dramatic religious acts and extreme religious choices (such as Julia must make about marrying Charles) to be simply contrived; but rather, these reflect with some accuracy an older form of Catholicism fading more and more into the realm of historical otherness. Furthermore, had he not dramatized such extreme choices, Waugh would not have expressed strongly enough what he feels is at stake for the modern reader of *Brideshead*. In *Brideshead*, Waugh resists a prevailing discourse of bourgeois individualism and materialism (most obviously embodied in Rex and Hooper) which he sees beneath the ruinous transformations of the modern world. Waugh resists this discourse by asserting a counter-discourse of rich, vividly realistic prose enshrining aristocratic, aesthetic, and religious values.

Yet, even more radical than a dramatic portrayal of difficult personal choices, more radical than Waugh's intended Catholic apologia, "an attempt to trace the workings of the divine purpose in a pagan world" (Waugh's dust jacket comment), *Brideshead Revisited* represents, through its characters and mode of narration, the awareness of an historical subjectivity brought about by confrontation with the disruptive forces in modern mass culture. Caught in the pull between "monastic rule" and the world, between Catholic family tradition and individual absorption into broader social relations, the Marchmain family represents a site of that unique modern struggle between competing modes of subjectivity. The characters are lured by the world's possibilities, held back by family tradition; they are compelled by the forces of history, haunted by the forces of memory.

In other words, for many of the characters memory is mingled with an historical sensibility,

producing a disturbing self-consciousness which they try to suppress and whose roots are fixed deep in the tenacious ground of childhood memory. Michel Foucault states that "Since memory is actually a very important factor in struggle, if one controls people's memory, one controls their dynamism." As we see especially with Julia and Sebastian, a Catholic identity, straining outward from childhood memory, operates as the irrepressible controlling factor in their struggle for self-control. For Julia and Sebastian (and for most of the Marchmain family), these early memories locate their entry into the symbolic realm of their Catholic family heritage where language, behavior patterns, social relations, rituals, are all, in turn, rooted in the ancient collective memory of Catholic culture. As children, their intimate link to this lived tradition of memory was forged by Lady Marchmain and Nanny Hawkins, the two primary preservers of family and faith in the novel. From them, Julia first learns the word that signifies the sundering of this vital link to family tradition—sin: "A word from so long ago, from Nanny Hawkins stitching by the hearth and the nightlight burning before the Sacred Heart. Cordelia and me with the catechism, in Mummy's room, before luncheon on Sundays."

Separated from this context, Julia, Sebastian, and also Lord Marchmain go along rudderless through life, until the "twitch upon the thread," the force of memory, recalls them to a repressed identity firmly interiorized during their youth (though admittedly for Lord Marchmain this identity is not rooted in childhood memory but was simply chosen and later abandoned). Cara's assessment of Sebastian and Lord Marchmain is therefore only half right. Both in a sense refuse to grow up, but Sebastian's is a selective memory of childhood: he suppresses his early bonds of memory to the Catholic tradition and chooses to remember only a time of playful frolic, symbolized by his toy bear. Lord Marchmain avoids more than just a loss of youthful freedom; he specifically avoids any memory of the Catholic identity he chose, with all its resulting obligations. Sebastian, Julia, and Lord Marchmain all know that to maintain their Catholic heritage consciously and deliberately demands a hard sacrifice of personal responsibility. To remember and protect the trappings of their Catholic family identity is an extremely difficult task considering the combined demands of their exclusive religion and their aristocratic status. Together, both of these factors create and intensify the sense of isolation they feel at Brideshead.

When memories finally do resurface, as in Julia's case, they are accompanied by a tremendous weight of self-consciousness, a traumatic awareness of how the modern world has taken its toll on her, sundering her vital link to a meaningful family tradition and leaving her a torn, isolated individual without an identity:

> Past and future; the years when I was trying to be a good wife, in the cigar smoke, while time crept on and the counters clicked on the backgammon board, and the man who was 'dummy' at the men's table filled the glasses; when I was trying to bear his child, torn in pieces by something already dead; putting him away, forgetting him, finding you, the past two years with you, all the future with you, all the future with or without you, war coming, world ending—sin.

Julia's dilemma can be more clearly defined by a comment from Nicholas Kostis on the force of memory in *Brideshead:* "Memories are but intermittances, momentary enchantments which are less an inner substance or property of the individual than a force from without which imposes itself on the individual and crushes him between past and future, leaving him more with the terror of his own absence than with the presence of a consoling reality." The novel asserts that without the consoling reality of a memorial consciousness linked to a common tradition, the individual is left with an empty personal history of discontinuous attempts to ground identity. Indeed, the possibility of reconstructing a kind of Catholic tribal life with a shared and enduring memory seems closed down for all the characters at the end of the story. Each embarks on a private quest for those sites of memory that re-link them to their origins and allow them to understand their history and their historical subjectivity. These sites of memory represent for the characters an image of historical difference through which they seek to retrace an unrecoverable identity, or as Pierre Nora states, "the decipherment of what we are in the light of what we are no longer."

By "revisiting" these sites, rituals, and trappings of memory, the characters represent those modern historical subjects who perceive their historical progress from ancient communities of memory, bound in devotion to the rituals of tradition, to fragmented modern communities whose individual members must maintain for themselves the historical signs that link present identity to a past communal or traditional identity. However, at the end of the novel, the characters are represented not merely as individuals who now try to comprehend who they are "in the light of what they are no longer," but also as individuals attempting to rein-scribe themselves in these sites of memory, seeking to revitalize there a sense of community and tradition that lives on in individual memory. Sebastian tries to re-link himself to past memory at a monastery where a Catholic communal tradition survives. Through Nanny Hawkins we learn that Julia and Cordelia plan to return to Brideshead after the war, and there we expect them to reconstitute what they can of a Catholic family tradition.

In this story about the extinguishing and relighting of a beaten-copper lamp, a story about the gradual extinguishing of a family tradition, a Catholic aristocratic identity, with the religious and aesthetic values they stand for, the power of memory represents the light of the lamp that Waugh will not allow to be extinguished or kept hidden. The power of memory is the primary agent which motivates the characters' lives; memory perpetuates a level of subjectivity that replays itself in their lives, re-emerging in the same and in different contexts uncontrollably.

The novel records, therefore, not just the nostalgia of outsiders trying to get back in and return to a certain origin, but also an obsession with preserving the outward signs and historical traces of this origin. Through Charles we realize how preoccupied the novel is with historicizing memory; that is, making memory the object of historical study, enshrining in an almost fetishistic manner each place, gesture, image, and object that tells the story of memory. One perfectly encapsulated example of this is Charles's reflection on the diamond-studded tortoise Julia receives from Rex:

> this slightly obscene object. . . became a memorable part of the evening, one of those needle-hooks of experience which catch the attention when larger matters are at stake, and remain in the mind when they are forgotten, so that years later it is a bit of gilding, or a certain smell, or the tone of a clock's striking which recalls one to a tragedy.

Charles the artist/storyteller is more accurately Charles the historian who, to preserve textually his own memory and the memory of Brideshead, depends entirely on the materiality of the trace, the visibility of the image. But most especially, to take in Waugh's more specific purposes, Charles's history text depends on the immediacy of those images and signs that sustain a link to a tradition of memory, a religious faith, a cultural heritage. As an example, Charles's paintings of Marchmain House and other doomed old houses represent a type of history writing within his larger historical narrative wherein he records with a fetishistic realism the disappearing sites of aristocratic life and values.

Lord Marchmain's deathbed sign is also a prized piece of historical evidence in Charles's historical narrative. Charles eagerly yearns for this sign, and his anticipation reflects a larger obsession seen throughout the novel with recording all the material indicators of inner dynamics and values, all the scenery and gestures that made the drama real. What is most significant, though, about Lord Marchmain's sign is that he finally gives it only after recounting his memories of Brideshead family history as once told to him by Aunt Julia and the field workers—"unlettered men" with "long memories." Lord Marchmain's deathbed repentance marks his return to an ancient family heritage; the last of the knights of the old guard returns to the historical site of his ancestral memory, stretching back before Henry VIII and the Reformation, back to the time of Agincourt. Lord Marchmain yields to the spell of memory which increasingly takes control of his consciousness, as his broken, spontaneous narrative seems to indicate. In his last remaining days he feels compelled to pass on his family story orally. Yet he fully recognizes his link to family tradition and memory only when he submits to the power of memory by marking himself with a sign of its dominance.

This act, however, does not simply reaffirm the need for a radical relationship to the transcendent. Again, a purely religious interpretation is insufficient to account for what motivates a relighting of the lamp in each of the characters. Religious motivations lose their primacy and autonomy when we consider how they are inextricably tied to the novel's politics of identity preservation. Lord Marchmain's sign expresses his fidelity to a Catholic family identity and history, while it simultaneously refutes his personal history of resistance to the work of sustaining this identity. The sign of the cross which he makes on his deathbed is both a private and a public gesture, a final attempt to reclaim his position as keeper and teacher of a family faith and memory. The sign tells a story of how he personally accepts his subjectivity to tradition and memory, of how through this sign he inscribes himself within the history of his family's faith tradition. He thereby helps to perpetuate a living history marked by similar signs, rituals, symbols, social practices—all maintained as part of a common Catholic memory.

In the task of preserving memory and identity, Charles's narrative performs an archival function: it is absorbed in the work of recording, remembering, and meticulously reconstituting each sign and site of memory that tells of his own story and the story of Brideshead. Moreover, the history recorded in Charles's narrative is about the merging of his personal story with the history of Brideshead. It is this integral bond between storyteller and story, between the archivist and his historical material, that makes Charles a representative of the modern historian as described by Pierre Nora. According to Nora, the role of the old historian was that of "an erudite transparency, a vehicle of transmission, a bridge stretched as lightly as possible between the raw materiality of the document and its inscription in memory—ultimately, an absence obsessed with objectivity. But with the disintegration of history-memory, a new type of historian emerges who, unlike his precursors, is ready to confess the intimate relation he maintains to his subject. Better still, he is ready to proclaim it, deepen it, make of it not the obstacle but the means of his understanding." Accordingly, the fictional history that is *Brideshead Revisited* is also the personalized document of Charles Ryder; it is the historical novel into which he writes himself and records his memories.

Charles preserves and legitimates his memory through an historical narrative that anchors, condenses, and expresses an identity born of these memories, an identity which has intersected with the memory, lives, and religious heritage of the Marchmain family. In addition, Waugh represents both Charles and the Marchmains as having intersected with a modern world that sweeps them up in the historical process summarized so well by Marx in the *Communist Manifesto:*

> All fixed, fast-frozen relations, with their train of ancient and venerable prejudices and opinions, are swept away, all new-formed ones become antiquated before they can ossify. All that is solid melts into air, all that is holy is profaned, and men at last are forced to face. . . the real condition of their lives and their relations with their fellow men.

The novel encloses this moment of intersection where memory and history meet, where an identity once sustained within a living tradition of memory becomes distanced from itself, other than itself—the moment when a subject realizes he is an historical subject, a split, fragmented subject, who must go in search of his origins in memory. Rather, he must preserve those originary sites of memory with all their symbolic excess. These function as the core of an historical subjectivity whose formations and deformations in the modern historical process mark a path of difference along which identity can be traced, represented, and preserved. Like the modern individual, the text of *Brideshead* is preoccupied with the questions of who we once were, what we have become, and how we have changed.

Within the novel we see various historical, literary, and aesthetic modes of preserving memory: the story told by Capt. Ryder, Lord Marchmain's recollections, Charles's architectural paintings, Mr. Samgrass's biography of Lady Marchmain's brothers, the "new house" at Brideshead containing the historical remnants (the original stones) of the old castle. The realistic, factual quality of these "texts," both in themselves and as the novel presents them, suggests an attempt to materialize the immaterial, to stop time and forgetting through the concretion of memory. At the same time, the living quality of these memory texts entices others to share in their virtual reality. Also, the rich, pictorial language of *Brideshead* attests to this desire to materialize memory, as if Waugh were demanding that each word and image be given visual and audible reality—a feat nearly accomplished in the exhaustive and meticulously exact PBS television version of *Brideshead Revisited.*

Through Charles, the text hearkens back to a time when an aristocratic Catholic culture sustained itself and expressed an identity through a collective memory and through gradually evolving but always self-enclosed, self-referential signs, rituals, images, and structures (such as the house at Brideshead, the chapel, the Catholic Mass, Catholic family life, and the perpetually burning sanctuary lamp). But also, through the two different personae of Charles and Capt. Ryder, the text highlights the historical distancing and rapid transformations wrought by the modern world. As a result of these modern changes, the text gives the central role to the operations of the historian—Charles Ryder—whose intimate involvement with the Marchmain family allows him to record accurately, to take inventory, and thus provide a means to understand the historical transformations of this family and its Catholic heritage. Moreover, because of his intimate relation to his subject, both Charles the historian and his historical narrative represent sites of memory; what Charles records is not merely history, it is the means of his own understanding and the ground of his identity.

Through Charles, the novel suggests that what was once the province of a collective tradition and memory is now dispersed and maintained within individuals who may at times gather to share memory and enact rituals, but are ultimately absorbed by the larger collective of modern society. Tribal life and memory are gone; the modern world sweeps them into its vortex, and the way is marked only by historical traces, by signs and sites of memory, which individuals and protective enclaves must dutifully preserve for themselves to defend and maintain a specific identity.

Source: David Rothstein, "*Brideshead Revisited* and the Modern Historicization of Memory," in *Studies in the Novel,* Vol. 25, No. 3, Fall 1993, pp. 318–31.

Sources

Burdett, Paul S., Jr., "Author Evelyn Waugh Served Honorably in the British Army as an SAS Commando," in *World War II,* Vol. 14, No. 1, May 1999, p. 16.

Carens, James F., *The Satiric Art of Evelyn Waugh,* University of Washington Press, 1966, pp. 98–110.

Fussell, Paul, "The Genesis of a Snob," in *New Republic,* Vol. 187, No. 3542, December 6, 1982, pp. 38–39.

Hutchens, John K., "Evelyn Waugh's Finest Novel," in *New York Times,* December 30, 1945.

Kermode, Frank, "Mr. Waugh's Cities," in *Encounter,* Vol. 15, No. 5, November, 1960, pp. 63–66, 68–70.

Lynch, Richard P., "Evelyn Waugh's Early Novels: the Limits of Fiction," in *Papers on Language and Literature,* Vol. 30, No. 4, Fall 1994, pp. 373–86.

Ulanov, Barry, "The Ordeal of Evelyn Waugh," in *The Vision Obscured: Perceptions of Some Twentieth-Century Catholic Novelists,* edited by Melvin J. Friedman, Fordham University Press, 1970, pp. 79–93.

Further Reading

Allitt, Patrick, *Catholic Converts,* Cornell University Press, 2000.
> Waugh is among a significant group of British and American intellectuals who, during the nineteenth and the early twentieth centuries, converted to Catholicism. This recently published book is an account of the impact these converts had on the Catholic Church.

Cannadine, David, *The Decline and Fall of the British Aristocracy,* Vintage Books, 1999.
> This book tracks the British aristocracy from its supremacy in the 1870s to the 1930s, when it had lost a generation of sons to World War I and much of its wealth as well.

Stannard, Martin, ed., *Evelyn Waugh,* Routledge, 1997.
> This text is one of the major biographies of Waugh, covering his life from the 1920s through to his death.

Wykes, David, *Evelyn Waugh: A Literary Life,* St. Martin's Press, 1999.
> Wykes's book explores how Waugh's life affected his writing, but this is more a work of literary criticism than a biography.

The Death of the Heart

Elizabeth Bowen

1938

Published in 1938, *The Death of the Heart* is Elizabeth Bowen's most well-known and popular novel. She was a prolific writer, and by the time she had published this, her sixth novel, her writing career had been fifteen years in the making. By this time, Bowen had nine other published books, the Irish Academy of Letters had elected her a member, and critics were comparing her to such celebrated writers as Virginia Woolf, E. M. Forster, Henry James, and Jane Austen.

The Death of the Heart is the story of an orphaned sixteen-year-old girl, Portia, whose half-brother and his wife reluctantly take her into their luxurious but emotionally sterile London home after the deaths of her parents. Bowen exposes a segment of English society between World War I and World War II that is stifling and almost completely lacking in compassion. Portia is lost in Thomas and Anna Quayne's world so she seeks solace and love in Eddie, Anna's ne'er-do-well friend and protégé. Her innocence and naiveté are a challenge to the Quaynes and their friends, who find her eagerness to fit in and her keen observations unsettling.

Critics note that Bowen's background is reflected in many of her books, including *The Death of the Heart*. She was born in Ireland but to landed gentry with strong ties to Protestant England and spent much of her childhood moving from place to place and living with a variety of relatives. Her formative experiences as an outsider gave her a platform from which she could tell, with particularly keen perception, the story of a girl who is never quite at home.

Author Biography

Elizabeth Bowen's early years—while not quite as grim as those of Portia, the main character in her most well-regarded novel, *The Death of the Heart*—were unstable. She found herself at various times being raised by a group of aunts. On occasion, Bowen moved from house to house, similar to the treks from hotel to hotel that Portia and her parents make across France and Switzerland.

Bowen was born June 7, 1899, in Dublin, Ireland, into a wealthy and socially prominent family with ties to England. She was her parents' only child. When Bowen was seven, her father was hospitalized for a mental condition. She and her mother moved to England and spent the next five years moving from villa to villa on the Kent coast. While this could have been a lonely existence, both her parents came from large extended families, and an Anglo-Irish network of adults and children surrounded Bowen during this period in her life. One of her closest relatives was Audrey Fiennes, a cousin about her age. Together with Fiennes, Bowen began to express her imaginative gifts, creating stories about make-believe families.

By 1912, Bowen's father had recuperated enough that he was making regular visits to Kent to see his wife and daughter. Later that year, however, tragedy struck the family when Bowen's mother was diagnosed with cancer and died. Once again, the extended family helped take care of Bowen.

In 1918, Bowen's father remarried, and his new wife's brother, who was in the publishing industry, gave Bowen insight and help with her nascent writing efforts. In 1923, she published her first collection of short stories, *Encounters,* to high praise and married Alan Cameron. Bowen and Cameron's marriage was, by all accounts, caring but not passionate, and she allegedly engaged in a number of affairs during her twenty-eight-year marriage. In 1925, the couple moved to Oxford, where Bowen met a number of intellectuals, as well as the novelist Rose Macaulay, who took the young writer under her wing and introduced her to editors, publishers, and literary agents. In 1926, Bowen published a second volume of short stories, and by 1929 Bowen had published her first two novels.

By the early 1930s, Bowen was well on her way to a hugely successful literary career. She became friends with such luminaries as Virginia Woolf, and in 1937, the Irish Academy of Letters

Elizabeth Bowen

elected her to its ranks. By the time *The Death of the Heart* was published in 1938, critics were comparing Bowen to such celebrated writers as Woolf, E. M. Forster, Henry James, and Jane Austen.

After her husband's death, Bowen spent much time in the United States, teaching at universities and lecturing. During the last years of her life, she suffered from various respiratory illnesses, and on February 22, 1973, she died in London of lung cancer.

Plot Summary

Part One: The World

In the opening of *The Death of the Heart,* Anna and her good friend St. Quentin walk through the park in the winter while Anna relates the story of how sixteen-year-old Portia has come to live with her and her husband, Portia's older half-brother, Thomas. Anna is especially vexed because she has found Portia's diary and read some of it, and it is not complimentary to Anna. The arrangement made by Portia's father, Mr. Quayne, that Anna and Thomas should take care of Portia, is not going well.

Portia's background is then revealed. She is the love child of Mr. Quayne and his former mistress, Irene. When Mr. Quayne told his first wife about Irene and the child, she insisted that he marry Irene. He did so, and they moved to southern France, where Portia was born.

Anna and Thomas take Portia out to watch a Marx Brothers film. Portia does not find it very amusing but is grateful for the evening out with them. As they wait for a taxi home, they run into Major Brutt, a friend of Anna's former lover, Robert Pidgeon.

Portia and her classmate Lilian walk to school together, as they usually do. At the school, Portia secretly reads a letter given to her by Eddie, a friend of Anna's. The school head disciplines her when she is caught reading the letter. Portia obviously feels out of place at this school and worries about making mistakes. Lilian shows Portia the letters she still gets from the cello teacher, Miss Hebner, with whom she fell in love the previous year.

Anna has convinced Thomas to give Eddie a job because she feels that it will help to settle him. But she has to tell Eddie to stop sending her flowers and coming by the house, especially now that he is working for Thomas' firm.

The servant Matchett goes up to Portia's room, after she's turned off the lights, to talk with her and say good night. She tells Portia about the day Portia was born, and that Mrs. Quayne meant "to do right" as opposed to doing good when she kicked Mr. Quayne out of the house and made him marry Irene. Matchett finds Eddie's letter under Portia's pillow and warns Portia that Eddie is usually up to no good.

Major Brutt is lonely, so he decides to drop by Thomas and Anna's. They are not the type to encourage drop-ins, so Thomas is quite taken aback when he sees Brutt in his front hall but invites him in anyway. Portia and Eddie come home from a trip to the zoo together; they have started seeing each other but are trying to keep this a secret. Thomas notices their demeanor but says nothing.

Portia and Eddie go to have tea after running into Major Brutt and Thomas at the Windsor Terrace house. Eddie stresses to Portia that no one should know of her relationship with him. She gives her diary to Eddie at tea. He makes her promise never to write anything about them in her diary because he knows that Anna reads the diary.

In her diary, Portia writes mostly of her school and of the various things that happen around the household. She leaves out a few visits with Eddie but includes the time she goes over to his flat and shares dinner with him. Matchett acts coolly toward

Portia probably because of her relationship with Eddie. Thomas asks Portia a few probing questions about Eddie, but she doesn't say much.

Thomas and Anna are leaving soon for a vacation in Capri, but they wait awhile before telling Portia about it because they don't want her with them and haven't figured out what to do with her. Eventually, Portia hears from Matchett that she will be staying at the seashore with Anna's former nanny, Mrs. Heccomb, while Thomas and Anna are in Capri, and the staff spring-cleans the house.

Part Two: The Flesh

Portia arrives in Seale-on-Sea where she will stay with Mrs. Heccomb while Thomas and Anna are in Capri. Mrs. Heccomb's seaside house is called Waikiki, and the household is comprised of her stepson Dickie, stepdaughter Daphne, and their many friends.

Portia receives three letters her second day at Seale-on-Sea, one of which is from Eddie, who says he misses her and muses about coming to see her at the Heccombs' house. Portia goes shopping with Mrs. Heccomb and enjoys herself immensely. She investigates which room in the house might be suitable for Eddie if he comes to visit. She writes him to say she has found a good room and will ask about his visit in the next day or so. On Saturday night, the family holds one of its frequent parties. Portia dances with a number of men—something new for her.

Portia becomes aware of how stifling London and her half-brother's home are. Waikiki seems to be filled with "spontaneous living." She asks Daphne, while a group is out walking, if she may invite Eddie to Seale-on-Sea for the weekend. The group is immediately impressed that she has a boyfriend, and Daphne agrees to ask her mother about the arrangements. Mrs. Heccomb agrees and begins to fix up a room for Eddie. Eddie's letter to Portia tells her that he is unsure about when he can make it to Seale-on-Sea and that he will not be sure until the last moment.

On Friday morning, Portia receives a letter from Eddie saying that he will be there Saturday. When he arrives, Mrs. Heccomb has tea ready; she is obviously a bit disappointed in Eddie's countenance, but he is polite and charming. He and Portia take a walk, and he reports that she should be frightened of him because of his bad behavior. Later that evening, Portia and Eddie accompany Daphne and Dickie and their dates to the movies where, when Dickie ignites his cigarette lighter, they can all see that Eddie and Daphne are holding hands.

The next day, Portia asks Eddie about the night before when he was holding Daphne's hand. He responds that it didn't mean anything. They have an argument, but Portia tries to make up with him, apologizing for being a "disappointment." Later, Portia talks with Daphne about Eddie's behavior at the movies. Daphne is intent on warning her about just what kind of person Eddie is, but Portia does not want to hear this. Later, Portia and Eddie take a walk in the woods. They have a conversation about how they feel about each other. He says he has been accused of being a vicious person, and she immediately begs him not to feel that way. She begins frantically to kiss him, and he warns her about himself, that he will "drown" her.

They take a bus to the Pavilion for tea where they meet with Daphne and Dickie and all of the friends Portia has made while at Seale-on-Sea. Eventually, Eddie gets very drunk and must figure out a way to get back to Waikiki to get his luggage and then find his way back to the train station. Dickie becomes angered by Eddie's behavior, and gathers everyone up to leave. Eddie follows Portia out onto the balcony where he begins to sob uncontrollably. In her diary, Portia relates that Waikiki is tense after Eddie's departure. She asks Dickie what he thinks of Eddie, and he replies that he is "something of a Lothario."

Part Three: The Devil

Portia returns from Seale-on-Sea to London. Matchett comments on Portia's "color" and that she seems to be speaking up more than before she went away. Portia is frantic when Matchett tells her that Eddie called the day before.

The next afternoon, Anna and Thomas return from Capri. Anna thinks about the cache of letters she still keeps from when she and Robert Pidgeon were lovers. Also, she thinks about how Portia makes her feel "like a tap that won't turn on."

A week later, Portia comes home to find Eddie and Anna having tea. They invite her to join them and bring up the subject of her time spent at Seale-on-Sea, but she spends the tea daydreaming and remembering when she ran into St. Quentin Miller on the street a few days prior. Miller let drop that Anna has been reading Portia's diary, news that stunned Portia. Ever since then, she has not been able to "confront anyone with candor."

Eddie calls Anna to say that Portia has told him that Anna has read her diary. Anna is furious, pri-marily because she is entertaining Major Brutt and a couple she thinks might be able to help him find a job. After the couple leaves, she confides in Major Brutt her concerns about Eddie and his becoming close to Portia, asking Major Brutt if he thinks Portia is happy. He says yes but suggests that Anna might have a word with Portia about Eddie and tell Eddie to leave Portia alone.

Later that same afternoon, Eddie and Portia meet at Covent Gardens. Portia is upset that Anna knows about her diary and is convinced that Eddie is the one who told Anna about it; Eddie says he did not. He is upset because Portia admits that the diary does contain some writing about their relationship, and Anna has probably read about them.

After Eddie tells Portia that she has changed and that he is no longer happy being with her, she flees his apartment and ends up at the Karachi Hotel where Major Brutt is staying. She tells him that she is never returning to Anna and Thomas' household. She asks Major Brut if she can marry him, stressing that she could cook and clean for him, and that they would not have to live in a hotel. He says he is flattered, but convinces Portia to let him call the Quaynes to arrange for her to return to them.

Back at the house, Anna, Thomas, and St. Quentin Miller are having dinner, aware that Portia is late. Anna takes a call in the middle of dinner from Major Brutt, who tells her that Portia is with him but does not wish to come home. The three adults continue to sit around the table, arguing about Portia, until St. Quentin admits telling Portia about Anna reading her diary, and Anna admits reading the diary as well as discussing it with Eddie. They must decide what is the best way to pick up Portia and eventually hit upon the idea of having Matchett fetch her from Major Brutt's hotel. Matchett leaves in a taxi, and the book ends with her entering the Hotel Karachi to bring Portia back home to the Quaynes.

Characters

Cecil Bowers

Cecil is a friend of the Heccomb family who is brought to Daphne and Dickie's Saturday night party for Portia. Cecil and Portia become good friends while Portia is at Seale-on-Sea.

Media Adaptations

- In 1985, Granada Television (United Kingdom) produced a television movie version of *The Death of the Heart,* starring JoJo Cole as Portia, Wendy Hiller as Matchett, Patricia Hodge as Anna, and Miranda Richardson as Daphne.

Major Eric "E. J." Brutt

Major Brutt is a lonely, retired soldier. Anna, along with Thomas and Portia, runs into him after the movies, and he mistakenly calls her Miss Fellowes, her maiden name. Major Brutt remembers Anna from before her marriage when she was with her lover, Robert Pidgeon. The family invites him back to the house for a drink, and he visits them on a number of other occasions although both Anna and Thomas are snippy about him behind his back. Portia likes him a great deal, and he gives her puzzles as gifts. After Eddie rejects her and she runs away from home, Portia ends up at his hotel.

Eddie

Eddie is twenty-three, charming, self-centered, a heavy drinker, and a ladies' man. He can swing from one emotional extreme to the other in a matter of minutes. He encourages Portia to fall in love with him even though he has no intention of honestly returning her affections. Early in the novel he claims to be in love with Anna and constantly visits the house to flirt with her. Anna finds a job for Eddie in Thomas' advertising firm because she believes him to be clever but in need of something to settle him down.

Eddie first encourages Portia's affections when he writes a letter to her, thanking her for an insignificant courtesy and adds that he is lonely and wants to be her friend because he sees that she is lonely, too. They begin to meet secretly because they know that no one approves of the two of them being together. Portia feels that no one understands Eddie. She begins to fall in love and shares her diary with him. She invites him to the seashore while she is there but is shocked when she sees him holding hands with Daphne in the movie theater. He tells her he no longer cares for her, primarily because he is simply overwhelmed by her innocence and eagerness for love. This statement prompts her to run away to Major Brutt's hotel room.

Daphne Heccomb

Daphne is Mrs. Heccomb's stepdaughter and has a job at a library. She lives at home with her brother and Mrs. Heccomb to help with the expenses. She is popular and full of spontaneity. Portia discovers Daphne and Eddie holding hands at the movie theater, but Daphne assures her that it was nothing—although she warns Portia to beware of Eddie.

Dickie Heccomb

Dickie is Mrs. Heccomb's stepson. He has a job at a bank and lives at home, helping his stepmother with the expenses. It is his cigarette lighter that illuminates Eddie holding hands with Daphne at the move theater.

Mrs. Heccomb

Mrs. Heccomb takes care of Portia at her home in Seale-on-Sea while Thomas and Anna are in Capri. She was once Anna's governess. She married a physician, who died and left her very little to live on. To make a little extra money, she paints lamp shades and rents out her house in the summer. The family life at Waikiki, Mrs. Heccomb's seaside villa, is lively and unrestricted—in stark contrast to Anna and Thomas' grim home in London. Mrs. Heccomb's two children, Daphne and Dickie, are popular and energetic and often have large spontaneous dance parties at the villa.

Lilian

Lilian is Portia's schoolmate, her only friend close to her in age. She has already started to get a womanly figure and to attract looks from men. She is at Miss Paullie's school because she fell in love with the female cello teacher at a previous school.

R. Matchett

Matchett is a servant in Thomas and Anna's house, coming from the first Mrs. Quayne's household after her death. She is very proper and runs the house with a sense of the absolute. But she is also sympathetic to Portia's situation. On evenings when Thomas and Anna are out, Matchett comes up to Portia's room to tuck her in for the night and to share stories about Portia's father when he lived with the first Mrs. Quayne.

One night, Matchett finds one of Eddie's letters to Portia under Portia's pillow. While she does not read the letter, she makes clear to Portia that she disapproves of Eddie and thinks he is nothing but trouble for a girl as inexperienced as Portia. Because of her relationship with Portia, Thomas and Anna choose Matchett to bring Portia back after she has run away.

St. Quentin Miller

St. Quentin Miller is a close friend of Anna's and a writer of some fame. He is aloof and somewhat cold and counts Anna one of his few friends. He makes vague references to the fact that he is so distant from others because in the past he has found that becoming intimate with another person is too painful. He is responsible for inadvertently telling Portia that Anna has read her diary.

Miss Paullie

Miss Paullie is the head of the school Portia attends. It is a very expensive school but seems to be especially for girls who have not done well at other schools. Miss Paullie holds classes in her father's huge house, where he also sees patients as a physician. She is strict and has very rigid codes of conduct for the girls.

Robert Pidgeon

Robert Pidgeon was a lover of Anna's before she married Thomas. She keeps his letters to her, of which Thomas is aware. The reason for Robert and Anna's breakup is not clear but has something to do with both his and Anna's inability to be truly intimate. Anna and Major Brutt see Robert as exceptionally capable, and he is well thought of. Anna still reads his old love letters.

Anna Quayne

Anna is Thomas' wife and is currently thirty-four. She and Thomas tried to have children but she miscarried twice, and she has now decided that she doesn't want children. Their relationship seems tense, and she is in control of just how close they are to each other. Anna does not like Portia and is almost cruel to her, but puts up with her living at their house because this is the right thing to do. She is unsympathetic toward everyone, most of all Portia, and is unable to imagine herself in anyone else's place. Both she and Thomas speak ill of many of their friends behind their backs. One of her closest friends is St. Quentin Miller, but she is also very attached to Eddie and has found him a job at Thomas' firm.

Irene Quayne

Irene is Mr. Quayne's second wife, considerably younger than he is, and Portia's mother. She and Mr. Quayne had an affair after being introduced to each other by mutual friends, and they married once she became pregnant with Portia. She dies in Switzerland after Mr. Quayne's death, and her sister sends the letter about Portia to the Quaynes in London. Portia has many memories of moving from one cheap hotel room to another in Switzerland with her mother and of the closeness they shared.

Mr. Quayne

Mr. Quayne is Portia and Thomas' father. He once ran a small business, but the first Mrs. Quayne had money, and she urged him to retire early to a house she had bought. Mr. Quayne is depicted as a weak man who has been led around by his wife. He was about fifty-seven and living a very orderly life when his affair with Irene began in London. At that time, he had had his first child, Thomas, with the first Mrs. Quayne, who, upon being told of the affair, calmly insisted upon a divorce and upon Mr. Quayne's marriage to Irene. Before he dies, Mr. Quayne writes a letter asking that, if Irene should also die before Portia becomes an adult, Anna and Thomas take care of Portia, at least for a year.

Mrs. Quayne

Mrs. Quayne is Thomas' mother and Mr. Quayne's first wife, and she has a substantial amount of money. When Mr. Quayne tells her of his affair with Irene, and that Irene is pregnant, she very calmly arranges the entire series of events that follows: her divorce from Mr. Quayne; the packing of his bags; Thomas' driving him to the train station; and even Mr. Quayne's marriage to Irene. When Matchett speaks of her former employer to Portia, she notes that Mrs. Quayne meant "to do right," as opposed to doing good when she kicked Mr. Quayne out of the house and made him marry Irene.

Portia Quayne

Portia is the sixteen-year-old love child of Mr. Quayne and Irene Quayne (the second Mrs. Quayne), and was born in France soon after their marriage. Her childhood has been spent traveling around Switzerland from one cheap hotel room to another. After her father and mother die, Portia moves to the London house of her half-brother, Thomas, and his wife, Anna. The childless couple takes in the orphan Portia because it is the right thing to do, but they take no joy in her company and find her a disruption to their sterile household. She is as eager as a puppy to fit in and learn the ways of their world, but her innocence startles them.

Portia keeps a diary, which Anna reads, learning that Portia has portrayed her and others in a less than flattering light. Realizing that Anna has read her diary is one of the events that precipitates Portia's running away from home toward the end of the book.

Portia falls in love with Eddie, a friend of Anna's who is a callous, self-centered Lothario (a man who likes to seduce women). He encourages her to consider him the focus of her life, but her innocence and eagerness for love frighten him, and he eventually tells her that he no longer loves her. His rejection of her is one of the other events that launches Portia's desperate attempt to run away.

Thomas Quayne

Thomas is Portia's older half-brother, the son of Mr. Quayne and the first Mrs. Quayne. He has few brotherly feelings toward Portia because he is still hurting from the fracture Portia's birth created in his family. He has been married to Anna for eight years, lives in a nice house in London, and is a partner in his own advertising firm, Quayne and Merrett.

Thomas' marriage to Anna appears, on most occasions, to be very cold and passionless. As well, his character gives the impression of being weak when dealing with his wife. For example, when St. Quentin Miller, a friend of Anna's, comes for tea, Thomas feels that he is not welcome and stays down in his library until Miller has left the house.

Themes

The Outsider

Anna and Thomas Quayne live in an insular world, comfortable knowing what will happen from one day to the next. Into their lives comes Portia, the daughter of Thomas' father and his mistress (later his second wife), Irene. Portia's very presence is a source of discomfort to the couple, and she enters their house as the consummate outsider. She is an orphaned love child in a childless household

where two miscarriages have occurred. Even before she came to London, Portia was an outsider, banned to the continent by her father's first wife, doomed to wander from cheap hotel to cheap hotel.

In Anna and Thomas' eyes, Portia is in need of housebreaking, like a young puppy, unschooled in the ways of their society. When Matchett asks Anna where Portia will eat, Anna responds that Portia will eat downstairs with the rest of the family. "Surely. She's got to learn to," Anna says, as if Portia must be trained in how to eat in a familial setting after so many years eating in hotel dining rooms.

Throughout the book, Portia is a keen observer, always on the lookout for clues as to what is the right thing to say and do. Often, she is confused about her position in the Quayne household and is overly deferential in her struggle to know what is correct behavior. For example, when Anna and St. Quentin arrive for tea, Portia behaves almost as though she is the maid, offering to take coats and put away hats. She is desperate to find a place for herself in this new world.

Even the language people speak in London is foreign to Portia. She asks herself, "for what reason people said what they did not mean, and did not say what they meant?"

Family

Portia is an orphan from a family that is barely legitimate, wrapped in shame. Her first sixteen years are hardly what most would call normal, moving from hotel room to hotel room, never attending school or making a steady set of friends. She is more like a mother to her own mother, offering tea and comfort after Irene has a crying spell and helping her mother to the hospital when she becomes ill.

Living with Thomas and Anna does not make Portia part of their family even though Thomas is her half-brother. Bowen describes the Quayne's house in intimidating terms, a large home with gleaming marble and ivory-painted walls, and a fire in the hearth that casts a "hard glow." Portia is glad when she comes back to the house and no one is home yet. Anna, as the woman of the house, could go up to say good-night to Portia, but this small sign of compassion is left up to Matchett, the crusty old servant who knew Portia's father before Portia was born.

Offering normal familial attention and love to Portia is simply beyond the capabilities of Anna and Thomas. Thomas is still stinging from the shame he first felt sixteen years ago when his mother kicked his father out of their house, forcing him to marry Irene, then pregnant with Portia. And Anna never feels close to the girl, asking Thomas, "would you really like me to love her?. . . No, you'd only like me to seem to love her." Instead of taking her with them on their trip to Capri, Anna and Thomas pack her off again, only a few months after she has arrived at their house, to stay with Anna's former nanny at the beach. And their concern about her relationship with Eddie is slight. They seem only to be concerned about how it affects them, and think nothing of her sneaking off to see him. When Portia is very late the final evening of the novel, their response is negligible. Anna responds more forcefully to a perceived slight by Lilian's mother, and the couple is truly baffled as to who should go get Portia when she has been discovered at Major Brutt's hotel.

Coming-of-Age

Portia and the adults around her seem to be from two distinct countries, but this sense can be attributed primarily to their different generations. Portia has seen little of the world while the Quaynes and their friends have lived through World War I, which left millions dead and changed how people thought about society and humanity altogether. Anna does not quite know how to treat Portia, so she enforces her opinions and choices on Portia without much consultation. Surprisingly, Matchett chides Anna when she decides that Portia should not wear the dark clothes she owns when she comes to London and selects brightly colored clothes for her. She also stands up to Anna when she questions the condition and contents of Portia's room.

Portia is struggling to grow up but without much guidance from most of the adults around her. Lacking this guidance, she falls for Eddie, the one person who pays her any attention. Even though he is twenty-three, Eddie is barely an adult himself. He is self-centered and moody, but Portia so desperately wants to please somebody that she ignores this and sees only that Eddie, like her, seems to be misunderstood. This bonds them and fulfills her immature image of what love should be—a relationship that creates an exclusive world of fantasy, away from the realities of the day-to-day. "Oh no!. . . You are my perfect Eddie," she tells him when he begins to talk about his bad side.

As well, Portia is trying to develop her own sense of who she is. Even though Eddie demands that she never change, Portia still has a sense that this cannot be true. "I feel everyone waiting;. . . I

Topics for Further Study

- In *The Death of the Heart,* Anna has a job doing interior design before she is married to Thomas. Research the status of British women in the 1930s and whether it was typical for a young woman from a wealthy background to have a career. What kinds of work did women do in 1930s England? How did this compare to the United States in the 1930s?

- In the novel, Portia comes to London with little or no formal education. Anna and Thomas put her in a school that appears to be for wealthy girls who have not done well at school. Investigate how women and girls were educated in England in the 1930s. Were there publicly supported schools for girls or only private and church-supported institutions? What subjects did the schools teach? How many girls continued their education at universities and colleges?

- Choose one chapter from *The Death of the Heart* that you find particularly interesting; adapt this chapter as a scene in a play. Act out the scene with a group of students. What insight can be gained about the characters and their dynamics from this exercise? In what ways are the events of this chapter significant to the novel as a whole?

- In *The Death of the Heart,* Portia runs away because she is upset by how Anna, Eddie, and others have treated her. Choose another literary work that features a teenage runaway and compare and contrast the works. Possible choices include *The Catcher in the Rye,* by J. D. Salinger; *Rite of Passage,* by Richard Wright; and *A Girl Named Disaster,* by Nancy Farmer. Present your findings in a Venn diagram or an essay.

cannot stay as I am. They will all expect something in a year or two more." She feels the pressure to become an adult even as she struggles to find her place as an adolescent. And she does change, as Matchett notices, when she returns from Seale-on-Sea more talkative and with more "color."

Death

The Death of the Heart is filled with symbolic deaths, as well as actual deaths. Both of Portia's parents have died, and the first Mrs. Quayne, Thomas' mother, has died, allowing Matchett (who was her servant) to move in with Thomas and his wife as their housekeeper. The novel's title indicates that something will die in the story; indeed, critics have noted that, through the deception of the adults around her, Portia's naiveté and innocence are dead by the end of the book. In one of the novel's final scenes, Portia asks Major Brutt to marry her, assuring him that she can cook and keep a good house. Her romantic ideals of love have been reduced considerably, even killed. At the start of the novel, even nature is pictured as dead. Bowen uses words such as "brittle," "pallid," and "black walks" to describe the park near the Quayne's house, setting the stage for a society where emotion has frozen and died.

Secrets

Secrets play a critical role in *The Death of the Heart*. Portia's life is launched by a secret love affair between Mr. Quayne and Irene, and their marriage remains a secret of sorts due to the fact that they are banished from England and never allowed to establish roots as a real family might. When Anna tells St. Quentin of Portia's origins, she does so in a conspiratorial manner, away from the house. And when Major Brutt asks about Portia's family ("Can your people spare you?"), she stumbles and can't get out the words to describe her situation.

Portia keeps a diary and is horrified when she discovers that Anna has read it and has discussed its contents with others. Her writing was to remain a secret, except to Eddie, to whom she trustingly gives the diary. But even with Eddie she thinks twice about exposing her background and history and wonders what he would think of her unusual vagabond life before she arrived in London. And, of course, her relationship with Eddie is a secret, and he demands that she not include one word of it in her diary, lest Anna discover their secret liaisons at the zoo, the park, and his apartment.

Anna keeps secrets, as well. Thomas knows that she still keeps Robert Pidgeon's letters, but he most likely does not know how she still thinks of him. And her relationships with St. Quentin and Eddie are strictly out-of-bounds for her husband; he is not even welcome to have tea with Anna and St. Quentin and stays hidden in his library until her friend leaves. Questions arise, in fact, about whether these two men are her lovers or have been

at some time, but Bowen is somewhat vague about the status of these connections.

Style

Point-of-View

The story in *The Death of the Heart* is told from numerous viewpoints. The primary narrator is generally omniscient, as if looking over the story from above, and speaks with an authoritative voice. This narrator sets the stage, for example, when each of the three parts of the book begins, describing the park in parts one and two, and the Quayne's house in part three. As well, this narrator describes characters' thoughts in a way that is clearer than the characters themselves could. Daphne's first impression of Portia is negatively colored by her association with Anna, and the narrator comments, "It was clear that her manner to Portia could not be less aggressive until she had stopped associating her with Anna." Daphne's thoughts and feelings are available to the narrator, perhaps more so than to Daphne herself.

Much of the story, as well, is told directly through the eyes of many of its characters. For example, parts of the book are Portia's diary entries where the story is told completely through her eyes; everything is filtered through her sensibilities and feelings. Here, Bowen can dabble in a bit of irony, as when Portia writes of Thomas asking her about Eddie. "I hope he is polite.. . . does he try it on?" Thomas asks her. She has no idea that Thomas is asking, in a veiled way, whether Eddie has tried to kiss Portia, or attempted more fondling. Thomas drops that line of questioning when she says she doesn't know what he means.

Occasionally, the narration shifts suddenly from the third-person into the first-person narrative point-of-view. At one point, when Anna is alone, thinking about how she cannot seem to understand people, the story is narrated from the third person omniscient point-of-view: "There seemed to be some way she did not know of by which people managed to understand each other." Then, suddenly, in the next paragraph, the reader is in Anna's head, and the writing has shifted to the first person point-of-view: "All I said to Thomas was, get off my quilt."

Setting

Bowen's descriptions of the novel's various settings contribute to the tone of the story, and she is careful to offer detailed pictures of the characters' surroundings. The house the Quayne's live in is a huge, grand house on Windsor Terrace, filled with the best furniture, drapes, and rugs. Anna is attentive to every detail of how the house looks, complaining when Portia does not maintain her room as Anna believes it should be maintained, and reprimanding Thomas for placing a glass in his library where it does not belong. Everything is "set" in the Quayne household, always in its proper place. Portia is used to the noise of a hotel, and the house is almost too quiet for her.

In contrast, Mrs. Heccomb's house in Seale-on-Sea, named Waikiki, has a much more fluid atmosphere. Its name is informal and exotic, and her children are forever involved in moving the furniture around for a party or other event. The house is right on the beach, with many windows, and is filled with lampshades hand-painted by Mrs. Heccomb and comfortable but aging furniture. A radio is usually playing loudly, and Mrs. Heccomb's two adult children are as rambunctious as puppies, tumbling up and down the stairs. Portia can hear the household in the morning, bathing and getting ready for the day.

Hotels as homes appear in the novel in two important ways: the different hotels that Portia and her parents lived in, and the Karachi Hotel where Major Brutt lives. Portia thinks fondly of the hotels she has lived in even though they offered her a less physically comfortable lifestyle than she now has at the Quayne's. "We used to make up stories about people at dinner, and it was fun to watch people come and go," she tells Thomas. And, when Portia is overwhelmed by Anna and Eddie's deceptions, she ends up at Major Brutt's hotel, maybe because hotels are the settings she knows best and in which she feels the most comfortable.

Structure

The Death of the Heart is divided into three parts of similar length, and each of these parts is, in turn, divided into chapters. Each part takes place where Portia is during a season: Part one is set in London during the winter; in part two, Portia moves to Seale-on-Sea for the spring; and in part three, she is back again in London with summer coming.

The three parts of the book are entitled, "The World," "The Flesh," and "The Devil," considered among Christians to be the three things humans must fight against if they are to remain virtuous. In fact, these three things appear in the Anglican Book of Common Prayer. The world signifies those things not associated with religion; the flesh stands for the pursuit of sensual pleasures; and the devil represents temptations to evil, such as theft and lying.

In the novel's three parts, Portia undergoes experiences that can be associated with these three titles. In "The World," she first comes to London, a new and strange world for her. In "The Flesh," she first kisses Eddie and, as well, witnesses him holding hands with Daphne. In "The Devil," further deception is exposed when she finds out about Anna reading her diary and sharing its contents with others.

Historical Context

The Inter-War Years

The period between World War I and World War II (1918–1939) was an era in which many people became disenchanted with society, politics, and traditional institutions. The carnage of the First World War had disillusioned many British, who once felt that the new century would be the start of a fresh and prosperous period for humanity in general and the United Kingdom specifically. This may be one reason why, in *The Death of the Heart*, the Quayne household seems isolated from most of the local and world events occurring in the 1930s.

In the 1930s, under Hitler, Germany was rearming itself in preparation for aggression against its neighbors. But Britain's foreign policy became stagnant and the government was unwilling to address the coming international crises; there were simply too many problems to worry about at home. The working class had begun to unionize, and labor relations had deteriorated. In the 1926 General Strike, two million workers had struck over plans to reduce wages and lengthen working hours. The General Strike itself failed, but the trade unions did realize that winning at the ballot box would give them real power to change the country.

The Depression

The worldwide economic depression, which began with the stock market crash of 1929, had a debilitating affect on Britain's economy. Even though there were signs of recovery by the mid-1930s, Britain still had an unemployment crisis and was experiencing a decline in its traditional export industries, making it difficult for the country to pay for its imports of foods and raw materials. But, while these traditional export industries, such as coal mining and cotton manufacturing, remained

Compare
&
Contrast

- **1930s:** Women in England, like Daphne and her friends, are enjoying the first decade of equal voting rights with men, granted to them in 1928.

  Today: With the 1997 general election, 120 women are now Members of Parliament, double the number elected in the previous general election in 1992. There are currently 12 women in the Prime Minister's Cabinet and 16 women in ministerial positions.

- **1930s:** Women are just beginning to see the possibilities of working outside the home in England. During World War I, more than a million women took over jobs left vacant by men who were fighting, but the government was under pressure by the unions to see that these jobs reverted to men when the war was over. The 1920s and 1930s, however, saw the increased acceptance of women working in shops, offices, factories, and light industry. By the 1930s, it is common to see young working women, such as Daphne, out on the town for an evening of dining and movies.

  Today: Women make up 45 percent of the workforce in the United Kingdom, and Britain employs more women than any other European country. Not only are women in positions throughout government, education, medicine, business, and other professions, but they account for about 35 percent of new business ventures.

- **1930s:** Upper-class women such as Anna regularly have "low tea" with friends in the afternoon each day, a small meal to tide one over until the larger evening meal. In addition to drinking tea, participants eat thin crustless sandwiches, shrimp or fish patés, toasted breads with jams, and pastries such as scones and crumpets. Commercial tea rooms are also increasingly popular, especially among young women such as Portia, who meets with Eddie early in their relationship at Madame Tussaud's for afternoon tea.

  Today: Teatime still is observed in England and Commonwealth countries, and the popularity of tea rooms in the United States has blossomed—although many label the small afternoon meal incorrectly as "high tea," which is actually a heavier, later meal, meant to pose as dinner. While tea and scones are still served at these tea rooms, some are expanding their menus to include champagne and strawberries, considered an American touch to the meal.

- **1930s:** Only well-to-do families can afford the time and money spent on vacations abroad, such Anna and Thomas Quayne's trip to Capri.

  Today: Six in ten British residents take at least one long holiday a year, either in Britain or abroad, and British spending on international vacation travel is increasing.

depressed, other industries, such as electrical engineering, automobile manufacture, and industrial chemistry, were strengthening.

The City of London

In the 1930s, the depression and the growing unease about what was happening in Germany had a sobering effect on the atmosphere of the city of London. Dance halls, which were so popular during World War I and immediately afterwards, became less prominent. The skyline of London had changed only gradually since the 1600s, giving London a sense of permanence and history. Public transport

expanded a great deal in the first quarter of the century in and around London with the establishment of tramlines and omnibus routes. After World War I, a great expansion in railway lines occurred, making access to London easier for those who lived in the suburban and rural regions around the city.

Struggles over Women's Rights

The 1920s introduced major social changes in Britain, including equal rights for women—but only after a long period of struggle.

Emmeline Pankhurst led the fight for women's voting rights in Britain, establishing the Women's

Franchise League in 1889 and assisting with the organization in 1903 of the National Women's Social and Political Union. Their bold program, demanding full voting rights for women, led them to stage parades and to engage in such violent forms of protest as window breaking. The police subjected Pankhurst and her followers to rough treatment, and occasionally they found themselves in jail for their activities.

Women in Britain were first granted the right to vote in 1918 but this included only women who were at least 30 years old and householders (meaning "wives"). Women finally received equal voting privileges to men in 1928, the year of Pankhurst's death.

Far more women worked in the 1920s and 1930s than had before World War I, and the average age of marriage rose sharply. Jobs opened up for women in shops and the new light industrial factories. It even became not uncommon to see women smoking in public. While women's colleges had been grudgingly allowed at Oxford and Cambridge since the 1870s, women could not take degrees at Oxford until 1921 and at Cambridge until 1948.

Critical Overview

Critics have responded to *The Death of the Heart* primarily in two ways: by discussing the implications of the author's childhood experiences *vis-à-vis* the motherless outsider in the novel; and by examining the conflict between innocence and experience threaded throughout the book.

Bowen grew up in a privileged Anglo-Irish family in Ireland, not really English but isolated by her English ties from the country in which she lived. According to Martha Henn in *Feminist Writers,* "she occupied a class position that put her at odds with most of her fellow Irish." As Richard Tillinghast notes in "The House, the Hotel, & the Child," "the Anglo-Irish were always, from the sixteenth century on, to some degree rootless and insecure in the country they governed." This tension is due to the fact that the Protestant ruling class owned land taken by force from the Irish Catholic population by their ancestors. This sense of uneasiness extends to Bowen's characters, according to Tillinghast. "The attenuation and malaise one feels among Bowen's characters springs, historically, from the growing isolation of the Anglo-

Irish." Bowen's relatives are strangers in a country where the Irish, in the early part of the twentieth century, are increasingly focused on struggles for Irish national independence from Britain.

This link between Bowen's own sense of cultural rootlessness and her most prominent character, the outsider, is also echoed by Sean O'Faolain in *The Vanishing Hero,* where he writes, "Elizabeth Bowen is detached by birth from that society she describes. She is an Irishwoman, at least one sea apart from English traditions." Bowen depicts Portia as a young woman without a country, traveling throughout Europe as a vagabond, expelled from England by no fault of her own. While she does have ties to England, as did Bowen, Portia arrives in London a foreigner with the ability and necessity to watch carefully the behavior of those around her. Tillinghast notes, "This outsider's point of view—cold-eyed, unillusioned—places Portia beyond the cozy circle of civilized mutual accommodation practiced by Anna and Thomas, and thus makes their visitor a dangerous presence."

In addition, Bowen's outsider status extended beyond merely the political; she lost her father to mental illness when she was about six years old and her mother to cancer when she was thirteen. The job of raising her fell to a battery of relatives, and home was a series of villas on the English coast. According to Henn, "Bowen believed that fiction is rooted in the experiences of the author's life, but at the same time she rejected the overtly autobiographical or confessional impulse."

However, critics cannot help but notice that a major theme in much of her writing, including *The Death of the Heart,* is of the motherless girl, lacking any guiding adult hands. Edwin J. Kenney, Jr., notes in *Elizabeth Bowen,* that she showed an interest in her own history "as a motherless only child" by writing three nonfiction accounts of her experiences, as well as including in her novels "the dislocated child who is urgently seeking an identity as a means of survival."

Critics have also noted Bowen's efforts to understand the relationship between innocence and experience. Kenney argues that her interest in the role of innocence is clearly seen by the fact that one of her recurring themes is "man's primary need for an illusion" and the eventual "loss of innocence, the acquisition of knowledge through loss, and the entrance into selfhood."

Portia's story in *The Death of the Heart* is one of trying to understand who and what she is, taking on and shedding illusions—such as the illusion of love with Eddie—and moving from one stage of her life to another. According to Robert Rubens in *The Contemporary Review:*

> *The Death of the Heart* is not only a crushing portrayal of the destruction of innocence, but a disillusioned warning that in the modern world innocence must be lost, that we all must compromise.

In 1998, the editorial board of the Modern Library cited *The Death of the Heart* among the one hundred best English language books of the twentieth century.

Criticism

Susan Sanderson

Sanderson holds a master of fine arts degree in fiction writing and is an independent writer. In this essay, she examines how Bowen uses indoor settings in a particular way to shed light on Portia's frame of mind.

Critics have noticed Elizabeth Bowen's interest in placing her characters in natural and garden-like settings in *The Death of the Heart,* especially to highlight their innocence and naiveté. Paul A. Parrish, in "The Loss of Eden: Four Novels of Elizabeth Bowen," argues that Bowen has Eddie and Portia meet at the seaside and later in the woods because "the country has an obvious unreality because it's not the kind of life they know." Portia finds it easier to maintain her fantasies about the possibilities of Eddie's love in a place that is so different from London and her half-brother's imposing mansion. Parrish adds, in fact, "the scenes which unite the elements of nature, love, and idealism are themselves reminiscent of the Edenic myth and the Garden." Edwin J. Kenney, Jr., in *Elizabeth Bowen,* reiterates the connection between nature and Bowen's concern with loss of innocence as a theme, noting that her concern "often finds its expression in allusions to the story of the early life of man, the story of the fall from the garden of Eden."

But certainly of equal interest are the indoor settings in which Bowen places her characters. In *The Death of the Heart,* there are four primary indoor settings in which Bowen places Portia: her half-brother's house on Windsor Terrace in London; Mrs. Heccomb's seaside villa, Waikiki; movie theaters; and hotels. Bowen allows Portia's character to react differently to each of these settings,

further illuminating the young girl's motivations and feelings.

Portia, as the love child of Mr. Quayne and his mistress, Irene (who later became the second Mrs. Quayne), was reared in a series of hotels and other temporary shelters. The only memories of love and familial warmth Portia has are of herself and Irene in these hotels, sharing cups of tea and eating chocolates, pulling an eiderdown comforter over themselves to stay warm, and making up entertaining stories about the other guests while they dine. But the London society she lands in, after the deaths of her parents, disdains hotels and refers to them only in pejorative tones. Anna intimates that Portia will have to be taught how to have dinner in polite company, and when Miss Paullie catches Portia reading Eddie's letter during class, she not only scolds her for the letter but also for keeping her handbag next to her desk instead of leaving it in the cloakroom. "To carry your bag about with you indoors is a hotel habit, you know," she chides.

It should come as no surprise that, after Portia is betrayed by Anna reading her diary, wounded by Eddie's announcement that he no longer loves her, and struck by her realization that most of the adults in her life have been viciously criticizing her, she finds herself at a hotel. Even though she is frightened and upset, looking like "a wild creature just old enough to know that it must dread humans," according to Major Brutt when he sees her in his hotel's lobby, she somehow finds her way to a hotel. With her heart broken and her innocence shed, Portia speaks openly, unlike she has ever spoken before in London, about Anna and Eddie and all the others who have disappointed her. She has been completely disabused of her fantasies about love— so much so that she offers to marry Major Brutt, a man who is a good thirty years older, promising that she would make him a good home. A hotel is where Portia comes to rest for a moment, to feel safe, before she is forced to go back out into the world, back to Anna and Thomas' house.

Movie houses seem to hold a special dread for Portia, almost as if they represent the crassness of the world in conflict with her innocence and inexperience. The first time she goes to a movie theater, she is with Anna and Thomas, and "the screen threw its tricky light on her relaxed profile; she sat almost appalled." This moment, for Portia, with its uncomfortableness, foreshadows an even more horrid evening when she goes to the movies at Seale-on-Sea with Eddie and Daphne and her other friends. There, illuminated for her in the darkness of the theater by a friend's cigarette lighter, is Eddie's mockery of her love for him—he and Daphne are holding hands. Eddie later tries to pass it off as just a silly thing he did, but this is the first break in Portia's fantasy about their love. Even as they occur in places that portray fantasy worlds, these experiences in movie houses underscore just how unprepared Portia is for the "real" world.

Thomas and Anna's relationship is tense, and that tension is everywhere in their house on Windsor Terrace. The house is filled with a heavy silence, unlike the chatter and sounds of living Portia is accustomed to hearing through the walls of hotels. This is a home where she feels very much not at home, and Bowen's descriptions of the place and how Portia behaves in it make that perfectly clear. In her diary, Portia writes, "When Thomas comes in he looks as though he was smelling something he thought he might not be let eat. This house makes a smell of feeling." And when the housemaid Matchett, the only person in the house who seems to care for her at all, asks her to share some tea, Portia later remembers that Matchett said she looked like a ghost. Portia writes in her diary, "But really it is this house that is like that."

Further displaying just how uncomfortable she feels at Windsor Terrace, and how much an outsider she thinks she is, Portia behaves in the manner of a skittish cat or of someone who is about to be found out. When Anna and St. Quentin come into the house for tea, Portia offers to take their coats and hats. A few minutes later, to compound this sense of submissiveness, Bowen has Portia slink out of the room:

> Then, holding herself so erect that she quivered, taking long, soft steps on the balls of her feet, and at the same time with an orphaned unostentation, she started making towards the door. She moved crabwise, as though the others were royalty, never quite turning her back on them.

When she visits her brother in his library, she displays no sense of relief being with him, even though he is a blood relative. She offers to refill his cigarette case, as if she were his valet, and folds herself up in a chair, as if attempting to take up the smallest possible piece of real estate inside the house.

But when Portia goes to stay with Mrs. Heccomb and her adult children at Seale-on-Sea, just after leaving Anna and Thomas's house in London, her entire demeanor changes, reflecting the relaxed, casual air that pervades the house named Waikiki. Over the weeks she spends in the Heccombs' light-

> " Movie houses seem to hold a special dread for Portia, almost as if they represent the crassness of the world in conflict with her innocence and inexperience. The first time she goes to a movie theater, she is with Anna and Thomas, and 'the screen threw its tricky light on her relaxed profile; she sat almost appalled.'"

filled home by the sea, she comes out of her shell and discovers new aspects of herself. The first evening Portia is at Waikiki, she is still performing her "crabwise" walk. "Portia, as unostentatiously as possible, edged round the room to stand beside Mrs. Heccomb." And, while she does permit herself to do a little exploring around the house the next morning, she is still cautious. "Before stepping over the wall. . . Portia glanced back at the Waikiki windows. But no one watched her; no one seemed to object."

However, by the time the first week is out, she has helped roll back the carpeting at Waikiki for a party and has danced, for the first time, with a boy. Portia realizes then that "something edited life in the Quayne's house," and that "the uneditedness of life here at Waikiki made for behaviour that was. . . frank." The house is "the fount of spontaneous living." She is beginning to question not only how the new people she is meeting live, but how all of the other people she knows live, including Thomas, Anna, and Eddie.

But all of this does not mean that Portia has shed her naiveté at Waikiki. Indeed, one of her Seale-on-Sea friends, Cecil, comments to her that he can tell she is "so young." And when a family friend of the Heccombs' comes by for a visit, he asks Portia, "How's the child of the house?" Portia is stunned, as well, while in Seale-on-Sea, by Eddie's behavior with Daphne at the movie house, and by Daphne's irritation with her afterwards, when Portia tries to find out what is going on. Even though the atmosphere at Waikiki to Portia is "life at its highest voltage," she still has yet to encounter the complete destruction of her innocence, which will come later, at the hands of Eddie and Anna and St. Quentin.

Source: Susan Sanderson, Critical Essay on *The Death of the Heart,* in *Novels for Students,* The Gale Group, 2002.

Allan E. Austin

In the following essay excerpt, Austin provides an overview of The Death of the Heart, *and praises Bowen for skillfully blending the maturation of Portia with the revitalization of the Quaynes' marriage.*

No Bowen novel has a more comically dramatic opening situation than *The Death of the Heart.* Into the adjusted, unemotional, childless, eight-year marriage of Anna and Thomas Quayne drops Portia, age fifteen, Thomas's half-sister. The Quaynes open the door of their expensive, overly ordered Regent's Park home with little enthusiasm to this newly orphaned child who was conceived in adultery. They are somewhat sustained by the possibility she may be shifted to other relatives after they have had her a year as the elder Mr. Quayne has beseeched them to do. The narrative culminates in a series of shocks: Portia is galvanized into action which, in turn, rebounds upon the Quaynes. By the end of the novel, considerable readjustment at 2 Windsor Terrace seems to be in the offing, and Portia's visit is quite likely a permanent one.

Though much of this "double-stranded" book records Portia's growth and her necessary loss of innocence, the more basic issue is the revitalization, perhaps simply the vitalization, of the moribund marriage. Much of this novel's brilliance results from the skillful blending of these two concerns and their subsidiary matters. This is Miss Bowen's most successful novel, artistically and commercially; and, along with *The Heat of the Day,* it constitutes the peak of her achievement.

The Quaynes have been living more of an arrangement than a marriage, for each came to it as an emotional cripple. Anna wed on the rebound from the one great love of her life, Robert Pidgeon. Though he dropped her, she has never come to terms with this romantic interlude; she harbors Pidgeon in the recesses of her mind in the same way that she has his letters secreted in a secret drawer of her desk. From her viewpoint, Thomas offered a quiet, undemanding, comfortable marriage, largely because of his passionless nature. Her hopes of establishing a

normal role as a mother have long since vanished with her failure to terminate her pregnancies: her disappointment and her consequent adjustment to childlessness contribute to her stiffness toward Portia. She has settled down to find satisfaction in safe male admirers who can entertain and flatter her but who require no physical reward. Three such bachelors are on the scene during the course of the novel: St. Quentin Martin, an urbane novelist; Eddie, a bright young man employed at Thomas's advertising agency; and latterly, Major Brutt, an older gentleman, a friend of Pidgeon, and recently returned to England and out of touch. As with several other characters in the novel, Anna's appearance belies her inner being; for beneath her brittle sophistication lies an insecure woman who has never risked much for fear of being something less than the best. She is a dabbler.

Thomas originally wed Anna because she was pleasant, self-possessed, and seemingly unconcerned with emotion: in short, she was an ideal marital companion for a man who found the opposite sex a source of anxiety and who abhorred thoughts of intimacy. Marriage for both partners, then, came as a source of relief and as an opportunity to live a quiet life. However, following the ceremony, Thomas experienced the unanticipated; he fell passionately in love with Anna; but assuming her allegiance to their tacit agreement of quietude, he suffers his pent-up feelings privately. In Bowen terms, both are failing to exercise their full emotional potential and will not likely do so unless their current roles are altered. Clearly, this function is to be played by Portia.

The story opens upon Anna and St. Quentin strolling in a winter landscape. She tells him she has been reading Portia's diary which she came across accidentally, for Portia's record of her days at 2 Windsor Terrace has quite unsettled Anna. It is, she says, "completely distorted and distorting. As I read I thought either this girl or I are mad." Portia has seemingly missed nothing, though "There's certainly not a thing she does not misconstruct." Standing on a bridge in Regent's Park, "their figures sexless and stiff," Anna and her companion watch swans "in slow indignation" swim down cracks in the frozen surface of the lake." Fittingly, Portia becomes associated with bird imagery; and her initial condition is not unlike that of the swans. Because Portia does not learn of Anna's acquaintance with her diary until Part III of the novel, repercussions do not come until then. Most of Part I is devoted to characterizing life at Windsor Terrace and to explaining Portia's background.

When Portia's father, the senior Thomas Quayne, was fifty-seven, he had "lost his head completely" and had begun an affair with a woman named Irene, twenty-nine. As Anna explains his situation to St. Quentin: "He and [Mrs. Quayne] had married so young—though Thomas, for some reason, was not born for quite a number of years—that he had almost no time to be silly in. Also, I think, she must have hypnotised him into being a good deal steadier than he felt. At the same time she was a woman who thought all men are great boys at heart, and she took every care to keep him one."

Mr. Quayne is another instance of retarded adult innocence and of the need, at whatever the risk, for youthful excess. When Irene becomes pregnant, Mr. Quayne tells his wife; and "Mrs. Quayne [is] quite as splendid as ever. . ." She becomes "all heroic reserve," calms her husband, packs him off to Irene, starts divorce proceedings, and settles down to enjoy her house and garden in contented peace. Like hopeless babies, Mr. Quayne and his bride retire to the south of France and begin a wandering existence in cheap hotels. He suffers because the growing Portia has no proper life; and during a trip to London, he secretly inspects Windsor Terrace and envisions his daughter sharing the normal family life it suggests to him. After he dies, Portia and her mother continue the transient existence; but, when Irene suddenly dies after an operation, Portia becomes her father's legacy to Regent's Park.

An inside view of the Quayne affair is provided by an older servant, Matchett, who had worked for Thomas's mother before coming to Anna along with her mother-in-law's good furniture when she had died. Matchett, stolid and humorless, but Portia's only source of affection, makes a distinction between the right action and the good one. In her view, Mrs. Thomas Quayne "meant to do right." She explains to Portia, "Sacrificers . . . are not the ones to pity. The ones to pity are those that they sacrifice." She has been a great admirer of Portia's father who, in her estimation, was unlike his wife in being honest and natural. She views Mrs. Quayne as a role player who was prepared to maintain her concept of herself at whatever cost to anyone else. In the light of Matchett's views, we see that Thomas and Anna are also doing the "right" rather than the good thing by Portia.

This background detail helps to account for Anna's report that she and Portia "are on such curious terms—when I ever do take a line, she never knows what it is." Quite evidently, feelings must

> **" Mr. Quayne is another instance of retarded adult innocence and of the need, at whatever the risk, for youthful excess."**

come to replace manners. That Portia, however, has two left feet because of her inexperience is humorously brought out in scenes at her private school for girls where she is decidedly unsuccessful in coping with the established decorum: "she had not learnt that one must learn. . ." Small wonder she feels all of London threatening her:

> She had watched life, since she came to London, with a sort of despair—motivated and busy always, always progressing: even people pausing on bridges seemed to pause with a purpose; no bird seemed to pursue a quite aimless flight. The spring of the works seemed unfounded only by her. . . . She could not believe there was not a plan of the whole set-up in every head but her own . . . nothing was not weighed down by significance. In her home life (her new home life) with its puzzles, she saw dissimulation always on guard; she asked herself humbly for what reason people said what they did not mean, and did not say what they meant. She felt most certain to find the clue when she felt the frenzy behind the clever remark.

Having a modest relationship with Anna and Thomas, and a closer but milder one with Matchett, Portia grabs rather eagerly at the interest shown in her by the irresponsible Eddie. From the viewpoint of the contemporary British novel, Eddie is an interesting creation because he so evidently anticipates Kingsley Amis's Lucky Jim; for, like him, Eddie comes from a modest background and is seeking to locate himself in the Establishment, in which he does not believe. A very conscious role player, Eddie prefigures Lucky Jim in his habits of face making and mimicry.

The relationship between Portia and Eddie is undemandingly comfortable from his viewpoint. He takes joy in her childlike innocence, and he feels she is the one person with whom he need not assume an interminable pose. Eddie, as it develops, misjudges in assuming that Portia will place no demands upon him. Really a very self-centered being, he is concerned with his welfare and per-

What Do I Read Next?

- *Coming Home* (1995), by Rosamunde Pilcher, tells the story of fourteen-year-old Judith Dunbar, who stays in England at Saint Ursula's boarding school when her mother and younger sister leave to join her father in Singapore. She and a friend grow up under the looming threat of World War II, which will eventually change their lives and the lives of those they love most.

- Muriel Spark's novel *The Girls of Slender Means* (1963), tells the World War II story of a boarding house founded for "the Pecuniary Convenience and Social Protection of Ladies of Slender Means below the Age of Thirty Years." The boarding house's residents go to their jobs, dream of marriage, gossip, and maintain a facade that life and the world are still normal despite the war.

- Radclyffe Hall's novel *The Well of Loneliness* (1928) tells the story of Stephen Mary Gordon. Given a male name by her father, who had des- perately wanted a son, young Stephen learns to hunt and shoot and ride horses. She develops an intimate but disastrous relationship with another woman that challenges an English society that values and reinforces conformity and accept- ability. Overwhelmed by grief and loneliness, she seeks escape in her work as a writer and as a World War I ambulance driver.

- *The Last September* (1929), by Elizabeth Bowen, set in 1920, is the story of Lois Farquar, who lives with her uncle and aunt, members of the Anglo-Irish aristocracy in County Cork, in a "big house" modeled on Bowen's own family estate in Ireland. The demise of British rule in Ireland is just around the corner, and the family attempts to deal with the end of an era.

- Elizabeth Bowen's *Bowen's Court* (1942) is a nonfiction history of the ancestral house where she spent her summers as a child, and which she inherited after her father died.

---

sonal freedom; but his surface superciliousness re- ally cloaks despair. An "experienced innocent," Eddie bears a resemblance to Emmeline of *To the North* in his unwillingness to adjust to the none- denic facts of life, or at least in his unwillingness to adjust without exacting his own price from the world. He seeks to punish and to travesty love be- cause it cannot be what he longs for it to be; he sees only himself as reality since he is the only person he is prepared to trust. Portia, from his viewpoint, is really a new lease on the impossible life; with her, he seeks to sustain the innocence of adolescent love, the state which holds out to him the possibility of beautiful fulfillment so long as it is never tested. Portia, of course, has no such in- sight as his; but she discovers soon enough Ed- die's unwillingness to allow their affair to progress, and she is left pondering his distress over her unwillingness to sustain their status quo and her desire to grow up.

Part II, "The Flesh," shifts to a contrasting set- ting, one which offers Portia an alternate kind of life with its own range of new characters and ex- periences. Anna, feeling the need of a vacation, whisks Thomas to Capri; Portia is sent to the sea- side at Seale to live with Anna's one-time gov- erness, the widowed Mrs. Heccomb and her two working step-children, Dickie and Daphne. Home is called Wakiki (which is intended to give this se- quence overtones of undemanding, irresponsible Pacific Island life), and the household is the an- tithesis of the highly mannered Windsor Terrace. Wakiki is sustained by blasting radios and by con- versation conducted by shouting above them; all is "pushing and frank," though neurotically proper. Portia discovers "the upright rudeness of the prim- itive state—than which nothing is more rigid." Life at Windsor Terrace is "edited," but that at Wakiki is the reverse. The contrast recalls that between the stately home in *The Last September* and the huts of the army families.

More at home at Wakiki but still reticent, Portia falls in with the crowd presided over by Daphne and Dickie. Portia soon becomes anxious to invite Eddie for a weekend; and Mrs. Heccomb, assured that Eddie is well known to Anna, assumes his visit will be quite proper. Portia awaits his coming anxiously, for she has decided on the reality of Seale and wishes him to confirm it for her. Eddie has hardly arrived, however, before he declares it "unreal"; for in his self-conscious state he is well aware Wakiki is the unexamined life. The only member of the Seale crown who is at all introspective is barely tolerated—is considered ineffectual and labeled "a cissie."

Unknowingly betrayed in London by Anna, Portia is to know betrayal in Seale through Eddie. Sitting between Portia and Daphne at a Saturday night movie, Eddie ends up, as Portia discovers, holding Daphne's hand. Since Eddie has been introduced into the crowd as Portia's friend, she finds this experience painful. When she is alone with Eddie the next day, she challenges his conduct. The episode, he explains, is innocent enough in his view and was intended to lead to nothing further; but this view is not easily conveyed to Portia. In fairness to Eddie, it must be said that he has warned Portia not to get serious with him and to make demands: "Never *be* potty about me: I can't do anything for you." Furthermore, Eddie anticipates what St. Quentin later elaborates for Portia when he says, "Don't you know how dreadful the things you say are?"

In her diary Portia views Seale to London's disadvantage: "In London I do not know what anybody is doing, there are no things I can watch people do. Though things have hurt me since I was left behind here, I would rather stay with the things here than go back to where I do not know what will happen." Even Portia feels the great temptation of comfort, of seeking out an effortless stasis. However, she must return to London to be greeted by Matchett, who observes, "I can't see that this change has done you harm. Nor the shake-up either; you were getting too quiet."

When Thomas and Anna return, it is evident they have not changed. Having been greeted warmly by Portia in the front hall, Anna cannot wait to go up to her bath; and Thomas, claiming a headache, quickly vanishes into his study. Later, Thomas observes to Anna, "Portia gave us a welcome"; and she replies, "It was we who were not adequate." But Anna remains prepared with her justifications: "let's face it—whoever is adequate? We all create situations each other can't live up to, then

break our hearts at them because they don't." This statement proves a telling one in the light of ensuing action. Though aware of their inadequacy in dealing with Portia, the Quaynes seem prepared to let matters drift. In the Bowen world, they are riding for an upset.

Critics generally agree that the "devil" of the final section is St. Quentin since he imparts to Portia the "forbidden" knowledge that Anna has been reading her diary. However, the devil may more properly be viewed as a situation rather than a person; for a comment Major Brutt makes to Anna provides the clue: "that's the devil, you know, about not having a fixed address." This statement assesses the root of the trouble, for what Portia ultimately feels is a lack of any sense of permanency. Her efforts at the close are directed toward finding a sanctuary; and, in a rather roundabout manner, she probably succeeds.

After learning from St. Quentin of Anna's having read the diary, Portia telephones Eddie to tell him, and he in turn calls Anna; and, though his position with both Thomas and Anna is insecure, he conveys his displeasure. When five days later, Portia arrives home to find Anna and Eddie tête-à-tête over tea, she is convinced they have been talking and laughing together about her. Two days later, when Portia walks out on Windsor Terrace, the time lapse, observes the narrator, is "long enough for the sense of two allied betrayals to push up a full growth, like a double tree. . ." Portia leaves her home after having arranged to meet Eddie; and, unbeknownst to him, she is intent on living with him. After Eddie has been more or less forced into taking her to his apartment and after he has reiterated his earlier claim that she does not know the ropes and has "a completely lunatic set of values" and that he simply cannot risk harboring her, she departs prepared to play her final card. She goes to Major Brutt, tells him she has "nowhere to be," and informs the poor dazed man that she wishes to marry him. She rather cruelly seeks to enlist him as an ally by telling him that Anna also laughs at him. When he insists that he must call Windsor Terrace, Portia tells him that Thomas and Anna will not know what to do; and she instructs him to say that her return will depend on their doing "the right thing."

Meanwhile, Portia's absence has been noted by the Quaynes and St. Quentin, their dinner guest. The air is already tense, and Anna and Thomas have already begun unburdening themselves to each other when the Major's call comes. Thomas now learns about the diary, and the scene which this disclosure threatens is just barely avoided as they turn their attention to the question of "the right thing." They quickly enough reject any thoughts of having Portia come across town alone in a taxi or of her being escorted home by Major Brutt. The importance of the issue they do not doubt; Anna points out: "It's not simply a question of getting her home this evening; it's a question of all three going on living here. . . yes, this is a situation. She's created it."

When St. Quentin initiates an important train of thought by suggesting that Anna and Thomas "are both unnaturally conscious of [Portia]. . .", Anna seeks to put herself in Portia's place and to express what her feelings must be: "Frantic, frantic desire to be handled with feeling, and, at the same time, to be let alone. Wish to be asked how I felt, great wish to be taken for granted—." The right act, really the good act, the natural thing, they decide is "something quite obvious. Something with no fuss." When Portia is normally brought home, Matchett brings her; so they dispatch Matchett and also decide against calling Major Brutt. Thomas says, "This is a *coup* or nothing."

Miss Bowen implies in her closing passage that life at Windsor Terrace will be better, but she once more avoids suggesting any miraculous change. Anna has already shown a humanitarian side, one that Portia is unaware of, in her efforts to find employment for Major Brutt, whose worth she recognizes. And she has also and most importantly come to terms with her harbored past feelings for Pidgeon. She admits to herself, as she never previously has, and tells Major Brutt as much, that Pidgeon did not really care for her, that their affair came to nothing because neither trusted the other. And she and Thomas have talked, as Thomas earlier complained they never did. Having "saved" Portia by pulling her back from a speeding car on one of their recent strolls in the park, he now appears committed to saving her in another sense. Emphasized at the very close, and clearly intended to contrast with the frigid landscape of the opening, is a description of the spring evening with its "intimation of summer coming. . ." And the piano music issuing from an open window as the curtain falls hints at the new harmony seemingly to be realized at Windsor Terrace.

Source: Allan E. Austin, "The Disruptive Children," in *Elizabeth Bowen,* Twayne Publishers, Inc., 1971, pp. 47–66.

Sources

Dunleavy, Janet E., "Elizabeth Bowen," in *Dictionary of Literary Biography,* Vol. 15: *British Novelists, 1930–1959, Part 1: A-L,* Gale Research, 1983, pp. 33–46.

Henn, Martha, "Bowen, Elizabeth Dorothea Cole," in *Feminist Writers,* edited by Pamela Kester-Shelton, St. James Press, 1996, pp. 57–60.

Kenney, Edwin J., Jr., in *Elizabeth Bowen,* Bucknell University Press, 1975, p. 18.

Kilfeather, Siobhán, "Elizabeth Bowen," in *British Writers,* Charles Scribner's Sons, 1992, pp. 77–96.

O'Faolain, Sean, "Elizabeth Bowen; or, Romance Does Not Pay," in *The Vanishing Hero: Studies in Novelists of the Twenties,* Eyre and Spottiswoode, 1956, pp. 167–90.

Parrish, Paul A., "The Loss of Eden: Four Novels of Elizabeth Bowen," in *Critique: Studies in Modern Fiction,* Vol. XV, No. 1, 1973, pp. 86–100.

Rubens, Robert, "Elizabeth Bowen: A Woman of Wisdom," in *Contemporary Review,* Vol. 268, No. 1565, June 1996, pp. 304–07.

Tillinghast, Richard, "Elizabeth Bowen: The House, the Hotel & the Child," in *New Criterion,* Vol. 13, No. 4, December 1994, pp. 24–33.

Further Reading

Bloom, Harold, ed., *Elizabeth Bowen,* Chelsea House Publishers, 1992.
    This is a collection of critical essays on the writings of Elizabeth Bowen, edited by the esteemed critic and academician Harold Bloom.

Bowen, Elizabeth, Graham Greene, and V. S. Pritchett, *Why Do I Write?: An Exchange of Views between Elizabeth Bowen, Graham Greene, and V. S. Pritchett,* M. S. G. Haskell House, 1975.
    This volume includes letters between these three literary giants on the subject of how writers live and what they think about as they go about their work.

Halperin, John, *Eminent Georgians: The Lives of King George V, Elizabeth Bowen, St. John Philby, and Nancy Astor,* St. Martin's Press, Inc., 1998.
    John Halperin traces the impact these leading figures had in England between the two great wars, and examines the world of intrigue below the glittering surface of British society in the 1920s and 1930s.

Walshe, Eibhear, ed., *Elizabeth Bowen Remembered: The Farahy Addresses,* Four Courts Press, 1998.
    Drawn from the annual lectures at the church in Farahy, in North Cork, where Bowen is buried, these essays provide insight into the life, fiction, and beliefs of the Anglo-Irish writer Elizabeth Bowen.

The Kitchen God's Wife

Amy Tan
1991

Amy Tan wrote *The Kitchen God's Wife* about her mother, Daisy. Most of Winnie's story in the novel is drawn from Daisy's life, including the difficult life and marriage she left behind in pre-communist China. The presentation of Winnie's story, as she tells her story to Pearl, is reminiscent of the oral tradition. Tan, like Pearl, had never given much thought to her mother's life in China, and she was amazed at what she learned.

When Tan started on her second novel, she wanted to avoid rehashing material and ideas from her successful first novel, *The Joy Luck Club*. She sequestered herself with soothing music and incense, realizing that solitude was her surest path to the next novel. Although she tried numerous times to write about something different, the story in *The Kitchen God's Wife* cried out to be told, and Tan realized that the pursuit of diversity was not a good reason to write about one topic over another. Her mother's eagerness to have her story fictionalized was also a major influence.

And so, *The Kitchen God's Wife* shares certain themes with *The Joy Luck Club*. Both *The Joy Luck Club* and *The Kitchen God's Wife* portray strained relationships between immigrant mothers and their American daughters. The theme of alienation also appears in both works. Despite its similarities to the first novel, the second novel won applause from Tan's readers and critics. Her novels contain a multitude of stories that converge into a cohesive work, and Tan is admired for her ability to move from the past to the present in her storytelling.

Amy Tan

Author Biography

Amy Tan was born in 1952 to first-generation Chinese-American parents. At her birth, Tan was given the Chinese name An-Mai, meaning "Blessing of America." Her father, John, was an electrical engineer and a volunteer Baptist minister who came to America in 1947. Her mother, Daisy, was a medical technician who had fled China in 1949 to escape an unhappy arranged marriage, leaving three daughters behind. In 1967, Tan's older brother, Peter, died of brain cancer, and, within a year, her father died of the same illness. After consulting a Chinese fortune teller, Daisy left the "evil" house and took her surviving children, Amy and John, to Europe.

The Tans settled in Switzerland, where Amy completed high school. It was an unhappy time for her; she felt like an outsider and was still grieving and angry over the losses in her family. Because being upright had not saved her brother and father, Tan decided to be rebellious and wild. Her friends were drug dealers, and she almost eloped to Australia with a mental patient who claimed to be a German army deserter.

When the Tans moved to Oregon, Daisy chose a college for her daughter and planned her pre-med curriculum. She was deeply disappointed when her daughter changed her major to English. In 1970, Tan moved to California to be closer to her boyfriend, Lou DiMattei. She transferred to San Jose State University and graduated in 1973. The next year, she and DiMattei married, and she received her Master's degree in English and linguistics.

As a freelance technical writer, Tan was highly successful, but she routinely worked ninety-hour weeks. Seeking to cure her compulsive working, she took up jazz piano and joined a writers' group. She took a trip to China with her mother in 1987 to connect with her Chinese heritage, an element that was lacking in her childhood. She soon realized that her best writing came from her Chinese-American perspective. Her short stories were published, and a planned collection of short fiction soon became the enormously popular *The Joy Luck Club,* published in 1989. The novel stayed on the *New York Times* bestseller list for nine months and received the 1989 Bay Area Book Reviewers Award for Best Fiction and the American Library Association's Best Book for Young Adult Readers Award. The novel was also a finalist for the National Book Award and the National Book Critics Circle Award.

When *The Kitchen God's Wife* was published in 1991, critics and readers praised the novel as being at least as good as the first one. Her first two novels established Tan as a serious writer whose unique perspective and storytelling ability captivate readers and impress critics. Although both novels center on mother-daughter relationships and intergenerational conflicts, Tan is resistant to being dubbed an expert on family relationships. Further, she does not want to be categorized as an ethnic writer because she seeks to portray universal themes and wants critics to evaluate her work on its merits, rather than as sub-genre writing.

Plot Summary

Chapters One–Two

The first two chapters of *The Kitchen God's Wife* are narrated by Pearl Brandt, the daughter of Winnie Louie, a Chinese woman who immigrated to the United States in adulthood. Winnie has convinced Pearl to attend an engagement banquet for her cousin in San Francisco. Reluctantly, Pearl agrees and then stays in the city an extra day to attend the funeral of Auntie Du.

During the engagement banquet, Winnie's close friend Helen tells Pearl she (Helen) has a brain tumor and will be forced to reveal Pearl's secret (that she has multiple sclerosis) to her mother unless she tells her herself. She hints that her mother also has secrets she may share with her daughter.

The relationship between Winnie and Pearl is strained because the Americanized daughter and her immigrant mother have little in common. The one thing they both understand is their grief, years previously, over the loss of Pearl's father, Jimmy, who was Winnie's great love. At the funeral for Auntie Du, Pearl has a breakthrough in which she finally cries for Jimmy. In her will, Auntie Du leaves Pearl her altar to the Kitchen God, a minor deity who, as a mortal, was an abusive husband to his virtuous wife. As a deity, he reports to the Jade Emperor about who has been good and who has been bad.

Chapters Three–Ten

Helen has told Winnie, too, of her illness and of the need to bring secrets into the open, so Winnie asks her daughter to sit with her in the kitchen while she tells all of her secrets. Chapters three through twenty-four are told from Winnie's point of view.

Winnie begins her story by describing her mother, the vain second wife of her wealthy father. When Winnie is six, her mother takes her on a fun-filled trip into the city, where they share wonderful experiences and see exciting things. The next day, Winnie's mother mysteriously disappears, and Winnie is sent to live with an uncle and his family so as not to remind her father of his missing wife. Winnie is unhappy in the new family because they are not as wealthy and treat her like a guest instead of like a family member. She makes friends with her cousin Peanut, a girl about the same age as Winnie. The two grow into adolescence together, carrying on like sisters.

During a New Year's festival, Winnie and Peanut go in search of trinkets and fortunes when they meet a charming young man named Wen Fu. He flirts with Peanut and later courts her. Winnie is suspicious of Wen Fu but says nothing. When Wen Fu finds out that Winnie's family is much wealthier than Peanut's, he proposes to Winnie. Despite Peanut's initial resentment, Winnie accepts and seeks her father's approval for the match. He agrees and explains to his daughter that when she is a wife, she will have to be obedient. He then sends one of his wives into town with Winnie to buy things for her dowry. It is a spectacular spending spree, and Winnie cannot believe the expense being put into her dowry. She later learns that the other daughters were given dowries ten times the size of hers and that her father knew that Wen Fu was from a questionable family.

Soon after the marriage, Wen Fu signs up with the military, as China recruits men to defend their country against the invading Japanese. The newlyweds move to Hangchow where Wen Fu trains as a member of the American Volunteer Group led by American pilot Claire Chennault. Winnie eventually discovers that her husband was only accepted because he used his deceased brother's name and credentials and that he is a coward who retreats when his fleet engages in air battle. Because of his social standing, however, no one challenges him. Wen Fu becomes abusive toward his new wife, often humiliating her sexually. Still, she tries to be a good wife, and her developing friendship with Helen, the wife of another pilot (Long Jiaguo), becomes her only supportive relationship.

Chapters Eleven–Nineteen

The pilots begin to fly in battle, and their numbers begin to dwindle. Finally, Wen Fu, Winnie, Helen, and Jiaguo flee to distant parts of the country with the air force group. Along the way, they learn of the terrible defeats China is suffering, and they feel fortunate to be alive. Traveling in her last months of pregnancy, Winnie anticipates the birth of her first child and is heartbroken when the baby girl is stillborn. Meanwhile, Wen Fu has become even crueler, especially after he suffers an injury in an auto accident that is his fault. At a military party, Winnie meets a Chinese-American man named Jimmy Louie, and she is immediately drawn to him. They dance and then go their separate ways.

Winnie gives birth to a second daughter, who becomes very ill months later. She goes to get the doctor, who is playing mah jongg with Wen Fu. Wen Fu refuses to let the doctor tend to his daughter, and she dies. When Winnie becomes pregnant again, she has a boy, and she vows that he will never be like his father. She ends several subsequent pregnancies by abortion because she cannot bear the idea of carrying another of Wen Fu's children. Her attempts to secure a divorce from him only anger him, causing him, more than once, to tear up the papers and rape her.

Chapters Twenty–Twenty-Six

After the war, Winnie and Wen Fu part ways with Helen and Jiaguo. Winnie looks forward to getting back to her family and telling her father how terribly Wen Fu has treated her. When they arrive, however, Winnie's father is a frail man who, having suffered a stroke, is unable to speak. Wen Fu's family moves in and begins selling off the old man's precious belongings, as he sits powerless to stop them. Unable to stand her life any longer, Winnie seeks out Peanut, who has escaped her own unhappy marriage. On her way to see Peanut, Winnie runs into Jimmy, and they sit and talk. Winnie sends her son to live with Helen and Jiaguo until she can get away from Wen Fu, but the child dies during a plague while he is away.

When Winnie's escape plans fall through, Jimmy suggests that she come and live with him. She does, but when word reaches Wen Fu, Jimmy is sent out of the country. He promises to come back for Winnie in two years. For her part in the incident, Winnie is arrested for deserting her husband and causing her son's death, and she is given the choice between prison and returning to Wen Fu. She chooses prison but is released early thanks to Helen and Auntie Du. She immediately contacts Jimmy, and he asks her to come to America and be his wife. She makes plans to flee the country, including tricking Wen Fu and his new wife into signing divorce papers. Wen Fu finds her, tears up the papers, rapes her, and steals her tickets. Helen arrives and helps Winnie overpower him. They throw his pants out the window and retrieve the tickets. Winnie arrives safely in America just before the communists take over and no one is allowed to leave China. A little less than nine months later, Pearl is born, meaning that her father is probably Wen Fu, not Jimmy.

In response to this dramatic story, Pearl tells her mother about her disease. Winnie promises to help Pearl fight the disease and wonders if it is somehow Wen Fu's fault. Later, Helen reveals that she does not really have a brain tumor. She made up the story so that Winnie and Pearl would tell each other their secrets. Winnie buys a new deity for the Kitchen God's altar, only this one is a woman. She names her Sorrowfree and prays to her for her daughter's health.

Characters

Cleo Brandt

Cleo is Pearl and Phil's three-year-old daughter. She calls her Chinese grandma "Ha-bu."

Pearl Brandt

Pearl is Winnie's forty-year-old daughter. She lives fifty miles away from Winnie with her husband, Phil, and their two daughters. She does not feel the same impulse to be with her family for gatherings as her mother does, but she feels a sense of duty to be present.

Pearl works as a linguist and speech therapist for mentally challenged children. She has been diagnosed with multiple sclerosis but has not told her mother. She has, however, told Helen, who claims to be dying and thus insists that Pearl tell her secret to her mother.

Although Pearl has always believed that Jimmy was her father, she learns from her mother's story that her father is probably Wen Fu.

Phil Brandt

Phil is Pearl's husband. Phil is a forty-three-year-old Caucasian man who has difficulty understanding the Chinese customs and expectations of his mother-in-law. Still, he has come to have affection for the quirky woman, even though she often exasperates him. He is a pathologist and feels powerless to do anything to help his wife with her multiple sclerosis.

Tessa Brandt

Tessa is Pearl and Phil's eight-year-old daughter. Pearl was diagnosed with multiple sclerosis a year after Tessa's birth. She, too, calls her Chinese grandma "Ha-bu."

Mary Kwong Cheu

Hulan and Henry's daughter, Mary is responsible for introducing Pearl and Phil. Although she thinks of herself as one of Pearl's best friends, Pearl now only tolerates her. They have known each other for a very long time, and Mary's husband went to medical school with Phil. For this reason, Mary and her husband know about Pearl's illness.

Auntie Du Ching

Hulan's aunt, Auntie Du, is outspoken but very gentle. In a bold act, she saves her money and escapes the Japanese in order to meet up with Hulan in Kunming. It is she who arranges for Winnie's release from prison, although she allows Hulan's new husband to believe he managed it. When Auntie Du comes to America, Winnie takes care of her until her death. When she dies, she leaves Pearl her Kitchen God altar.

Danru

Danru is Winnie's third child and only son. His name means "nonchalance." Winnie swears that she will not allow him to become like his father. As Winnie plans her escape, she sends Danru to stay with Helen so that Wen Fu cannot get to him. While away, the child dies in an epidemic.

Wen Fu

Wen Fu is Winnie's abusive and domineering first husband. While planning to marry Peanut, he discovers that Winnie's family is wealthier and turns his attention to her. As a husband, he is verbally and physically abusive and enjoys frightening and humiliating Winnie. He is a coward, a womanizer, and a schemer.

When the war effort is underway, Wen Fu enlists in the air force and joins the group led by American pilot Claire Chennault. Winnie later discovers that Wen Fu was only accepted because he used his deceased brother's name and credentials. He becomes extremely violent after an auto accident claims one of his eyes, and each time Winnie tries to get a divorce he flies into a rage. Only when Winnie hears the news that he is dead does she feel completely free.

Gan

One of the pilots in Wen Fu's squadron, Gan is kind to Winnie and compliments her often. He is a gentleman who gives Winnie her first experience of feeling valued by a man.

Jiang Huazheng

Known affectionately as "Peanut," Jiang is Winnie's cousin and becomes a sister figure as the girls grow into adolescence. She thinks of herself as worldly and rebellious, wearing makeup and kissing Wen Fu when he visits her. Hoping for a wealthy husband who lives far away, she pays a fortune-teller to drive away any local suitors. Ironically, her marriage turns out so badly that she joins the communists, runs away from her husband, and later provides a place for other runaway wives to stay.

Long Jiaguo

Long Jiaguo is Hulan's first husband. He is a pilot in the same group as Wen Fu, although Long Jiaguo is Wen Fu's superior. He is even-tempered, reasonable, and dominated by his wife.

Henry Kwong

Henry is Hulan's second husband.

Media Adaptations

- Audio adaptations have been made by Dove Entertainment (abridged and unabridged), in 1991 and (with *The Joy Luck Club*) 1998.

Hulan Kwong

Hulan (who is called Helen in America) is Winnie's oldest and dearest friend. In fact, they call each other sisters. Until Pearl hears Winnie's story, she believes that Hulan is her aunt.

Hulan co-owns the flower shop in Chinatown with Winnie. She is brash and uneducated, and her first marriage is unconventional in that she is usually the one in control. Her friendship with Winnie is unbreakable, although they often argue.

Roger Kwong

Roger is Hulan and Henry's son. He is called "Bao-bao." Already divorced twice and having recently broken an engagement, he is newly engaged at the beginning of the novel. It is his engagement banquet that brings Pearl to San Francisco.

Jimmy Louie

Winnie's great love, Jimmy is a Chinese-American man who acts as a translator for the military. He and Winnie meet at a military dance, and when they meet again by chance, they begin to make plans together. He is a kind man who becomes a Baptist minister in the United States. When Winnie is released from prison, he asks her to join him in America and be his wife.

Jimmy dies of stomach cancer when Pearl is fourteen years old. His death leaves an emotional scar on both Winnie and Pearl. Winnie theorizes that his death was the result of being a minister and swallowing everyone else's problems for so many years. It is not until Auntie Du's funeral that Pearl is able to tap her unexpressed grief and finally cry for the loss of the wonderful man she knew as her father.

Samuel Louie

Winnie's son is a few years younger than Pearl. He lives in New Jersey.

Winnie Louie

Winnie, known as Jiang Weili in China, is Pearl's mother. The majority of the novel comprises the incredible story of her arduous childhood and young womanhood in China, before she escaped her abusive husband and came to America. She was born into a wealthy family to her father's second wife, who doted on Winnie until her mysterious disappearance when Winnie was only six. Winnie marries a man she hardly knows and endures many trials and much suffering, including the loss of three children.

When Winnie flees to the United States, she marries Jimmy Louie, a kind Chinese-American man she met in China. She is a superstitious woman who adheres to many of the traditional Chinese beliefs. As a parent, she is demanding, warning her daughter of the dangers of blue eye shadow and certain boys. Her experiences in China have taken her from naivete and dependence to wisdom and self-confidence. When she finally shares her story with her daughter, they are able to relate to each other in a meaningful way. Her character represents the triumph of the human spirit, the commitment to survival, and the ability to endure tremendous hardship and create a new life for oneself. Having always identified with the Kitchen God's wife, Winnie "corrects" the myth at the end of the novel by replacing the Kitchen God (who had been an abusive and cruel mortal) with a female deity, whom she names "Sorrowfree."

San Ma

San Ma is Winnie's father's third wife. She takes Winnie shopping for her dowry and takes care of her husband when his health fails.

Min

Min is a concubine whom Wen Fu brings home for his pleasure while Winnie gives birth to Danru. She is illiterate and a performer. Winnie befriends her.

Mochou

Mochou is Winnie's first child, a stillborn girl. Her name means "Sorrowfree," the name Winnie later gives her new deity.

Peanut

See Jiang Huazheng

Jiang Sao-yen

Jiang Sao-yen is Winnie's father, a successful businessman who made his fortune in textiles. He has several wives and many children. He approves Winnie's marriage to Wen Fu, even though he apparently knows the family is not honorable. Late in life, he suffers a stroke and is unable to speak. His weakened health is the only thing that saves him from being executed by the Communists. When his daughter returns with Wen Fu, he understands that she is trying to escape and nods to show her where he has gold hidden. Winnie learns that he has died while she is in prison.

Uncle

This is Winnie's uncle, the younger brother of Jiang Sao-yen. Because of his lack of success, his older brother gives him a textile factory to manage. When Winnie's mother disappears, Winnie is sent to live with Uncle and his family.

Winnie's Mother

Her name is never given in the novel, but she is the second wife of Jiang Sao-yen. When she marries him, she occupies the second-wife position to replace the previous second wife, who committed suicide. She is a vain woman who takes her little daughter on a fun-filled day in town the day before she mysteriously disappears.

Yiku

Winnie's second daughter, Yiku's name means "sorrow over bitterness," and she dies in infancy when Wen Fu refuses to release the doctor from a game of mah jong to check on her.

Themes

Duty

A central element in Eastern culture is duty, and Winnie exhibits this sense of responsibility throughout her life. When Wen Fu proposes marriage, she is both eager to leave her uncle's house and aware of her duty to marry. Her father talks to her after he has approved the union and reminds her that, as a wife, her duty will be to honor and obey her husband. She soon realizes that Wen Fu is an evil and sadistic man, but her duty (and lack of power to leave) forces her to stay with him. As an adult in America, Winnie dutifully takes care of Auntie Du in her old age.

Topics For Further Study

- Winnie Louie's life in China was difficult and tumultuous. Research China in the 1940s with special attention to political events. Pretend you are a simple villager and write a two-week diary in which you make the decision either to stay in China or to leave before the Communists claim power.

- Study Chinese visual arts and prepare an overview of how they did and did not change over the course of the twentieth century. Given the historical context, try to account for the changes as well as the adherence to tradition.

- Review Chinese religious belief systems and consider how they would respond to one of the following modern-day issues: genetic manipulation, space exploration, or racial tensions. Write an essay in which you present three different possible responses to one of these issues, based on what you have learned about Chinese religions.

- The role of women in China has changed since the events of Winnie Louie's life. Hold a debate on the following topic: During the twentieth century, women's roles in the United States changed in much the same manner as women's roles in China changed, and women's rise in status in the two countries is comparable.

- Provide three compelling and well-supported reasons why Japan was determined to claim Chinese land in the 1930s and 1940s. Consider areas such as military strategy, imperialism, resources, and the historical relationship between the two nations.

- *The Kitchen God's Wife* is a novel of conflict—interpersonal conflict, international conflict, and intergenerational conflict. Draw five examples of conflict from the novel and determine what you believe the root cause to be in each case. Can you think of possible ways to resolve any or all of these conflicts, or are they unable to be resolved?

Although she is fully assimilated into Western culture, Pearl also recognizes the importance of duty, although to a lesser degree. She attends family gatherings only out of duty, as is typical for many Americans. Pearl is uncertain why she continues to fulfill family obligations that she has come to resent. She also perceives a sense of duty in her husband as she notices that their arguments become less petty after the birth of their first child. She comments in chapter one that this is "perhaps because Phil developed a sense of duty toward the baby, as well as to me, or at least to my medical condition."

Luck

Winnie makes frequent references to luck. She believes that luck plays a major role in people's lives and that people have the power to improve their luck. By the same token, people can do things—intentionally or unintentionally—to attract bad luck. This is illustrated in the idea of *daomei*, which asserts that negative thoughts can become self-fulfilling prophecies. Winnie imagines her husband dying while engaged in air battle, and he returns wounded, filling her with guilt for having made it happen. The Chinese New Year is considered a time when people can change their luck, so they perform rituals and visit fortune-tellers to discover their lucky days and numbers. Even minor domestic occurrences are regarded as having an effect on luck. One of Uncle's wives reprimands a cook for cutting squid the wrong way because it will not form good-luck balls. Another example is the Kitchen God, whose role as a minor deity is to report to the Jade Emperor all those who have behaved well and who have behaved badly. This determines who receives good luck and who receives bad luck. To gain the Kitchen God's favor and manipulate their chances of being blessed with good luck, people offer him gifts and burn incense in his honor.

Winnie also believes that some people are lucky throughout their lives and that Helen is one of them. She states in chapter three:

> Helen thinks all her decisions are always right, but really, she is only lucky. For over fifty years I have seen this happen, how her foolish thinking turns into good fortune.. . . Even though Helen is not smart, even though she was born poor, even though she has never been pretty, she has always had luck pour onto her plate.

Situations can also be a source of bad luck. When Winnie's mother marries Jiang, she occupies the position as second wife to replace a wife who killed herself. Because of the circumstances, the second wife's place is considered bad luck, and Winnie's mother's mysterious disappearance seems to confirm this. Early in their relationship, Helen tells Winnie that the city of Loyang was once famous for having one hundred thousand statues of Buddha. Now, however, the Buddhas' heads have been cut off, so if the air force sends them there, a place filled with wounded Buddhas, it can only mean tragic luck.

Conflict

Conflict exists at every level in the novel, ranging from mother-daughter conflicts to international warfare. Winnie experiences conflict with her cruel husband. The conflict between Winnie and Helen is so embedded in their relationship, it is not a threat to their longstanding friendship. Pearl is in cultural and generational conflict with her immigrant mother.

The Japanese invasion of China provides a backdrop of terrifying conflict that is present throughout most of Winnie's young womanhood. Winnie, Helen, and the others in their group hear horrific stories of wartime violence and bloodshed. At the same time, China was enduring internal political conflict. Winnie comments in chapter nine:

> That's how everything was in China then. Too busy fighting each other to fight together. And not just the Americans and the Chinese. The old revolutionaries, the new revolutionaries, the Kuomintang [Nationalists] and the Communists, the warlords, the bandits, and the students—gwah! gwah! gwah!—everybody squabbling, like old roosters claiming the same sunrise.

Patriarchal Society

The Kitchen God's Wife illustrates several facets of the humble status of women in Chinese society in the early twentieth century. The arranged marriage demonstrates the woman's lack of control over her own life and her inability to pursue any other course than that which is expected of her. Wen Fu's proposal is approved by Winnie's father after which Winnie must submit to Wen Fu's cruel whims. His family rapidly depletes her dowry, and she is powerless to object. Her story is unusual, however, because she ultimately escapes by fleeing China and going to America. Her discovery of a group of runaway wives suggests hope because she is not alone in her willingness to take risks to live differently.

Women were not considered suitable for a thorough education because as domestic figures they were not expected to voice opinions or engage in intellectual discussions. In chapter five, Winnie recalls that her grandfather did not want to send her mother away to school:

> That was the modern thought—educate sons, educate daughters a little to prove you were not too feudal-thinking. But Gung-gung did not want to send her to France, or England, or America.. . . Why should he educate a daughter only to turn her into a girl he did not like?"

Style

First-Person Narration

The Kitchen God's Wife is an interesting example of a first-person narrative because of its complexity. The story is told from both Pearl's and Winnie's points of view, and Winnie talks about both the past and the present. The structure of the novel, with the mother and daughter as the speakers, suggests indirect communication between the two of them through the reader. Of course, by the end of the novel, this has become direct communication as the two women share the secrets they have hidden from each other.

As Winnie tells her life story to her daughter, she occasionally makes a reference to contemporary life or asks Pearl a question, which reminds the reader that the story is being told by Winnie to her daughter as they sit in Winnie's kitchen. The tone is confessional and reminiscent of the oral tradition as Winnie relates events of the past with the wisdom of the present. Critics commend Tan's ability to create unique voices for Pearl and Winnie. When Winnie speaks, her syntax, word choice, and idioms all support the realism of the speaker. In contrast, when Pearl speaks, the text reads just as if a typical American were speaking.

Roman à Clef

Because Winnie's story is drawn heavily from Tan's mother's life, the inclusion of actual historical events and figures is not surprising. In fact, the historical context is so striking and real, the novel can be considered a roman à clef, which is a novel in which real people and events are presented in a fictional context. Examples of this type of novel include Margaret Mitchell's *Gone with the Wind* and Victor Hugo's *Les Miserables.*

There are many real events and people in the novel. Winnie, of course, is based on Daisy Tan, the author's mother. Wen Fu is based on Daisy's first husband. The social context of the novel, with its patriarchy and arranged marriages, is an accurate depiction of what life was like in China at that time. The details of the war, from the stories of cities bombed by the Japanese to the character of Claire Chennault, are drawn directly from history.

Detailed Descriptions

In *The Kitchen God's Wife,* Tan includes lots of domestic details and descriptions of landscapes to give the reader a strong sense of the characters' lives. This serves two purposes: first, it draws the reader into the story and brings the characters and scenes to life; second, it provides much-needed context for Western readers, to whom the characters and their surroundings are unfamiliar. Domestic details include food preparation, the importance of good sewing needles, and the social separation between men and women in the home. At night, the men play cards and smoke while the women attend to household duties or sit quietly. Each time the pilots and their wives move, Tan presents rich descriptions of the landscapes, including ponds, trees, rolling hills, and the darkness of night.

Tan also includes a great deal of sensory detail. This type of detail helps create vivid atmosphere and appeals to the universal experiences of seeing, hearing, feeling, tasting, and smelling. In chapter one, Pearl visits her mother in her flower shop:

> I open the door and bells jangle. I'm instantly engulfed in the pungent smell of gardenias, a scent I've always associated with funeral parlors. The place is dimly lit, with only one fluorescent tube hanging over the cash register.

In this short excerpt, Tan includes sound, smell, and sight, describing fully the experience of walking into the flower shop. Tan also shows how a sensory experience can have an emotional impact, as when Pearl and her family stay at Winnie's

house before Auntie Du's funeral. Pearl and Winnie have said good night, and Pearl notes, "I hold my breath. There is only silence. And finally, I hear her slippers slowly padding down the hallway, each soft shuffle breaking my heart." Later, Winnie explains that she can no longer stand the taste of eels because of an experience during the war. She and her group had left Nanking, and as they were enjoying the delicacy of white eels, Nanking was ravaged and its people brutalized. Because of her overwhelming guilt, she can never eat eels again. She wonders in chapter thirteen, "Why do some memories live only in your tongue or in your nose? Why do others always stay in your heart?"

Literary Devices

Perhaps Tan's education in English accounts for her use of a wide variety of literary devices. Inventive similes intrigue the reader, as in chapter one, when Pearl thinks, "I've always found [funeral] wreaths hideously sad, like decorative lifesavers thrown out too late." As Winnie tells her story, there are occasional instances of foreshadowing. In chapter eight, she remarks, "Of course, maybe my marriage never really had a chance.. . . But without the worries Peanut put in my head, maybe I would have found a few moments of happiness before all the truth came out." Some of the Chinese words are examples of onomatopoeia, such as the fish called the "wah-wah yu," named for the sound it makes, which resembles a baby crying.

Historical Context

Political Climate

Winnie's story takes place in pre-communist China when China endured internal struggles between the Nationalists and the Communists, in addition to attacks by Japan. Because China had grown wealthy under Nationalist rule, Japan was eager to claim it. While defending their country, members of the Nationalist and Communist parties joined forces. Japan invaded Manchuria in 1931 and attacked the rest of the country in 1937. That year, Chiang Kai-shek, the Nationalist leader, recruited American pilot Claire Chennault out of retirement to train pilots with little military experience. Despite cynicism about the project, Chennault's squadron soon became a respected military force. In *The Kitchen God's Wife,* Winnie meets Chennault in Hangchow, and she comments

Compare & Contrast

- **1930s:** In China, marriage is arranged to provide the husband's family with the most wealthy or powerful relations possible. Often, either the couple has never met or they have known each other for only a short time. The woman has no say and is expected to comply with her father's wishes regarding her groom. Once married, she and her children became subordinates to her husband. Divorce is extremely rare because both parties have to agree to it.

  Today: In America, marriage is entered willingly by both parties. Generally, men and women take time to get to know each other before deciding to get married, and the decision rests solely with the bride and groom. Marriage is often egalitarian, with both people involved equally and both people voicing opinions, ideas, and needs. Divorce is extremely common.

- **1930s:** In China, the bond between a mother and daughter is considered sacred and unbreakable even if the relationship is strained. The clan and family mentality shapes adult relationships.

  Today: In America, the bond between a mother and her adult daughter is sometimes cherished and nurtured and sometimes non-existent. While many mothers and daughters enjoy the changing nature of their relationship and come to enjoy each other's company as adults, the individualism of American culture often leads to distant relationships among family members.

- **1930s:** In China, the political climate is threatening and unstable. Conflicts emerge from within and without. People live in fear and uncertainty.

  Today: In America, the political climate is stable. There are regular elections in which citizens have the opportunity to make choices about their governments, and political parties have a formal process for seeking power. Still, low voter turnout is a consistent source of disappointment to candidates and party leaders.

---

on the Chinese name he has been given, which sounds very much like his American name and means "noisy lightning."

War ravaged China until 1942 when Japanese defeat was imminent. With the external threat diminished, the Communist Party soon reemerged in a struggle for power. This was called the Liberation War, and it lasted from 1946 to 1949, ending with Nationalist leader Chiang Kai-shek's retreat to Taiwan. Fearing Communist rule, many people fled the country just before it officially became the People's Republic of China.

Superstition and Religion

In *The Kitchen God's Wife,* many characters hold syncretic, or combined, beliefs, which represent a blend of Taoism, Buddhism, Confucianism, and popular lore. At the center of syncretism is the individual's impulse to master his or her fate. This is reflected in the belief that one's thoughts and actions, intentional or not, make a difference in what happens. *Daomei,* for example, is the belief that negative thoughts and feelings bring about unlucky events. Winnie imagines her husband dying in battle and is filled with guilt when he returns injured. Even before Pearl hears her mother's story, she knows how important *daomei* is to Winnie. Pearl thinks that if she tells her mother about her multiple sclerosis, Winnie will somehow blame herself for Pearl's illness.

Superstition plays a major role in many of the characters' lives. The altar to the Kitchen God is a way to influence the deity to bring good luck to the family, a practice that goes back as far as the eighth century B.C. People believe that if they behave properly and offer gifts, the Kitchen God will take good reports of them to the Jade Emperor. The Chinese New Year involves various rituals that are intended to bring about good luck in the coming year. People consult fortune-tellers and astrologers regarding what can be expected. If the news is bad, fortune-tellers provide corrective practices or rituals that individuals can perform to change their luck. In the novel, Peanut does not like what the fortune-teller says about her marriage prospects, so she has the fortune-teller change things. Winnie believes that the husband Peanut should have had was Wen Fu, who married her instead.

Marriage and Women

According to Chinese tradition at the time of Winnie's youth, marriages were arranged to make a good match for the families. This meant that little attention was given to whether the pairing was suitable for the bride and groom. Men sought to marry into wealthy or powerful families that could improve their social standing. As for women, their needs and desires were of no consequence. The bigger the dowry a young wife brought to her new family, the better. It was the father's responsibility to approve the match, making sure that his daughter was marrying into a respectable family. In *The Kitchen God's Wife,* Winnie's father approves her marriage to Wen Fu, explaining to her that once she is married, her opinions will be of no value. Instead, she is expected to think only of her husband's wishes. Later, when she realizes that her father knew what kind of people Wen Fu's family were, she understands that by letting her marry Wen Fu, her father was demonstrating that she was of little value.

Once married, a woman was placed at the bottom of the hierarchy of her husband's household. Men had multiple wives, and the older wives were more powerful than the newer wives. At the top of the hierarchy was the man, who was granted complete control over his wives and children. In abusive situations, there was nothing women or children could do. Although *The Kitchen God's Wife* is based on Tan's mother's story, there is one important episode that was completely changed. In reality, Daisy's mother did not simply disappear one day but was widowed at a young age before her husband had been able to take a good-paying job. She was raped and then taken as a concubine into the dead man's family where she endured humiliation and shame. To preserve her son's honor, she abandoned him so that he would not be associated with her. She then took her daughter and fled to Shanghai. On New Year's Eve, she committed suicide by hiding a lethal dose of opium in her rice cake. Daisy told Tan this story to show how vul-

nerable and powerless women were in early twentieth-century China.

Critical Overview

After the success Tan enjoyed from her first novel, the challenge of releasing a second novel was daunting. The much-anticipated publication of *The Kitchen God's Wife,* captured the attention of readers and critics alike. Response was overwhelmingly positive as readers found themselves swept up in the drama and detailed storytelling that had made *The Joy Luck Club* so impressive.

While critics can be harsh on authors whose second books are noticeably weaker than their first, reviewers declared *The Kitchen God's Wife* at least as good as *The Joy Luck Club.* In fact, Wendy Law-Yone of *Washington Post Book World* declared *The Kitchen God's Wife* "bigger, bolder, and, I have to say, better" than Tan's first novel. Similarly, Pico Iyer of *Time* commented that "Tan has transcended herself again." In *Women's Review of Books,* critic Helen Yglesias expressed her certainty that "readers who loved the first [book] will surely love the second, since both tell the same story—and this time around Tan has executed the work better in conception, in design, in detail and in sheer pleasure for the reader." Reviewers found that by focusing on one woman's story (rather than a group of four, as in *The Joy Luck Club*), the novel exhibits more unity and compels the reader to feel more compassion.

Critics were generally impressed with Tan's techniques in *The Kitchen God's Wife.* Yglesias noted, "Amy Tan commands an intriguing style, which, along with her highly specialized subject matter, makes for a unique contribution to contemporary writing.. . . Tan is gifted with a quirky style, a broad historical sense, and great energy as a storyteller." Many reviewers were especially taken with Tan's inclusion of details in creating the novel's settings and the characters' daily lives. "It is in its details that *The Kitchen God's Wife* excels," wrote Yglesias, adding, "Tan weaves trivia into rich and illuminating character portrayal, treasures that literally appear on every page." In *Belles Lettres,* Scarlet Cheng wrote, "Tan captures beautifully this helter-skelter period in China."

Criticism is divided on the subjects of characterization and plot structure. Elgy Gillespie of *San Francisco Review of Books* found that although the

Amy Tan and her mother, Tu Ching "Daisy" Tan, on whose experiences the novel is based

characters are sometimes exaggerated, the dialogue brings each one to life. Christopher Lehmann-Haupt of *New York Times Book Review,* however, concluded that the portrayal of Wen Fu, Winnie's first husband, undermines the novel. He declared that

> the novel's fairy tale quality also works against it, particularly in the character of Winnie's evil husband, Wen Fu, a man of such one-dimensional malevolence that one can only regard him as a caricature. . . . There is no accounting for Wen Fu, and this inexplicability shrinks Ms. Tan's story to the moral dimension of pop fiction.

Lehmann-Haupt concluded, "Where Ms. Tan writes about contemporary Chinese Americans, her portraits are often witty and complex. . . . But the plight of a maiden victimized by an arranged marriage seems very old stuff. Amy Tan can probably do better. One hopes that she soon will." A few critics found the novel's structure arduous, as the narrative switches back and forth from past to present. Robb Forman Dew of *New York Times Book Review* wrote:

> It is irritating each time she insists on bringing us back from Winnie's mesmerizing tale. Whenever Winnie halts her narrative to ask her daughter some question whose answer we only infer—Pearl does not speak—Ms. Tan challenges our suspension of disbelief. But never mind. . . . Don't worry about the ob-

stacle of the framework of this novel, simply give yourself over to the world Ms. Tan creates for you. It's the story she tells that really matters.

Critics admired the poignant and moving storytelling and the bittersweet humor of the novel. Charles Solomon of *Los Angeles Times Book Review* found that the novel shows how "shared afflictions can create ties between people closer than blood relationships." Dew introduced his discussion of Tan's novel by stating, "Within the peculiar construction of Amy Tan's second novel is a harrowing, compelling, and at times bitterly humorous tale in which an entire world unfolds in a Tolstoyan tide of event and detail." Sabine Durrant of London *Times* described the book as "gripping" and "enchanting," while Charles Foran of Toronto *Globe and Mail* deemed it "a fine novel" carried by its "exuberant storytelling and rich drama."

Commenting on *The Kitchen God's Wife*'s bestselling status, Gillespie discouraged readers from assuming that the book lacks literary merit. Gillespie noted, "It is. . . quite possible for a bestseller to be an estimable piece of writing as well as a ripping read." Similarly, Judith Caesar of *North Dakota Quarterly* explained:

> Under the outward layer of a highly readable popular novel, Tan has written an extremely complex postmodern literary novel that challenges the dominant

narratives of contemporary American society, particularly our ideas of who matters and who does not, of whose version is 'true' and whose is not, and indeed of how one can find what is true.

The result of Tan's mainstream appeal, Gillespie added, is that many Americans gain "an education for the heart," having learned about the forgotten millions who suffered throughout Chinese history and "how, why, and from where Chinese-American society evolved." In the same vein, Caesar wrote, "Tan verifies the reality of a world outside the American experience as nevertheless part of the human experience and questions the sense of entitlement and cultural superiority that allows Americans to dismiss the sufferings of foreigners." Gillespie declared that Tan's achievement in this sense is significant: "All this is the most important job of fiction, of course; and since Chinese women lived lives not just of forgotten obscurity, but of hermetically sealed oblivion, Tan is handing us a key with no price tag and letting us open the brass-bolted door."

Criticism

Jennifer Bussey

Bussey holds a master's degree in interdisciplinary studies and a bachelor's degree in English literature. She is an independent writer specializing in literature. In the following essay, she discusses the tension between Eastern culture and Western culture in Tan's novel.

Amy Tan's *The Kitchen God's Wife* has been compared in various ways to Tan's first novel, *The Joy Luck Club.* Both novels have garnered the praise of critics and readers, most of whom cannot help but notice the similarities between the two books. Perhaps the most obvious similarity is the theme of mother-daughter conflict as the result of Americanized daughters having so little in common with their immigrant mothers. This tension—really a tension between Eastern and Western cultures—is at the heart of *The Kitchen God's Wife,* in which Pearl has trouble relating to her mother, Winnie. The plot development, however, takes these two characters from distance to understanding and respect. The story is about how secrets create distance in the relationships that should be closest. Once Winnie has told Pearl all of her secrets from her life in China, Pearl is free to tell Winnie her own secret—that she has multiple sclerosis. With insight into each other's struggles, these two

> "The plot development, however, takes these two characters from distance to understanding and respect. The story is about how secrets create distance in the relationships that should be closest."

women come to common ground in a very unexpected way, and they do so without compromising their distinctly Eastern (Winnie) and Western (Pearl) identities.

Winnie, although she lives in the United States, is still very much a Chinese woman. She lives in San Francisco and co-owns a flower shop in Chinatown with her lifelong friend, Helen. She has found a place in America where she can still feel like she is in her element and resist assimilating without sacrifice. She is displaced; after all, she left China to escape her husband, not because she didn't love her country. She has built a life for herself in America, but that life is deeply rooted in her friends and family, who are also Chinese. Many of them are figures from her stormy past and thus perhaps represent the best of the life she led in China.

Winnie resists becoming Americanized and often scoffs at Western ways of doing things. Describing her uncle, she says that every year he took up a new hobby such as growing flowers. She remarks in chapter six, "He always called it 'hobby,' just like the English, no Chinese word for doing something only to waste time, waste money." In chapter twelve, she describes putting on her coat and shoes to walk into town, three or four *li* away. She explains to Pearl that a *li* is about a half-mile, adding, "'And I had to walk that distance. I wasn't like you, getting into a car to go two blocks to the grocery store.'" Similarly, she describes the truck that carried her and the air force group across the country. It pulled a tank of gas behind it because "that was the only way to get to Kunming back then. We didn't have gas stations every ten miles, no such thing. And we did not travel on big highways, with seventy-mile-an-hour speed limits." Winnie means only to express her pride in her native land and to emphasize how difficult life was for her then, especially compared to Pearl's life of convenience. In chapter thirteen, she remarks:

> We didn't complain too much. Chinese people know how to adapt to almost anything. It didn't matter what your background was, rich or poor. We always knew: Our situation could change any minute. You're lucky you were born in this country. You never had to think that way.

Of course, the irony in Winnie's statement is that she has not adapted to American life. Perhaps this is simply a choice, not a matter of not knowing how to adapt; she simply chooses to live as Chinese a life as she can.

Many of Winnie's characteristics point to her Chinese heritage and lifestyle. Her reliance on superstition and luck is a critical part of her thinking. Despite marrying a Baptist minister, she adheres to the religion of her past, complete with household deities, like the Kitchen God, and ghosts. Her daughter Pearl recalls a childhood memory of seeing a ghost swirl out of a jack-o-lantern's mouth. She told her mother, who immediately began searching for the ghost. Winnie's father, on the other hand, explained that there are no such things as ghosts, and that the only ghost is the Holy Ghost, who would never try to scare children. Pearl remarks,

> I was not comforted by his answer, because my mother had then stared at me, as if I had betrayed her and made her look like a fool. That's how things were. She was always trying to suppress certain beliefs that did not coincide with my father's Christian ones, but sometimes they popped out anyway.

This memory reveals another important side of Winnie's character, which is her driving sense of duty. From her first days as Wen Fu's bride, she understood that her role was to obey and please her husband. Even as the wife of a different man in America, she still tries to suppress her own religious beliefs in favor of her husband's. When Auntie Du comes to America, Winnie considers it her duty to take care of the old woman until her death.

In Winnie's language and conduct, she exhibits many characteristics of Eastern culture. She is subtle and often talks around what she means to say, a method of communication that is lost on her daughter. Other Chinese people of Winnie's generation, however, understand exactly what is being said, even when someone is speaking indirectly. Persuading her daughter to stay for Auntie Du's funeral, Winnie tells Pearl that Auntie Du was always proud of her. Winnie knows that what Auntie Du meant by this was that she loved Pearl. Winnie is often aware of the differences in the Chinese and English languages. Just as she states that there is no Chinese word for *hobby,* she describes her relationship with Helen in chapter three by saying, "And yet we are closer perhaps than sisters, related by fate, joined by debts. I have kept her secrets. She has kept mine. And we have a kind of loyalty that has no word in this country." Winnie also speaks in metaphors and similes that draw from nature, which is regarded as consistent with Eastern expression. In chapter three, for example, she comments, "If I try to say what happened, my story would not flow forward like a river from the beginning to the end, everything connected, the lake to the sea."

Pearl, in contrast to Winnie, is representative of the Western sensibility. Although she is only one generation removed from China, she has lived her entire life in America. She and her Anglo husband and their two daughters live in the city and lead typical middle-class American lives. She is a linguist who works with mentally challenged children, and he is a pathologist. She enjoys a satisfying marriage in which she and her husband share power, and she is comfortable with keeping a comfortable distance between herself and her family in San Francisco. Pearl is so unfamiliar with the nuances of Chinese conduct and culture that she sometimes missteps in the presence of the older members of her family. She speaks only a little Mandarin and is uncertain about what happens at a Buddhist funeral. Because her life experience has been so different from her mother's, the two have little common ground on which to build a relationship.

In the landscape of her extended family, Pearl is the bridge between life in China and life in America. Had she not been given the opportunity to learn about her mother's painful and dramatic past, it is likely that Pearl's daughters would have no connection whatsoever to their Chinese roots. The Kitchen God's altar would be, as suggested by Pearl's husband, Phil, nothing but a dollhouse for their playtime until they grew tired of it.

While Winnie talks around topics, Pearl is a typical American in that she believes in talking plainly about what needs to be said. When Winnie expresses her wish that Helen had been more helpful in caring for Auntie Du, Pearl simply suggests that she tell Helen how she feels. At the same time, when Pearl talks to her mother, she tends to avoid certain topics and maintains a polite distance in their conversations. This is not the direct approach she advocates, but she understands that her mother's communication is different than her own and tries to "meet her halfway."

Tan intersperses numerous reminders of how different Eastern and Western cultures are. This serves to keep the theme close to the surface without placing all the weight of the theme on the mother-daughter relationship. After the funeral, for example, Pearl, Phil, and their girls are back at Winnie's house. Phil is anxious to get started on the drive back home (the Western way), but Winnie is unconcerned with his impatience and continues to talk to her daughter. When Winnie tells the story of the Kitchen God in chapter two, she tries to explain his status by comparing him to a store manager, who is "important, but still many, many bosses above him." Pearl notices Phil chuckling at Winnie's attempts to provide an American context, and she wonders if that is how her mother thinks of Chinese deities or if her comparison is strictly for their benefit. Later in the conversation, Phil likens the Kitchen God to Santa Claus because he reports on who has been good and who has been bad. Winnie responds, "'He is not Santa Claus. More like a spy—FBI agent, CIA, Mafia, worse than IRS, that kind of person!'"

In their expression of affection, the Western characters are much more demonstrative than the Eastern characters. When Pearl first sees her mother after arriving in town for the banquet, the two begin a superficial conversation. Pearl thinks, "Although we have not seen each other since Christmas, almost a month ago, we do none of the casual hugs and kisses Phil and I exchange when we see his parents and friends." In chapter seven, Winnie describes seeing her father after twelve years of absence, when she comes seeking his approval for her marriage. She says, "'Of course, he did not hug me and kiss me, not the way you Americans do when you have been reunited after five minutes' separation. We did not even talk very long after my aunties left.'"

As the story closes, Winnie and Pearl have come to better understand each other's personal struggles and, as a result, regard each other with more compassion and respect. By portraying, in these two characters, the Eastern and Western sides of her own identity, Tan allows the reader to see how the two cultures clash but also how they can coexist. Many critics credit Tan with opening American readers to the beauty and depth of Chinese culture and thus paving the way for other Asian-American writers. In a sense, the bridge created between Winnie and Pearl is a bridge that takes American readers to an understanding and appreciation of Eastern belief, thought, and behavior.

Source: Jennifer Bussey, Critical Essay on *The Kitchen God's Wife,* in *Novels for Students,* The Gale Group, 2002.

Judith Caesar

In the following essay, Caesar asserts that The Kitchen God's Wife *is "an extremely complex postmodern literary novel that challenges the dominant narratives of contemporary American society, particularly our ideas of who matters and who does not."*

If, as Jean-Francois Lyotard says, a "master narrative" is required to legitimate artistic expression, for the past thirty years the legitimizing narrative of mainstream American literary realism has been the quest for personal fulfillment. The increasingly stagnant, if not outright polluted, mainstream has produced novel after novel concerning the mid-life crises (and sometimes accompanying marital infidelities) of self-centered American men, with even the once rich Jewish and Southern literary traditions now given over to novels like Bernard Malamud's *Dubin's Lives,* Walker Percy's *The Second Coming,* and Reynolds Price's *Blue Calhoun,* all concerning a middle-aged (and in the first two instances, wealthy) white man's discontent. All are a far cry from the writers' earlier ethical and philosophical concerns. The consideration of the reflective person's stance toward questions of political and social justice, central to the 19th-and early 20th-century novel from Charles Dickens' *Bleak House* to Ernest Hemingway's *For Whom the Bell Tolls,* seems to have become limited to experimental postmodern novels (E. L. Doctorow's *Ragtime,* Thomas Pynchon's *Vineland*) and to the kinds of essays on domestic politics, international affairs, and human rights that appear in *The New Yorker, Harpers',* and *The Nation.* Worse, American literary realism's concentration on the purely personal has led to a delegitimation of other experience, namely, the experience of introspective and articulate people who have lived lives devastated by social and political forces outside their control. These people are relegated to inarticulate images on the television screen—in Sarajevo, in Somalia, in the Middle East, in Thailand, and in China. These people, then, whose real stories and histories remain untold to the American public, become less "real" than many of the characters who populate American literary fiction.

In this context, it is very significant that the supposedly "popular" novels of minority American

> [Tan] creates her own narrative by seeming to affirm popular American assumptions in the formula of the popular novel and then undermining that very narrative in a complex political allegory that questions the basic American (indeed Western) concepts of truth and rationality."

women—Alice Walker, Toni Morrison, Maxine Hong Kingston, Louise Erdrich, and now Amy Tan—seem to be reaching a larger audience than much mainstream literary realism. In part, this is because all five can create such an engaging and often witty surface and because all seem to deal with the popular topics of TV talk shows: spouse abuse, recovering from divorce, finding one's roots, etc. And of course all are hyphenated Americans of some sort, a fact which engages the curiosity of readers who do not share the writers' backgrounds. (Chicana and Native American writers like Sandra Cisneros and Leslie Silko, who use more experimental techniques and deal with a wider range of subject matter, have yet to reach the Waldenbooks reader.)

Yet Tan, for one, does much more than articulate popular media issues. She causes us to question the very basis of how we know what we know. She creates her own narrative by seeming to affirm popular American assumptions in the formula of the popular novel and then undermining that very narrative in a complex political allegory that questions the basic American (indeed Western) concepts of truth and rationality.

In keeping with this subtly deceptive plan, *The Kitchen God's Wife* seems at first like a lively but somewhat clichéd popular novel, a modern pseudo-feminist retelling of the folklore story of the abused wife (patient Griselda in the West, the kitchen god's wife in the East) who wins her husband's love by passing all his tests or his remorse by her generosity of spirit. What makes it modern is that

the abused wife is angry at her ill treatment and seemingly "finds herself" in that anger. The women, moreover, are the "good guys" while the men seem quite unrelievedly evil, with the exception of the male rescuer. It seems, in short, to be a type of formula novel which provides women readers with clear heroines, heroes, and villains, all without disrupting the Gothic romance's illusion of rescue by "the right man." Jiang Weili, the narrator of the central three-fourths of the novel, endures the most horrifying abuse from her brutal husband, Wen Fu, while traditional Chinese society not only fails to intervene but colludes in her victimization. The only twist seems to be that instead of winning her husband's love, Weili is rescued by a handsome prince, in this case, Jimmy Louie, a Chinese-American soldier who marries her and takes her back to the United States. In fact, one can see the novel as a rather smug indictment of the misery of women in traditional Chinese society in contrast to American society's enlightened feminism. Moreover, the story that frames the story, that of Jiang Weili's daughter Pearl and her relationship with her mother, seems like yet another story about returning to one's roots to discover some less complicated identity. In short, there seems little here to challenge conventional American thinking.

Yet nothing in the novel is as it seems. Certainly, in the beginning, nothing is as it seems to Weili's American-born daughter Pearl, who narrates the opening chapters of the novel and embodies the American sensibility in all its directness and in all its limitations. Like well-meaning Americans in China, Pearl makes cultural gaffes in dealing with the older Chinese-American community and even with her mother because she doesn't seem to understand the differences between outer display and actual feeling or the realm of implied meanings that are so much a part of Chinese tradition. Thus, at the funeral of elderly Grand Auntie Du which opens the novel, Pearl sees a group of sobbing women in threadbare padded jackets and takes them for recent immigrants from China, Grand Auntie Du's "real friends," when in fact they are Vietnamese professional mourners. Worse, with all the confidence of American pop psychology, Pearl advises her mother to speak frankly to her contemporary, Auntie Helen, about her feelings that Auntie Helen should be sharing more in Grand Auntie Du's care. Pearl says,

"Why don't you just tell Auntie Helen how you feel and stop complaining?" This is what Phil [Pearl's Anglo husband] had suggested I say, a perfectly reasonable way to get my mother to realize what was

What Do I Read Next?

- Patricia P. Chu's *Assimilating Asians: Gendered Strategies of Authorship in Asian America (New Americanists)*, (2000) explores the increasingly important role of Asian authors in America and the ways in which they employ traditionally Western techniques to tell their stories. Chu also examines the ways in which female authors differ from male authors.

- *Typical American,* Gish Jen's 1991 novel, relates the story of three Chinese immigrants who make new lives for themselves in America. They soon find that their beliefs, values, and expectations change as they become immersed in their new culture.

- Maxine Hong Kingston's *The Woman Warrior: Memoirs of a Girlhood among Ghosts* (1976) is considered a precursor to Tan's fiction. It is an intense and bitter story of a Chinese-American girl growing up in California, caught between the world of Caucasian "ghosts" and her mother's "talk-stories" about China.

- Amy Tan's *The Joy Luck Club* (1989) presents the lives of four Chinese women living in America who recall their troubled and dramatic lives in their native land. Because of their altogether different life experiences, the women's daughters have difficulty relating to them. This novel was made into a successful movie in 1993 by Hollywood Pictures.

- Ben Fong-Torres' *The Rice Room: Growing Up Chinese-American—From Number Two Son to Rock'N'Roll* (1994) is the author's account of growing up Chinese American. Although expected to adhere to his Chinese heritage, Fong-Torres wanted nothing more than to assimilate into American culture.

- Anzia Yezierska's novel *Bread Givers: A Struggle between a Father of the Old World and a Daughter of the New World* (1925) is the story of Sara Smolinksy, a young Jewish girl struggling to free herself of the traditional expectations of women in Orthodox Jewish society. When she sees her father, a rabbi, marry her sisters into unhappy marriages, she runs away to make a new life for herself.

---

making her miserable so she could finally take positive action.

Of course, Pearl doesn't realize that her mother is quietly boasting to Pearl about her own dutifulness and implying that more could be expected of Pearl as well. Thus, Pearl is shocked when her mother is so profoundly offended that she will barely speak to her for a month.

She knows her mother as Winnie Louie, her American name, her kindly but often inexplicably crotchety mother to whom she is bound by sometimes tiresome traditions that don't seem to apply to other Americans. She doesn't realize until the end of the novel that her mother is also Jiang Weili, a woman brought up in China who has survived both a disastrous marriage and the invasion and occupation of her country by a brutal enemy army. And because she doesn't know who her mother is,

Pearl also doesn't know that she herself is not the daughter of the kindly Jimmy Louie but of Wen Fu, the brutal first husband. This is but one of the novel's pattern of multiple and mistaken identities that suggests the ambiguity of all knowledge and the incompleteness of the official (legitimate) narrative.

In particular, the novel explores the incompleteness of the American narrative, an incompleteness that comes from a refusal to see the validity of the knowledge of other cultures or of the experiences of people who are not Americans. Pearl, with her confident American knowledge of the way things are, her faulty Mandarin, and her imperviousness to implied meanings, misses much of what is going on beneath the surface, although she is sensitive enough sometimes to realize that there are some things she doesn't under-

---

stand: ". . . apparently, there's a lot I don't know about my mother and Auntie Helen," she thinks at one point. Since the bulk of the novel is Weili's story, it would seem that one of the purposes of having Pearl as the initial narrator is not only to contrast the American sensibility with the Chinese, but to alert the American reader to the subtext beneath Jiang Weili's story as well. Although the reader would first identify with the American, Pearl, it is very clear that Pearl doesn't know all that needs to be known.

Weili's story is also much more than it would first seem to an American reader. Most obviously, Jiang Weili's is the story of a progressively more violent and degrading marriage set against the backdrop of the Japanese invasion of China. Weili is married off to a man of a socially "suitable" family, although both her father and her aunts and uncles clearly have a sense of the man's flawed character. Because they know something of his deceptiveness, if not his outright cruelty, they marry Weili to him and not her favored cousin, nicknamed Peanut, who had wanted to marry her. Wen Fu proves to be a sexual sadist who delights in humiliation games, a liar who uses his dead brother's diplomas to become an officer in the Nationalist air force (another confused identity), and a coward who manages to save his own life throughout the war by deserting his fellow pilots whenever they encounter Japanese aircraft. Because of Wen Fu's social position, however, no one acknowledges any of these failings.

As the war continues and the Nationalist army flees from Shanghai to Nanjing and finally to Kunming, so Wen Fu degenerates. He refuses to leave a card game to get a doctor for his sick daughter, and then he publicly blames Weili when the child dies. He brings a concubine into the house and then discards her when she becomes pregnant. He forces Weili to "admit" publicly to being a prostitute, despite her very obvious fidelity. He is the enemy of whatever is life-affirming and generous (Weili's maternal responses to save her child, her sisterly desire to help the ignorant concubine) disguised as patriarchal morality. Throughout all of this abuse, no one interferes; in fact, when Weili tries to run away from Wen Fu, her friends Hulan (later Helen) and Auntie Du tell him her hiding place. The increasing viciousness of Wen Fu parallels the increasing closeness of the Japanese army, so that by the time Weili has run away and been brought back to a still more degraded life, the Japanese are bombing Kunming.

The parallel between the victimization of Weili and the Japanese conquest of China is further emphasized by the fact that old Jiang, Weili's father, has collaborated with the Japanese, betraying his country in the same way he betrayed his daughter. His pattern of ineffectual resistance and subsequent capitulation, moreover, continues throughout the novel. He throws a teacup against a priceless painting to show that he would rather destroy China's heritage than betray it—and then accedes to Japanese demands; in Shanghai, when both he and Weili are Wen Fu's victims, he gives Weili the money with which to leave Wen Fu—and then is too ill to help her when Wen Fu accuses her of theft and has her imprisoned.

Even at this level of the political allegory, however, there is little in equating Chinese patriarchy with Japanese expansionism and imperialism that would discomfort or challenge an American reader. It is still "those people" who have done these terrible things, not "us." Yet it is not so comforting if one carries the political allegory to its logical conclusions. Weili's victimization couldn't have taken place if Chinese society had not condoned it to such an extent that even her best friends didn't want to blemish their reputations by helping her escape—at least until the very end of the novel, when they try to get her out of jail (ineffectually, it turns out) by saying that they had witnessed her divorce. These friends, who later join her in the United States, are not all that different from the United States itself, which, as Tan points out, helped to keep the Japanese war machine running by supplying the Japanese with oil and scrap metal all through the 1930s and later helped China only after the United States itself was under attack. Hulan thinks that she freed Weili through her second husband's influence with the Nationalist government; in fact, it is Weili's cousin Peanut, now a communist cadre who runs a shelter for abused wives, who gets Weili out of prison because Nationalist officials in charge of Weili's case fear reprisals from the communists. If Weili is China, then it is a communist who helps to liberate her, although the liberation is far from complete.

Moreover, if we interpret the novel as a fairly literal political allegory, there is yet another disturbing implication. Wen Fu is never punished. When Weili finally gets word of his death, she learns that he has died an old man, surrounded by his family and respected by his community—the very definition of a righteous man's proper death in Chinese tradition. In contrast, Weili's good husband Jimmy Louie dies relatively young and in great pain, seemingly denied by Pearl, the daughter whom he raised. The pain and prematurity of Jimmy's death is one reason it so haunts Weili. Weili, furthermore, is eking out a living in a foreign country (America), widowed and at least, as the book opens, culturally estranged from her children. One could see this as paralleling the fact that all the former imperial powers—Japan among them—are both more prosperous and more respected than their former victims. To cite the most literal sort of example, the Western media tends to blame the human rights abuses and the political unrest in China and the rest of the former colonial world on the ideological systems that ejected the colonial powers, not on the after-effects of imperialism itself. And the crimes of imperialism did go unpunished. The war crimes trials after World War II focused on the Japanese abuse of western POWs, not on the Japanese imprisonment and massacre of millions of Chinese civilians.

One reason for Tan's equation of imperialism and patriarchy is essentially rhetorical. It is easier for an American audience to sympathize with the victims of patriarchy than with the victims of imperialism. Many American women have been the victims of patriarchy, after all, while very few have been the victims of imperialism. We have not had our country invaded and occupied by a foreign army or had laws imposed on us by people who didn't know our language or culture—except, of course, for Native Americans. The type of suffering Weili endures, moreover, is primarily emotional and psychological rather than physical. She is humiliated and exploited; she cannot even complain about her plight. But she is not being starved, beaten, or tortured at a time when millions of her countrymen (and women) were, as Weili herself points out. Weili's suffering is that of a middle-class woman married to a bully. An American reader can identify with this, at least to some degree; and once one has done this, one can begin to get a sense of the type of suffering that Tan suggests only metaphorically or seemingly incidentally—the Nanjing massacre, for instance. Then other events fit into place. Weili and Wen Fu's children die, one the direct victim of Wen Fu's neglect, two the indirect victims of the Japanese. Tan's presentation helps to legitimize a narrative of suffering otherwise so far outside the American experience that it could seem beyond our capacity for empathy.

But there are more complex philosophical reasons for linking imperialism and patriarchy. For one thing, they both shape the "legitimate" printed narratives of Weili's story. To the Shanghai press covering Weili's case, Wen Fu is a war hero whose wife has been seduced and corrupted by a lecherous American. In this patriarchal narrative, Weili wants to escape Wen Fu not because she has been abused, but because she is "crazy for American sex." This is as true as the printed leaflets the Japanese drop on Nanjing, explaining that civilians will not be harmed.

Behind these official narratives is the assumption that some people's suffering is more significant than other people's sufferings. The Chinese historian Szuma Chien once ironically remarked that some deaths are as heavy as Mount Tai, while others are lighter than a feather—that is, in official versions of events. Thus, the honor of men is more important than the dignity of women, and the deaths of ordinary Chinese simply aren't important at all. This assumption isn't merely Oriental, moreover, since it underlies the current American narrative that the personal emotional crisis of an American is the only suffering interesting enough to write about. The official narratives are used to ignore or justify the sufferings of the powerless.

Consequently, all the official facts in Tan's novel are questionable. Weili's divorce is officially valid when Wen Fu holds a gun to her head and makes her sign the paper, but it can be made invalid by her ex-husband's tearing up the paper. What is a divorce and what does it mean under those circumstances? Weili can be "officially" a thief for taking the gold her father gave her, and then later be "officially" innocent when her imprisonment is termed an "error of the court." Even Pearl's official American knowledge that World War II began with the bombing of Pearl Harbor is questionable, since, as Weili points out, it began for China with the Japanese invasion of Manchuria. (Or did it begin even earlier, with the German concession of the Shantung peninsula to the Japanese?) The Western narrative is at best an incomplete truth. When does a divorce or a war begin or end?

The narrative structure of the novel also suggests the problematic nature of truth. As Edward Said has pointed out in *Culture and Imperialism,* the narrative structure of the classic 19th-century realistic novel, with its omniscient narrator or reliable first-person narrator, helped to underscore the idea of an authoritative and "correct" version of events. Despite the polyphonic narrations of the high modernist novel, the 20th-century popular novel has generally preserved the 19th-century technique, as has much of contemporary literary realism. The modernist novel, moreover, focuses on the psychological and philosophical implications of competing narratives (*Mrs. Dalloway, As I Lay Dying,* etc.), not on their political implication. Much contemporary fiction thus tends to confirm the value of Americanness over foreignness, a kind of contemporary imperialism. (Think, for example, of Cormac McCarthy's National Book Award-winning *All the Pretty Horses* in which the good guys are all American men and the bad guys either Mexican or female. Consider how different it would be if any of the Mexican or women characters gave their version of events.) In contrast, Tan has two narrators and three versions of events—Pearl's, Weili's, and Hulan's, all of which seem credible in some respects.

While Tan's use of a polyphonic narrative is significant in itself, perhaps more significant is who speaks. Through much of the novel, after all, it is an elderly Chinese immigrant whose syntax and word choice reflect the patterns of Chinese-accented English, a speech pattern marginalized and mocked by contemporary mainstream American society. Tan helps to give this voice a validity and dignity in the same way that Walker and Morrison have helped to legitimize African American speech. She has made the sufferings of those who speak in this voice "as heavy as Mount Tai."

The details of the novel confirm both the validity of these Chinese women's experience and the subjective nature of truth. What Hulan remembers is different from what Weili remembers, yet Hulan's insights are given sudden credibility when she tells Pearl, "You know how she [Weili] is, very hard to thank. . .", and we realize how very true this is of both Weili and Pearl. Just as Pearl rejects her "cousin" Mary's comforting casseroles when Mary learns of Pearl's illness, Weili would indeed be repelled by the idea of being indebted to Hulan in any way. We also realize the extent to which Hulan's behavior, which Weili had interpreted as simply contrary and obstructive, was well intended. What is interesting here is that in personal relationships, unlike political ones, conflicting versions of the truth are not necessarily divisive, since neither version is used as a means of control or suppression. Thus even the quarrels between Winnie (once Weili) and Helen (once Hulan) are not precisely quarrels at all. Pearl observes,

> I watch them continue to argue, although perhaps it is not arguing. They are remembering together, dreaming together.

Tan also contradicts this idea of a rational Western truth through the pattern of double and shifting identities of her characters and by her clear indications that the commonly accepted criteria for determining identity are sometimes irrelevant. Tan shows a world of multiple and contradictory truths, truth as a series of Chinese boxes, not a unitary truth to be "discovered" in the Western sense. Tan's is not even a Western "postmodernist" truth of multiple linear narratives, but of contradictory truths and partial truths intermixed in layers of meaning. Through the contradictions in Winnie's (Weili's) character, we see that a complete person can be both large-spirited and petty, loving and distant. Indeed, self-knowledge consists of acknowledging these seemingly contradictory traits. At one point Weili tells Pearl,

> I have told you about the early days of my marriage so you can understand why I became strong and weak at the same time. Maybe according to your American mind, you cannot be both, that would be a contradiction. But according to my life, I had to be both.

The simultaneous existence of these opposites is indeed very different from what our American minds tell us is rational, and thus it calls into question the validity of that rationality.

Moreover, none of the characters is precisely what they seem, even concerning the most common determiner of identity, family relationships. Consider, for instance, the ways in which the characters seem to be related but aren't. Pearl calls Hulan "auntie" and thinks of Hulan's children Bao-Bao and Mary as her cousins. Indeed, Winnie and Helen, with all their feuding and tenderness, act like sisters. And Pearl is as exasperated and yet connected to the "cousins" as she would be with any blood relative, a relationship Tan underscores by using them as foils to Pearl. Pearl has believed the "official version" that Helen is the widow of Winnie's younger brother, but she learns very early in her mother's story that Helen is "merely" a person she has known ever since her youth.

Thus it is not surprising that Pearl's discovery of her parentage, her "real identity" does not have the significance the episode's placement in the novel would seem to grant it. Finally, the great climatic revelation that Wen Fu is Pearl's "real" father seems to be irrelevant after all. It is the pattern formed by all the revelations leading up to it that is important. That Jimmy Louie is Pearl's "real" father is simply one more item in the list of things that seems true, isn't true, and finally is in a larger sense as true as any of the novel's other ambiguous truths. And on the level of character, it doesn't matter either. Pearl is not at all like Wen Fu, as Winnie points out. Ancestry and blood relationship finally do not matter very much—a very non-Chinese idea in a very non-American narrative.

Meaning and truth exist in layers, and what is true on the surface is contradicted by another truth underneath, which is in turn contradicted by a third layer. And all are "true." We see this kind of paradox even in the names of minor characters. Pearl's cousin Roger is named Bao-Bao, "precious baby," because his parents were so happy to finally have a child, but the nickname sticks as he grows up because it becomes a sarcastic description of his superficial and immature behavior. The only one of the Chinese-American characters to have a Chinese name, he speaks like a cartoon of an American and gets married and divorced as carelessly as a character in a Woody Allen comedy. Is it then because he is so American that he is so superficial? In fact, in his self-centeredness and sexual inconstancy, he seems like a comic and relatively benign version of Wen Fu. He's a beloved precious baby who has become a spoiled precious baby whose faults are equally American and Chinese.

In this context, it is not surprising that nationality doesn't matter very much in determining the identity of both Weili and Pearl either. It merely determines their modes of expression. Pearl is very much an American version of Weili. Like Weili, she is a concerned and loving mother, she faces difficulties (her multiple sclerosis, for example) with such stoicism that she cuts herself off from both her husband and her mother, she is witty and critical, and she is willing to let things be understood without spelling them out. Yet in her manners and beliefs, she is an American. When, at the end, she accepts her mother's herbal cures and the offering to Lady Sorrowfree, she does so as an acceptance of her mother's solicitude, not her beliefs. She hasn't found a "Chinese identity" in the way the characters in *Song of Solomon* and *The Color Purple* find an African identity; instead she has found a closer relationship with her mother and an insight into the seemingly conflicting layers of reality in the world around her, beginning with the multiple identities of her mother and the Chinese "relatives" whom she thought she knew. Personal identity, like both personal and political truth, is many-layered and elusive, something accepted rather than discovered.

Under the outward layer of a highly readable popular novel, Tan has written an extremely complex postmodern literary novel that challenges the dominant narratives of contemporary American so-

Communist Chinese leader Mao Zedong

ciety, particularly our ideas of who matters and who does not, of whose version is "true" and whose is not, and indeed of how one can find what is true. Through the voices of characters like Weili and Hulan, Tan presents a world in which complex and intelligent people must find a way of accommodating hostile political and social forces against which they are powerless to rebel—a type of suffering from which most American readers have been sheltered. Thus, Tan verifies the reality of a world outside the American experience as nevertheless part of the human experience and questions the sense of entitlement and cultural superiority that allows Americans to dismiss the sufferings of foreigners. This sense of entitlement, the idea that "our" deaths are as heavy as Mount Tai and "their" deaths are light as feathers underlies the callousness of all imperial narratives—the novels of contemporary America, as well as narratives of the Imperial China of which Szuma Chien wrote and of patriarchal China and Imperial Japan, of which Jiang Weili speaks. By making us question the validity of American knowledge and the "otherness" of what Americans consider foreign, Amy Tan has helped to enlarge the American narrative.

Source: Judith Caesar, "Patriarchy, Imperialism, and Knowledge in *The Kitchen God's Wife*," in *North Dakota Quarterly,* Vol. 62, No. 4, Fall, 1995, pp. 164–74.

Tan displays superb
storytelling—spinning personae
and situations that are credible
and compelling. But more, she
has the courage to share heartfelt
sorrow and grief, to acknowledge
human imperfection and fate's
ambiguities."

Scarlet Cheng

In the following review, Cheng lauds The
Kitchen God's Wife, *stating, "The ending, with its
extraordinary convergence of all that has gone on
before, is a marvel."*

Yes, it's true: Amy Tan has done it again—with
searing clarity of vision she has spun a tale that
lyrically weaves past and present, myth and memory. And she has written a true novel this time, one
sustained story that lasts all of some four hundred
pages.

For the many who read her first book, *The Joy
Luck Club,* the second opens on familiar territory—
Pearl is the grown daughter of a very Chinese
mother, Winnie, who speaks English with the
snappy cadence and salty metaphors of her native
tongue and whose way of thinking—of linking the
visible and the invisible worlds—has come with her
across the Pacific to the San Francisco Bay Area.

While Winnie still lives in Chinatown, Pearl is
living fifty miles outside the city with a Caucasian
husband and two Americanized little girls. They
come together for a cousin's engagement dinner
and for an aunt's funeral. Each has been guarding
a secret: Pearl has multiple sclerosis; Winnie a
checkered past she tried to leave behind in China.

But meddlesome Aunt Helen takes it on herself to set the record straight. When she nags Pearl
to reveal her illness, Pearl protests that she does not
want to worry her mother.

"This is her right to worry," says Aunt Helen. "She
is your mother."

"But she shouldn't have to worry about something
that isn't really a problem."

"That's why you should tell her now. No more problem after that."

"But then she'll wonder why we kept this a secret
from her. She'll think it's worse than it is."

"Maybe she has some secrets too." She smiles, then
laughs at what must be a private joke. "Your mother,
oh yes, plenty of secrets!"

Winnie does have plenty of secrets, and revealing them takes most of the book. While both
mother and daughter learn to share what has been
locked deep inside, this is really Winnie's story.
She tells of the turns of fate she suffered in a China
that was attempting to modernize but was still fundamentally feudal and often brutal to women.

First Winnie (Weili in her other life) conjures
up the romantic memory of her own mother, the
first of the moderns of Chinese society to have unbound feet. "When my mother was eight years old,"
Winnie recalls, "her feet were already unbound,
and some people say that's why she ran wild." Her
mother received an education, which some later
called "bad." But Winnie says, "If you were to ask
me, what happened to my mother was not a bad
education but bad fate. Her education only made
her unhappy thinking about it—that no matter how
much she changed her life, she could not change
the world that surrounded her."

Her bad fate was to fall in love with one man
but be forced to marry another. Then one day she
mysteriously disappears, and her young daughter is
dispatched to be raised by relatives on a remote island. Weili grows up dreaming for her disgraced
fate to change. When she gets matched to the dashing young Wen Fu, a man from a well-to-do family, she believes that it has. But as soon as she is
married, her in-laws make off with her immense
dowry, and her groom turns out to be a selfish brute
whose behavior gets progressively worse.

As one of the first pilots for the Chinese Air
Force, Wen Fu is transferred from training camp to
military base and finally to Kunming, the Kuom-
ingtang stronghold towards the end of the war.
Weili naturally moved with him, trying to maintain
the semblance of home, preparing special meals
and treats purchased with the dowry money that
was, fortunately, banked in her own name.

In such ways Weili and her friend Hulan, both
alternately foolish and valiant, seek happiness even
as the world around them is collapsing. Tan captures beautifully this helter-skelter period in China,
when many lived on the run, never knowing how
long they would be in one place—or one piece, as
the Japanese battered cities with aerial raids.

It seems that Weili endures one humiliation, only to have greater sorrow come to crush her. She is physically beaten, her babies die, and more, much more. Yet this woman grows less foolish, more resilient, until she finds the courage to grasp her own happiness.

The ending, with its extraordinary convergence of all that has gone on before, is a marvel.

At a recent appearance in Washington, D.C., Amy Tan said, "I always find that it's necessary to write with some reader in mind, and for me, that someone is always my mother." In a haunting way, she has also successfully taken on her mother's voice in *The Kitchen God's Wife*—or, at least, the voice of someone of her mother's generation who lived through the tumultuous period of history her mother did. In addition to this remarkable mediumship, Tan displays superb storytelling—spinning personae and situations that are credible and compelling. But more, she has the courage to share heartfelt sorrow and grief, to acknowledge human imperfection and fate's ambiguities. Tan shows us that a life can encompass all that—grief, imperfection, ambiguity—and still add up to triumph, a triumph of the spirit, of the human soul to endure, to show compassion, and to hold fast to dreams.

Source: Scarlet Cheng, "Amy Tan Redux," in *Belles Lettres*, Vol. 7, No. 1, Fall 1991, pp. 15, 19.

Sources

Caesar, Judith, "Patriarchy, Imperialism, and Knowledge," in *North Dakota Quarterly*, Vol. 62, No. 4, Fall 1994–1995, pp. 164–74.

Cheng, Scarlet, "Amy Tan Redux," in *Belles Lettres*, Vol. 7, No. 1, Fall 1991, pp. 15, 19.

Dew, Robb Forman, "Pangs of an Abandoned Child," in *New York Times Book Review*, June 16, 1991, p. 9.

Durrant, Sabine, Review of *The Kitchen God's Wife*, in *Times* (London), July 11, 1991, p. 16.

Foran, Charles, Review of *The Kitchen God's Wife*, in *Globe and Mail* (Toronto), June 29, 1991, p. C8.

Gillespie, Elgy, "Amy, Angst, and the Second Novel," in *San Francisco Review of Books*, Vol. 16, No. 1, Summer 1991, pp. 33–34.

Iyer, Pico, "Fresh Voices above the Noisy Din: New Works by Four Chinese-American Writers Splendidly Illustrate the Frustrations, Humor, and Eternal Wonder of the Immigrant's Life," in *Time*, June 3, 1991, p. 67.

Law-Yone, Wendy, Review of *The Kitchen God's Wife*, in *Washington Post Book World*, June 16, 1991, pp. 1–2.

Lehmann-Haupt, Christopher, "Books of the Times: Mother and Daughter, Each with Her Secret," in *New York Times Book Review*, June 20, 1991.

Solomon, Charles, Review of *The Kitchen God's Wife*, in *Los Angeles Times Book Review*, July 5, 1992, p. 10.

Yglesias, Helen, Review of *The Kitchen God's Wife*, in *Women's Review of Books*, September 1991, pp. 1, 3–4.

Further Reading

Bloom, Harold, ed., *Amy Tan*, Chelsea House, 2000.
Respected literary critic, Harold Bloom, provides an overview of Tan's life and her work in and impact on contemporary American literature.

Ching, Julia, *Chinese Religions*, Orbis Books, 1993.
Ching presents the history and development of Chinese religious thought in three parts: indigenous religions, foreign religions, and syncretism. The author presents insightful comparisons rather than a cursory handling of each belief system.

Fitzgerald, Penelope, "Luck Dispensers," in *London Review of Books*, Vol. 13, No. 13, July 11, 1991, p. 19.
In this review of Tan's novel, Fitzgerald discusses the story of the Kitchen God's wife and states that the book's strength comes from its depiction of the attitudes of the older Chinese-American generation.

Huntley, E. D., *Amy Tan: A Critical Companion*, Greenwood Press, 1998.
Huntley discusses *The Joy Luck Club*, *The Kitchen God's Wife*, and *The Hundred Secret Senses*, commenting on Tan's expert use of setting, themes, plot structure, characterization, and literary techniques. This book is written by a literary scholar specifically for the high school English student.

Tung, May Pao-May, *Chinese Americans and Their Immigrant Parents: Conflict, Identity, and Values*, Haworth Press, 2000.
This book presents an analytical view of the struggles between Chinese Americans, who are profoundly affected by American culture, and their Chinese parents, who are shaped by their Chinese heritage.

Wong, Shawn, *Asian American Literature: A Brief Introduction and Anthology (HarperCollins Literary Mosaic)*, Addison-Wesley, 1995.
Wong offers a compilation of Asian-American literature divided into sections of Memoirs and Nonfiction, Fiction, Poetry, and Drama.

The Member of the Wedding

Carson McCullers

1946

Regarded by many critics as Carson McCullers's most accessible work, *The Member of the Wedding* is a sensitive portrayal of twelve-year-old Frankie Addams. McCullers was able to finish the novel with the help of a Guggenheim Fellowship, a National Institute of Arts and Letters grant, and several summers at Yaddo, a writers' colony in New York. Much of the material for the novel is autobiographical. The town in which Frankie lives is based on McCullers's hometown of Columbus, Georgia. McCullers's father, like Frankie's, was a jeweler, and her family had employed African-American servants in her childhood home. Many of Frankie's feelings of awkwardness are drawn from McCullers's own memories of what it was like to be twelve years old. She, like Frankie, felt like a gangly misfit whose tomboyish ways made it difficult to fit in with boys or girls her age.

At the urging of her friend Tennessee Williams, McCullers's adapted the novel into a play. The play was highly successful, opening on Broadway in 1950 and lasting for fourteen months and 501 performances. In addition, the play received a number of prestigious awards. Despite the popular and critical success of the play, most critics agree that some of the insight into the characters is lost on the stage. It is just such insights, along with believable characters, a smooth writing style, and an unsentimental tone that continue to impress readers and critics alike.

Author Biography

Carson McCullers was born Lula Carson Smith on February 19, 1917, in Columbus, Georgia. McCullers's mother had early intuitions that her daughter was destined for greatness. Consequently, as a child, McCullers was lavished with attention by her mother to the exclusion of her two other siblings. Her musical ability became apparent at an early age, and when she graduated from high school, she was sent to the prestigious Juilliard School of Music in New York City. Because her family could not afford such an expensive school, they sold a family heirloom ring to pay the tuition. Before she enrolled, however, McCullers's roommate lost all of their money, and McCullers was forced to take odd jobs instead of attending Juilliard. She enrolled in writing classes at Columbia and New York University where her ability to write compelling fiction developed.

In 1936, McCullers met an army corporal named James Reeves McCullers. They married the following year, beginning a tumultuous marriage. Her writing career took off in 1939 with the publication of her critically acclaimed novel *The Heart Is a Lonely Hunter.* That same year, McCullers began writing *The Member of the Wedding,* a novel she would work on for seven years. Her other works include *The Ballad of the Sad Cafe* and *Reflections in a Golden Eye.*

McCullers and her husband separated and reconciled numerous times. In addition, the mid-1940s brought the beginning of McCullers's health problems, including recurrent influenza and pleurisy. Her failing health did not stop the couple from traveling extensively around Europe, however, until she suffered a debilitating stroke at the age of thirty. In 1948, she attempted suicide. By 1953, when her husband tried to talk her into a double suicide, she was no longer interested in taking her life so she left him in France to return home. Soon after, he killed himself.

Unable to write much in the last years of her life because of further strokes, McCullers became quite eccentric, opting to wear white almost constantly. She often gave interviews wearing white nightgowns and tennis shoes. She underwent surgeries to repair damage from strokes, a heart attack, and a broken hip, and she had a cancerous breast removed. On August 15, 1967, McCullers suffered from a massive brain hemorrhage and fell into a forty-seven-day coma. She died on September 28

Carson McCullers

and is buried beside her mother in Oak Hill Cemetery in Nyack, New York.

Plot Summary

Part One

Frankie Addams is an awkward twelve-year-old tomboy who is out of school for the summer. She lives with her widower father (her mother died in childbirth) and an African-American housekeeper named Berenice. Her father, who is seldom home, runs a successful jewelry store in the small mill town where they live. Berenice, as a result, is closer to a parental figure for Frankie than is her father. Frankie's six-year-old cousin, John Henry, often spends the days and nights with Frankie. Frankie feels like a misfit because she is so tall, has cropped hair, and is no longer included in the group of slightly older neighborhood girls. At the same time, she is at a point in her adolescence where she begins struggling with her identity and self-esteem.

Frankie reads about the events of World War II and imagines the adventures of soldiers all over the world. She wants to be a part of it because she desperately wants to be a part of something she can easily define. Her brother, Jarvis, is stationed in

Alaska in the army. When he returns home briefly to announce his upcoming wedding, Frankie is elated. Through a combination of wishful thinking and youthful naiveté, she becomes convinced that she will go with her brother and his bride on their honeymoon, then live with them wherever they go afterward. Believing that she has solved the problem of not belonging anywhere, she begins planning for her new life.

Part Two

The day before the wedding, Frankie puts on her pink dress, stockings, lipstick, and perfume and goes into town. Instead of Frankie, she starts calling herself F. Jasmine. She feels the need to see all the familiar sights for the last time, and along the way she tells everyone who will listen about her plans to leave the town and live with her brother. When she meets a red-haired soldier, he invites her to the Blue Moon, a local bar and hotel. He does not seem to realize how young she is, and he buys her a beer. As she is leaving, he asks her for a date that night, and she hesitantly agrees. Before returning home, she stops to buy a dress to wear to the wedding after visiting her father in his jewelry store.

Frankie learns that her Uncle Charles has died but is relieved that this will not change her family's plans to attend the wedding the next day. Later, she and Berenice and John Henry sit at the table eating dinner and playing cards, and they begin talking about Berenice's life, love, and the pains of growing older. Frankie decides to visit Berenice's mother, Big Mama, who is a fortune-teller, and then goes to meet the soldier. When he sees her, he suggests that they go up to his room. Frankie is uneasy but agrees. When the soldier makes advances toward her, she hits him over the head with a glass pitcher and escapes. When she arrives home, she says nothing of the incident and is sent to bed. The family must rise early the next morning to catch a bus to the wedding.

Part Three

The day of the wedding goes by in a blur for Frankie. She never has a chance to talk to her brother or to his bride about her desire to go with them, and when she gets in the honeymoon car after the wedding, her father pulls her out. Frankie screams after the car, "Take me! Take me!" When she gets home, Frankie makes a half-hearted attempt to run away, but her father finds her.

A year later, Frankie (who is now called Frances) is helping her family prepare to move to another house. Berenice will not be going with them, as she has decided to marry her suitor, T. T.; and John Henry has died of meningitis. Frankie is now more mature, however, and is able to handle unexpected changes. She has a new friend named Mary, a girl her own age with similar interests.

Characters

Frances Addams

Frances, who is most often referred to as Frankie, is the main character and a twelve-year-old tomboy who feels that she does not belong anywhere. She is tall for her age and feels awkward and ugly. She keeps her hair short, wears boyish clothes, and enjoys knife-throwing.

Out of school for the summer, she spends most of her time at home with Berenice and John Henry. She is restless and bored with her hometown, and she dreams of a more exciting life. Wanting desperately to be a part of something, she wishes she could go fight in the war. When Frankie learns that her brother, who is in the army, is getting married, she sees the solution to her problems. She imagines that she will accompany the couple on their honeymoon and then live with them wherever they go afterward. Her limited experience of the world prevents her from understanding how inappropriate and impractical her plan is.

Frankie's relationships are atypical of those of a girl her age. Her relationship with Berenice is loving, but the two often argue. Even though Berenice is a mother figure, Frankie knows that she is hired help, which ultimately gives Frankie the upper hand. Her relationship with John Henry is superficial because of the difference in their ages. They are playmates, and she calls on him when she does not want to be alone. Her lack of genuine feeling for him is evident when he dies. She is surprised but not devastated. Frankie and her father have a friendly relationship, but they do not share a deep parent-child bond. It is obvious that her father does not discuss important issues such as sex, death, and love with her. Not until the end of the story, when Frankie begins a friendship with Mary, does Frankie enjoy a "normal" friendship.

Jarvis Addams

Jarvis is Frankie's older brother. He is described as blond and handsome. Jarvis is in the army and is stationed in Alaska but comes home briefly to announce his upcoming wedding. Jarvis is not a fully developed character; he is simply the vehicle in Frankie's fantasy about escaping her hometown.

Royal Quincy Addams

Royal Quincy Addams is Frankie's father. He owns a successful jewelry store in town and earns a middle-class living for himself and Frankie. He is seldom home, and, although a congenial man, he does not share a deep bond with Frankie. When Frankie attempts to go with the bride and groom by getting in the wedding car, it is Mr. Addams who pulls her out of the car.

Big Mama

Big Mama is Berenice's elderly mother. Bedridden since she hurt her back many years ago, she is said to have developed "second sight." People often come to her to have their fortunes told, and Frankie decides to visit her. Big Mama (who is actually a slight woman) tells Frankie that she will marry a light-haired, blue-eyed boy and that there is a trip in her near future. Frankie is upset to hear Big Mama say that this trip (which Frankie assumes means the trip to the wedding the next day) will end with Frankie back in her hometown.

Berenice Sadie Brown

Berenice has been the Addams' African-American cook for most of Frankie's life. Her skin is very dark, and she is short and broad. She wears her hair in greased plaits and has a glass eye that is bright blue. Because Frankie's mother is dead, Berenice develops a somewhat motherly relationship with the girl. She offers advice, tells stories, and puts up with Frankie's moodiness although her position as a servant prevents her from being much of a disciplinarian.

Berenice is open and reacts to questions and situations with homespun wisdom. She has been married four times (first when she was only thirteen), but she never loses her belief in love. Her first husband, Ludie Freedman, was the love of her life. When he died, she was devastated, and each of her subsequent marriages was an attempt to reclaim the happiness she once enjoyed with Ludie. Instead, she ended up in destructive relationships with abusive and alcoholic men, the last of whom gouged out her eye. At the time of the story, she is not married, although T. T. Williams is interested in her.

In a conversation with Frankie and John Henry, Berenice reveals how difficult it is to be an African-American woman of the time. She explains

Media Adaptations

- At the encouragement of Tennessee Williams, McCullers adapted *The Member of the Wedding* for the stage. The play opened on Broadway in 1950 and was very successful. It ran for fourteen months and over five hundred performances. For this play, McCullers won the New York Drama Critics Circle Award, the Donaldson Award for Best Drama of the Year, and the Gold Medal of the Theatre Club.

- A film adaptation was made in 1952. Produced by Columbia Pictures, it earned a 1953 Academy Award nomination for best actress for Julie Harris (who played Frankie). Brandon de Wilde (who played John Henry) won a 1953 Special Golden Globe for best juvenile actor.

- Two television movies have been based on the novel. A 1982 version was performed on "NBC Live Theater," and, in 1997, Hallmark Home Entertainment produced a television movie starring Anna Paquin as Frankie and Alfre Woodard as Berenice.

- In 1987, DH Audio released an audio adaptation with Tammy Grimes as the reader.

to the children that her options are limited and that she is constantly judged by her appearance. She dreams of a world in which everyone is the same color, and there is no war. This sense of optimism may be the reason why, in the end, she agrees to marry T. T. Williams.

Honey Camden Brown

Honey is Berenice's foster brother, who lives with Big Mama. When the army would not accept him, he took a job in a gravel pit until he suffered an internal injury; now he does not work. He is a stylish dresser who is intelligent and well spoken when he chooses to be. Because of his light skin, Frankie tells him he should go to Cuba and live there (apparently because he would face less prejudice there since he looks like most Cubans). Perhaps because he is unable to find a suitable place in the community, he is a rebel who is disrespectful. He eventually goes to jail when he threatens his marijuana dealer.

Uncle Charles

Uncle Charles is Frankie's uncle, who dies just before the wedding. Frankie remembers visiting him after he fell ill, and the sight of the sickly man frightened her. When he dies, Frankie is relieved that his death will not interfere with the wedding plans.

Frankie

See Frances Addams.

Janice

Janice is Jarvis's bride. She is a petite brunette, whom Frankie thinks is beautiful. On the day of the wedding, Janice tells Frankie how delighted she is to have a younger sister.

Mary Littlejohn

Introduced at the end of the book, Mary is Frankie's new best friend. They meet at a raffle and become instant friends. Mary has brown eyes and long blonde braids, and she loves art and poetry.

The Red-Haired Soldier

Frankie meets the red-haired soldier when she is dressed up in her pink dress and telling everyone in town about her plans to leave with her brother and his bride. The soldier is stationed nearby and is on a three-day pass. He does not seem to realize how young Frankie is; he may be drunk when Frankie first meets him, and it is dark the second time. He buys Frankie a beer and asks for a date. When Frankie meets him for the date, he asks her up to his room and makes advances. Confused and frightened, Frankie hits him over the head with a glass pitcher and escapes.

John Henry West

John Henry is Frankie's six-year-old cousin. He lives nearby and spends lots of time with Frankie and Berenice. He wears gold-rimmed glasses and a small lead donkey around his neck. John Henry is small yet unusually mature and sensitive for his age and is somewhat effeminate. He enjoys cooking with Berenice, and he likes to dress up in Frankie's costume dresses and heels. While most boys his age are playing in the dirt and roughhousing, John Henry is content to play cards or draw pictures.

In the last pages of the book (during the year that has passed unnarrated near the end of the book), McCullers explains that John Henry had a terrible headache one day. Neither Berenice nor Frankie thought much of it, but within ten days John Henry is dead of meningitis. His last days are described as having been full of suffering.

The character of John Henry, along with the character of Dill in *To Kill a Mockingbird,* has been the subject of some interesting speculation. Some critics and scholars suspect that both characters are based on the author Truman Capote as a child.

T. T. Williams

T. T. is Berenice's current suitor, a large man who is older than she is. He runs a successful restaurant and is a good man, but Berenice says he does not make her "shiver." He is polite and friendly, and in the end Berenice agrees to marry him.

Themes

Identity and Self

Twelve-year-old Frankie is entering the phase of her adolescence in which she undergoes dramatic changes and begins seriously considering who she is as a person and who she will become. McCullers describes Frankie's unrest in part one, writing:

> Very early in the morning she would sometimes go out into the yard and stand for a long time looking at the sunrise sky. And it was as though a question came into her heart, and the sky did not answer. Things she had never noticed much before began to hurt her: home lights watched from the evening sidewalks, an unknown voice in the alley. She would stare at the lights and listen to the voice, and something inside her stiffened and waited. But the lights would darken, the voice fall silent, and though she waited, that was all. She was afraid of these things that made her suddenly wonder who she was, and what she was going to be in the world, and why she was standing at that minute, seeing a light, or listening or staring up at the sky: alone.

Frankie is exceptionally tall for her age, which makes her feel gawky and clumsy. She is a tomboy who wears boyish clothes and has shortly cropped hair, and when she looks at herself in the mirror, she sees only ugliness. Her self-esteem is low, as indicated in the following excerpt from part one:

> This was the summer when Frankie was sick and tired of being Frankie. She hated herself, and had become a loafer and a big no-good who hung around the summer kitchen: dirty and greedy and mean and sad.

No longer interested in many of the activities that once entertained her, Frankie finds herself torn between the worlds of childhood and adulthood. As the story progresses, the reader can see how her sense of identity changes each time she changes her name. In the beginning, she is Frankie, which suits her tomboy identity. When she decides to join her brother and his bride, she decides to be F. Jasmine so that her name (Jasmine) will sound more like their names, Jarvis and Janice. She attempts to identify herself with them by changing her name. By the end, however, she has decided to be called Frances, her given name. This choice indicates her coming to terms with herself as a maturing young woman who can determine her own identity within the parameters of social expectations.

The Need to Belong

McCullers's theme of belonging is the other side of her theme of identity. While identity asks the question, "Who am I as an individual?" the need to belong asks the question, "Who am I in relation to others?" From the first paragraph, McCullers makes this theme clear:

> This was the summer when for a long time she had not been a member. She belonged to no club and was a member of nothing in the world. Frankie had become an unjoined person who hung around in doorways, and she was afraid.

She is not welcome in the summer club formed by a group of neighborhood girls who are a few years older. Although she was a sort of junior member of the group in the past, the older girls are no longer interested in having Frankie around them. In addition, she lacks the sense of family that often anchors adolescents as they navigate these troubling years. The closest thing she has to a family unit is the trio formed by herself, Berenice, and John Henry.

Frankie is disappointed that she cannot be a part of the war in some way. McCullers writes, "She wanted to be a boy and go to war as a Marine." Because of her age and gender, she cannot join the military. She plans to donate blood so that her blood will run in the veins of soldiers all over the world. By doing this, she thinks, she will feel like a part of the war. When the Red Cross refuses to take her blood because of her young age, Frankie is disappointed and angry, and she generalizes her feelings to include the rest of the world that "seemed somehow separate from herself."

When Frankie hears that her brother plans to marry a local girl, she imagines herself as a member of the wedding and of their new family. In her mind, she aligns herself with the bride and groom at such an intimate level that she plans to accompany them on their honeymoon and then go with

Topics for Further Study

- Read what three major psychologists have to say about adolescence. Apply these theories to the character of Frankie to determine in what ways she fits the patterns suggested by psychologists and in what ways she is unusual.

- Research the role of African-American servants in white Southern households in the early-to mid-twentieth century. Create a class presentation to relate your findings and personal comments. Lead a discussion about the progress against discrimination made by African Americans in the latter half of the century.

- Compare the African-American characters in *The Member of the Wedding* with African-American characters in one of the following: *Gone with the Wind, Uncle Tom's Cabin, Huckleberry Finn,* or *To Kill a Mockingbird.*

- Music was an important part of McCullers's life, and she uses musical references and imagery throughout the novel. Imagine that you are a guest lecturer at a school for music, and your objective is to interest the students in literature. Prepare a lecture in which you use *The Member of the Wedding* to teach students how music and literature can complement each other. Be sure to demonstrate how an understanding of music gives insight into the book.

them wherever they live. She believes that everyone is part of a "we," and she declares that Jarvis and Janice are "the we of me." Her desperation to belong somewhere and her naiveté prevent her from understanding the inappropriateness and impracticality of her plan.

Style

Similes

Part of the appeal of McCullers's writing style is her use of unexpected similes. As a preadolescent, Frankie looks for new ways to understand familiar things and also reaches for ways to understand and express experiences and feelings that are new to her. In this situation, similes are a natural form of expression.

Frankie associates her longing to go somewhere interesting with what she imagines her brother's life is like. In part one, McCullers writes, "Frankie had not seen her brother for a long, long time, and his face had become masked and changing, like a face seen under water." Later, Frankie thinks about the people at the freak show, and the Fat Lady is described as having fat that "was like loose-powdered dough which she kept slapping and working with her hands." This is a highly visual simile that is drawn from Frankie's domestic experience, as the reader soon encounters a scene in which Berenice and John Henry are working with biscuit dough. Similarly, in part two, the hot afternoon air is described as "thick and sticky as hot syrup." The fragility of John Henry is expressed in a scene in which Frankie goes to visit him in the evening, and he is standing on his porch. McCullers writes, "John Henry was leaning against the banisters of his front porch, with a lighted window behind him, so that he looked like a little black paper doll on a piece of yellow paper." In each case, McCullers is demonstrating Frankie's ability to see familiar things in new ways although she is forced to reinterpret sights and feelings in terms of her limited experiences.

Symbolism

McCullers's flair for allegory is evident in *The Member of the Wedding*. Readers looking for symbolism find the text rich with symbolic elements. The backdrop of the war symbolizes Frankie's inner turmoil as she is forced to leave childhood behind and enter adulthood. In part one, McCullers explains:

> Frankie stood looking up and down the four walls of the room. She thought of the world, and it was fast and loose and turning, faster and looser and bigger than ever it had been before. The pictures of the War sprang out and clashed together in her mind. She saw bright flowered islands and a land by the northern sea with the gray waves on the shore. Bombed eyes and the shuffle of soldiers' feet. Tanks and a plane, wing broken, burning and downward-falling in a desert sky. The world was cracked by the loud battles and turning a thousand miles a minute.

Frankie reads about the war in the newspapers and applies her active imagination to the events of the war. She wants to somehow be a part of it and plans to donate lots of blood so that her blood will

be in soldiers all over the world. Frankie is too young, however, to realize that her preoccupation with the war is driven by her own uncertainty in how to handle the changes taking place in her and the unspoken expectations society places on her. She is unsettled, and her private pain is mirrored in the war efforts.

Frankie's closest relationships are with John Henry and Berenice, each of whom symbolizes an important aspect of the crossroads at which Frankie finds herself. John Henry is only six years old, yet he is her playmate. He represents the childhood simplicity she is uncomfortable leaving behind while Berenice represents the feminine wisdom and nurturing toward which Frankie feels she should be moving. Berenice is not an educated woman, rather her wisdom derives from life experience, something Frankie knows she lacks. Berenice's life experiences have been mostly difficult and painful, making Frankie less than enthusiastic about entering womanhood. At the same time, Berenice's unflagging optimism symbolizes hope for the future.

Historical Context

World War II

Although the exact date of the story is not given, the events described indicate that it takes place near the end of World War II. In part one, Berenice mentions to Frankie that she read that the French were driving the Germans out of Paris. The liberation of Paris took place on August 25, 1944. McCullers mentions that Frankie reads the war news as she thinks about the summer. Describing the summer, she writes, "It was the summer when Patton was chasing the Germans across France. And they were fighting, too, in Russia and Saipan." These references indicate the summer of 1944.

Jarvis, Frankie's brother, is in the army and is stationed in Alaska. In 1942, while the Battle of Midway waged in the South Pacific, the Japanese took control of two Aleutian Islands (in southwest Alaska). This victory was less strategic than it was psychological, as the Americans were terrified at the prospect of having the enemy on the continent. In 1943, the American military began a fifteen-month battle to reclaim the land, which they eventually won. There is also a reference to Jarvis and his bride going to Luxembourg, a formerly Nazi-occupied country. After the Allies freed Luxembourg in September of 1944, American military personnel were sent to aid in peacekeeping.

Compare & Contrast

- **1942:** In small towns, boys and girls amuse themselves by playing with friends and family members of about the same age. They often play outdoor games such as softball, tag, and hide-and-seek. Other common pastimes include performing skits; dressing up in silly outfits or grownups' clothing; exploring nearby trails, woods, or creeks; and setting up lemonade or snow-cone stands to make a little money.

  Today: In small towns and big cities alike, children and adolescents entertain themselves with television, videos, computers, video games, music, and reading.

- **1942:** Many middle-class white families employ African Americans as domestic help. Women are often housekeepers who also help with child rearing and thus become a part of the family dynamics. For many African-American women (like Berenice), this is their best opportunity for work. Men are employed less frequently but are sometimes paid to perform tasks such as household repairs, yard work, and wood chopping.

  Today: Only the wealthiest households employ servants, and they may be of any race. While many people hire maid services, the relationship is nothing at all like the relationships with live-in housekeepers of the past. African Americans have opportunities to work in all types of jobs, and the law protects their right to do so.

- **1942:** Adolescents in small- to medium-sized towns look forward to growing old enough to leave their hometowns and see what life is like in the larger world. Having grown up in communities where everyone knows them and they know everyone, they look forward to meeting new people and experiencing new things.

  Today: Adolescents in small- to medium-sized towns feel the same way adolescents in the past felt about their hometowns. The modern media make life outside small-town city limits seem glamorous and exciting, and the ability to communicate with people all over the world via the Internet intensifies the desire to see the world. In addition, bigger cities often offer more opportunities for advanced education, better careers, and higher pay. Among teenagers, it is considered very sophisticated to be bored and frustrated by their hometowns.

Because there is an army base near Frankie's hometown, she is accustomed to the sight of soldiers on leave. In part two, McCullers comments that when Frankie went into town during the summers, "she browsed the counters of the ten-cent store, or sat on the front row of the Palace show, or hung around her father's store, or stood on street corners watching soldiers." To Frankie, the presence of uniformed military men is a familiar sight. Her tendency to glamorize them, however, almost gets her into trouble when she goes to the red-haired soldier's room.

Southern Gothic

McCullers is among the writers associated with the southern gothic style of writing. This style features settings in the American South and char-

acters that are bizarre, grotesque, and outcast. Although the novels do not take place in drafty castles, mazes, and dark woods (settings tied with gothic literature), the same themes derived from these settings appear in southern gothic writing. These themes include isolation, confusion, and the search for meaning. McCullers' *The Heart Is a Lonely Hunter* and *Reflections in a Golden Eye* are especially known for representing this sub-genre because of their unusual casts of characters. Although *The Member of the Wedding* is less strongly associated with southern gothic writing, certain elements (such as Frankie's interest in the people in the freak show) fit this writing style. Some critics note that McCullers' work differs somewhat from the writing of other southern gothic authors in that she portrays her misfit characters with sensitivity

Julie Harris (left) as Frankie Addams, Ethel Waters as Berenice Sadie Brown, and Brandon de Wilde as John Henry in the Broadway adaptation of the novel

and compassion for their situations. She once said that spiritual isolation was at the center of her novels, and this theme, consistent with the southern gothic tradition, is apparent in *The Member of the Wedding.*

Other writers associated with southern gothic writing include Tennessee Williams, Flannery O'Connor, William Faulkner, Katherine Anne Porter, and Truman Capote.

Critical Overview

McCullers is ranked among the most respected writers in the southern tradition. She is often compared with William Faulkner, Flannery O'Connor, Eudora Welty, and Tennessee Williams. Today, critics continue to revisit her few novels as important writings. Critics consistently praise *The Heart Is a Lonely Hunter, The Ballad of the Sad Cafe,* and *The Member of the Wedding* as her best works.

While most critics praise *The Member of the Wedding,* others claim that McCullers ends the story with plot developments that are too convenient. Louis D. Rubin Jr. of the *Virginia Quarterly*

Review finds Frankie's sudden acceptance of womanhood unrealistic and John Henry's death gratuitous and contrived. Edmund Wilson of the *New Yorker* writes in 1946 that the book was "utterly pointless" and lacked a sense of drama. It was this review that so incensed McCullers that she was inclined to take Tennessee Williams's advice and adapt the novel as a play.

Lawrence Graver, in *American Writers,* explores the structure of *The Member of the Wedding.* He observes that the novel is divided into three parts, a structure that calls attention to the rhythm of the novel. He explains,

> In Mrs. McCullers' book, the rhythm. . . follows the familiar journey of adolescent initiation: the stirrings of dissatisfaction, jubilant hope founded on misplaced idealism, and disillusionment accompanied by a new wisdom about the limits of human life.

Other critics have likened this three-part structure to that of a sonata, a type of musical piece that often has three parts. Based on biographical information about McCullers, these commentators believe that in *The Member of the Wedding* the author bridges her passion for music with her passion for writing.

The character of Frankie continues to be scrutinized as a portrayal of adolescent angst in the South. Judith Everson, in *Dictionary of Literary Biography, Volume 173: American Novelists Since World War II,* observes that Frankie is "an adolescent 'everyman' in her awkward, agonized movement toward maturation. Yet at the same time, as feminist critics remind readers, she bears the special burden of girlhood, which complicates her transition to adult status." In this respect especially, the book is often compared to *The Heart Is a Lonely Hunter,* a book that features another adolescent tomboy, Mick Kelly. According to Louise Westling of *Southern Humanities Review,* both characters dramatize "the crisis of identity which faces ambitious girls as they leave childhood and stumble into an understanding of what the world expects them to become."

Rubin writes that he finds the character of Frankie the more realistic of the two. He explains, "Frankie Addams is the most appealing of Mrs. McCullers' people; I like her better than Mick Kelly because she is less strident—less written, I think, to a thesis." He adds that "her struggles with pre-adolescence are entirely convincing and wondrously done—up to a point." Rubin believes that when Frankie and Berenice have their "surrealistic, mystic visions of pain and misery" after the piano tuner begins working, Frankie's character loses her realism. He maintains that, at this point, the novel "drops off the deep end into distortion for the sake of distortion."

Most critics point to *The Member of the Wedding* as McCullers's most realistic and most accessible novel. The book is praised for its writing style, depth, tone, and insight. Graver declares, "The novel is one of the few sentimental comedies to escape the charge of being maudlin; stylistically, it is the freshest and most inventive of her novels and stories." A contributor to *Feminist Writers* explains the importance of the novel by praising McCullers for her "analysis of maturation, race, and gender in *The Member of the Wedding,* perhaps her most perfect novel. . . In *The Member of the Wedding,* McCullers brings to the forefront a world too often seen as unimportant—a black woman, a clumsy, masculine girl, and a young, feminine boy." In a 1946 article, George Dangerfield of *Saturday Review of Literature* comments on the book's "utmost delicacy and balance." In the *New York Times,* Isa Kapp expresses her delight in McCullers's language, citing its "freshness, quaintness, and gentleness." Fifteen years after the novel's publication, Rumer Godden, in *New York Herald Tribune Books,* calls it a masterpiece, adding that the book has retained its appeal and become "universally popular."

Criticism

Jennifer Bussey

Bussey holds a master's degree in interdisciplinary studies and a bachelor's degree in English literature. She is an independent writer specializing in literature. In the following essay, she reviews six of the symbolic elements used by McCullers in her novel.

Carson McCullers's writing is often analyzed in terms of its symbolic content. In *The Member of the Wedding,* she relates an accessible story that is rich with symbolism, which gives the novel greater depth. Symbolic uses of colors, seasons, the family kitchen, the Frankie-Berenice-John Henry triad, names, and music give the reader greater insight into Frankie's character. McCullers uses these symbolic elements in such a way that they do not intrude upon the story or seem superimposed on the narrative; rather, they flow naturally from the story while encouraging the reader to investigate them further.

Throughout *The Member of the Wedding,* McCullers uses colors to describe sights, sounds, and feelings. Certain colors are used with greater frequency than others, however, and these colors are significant in the context of Frankie's perceptions. In part one, green is used to describe summer, trees, a dream, a distant island, moths, vines, and spring sweetness. The first line of the book reads, "It happened that green and crazy summer when Frankie was twelve years old." The color green comes to represent Frankie's experience of this awkward and uncomfortable summer; and she sees green everywhere. Green represents her dissatisfaction and her feelings of being stuck. She marvels at the pale green moths, which have the ability to go anywhere they like, yet continue to return to the same window every night.

In part two and to a lesser degree in part three, the color blue becomes significant. It describes windows, Frankie's pajamas, her father's shirt, evenings, the sky, Berenice's cigarette smoke, fields, and Berenice's wedding outfit. Also, the name of the bar where she meets with the red-haired soldier is the Blue Moon, and it is filled with blue neon lights. Blue represents Frankie's uneasy

> Each symbol—colors, seasons, the kitchen, the Frankie-Berenice-John Henry triad, names, and music—gives the reader another pathway of insight into Frankie's confused psyche."

awareness that she is growing older. While it is familiar (pajamas, her father's shirt, the sky), it also is associated with new experiences (the bar, the conversation she has with Berenice when Berenice has a cigarette). Blue is a color of transition and of adulthood.

Finally, the color gray appears frequently in parts two and three. Besides Frankie's eyes, all of the following are gray: the ocean, Frankie's father's pants, dawn, sidewalks, streets, the kitchen, the curtain in her father's store, John Henry's finger, the air, and John Henry's presence in the kitchen after his death. Gray is drab and boring, which is how Frankie sees her hometown and her life in it. It is similar to green in that it represents the familiar trappings of her daily existence, but it has a more ethereal quality because it describes the distant ocean, the air, and John Henry's ghostly presence. Gray represents what Frankie leaves behind. At the end of the book, she is more likely to see the ocean as blue, the dawn in glowing colors, and the air as a refreshing, life-giving color.

McCullers's use of seasonal symbolism is unusual in that it reverses the usual portrayals of summer and winter. Frankie strongly dislikes summer and is drawn to the winter. She identifies the summer as the period in her life when she is most dissatisfied and confused. She calls it "crazy" and finds it stifling and restricting while most children find the summer liberating and fun. Frankie dreams about going to the wedding at Winter Hill and when she describes her version of a perfect world, she says she would change the seasons, "leaving out summer altogether, and adding much snow."

Winter is normally associated with the final years of a person's life while summer represents youth and vitality. Here, however, Frankie is disgusted with summer because of her current unrest and frustration while winter seems distant and

pleasant. Winter symbolizes where Frankie wants to go and who she wants to be, but her lack of reference to autumn suggests that she is uncertain how to get there from where she is.

Much of the book takes place in the Addams' small, square kitchen, which represents safety and security. The kitchen is normally the warmest, coziest part of a home. It is not only where Frankie eats meals with Berenice and John Henry, but it is also where they sit at the table and talk and play cards. Berenice is Frankie's maternal figure, and John Henry is her childish, non-threatening playmate. When she ventures out into town, she returns to the kitchen to talk to her "family." When she decides to go live with her brother, she tells of her plans while she is in the kitchen. The lengthy scene in which she and Berenice talk about life and love takes place in the kitchen, and at the end of this scene, Frankie climbs up into Berenice's lap for comfort. At the end of the novel, Frankie has established her own footing as she enters her teenage years, and she is able to leave the kitchen (and Berenice and John Henry) in her past.

The characters of Berenice and John Henry are symbolic as well. John Henry is six years old and relatively carefree so he represents childhood. Berenice is world-wise, having been married four times and lived with oppression. Still, she remains optimistic about the future, so she represents Frankie's future as a worldly woman with a life of possibilities before her. Frankie is struggling with the precarious transition from childhood to adulthood so her relationships with John Henry and Berenice are important. They represent the two stages of life she must bridge. In the end, she must let go of Berenice when she and her father move because Berenice has decided to marry T. T. Williams and get on with her own life. Frankie has also lost John Henry to meningitis. While many readers find his death unexpected, his passing is highly symbolic of the passing of Frankie's childhood years. Standing in the kitchen, she feels that she can sense his presence. She will not forget her childhood years, but she realizes that they are in her past.

As Frankie moves gradually toward accepting her own maturation, she changes her name twice. McCullers uses the words of Berenice to call attention to the importance of names: "Because things accumulate around your name. You have a name and one thing after another happens to you, and you behave in various ways and do things, so that soon the name begins to have a meaning."

First, she is Frankie, the gawky tomboy who likes to throw knives and play with her teepee. When she puts on her pink dress to go into town, she becomes F. Jasmine. The name Jasmine sounds better with Jarvis and Janice, her brother and his bride, with whom she plans to live. It also sounds more romantic and mature. When she is prevented from living with her brother, she comes to accept a more realistic view of herself and her life. At this point, she goes by Frances, her given name. It is a more feminine name than Frankie, and it is her real name; the decision to use it signifies her acceptance that she must be herself to be comfortable in the world, even if she is still in the process of exploring her identity.

Music figures prominently throughout the story, and its use is symbolic of Frankie's inner turmoil. Visiting John Henry one evening, she overhears someone playing blues on a horn. She is swept up in the music and is disturbed when the music suddenly stops. She tells John Henry that it will resume in a minute, but it never does. When she and Berenice and John Henry are talking in the kitchen, Frankie is torn apart by the incomplete scales of someone tuning a piano in a nearby house. The tuner keeps playing seven notes but never the eighth, and often strikes a single note several times. The cacophony of this is too much for Frankie to bear.

Unfinished music disturbs Frankie deeply because it seems to confirm her sense that the world is unpredictable and that is does not always finish things on its own. It mirrors the feelings she is unable to understand or express. The scene with the piano tuner comes the evening before the wedding and so foreshadows the ultimate incompleteness of Frankie's plans to leave home. Such musical references symbolize the confusion and chaos Frankie associates with the world to which she feels she does not belong.

In other instances, however, music has the ability to calm and reassure her. Describing the summertime interactions of Frankie, Berenice, and John Henry, McCullers writes in part two,

> Often in the dark, that August, they would all at once begin to sing a Christmas carol, or a song like the 'Slitbelly Blues.' Sometimes they knew in advance what they would sing, and they would agree on the tune among themselves. Or again, they would disagree and start off on three different songs at once, until at last the tunes began to merge and they sang a special music that the three of them made together.

Here, music clearly represents order and comfort for Frankie because even when she and her closest companions disagree, music enables them to harmonize.

McCullers's creation of the character of Frankie is thorough and artful. Not only does she present straightforward experiences, feelings, and reactions, but she also deepens her main character with her skillful use of symbolism. Each symbol—colors, seasons, the kitchen, the Frankie-Berenice-John Henry triad, names, and music—gives the reader another pathway of insight into Frankie's confused psyche. In the end, the reader not only understands the character better but also has a better idea of who she will become, which is what Frankie seeks to know herself. Further, a deeper understanding of Frankie as a typical angst-ridden adolescent enables the reader to better understand the human experience in general.

Source: Jennifer Bussey, Critical Essay on *The Member of the Wedding,* in *Novels for Students,* The Gale Group, 2002.

Barbara A. White

In the following essay, White interprets The Member of the Wedding *within the contexts of gender and initiation into adolescence.*

Carson McCullers's *The Member of the Wedding* (1946) takes place in a small southern town where the protagonist, Frankie Addams, lives with her father. During the hot August of the novel Frankie spends her time in the Addamses' kitchen with the black cook, Berenice, and her six-year-old cousin, John Henry. She becomes enchanted with her brother's approaching wedding, decides to join the wedding and the honeymoon, and is disillusioned when her plan fails.

Although Frankie is only "twelve and five-sixths years old," there is much about her which will immediately seem familiar. She makes her appearance dressed as a boy, though she also douses herself with Sweet Serenade perfume; she hesitates on the threshold of the kitchen, being "an unjoined person who hung around in doorways." In the first few pages of the novel we learn that Frankie fears the future and resists even the knowledge of sex, which she calls "nasty lies about married people." Her hometown might just as well be North Dormer or Buena Vista, for Frankie wants out: "I've been ready to leave this town so long. . . . I wish I had a hundred dollars and could just light out and never see this town again."

In light of Frankie's resemblance to her predecessors in the novel of adolescence, it is surprising that a well-read critic like Edmund Wilson

> This decision which confronts her, 'the decision to be a woman at all,' accounts in large part for Frankie's fear and forms a major thematic concern of *The Member of the Wedding.*

could not determine what the novel is about. Wilson, in a review which infuriated McCullers, declared that "the whole story seems utterly pointless." McCullers had the same problem when she tried to market her dramatic version of *Member:* "Few [producers] seemed to know what the play was really about." Subsequent readers have turned to her other works in attempt to explain *Member.* Since one of McCullers's continuing themes is spiritual isolation, most critics interpret Frankie's fear of the future as the universal fear of separate identity and her attempt to join her brother's wedding as representative of all people's struggle to overcome their final separateness from other humans. Thus Frankie becomes a "symbol of spiritual loneliness."

Alternatively, Frankie is thought to symbolize the grotesqueness of the human condition. If Carson McCullers writes about isolation, she also includes in her novels a large number of "freaks": deaf-mutes, alcoholics, idiots, hunch-backed dwarves, etc. Frankie, having seen such beings as the Giant, the Pin Head, and the Alligator Boy at the fair, worries that she herself may become a freak; she calculates that if she continues growing at her present rate she will be over nine feet tall. Some readers have taken Frankie's fear literally and regarded *Member* as another examination by McCullers of the "freakish and perverse." Frankie becomes a "little monster" illustrating the general wretchedness of humanity.

Neither the "freak" nor the "spiritual isolation" approach turns out to be helpful in interpreting *The Member of the Wedding.* It is difficult to understand just what is "freakish" about Frankie; if she occasionally lies and steals and dresses up in garish costumes, so does Huckleberry Finn, nobody's idea of a freak. Frankie makes a more promising symbol of spiritual isolation, but isolation is only

one theme of *Member* and does not in itself allow us to account for the rich detail of the novel. The eagerness of critics to make her symbolic suggests some anxiety over the subject of female adolescence. To some extent we can see this anxiety operating in critical reaction to Wharton's *Summer* and Suckow's fiction. *Summer* was thought to be about New England life or Lawyer Royall, anything but a girl growing up; Suckow's novels were labelled too domestic and too "intrinsically feminine." But *Summer* and Suckow could easily be ignored—*Summer* relegated to the position of a "minor" novel in Wharton's oeuvre and Suckow dismissed altogether. *The Member of the Wedding,* as the long-awaited novel of a young "genius," invited more extensive critical response. Interestingly, the major part of this response has been barely concealed disappointment at the subject of McCullers's novel, a feeling that it deals with only "a narrow corner of human existence." Although, as I noted in my preface, male initiation is considered a significant subject for novelists to treat, female initiation is not perceived as equally "universal." Thus most critics have tried to make *Member* about something other than female adolescence, such as isolation or freakdom; they have avoided any discussion of the gender of the protagonist.

Not surprisingly, it was Leslie Fiedler who introduced the question of gender when he characterized Frankie as one of McCullers's "boy-girls," her "transvestite Huckleberry Finns." Once we have seen how McCullers portrays Frankie's adolescence, I will return to criticism of *The Member of the Wedding* and show how Fiedler also set a precedent in sexist interpretation of McCullers's "boy-girls," whereby her literary reputation is disparaged; for now the point is that Frankie's gender has at least been admitted as relevant. Taking his cue from Fiedler, Chester Eisinger says:

> The adolescent girl, in Mrs. McCullers's fiction, has the problem not only of sex awareness but of sex determination. It is not the responsibility of womanhood that she reluctantly must take up but the decision to be a woman at all that she must make. She is, then sexless, hovering between the two sexes.

This decision which confronts her, "the decision to be a woman at all," accounts in large part for Frankie's fear and forms a major thematic concern of *The Member of the Wedding.* Eisinger's term "sexless" has no meaning, since Frankie's "sex determination" was made at birth; however, she is "hovering between the two sexes" in the sense that she is a girl who does not want to relinquish the privileges of boys. Like Ruth Suckow's heroines,

Frankie exists in a divided state: while she hesitates to stay in childhood, she cannot fulfill her desire to be "grown-up" without accepting her identity as female, and she already suspects that her gender will be confining. Frankie thus vacillates between striving for adult status and resisting it.

Frankie's reluctance to remain a child is shown in her outrage at being given a doll by her brother Jarvis and his fiancée. She also resents being addressed as a child and peppers her own language with such grown-up phrases as "sick unto death" and "irony of fate." The most obvious sign of Frankie's projected change of identity from child to adult is her revision of her name from "Frankie" to "F. Jasmine." While "Frankie" is a child's name, "F. Jasmine" sounds older. Frankie chooses "Jasmine" partly because the initial "Ja" matches the "Ja" of Jarvis and Janice, but "Jasmine," associated with sweet fragrance and pale yellow flowers, has obvious, romantic, "feminine" connotations. Growing up necessitates shedding a "masculine" name, clothing, and activities for "feminine" ones.

In many ways Frankie wants to make this change. When she becomes F. Jasmine she vows to give up being "rough and greedy." Most important, she attempts to change her appearance. Apart from her name, Frankie's most obvious "tomboy" badges are her crewcut and her typical costume of shorts, undervest, and cowboy hat. As F. Jasmine she wears a pink organdy dress, heavy lipstick, and Sweet Serenade perfume. She cannot alter her hair style immediately but she knows what women "should" look like; "I ought to have long bright yellow hair," Frankie thinks.

Frankie's avatar, Mick Kelly of McCullers's *The Heart Is a Lonely Hunter* (1940), undergoes the same transformation. At first Mick resists her older sisters when they try to make her stop wearing "those silly boys' clothes." In a passage reminiscent of Jo March's pulling off her hair net, she exclaims:

> "I wear shorts because I don't want to wear your old hand-me-downs. I don't want to be like either of you and I don't want to look like either of you. And I won't. That's why I wear shorts. I'd rather be a boy any day."

But eventually Mick practices dressing up in her older sisters' evening gowns. She decides she is too old to wear shorts and switches permanently to skirts.

Both Mick's and Frankie's attempts to imitate the dress of adult women are confused and naive. The pleats and hem of Mick's skirt have come out,

What Do I Read Next?

- Noted literary scholar Harold Bloom and William Golding compiled *Carson McCullers (Modern Critical Views)* (1986) to provide a wide range of critical viewpoints for students of McCullers's work. In addition to considering her career as a whole, the authors comment on individual works.

- In the Pulitzer Prize-winning novel *To Kill a Mockingbird* (1960), Harper Lee tells the story of eight-year-old Scout and her older brother Jem growing up in the South during the Depression. Their attorney father takes an unpopular stance when he agrees to represent an African-American man accused of raping a poor white woman.

- McCullers's critically acclaimed *The Heart Is a Lonely Hunter* (1940) is the story of John Singer, a deaf-mute living in a southern mill town in the 1930s. The novel explores themes of loneliness, morality, and intolerance as it presents the lives of five characters.

- Tennessee Williams's play *The Glass Menagerie* (1944) tells the story of the members of a southern family who are facing their individual problems along with the problems of modern life.

and to other characters in the novel she still looks as much like a boy as a girl. For her brother's wedding Frankie buys a cheap orange satin evening dress and silver slippers, revealing that she does not yet understand society's division of women into "nice" (pink organdy) and "not nice" (orange satin). Furthermore, as Berenice points out, a woman's evening dress and the brown crust on Frankie's elbows do not mix. Even the new "feminine" name "F. Jasmine" is ambiguous because it is generally a male practice to use an initial and a middle name. One might conclude that Frankie is unconsciously subverting her outward attempt to become more womanly.

But even if Frankie approaches the "feminine" art of self-decoration with ambivalence, it is significant that she cares about her appearance. Frankie dislikes what she considers her "dark ugly mug"; as we noted earlier, she worries that she is too tall and will be a nine-foot freak. Her preoccupation with freaks has been linked to her fear of isolation; however, to Frankie the true horror of freakdom is the horror of being an *ugly woman,* of not being able to live up to the name "Jasmine." Frankie's questions to Berenice "Do you think I will grow into a Freak?" and "Do you think I will be pretty?" are joined together, and her association of looks and male approval becomes clear when she tells Berenice she doubts that freaks ever get married.

Since marriage has traditionally been woman's fate, it is logical that in contemplating growing up Frankie should turn to thoughts of love, sex, and marriage. The younger Frankie had scorned love and left it out of her homemade shows; preferring movies about criminals, cowboys, and war, she caused a disturbance when the local theatre showed *Camille.* But now she recalls the time when she committed a "queer sin" with the neighbor boy Barney MacKean and the time when she surprised one of the Addams's boarders in bed with his wife "having a fit." She thinks about love and becomes fascinated with her brother's wedding. If the wedding provides an opportunity for Frankie to escape her loneliness and become a "member" of something, it is also the marriage of a man and a woman, and in her obsession with a wedding, Frankie anticipates her own destiny. Instead of stopping her ears as she used to when Berenice talked of love and marriage, Frankie now encourages Berenice and listens to her carefully.

Whatever difficulties Frankie has in making the "decision to be a woman" cannot be attributed to her lack of a mother because Berenice performs a motherly function in initiating Frankie into her expected role. Berenice correctly interprets Frankie's concern with the wedding as concern with her own future as a woman. Thus Berenice suggests that Frankie acquire a "nice little white boy beau." Berenice's advice to Frankie is a classic compression of traditional "womanly wisdom." She says: "Now you belong to change from being so rough and greedy and big. You ought to fix yourself up nice in your dresses. And speak sweetly and act sly." In three sentences Berenice has summarized the major traits girls are taught to cultivate in preparation for their relationships with men: "object" orientation ("fix yourself up nice"), passivity and submission ("speak sweetly"), and calculation and trickery ("act sly"). No real mother could do a more thorough job of socialization.

Critics have been unanimous in viewing Berenice as a positive influence on Frankie. They consider her wise and spiritual, a mouthpiece for McCullers and the "Socrates of the novel." However, McCullers presents Berenice as a completely man-oriented woman. For her to talk about her life means to talk about her four previous husbands and current beau. Berenice communicates to Frankie pride in the number of men one can attract. When John Henry asks her how many beaus she "caught," she replies: "Lamb, how many hairs is in these plaits? You talking to Berenice Sadie Brown." Berenice feels proud that men "treat" her, that she doesn't have to "pay her own way." Besides, the company of men is preferable to that of women; she proclaims, "I'm not the kind of person to go around with crowds of womens."

It is surprising how much Berenice resembles a mother who has been the object of much vituperation from critics, Amanda Wingfield of Tennessee Williams's *The Glass Menagerie* (1944). In this play by McCullers's close friend, Amanda tries to transform her shy daughter into a southern belle. Berenice is in most ways a more attractive character than Amanda; yet her cataloging of her past in terms of beaus is much like Amanda's in terms of "gentlemen callers," and her advice to her reluctant young charge is exactly the same as Amanda's to her daughter.

Much of the humor in *The Member of the Wedding* involves the young and unworldly Frankie and John Henry, but we are not allowed to forget that Berenice also is limited in her perceptions. For instance, Frankie asks Berenice why she married at the youthful age of thirteen (Frankie is almost thirteen herself). Berenice responds, "Because I wanted to. I were thirteen years old and I haven't growed a inch since." Frankie, who we know worries about her height, asks, "Does marrying really stop your growth?" "It certainy [sic] do," replies Berenice, unaware of the implications of her statement. In this case, the author has distanced herself from Berenice, creating an irony involving her.

Furthermore, the Berenice who in the middle of the novel rejects Frankie's advice that she marry her latest beau, T. T. Williams, ends up by taking it. Frankie tells Berenice to "quit worrying about beaus and be content with T. T. I bet you are forty years old. It is time for you to settle down." Berenice asserts that she will not marry T. T. because he doesn't "make her shiver." She rebukes Frankie, saying, "I got many a long year ahead of me before I resign myself to a corner." But finally Berenice decides that she "might as well" marry T. T. In other words, her experience in the novel is not at a level above Frankie's but parallels it. Berenice, like Frankie, hates sleeping alone, and she submits, resigning herself to a corner, just as Frankie finally gives up her dreams and accepts the role marked out for her.

Even with Berenice's tutelage and her own desire to be treated as an adult, Frankie fears growing up. It is not simply that she might fail to meet the standards of womanhood (be the proper height, be pretty, etc.)—Frankie feels especially afraid when she "thinks about the world." She reads the war news in the paper and wants

> to be a boy and go to war as a Marine. She thought about flying aeroplanes and winning gold medals for bravery. But she could not join the war, and this made her sometimes feel restless and blue. . . .To think about the world for very long made her afraid. She was not afraid of Germans or bombs or Japanese. She was afraid because in the war they would not include her, and because the world seemed somehow separate from herself.

She envies the soldiers she sees in town for their mobility, the opportunity they have to travel and see the world—in other words, to gain experience. Frankie feels left out. When she wonders "who she was, and what she was going to be in the world," she gets a "queer tightness in her chest."

No doubt many a boy has had the same thirst for adventure and felt frustrated by his youth. But it is not just a question of youth for Frankie, any more than it is for Richard Wright's Bigger Thomas. When he sees a plane overhead, Bigger tells his friend Gus, "I could fly one of them things if I had a chance." "If you wasn't black and if you had some money and if they'd let you go to that aviation school," replies Gus. The youthful Bigger feels the same tightness as Frankie, "like somebody's poking a red-hot iron down my throat. . . . It's just like living in jail. Half the time I feel like I'm on the outside of the world peeping in."

One might conclude that Wright's novel is a "parable of the essential loneliness of man," but, so far as I know, no one has ventured this interpretation of *Native Son.* Bigger's problem, like Frankie's, is not isolation but exclusion. It is true that Frankie resolves her "sexual ambiguity," as one critic puts it, and takes a "definite step toward assuming her feminine nature" when she finally gives up wanting to be a pilot. The question is why

"feminine nature" (or dark skin) precludes being a pilot. Whenever Frankie senses that becoming a woman entails renunciation, she feels the tightness in her chest and rebels.

McCullers endows Mick Kelly with the same desires as Frankie. Mick would also like to fight the Fascists—she imagines dressing as a boy and being accepted in the army. Like Frankie, Mick wants to see the world; she spends her time at the library poring over *National Geographic* magazines. But Mick's first love is music, and above all things she wants to be a composer. It seems initially that she has to give up her goal for purely economic reasons: her parents cannot afford a piano or music lessons, and she must work to help support the family. However, just as Bigger's friend Gus puts race first and money second in listing the obstacles to Bigger's becoming a pilot, McCullers reveals that the primary check to Mick's dream is her gender.

Mick has a friend, Harry Minowitz, whose function in the novel is to serve both as the agent of her sexual initiation and as a contrast to her. Mick and Harry, as a poor girl and a poor boy, resemble Ruth Suckow's Daisy and Gerald with their very different prospects for the future. Although Harry must work to support his widowed mother, he can find a high-paying part-time job; thus he can finish studying mechanics at the local high school. Mick comments:

> "A boy has a better advantage like that than a girl. I mean a boy can usually get some part-time job that don't take him out of school and leaves him time for other things. But the're [sic] not jobs like that for girls. When a girl wants a job she has to quit school and work full-time."

After Harry and Mick have sex, Harry leaves town, either because he feels guilty or because he wants to avoid being "tied down." We are not informed of Harry's ultimate fate, but he can support himself as a skilled mechanic and has at least escaped the small town to which Mick feels bound. Mick's tiring full-time job at Woolworth's puts an end to her dreams of a musical career. She is cut off from her "inner room," the "good private place where she could go and be by herself and study. . . music," and feels trapped and cheated.

This sense of being trapped is developed in greater detail in *The Member of the Wedding* where the very setting of the novel is designed to reflect Frankie's feelings of being limited and restricted. The Addamses' kitchen, where Frankie spends most of her time, seems to her "sad and ugly" and is most often described by McCullers as "gray." The walls are covered with John Henry's "queer" drawings which no one can decipher. The kitchen is a place where "nothing happens" and, often, nothing even moves. Time passes slowly there (McCullers reinforces this impression by noting frequently that "it was only six" or "only half-past six"), and Frankie, Berenice, and John Henry "say the same things over and over" until the words seem to rhyme. In attempt to classify *Member* as a Gothic novel one critic contends that the Addamses' kitchen parallels the "old dank dungeon" of the classic Gothic romance. Certainly to Frankie it seems a kind of prison.

Frankie cannot find relief beyond the kitchen, for the outside atmosphere is just as stifling. The connotations of hot and cold in Wharton's *Summer* are reversed in *The Member of the Wedding.* In *Member,* as in her other novels, McCullers uses heat to suggest boredom and restriction and cold to suggest liberation. Frankie dreams of snow and ice; Jarvis and Janice blend with her ideals because he was stationed in Alaska and she comes from a town called Winter Hill. But the reality of Frankie's environment is deadening heat. The town turns "black and shrunken under the glare of the sun," and the sidewalks seem to be on fire. The atmosphere is motionless as well as hot. "The world seemed to die each afternoon and nothing moved any longer. At last the summer was like a green sick dream, or like a silent crazy jungle under glass." McCullers's references to heat and stasis create an effect of constriction, almost suffocation, that parallels Frankie's feeling of tightness in her chest. Even the sunlight crosses her backyard "like the bars of a bright, strange jail."

Frankie tries to communicate her feeling of being trapped to Berenice, who expresses it eloquently:

> "We all of us somehow caught. We born this way or that way and we don't know why. But we caught anyhow. I born Berenice. You born Frankie. John Henry born John Henry. And maybe we wants to widen and bust free. But no matter what we do we still caught."

Almost everyone who has written about *Member* notes that Berenice is describing people being "caught" in their own individual identities and being ultimately isolated. It is usually forgotten, however, that Berenice goes on to define a special way of being caught. She says she is caught worse

> "because I'm black. . . .Because I am colored. Everybody is caught one way or another, but they done drawn completely extra bounds around all colored people. They done squeezed us off in one corner by

ourself. So we caught that firstway I was telling you, as all human beings is caught. And we caught as colored people also. Sometimes a boy like Honey [Berenice's foster brother] feel like he just can't breathe no more. He feel like he got to break something or break himself. Sometimes it just about more than he can stand. He just feels desperate like."

Frankie's responses to Berenice are significant. To the first statement she says she "doesn't know" but to the second that she knows how Honey feels. "Sometimes I feel like I want to break something, too. I feel like I wish I could just tear down the whole town." In other words, Frankie believes she is caught in a special way other than the first one Berenice explained. Berenice, having accepted the female role, does not mention the "extra bounds" drawn around women, but Frankie feels them keenly.

Honey Brown, who "just can't breathe no more," is Frankie's double in the novel. Frankie feels a kinship with him because she senses that he is in the same divided state that she is. On the one hand, Honey works hard studying music and French; on the other, he "suddenly run[s] hog-wild all over Sugarville and tear[s] around for several days, until his friends bring him home more dead than living." Although he can talk "like a white schoolteacher," he often adopts his expected role with a vengeance, speaking in a "colored jumble" that even his family cannot understand. Honey spends only part of his energy trying to overcome or protesting the limitations placed on him; the rest of the time he accepts society's label of "inferior" and punishes himself.

Frankie exhibits this same psychology. She frequently "hates herself," and her attempts at rebellion against the female role are mainly symbolic. As Simone de Beauvoir puts it, the young girl "is too much divided against herself to join battle with the world; she limits herself to a flight from reality or a symbolic struggle against it." De Beauvoir mentions four common forms of "symbolic struggle": odd eating habits, kleptomania, self-mutilation, and running away from home. While Frankie never carries these behaviors to extremes, she indulges in all four types. She eats "greedily," pilfers from the five-and-ten, hacks at her foot with a knife, and tries to run away. It is characteristic of these acts that, like Honey's rampages, they are ineffective—the young girl is "struggling in her cage rather than trying to get out of it." At the end of the novel we find Honey in an actual prison and Frankie in a jail of her own.

Frankie's principal "flight from reality" is her creation of a fantasy world. The adult Honey laughs at her solution to racism, that he go to Cuba and pass as a Cuban. But Frankie still deals with her feeling of being trapped by escaping to the haven of her dreams where she can fly airplanes and see the whole world. Her favorite pastime with Berenice and John Henry is their game of criticizing God and putting themselves in the position of creator. Frankie agrees with the basic modifications Berenice would make. The world would be "just and reasonable": there would be no separate colored people, no killed Jews, and no hunger. Frankie makes a major addition, however. "She planned it so that people could instantly change back and forth from boys to girls, whichever way they felt like and wanted." This plan provides a neat symbolic solution to Frankie's conflicts.

To many commentators on McCullers's work, however, Frankie's dream is an "abnormal" one; a product of the author's "homosexual sensibility." We saw earlier that Leslie Fiedler initiated discussion of gender in McCullers's fiction when he referred to Frankie and Mick as "boy-girl" characters. This point might have led to recognition of McCullers's portrayal of the conflict between a woman's humanity and her destiny as a woman; but Fiedler went on, in a disapproving tone, to call the "tomboy image" "lesbian" and argue that McCullers is "projecting in her neo-tomboys, ambiguous and epicene, the homosexual's. . . uneasiness before heterosexual passion." Fiedler ends up in the absurd position of contending that Frankie and Berenice are having a "homosexual romance."

Some critics have tried to preserve Fiedler's basic argument by giving Frankie a more appropriate lover. They see her relationship at the end of the novel with her newfound friend, Mary Littlejohn, as "latently homosexual"; Mary's name fits conveniently with this theory—she is a "little John," a "surrogate male lover." Other critics influenced by Fiedler take Frankie's refusal to recognize "the facts of life" as evidence of different sexual "abnormalities." Perhaps she wants to join her brother's wedding so that she can commit incest; perhaps she is really "asexual" (to Ihab Hassan, McCullers's "men-women freaks" are "all bisexual, which is to say a-sexual"). The critics who have followed Fiedler's lead leave as many questions unanswered as he does. We never learn what a "homosexual sensibility" might be and how it is "abnormal," what the "tomboy image" has to do with lesbianism, how "bisexual" and "a-sexual" are the same. Because so many terms remain unde-

fined, discussion of sex and gender in McCullers's fiction has been hopelessly confused.

At issue seems to be McCullers's endorsement of androgyny in her fiction. Frankie and Mick are only two among many androgynous characters, including Singer and Biff Brannon in *The Heart Is a Lonely Hunter,* Captain Penderton in *Reflections in a Golden Eye* (1941), and Amelia in *Ballad of the Sad Café* (1943). These characters are McCullers's most sympathetic, and they often seem to speak for her. Biff Brannon, when he sees Mick looking as much like a boy as a girl, thinks to himself:

> And on that subject why was it that the smartest people mostly missed that point? By nature all people are of both sexes. So that marriage and the bed is not all by any means. The proof? Real youth and old age. Because often old men's voices grow high and reedy and they take on a mincing walk. And old women sometimes grow fat and their voices get rough and deep and they grow dark little mustaches. And he even proved it himself—the part of him that sometimes wished he was a mother and that Mick and Baby were his kids.

Biff, who is one of the strongest and most self-sufficient characters in McCullers's fiction, is shown becoming so after his wife dies. He takes over some of her "feminine" habits, discarding the clearly defined role which had previously confined him. If McCullers implies any solution besides racial equality to the social injustice and personal isolation and despair she portrays in her novels, it is a move toward the loosening of conventional gender roles, toward the more androgynous world Frankie envisions when she wishes people could "change back and forth from boys to girls."

But the critics who discuss McCullers's androgynous characters conclude that "there is something frightening about them." McCullers fails to present women who are happily female and "men who are men (i.e., Gary Cooper)," and Biff Brannon is a "sexual deviate." The next step is devaluation of McCullers's reputation as a writer. Fiedler dismisses her as a "chic" writer supported by New York homosexuals. A. S. Knowles less readily equates androgyny and homosexuality but finds either one "frightening." In his reassessment of McCullers's literary reputation Knowles expresses distaste for the "By nature all people are of both sexes" passage quoted above; he is horrified that McCullers actually "means what she seems to be saying" in this passage. He concludes that McCullers links "sensitivity" with "sexual abnormality" and is thus a less important novelist than she first appeared to be.

Ironically, the recognition of the importance of gender in McCullers's fiction has been no more productive than the ignoring of gender and search for "universal" themes we noted earlier. The main import of the Fiedler approach is a sinister message for potential novelists. If the "universalist" critics imply that novelists should avoid writing about female adolescence because it is not universal enough, the Fiedlerites proclaim loudly, "Do not write about female adolescence if you criticize the current gender system. Those who criticize the gender system are homosexuals, and homosexuals cannot be important novelists."

The universalists have tried to produce comprehensive interpretations of *The Member of the Wedding,* but to the Fiedlerites a fuller understanding of the novel seems to have been a secondary concern. The readings they have come up with are distorted and partial; we are left to figure out for ourselves why Frankie Addams should be lusting after Berenice or her brother. Frankie's attitude toward sex provides a specific example where both critical approaches have resulted in misreadings. Everyone recognizes that Frankie resists even the knowledge of sexual intercourse. It is not only that she does not understand, or try to understand, such incidents mentioned earlier as her "sin" with Barney MacKean and her glimpse of the boarder "having a fit"; she also conveniently "forgets" both incidents. After Frankie has misinterpreted the purpose of her date with a soldier and has had to fend off his advances, she fleetingly remembers these earlier bits of knowledge. But, significantly, she does not "let these separate glimpses fall together"; she prefers to think of the soldier as an anomaly, a "crazy man."

To the Fiedlerites, as we have seen, Frankie's resistance means that she is a lesbian or a "deviate." To the universalists it is either "pointless" or symbolic of the course of initiation in the modern world—Frankie's failure to gain "insight into sexual experience" shows that initiation no longer entails knowledge and commitment. In fact, there is no evidence in *The Member of the Wedding* that Frankie is homosexual (or heterosexual, bisexual, or asexual). In the play she adapted from the novel McCullers presents Frankie in the last scene swooning over Barney MacKean, the boy she previously hated. In the novel we are given no clue as to what her sexual preference will eventually be. But Frankie does not fail to gain insight into heterosexual experience. Although she manages for a while to keep her "separate glimpses" of sex from falling together, near the end of the novel she gets a sudden flash of understanding. Significantly, her moment of recognition comes after her plan to join the wedding has failed; it is associated with her consequent feelings of helplessness and resignation—she "might as well" ask the soldier to marry her.

Frankie's attitude toward sex is not unusual. The adolescent heroines we have met [throughout *Growing Up Female*], even the sensuous Charity Royall, fear and resist sexual experience; as we will see, resistance to sex is almost universal in novels of female adolescence. The reason is always the same: adolescent heroines view sex as domination by a man (not until very recently are they even aware of the possibility of sex with women). They may, like Mick Kelly, worry about losing their virginity (the woman is traditionally spoken of as "losing" her virginity when she "submits" or "yields" to a man); but they fear most strongly, as Mick does, losing their autonomy.

In his survey of novels of adolescence James Johnson puzzles over Frankie's encounter with the soldier, wondering why her experience lacks the "positive quality" of Stephen Dedalus's sexual initiation. If we look at Stephen's first sexual experience in *A Portrait of the Artist as a Young Man,* we find that his behavior is the opposite of Frankie's. Stephen, hardly the "man's man," Gary Cooper, "suddenly become[s] strong and fearless and sure of himself." Frankie, on the other hand, does not "know how to refuse" the soldier's invitation to his room; she thinks she is unable to leave, and when he grabs her, she feels "paralyzed." In other words, Stephen receives a sudden influx of power, while Frankie feels loss of power.

McCullers treats an adolescent girl's association of sexual intercourse with male domination and loss of personal choice and power in an early short story entitled "Like That." The thirteen-year-old narrator of the story, an early version of Mick and Frankie, bemoans the change that has come over her older sister. Previously she and Sis had had fun together, but one night after a date with her boyfriend, Sis began to act differently. The present Sis has lost weight, cries a lot, and spends her time sitting by herself or writing her boyfriend. The unnamed narrator, whom I will call N., declares, "I wouldn't like any boy in the world as much as she does Tuck. I'd never let any boy or any thing make me act like she does." She thinks of Sis as "dead."

Although N. does not understand the cause of Sis's behavior, she associates the change with her sister's first menstruation which she had "forgotten" for several years because she "hadn't wanted to remember." N. thus connects becoming a woman with giving up of self and being oriented toward and dominated by a man. N. does not want to let "anything really change me," so she either conveniently "forgets" or refuses to listen to information about sex. N. concludes:

> One afternoon the kids all got quiet in the gym basement and then started telling certain things—about being married and all—I got up quick so I wouldn't hear and went up and played basketball. And when some of the kids said they were going to start wearing lipstick and stockings I said I wouldn't for a hundred dollars. You see I'd never be like Sis is now. I wouldn't. Anybody could know that if they knew me. I just wouldn't, that's all. I don't want to grow up—if it's like that.

N. seems more conscious than Frankie of her motives in avoiding discussion of sexual facts and "forgetting" those facts she cannot avoid. McCullers has Frankie express her conflicts in fantasies, as with her dream of a world where people could instantly change sexes. Frankie knows this dream is impossible. She finds society's condemnation of androgyny, which we saw expressed by literary critics, reflected in her own world; after all, one of the freaks at the fair is the Half-Man Half-Woman. Frankie thus projects all her desires and fears into a fantasy that she imagines might be more socially acceptable—she will join her brother and his fiancée and become "a member of the wedding." Those readers who have stressed the theme of spiritual isolation in McCullers's works have noted that joining the wedding would allow Frankie to escape her own separate identity, to become, as Frankie says, a "we" person instead of an "I" person. But paradoxically, Frankie's plan to join the wedding is also a desperate attempt to *preserve* her identity. Her wedding fantasy is a symbolic way of resolving her conflict of wanting to be an adult but not wanting to be a woman, not wanting to "grow up—if it's like that."

Weddings are, traditionally, the destiny of girls, and with marriage a girl officially becomes an adult. But Frankie has changed her female destiny, for this wedding does not entail any of the restrictions that she has perceived in womanhood. Her proposed marriage is not to one man because in her society that implies submission; the marriage is for the same reason sexless. Nor does Frankie attempt to acquire in her brother and sister-in-law a new set of parents, for then she would be a child again. Frankie dreams of being neither a *wife* nor a *child* but an adult *equal*. In reality Frankie is already a member of something—she has "the terrible summer *we* of her and John Henry and

Berenice"; but "that was the last *we* in the world she wanted," because a black woman and a child do not raise her status. Her brother Jarvis is a soldier, one of those envied beings who gets to see the world; his fiancée, whom Frankie has met only briefly, at least has the distinction of being "small and pretty." According to Frankie's plan, the three JA's will travel together. She will no longer be trapped in her kitchen but can climb glaciers in Alaska and ride camels in Africa. Frankie will be able to fly planes and win medals, and all three JA's will be equally famous and successful. This fantasy makes Frankie feel "lightness" in place of that old constriction in her chest; it gives her a sense of "power" and "entitlement."

But Frankie's plan to join the wedding is a nonrealistic way of solving her conflict, a "flight from reality" more elaborately imagined than the ones Simone de Beauvoir describes. When Frankie is dragged screaming from the honeymoon car, her dream is crushed. She realizes that "all that came about [at the wedding] occurred in a world beyond her power"; she feels powerless. When she runs away from home after the wedding, Frankie merely goes through the motions of protest and attempted escape. She knows before she reaches the street corner that her father has awakened and will soon be after her. Her plan of hopping a box-car seems unreal even to her. "It is easy to talk about hopping a freight train, but how did bums and people really do it?" She admits to herself that she is "too scared to go into the world alone."

Frankie now resigns herself—the world seems too "enormous" and "powerful" for her to fight. "Between herself and all the places there was a space like an enormous canyon she could not hope to bridge or cross." When Frankie suddenly puts together the sexual facts she previously refused to connect and thinks she might as well ask the soldier to marry her, we realize that she is giving up her rebellion and submitting to her female fate. At this point the jail image, part of the motif of constriction in the novel, recurs. Frankie wishes the policeman who comes to fetch her would take her to jail, for "it was better to be in a jail where you could bang the walls than in a jail you could not see."

Had McCullers ended *The Member of the Wedding* here, it would have been difficult for anyone to see the novel as "cute" and "sentimental," a *Tom Sawyer* as opposed to McCullers's *Huckleberry Finn, The Heart Is a Lonely Hunter.* However, she includes a few pages showing Frankie several months later. John Henry has died of meningitis,

Honey is in jail, Berenice plans to marry T. T., but Frankie is content. She has found a friend and model in the older Mary Littlejohn, a modern good good girl with long blonde hair, pale white complexion, and ladylike habits; Mary encourages Frankie to collect paintings by Michelangelo and read Tennyson. The novel ends as Frankie, with "an instant shock of happiness," hears Mary at the front door.

Twentieth-century novelists rarely leave their characters in a state of euphoria, and those critics who have not thereby consigned *Member* to the rank of sentimental popular novels about adolescence have tended to focus on Frankie's "successful" initiation. That is, the "happy ending" means that Frankie is "accepting reality and responsibility." Louise Gossett contends that McCullers often leaves adults "physically and emotionally ruined" but "brings her adolescents to a healthy measure of maturity." Her adolescents'

> ability to achieve wholeness distinguishes their growth from that of many young people in twentieth century literature about the suffering adolescent. The struggle of the adolescent who appears in the fiction of William Goyen or Truman Capote injures or defeats him with a deadly finality. Mrs. McCullers prefers to educate rather than to destroy her adolescents.

Unlike these other adolescent protagonists, Frankie is not "injured or crippled emotionally" by her experiences.

Indeed, Frankie does not retreat to a fantasy world (Joel Knox of Capote's *Other Voices, Other Rooms*), end up in a mental institution (Holden Caulfield), or commit suicide (Peyton Loftis of Styron's *Lie Down in Darkness*). But the very point of McCullers's epilogue is to show that, while Frankie has "adjusted" to growing up and is undergoing a "normal" adolescence, she has been severely "crippled." Frankie has not merely replaced her old aspirations with new ones just as impossible; she has changed the very nature of her dreams. Frankie's old dreams, of flying planes, of being able to switch genders whenever she wished, of joining the wedding, were protests against the secondary status of women. They were projections of her desire to be an autonomous adult. Now Frankie, or Frances, as she is finally called, wants to write poetry and travel with Mary Littlejohn. Her new dreams are socially acceptable and easily within her reach. Although she will not climb glaciers and ride camels with Mary Littlejohn, she may tour Europe under the aegis of Mary and her mother. It is permissible for Frankie to go "around the world" but not into it.

Frankie now lives in a permanent "daytime" state, or what Mick Kelly would call the "outside room." To Mick her "outside room" is "school and the family and the things that happened every day" and her "inside room" a "very private place" full of "plans" and "music"—in other words, her inner self. When Mick gives up composing to work at the five-and-ten and stops resisting womanhood to become "ladylike and delicate," she is barred from the inside room: she loses her self. Although we leave Frankie at a younger age, it is clear that she has already sacrificed her "inner room." Her life is "filled with. . . school and Mary Littlejohn" (the outside room), and her summer of plans is almost forgotten. The very kitchen where Frankie thought about "who she was" and resisted "what she was going to be in the world" has been whitewashed.

Immediately after Honey's imprisonment and John Henry's death Frankie would feel a "hush" when she thought of them, and she had nightmares about John Henry. "But the dreams came only once or twice" and "it was seldom now that she felt his presence." Although Berenice appears in the last few pages of the novel, Frankie hardly feels her presence either; she ignores her in anticipation of being with Mary Littlejohn and seems indifferent to Berenice's departure. The fates of Berenice, Honey, and John Henry reflect on Frankie's own situation. The formerly lively Berenice, who once towered over the Addamses' kitchen, is subdued; she sits sad and "idle" in a chair, "her limp arms hanging at her sides." Honey is in prison as the result of drugging himself. John Henry's death seems fitting. Through most of the novel, as Frankie vacillated between childhood and adulthood, she alternately avoided and clung to him. Now, as part of her childhood and her "inner room," he is appropriately dead.

In reporting John Henry's death McCullers juxtaposes accounts of his terrible suffering with descriptions of the "golden" autumn weather—the chilled air and the clear green-blue sky filled with light. The effect is to make Frankie seem a bit callous, for the cool weather reflects her joyous mood; she can hardly feel John Henry's death. Like Edith Wharton's *Summer*, *The Member of the Wedding* portrays an adolescent girl's hot summer, which at the very end of the novel gives way to a chilly autumn. But the passage to autumn has a different import in McCullers's novel. Although Frankie, unlike Charity, loves the cold, there is no glimmer of promise in *Member* because Frankie has not experienced any of the positive growth Charity has. The seasonal motif suggests the possibility of renewal;

perhaps "spring will return" for Frankie as well as Charity, but Berenice, Honey, and John Henry are irrevocably lost. At the end of *The Member of the Wedding* Frankie seems better off than Charity. She is certainly happy, having released the tension of not "belonging"; but the final irony of the novel is that having gained her membership, Frankie has lost her self.

McCullers does not blame Frankie, any more than she does Mick, for this loss of self. As the critical comments stressing her new "maturity" imply, Frankie has done exactly what has been expected of her, what she has been educated to do. In this context Louise Gossett's remarks on her environment seem ironic. Frankie's environment, says Gossett, is less menacing than Holden Caulfield's:

> His displacement is more radical than Frankie's because his society has no place for him, whereas the community of Frankie or of Mick, less large and competitive, defines what is acceptable in the stages through which the girls grow and also superintends their progress.

It is, of course, the problem rather than the solution that Frankie's and Mick's society has a "place" for them and "superintends" them into it. That same society has a place for Honey Brown.

The Member of the Wedding is less a novel of initiation into "acceptance of *human* limits" than a novel of initiation into acceptance of *female* limits. Frankie's desire to be a soldier or a pilot, or Mick's to be an inventor or a composer, could be fulfilled by a boy; these goals are simply defined as unacceptable for girls. Nor is Frankie's ambition to travel and gain experience in the world unattainable for a boy. Gossett's comparison of Frankie with Holden Caulfield has relevance here. Holden's basic conflict resembles Frankie's—he does not want to remain a child but has reservations about the "phoniness" of adults (he projects these doubts into his dream of being "catcher in the rye" and catching children before they fall over the "cliff" into adulthood). But if Holden's "displacement" appears greater than Frankie's, it is merely a measure of his greater freedom. He can at least venture into the world and test it by experience. James Johnson includes Frankie and Holden as examples of modern adolescent characters who flee their homes and undertake journeys. Yet Frankie's hour of running away hardly measures up to Holden's experience or that of Johnson's other examples, Eugene Gant, Nick Adams, or Stephen Dedalus, all inveterate wanderers.

The barriers to Frankie's entering the world are not solely external, any more than they are for Ruth Suckow's adolescent heroines. Frankie and Mick are "protected" (that is, banned) from experience in the way of Suckow's "nice girls," and Mick especially is expected to preserve close ties to the family. But, in large part, the girls fail to journey into the world because of their own passivity. Frankie and Mick, like Marjorie Schoessel, wait for "something to happen" to them—they do not think in terms of making something happen. They dream but seldom act. Even Frankie's desire to be a "member" stresses identification with the world rather than participation in it. When Frankie tries to run away from home, she discovers that she does not have the necessary resources to leave by herself. The details of "hopping a freight," for instance, lie outside the realm of her preparatory experience. She does not have to be prevented from hopping freights; her greatest restriction is that she does not know how or really want to.

Frankie's and Mick's passivity becomes striking when we compare them with the male adolescent protagonist of one of McCullers's early versions of *The Heart Is a Lonely Hunter*. Andrew has the same background as Frankie and Mick; he lives in a small Georgia town with a jeweller father, a sister Sara, a little sister Mick, and a black cook Vitalis. Interestingly, much of this draft deals with Andrew's recollections of his sister Sara's troubled adolescence and her attempts to "try to act like a boy" and run away from home. McCullers had not yet determined her true focus, the adolescent girl, and this early draft is confused because the protagonist, Andrew, is not really the center of interest. We discover enough about him, however, to see how his character and fate differ from that of Sara-Mick-Frankie.

Andrew resembles the female adolescent in being "lonesome" and apprehensive about the future. "He was getting to be a man and he did not know what was going to come. And always he was hungry and always he felt that something was just about to happen." The difference is that Andrew himself causes the event to happen. He takes a walk by Vitalis's house, says he is hungry, follows her into the house, and seduces her. Afterwards, Andrew feels guilty and leaves town permanently for New York City. It seems to him that his experience with Vitalis was "accidental," but it is clear from his seeking her out and claiming to be hungry that he at least unconsciously sought sexual contact. Although Andrew's experience involves some loss of control, as his bodily desires overcome his conscious plans, it contrasts with Mick's and Frankie's in that Andrew acts throughout. It is he who has the desire, seeks out Vitalis, and initiates the sexual encounter. He makes a decision to leave town and then follows through with his decision.

Andrew is an early version of Harry Minowitz, and his two sisters later merge into the figure of Mick Kelly. In *The Heart Is a Lonely Hunter* Harry will be presented as more active than Mick; his situation will also differ from hers in terms of his greater economic opportunity and freedom of movement. Still, Harry ends up a minor character, his function being to highlight the restrictions placed on Mick. Like Ruth Suckow, McCullers includes male adolescents in her fiction but reserves center stage for girls. Not until their last novels, Suckow's *The John Wood Case* (1959) and Mc-Cullers's *Clock Without Hands* (1961), do they make a boy the protagonist, and they do not provide him with a female counterpart.

Source: Barbara A. White, "Loss of Self in *The Member of the Wedding*," in *Carson McCullers,* edited by Harold Bloom, Modern Critical Views, Chelsea House Publishers, 1986, pp. 125–42.

Sources

Brantley, Jennifer, "McCullers, (Lula) Carson," in *Feminist Writers,* St. James Press, 1996, pp. 319–20.

Dangerfield, George, Review, in *Saturday Review of Literature,* March 30, 1946.

Everson, Judith L., "Carson McCullers," in *Dictionary of Literary Biography,* Volume 173: *American Novelists Since World War II,* Gale Research, 1996, pp. 148–69.

Godden, Rumer, Review, in *New York Herald Tribune Books,* September 17, 1961.

Graver, Lawrence, "Carson McCullers," in *American Writers, Volume 2,* Charles Scribner's Sons, 1974.

Kapp, Isa, Review, in *New York Times,* March 24, 1946.

Kiernan, Robert F., "Carson McCullers," in *Concise Dictionary of American Literary Biography: The New Consciousness, 1941–1968,* Gale Research, 1987, pp. 347–57.

McElroy, Lorie, "Carson McCullers," in *Authors and Artists for Young Adults,* Vol. 21, The Gale Group, 1999, pp. 153–62.

Millichap, Joseph R., "McCullers, (Lula) Carson (Smith)," in *St. James Guide to Young Adult Writers,* St. James Press, 1999, pp. 565–67.

Moss, Joyce, and George Wilson, eds., "Carson McCullers: *The Member of the Wedding,*" in *Literature and Its Times,* Vol. 4, Gale Research, 1997.

Rubin, Louis D., Jr., "Carson McCullers: The Aesthetic of Pain," in *Virginia Quarterly Review,* Vol. 53, No. 2, Spring 1977, pp. 265–83.

Torsney, Cheryl B., "Carson McCullers," in *Modern American Women Writers,* Charles Scribner's Sons, 1991.

Westling, Louise, "Carson McCullers's Tomboys," in *Southern Humanities Review,* Vol. 14, No. 4, Fall 1980, pp. 339–50.

Wilson, Edmund, Review, in *New Yorker,* March 30, 1946.

Further Reading

Andrews, William L., ed., *The Literature of the American South: A Norton Anthology,* W. W. Norton & Co., 1997.
    Andrews collects writing of the American South from the seventeenth century to the present. This anthology contains poetry, sermons, short fiction, songs, excerpts from novels, criticism, and nonfiction.

Carr, Virginia Spence, *The Lonely Hunter: A Biography of Carson McCullers,* Carroll & Graf, 1985.
    Originally published in 1975, this biography presents the tragic events and circumstances of McCullers's life. Carr demonstrates how these events influenced McCullers's fiction.

McCullers, Carson, *Collected Stories: Including "The Member of the Wedding" and "The Ballad of the Sad Cafe,"* Houghton Mifflin, 1998.
    This book contains McCullers's short works including the short novel *The Member of the Wedding.* At more than four hundred pages, this book allows the student of McCullers's writing to compare and contrast the author's works.

O'Connor, Flannery, *The Complete Stories,* Noonday Press, 1996.
    Flannery O'Connor is an important female writer in the southern tradition. Although she wrote novels, she is best known for her short stories, which are collected fully in this book.

Welty, Eudora, *Collected Stories of Eudora Welty,* Harcourt Brace, 1982.
    Eudora Welty remains one of the dominant literary figures of the American South. She is known primarily for her short fiction, and this collection provides a thorough introduction to Welty's writing.

Moll Flanders

Daniel Defoe
1722

Daniel Defoe published *Moll Flanders* in 1722 after a long career of writing nonfiction. Many critics have speculated that Defoe's story of a beautiful and greedy woman who turns to crime is not a novel in the true sense but a work combining biography and fiction. Defoe (and others) wrote numerous accounts of various women in early eighteenth-century London named Moll who made their fame as thieves and pickpockets, and the criminal records of that period in London reveal the accounts of women who were arrested for stealing. Many critics and historians argue that a woman named Elizabeth Atkins, a notorious thief who died in prison in 1723, was one of Defoe's inspirations for the character of Moll Flanders.

Whatever the sources of Defoe's popular work may have been, the novel has endured nearly three hundred years of changing tastes and mores and has secured its author's position as one of the most well-respected English writers and, some say, as the father of the novel form.

Author Biography

Looking over the full life of Daniel Defoe, there seems to be little that the Englishman did not attempt or experience. He was a trainee for the ministry, a poet, a businessman, a shopkeeper, a historian, an investor, a soldier, and a writer of fictional works as well as political and social tracts. Many of his business dealings put him on the brink of fi-

Daniel Defoe

nancial failure, and a number of his writings landed him in jail. His political writings, though, were ultimately so well-regarded and widely quoted that, according to Paula R. Backscheider in *The Dictionary of Literary Biography,* "echoes of them exist in, for instance, the United States Constitution." In spite of this, Defoe is currently best known for his works of fiction, including *Moll Flanders.*

Defoe is believed to have been born around 1660 to James and Alice Foe in London, England. While the family was solidly middle-class, Defoe grew up in hardship, primarily because of his father's religious views. James Foe was a Nonconformist, a Protestant who refused to conform to the tenets of the restored Church of England (Anglican). Because of this, his son could not attend Oxford or Cambridge but was able to attend one of the many dissenting academies set up in England, to be trained for the ministry.

Defoe decided in the early 1680s that he was much more interested in business than in religion. He first became a hosiery merchant, then he invested in a variety of ventures, including the diving bell, civet cats, international shipping, and property. In 1691, he went bankrupt but was able to settle with his creditors, and soon thereafter he started a brick business.

Amid all of these efforts, Defoe found time to fight with the Duke of Monmouth in an unsuccessful attempt to establish a Protestant monarchy in England. In 1700, he published a poem entitled "A True-Born Englishman", a satire on those who mocked King William because he was Dutch. According to Backscheider, this became the most popular poem of the early eighteenth century.

Defoe eventually began writing for a variety of publications and enjoyed a career writing on almost every conceivable topic. In 1702, he published a pamphlet entitled *The Shortest Way with the Dissenters,* angering nearly everyone and landing him in jail for seditious libel. He wrote successfully for an assortment of political and religious causes—some diametrically opposed to each other—and both in support of and against the current government and ruler. He is reputed to be one of the most prolific writers of nonfiction in the English language to this day.

In 1719, Defoe published *Robinson Crusoe,* supposedly based on the adventures of Alexander Selkirk (a Scottish sailor and castaway). Defoe used a style of writing in which he took supposedly true events and fictionalized them in an attempt to appeal to a broad audience. In 1722, he published *Moll Flanders,* purportedly taken from the exploits of an infamous female pickpocket of the day.

Although historians disagree as to the exact number of books, articles, pamphlets, poems, and other pieces attributable to Defoe, more than five hundred works have been credited to him. Defoe continued writing almost up to his death at the approximate age of seventy on April 26, 1731, in London.

Plot Summary

The Preface

Defoe's narrator opens *Moll Flanders* as the person who has edited Moll's first-person story of her life. He implores the novel's readers to learn something from his story of a woman drawn to crime and to pay attention less to the fabulous tales of misdeeds and felonies and more to the moral of the story.

Section One

Moll Flanders relates the circumstances of her birth at London's Newgate Prison to a woman imprisoned for stealing cloth. She is reared by gypsies until she is three years old when she is transferred to a home run by a woman she refers to as the nurse, who schools Moll in needlework and manners.

By the time Moll is eight, she knows that she does not intend to become a servant, even though that is what is expected of her by the town authorities, given her lack of financial means. She decides, instead, to become a "gentlewoman," like a neighbor who seems to earn her living by needlework but is actually a prostitute. Moll's innocence and energy amuse the nurse, and she decides to keep Moll around as her assistant.

Moll, because she is pretty and clever, becomes a favorite of the wealthy ladies in town, and they enjoy visiting with her and giving her money for her living expenses. Her needlework is earning her money as well.

When Moll is fourteen, the nurse dies, and Moll is taken in by one of the wealthy women. The two brothers in the new family begin to take notice of her because she is becoming a woman. The elder brother, through flattery, succeeds in getting Moll to sleep with him. He offers to keep her as his mistress and to eventually marry her. They must keep their relationship a secret.

Meanwhile, the younger brother, Robin, makes it clear that he finds Moll very attractive and wishes to marry her. Moll expresses her concern to the elder brother, who says she must accept Robin's attentions. Moll eventually realizes that she is in a bad situation and that to protect her own and the elder brother's reputations, she must marry Robin. The family approves of the match because they are impressed that Moll is reluctant to marry Robin, meaning that she is not a fortune hunter. Moll and Robin live together for five years and have two children. Robin dies, and the children go to his parents. Moll is "left loose upon the world" and acts the part of the beautiful, young widow, attending parties and living a wild life.

Section Two

Eventually Moll finds a new husband, the draper, who is a rake and is arrested for his debts. He breaks out of prison and escapes to France. Moll finds herself in a tight situation again, gives herself the name of Mrs. Flanders, and changes her address.

She moves in with a woman (a captain's widow) who gets married soon after, leaving Moll on her own again. Moll, with the help of her former roommate, devises a scheme in which rumors are spread that Moll has a huge fortune. She re-

ceives quite a few suitors and is able to choose one based upon how much he loves her. After they are married, she reveals that she does not have quite as much money as was rumored, but she is not to blame because she herself never said anything about her finances. Her suitor confesses that his finances aren't quite what he had suggested either and says that, to save money, they must live at his plantation in Virginia.

Moll and her new husband live together for a number of years in Virginia and have three children. Eventually, through discussions with her mother-in-law, Moll comes to the horrible realization that the woman is her mother, thus making her husband her brother. Moll's mother urges her to cover up the entire affair, but Moll insists that she cannot. The mother promises Moll that she will secretly leave an inheritance for her, separate from her brother/husband's if she buries this problem and stays in Virginia, but Moll decides to break the news to him. He attempts suicide and becomes ill at the news, but agrees that she should leave.

Section Three

When Moll arrives in England, she realizes that her cargo has been destroyed and that she is beginning life again with very little money and few possessions. She goes to Bath, thinking that the fashionable resort will be a good place to find a new husband, but the men there only want mistresses. Moll spends platonic time with the gentleman in Bath, a wealthy man whose wife is mentally ill, and eventually accepts money from him.

The gentleman becomes quite ill while on a trip away from Bath and asks Moll to come and nurse him back to health, which she does. They stay together for two years in a platonic relationship until a night of much wine, after which Moll becomes his mistress for six years. All is well until the gentleman becomes ill again. He escapes death but ends their relationship.

Section Four

Moll is now forty-two years old, no longer a young woman. She is interested in finding a husband again. Moll goes to Lancashire and meets with a north-country woman who claims that her brother, Jemy, is wealthy and interested in marriage. Jemy and Moll marry, but they soon discover that, though they do sincerely love one another, neither has any fortune to bring to the marriage. Moll also discovers that Jemy and the north-country woman are former lovers and had planned this scheme to claim Moll's supposed fortune. Jemy leaves, but he and Moll promise that they will someday meet up again.

Moll returns to London where she discovers that she is again pregnant. She moves to a house run by a midwife of questionable background. In the meantime, her bank clerk friend is pressuring her through letters to marry him and offering status reports on his efforts at securing a divorce.

After she has her baby and finds a home for it, Moll marries the bank clerk. They live a comfortable life for about five years. But the bank clerk dies from grief when he loses most of their money. Moll is again out on the street with little money and two children.

Section Five

Moll begins stealing to make a living. She does not know where or how to sell the things she steals, so she visits her old friend, the midwife, whom she also calls the governess. The governess is impressed with Moll's thieving skills and talks her into stealing full-time.

Moll becomes quite accomplished at stealing and is well-known around town for her exploits. She and her partners concoct various schemes, including using a house fire to distract the owners from their property and striking a deal with a customs official over some illegal Flemish lace. Moll always comes out safe, but her accomplices are usually caught and sent to prison or executed. Moll protects her identity, even from her partners, by disguises and also by changing her name and where she lives. The governess continues encouraging her to steal and is sharing in the plunder.

Moll goes to a fair and meets the baron, who has been drinking too much. They end up sleeping together, and Moll steals from him after he passes out. The governess knows the man and develops a scheme whereby he pays for the return of his stolen goods in exchange for her keeping quiet about how they came to be stolen. Moll becomes his mistress for a year during which time Moll does not steal.

After this relationship ends, Moll begins stealing again. She becomes very wealthy, thanks to her thievery, but she does not want to stop. She is proud that she is so well-known and successful. This is her undoing; she is caught trying to remove some valuable cloth from a home and is sent to Newgate Prison.

Section Six

While Moll is at Newgate Prison, she hears that Jemy has been brought in for being a high-wayman. Moll is tried and sentenced to death. Both she and the governess repent of their sins.

Moll's minister somehow secures a reprieve of her death sentence, and Moll is condemned to "transportation"; she must board a ship to America and become a slave for five years. She contrives a way to meet with Jemy. He reluctantly agrees that going to America may be better than death, and plans to seek a "transport" sentence as well.

The governess, through various dealings with the ship's captain and others, arranges to have Moll and Jemy sent to America but released from their obligations once there. Moll arranges to have tools and other supplies shipped with them so that she and Jemy can set themselves up as plantation owners.

Section Seven

Once in America, Moll discovers that her brother/husband and son are still living nearby. She desires to see them and also to see if her now-dead mother has left her any inheritance, but she does not want Jemy to know anything about her past life. She and Jemy end up buying a piece of land in southern Maryland.

Moll goes to see her brother/husband and her son in Virginia. She and her son have a joyous reunion, but she learns that her brother/husband is ill and nearly deaf. Moll discovers that her mother did leave her a small plantation that produces a yearly income. Moll does not tell her son of Jemy and does not give Jemy the entire truth of what she has been doing in Virginia.

A year later, Moll returns to Virginia to collect the income on her inherited land, whereupon she learns from her son that her brother/husband is dead. She mentions to her son that she may now want to marry again. Ultimately, she lets her son know about Jemy and gives Jemy all of the background on her previous life in Virginia. Jemy is not disturbed, and they continue to live well and prosper, returning to England "to spend the remainder of our years in sincere penitence for the wicked lives we have lived."

Characters

The Bank Clerk

Moll meets the bank clerk just before she is about to go to Lancashire and feels that she needs someone to hold her money in London while she is away. He almost immediately expresses romantic interest in her, telling Moll that his wife is a whore. Moll likes him, noting that he is a stable man, but she puts off his advances for some time, until he is able to divorce his wife. They eventually marry, have children, and live happily until the bank clerk dies from grief over losing most of the family's money.

The Draper

The draper is Moll's second husband. During her marriage to him, Moll says she "had the pleasure of seeing a great deal of my money spent upon myself." The draper ends up in prison for failing to pay his debts but escapes and flees to France, leaving Moll with "a husband, and no husband." Because of the draper's bad credit, Moll changes her name to Mrs. Flanders and moves to the Mint, a neighborhood where debtors find legal sanctuary.

The Elder Brother

The elder brother is Moll's first love, a handsome but tricky young man. His mother and sisters find Moll clever and ask her to live with them after the woman who originally took in Moll dies. The elder brother flatters Moll and eventually gets her into his bed with promises of marriage and gifts. But he considers Moll his mistress and has no intentions of marrying her. Eventually, he tires of Moll and creates a series of deceptions, putting Moll into a position where she must marry his brother, Robin. On Robin and Moll's wedding night, the elder brother gets Robin drunk so that he will not know that Moll is not a virgin.

Moll Flanders

Moll Flanders, the heroine and first-person narrator of the novel, was born in Newgate Prison to a thief who would have been hung had she not been pregnant with Moll. While Moll is still an infant, her mother is sentenced to "transportation" and sent to America to work on a plantation, making Moll an orphan. Moll spends her childhood living first with gypsies, then with a woman who takes in orphans, and finally with a family who enjoys her company.

Moll is a beautiful woman. She uses her beauty and cleverness to avoid servitude and poverty. She is forever seeking a rich husband and thinking up ways to acquire money. When she reaches middle-age and realizes that her beauty has faded, she finds herself in dire financial straights. Her solution is to turn to stealing to support herself. While she states throughout the book that she is sorry for the crimes

Media Adaptations

- In 1965, Paramount adapted *Moll Flanders* as a film entitled *The Amorous Adventures of Moll Flanders,* starring Kim Novak and Richard Johnson, and directed by Terence Young. It is available as a video in VHS format.

- In 1996, Robin Wright, Morgan Freeman, and Stockard Channing starred in a big-screen version of the novel titled simply *Moll Flanders*, produced by MGM and directed by Pen Densham. It is available on MGM Video in VHS or DVD format.

- In 1975, the British Broadcasting Corporation produced *Moll Flanders* for the television screen, in two episodes.

- In 1981, Granada Television (U.K.) produced a four-part television version entitled Fortunes and Misfortunes of Moll Flanders, starring Alex Kingston as Moll Flanders and directed by David Atwood. It is available as a videotape in VHS format from Anchor Bay Entertainment.

she has committed, she blames others for forcing her to choose such a life. Despite her dangerous life, she seems always to be the lucky one: while her partners in crime often meet violent ends and her husbands either die or run into trouble, Moll is always left standing.

Moll is married a total of five times and has many lovers. Her first husband, Robin, is not her choice, but she has a contented, five-year marriage with him, producing two children before he dies. Her second husband is a draper by trade and careless with money. He is forced to leave England after escaping from debtors' prison. Theoretically, Moll continues to be married to this man throughout the book.

Moll's third husband ends up being her brother, whom she leaves after discovering this unsavory fact. She and her fourth husband, a highwayman, agree to separate when they find out they have lied to each other about their individual wealth. Her fifth husband is a bank clerk who dies after losing all of the family's money. After his death, Moll is destitute, and turns to picking pockets and other crimes to survive.

Moll eventually ends up in her birthplace, Newgate Prison, after she is caught stealing expensive cloth from a home. Her luck never seems to leave her, however, and her death sentence is commuted to "transportation," as her mother's had been. She connects up with her fourth husband, Jemy, and they move to Virginia to start a plantation together. She finishes the novel a prosperous woman in her sixties, still living with Jemy.

Moll reports that she changes her name a number of times (but usually does not indicate to what name), usually to protect her identity. She is known as Mrs. Flanders when living in the Mint neighborhood and, when she is living with the rich matron who takes her in after the nurse dies, she is called Mrs. Betty, or Betty. This term was used in the eighteenth century to indicate both a servant and female promiscuity.

The Gentleman in Bath

Moll meets the gentleman after returning, nearly destitute, to England from Virginia. The gentleman is married but claims his wife is crazy. He meets Moll in the fashionable resort town of Bath where he becomes quite enamored of her and wishes to help her financially. She refuses at first, but in time she does accept money from him as a gift. He leaves Bath, becomes ill, and asks Moll to nurse him back to health. She does, and they stay together for two years in a platonic relationship. One night, after drinking too much wine, Moll becomes his mistress. She has a child by him, and he provides for their care with an apartment and other necessities. Moll remains his mistress for about six years until the gentleman gets sick again, almost dies, and, in a moment of remorsefulness, ends his affair with Moll.

The Governess

The governess serves as Moll's midwife when she is pregnant (probably with Jemy's child). The governess runs a shady establishment, mostly catering to whores who need a place to stay during their pregnancies.

Later in the novel, Moll returns to the governess after Moll performs her first few thefts, unsure how to sell the items she has stolen. As it turns out, the governess is a pawnbroker and, seeing that Moll is an especially talented thief, encourages her

to continue her crimes. She and Moll work together until Moll is caught and sent to Newgate Prison. This so unsettles the governess that she becomes remorseful about her life and sends a minister to Moll in prison to help her recognize the evil of her ways. But the governess also tries to bribe prison officials to help Moll and works a few deals to get Moll and Jemy's legal situation smoothed out.

Humphrey

Humphrey is Moll's son, born to Moll and her brother in Virginia. When Moll returns to Virginia with Jemy, she contacts her family there, and Humphrey responds to her letter. Their reunion is joyous, and Humphrey heaps gifts and money upon Moll. He arranges to help manage the land Moll's mother has left her, and Moll visits him whenever she returns to her brother's plantation to pick up her annual income from the land.

James

See Jemy

Jemy

Jemy is Moll's fourth husband, and she often refers to him as her "Lancashire husband." A north-country woman claiming to be Jemy's sister introduces them to each other, representing Jemy as a gentleman with land and money and believing rumors that Moll is also fabulously wealthy. Moll and Jemy marry but soon discover the truth—that neither of them has any money. Moll also finds out that this arrangement was unsavory from the start; the woman who claimed to be his sister is actually his former lover and was to have received a fee for the match.

Moll and Jemy truly love each other and do not really want to separate. Jemy believes the parting is necessary but tells Moll he will try to make some money farming in Ireland and then will contact her. She tries to convince him to go with her to Virginia to start a plantation, but he is not interested. They part, promising to keep in touch.

Moll briefly sees Jemy again later in the novel, and saves his life by convincing a mob that he is not the highwayman they suspect him to be. She ultimately connects up with him for good toward the end of the book when he is brought to Newgate Prison for highway robbery. She successfully persuades him to get his sentence commuted to "transportation," like hers, so they can leave together for Virginia and start a plantation together. In America, they become quite prosperous and return to England to live out their days together.

Novels for Students

Moll's Brother/Husband

After planting gossip to make Moll's suitors believe that she is wealthy, Moll and a friend successfully attract a man of means. This man becomes Moll's third husband and, upon discovering that Moll has no wealth, he insists they move to Virginia to live more cheaply. There, after bearing him three children, Moll discovers that she is her husband's sister through conversations with his mother.

Eventually, against the wishes of her mother-in-law, Moll tells her brother what she has learned. He agrees that she must return to England. Moll sees him again when she returns to Virginia in her sixties. He is ill and nearly blind, and does not recognize her.

Moll's Mother

Moll's mother appears twice in the book. Early in the novel, she is mentioned as being in Newgate Prison, where she gives birth to Moll. Soon after Moll's birth, she is sent to Virginia as punishment for her thieving.

In Virginia, Moll's mother serves first as a slave, then eventually marries her master and bears him two children—one of whom becomes Moll's third husband. Later in the novel when Moll moves to Virginia with this husband, she discovers his mother is also her mother. Moll keeps this information secret for a few years, but finally tells her mother what she knows. Moll's mother, like Moll, is horrified, but begs Moll to cover up the secret and continue living with her son as his wife, for the sake of the family. She promises Moll that she will leave her an inheritance apart from what she leaves her son, which she does.

The Nurse

The nurse takes in Moll when she is a young orphan and promises the town authorities that she will be responsible for her. At her home, The Nurse educates orphans and teaches them useful skills, in preparation for their lives as servants. She prevents Moll from having to become a servant by keeping her in the house as her assistant. The Nurse dies when Moll is about fourteen years old.

Robin

Robin is Moll's first husband, a man who truly loves and respects her. Moll is not interested in marrying him but has no choice, thanks to the scheming of his elder brother. Robin and Moll have a solid marriage, despite the fact that she does not find him attractive, and she bears him two children. After being married only five years, Robin dies, and his parents take the children from Moll.

Themes

Money

Truly, in *Moll Flanders,* money makes the world go around. Hardly a page goes by in the novel without a mention of money. Moll's money worries begin at the age of eight when Moll must figure out a way to avoid being placed in servitude. To do this, she tells the nurse who has taken her in that she can work, and that eventually she will earn her own way in the world. When the nurse expresses doubt that Moll can really earn her keep, Moll responds, "I will work harder, says I, and you shall have it all."

Though Moll is easily flattered by men commenting on her beauty, she is even more flattered at their attentions if the men are wealthy. When she and the elder brother are discussing their future, he shows her a purse full of coins that he claims he will give her every year until they are married, in essence for remaining his mistress. Moll's "colour came and went, at the sight of the purse," and at the thought of the money he had promised her.

Moll complains after the death of her first husband that no one in the city appreciates a beautiful, well-mannered woman, and that the only thing a man is looking for in a wife is her ability to bring money into the relationship. She notes that "money only made a woman agreeable" when she wanted to become a wife, and that only whores and mistresses are chosen because of their personal and physical qualities—and, of course, these relationships are built upon money, as well.

Ultimately, most of Moll's actions are precipitated by the need or desire for money. She searches for husbands who have money and usually tries to give them the mistaken impression that she is wealthy. She plots and schemes because she believes that all that matters in life is the acquisition of wealth. Even when she becomes the richest thief in all of England and her fame threatens her ability to continue stealing, she cannot stop her hunt for more money. Her greed is ultimately her downfall, for she gets sloppy and is caught stealing from a house where she cannot pretend to have been shopping.

Sexuality

Defoe is not shy about making clear that Moll is fairly free with sexual favors, and that they are

Topics for Further Study

- Create a time line showing the major political, religious, social, scientific, and cultural events that occurred while Moll Flanders and Daniel Defoe lived (the late 1600s through the early 1700s).

- Elizabeth Frye was an English prison reform activist who lived from 1780 to 1845. She especially worked to improve conditions for female prisoners at Newgate Prison. Investigate the prison reform movement in England and find out its history. Were there any prison reformers working during the time Moll Flanders was in Newgate? What were the typical conditions at a prison such as Newgate?

- Syphilis and other venereal diseases were common in London during the late seventeenth and early eighteenth centuries. Research the prevalence of these diseases and how it compares to their current prevalence in London and in the United States. Examine how venereal diseases were treated during the time of *Moll Flanders* and how this compares to current treatments.

- Choose an episode from *Moll Flanders* that you especially like, and write a script for a soap opera featuring the episode. Update the characters, setting, and events as you think appropriate to a present-day story.

---

often tied to receiving money. In fact, on the novel's original frontispiece, Defoe states that Moll is "twelve year a whore." She loses her virginity to the elder brother and remains his mistress in return for a promise of marriage and money. Although she and the gentleman she meets in Bath both insist on remaining platonic companions, she eventually initiates sex one night after they have shared a large amount of wine: "Thus the government of our virtue was broken, and I exchang'd the place of friend for that unmusical harsh-sounding title of whore." They go on to have a long affair, and he supports her financially for a number of years.

One of the more dramatic uses of Moll's sexuality comes after Moll has had good success as a pickpocket. She goes to a fair to see if she can lift any gold watches and meets up with a baron. They end up in bed together that evening, and because he is so drunk, she is able to relieve him of his money and jewelry. The next day, the governess concocts a scheme in which she and Moll sell back to the baron his own stolen valuables and Moll becomes his mistress for a year. This saves Moll the trouble of having to steal for her living for a while.

Secrets and Lies

Moll's life is filled with secrets and lies. She is cagey from the beginning as to her real name. She begins her story indicating that she has lived under a variety of names, but that the book's readers should refer to her as Moll Flanders "till I dare own who I have been, as well as who I am." Nearly every time she moves from one relationship to another, she gives a fabricated name to her latest beau; but oddly enough, she rarely reveals what that new name is in the text of the book.

Moll is also fond of disguises and uses them frequently in her career as a pickpocket. She disguises herself as a widow, as a woman of means, as a man, and as a beggar to confuse those from whom she is stealing. In one humorous instance, she dresses as a widow and comes just short of committing a theft but is nearly taken for the actual thief, who is also dressed as a widow.

Moll is never totally open about her past with any of her lovers. For example, she marries her first husband because she must lie about her relationship with his brother, and she catches her third husband because she and a friend spread gossip around town that she is a wealthy widow. In fact, Moll seems fairly comfortable with presenting herself to nearly every man as someone she is not, excusing her behavior as necessary given the treachery of men in general. She never reveals to husbands three, four, and five that she is still legally married to her second husband. And when she does marry, she usually keeps what money she has a secret. For example, even when she and Jemy, the love of her life, reunite and move to Virginia, she secretly keeps a healthy sum of her wealth back in London, managed by the governess.

Perseverance and Ambition

The story of Moll Flanders is the story of a woman who is nothing if not persistent in her quest to become independent and financially comfortable. From an early age she sets her sights on becoming something more than just a servant girl, pleading with the nurse to let her learn how to make money as a seamstress. Even though Moll spends much of her time in the book pursuing marriage, she is adamant that women should not have to settle for just any man. "Nothing is more certain than that the ladies always gain of the men by keeping their ground," she admonishes.

With every fall from fortune Moll suffers, she has a plan that will put her back on her feet. She is able to survey her situation quickly and come up with a solution—although, granted, her solutions are not always legal and ethical, and they usually require a heavy dose of luck. When she is young and living with a wealthy family, she realizes that she must be even more beautiful and talented than the sisters. To that end, she learns French and dancing by listening in on their lessons. When she discovers that she has been married to her brother and has borne his children, she devises a plan whereby she is able to get on a ship for England and make a new start. When Moll, by her own reckoning, is forced into a life of crime, she becomes the best-known and richest thief in England. And even when she is faced with the gallows, somehow she comes out of the situation fine, sailing back to America with her only true love and a cargo hold filled with tools and equipment that will make her a rich plantation owner.

Crime and Remorse

On the whole, *Moll Flanders* is a book about crime. Moll turns to crime after her affair with the gentleman in Bath leaves her destitute and aimlessly wandering around London. Her looks are gone and, in a daze, she steals a bundle of silver goods. Not knowing how to sell the items, she returns to her old friend, the governess, who, as it happens, is a pawnbroker and encourages Moll to pursue stealing as an occupation.

Moll seems to enjoy her occupation and excels in it. In fact, her vanity about her beauty is transferred to a sort of pride in being a great criminal, and she is always prompted to do more when the governess reminds her of how famous she is. Moll dabbles in a few other areas outside of theft and picking pockets, but she realizes that theft is her strong suit and wisely does not venture far from it.

Whether Moll is a hardened criminal is open for debate. She steals valuables from children and then transfers the blame for her act to their parents, who either should not have dressed them so well or should not have let them out by themselves.

Throughout the section in which Moll is stealing, she vacillates from blaming her victim or society for putting her in a position where she must steal to urging the reader to learn something about remorse from her story of sin. Moll claims to be penitent just before her death sentence is commuted to "transportation," as does the governess, stricken with grief over Moll's fate. But soon after Moll realizes that she will not die in prison, she begins to scheme again with the governess to make her sentence a bit easier—although she does not accept the governess's offer to avoid completely the forced trip to America.

Style

Picaresque Novel

Moll Flanders is considered an example of a picaresque novel. These novels usually employ a first-person narrator recounting the adventures of a scoundrel or low-class adventurer who moves from place to place and from one social environment to another in an effort to survive. The construction of these novels, like that of *Moll Flanders,* is typically episodic, and the hero or heroine is a cynical and amoral rascal who lives by his or her wits.

Structure

Defoe did not use chapter or section divisions to break up the work. The action moves chronologically, though, and is divided into close to one hundred different episodes. Defoe covers long periods of time with sweeping statements, as when Moll refers to her first marriage by saying, "It concerns the story in hand very little to enter into the farther particulars of the family, . . . for the five years I liv'd with this husband."

Defoe begins the novel with a preface in which he claims that the story is more of a "private history" than a novel. He urges the reader to be more interested in the parts where Moll is remorseful about her crimes than in the crimes themselves, and he recommends the book "as a work from every part of which something may be learned."

Point-of-View

Defoe wrote the novel in the first person, with Moll telling the story of her life. This form brings Moll close to readers, as if she is speaking directly to them. As well, Moll tells her story from the vantage point of being nearly seventy years old and being, purportedly, repentant. She pauses occasionally in the action to speak from her position as a penitent seventy-year-old and cautions about particular behaviors and choices.

Hero/Heroine

Moll is not a typical heroine because she is not someone whose behavior is admirable. Very often her actions are morally reprehensible and open to condemnation. Her integrity, at the very least, is suspect. But she is the heroine of her own story, nonetheless, because she does capture some of the qualities of the traditional heroine: one who is brave in the face of adversity, successfully challenges the status quo, and progresses through the novel with a certain amount of fortitude and purpose. Moll's life is victorious, in a way, because in the end she both gets what she wants *and* appears sorry for the damage she has caused.

Romantic Tone

Defoe has written *Moll Flanders* in an exaggerated fashion, developing a protagonist in Moll who is, for example, not only a good thief but also the richest and most famous thief in the country. She marries not one or two men, but five, one of whom—almost beyond belief—just happens to be her long-lost brother. The novel is written with a romantic tone, meaning that actions are exaggerated and larger than life, not that people fall in love. The novel is almost soap opera-like given the amazing things that happen to Moll.

Foreshadowing

Defoe occasionally uses foreshadowing, a writing technique that creates the expectation of something happening later in the work. When she looks for a husband after the draper leaves her, Moll encounters a group of hard-drinking and hard-living rogues who try to interest her in a bit of fun, but she responds, "I was not wicked enough for such fellows as these yet." When Jemy and Moll break up because they have no money, she makes it clear that he will show up again later, noting, "But I shall have more to say of him hereafter."

Historical Context

The American Colonies and the English Economy

In the novel, Moll sails to Virginia twice: first as the wife of a plantation owner, and second as a convicted criminal sentenced to serve time as a

slave. In the late seventeenth century and early eighteenth century, Virginia was an English colony, evidence of expanding English overseas interests in the name of trade and political power. Settled in the early 1600s, Virginia was a thriving and important complement to England's economy by the early 1700s.

During this period, wealth came progressively more from merchants' capital, creating a powerful and prosperous business class. Business was booming in England, fostering an attitude that there was lots of money to be made. England's major manufactured export product during this period was cloth, which, along with other manufactured goods, was shipped to the American colonies in exchange for an increasingly valuable commodity, tobacco.

The Role of Women

While the philosophy of the eighteenth century Enlightenment period addressed such issues as individual liberties, social welfare, economic liberty, and education, these concerns did not translate into major changes for women between the late 1600s and early 1700s. In fact, there are indications that the status of women declined during this period; in 1600, more than two-thirds of the businesses in London were reported to be owned by women, but by the end of the eighteenth century, that rate had been reduced to only ten percent.

Because the English economy at this time was based on the family unit, financial success determined that most people live within a family unit. In such an environment, society looked upon individuals who lived outside of a family unit with suspicion and assumed they were probably criminals, beggars, or prostitutes. Moll, when she finds herself in particularly difficult situations, frequently bemoans the fact that she does not have any family or friends whose household she could join. Essentially, her eternal search for a husband is a search for a family unit of her own.

Working-class women were expected to participate in the labor force as early as their sixth birthday. If a child was an orphan without anyone willing to provide financial support, as Moll's nurse did for her, the authorities expected the orphan to go into "service," usually household work for young girls. Women could rarely marry without a dowry, an amount of money that went to the husband as a sort of investment in the family economic unit.

Women of laboring families, married or single, worked in low-status jobs. Middle-and upper-

Compare & Contrast

- **1700s:** London's population reaches 550,000, up from 450,000 in 1660. Despite losing as many as 100,000 citizens to the Great Plague in 1665, and the destruction of much of the city in 1666 during the three-day Great Fire, London is now the largest city in Europe. Rebuilding London after the Great Fire takes place quickly and haphazardly.

  Today: London now boasts about seven million people within its six hundred and twenty square miles and is still the largest city in Europe. Major historical buildings, such as the Royal Opera House and the British Museum, are being renovated.

- **1700s:** Middle- and upper-class English women have more economic options than lower-class women; however, women are increasingly excluded from productive work as their social status increases. Opportunities in areas such as teaching are growing, but trade guilds and apprenticeships exclude women in large numbers while some formerly female professions, such as midwifery, are being crowded out by new male health-care professionals.

  Today: Women make up 45 percent of the workforce in the United Kingdom, and Britain employs more women than any other European country. Not only are women found in positions throughout government, education, medicine, business, and other professions, but they account for about 35 percent of new business ventures.

- **1700s:** Black slaves comprise 24 percent of the Virginia colony's population in 1715, up from less than 5 percent in 1671. Slavery is not abolished in Virginia until after the United States Civil War.

  Today: U.S. Census 2000 reports for the state of Virginia show that African Americans comprise about 20 percent of the total population.

- **Early 1700s:** The English criminal Jack Sheppard is famous for his astonishing escapes from custody, particularly his 1724 escape from Newgate Prison. His exploits became the subject of numerous narratives and plays, some attributed to Daniel Defoe, and he is the hero of William Harris Ainsworth's 1839 novel *Jack Sheppard.*

  Today: Newgate Prison was demolished in 1902, and today the front iron doors of the prison can be viewed in the Museum of London.

---

class women had more economic options although by the seventeenth century, as a woman's status increased, her ability to secure productive work diminished as she was not expected to be in a situation where she would have to work.

Many progressive Englishmen of the day believed that education was a paramount requirement for a civilized society; educational opportunities were extended to middle- and upper-class women in addition to men. But existing attitudes dictated that only men receive instruction in the more intellectual subjects such as philosophy and science, and that women should study subjects that would contribute to their moral development and to their desirability as marriage prospects. These subjects included singing, dancing, and languages, as demonstrated by the young girls in the household of Moll's first husband, Robin. Moll listens in on these lessons, giving her an edge that most girls in her economic status did not have.

Critical Overview

When *Moll Flanders* was published in 1722, most reactions to it focused on one of two points: which of the numerous infamous female pickpockets of the day Defoe was writing about when he created Moll, or the base nature of the story itself. On the

Robin Wright Penn as Moll in the 1996 film version of the novel

latter count, a famous anonymous couplet, appearing in a 1729 edition of *The Flying Post; or Weekly Medley,* indicated that only members of the lower classes were reading Defoe's hugely popular book:

> Down in the kitchen, honest Dick and Doll Are studying Colonel Jack and Flanders Moll.

However, many have pointed out that, given the popularity of the work, more than just servants were buying copies of the novel. As to its reception and popularity, Maximillian Novak points out in *The Dictionary of Literary Biography,* "Although there were numerous chapbook versions of Moll Flanders, it was not the kind of work that was sufficiently 'polite' or proper for either the eighteenth or for most of the nineteenth century."

According to Edward H. Kelly in his foreword to the Norton Critical Edition of *Moll Flanders,* "the novel was often dismissed by nineteenth-century critics and biographers as unimportant, 'secondary,' or immoral." Two critics of the nineteenth century found little to like about Defoe and his *Moll Flanders.* W. C. Roscoe in an 1856 issue of the *National Review* condemns Defoe for writing with little imagination and with too few attempts to delve into the interiors of his characters. Roscoe charges that Defoe "abides in the concrete; he has no analytical perception whatever. Never was there a man to whom a yellow primrose was

less or anything more than a yellow primrose." Specifically about Moll, Roscoe writes, "We must use our own insight and judgment if we wish to know what really was the interior character of Moll Flanders, just as we must have done had we met her in life—not altogether a pleasant sort of person." Leslie Stephen, writing in his book *Hours in a Library,* picks up on Roscoe's sentiments, writing that Defoe accumulates merely facts in many of his novels, and that the story of Moll Flanders should not claim "any higher interest than that which belongs to the ordinary police report, given with infinite fulness and vivacity of detail."

Twentieth-century critics are considerably kinder to Defoe, possibly because of the passing of the Victorian Age and the introduction of less rigid concepts about the inclusion of sex and antisocial behavior in literature. Virginia Woolf was the daughter of the critic Leslie Stephen, and her impressions of Moll Flanders could not have been more different than her father's. In *The Common Reader,* Woolf praises Defoe's "peculiar genius" for creating a complicated "woman of her own account." And she directly confronts her father's earlier charge that Defoe was a writer little interested in the interior psychology of Moll Flanders, arguing that "the list of qualities and graces of this seasoned old sinner is by no means exhausted."

Moll's psychological underpinnings are of continuing concern for the contemporary critic, and increasingly most do not charge Defoe with being deficient in how he portrays his heroine. Ian Watt, writing in his book *The Rise of the Novel: Studies in Defoe, Richardson, and Fielding,* is confident that Defoe gives Moll Flanders plenty of reasons to behave as she does and that her personality is much more than one-dimensional. "Defoe makes us admire the speed and resolution of Moll's reactions to profit or danger; and if there are no detailed psychological analyses, it is because they would be wholly superfluous," he argues. According to Watt, the perception that Moll is a one-dimensional character rests in the fact of when the novel was written. "We place Defoe's novels in a very different context from that of their own time; we take novels much more seriously now, and we judge his by the more exacting literary standards of today," writes Watt. This has caused many readers of *Moll Flanders,* in fact, to see irony where there was none intended by Defoe.

Despite the differing interpretations of Defoe's *Moll Flanders,* critics almost universally respect the author for his part in developing the modern novel form. In fact, Defoe is commonly known as the "father of the English novel."

Criticism

Susan Sanderson

Sanderson holds a master of fine arts degree in fiction writing and is an independent writer. In this essay, she argues that Defoe wrote his novel less as a book addressing Moll's soul and more as an entertaining book addressing Moll's social and economic success.

In Defoe's *Moll Flanders,* mind-boggling things happen to the book's heroine: events align to create amazing coincidences; consequences that might prove pesky in future episodes simply disappear; the heroine freely employs disguises and changes her name; and, though numerous trials and tribulations befall her, the heroine still rises above the fray to become a success. Sound familiar?

Give Moll a different set of clothes and move her to an anonymous mid-sized American city, and you have the basis for a character in a hugely successful soap opera. Defoe's novel, an enormously popular success in eighteenth-century England, is a story with a two-faceted appeal—the story of the

spunky girl that audiences love to hate. On one hand, she is wicked and participates in activities no self-respecting woman would ever dream of; but, on the other hand, she ultimately achieves independence, finds happiness with her one true love, and lives out her final days in spiritual accomplishment.

Why would Defoe, a man raised on the tenets of conservative Protestantism, write such a book? Was it really, as his narrator claims in the preface, "a work from every part of which something may be learned, and some just and religious inference is drawn"? Or is it a story less concerned with the spiritual and moral saving of Moll's soul and more with her financial recovery and ultimate success?

The same features that drew readers to *Moll Flanders* three hundred years ago still draw viewers to similar stories on television. And similar to the denials many people make today that they never watch such popular television shows as *Dallas* or *All My Children,* many made claims in the eighteenth century that Defoe's work was vulgar and lewd, and therefore not fit reading for honorable men and women. But *someone* was reading and enjoying Moll Flanders's exploits, just as viewers today still enjoy stories of remarkable coincidence and lusty heroines, stories filled with lessons of romantic and financial success built on (not necessarily legal or ethical) hard work and audacity.

Even the most casual reading of *Moll Flanders* reveals a romantic world where nearly everything ultimately works in the heroine's favor. First are the series of remarkable coincidences that occur around Moll—some positive, some not so positive, but all placed in a way that turns the tide of events ultimately to Moll's benefit. Moll, through trickery, catches a husband whom she discovers later to be her half-brother. While this is, indeed, horrible news, and Moll is appropriately shocked, this ugly chapter of her life plants the seeds for her successful return to America—a return whose punishment aspect is muted considerably by Moll's ability to buy her and Jemy's way out of servitude. Would she really so happily consider traveling to Virginia after her death sentence commutation if she were not hoping to take possession of whatever valuable inheritance her mother had promised her? When she urges Jemy to seek a reprieve of his death sentence and join her in America, she assures him that death would be much worse than moving to Virginia, for "you do not know the place so well as I do."

Moll's relationship with Jemy is filled with a series of even more coincidences, all paving the

> Defoe's novel, written during a period of economic expansion and mercantile opportunity, is a lesson in financial boot-strapping and self-sufficiency, couched in an entertaining tale of one woman's climb up the socio-economic ladder."

way to her eventual financial and romantic success with him. A number of years after she and Jemy have separated (because of their impoverished situations), Moll is freshly married again when she just happens to look out a window. She sees Jemy, who later leaves in a hurry, obviously due to his criminal occupation. When a mob comes by the next day, looking for Jemy as one of the highwaymen who recently robbed a coach, Moll vouches for him, swearing that he is an upstanding gentleman and not a villain. The next time she sees him is years later when they both just happen to be at Newgate Prison at the same time. She is able to persuade him to sail to America with her, primarily because she saved his life when she lied to the mob. "It was you that saved my life at that time, and I am glad I owe my life to you, for I will pay my debt to you now," Jemy promises.

Another resemblance to soap-opera style is the way Defoe creates difficulties for Moll and then simply drops them to move ahead in the story. E. M. Forster in his book *Aspects of the Novel* notes Defoe's tendency to toss away aspects of Moll's life, especially the mysterious disappearance of most of her children. "[S]tray threads [are] left about," according to Forster, "on the chance of the writer wanting to pick them up afterwards: Moll's early batch of children, for instance." While Defoe does mention in the book's preface the possibility of a sequel to the novel, as he did in *Robinson Crusoe*, the childrens' vanishing act could be simply a technique used by the author to both move the action along more quickly and smooth out the way for more bawdy adventures where the presence of children would be inconvenient, as well as dis-

tracting. When Moll does speak of her missing children, it is usually to recount that they were "happily" taken off her hands. Only two children seem to capture Moll's attention: the child she bears after her marriage to Jemy, and therefore most likely his child; and Humphrey, one of the children she has with her brother. Humphrey is the one who greets her in Virginia with loving tears and gifts of land and money.

But Defoe does more than create remarkable coincidences and sweep away troublesome details; Moll shares with her contemporary soap opera sisters a love of disguises. Moll is especially fond of dressing to deceive during her twelve-year criminal career, employing the costumes of a beggar, a widow, a wealthy gentlewoman, and a man. In a gambling house she pretends to be an innocent bystander who knows nothing about wagering and comes out of the afternoon a bit richer. In addition to simply changing her attire, Moll changes her name several times and, indeed, her identity. For example, after her marriage to the draper ends, Moll realizes that being the former wife of an escaped debtor has its problems. To combat this she moves to a different neighborhood, changes her name and, with the help of a friend, spreads gossip that she is a wealthy widow.

The character of the wealthy widow is one of her favorites. In fact, she often does not tell her male friends her real name and, even with Jemy, is not completely up front about her identity and her finances. She is proud of her ability to create a secret identity and to keep secrets when necessary. While most men might believe that women cannot keep secrets, Moll disagrees, and points to her life as evidence: "[F]or let them say what they please of our sex not being about to keep a secret, my life is a plain conviction to me of the contrary."

Ultimately, such a character must do more than run around wearing disguises and getting into trouble. For the audience to love her, she must, in the end, be a success, or the wicked and sinful things in which she has engaged will all be for nothing. Here is where Defoe excels because Moll Flanders, despite her sinful behavior, is nothing if not a tremendous success—in her love life, in her personal finances, and in her heart. She has risen from penury, born an orphan at Newgate Prison, to well beyond her original station in life. Her entire life is a concerted effort to avoid becoming anyone's servant, as Virginia Woolf notes in an essay in *The Common Reader,* "a woman on her own account." Moll becomes, by the end of the novel, a woman of independent means, beholden to no one, and, according to Woolf, "we admire Moll Flanders far more than we blame her."

Moll's tale, then, is more a story of the restitution of her self and less a story about the restitution of her soul, as Defoe might have his audience believe from his preface. Early in her prison experience, Moll tries to repent, but, in her own words, "that repentance yielded me no satisfaction, no peace" because she was sorry only for the punishment and not for the sin. Interestingly enough, though, when she does face the actual prospect of dying for her crime, she then believes she has truly succeeded in producing a real sense of repentance, although she is incapable of saying exactly what that is. "Indeed, those impressions are not to be explain'd by words, or if they are I am not mistress of words enough to express them," she says, an odd statement from someone who has put the last fifty or so years of her life into words.

Moll's life after declaring her repentance is not *precisely* like her previous life, but it certainly shares many of the same qualities. For example, to see Jemy and encourage him to follow her to America, she must again disguise herself. In addition, Moll has numerous discussions with Jemy and the governess concerning schemes to bribe their way out of the sentence of slavery and exile to America. And when she lands in America, Moll is obsessed with visiting her brother/husband's plantation to see if their mother has left her an inheritance. Moll prevents Jemy from learning anything about her inherited plantation until she is in a strong financial position—and even then she softens the news of her plantation and her sordid past with a huge bounty of expensive gifts shipped in from England.

Defoe's novel, written during a period of economic expansion and mercantile opportunity, is a lesson in financial boot-strapping and self-sufficiency, couched in an entertaining tale of one woman's climb up the socio-economic ladder. Pretending to frame it in cautionary language about avoiding the slippery slope of avarice and other transgressions, Defoe challenges anyone to "cast any reproach upon it, or our design in publishing it." He argues in the preface that

> there is not a wicked action in any part of it, but is first or last rendered unhappy and unfortunate; there is not a superlative villain brought upon the stage, but either he is brought to an unhappy end, or brought to be a penitent.

What Do I Read Next?

- The setting is London in the 1750s in Paula Allardyce's novel *Miss Philadelphia Smith* (1977). This romantic novel looks at class differences on a London street that is divided between the odd-numbered houses of the wealthy and the even-numbered houses of the middle-class. Philadelphia Smith lives in an even-numbered cottage and attracts the attention of a wealthy rake whose family lives on the odd-numbered side of the street.

- *Jack Sheppard,* written by William Harrison Ainsworth in 1839, is a novel that, like *Moll Flanders,* greatly romanticizes crime and criminals. In what is considered one of the "Newgate novels," named for the famous English prison, Ainsworth tells the story of Sheppard, a real-life burglar and jail-breaker.

- *Soldiers of Fortune* (1962), by Peter Bourne, gives a profile of the colonists of Virginia as they make the hard trip across the Atlantic Ocean. Their stories and others offer a panorama of English history and America's first colonists.

- *Roxana: The Fortunate Mistress* (1724) is Daniel Defoe's last and darkest novel. It is the purported autobiography of a woman, the mistress of rich and powerful men, who has traded her virtue for survival and then for fame and fortune.

But in the end, Moll is allowed to live out the last days of her life a wealthy woman, living with a man who may or may not be her legal husband, and her penance and punishment for her past life is indeed suspect.

Moll is a poster child for a sort of soap-opera-type heroine who, through grit and determination, pulls herself up by her own bootstraps and offers her life as a lesson in how to "begin the world upon a new foundation; . . . [and] live as new people in a new world." This is a story people have loved to hear throughout the ages, one much more

A prisoner sitting in a cell in London's Newgate Prison

powerful than a tale of sin and punishment and failure.

Source: Susan Sanderson, Critical Essay on *Moll Flanders,* in *Novels for Students,* The Gale Group, 2002.

John J. Richetti

In the following essay excerpt, Richetti focuses on Defoe's characterization of Moll Flanders, especially her moral ambiguity.

Critics have always recognized that Defoe's strong suit is the richly particularized incident, his weakness developing connections between epi-sodes. At first glance, *Moll Flanders* (1722) looks like the most formlessly episodic of Defoe's books, with over a hundred separate scenes tied together by rapid synopses of other events. And yet most critics would agree that Moll is Defoe's most memorable character, her story the most widely read and highly regarded of Defoe's fictions in the last fifty years. Where Jack seems a shadowy figure, an excuse for stringing adventures together, Moll has struck many readers as profoundly real. Her concreteness may be partially the result of her narrative's narrower setting; she spends most of her time in and around London. But a more important reason for the relative depth and unity of characteri-zation Defoe achieves lies in her gender. As a woman of no fixed social position and limited financial possibilities, she has a unifying and recurring problem: female survival in a masculine world. But richly varied as they are, the episodes in *Moll Flanders* are not a plot in any strict sense; they do not all fit together like a jigsaw puzzle, and one could safely omit some or rearrange others. Taken as a whole, however, they do have a degree of continuity, evoking much more convincingly than *Colonel Jack* a dense tangle of sexual, economic, and moral relationships between self and society.

Like all Defoe's books, *Moll Flanders* has its origin in a popular genre. A criminal biography, based loosely on the lives of two famous thieves, Moll King and Callico Sarah, the book pretends to be a documentary, like *Colonel Jack,* crowded with a variety of incidents in actual places: *The Fortunes and Misfortunes of the Famous Moll Flanders, who was born in Newgate, and during a life of continu'd variety for threescore years, besides her childhood, was twelve year a whore, five times a wife (whereof once to her own brother) twelve year a thief, eight year a transported felon in Virginia, at last grew rich, liv'd honest, and died a penitent, written from her own memorandums.* Although it is far more detailed and complicated than they are, *Moll Flanders* has important affinities with the criminal narratives it imitates. Much of the moral ambiguity in *Moll Flanders* derives from its origins in criminal biography, for as a literary and moral type, the criminal in the early eighteenth century (and now, perhaps) excites a mixture of moral disgust and fascination. Thus, Defoe's characterization of the infamous Jonathan Wild in his 1725 biography stresses Wild's singular, even unique courage: "It must be allowed to Jonathan's fame, that as he steered among rocks and dangerous shoals, so he was a bold pilot; he ventured in and always got out in a manner equally superior; no man ever did the like before him, and I say no man will attempt to do the like after him." To write about a criminal, of course, requires some justification; the subject has to deserve the limelight by being a monster of vice (like Jonathan Wild) or sometimes by being the best at the trade, never just a run-of-the-mill criminal. For example, Moll is hardly modest about her accomplishments as a thief. "I grew the greatest artist of my time, and work'd myself out of every danger," she brags, and goes on to note that where other thieves were in Newgate prison after six months, she worked for more than five years "and the people at Newgate, did not so much as know me; they had heard much of me indeed, and often expected me there; but I always got off, tho' many times in the extreamest danger." Even as Moll records with shame her "hardening" in crime, she still reports her unparalleled success at it, celebrating her fame even as she deplores its cause: "I grew more harden'd and audacious than ever, and the success I had, made my name as famous as any thief of my sort ever had been at Newgate, and in the Old-Bayly."

This blend of repentance and celebration is entirely typical of criminal biography, and it can be seen in cruder fashion in Defoe's own criminal biographies. For example, *The History of the remarkable Life of John Sheppard* (1724) validates as fact the incredible events of Sheppard's career as housebreaker and escape artist: "His history will astonish! and is not compos'd of fiction, fable, or stories plac'd at York, Rome, or Jamaica, but facts done at your doors, facts unheard of, altogether new, incredible, and yet uncontestable." In due course, Defoe's narrator is implicitly contemptuous of Sheppard's vulgar fame: "His escape and his being so suddenly re-taken made such a noise in the town, that it was thought all the common people would have gone mad about him; there being not a potter to be had for love nor money, nor getting into an ale-house, for butchers, shoemakers and barbers, all engag'd in controversies, and wagers, about Sheppard." But the overall effect is mitigation of Sheppard's guilt by detailed, admiring examination of his criminal techniques. The officers at Newgate, the narrator concludes, are not to blame for Sheppard's escapes. "They are but men, and have had to deal with a creature something more than man, a Proteus, supernatural. Words cannot describe him, his actions and workmanship which are too visible, best testifie him." But Defoe describes that workmanship at some length, dwelling with evident satisfaction on the smallest particulars. Visiting the scene of the escape, the narrator reports: "Three screws are visibly taken off the lock, and the doors as strong as art could make them, forc'd open: The locks and bolts either wrench'd or broke, and the cases and other irons made for their security cut asunder: An iron spike broke off from the hatch in the chapel, which he fix'd in the wall and fasten'd his blanket to it, to drop on the leads of Mr. Bird's house; his stockings were found on the leads of Newgate; 'tis question'd whether sixty pounds will repair the damage done to the jayl."

In all his work, fiction and factual journalism, Defoe is powerfully drawn to precisely how trades and crafts operate. This elaboration of techniques

> Much of the moral ambiguity in *Moll Flanders* derives from its origins in criminal biography, for as a literary and moral type, the criminal in the early eighteenth century (and now, perhaps) excites a mixture of moral disgust and fascination."

has a momentum of its own that blurs moral considerations, and crime becomes in the telling another set of fascinating procedures perfectly executed by masters like Sheppard or, in another, less violent mode, like Moll Flanders. Moll's skills as a thief are more subtle than Sheppard's spectacular escapes, a matter of watching for opportunity, walking the city and taking advantage of the rich prizes there, mastering the arts of disguise and social impersonation. This is how a confederate teaches Moll the art of stealing gold watches from ladies:

> At length she put me to practise, she had shewn me her art, and I had several times unhook'd a watch from her own side with great dexterity; at last she show'd me a prize, and this was a young lady big with child who had a charming watch, the thing was to be done as she came out of church; she goes on one side of the lady, and pretends, just as she came to the steps, to fall, and fell against the lady with so much violence as put her into a great fright, and both cry'd out terribly; in the very moment that she jostl'd the lady, I had hold of the watch, and holding it the right way, the start she gave drew the hook out and she never felt it; I made off immediately, and left my schoolmistress to come out of her pretended fright gradually, and the lady too; and presently the watch was miss'd; ay, says my comrade, then it was those rogues that thrust me down, I warrant ye; I wonder the gentlewoman did not miss her watch before, then we might have taken them.

And yet the difference between the sketchy sensationalism of criminal biography and the novelistic fullness of *Moll Flanders* is also apparent. Even as Moll describes with obvious satisfaction how she mastered her trade, she also dwells on the moral and psychological significance of that satisfaction. Moll realizes, as she looks back, that this marks a new phase in her career. Drawn into crime by poverty, Moll continues in it even though she might well live honestly if poorly by her needle. "But practise had hardened me, and I grew audacious to the last degree; and the more so, because I had carried it on so long, and had never been taken; for in a word, my new partner in wickedness and I went on together so long, without being ever detected, that we not only grew bold, but we grew rich, and we had at one time one and twenty gold watches in our hands." Yet even as Moll deplores her moral condition, a note of irrepressible triumph is heard in those twenty-one gold watches, as her pleasure in remembering her triumphs mixes with tough-minded analysis of her moral failure.

As she herself warns, Moll is "but a very indifferent monitor," and readers are advised to construct their "own just reflections, which they will be more able to make effectual than I, who so soon forget myself." At the very end of her story, Moll wonders at the goodness of Providence, and the abhorrence of her past such wonder provokes, but breaks off the reflection: "I leave the reader to improve these thoughts, as no doubt they will see cause, and I go on to the fact." Characteristically, Moll is a sort of ironic chorus on the foolishness she has seen in her time, and her discourse is peppered with wry reflections. Women who run into marriage, for example, "are a sort of ladies that are to be pray'd for among the rest of distemper'd people; and to me they look like people that venture their whole estates in a lottery where there is a hundred thousand blanks to one prize." And Moll the underworld moralist views some of her old associates with compact sarcasm. She remembers with some distaste two thieves, a man and a woman, with whom she worked briefly. Clumsy and coarse in their larcenous techniques, they are caught in housebreaking, which Moll always avoids, and her sardonic summary reveals her own sense of propriety: "they were partners it seems in the trade they carried on; and partners in something else too. In short, they robb'd together, lay together, were taken together, and at last were hang'd together."

In other words, Moll Flanders is not the conventionally defiant and/or repentant criminal of popular biography but possesses a distinctive, individuated voice and a crafty intelligence. She sounds at times like the former pickpocket she is, speaking in a racy demotic style, capable of self-irony, double entendre, and word play. As Defoe arranges it, she is an old woman looking back on her life with complicated retrospection, repentant

of course but also undiminished in wit and spirit and in fact pretty satisfied with a good deal of her story. The reader is conscious, in effect, of two characters, one narrating, the other acting. Much of Defoe's specifically novelistic innovation in *Moll Flanders* lies in just this process of interpretation old Moll brings to her narrative. What we are reading is not simply a record of a character in action but a process of remembering and interpreting that action whereby character is revealed and developed in complex ways through the act of narration itself. Moreover, many of Moll's interpretations of her life as she narrates it are open to question, morally inconsistent and thereby revealing (like the mixture of pride and repentance noted above) but also endearingly human. To an important extent, this tendency to ethical neutrality is the result of Defoe's realism which, as Ian Watt notes, subordinates "any coherent ulterior significance to the illusion that the text represents the authentic lucubrations of an historical person."

But this ethically neutral realism is accompanied, as always in Defoe's fictions, by elaborate didactic claims. The preface stresses that this is an expurgated autobiography, with Moll's saltier language cleaned up and "some of the vicious part of her life, which cou'd not be modestly told," left out. In spite of what it calls the book's "infinite variety," the preface claims that everything in it conforms to poetic justice: "there is not a wicked action in any part of it, but is first or last rendered unhappy and unfortunate: There is not a superlative villain brought upon the stage, but either he is brought to an unhappy end, or brought to be a penitent." The book is also, says the preface, a warning and an inspiration. Reading about Moll's criminal techniques will help honest people to beware of such thieves, and watching her "application to a sober life, and industrious management at last in Virginia" will teach the reader that "no case can be so low, so despicable, or so empty of prospect, but that an unwearied industry will go a great way to deliver us from it, will in time raise the meanest creature to appear again in the world, and give him a new cast for his life."

Whether Defoe wrote this preface is uncertain. But its promises of different satisfactions for readers of *Moll Flanders* point to the book's perennially fascinating ambiguities. As some recent critics have insisted, *Moll Flanders* is best understood, like *Robinson Crusoe*, as a version of spiritual autobiography, depicting in Moll a process of spiritual "hardening" dramatically resolved by her true repentance in Newgate. For G. A. Starr, the scattered, episodic quality of the narrative is unified by "a gradual, fairly systematic development of the heroine's spiritual condition." As she reviews her life of crime, Moll presents its roots in economic necessity and urges readers to remember "that a time of distress is a time of dreadful temptation, and all the strength to resist is taken away; poverty presses, the soul is made desperate by distress, and what can be done?" But mysterious forces cooperate with economic factors, and it is the devil who lays snares, who leaves on the counter top the unattended bundle that is Moll's first theft, who whispers in her ear, "take the bundle; be quick; do it this moment." Moll renders vividly her guilty fear and remorse after this initial theft, but "an evil counsellor within" pushes her on. Coming upon a child wearing a costly necklace. Moll leads her into an alley and is tempted to kill the child after lifting the jewelry: "Here, I say, the Devil put me upon killing the child in the dark alley, that it might not cry; but the very thought frighted me so that I was ready to drop down." The inner life Moll shows us has its darkly mysterious side, and this hastily suppressed glimpse of homicidal possibility suggests that her will for survival is instinctively ruthless.

Defoe seems to be marking the limits of self-knowledge and social and economic determinants, which can only explain so much. Temptations like these and Moll's subsequent settling into a criminal life illustrate progressive spiritual and moral decay and identify the narrative for some critics as spiritual autobiography. For other readers, Moll seems to embody an irrepressible individualism rather like Defoe's and to affirm the possibilities of triumphant survival in a hostile modern environment. Strictly speaking, these critical views are not opposed but describe the two different levels on which Defoe's book operates. Defoe clearly intended, however unsystematically, to portray Moll's life according to the Christian pattern of sin and repentance. Various factors, not the least of which may have been the haste with which he worked, made those intentions operate only fitfully or at least inefficiently and helped to produce something more like a novel than a spiritual autobiography.

Spiritual autobiography is necessarily single-minded, driving toward the moment of conversion, sifting experience for evidence of spiritual evolution or erosion. *Moll Flanders,* from its outset, is distracted from such Christian intensity by an interest in secular variety and psychological plenitude, the excitement of extreme situations Defoe's audience clearly wanted. Moreover, Defoe's char-

acteristic approach involves an almost consuming curiosity about experience in all its forms that tends to make his autobiographers only intermittently focused on their spiritual development. What Moll delivers most of the time is precisely what later novelists offer more self-consciously: the process whereby an individual gradually develops an identity in relation to society, coming to self-consciousness both within and against an external world, establishing a social self and discovering a private self that may diverge radically from that public identity. As Leo Braudy puts it very forcefully, the peculiar power of Defoe's novels appears to come from his "awakening to the implications of speaking in his own voice or masquerading in the voice of another," in the process grappling "with the problem of individuality and identity with an energy bordering on obsessiveness." With all its clumsiness and inconsistency and to some extent because of them, *Moll Flanders* conjures up a personality, a character claiming quite aggressively to be a unique individual with a history entirely her own, not simply a moral or social type. In that struggle for individuality, a matter of mere survival at times, an opposing external world is richly revealed, and Defoe's psychological realism is always rooted in a corresponding social realism.

From the beginning, Moll's narrative turns on that revealing struggle. She is born in Newgate prison, as the title page advertises, but her childhood and adolescence are hardly predicted by such birth. What Defoe promises his readers, after all, is something out of the ordinary, so Moll does not become as we might expect part of the urban underclass like Colonel Jack. As far as she can remember, she was kidnapped by gypsies and left at Colchester, in Essex, where she is raised by a poor woman paid by the local parish. When she is fourteen, her "nurse" dies, and she is adopted by an upper middle-class family. In these opening pages Moll is enmeshed in institutions like the rudimentary child welfare system of the time and the upper middle-class family, but she also actively resists their influence, an outsider somehow, different from other foster children in wanting to live by her needle rather than become a servant, precociously if innocently independent, conscious always as she tells us of her social difference even within the bosom of the wealthy family that takes her in. Thus, she absorbs the privileged education the daughters receive without being officially entitled to it: "as I was always with them, I learn'd as fast as they; and tho' the masters were not appointed to teach me, yet I learn'd by imitation and enquiry, all that they learn'd by instruction and direction." By her own account but also she insists by the "opinion of all that knew the family", Moll is the natural superior of these privileged girls: "and in some things, I had the advantage of my ladies, tho' they were my superiors; but they were all the gifts of nature, and which all their fortunes could not furnish."

In other words, Moll's history simultaneously dramatizes social inevitability and the personal freedom that operates to modify its effects. Carried along by circumstances and institutions, she exploits natural gifts that enable her to attract the attention of her adoptive family in the first place. Like all Defoe's heroes, self-made to some extent, she learns by "imitation and enquiry." In a sense, this opening set of events predicts the pattern of the rest of the book. Over and over, in increasingly difficult situations, Moll shows how she ultimately transformed limiting, nearly disastrous circumstances into opportunities for expansion and self-renewal. And yet, *Moll Flanders* is hardly schematic. Moll's early days in Colchester are a turbulent record of sexual awakening and betrayal. Seduced by the elder brother of the house, she is married off in due course to the younger, but before that dull outcome she has her moments of excitement and self-discovery. The exact nature of those moments is worth dwelling on, for they help explain how the book operates on two complementary levels.

Finding Moll alone one day, the elder brother impulsively kisses her and declares his love. Several days later, kissing her more violently on a bed, he gives Moll five guineas, repeating all this shortly after and giving her more gold. Here are Moll's reflections on these events:

> It will not be strange, if I now began to think, but alas! it was but with very little solid reflection: I had a most unbounded stock of vanity and pride, and but a very little stock of vertue; I did indeed cast sometimes with myself what my young master aim'd at, but thought of nothing but the fine words, and the gold; whether he intended to marry me, or not to marry me, seem'd a matter of no great consequence to me; nor did my thoughts so much as suggest to me the necessity of making any capitulation [i.e., striking a bargain] for myself, till he came to make a kind of formal proposal to me, as you shall hear presently.

> Thus I gave up myself to a readiness of being ruined without the least concern, and am a fair *memento* to all young women, whose vanity prevails over their vertue: Nothing was ever so stupid on both sides, had I acted as became me, and resisted as vertue and honour requir'd, this gentleman had either desisted his attacks, finding no room to expect the accomplishment of his design, or had made fair, and honourable

proposals of marriage; in which case, whoever had blam'd him, no body could have blam'd me. In short, if he had known me, and how easy the trifle he aim'd at, was to be had, he would have troubled his head no farther, but have given me four or five guineas, and have lain with me the next time he had come at me; and if I had known his thoughts, and how hard he thought I would be to be gain'd, I might have made my own terms with him; and if I had not capitulated for an immediate marriage, I might for a maintenance till marriage, and might have had what I would; for he was already rich to excess, besides what he had in expectation; but I seem'd wholly to have abandoned all such thoughts as these, and was taken up onely with the pride of my beauty, and of being belov'd by such a gentleman; as for the gold I spent whole hours in looking upon it; I told [i.e., counted] the guineas over and over a thousand times a day.

Highlighted here is the gap between Moll the actor and Moll the narrator. In her ironic, slightly brutal assessment of her young innocence, Moll reveals how she has changed since then, substituted a strategically precise (and coldly calculating) knowledge of human relationships for the spontaneous emotions and passionate involvement of her youth. And yet Moll is divided in the attitudes she projects, concerned about underlining the moral of her story, an illustration of vanity overcoming virtue, but revealing in her actual narrative mainly a disgust with her naivete rather than any moral regret. In the second paragraph, the relative formality and moral conclusiveness of the first sentence slide into the colloquial outburst "Nothing was ever so stupid on both sides." Moll outlines a self-protective, legalistic approach to human relationships. The ideal course would have been not so much moral as blamelessly advantageous: "whoever had blam'd him, no body could have blam'd me." In a crucial metaphor in the first paragraph, Moll speaks of her small "stock" of virtue and her huge "stock" of vanity and pride. The expression seems conventional enough here, but as the book proceeds the reader will see how Moll's moral and psychological reflections are governed by the mercantile materialism implicit in "stock." Her story turns on the problems of accumulating capital; her personality is formed in terms of assets and liabilities. And in fact as Moll remembers it, what thrilled her chiefly about the elder brother's advances was not the sex, hastily summarized, but the gold obsessively, erotically counted. As Defoe masterfully arranges it, young Moll's passion is compounded of various forms of excitement; her sexuality is inseparable from the thrilling prospect of money and social advancement. In fact, the scene's erotic center is Moll counting the gold over and over again, realizing instinctively the deeply sexual resonances of money and its power. To be sure, old Moll sees only the latter and disparages the sexual ("the trifle he aim'd at"), thus beginning a consistent and unifying refrain in the narrative.

In much Western literature, what often identifies female characters is a turbulent, compulsive sexuality. Granted a richer emotional life than men by a persistent patriarchal myth, women are both exalted and degraded in this sexual division of psychological labor. Their inner life can make them the moral superiors of men, more sensitive, caring and so on, but their emotional sensitivity frequently renders them sexually unstable, in early eighteenth-century drama and fiction quite often the victims of self-destructive romantic passion. One recent commentator on *Moll Flanders* explains this situation in economic terms. Excluded from meaningful economic activity by early modern capitalism, women "were endowed with a moral superiority to compensate for their economic diminution." What is striking about Defoe's version of this myth is his subversion of it. After this initial, in some ways quite conventional seduction by the elder brother (the sexual exploitation of servants and lower-class women by upper-class men was a popular literary subject as well as a social reality), Moll quickly acquires a cooler, infinitely more controlled personality, bent upon survival and prosperity, out to use sexuality as a means to those ends, no longer the helpless prey of her emotions. At least, that is what old Moll quickly jumps to in her narrative, the hasty summarizing of her next five years married to Robin, the younger brother, pointing to her impatience with a discarded younger self. "It concerns the story in hand very little, to enter into the farther particulars of the family, or of myself, for the five years that I liv'd with this husband; only to observe that I had two children by him, and that at the end of five year he died." Instead, Moll provides the first of what will be regular accountings of her financial condition. Only moderately profitable is her comment on this marriage's bottom line: "nor was I much mended by the match: Indeed I had preserv'd the elder brother's bonds to me, to pay me 500 (Pounds) which he offer'd me for my consent to marry his brother; and with this and what I had saved of the money he formerly gave me, and about as much more by my husband, left me a widow with about 1200 (Pounds) in my pocket."

Moll now embarks on a tangled set of adventures, in all of which her object is to marry profitably: "I had been trick'd once by *that cheat* call'd LOVE, but the game was over; I was resolv'd now to be married, or nothing, and to be well married, or not at all." Experience soon teaches her that in London marriages were "the consequences of politick schemes, for forming interests, and carrying on business, and that LOVE had no share, or but very little in the matter." In much of what follows, Defoe displays his characteristic fascination with duplicity and manipulation of others. In sequences too complicated for extensive summary, Moll learns to hold herself in reserve, to assume false names, to pretend to fortune in order to attract men, and in general to adapt her identity for self-advantage. What matters, above all, is self-control, keeping her true self secret and essentially apart, at least from men. A good half of the novel is, in fact, devoted to these adventures, which result in five sexual relationships, four of them marriages, one of them incestuous and one of them bigamous. The abilities Moll quickly acquires to manage these relationships have seemed to many readers to be fairly implausible if interesting in their obvious affinities with Defoe's own talents. The marriage market where Moll wheels and deals is not essentially different from markets Defoe knew at first hand, and Moll's conspiratorial alliances with other women in her campaigns to bag suitable husbands echo the political maneuvers in which he was still involved.

And yet Defoe's own published opinions about marriage were very far from Moll's calculating materialism. *Conjugal Lewdness; or Matrimonial Whoredom. A Treatise concerning the Use and Abuse of the Marriage Bed* (1727) is as eloquent in its praise of marriage as it is fiery in its denunciations of sexual and mercenary motives for entering into it. Defoe counsels caution, warning against the hell of an unhappy marriage: "HOUSEHOLD strife is a terrestrial Hell, at least, 'tis an emblem of real Hell." But he also labels marriage the summation of "all that can be called happy in the life of man." Clearly, *Moll Flanders* provided an opportunity to imagine a subversive marginality otherwise unavailable to Defoe. An insolated and embattled woman like Moll is to some extent a metaphor for that marginality rather than a plausible version of reality, her experience in the marriage market, like her criminal career afterwards, serving as a means for exploring normally forbidden possibilities of action and self-consciousness and perhaps for enjoying the play of strategy and counter-strategy, as well as the exhilaration of impersonation and social movement that are so important in Defoe's own personality.

But some critics contend that moral irony governs the book, that Defoe intended his readers to see Moll's views on marriage as abhorrent and to realize that Moll is inconsistent, untrue to the self-serving materialism she claims to live by. The case to be made for this reading is a good one. Even old Moll has to admit that she was not immune to lingering traces of passion. While she lived with her first husband, the younger brother of her seducer, 'I never was in bed with my husband, but I wish'd my self in the arms of his brother. . . I committed adultery and incest with him every day in my desires." By her own admission, Moll is frequently for all her tough talk betrayed by her emotions. First, she is "hurried on (by my fancy to a gentleman)" to marry her second husband, the shopkeeper who goes bankrupt and deserts her. Later, at Bath she becomes a wealthy man's mistress and her moral qualms are stilled by growing affection: "But these were thoughts of no weight, and whenever he came to me they vanish'd; for his company was so delightful, that there was no being melancholly when he was there." In similar fashion, Moll later agrees to marry the banker who has just divorced his unfaithful wife and proposed to her, but she is struck by sudden guilt. He little knows, she exclaims, that he is divorcing one whore to marry another, "that has lain with thirteen men, and has had a child since he saw me." Her resolution would warm the heart of the most sentimental women's magazine reader: "I'll be a true wife to him, and love him suitably to the strange excess of his passion for me; I will make him amends, if possible, by what he shall see, for the cheats and abuses I put upon him, which he does not see." Finally, Moll's most elaborate scheme for mercenary marriage collapses comically when she discovers that the new husband she thought was a rich Irish peer is a penniless fortune hunter. But when he leaves her the next day, her reaction is intense: "I eat but little, and after dinner I fell into a vehement fit of crying, every now and then, calling him by his name, which was James, O Jemy! said I, come back, come back, I'll give you all I have; I'll beg, I'll starve with you, and thus I run raving about the room several times."

Although there are times when Moll sounds like a female impersonator, she acquires skills at survival and manipulation by painfully repressing emotions that the book identifies as specifically female susceptibilities. At the least, Defoe tries to arrange a balance between the emotional melodrama that gives Moll's life shape and the artful manipulations by which she survives those psychological crises. Sometimes, he clearly falters in the attempt, and long stretches of Moll's marital career are really fascinated expositions of her cleverness as a sort of confidence woman, a skilled predator in the sexual jungle. "I play'd with this lover," she says and repeats an earlier image, "as an angle does with a trout: I found I had him fast on the hook, so I jested with his new proposal; and put him off." And yet as events show, Moll is herself being tricked and played with, by some of her male antagonists and ultimately by fate. Thanks to the disasters that follow Moll's manipulations and her own confessions of emotional vulnerability, a personality emerges rather different from the one Moll herself projects.

As the title page luridly advertises, Moll commits incest. But her marriage to the man who turns out to be her brother is the culmination of her first really elaborate and successful marital scheme. With the help of her female friend, a sea captain's wife, the first in a series of crucial female accomplices for Moll, she passes for a woman of fortune and attracts a number of suitors: "I who had a subtile game to play, had nothing now to do but to single out from them all the properest man that might be for my purpose; that is to say, the man who was most likely to depend upon the hear say of a fortune, and not enquire too far into the particulars; and unless I did this, I did nothing, for my case would not bear much enquiry." Even as Moll assumes an identity and undermines any sort of sincerity by her evasions and manipulations, she is ironically discovering an unlooked for biological identity, being cruelly manipulated by fate or at least by coincidence. Moreover, once she learns, in Virginia where she has gone to live with her new husband, that her mother-in-law is her mother and her husband her brother, the secrecy that she has chosen as a means of power is transformed into a hell of private anguish. "I resolv'd, that it was absolutely necessary to conceal it all, and not make the least discovery of it either to mother or husband; and thus I liv'd with the greatest pressure imaginable for three year more, but had no more children."

Moll's implausible resilience allows her to return to England hardly the worse for wear and to pick up her career as woman on the make. Defoe is not novelist enough to render the cumulative effects of emotional stress. What he does try to do some justice to is the coexistence in Moll of contradictory elements of controlling calculation and compelling emotion. Moll's life is at once a series of free choices and coercive circumstances, an attempt to balance various kinds of necessity, biological and social, with personal freedom. That attempt comes to a head in Moll's arrest and incarceration in Newgate prison, the most moving and significant sequence in the novel.

After several close calls in her fantastically successful career as a thief, Moll is finally caught in the act and with no real transition the episodic rush of narrative, with its high-spirited accumulation of tricks and disguises and its panorama of scenes and faces, slows to a melodramatic halt. Moll is, as she says, "fix'd indeed", for her narrative is suddenly restricted to one terrible location and the expansive forward movement of her criminal career is now shifted violently back to the past and the fate it has apparently fixed for her. Moll's narrative habits so far consist mainly of sketching her movements and rendering dialogue, giving us people and their interaction rather than the places they inhabit. What matters to her story are strategies and states of mind, and even exotic places like Virginia remain indistinct, mere stage backdrops. Unlike the London streets of her criminal career, which are diagramed to give the reader a sense of the swiftness and agility of Moll's movements, Newgate is solid rock, looming gigantically as a place of confinement, a palpable set of walls and an embodiment of inescapable, immovable circumstances. For almost the first time in her narrative, Moll attempts to describe a physical location, sliding from the fearful insight that she was destined for it, to a still half-boastful reminder of her skill in avoiding it, to her unique admission of its fateful force.

> I was carried to *Newgate;* that horrid place! my very blood chills at the mention of its name; the place, where so many of my comrades had been lock'd up, and from whence they went to the fatal tree [i.e., the gallows]; the place where my mother suffered so deeply, where I was brought into the world, and from whence I expected no redemption, but by an infamous death: To conclude, the place that had so long expected me, and which with so much art and success I had so long avoided. I was now fix'd indeed; 'tis impossible to describe the terror of my mind, when I was first brought in, and when I look'd round upon all the horrors of that dismal place: I look'd on myself as lost, and that I had nothing to think of, but of going out of the world, and that with the utmost infamy; the hellish noise, the roaring, swearing and clamour, the stench and nastiness, and all the dreadful croud of afflicting things that I saw there; joyn'd together to make the place seem an emblem of hell itself, and a kind of an entrance into it.

And yet that is hardly the worst aspect of Newgate, since Moll's (or Defoe's) powers of physical evocation are not great. Moll is plunged into fear

and trembling and thinks night and day "of gibbets and halters, evil spirits and devils. . . harrass'd between the dreadful apprehensions of death, and the terror of my conscience reproaching me with my past horrible life." But what Moll describes at greater length than this terror is the transformation that follows and cancels it. Heretofore, Moll has evaded the full consequences of her circumstances; her story is a testimonial to the powers of individualistic self-creation. But Newgate operates as the concentrated essence of an irresistible external world that erodes free will and individual agency, that determines personality and destroys freedom. In an unusually vivid image for the plainspoken Moll, she evokes the prison's compelling force. It operates "like the waters in the caveties, and hollows of mountains, which petrifies and turns into stone whatever they are suffer'd to drop upon," so her confinement in this enforced environment turns her "first stupid and senseless, then brutish and thoughtless, and at last raving mad." Moll is transformed, loses the identity she thought she had: "I scarce retain'd the habit and custom of good breeding and manners, which all along till now run thro' my conversation; so thoro' a degeneracy had possess'd me, that I was no more the same thing that I had been, than if I had never been otherwise than what I was now."

In the context of Defoe's fiction, this is a crucial moment. All his narratives challenge the notion of simple or stable identity. His characters record nothing less than the fluid and dynamic nature of personality, a matter of changing roles, wearing masks, responding to circumstances, and discovering new possibilities of self-expression. Up to now, Moll has defined herself by evading the restraint built into the idea of simple identity. Both as woman and as criminal, her survival has been a matter of reserving the truth about herself; and her identity, if she can be said to have any, lies in those repeated acts of deception and self-reservation. Those acts seem in stark contrast to this involuntary transformation into what Moll calls a "meer Newgate-Bird." But Defoe may have intended a profound irony. Without realizing it, Moll's immersion in crime past the point of necessity has "hardened" her in vice, slowly transformed her and eroded her powers of moral choice. Newgate is simply the culmination of that process, an accelerated revelation of the real Moll formed by a life of crime, "harden'd" in a sort of moral stupor long before she arrived in Newgate.

There are two events that restore Moll to self-consciousness. One, of course, is her spiritual conversion, the true repentance that is the climax of her spiritual autobiography. Condemned to death, Moll is visited by a minister who leads her to regret her past out of more than fear of earthly punishment. Responding to his prayers and entreaties, Moll repents out of concern for having offended God, conscious as never before of her eternal welfare. The experience, Moll admits, is impossible to render, just as the minister's methods and reasonings are beyond her powers of narration: "I am not able to repeat the excellent discourses of this extraordinary man; 'tis all that I am able to do to say, that he reviv'd my heart, and brought me into such a condition, that I never knew any thing in my life before: I was cover'd with shame and tears for things past, and yet had at the same time a secret surprizing joy at the prospect of being a true penitent." Moll, once again, leaves it to "the work of every sober reader to make just reflections" upon her religious conversion; she is "not mistress of words enough to express them." What she is able to describe very precisely is the other event that brings her out of her lethargy, the arrival in Newgate of her Lancashire husband, Jemy, along with two other captured highwaymen. Overwhelmed with grief for him, she tells us, Moll blames herself for his taking to a life of crime, and the result is a return to self-consciousness: "I bewail'd his misfortunes, and the ruin he was now come to, at such a rate, that I relish'd nothing now, as I did before, and the first reflections I made upon the horrid detestable life I had liv'd, began to return upon me, and as these things return'd my abhorrance of the place I was in, and of the way of living in it, return'd also; in a word, I was perfectly chang'd, and became another body." "Conscious guilt," as Moll calls it, restores her to herself, to what she calls the "thinking" that equals self-consciousness. "I began to think, and to think is one real advance from hell to heaven; all that hellish harden'd state and temper of soul. . . is but a deprivation of thought; he that is restor'd to his power of thinking is restor'd to himself"

This self-restoration precedes the spiritual conversion and is in effect a precondition for true repentance. Moll is restored to herself, we can say, by regaining her sense that she can exercise a controlling relationship with other people, and her rather (on the face of it) overstated guilt about Jemy marks the beginning of a revivifying connection with her past. As the last phase of her career begins, Moll resonstructs certain aspects of her past, no longer plunging ahead from episode to episode and improvising survival as she goes but revisiting and reintegrating past and present. Reprieved from execution and ordered "transported" to Virginia, she persuades the reluctant Jemy to come along and settles in Virginia with the help of carefully enumerated assets accumulated in her life of crime. Once there, she buys her freedom and establishes herself and Jemy as proprietors of a plantation, increasing her holdings when she discovers that her mother has died and left her an inheritance. This last she discovers by seeking out, in disguise, the son—Humphry, who is now a grown man—shed had with her brother-husband. The scene when she first glimpses her son is a fine moment but raises again the recurrent problem of psychological realism. When someone points Humphry out to her, Moll is deeply affected:

> you may guess, if you can, what a confus'd mixture of joy and fright possest my thoughts upon this occasion, for I immediately knew that this was no body else, but my own son. . . let any mother of children that reads this, consider it, and but think with what anguish of mind I restrain'd myself; what yearnings of soul I had in me to embrace him, and weep over him; and how I thought all my entrails turn'd within me, that my very bowels mov'd, and I knew not what to do; as I now know not how to express those agonies: When he went from me I stood gazing and trembling, and looking after him as long as I could see him; then sitting down on the grass, just at a place I had mark'd, I made as if I lay down to rest me, but turn'd from her [the woman who has identified Moll's son], and lying on my face wept, and kiss'd the ground that he had set his foot on.

By itself, this is convincing, especially in the care with which Moll disguises herself and hides her intense emotions, preserving something of her old cunning at self-concealment even as she reveals herself to the reader. But within the context of Moll's career as a mother in which she has more or less abandoned or carelessly disposed of a string of children such intensity may seem strangely inconsistent at best. And yet without giving Defoe more credit for novelistic sophistication than he deserves, the scene fits exactly into this last phase of Moll's career. Moll's intensity is a coherent reaction to her own maternal failures, and Humphry represents accumulated guilt as well as inexpressible joy. Moreover, the scene begins yet another sequence in which Moll can operate in her characteristically self-renewing way. As so often before, she has a secret and acquires a confidant to manipulate the secret to advantage. Only now her collaborator is her son and the secret links her joyfully and productively with a past rather than just concealing it. As she and Humphry huddle together and he hands over Moll's substantial inheritance, she looks up "with great thankfulness to the hand of Providence, which had done such wonders for me, who had been myself the greatest wonder of wickedness, perhaps that had been suffered to live in the world." The moral ambiguity in Moll's thanksgiving, with its irrepressible self-promotion, it a link with the unrepentant Moll of earlier times. For some readers, this particular inconsistency and adamant inability to become simply moral types are what make Defoe's characters a uniquely living collection.

Source: John J. Richetti, "Daniel Defoe," in *Twayne's English Author's Series Online,* G. K. Hall & Co., 1999.

Sources

Anonymous, Review in *The Flying Post; or, Weekly Medley,* March 1, 1729.

Backscheider, Paula R., "Daniel Defoe," in *Dictionary of Literary Biography,* Vol. 101: *British Prose Writers, 1660–1800, First Series,* edited by Donald T. Siebert, Gale Research, 1991, pp. 103–26.

Defoe, Daniel, *Moll Flanders,* W. W. Norton and Co., 1973.

Fielding, Penelope, "Moll Flanders," in *Reference Guide to English Literature,* 2d ed., Vol. 3, edited by D. L. Kirkpatrick, St. James Press, 1991, pp. 1719–20.

Forster, E. M., *Aspects of the Novel,* Harcourt, Brace, 1927, pp. 56–63.

Kelly, Edward H., Foreword, in *Moll Flanders,* W. W. Norton and Co., 1973, pp. vii–ix.

Novak, Maximillian E., "Daniel Defoe," in *Dictionary of Literary Biography,* Vol. 39: *British Novelists, 1660–1800, Part 1: A–L,* edited by Martin C. Battestin, Gale Research, 1985, pp. 143–66.

Richetti, John J., "Daniel Defoe," in *Twayne's English Authors Series,* G. K. Hall & Co., 1999.

Roscoe, W. C., "Defoe as a Novelist," in *National Review,* Vol. 3, No. 6, October 1856, pp. 380–410.

Stephen, Leslie, "Defoe's Novels," in *Hours in a Library,* Vol. 1, rev. ed., G. P. Putnam's Sons, 1894 (and reprinted by Putnam's, 1899), pp. 1–46.

Watt, Ian, "Defoe as Novelist: *Moll Flanders,*" in *The Rise of the Novel: Studies in Defoe, Richardson, and Fielding,* University of California Press, 1957, pp. 93–134.

Woolf, Virginia, "Defoe," in *The Common Reader,* First Series, Harcourt, Brace & World, 1925, pp. 89–97.

Further Reading

Backscheider, Paula R., *Daniel Defoe: His Life,* Johns Hopkins University Press, 1992.

In this highly regarded biography of Defoe, Backscheider reveals new information about Defoe's secret career as a double agent, his daring business ventures, and his cat-and-mouse games with those who wanted to control the press.

Defoe, Daniel, *A Journal of the Plague Year,* Oxford University Press, 1998.

This book was originally published the same year as *Moll Flanders* and is a compelling account of the Great Plague of 1665. In the book, Defoe scans the streets and alleyways of stricken London in an effort to record the extreme suffering of the victims of the Great Plague, which occurred during Defoe's early childhood. The book is both horrifying and sympathetic and offers a frightening vision of the city laid to waste.

Hay, Douglas, and Nicholas Rogers, *Eighteenth-Century English Society: Shuttles and Swords,* Oxford University Press, 1997.

Drawing on recent work on demography, labor, and law, this book covers the period 1688–1820 and focuses on the experience of the 80 percent of the population that made up England's "lower orders." The authors provide insights into food shortages, changes in poor relief, use of the criminal law, and the shifts in social power caused by industrialization that would bring about the birth of working-class radicalism.

Waller, Maureen, *1700: Scenes from London Life,* Four Walls, Eight Windows, 2000.

This book presents a huge amount of detail about daily life (and death) in eighteenth-century London, focusing on where people lived and worked, how they behaved, what they wore and ate, and how they suffered from illness and injury. The book is made up of vignettes drawn from the author's research and by excerpts from contemporary diarists, novelists, and commentators.

Nectar in a Sieve

Kamala Markandaya
1954

Nectar in a Sieve is Kamala Markandaya's first novel to be published although it is actually the third novel she wrote. It became a best-seller around the world and was translated into seventeen languages. In 1955, it was named a Notable Book by the American Library Association.

The novel was published in 1954, less than a decade after India won its independence from Britain. *Nectar in a Sieve* is clearly influenced by this event, portraying some of the problems encountered by the Indian people as they dealt with the changing times. Markandaya never mentions a specific time or place, however, which gives the story universality. Some of the struggles that the main character, Rukmani, faces are the result of the changing times, but they are the kinds of struggles (poverty, death, loss of tradition) that are experienced by many people for many reasons.

Far beyond its political context, the novel is appealing to modern readers for its sensitive and moving portrayal of the strength of a woman struggling with forces beyond her control. It is a story about the resilience of the human spirit and the importance of values.

Author Biography

Kamala Purnaiya Taylor, who often writes under the name Kamala Markandaya, was born in Bangalore, India, in 1924. Her family was Brahmin, the highest caste in Hindu society. Markandaya made an effort to know not just the city in which she lived, but also the rural areas. She was educated at the University of Madras in Chennai, India, and worked briefly for a weekly newspaper before emigrating to England in 1948. There she met her husband, with whom she lives today in London. They have one daughter.

Markandaya has made England her home, but she has made many visits to India over the years, returning to stay in touch with her culture and to find inspiration and information for her fiction. As a writer, Markandaya is respected for her accessible writing style and the range of experience expressed in her novels. Critics generally commend her portrayals of personal relationships, social consciousness, and the desire for independence.

While *Nectar in a Sieve* tells the story of a peasant woman facing an array of difficulties, Markandaya's other novels range in subject matter from the middle class to the urban poor to the struggle between Western and Indian ideas and ways of life. Because her own life does not include all of these experiences, Markandaya has been criticized by some Indian reviewers for a lack of true connection to the poor. Other critics accuse Markandaya of losing touch with her identity by living in England. Markandaya's response is that her adult life in England—her choice to be an outsider—gives her an objective perspective on her native culture.

Plot Summary

Part One

Nectar in a Sieve is a first-person narrative told by Rukmani, the widow of a poor tenant farmer in India during the early 1950s. She begins her story with her marriage to Nathan. The marriage is arranged, and because Rukmani is the fourth daughter and there is very little dowry, her best match is to a poor rice farmer. She begins her life with him and finds him to be very kind and loving. He is so understanding that he is not threatened by her ability to read and write.

Soon, she gives birth to their first child, a daughter named Irawaddy ("Ira"). She is worried, however, when many years pass and no more children come. Just prior to her mother's death, Rukmani meets the man caring for her mother, a Western doctor named Kennington ("Kenny"). She talks to him about her inability to conceive, and he helps

her. Rukmani never tells Nathan that the reason she gives birth to four sons in four years is because of Kenny's help. The family is very happy, despite having little food or money.

Years later, a tannery is built in the small village where Rukmani and her family live. While many villagers welcome it, Rukmani is resistant because of the changes it brings to the community. When her two oldest sons go to work in the tannery, she is forced to accept it.

Ira is now fourteen and old enough to marry. Rukmani has a matchmaker find a good husband, even though there is a small dowry. A favorable match is made, and Ira moves to the home of her husband.

Five years later, a terrible monsoon destroys Rukmani's home and rice paddy. For a long time, they survive on very little food. Unfortunately, Ira's husband returns her because she has failed to give him any children. Rukmani arranges for Kenny to provide infertility treatment for Ira, but Ira's husband has already taken another wife.

Rukmani gives birth to another child, a boy named Ruki. Ira nurtures him, and when lack of food threatens his life, Ira becomes a prostitute to earn money to feed him. Still, the child dies.

Meanwhile, Rukmani's sons have lost their jobs in the tannery and decide to answer a call for laborers on tea plantations on the island of Ceylon. Another of Rukmani's sons has taken a job far away as a servant.

When a drought hits, the family struggles once again. Rukmani and Nathan are forced to sell everything they have of value just to buy food for the family. When the rain finally comes, it is too late for that year's crop.

One of the neighbors' wives, Kunthi, arrives at Rukmani's house, demanding rice and threatening to tell Nathan about Rukmani's secret visits to Kenny. Afraid that Nathan will not understand that the visits were for Ira's infertility, Rukmani gives Kunthi some rice, even though it means that her own family will have too little. Rukmani learns that Kunthi also blackmails Nathan for rice, threatening to tell Rukmani that two of Kunthi's sons were fathered by Nathan.

One of Rukmani's sons is killed at the tannery for trying to steal a pelt to sell. Soon after, the paddies are finally harvested, and the family has money again. The youngest of Rukmani's sons, Selvam, breaks the news that he is not interested in a life of farming and has decided to accept a job with Kenny at the new hospital which is being built.

Ira becomes pregnant and gives birth to an albino child. Rukmani knows that, as hard as life would have been for Ira, it will be more difficult with an illegitimate child whose appearance frightens many of the villagers. Selvam loves the child and supports his sister.

The man who owns the land Nathan works informs them that he is selling the land to the tannery owner. Nathan is almost fifty years old and knows no other life but farming. Having few choices, Rukmani and Nathan decide to go find their son Murugan (who is a servant far away) and live with him and his wife.

Part Two

Rukmani and Nathan take the hundred-mile journey to find Murugan. When they arrive, they find that he changed jobs two years previously. When they go to find him, they meet his wife. She tells them that he has abandoned her, and now she must work as a housekeeper to support herself and her children. Rukmani and Nathan have no place to stay, and their possessions and money have been stolen, so they go to the temple where beggars are fed once every day and given a place to sleep. They meet a boy named Puli, who is a streetwise orphan. He shows them where they can break stones for money, and they eventually save enough to return home. Unfortunately, Nathan collapses before they leave and dies.

Rukmani returns to her village, bringing Puli with her, and stays with Selvam and Ira. She is exhausted upon arrival and simply tells them that Nathan died peacefully.

Characters

Arjun

Rukmani's first son, Arjun is an energetic boy who grows into an impassioned man. He and his brother Thambi go to work in the tannery, but when they organize the workers in an effort to demand more money, they lose their jobs. Because money beyond what the young men can earn locally is so necessary to a decent standard of living, he and Thambi take jobs on the distant island of Ceylon and are never seen again.

Biswas

Biswas is the moneylender in town and the only character who never seems to suffer from a lack of resources. Rukmani finds him untrust-

worthy and unpleasant because of his flippant manner of speaking and his suggestions that Rukmani and Kenny have an inappropriate relationship. Because Biswas has money, Rukmani sells him some of her garden produce, and she has no choice but to go to him when she has to sell her fine saris.

Ira

See Irawaddy

Irawaddy

Irawaddy ("Ira") is Rukmani's only daughter. She is beautiful, hard-working, and nurturing. She is married at the age of fourteen but fails to produce children and so is returned home. She cares for her baby brother Kuti in a maternal way, resorting to prostitution to earn money to feed him. Later, she becomes pregnant and gives birth to an albino son Sacrabani, whose abnormalities she seems not to see. She sees him with a mother's eyes and resents the hurtful comments made by some of the villagers.

Kali

Kali is the wife of a farmer who works a neighboring field. She is very gracious to Rukmani when she has her daughter, helping her through labor and taking care of the house while she recovers. Although she likes to exaggerate stories and is a bit gullible, Kali is likeable and loved by Rukmani. In later years, however, the women drift apart and when Kali arrives to see Ira's baby, she makes rude remarks. The years seem to have stripped her of her sensitivity and kindness.

Kennington

Kennington ("Kenny") is the white doctor in town who provides modern medical care for the poor people of the village. He is not there year-round, however; he explains that he can only stand to be there for certain spans of time. He becomes frustrated with many of the local customs and seeing so much poverty weakens his spirit. Kenny cares for Rukmani's mother in her last days and then addresses Rukmani's infertility problem. Rukmani is forever grateful, and Kenny becomes a friend of the family. When he visits, he sometimes brings milk or food. He helps one son secure a job as a servant in a distant city, and offers another son a job as an assistant in a new hospital that is being built.

Little is said about Kenny's own family, except that he has a wife and children whom he refuses to allow to restrict his "come and go" lifestyle. At one point in the novel, he tells Rukmani that his wife has left him. He seems saddened by this, but his is a solitary way of life, and he accepts loneliness. Kenny's calling is to treat the sick and help the poor as evidenced by the way he raises funds for the hospital while he is gone from the village.

Kenny

See Kennington

Kunthi

Kunthi is the wife of a neighbor. When Rukmani first arrives in the village, Kunthi is distant and rather unwelcoming. Still, Rukmani stays with her when she is in labor with her first child. When the tannery is built, Kunthi takes advantage of her good looks and attractive figure to make money by entertaining men. She soon gains a reputation and later loses her husband. On the brink of starvation, she resorts to blackmailing Rukmani and Nathan separately to take some of their precious rice. She blackmails Rukmani by threatening to tell Nathan about her secret trips at night to see Kenny. (Rukmani does not want her husband to know that the Western doctor is treating her for infertility.) She also blackmails Nathan by threatening to reveal to Rukmani that two of her sons are his. Her character and bleak circumstances have made her a pitiful and desperate woman.

Kuti

Rukmani's sixth son, Kuti is much younger than his siblings. He is born after his sister Ira returns home, and she cares for him like a mother. He is severely weakened by the lack of food brought on by the drought, and, even though Ira prostitutes herself to earn money to buy him food, he dies.

Murugan

Rukmani's third son, Murugan takes a job a hundred miles away as a servant. He rarely writes to his family, so when his parents try to find him, they discover that he left the job as a servant years previously. When they go to his house, they meet his wife, who tells them he abandoned her for a life of women and gambling and that he never writes.

Nathan

Nathan is Rukmani's husband. His real name is never given; Rukmani explains that she will simply call him by this name because it is inappropriate for a woman to call her husband anything but "husband."

Nathan is an extremely hard-working man who is dedicated to supporting his family to the best of his ability. Before he brings his new wife home, he builds a new mud hut for her with his own hands. He is poor and merely rents the farmland that he works, never earning enough to be able to buy his own land. His marriage to Rukmani is arranged, but he truly loves her and treats her with affection and respect. He does not discourage her reading and writing, and rarely discourages her from speaking her mind. He is a good companion for Rukmani because when she is stubborn or passionate about something, he advises her in a calm and wise way without discounting her feelings. He is equally loving to his children, and, although he is disappointed that none of his sons chooses to take up farming, he does not impede them in pursuing their goals.

Old Granny

Old Granny is a kind woman who sells guavas and peanuts on the street in town. She buys some of Rukmani's garden produce but also understands when Rukmani must sell it to those who can pay higher prices. When it is time for Ira to marry, Rukmani chooses Old Granny as the matchmaker. Despite Ira's small dowry, Old Granny is able to make a good match, and everyone in town is impressed. After Ira and her husband separate, Old Granny feels responsible for what happens to Ira. Although she has almost no money, she gives a rupee to Ira's albino baby. Old Granny is a poor woman who lives on the street. In the end, unable to survive the drought, she dies of starvation.

Puli

Puli is an orphan boy whose fingers are missing due to a disease. He is cunning, streetwise, and opportunistic. Rukmani and Nathan meet him when they go in search of their son, and Puli helps them find ways to make money to get back home. Puli agrees to go with Rukmani, who provides him with a home and medical care for his skin condition.

Raja

Rukmani's fourth son, Raja is killed by a watchman at the tannery after he is caught trying to steal a pelt to sell for money. The family is on the brink of starvation, so they assume he only meant to try to feed them.

Rukmani

The narrator of the story, Rukmani is the widow of a poor tenant farmer. She tells the story of how she came to marry him and of the many struggles they faced over the years. Rukmani is literate, which is unusual for a woman in her position, and she teaches her children to read and write. Sensitive and loving, Rukmani quickly adapts to life as a poor man's wife and helps with the work in the rice paddy. She also grows her own garden to provide additional food for her family or, when necessary, something she can sell in town for money. Rukmani never complains about the poverty in which she lives, but she is vocal when she does not agree with something that happens in her community. When the tannery comes, for example, she makes her disapproval very clear to her friends and family. Still, once she realizes that she cannot change something (like the presence of the tannery), she accepts it.

Rukmani loves her family above all else and worries about her children as they leave home. As much as she despises Ira's prostitution, she never loves her any less for doing it. When her sons announce that they are leaving the village to take jobs in distant places, she is saddened but makes no real effort to stop them.

Rukmani is also a religious woman, participating in the Hindu festivals and praying to the gods. She makes offerings to the gods and goddesses when she prays to them, as is the custom.

What is most striking about Rukmani is her acceptance of extraordinarily bad luck. Whether suffering a drought, a monsoon, or being stranded in an unfamiliar city with no money, she never allows herself to wallow in self-pity. She feels despair and frustration just as anyone would, but her reaction to crisis is to think of a plan to solve it. When necessary, she can be assertive and strong, such as when she fights her way to the front of the line for food at the temple.

Sacrabani

Sacrabani is Ira's albino son.

Selvam

Rukmani's fifth son, Selvam reads more than his siblings do. This is partly why Kenny chooses to train him as his assistant in the new hospital. After the hospital opens, Selvam begins seeing patients with minor ailments. He is very protective of his sister Ira and her baby and offers to care for them when Rukmani and Nathan lose their farmland.

Thambi

Rukmani's second son, Thambi joins his brother Arjun to work in the tannery and later in Ceylon.

Themes

Change

Rukmani experiences the changes typical of a young woman in her time. She marries a man she does not know, becomes a mother, and, as she has more children, learns to share limited resources with more people.

Other changes, however, prove more difficult to accept. When the tannery comes to her town, she is deeply resistant to its effects on the village and its people. She comments, "Change I had known before, and it had been gradual. . . . But the change that now came into my life, into all our lives, blasting its way into our village, seemed wrought in the twinkling of an eye." To her, the tannery is destructive to their peaceful way of life, causes prices to increase, and encourages people to choose wayward paths. Although she eventually takes her husband's advice to be flexible, she does so only because she has little choice.

Getting used to change becomes a necessity in Rukmani's life. By the end of the story, her sons have grown and started their own lives, leaving her with an all but empty household. After her married daughter is returned by her husband for not bearing children, Rukmani considers Nathan's advice to get used to it, because it is out of their control. She says:

> It is true, one gets used to anything. I had got used to the noise and the smell of the tannery; they no longer affected me. I had seen the slow, calm beauty of our village wilt in the blast from town, and I grieved no more; so now I accepted the future and Ira's lot in it, and thrust it from me; only sometimes when I was weak, or in sleep while my will lay dormant, I found myself rebellious, protesting, rejecting, and no longer calm.

Later, when Nathan loses his land, Rukmani faces the daunting prospect of a completely new lifestyle, begun when she is well into adulthood. Looking for one of their sons, Rukmani and Nathan confront the challenges and hardships of a large, unforgiving city. To make matters worse, their son is gone and they have lost all of their possessions and money, forcing them to devise a new plan to earn money for passage back to their village.

Topics for Further Study

- At the beginning of *Nectar in a Sieve,* Markandaya offers the following quotation from Samuel Taylor Coleridge: "Work without hope draws nectar in a sieve,/ And hope without an object cannot live." What is the significance of this quote to the novel as a whole? How does this quote shed light on the author's concerns, as expressed through the novel? What is the significance of this quote to your own life and your own culture?

- Learn more about Hinduism, paying special attention to traditional gender roles, rituals, dress, food, social customs, and core beliefs. What events in the novel are consistent with the beliefs and practices of Hinduism? What events demonstrate the importance of religion to the characters? In what ways is religion important to the story?

- Learn more about British colonization of India and about India's independence in 1947. Draw comparisons and contrasts between America's and India's fight for independence from the British.

- *Nectar in a Sieve* describes some of the effects of the clash between industrialization and agriculture. Do some research to learn about India's economy today. What percentage of India's people live in small villages and do agricultural work, and what percentage live in big cities? Is industry moving into small towns, as occurs in the book? Can you find information about continuing clashes between these two sectors of the economy?

Their lives are in complete upheaval, and Rukmani reacts by adapting and remaining as optimistic as possible, rather than by giving up altogether. When her husband dies, Rukmani must deal with the profound change of going from wife to widow. Markandaya demonstrates through these drastic changes that Rukmani's life is characterized by uncertainty and instability, but because she es-

tablishes constancy within herself, she is able to handle the many changes and surprises that come her way.

Adversity

Rukmani faces many difficulties in her adult life. From the time she arrives at her husband's humble mud hut, she knows that life will be more difficult than she imagined. Her new life requires hard work for little money and few comforts. She finds herself the wife of a poor tenant farmer, but takes comfort in the realization that she is happily married to a man who loves her deeply.

When many childless years pass after the birth of their daughter, Rukmani faces the possibility of carrying a social stigma. She solves her problem by visiting Kenny, the foreign doctor in town, whose new methods would not be acceptable to Rukmani's husband. Although she hates keeping secrets from him, she determines never to tell her husband how she came to bear five sons.

Rukmani faces the adversities of natural disaster when a monsoon destroys much of their home and floods the rice paddies on which their livelihood depends. She watches as her children either suffer cruel fates or leave the village to make their own lives. She and Nathan lose their land, and in the end she is a widow.

Markandaya shows, however, that Rukmani is not a woman who allows adversity to destroy her. She has enough in her life that fulfills her (children she loves, friends, and a happy marriage) to find the will to continue seeking improvement. While she is sometimes struck with despair, she never wallows in self-pity. At the end of the story, she is at peace with herself and her life. She is hopeful and cherishes her memories because she clings to the happiness in her past, rather than to the heartache.

Style

Figurative Language

Throughout *Nectar in a Sieve* Markandaya uses a variety of literary devices to bring her story to life. Her inclusion of insightful similes (a figure of speech used to compare two unlike things), well-designed allegories, and vibrant imagery enable Western readers to understand and enjoy this novel whose setting, people, and culture are completely unfamiliar. These devices also help the reader to connect with the events of the book through the universality of the experiences and images.

Markandaya frequently uses similes. When Rukmani recalls running through her garden when she was pregnant, she says, "I realized I must have looked like a water buffalo, running in such a frenzy." In an extended simile, Rukmani remarks,

> Nature is like a wild animal that you have trained to work for you. So long as you are vigilant and walk warily with thought and care, so long will it give you its aid; but look away for an instant, be heedless or forgetful, and it has you by the throat.

During the festival of Deepavali, Rukmani watches in wonder at the brilliant fireworks, noting, "Now and then a rocket would tear into the sky, break and pour out its riches like precious jewels into the darkness."

In a moving scene in which Nathan brings her outside to sit, Rukmani sees her own experience paralleled in the landscape. At this point, she is grateful for the blessings in her life, but is saddened because her children are becoming adults and leaving to start new lives. Markandaya creates a brilliant image, both melancholy and enchanting:

> He coaxed me out into the sunlight and we sat down together on the brown earth that was part of us, and we gazed at the paddy fields spreading rich and green before us, and they were indeed beautiful.. . . At one time there had been kingfishers here, flashing between the young shoots for our fish; and paddy birds; and sometimes, in the shallower reaches of the river, flamingoes, striding with ungainly precision among the water reeds, with plumage of a glory not of this earth. Now birds came no more.

Flashback

Rukmani tells her story in the past tense. She is a mature woman, remembering back to her childhood and relating the events of her life. From time to time, she interjects thoughtful observations that come from the reflective nature of her recollection. For example, she tells about the birth of her daughter, remembering how kind and helpful her friend Kali was. She observes,

> When I recall all the help Kali gave me with my first child, I am ashamed that I ever had such thoughts [that Kali did not understand what it was like to have only a daughter, because Kali had three sons already]: my only excuse is that thoughts come of their own accord, although afterwards we can chase them away.

Clearly, at the time of telling the story, Rukmani has chased away her resentful thoughts of her friend. Later, she thinks back on her years of motherhood, observing, "How quickly children grow! They are infants—you look away a minute and in that time they have left their babyhood behind."

Historical Context

India's Independence from Britain

The British had controlled India since the early 1800s, but on August 15, 1947, the Indian Independence Act established the self-sovereignty of India and Pakistan. Hindus lived in India, and Muslims lived in Pakistan, although people were free to travel between the two countries.

After British governmental power was dissolved, India's Constituent Assembly chose a republican constitutional form of government (very similar to the American system). A constitution was drafted, its length exceeding that of any existing body of law in the world. Among the provisions of the new constitution was the abolition of the ancient caste system, which had brought great disadvantages to millions of Indians. The first president was Rajendra Prasad, one of Mahatma Gandhi's (an Indian nationalist, moral and spiritual leader in India's struggle for independence from Great Britain) followers and an experienced politician. A cabinet was also formed, with Jawaharlal Nehru as the prime minister.

The first years of India's new government were both trying and dynamic. India chose to remain neutral during the tensions of the Cold War between the Soviet Union and the United States. This unwillingness to get involved made it difficult to acquire famine relief from the United States when a series of natural disasters (drought, earthquakes, and floods) ravaged India in 1950. The American government eventually approved famine relief in 1951, however, with terms that were acceptable to India's political leaders. Soon after, Nehru organized government programs to encourage birth control in an effort to curb overpopulation. He also designed a five-year plan to expand irrigation and hydroelectric programs for farming.

Daily Life in an Indian Village

In Indian villages, now as at the time of the novel, it is common for extended families to live in the same house or nearby. This arrangement requires patience and respect, as struggles over privacy, responsibilities, and resource allocation are a way of life. On the other hand, families are extremely close, which discourages members from going far away. Traditionally, a woman's role has

Compare
&
Contrast

- **1950s:** Girls in India are often subject to arranged marriages at a very young age. They are usually at least thirteen years old, and when they are younger, they often do not immediately move in with their husbands.

  Today: Although Indian women are gaining more freedom to choose their spouses, the practice of arranged marriage is still quite common. Families often adhere to this tradition to ensure that their children are marrying social equals. The tradition is such a central part of Indian culture that, occasionally, Indian families living in the United States arrange the marriages of their children.

- **1950s:** The diet of a farming family in India consists of rice, lentils, vegetables, and some dairy products. Such families eat little meat because of the expense and also because beef consumption is forbidden by the Hindu religion.

  Today: The diet of farming families has changed little over the years; most farming fam-

ilies consume part of what they grow. As in the past, most food grown in India is grown on small farms. Meat consumption is still minimal because of religious beliefs.

- **1950s:** In the novel, Rukmani mentions that the men building the tannery are well paid, earning two rupees per day. By modern conversion, this is the equivalent of approximately four cents; yet the standard of living is so low that this is plenty of money.

  Today: Since 1951, India has instituted a succession of five-year plans intended to breathe life into the economy. With the exception of drought periods (such as in 1979 and 1987), these plans have been successful. Between 1965 and 1980, the economy grew at an annual rate of almost five percent, and from 1982 to 1992, annual growth was over seven percent. This means that despite population concerns, India's economic situation has improved over the last fifty years.

been to maintain the home, rear the children, cook, and oversee religious and cultural observances. Men earn money to support the family and also teach their sons their trades so that one day they can take over the father's work.

Especially in the past, married couples were expected to have children; if they did not, they would lose social standing and respect. Further, without children, the couple would have limited prospects for the future. The arrival of a child was a celebratory event, but the arrival of a son was particularly joyous at the time of the novel. A son would learn his father's trade and assume the business responsibilities for his father while a daughter could not earn money for the family, yet required a dowry for marriage.

Hinduism

Hinduism is the prevalent religion in India, although Islam and Christianity are not uncommon.

Hinduism involves many rituals and the recognition of various gods and goddesses. Festivals such as Deepavali are an important part of Hinduism and provide a communal aspect of the religion to complement deeply personal practices, such as meditation and prayer. To Hindus, the cow is a sacred animal, so they do not eat beef or touch any part of a slaughtered cow. This is an important consideration with regard to the tannery in the novel because it explains why so many Muslims initially worked at the tannery and, in part, why Rukmani was disappointed that her sons went to work there.

Critical Overview

Upon its 1954 publication, *Nectar in a Sieve* was embraced by critics and readers alike. The book was praised for its sensitive and artful depiction of life in an Indian village as it changes in the wake

Man working in a tannery in India

of industrialization and modernization. Western readers found the book accessible, despite its unfamiliar physical and cultural setting. A contributor to *Contemporary Novelists* declared Markandaya "one of the best contemporary Indian novelists."

Critics note that although Markandaya wrote the book in English, the language never seems at odds with the themes or the characters' speech. This is an accomplishment because, although English is one of the official languages of India, it is not the language of daily life, especially the daily lives of poor people such as those portrayed in the book. Markandaya manages to write a distinctly Indian story in a Western language. William Dunlea of *Commonwealth* described Markandaya's use of English as "fresh and limpid, only slightly ornate in stylization."

Many critics were especially impressed by Markandaya's accurate portrayal of life in a rural Indian village. In a 1955 review, Donald Barr of the *New York Times Book Review* wrote, "*Nectar in a Sieve* has a wonderful, quiet authority over our sympathies because Kamala Markandaya is manifestly an authority on village life in India." He adds that, after all, "everything that is of final importance in life can happen in a village." Reviewers comment on how Markandaya makes village exis-

tence come to life in the minds and hearts of Western readers, allowing them to look inside the minds of people whose experiences are vastly different from their own. J. F. Muehl of *Saturday Review,* for example, noted,

> You read it because it answers so many real questions: What is the day-to-day life of the villager like? How does a village woman really think of herself? What goes through the minds of people who are starving?

Only a few of Markandaya's contemporaries found the book lacking. Dunlea, for example, commented, "*Nectar in a Sieve* is true without being revealing, promising but not remarkable." Most critics and readers, however, are drawn to the rich cultural landscape, the realistic characters, the well-wrought themes, and the lively language.

Since the publication of *Nectar in a Sieve,* Markandaya has written nine other novels, yet this one continues to be the subject of much critical analysis and acclaim. That female Indian writers today are compared and contrasted with Markandaya is further evidence of her staying power.

Criticism

Jennifer Bussey

Bussey holds a master's degree in interdisciplinary studies and a bachelor's degree in English literature. She is an independent writer specializing in literature. In the following essay, she explains why Western readers are likely to find that the hopelessness of the characters' situations in Markandaya's novel overshadows the book's positive message.

Although *Nectar in a Sieve* is an Indian story, it was written in English for Western readers, perhaps to give a glimpse into the hardships endured by people in Asia. The subject matter, however, threatens to distance readers from the work because of the pervasive hopelessness that runs throughout the novel. For Western readers, especially Americans, this bleakness may overshadow Markandaya's attempt to create a story about the triumph of the human spirit. Markandaya's portrayal of life for the rural poor in India may be accurate, but the absence of a single character who rises above his or her bleak prospects tends to eclipse the author's positive message. While some of the characters overcome adversity in some of its guises, they never overcome their hopeless situations, which is not a fate to which American readers are generally receptive. By reviewing the experiences of Rukmani, Nathan, their family, and other villagers, it will become clear that each character's life is marked by hopelessness. But, by briefly exploring the Eastern experience and mindset, it will also become clear that inner triumphs are possible, even amid unrelenting circumstances.

Prior to marrying Nathan, Rukmani lives a comfortable life. Her family is not wealthy, but they have the resources to live free of worries regarding food, clothing, or shelter. Her oldest sister had a handsome dowry and a grand feast for her wedding, which indicates that the family had at least a modest income. Rukmani is the fourth daughter, and although her dowry is small, she has something to offer her future husband.

Once Rukmani marries Nathan, a poor tenant farmer, however, her life becomes a series of hardships and heartaches. As the wife of a farmer, she soon learns to work very hard with her husband in the rice paddy. As hard as they work, their lifestyle remains very humble. She faces the real possibility of her family's starvation when the weather claims their crops. In fact, her youngest son does not survive a drought; he dies of weakness from malnutrition. Because she is poor, Rukmani must humble herself before a man she despises in an effort to sell her wedding sari and other nice clothes because she needs money to feed her family. Nathan does not earn enough money to save up and buy his own land, so when the landlord tells them to leave because he is selling the land to someone else, they have no recourse. Worse, they have no other means of supporting themselves. In search of their son, they find themselves helpless and lost in a strange city where their belongings and money are stolen. Having nowhere to go, they sleep in the temple at night with all the other beggars, and, having no income, perform backbreaking work in a quarry to earn the money to return home. In the end, Nathan dies before they begin their journey home, and Rukmani is left a widow. For Rukmani, life is constant struggle and worry about her children. For Nathan, even his life of relentless work is ultimately taken from him. They never get an opportunity to improve their condition, and they are forced to live day-to-day, reacting to each disaster as it comes.

Because Rukmani's children come from an impoverished family, their futures are limited and they suffer their own hardships. Ira, the daughter, seems to find the road to happiness and financial comfort

> " Without a single character to give the reader hope, the message seems to many Westerners to be that a life in dire poverty is a life in which no effort is worthwhile and no victories are possible."

when she marries a man who is the only son of a landowner. Five years later, however, she is returned to her parents because she has failed to produce any children. Ira becomes depressed until Rukmani gives birth to a son, whom Ira mothers. When the child's health declines steadily from lack of food, Ira resorts to prostitution to earn money to feed him. As if this were not tragic enough, her little brother dies anyway. Later, Ira becomes pregnant out of wedlock, a serious social stigma in Hindu society. The baby is born and he is albino, meaning that all by herself, Ira will have to raise a son who is the subject of ridicule and fear and will likely never marry.

Rukmani's sons also suffer cruel fates. Her two eldest sons take jobs in the tannery, which enables them to earn good money for the family but requires them to engage in a business that processes the remains of slaughtered cows, sacred animals to Hindus. When they lose their jobs, they decide to answer a call for workers in Ceylon. Although their culture encourages families to stay as close together as possible (especially sons, who have a choice), the call of money is too strong for them, and they never see their families again. Their story is sad because they grew up in a happy family with parents who loved each other, but the poverty was so distasteful to them that they were willing to sacrifice their relationships with that family for the sake of money.

The third son takes a job a hundred miles away, as a servant in a house owned by a wealthy female doctor. Rukmani and Nathan arrive only to find that he has left to take a job with higher wages. From there, he took up a life of women and gambling and abandoned his wife and children. This story shows that, for this man, as for his two older brothers, the

What Do I Read Next?

- Pearl Buck's Pulitzer Prize-winning *The Good Earth* (1931) portrays dramatic political and social change in China during the time of the last emperor's reign. Focusing on the farmer Wang Lung, Buck tells a memorable story of terror, destiny, hard work, humility, and ambition.

- Anita Desai is an Indian writer whose work is often discussed in relation to Markandaya's. *Diamond Dust: Stories* (2000) is Desai's collection of short stories in which her typical sense of setting and character is evident as she tells stories that are both riveting and serious.

- Markandaya's *A Silence of Desire* (1960) is considered by some to be her best novel. It is the story of a woman who discovers that she is ill and visits a faith healer without telling her husband. The novel deals with tensions between tradition and modernity and between logic and belief.

- Alan Paton's novel *Cry, the Beloved Country* (1948) centers on a Zulu pastor and his son. Set in tumultuous South Africa during the 1940s, the novel offers a sympathetic view of people caught in a time and place when racial injustice was common.

- *The God of Small Things* (1998) was Arundhati Roy's first novel. Set in India, it is the story of fraternal twins from a wealthy family. Roy explores themes of ethnic pride and shame, politics, and independence in a story that is mysterious and compelling.

- S. K. Wall's *Kamala Markandaya: "Nectar in a Sieve," a Stylistic Study* (1987) is an in-depth look at Markandaya's debut novel in terms of style. Wall explores how the author's particular telling of the story is important in the reader's reception of its events and characters.

---

lure of money was stronger than that of family or stability. First, he left his happy (but poor) family, then he left a job working for a generous and compassionate woman (the doctor), and then he sank into a life of gambling, forsaking his responsibility to his own immediate family.

Rukmani's fourth and sixth sons die; one is killed when he attempts to steal a pelt from the tannery to sell, and the other dies of malnutrition.

The fifth son takes a job as Kenny's assistant at the new hospital. Because his mother educated all the children to read and write, they could have found opportunities not open to everyone, but the fifth son is the only one who takes advantage of this. His seems to be the most promising story, but his job pays very little. It is unlikely that he will make a comfortable income in the career he has chosen. Besides, he seems to be punished for his decision when the construction of the hospital takes seven years to complete. Each of the children's stories is colored by the poverty and hopelessness of their collective situation, and in the end none of them seems to find a way out of it.

Markandaya's portrayal of the other villagers offers little hope that their futures will be brighter. Kunthi, a neighbor's wife, loses her husband when he learns that she has been prostituting herself to the tannery workers. She loses her beauty, her virtue, her reputation, and her friends, and has to resort to blackmail to get Rukmani and Nathan to give her food. She reasons that if she can only regain some of her health, she will be attractive enough to resume her work. Kali, another neighbor's wife, is a good friend to Rukmani when they are young. She is faithful, kind, and comforting to Rukmani in times of uncertainty and fear. In later years, however, she seems to have become insensitive and thoughtless. She makes rude, inappropriate remarks about the albino baby and is no longer welcome in Rukmani's house. The years of trial change her basic good character. Old Granny is an endearing character who sells fruit and peanuts to scrape out a meager living. She has no home and is forced to live on the street, but remains friendly and as generous as she is able to be. In the end, she dies of starvation on the street.

Without a single character to give the reader hope, the message seems to many Westerners to be that a life in dire poverty is a life in which no effort is worthwhile and no victories are possible. The best any of these characters hope for is to survive another day to face another misery. And the Western experience, both in literature and in life, has left Western readers unwilling to accept such a reality. Western readers, especially Americans, are drawn to stories of people who are in devastating situations yet find a way to a better life. Stories of underdogs who rise above their circumstances through hard work, cunning, good luck, and the kindness of others are popular and lasting in Western culture. Examples include the title characters in the American classic *Huckleberry Finn* by Mark Twain, the English classic *Oliver Twist* by Charles Dickens, and the character Jean Valjean in the French classic *Les Miserables* by Victor Hugo. These literary heroes are not wholly make-believe figures but are echoes of the Western experience. America (and to a lesser extent Western Europe) has offered to poor people opportunities for material advancement unparalleled in history. In the West, being born to poverty does not mean, necessarily, dying in poverty. Young nations rich in natural resources and capital, blessed not just with political but also with economic freedom, have provided countless routes to material comfort for many of those willing to work as hard as Markandaya's characters toil. Readers who have known nothing but opportunity find it difficult to understand or accept the kind of destitution that is not diminished, even by heroic effort. Unfortunately, many readers will miss the fact that Markandaya does have a positive message here.

The positive message of *Nectar in a Sieve* is grounded in the Eastern idea of an internal overcoming. Easterners are not accustomed to the ever-expanding material opportunities bestowed on Westerners. They are well acquainted with the grinding, unchanging poverty faced by Markandaya's characters. They know that, for some, the only ground on which victory is possible is the interior landscape of the mind and heart—a victory that is won by remaining, as Rukmani does, sane, loving, compassionate, gentle, and even hopeful in the face of every reason to be otherwise. This is an unfamiliar victory to Western readers, but surely a noteworthy one.

Source: Jennifer Bussey, Critical Essay on *Nectar in a Sieve,* in *Novels for Students,* The Gale Group, 2002.

Usha Pathania

In the following essay excerpt, Pathania provides an overview of Nectar in a Sieve, *and focuses on the relationship between Rukmani and Nathan.*

The depiction of man-woman relationship in Kamala Markandaya is different from what we have observed in the novels of Anita Desai. Her protagonists are strong-willed and courageous, but they do not suffer from the existentialist dilemma of saying the "Yes" or the great "No". They are often conformists who accept life and surrender themselves to its vagaries. Unlike the sophisticated heroines of Anita Desai, love means living for them. Hence, they cherish their relationship for the sense of security, companionship, belongingness and fulfilment it provides them in the face of cruel social, economic or political upheavals. The fictional world of Kamala Markandaya is no utopia. Disillusionment and despair; disappointment and frustration abound in the lives of her protagonists also. But they are no idealists; they know that all mortals are fallible; and believe that the great courage lies in "bending like grass" and not in saying the great "No." They are no relentless seekers of individual identity and thus, not afraid of involvement and surrender. They are, indeed, great heroic figures in their capacity to rise above their misfortunes. However, those who cannot adapt or adjust, face dissonance, disillusionment and disintegration in Kamala Markandaya's world also.

In *Nectar in a Sieve* Kamala Markandaya is mainly preoccupied with the sufferings of peasants in Colonial India. She, therefore, views the problem of human relationships in this novel, in the context of economic forces, social evils and vagaries of cruel nature. The novel also dramatises the tragedy of a traditional Indian village and a peasant family assaulted by industrialisation. Nevertheless depiction of human relationships is her cardinal concern.

Nectar in a Sieve is a woeful tale of the trials and turbulations [sic] of a peasant couple. Rukmani, the youngest of the four daughters of a village headman, is married to Nathan, "a tenant farmer who was poor in everything but in love and care for. . . his wife". Reconciled to her lot, she lives with her husband in a hut built by his own hands, and facing utter penury, she bears him children.

Rukmani and Nathan, like archetypal figures, Adam and Eve, are pitted against the forces of industrialisation, social evils and natural calamities. Despite the crushing weight of these forces, the ten-

> *Nectar in a Sieve*, thus, incorporates an ideal fulfilling man-woman relationship against the backdrop of a life full of harrowing experiences. The matrimonial bond between Rukmani and Nathan rests serenely on the solid foundation of trust, faith and understanding."

der human relationships between Nathan and Rukmani make *Nectar in a Sieve* a fictional epic on Indian life. These unsophisticated peasant characters become grand tragic figures because their matrimonial bond is characterised by understanding, self-sacrifice, and above all a deep faith in all humanities.

The relationship between Rukmani and Nathan is angelic and almost divine. Their life together, for the major part of it, is miserable, unhappy and disappointing, yet they face it with full confidence and trust in each other. Rukmani feels Nathan to be with her even after his death. The novel opens with Rukmani telling us: "Sometimes at night I think that my husband is with me again, coming gently through the mists, and we are tranquil together. Then morning comes, the wavering grey turns to gold, there is a stirring within as the sleepers awake, and he softly departs."

Nectar in a Sieve can be described as a novel about the economic implications of human relationships. The dwindling financial position of Rukmani's father forces him to marry her to a tenant farmer. The glaring disparity between the financial and social status of a village headman and a tenant farmer is obvious to Rukmani even at the tender age of twelve. Rukmani's three elder sisters were married in a befitting manner, but as luck would have it the headman is no longer of any consequence and hence Rukmani "without beauty and without dowry" is given away to Nathan—a tenant farmer. Everybody takes pity on her. She herself feels humiliated and has apprehensions about her future happiness:

> And when the religious ceremonies had been completed, we left, my husband and I. How well I remember the day, and the sudden sickness that overcame me when the moment for departure came! My mother in the doorway, no tears in her eyes but her face bloated with their weight. My father standing a little in front of her, waiting to see us safely on our way. . . and I was sick. Such a disgrace for me. "How shall I ever live it down," I remember thinking.

However, Nathan is immensely rich in regard to his love and care for his wife. His loving and caring ways make Rukmani overcome the disgrace and shame she felt at the time of her wedding. Nathan's limited financial resources and his landless status does not come in the way of their happiness and contentment. Rukmani says, "I haven't forgotten but the memory is not sour. My husband soothed and calmed me." It happens because he "was poor in everything but in love and care for me, his wife,. . . Our relatives, I know murmured "'A poor match,' they said and not always quietly. How little they knew any of them."

Unlike the couples in Anita Desai's novels, Rukmani and Nathan have mutual understanding. Right from the beginning a deep understanding exist between the two. Nathan is aware of her anguish and disappointment when the young bride come to his mud hut. He realises that she is used to better living. He makes sincere efforts to cheer her up, assuring her of better times to come. His loving concern and good conduct dispel her doubts and misgivings.

> This mud hut, nothing but mud and thatch was my home. . . I sank down. Nathan's face filled with concern as he came to hold me.
>
> He said, "Perhaps you are frightened at living here alone—but in a few years we can more—may be even buy a house such as your father's. You could like that?" There was something in his voice, a pleading a look on his face. . .
>
> "No" I said, "I am not frightened. It suits me quite well to live here.". . .
>
> "Such harvest as this" he said, sliding the grains about in his hand, "and you shall not want for anything beloved."

These are not mere hollow words to sooth and calm the agitated mind of Rukmani. Nathan's concern for Rukmani's happiness is genuine. He makes preparations for the welcome of his new bride. He builds, with his own hands, a sort of cozy nest where he plans to start a life of married bliss. There is a vast difference between the imposing house of an erstwhile village headman and his humble hut of mud and thatch. He, therefore, does not tell his wife that he himself with love and care, built her home. Kali reveals this to the amazement of Rukmani: "The fuss your husband made! Why, for weeks he was as brittle as a bamboo before it bursts into flame! He built your hut with his own hands. . . . He made our home himself, and I had felt only fear to live in it."

This love or consideration forms a solid foundation for a fulfilling relationship between the two. Rukmani's heart is filled with ecstasy; she is proud to have such a loving and sensitive husband. She frankly tells him: "I am glad, she told me, should I not be proud that you have built this house with your own hands?" There is no disappointment, she considers herself the most fulfilled woman, supremely blessed and perfectly contented in that Arcadian atmosphere. Nathan's humble hut and the green paddy fields become her most prized possessions:

> While the sun shines on you and the fields are green and beautiful to the eyes, and your husband sees beauty in you which no one has seen before and you have a good store of grain laid away for hard times, a roof over you and a sweet stirring in your body, what more can a woman ask for? My heart sang and my feet were light.

As Rukmani and Nathan evaluate each other positively, their relationship is strengthened with the passage of time. Rukmani loves, rather adores Nathan, because he is not a male chauvinist. Nathan, in her eyes, is an efficient, hardworking and loving husband who shows great patience towards his ignorant,—plain, child bride. She learns many household jobs from Kali and Janaki. Nathan does not snub her either for her plain looks or her lack of accomplishments. Unlike Gautama (in *Cry, The Peacock*), he does not belittle her for her ignorance. All this makes Rukmani confess: "For myself, I am glad I married 'beneath me' for a finer man no one could have had. . . I know, for I was ignorant of the simplest things. . . . Not one cross word or impatient look, and praise for whatever small success I achieved."

Admiration or regard for each other's qualities makes for a positive, reciprocal relationship, says Stott. If Rukmani is happy with Nathan, Nathan is equally proud of Rukmani whom he considers the best of all women. This opinion remains unchanged even after many years of married life. After Ira's wedding, on a Divali day, they all enjoy themselves in a carefree manner around the bonfire. Nathan abandons himself to the joy and gaiety of the mo-

ment and lifting up Rukmani he says "I am happy because life is good and the children are good, and you are the best of all."

Rukmani and Nathan have unflinching faith in each other. She considers him her friend and guide. All confusion and misery dispel under his steady assurances of a happier future. Rukmani is sad when her sons, Arjun and Thambi, leave for Ceylon to work there in tea-plantations. She cries bitterly and feels shattered at the thought of being separated from her sons. Nathan comforts her by diverting her mind to a bright future:

> "You brood too much" Nathan said, "and think only of your trials, not of the joys that are still with us. Look at our land—is it not beautiful? The fields are green and the grain is ripening. It will be a good harvest year, there will be plenty. . . .We may even make enough to visit our son—would not that be good?"

> Thus he sought to comfort me and after a time I was with him thinking pleasuringly of harvesting and of plucking the pumpkins swelling on the vine and visiting our son—and we made our plans.

Rukmani has an absolute trust in Nathan and does not take offence if he loses his temper or uses harsh words. She believes that he cannot be inconsiderate to her. She interprets his outburst of anger or impatience as the outcome of his concern for her welfare or his being distracted by something really beyond his control. Being unable to pay the amount they owed to the landlord, Nathan decides to sell everything including the seed for the next crop. Rukmani does not agree to this proposal. Nathan feels crossed and shouts at her: " 'Do you think I am blind and do not see or so stupid as to believe that crops are raised without seeds? Do you take me for a fool.'. . . He was not shouting at me but at the terrible choice forced upon us. . . . I thought, smothering my sobs, 'He is distracted and does not mean to be harsh.' "

At times devotion and trust; love and concern for each other make the spouses secretive. This tale of ideal conjugal relationship has its own share of lies, concealment and deceit. Nathan, like other mortals, falls a prey to the evil charms of Kunthi and sires her two sons. Nathan is mortally scared of Kunthi lest she might tell Rukmani about it. He is aware of the trauma it can cause to the innocent Rukmani. The fear of betrayal forces him to steal the rice that Rukmani has hidden underground. When Rukmani comes to know about the theft, she takes the children to task. Nathan can no longer bear it, he confesses his guilt, crying bitterly:

> "Kunthi took it all I swear it. She forced me, I did not want you to know."

"She has a strange power this woman," I said half to myself.

"Not strange," Nathan said, "I am the father of her sons. She would have told you and I was weak."

Nathan's frank confession of his clandestine relation with Kunthi is the cruelest surprise in Rukmani's life. She is torn asunder by a bewildering variety of negative emotions that come surging upon her one after the other. It is an unexpected turn of event revealing to her that Nathan is a fallible mortal: "Disbelief first; disillusionment; anger, reproach, pain. To find out, after so many years in such a cruel way Kali's words, 'She has fire in her body, men burn before and after.' My husband was one of those men. He has known her not once but twice."

Faithlessness on the part of the spouses is the rudest jolt to even the most fulfilling of matrimonial relationships. However, Rukmani's courage, self-control and level-headedness save her from being swept away by a sense of mortification. She feels cheated, but she does not give vent to her anguish because she also has feet of clay. She herself has practised concealment and deceit; of course for valid reasons, and has not been absolutely honest with Nathan about her relationship with Kenny, the doctor. In spite of her best intentions she has sinned by flouting the moral code of absolute honesty of deed and thought in matrimonial ties. That Kunthi is powerful, she knows herself because she has also been blackmailed by her into giving her the rice for not divulging her secret about Kenny. Nathan is Rukmani's most precious possession, and she does not want to lose him at any cost: "I need you," I cried to myself, "Nathan, my husband I cannot take the risk, because there is a risk since she is clever and I am not."

Nathan's uninhibited revelation hurt Rukmani, no doubt, but it infuses her with moral courage to be honest and open; to throw away the crushing weight of her foolish silences. She feels immensely relieved from Kunthi's sinister hold, and tells Nathan how Kunthi had extorted rice from her also. She feels more comfortable as: it seemed to me that a new peace came to us then, freed at last from the necessity for lies and concealment and deceit, with the fear of betrayal.

The Kunthi episode, though not moulded into a dramatic context, reveals an important fact about human ties. Howsoever intimate a relationship may be, there is much that remains unknown, unseen and untold to the individuals concerned. The complete knowledge of the deeds and personality of an individual is impossible even in the case of the most intimate of human bonds. Each one is an island. Thus a complete sharing of our life with each other, in the real sense of the term is a myth. Nevertheless the Kunthi episode is a touchstone of the real strength of the relationship between Rukmani and Nathan. It is an example of what sociologists term as "external stress" introduced into a relationship. These external factors can prove disruptive if the ties between two individuals are weak or shaky. A strong, healthy relationship of some duration has the capacity to adapt to such an extra-system load. By the time this unsavoury fact comes to light, Rukmani and Nathan are already happily adjusted with each other, and no dislocation is caused in their daily life or relationship.

Although Nathan and Rukmani are unsophisticated village folks, they understand the significance of their relationship with each other. They feel that united they stand, divided they fall. Together they have been able to bear the unequal strife between helpless peasantry and the menacing forces of an unjust social order, industrialisation and the blood-thirsty moods of wild nature. The ties between them are strengthened because of their mutual trust and empathy. They suffer together and try to mitigate each other's suffering. Their eviction from the land is the cruelest blow of all. Rukmani is terribly afflicted, she knows that a landless labour has nowhere to turn to. Nathan is also upset. But his presence by her side makes the misery bearable: together there was more strength. . . I knew neither could have borne it alone.

During the long years of togetherness Nathan and Rukmani achieve the coveted "interpersonal fusion" that makes them heroic and brave. The love, faith and trust they have for each other invest them with a stoic calm to face the worst in their life. They vacate their fields, and their hut—the mute spectators of their joys and miseries; prosperity and penury for thirty years. Rukmani feels dizzy, her "throat is dry. I lean against my husband, he is already leaning on me, together we achieve a kind of comfort." Once uprooted from the land, their life becomes a nightmare. On their way to their son's house in the city they first lose their meagre belongings and then the money they have. Penniless they reach his place, only to find out he has gone away. To earn money for their return they become stone-breakers. A tenure of thwarted hopes, deprivations, hunger and tragedies, takes toll of Nathan's life. Their last moments of togetherness are poignant and touching. They forget the gruesome realities of their unhappy existence,

Rural village in India

pangs of regret, repentance and sorrow and sit together enveloped in thoughts of joys and married bliss they had:

> Midnight, and as always before, his paroxysms eased. . .
>
> In the calm stillness I saw him open his eyes, his hand came to my face. . .
>
> "You must not cry my dearest. What has to be, has to be."
>
> "Hush," I said, "Rest and grow better."
>
> "I have only to stretch out my hand," he said, "to feel the coldness of death. Would you hold me when my time is come? I am at peace. Do not grieve."
>
> "If I grieve," I said, "it is not for you, but for myself, beloved, for how shall I endure to live without you, who are my love and my life?"
>
> "You are not alone," he said, "I live in my children" and was silent, and then I heard him murmur my name and bent down.
>
> "Have we not been happy together?"
>
> "Always my dearest always."
>
> "It is slipping away fast", he said.
>
> "Rest with me a little."

Nectar in a Sieve, thus, incorporates an ideal fulfilling man-woman relationship against the backdrop of a life full of harrowing experiences. The matrimonial bond between Rukmani and

Nathan rests serenely on the solid foundation of trust, faith and understanding. They are not sophisticated like Maya, Sita, Nirode or Nanda Kaul, but they have the wisdom to accept life and people as they are. Moreover, they prize their relationship with each other above everything else. "A woman's place is by her husband" is the strong conviction of Rukmani, she also believes in compromise and one's capacity to rise above his or her misfortunes. "What profit to bewail that which has always been and cannot change."

Source: Usha Pathania, "Harmony and Fulfilment," in *Human Bonds and Bondages: The Fiction of Anita Desai and Kamala Markandaya,* Kanishka Publishing House, 1992, pp. 54–63.

Usha Pathania

In the following essay excerpt, Pathania explores "the impact of money on filial ties" in Nectar in a Sieve.

The foregoing chapter dealt with the analysis of the filial bonds in the novels of Anita Desai. In her writing these ties, no matter whether stifling or fulfilling, continue to affect the sensibilities of her protagonists. Their severance is a painful experience. In Kamala Markandaya too, this relationship is significant. For her also, these equations persist in life. The basis of exchange between parents and

> *Nectar in a Sieve* depicts the life of a by-gone era with all its social norms and cultural attitudes. During those days, son always had a place of pride in the family. Parents loved their daughter, but they were proud of their sons."

children changes throughout the life cycle, depending on each side's circumstances, but its importance remains. External factors such as economic hardships and changing values and attitudes, very often, adversely affect these fundamental ties. Nevertheless, these bonds are sacred, powerful and enduring. Even when the solidarity is affected, these ties, in her novels, do not become a noose around one's neck. Kamala Markandaya favours greater freedom, trust and understanding between the parents and children. The filial ties, therefore, are no insufferable bondage for her characters. Their march towards autonomy is consistent, smooth and inevitable.

Nectar in a Sieve deals with human relationships in their variegated aspects. The chronicle of Rukmani and Nathan's life illuminates the multi-coloured, everchanging nature of filial ties. The children are the flesh and blood of their parents. Theoretically, this should make the ties strong and permanent. However, the hard facts of human existence, as depicted in the novel, highlight the impact of money on filial ties.

As sociologists like Graham A. Allan maintain, kin-relationships provide one with a sense of security. In *Nectar in a Sieve,* the social and financial status of Rukmani's father gives her a sense of confidence and makes her hopeful of a bright future. She is proud to be the daughter of a village headman. She is the youngest of the four daughters. Rukmani's mother worries about her dowry, as the earlier three marriages have squeezed them dry. Nevertheless, being a village headman's daughter, Rukmani is confident of her future happiness. In order to cheer her mother, she tells her: "I shall have a grand wedding. . . . Such that every-

body will remember when all else is a dream forgotten. . . . For is not my father head of the village? I knew this pleased my mother, for she would at once laugh and lose her look of worry." Her brother tells Rukmani that her father is no longer of consequence since the power now vests in the collector and the persons he appoints. This shocking revelation naturally frightens her. She feels insecure and anxious: "This was the first time I had ever heard that my father was of no consequence. It was as if a prop, on which I leaned, had been roughly kicked away and I felt frightened and refused to believe him."

Sociological research points out that "positive concern" for each other's happiness is mutual in filial bonds. However, this is also a proven fact that daughters feel more involved with their parents and show greater affection and consideration towards them. At the tender age of twelve, Rukmani displays considerable understanding of her parent's limitations. She is considerate towards them and does not want to hurt their feelings. She accepts their decision regarding her marriage ungrudgingly, as she does not wish any misery to her helpless parents. She remembers her wedding day when her mother in the "door way, no tears in her eyes but her face bloated with their weight" bids her farewell.

Rukmani's thwarted expectations of a suitable marriage could have created dissonance. However, she continues to be attached to her parents. She does not complain or show any resentment, for being married beneath her. "To reduce dissonance, people emphasize the positive aspects of the chosen object while emphasizing the negative and deemphasizing [sic] the positive aspects of the unchosen object." Rukmani appreciates the positive contribution of her parents towards her proper upbringing. She is proud of her father and appreciates his foresight, as she remarks: "It was my father who taught me to read and write. People said he did it because he wanted his children to be one cut above the rest, perhaps so, but I am certain that he also knew that it would be a solace to me in affliction, a joy amid tranquillity."

Loving and caring parents are believed to do anything for their children. Gifted with foresight at times, parents cultivate tastes and skills primarily for their children's sake. After her marriage with Nathan, an illiterate peasant, Rukmani's ability to read and write is of no avail. Nevertheless, she practises writing purposely so that, "when my child is ready, I will teach him too and I practised harder than ever lest my fingers should lose their skill."

The birth of her daughter does not weaken the attachment between Rukmani and her mother. She gets busy with her child and now finds the journey to her parent's house tiring. Yet she visits them though at longer intervals. "Since there was so much to be done in my own home; and my mother knowing that did not reproach me for the long intervals between my visits."

Parents care and pray for their children even when they are grown-up and can look after themselves. Rukmani's mother feels unhappy when, for many a year after Ira's birth, Rukmani does not bear a child. Despite her own failing health, she tries her best to help Rukmani. This concern on her mother's part profoundly impresses Rukmani, who many years, later vividly remembers and reproduces the words spoken by her mother on her death bed:

> When Ira was nearing six, my mother was afflicted with consumption, and was soon so feeble that she could not rise from her bed yet, in the midst of her pain, she could still think of me and one day she beckoned me near and placed in my hand a lingam—symbol of fertility.

> "Wear it," she said, "You will bear many sons. I see them, and what the dying, see will come to pass. . . . be assured, this is not illusion."

Rukmani and Nathan are the product of a culture where the birth of a son is a blessing and that of a daughter a sort of curse. Rukmani, though quite liberal in her views, is not free from this bias. As luck would have it, her first child is her daughter Irawaddy. She is sad when on uncovering the small form she finds it to be a girl's body. She tells, "I turned away and, despite myself, the tears came, tears of weakness and disappointment, for what woman wants a girl for her first born". Nathan does not express his disappointment, his behaviour, however, shows his preference for a son. Initially he pays scant attention to her, as he had wanted "a son to continue his line and walk beside him on the land, not a pulling infant who would take with her a dowry and leave nothing but a memory behind.

Nectar in a Sieve depicts the life of a by-gone era with all its social norms and cultural attitudes. During those days, son always had a place of pride in the family. Parents loved their daughter, but they were proud of their sons. Nathan, Rukmani and even her father are no exception. When Rukmani gives birth to her first son, Arjun, Nathan is besides himself with joy and celebrates the occasion by hosting a grand feast to the whole village:

> My husband was over-joyed at the arrival of son; not less so my father. . . .

> "Your mother would have been glad," he said, "she was always praying for you."

> "She knew," I told him, "she said I would have many sons."

> As for Nathan, nothing would do but that the whole village would know—as if they didn't already. On the tenth day from the birth he invited everybody to feast and rejoice with us in our good fortune.

Nectar in a Sieve stresses the fact that the preference for sons is often on theoretical grounds. Rukmani and Nathan are, no doubt, keen on having a son for various reasons, yet, the shock of getting a daughter as their first child is temporary. Daughters are equally dear to parents. They also love their parents no less than the sons. The discrimination between son and daughter disappears as the child starts responding to the parents. Nobody can ignore the loving advances of a child—whether a son or a daughter. Nathan is overwhelmed when Ira "at the age of ten months called him 'apa' which means father, he began to take lively interest in her."

Rukmani and Nathan are affectionate parents who inspire trust and confidence in the heart of their children. Ira accepts her parents' choice with her usual docility, but she frets at the thought of leaving her parents, the impending separation from them makes her sad. Once she asks a little wistfully: "How frequently I would be able to visit her, and although I knew such trips would have to be very rare since her future home lay some ten villages away. I assured her not a year would pass without my going to see her two or three times."

The real worth and strength of a relationship is judged in the times of need and adversity. Parental obligation is not over by simply marrying away their daughter. The prime concern of parents is to see their children happy and blessed with all the good things of life. Rukmani and Nathan bring up their daughter, Ira affectionately, and marry her well. Unfortunately, she is not destined to enjoy married bliss because of her being barren. She is abandoned by her husband and has to live with her parents. They are wise, understanding parents, who never, by word or deed, make her feel an unwanted burden.

All this, however, should not make one forget that jealousy and rivalry affect the most intimate human relationships. The children, howsoever, devoted they are, at times resent the parents enjoying or achieving something which is denied to them.

Ira has been deserted by her husband for her in-ability to conceive. Consequently, the advancing pregnancy of Rukmani is unpalatable for her. She envies her mother, and Rukmani is well aware of her resentful looks; "Sometimes I saw her looking at me with brooding, resentful eyes and despite my-self I could not help wondering if hatred lay be-hind her glance."

Financial implications often determine the na-ture and quality of interaction between the parents and children. The relationship between Ira and her parents in *Nectar in a Sieve* suggests that children are obedient, meek and submissive as long as the parents are responsive to their needs. When the children have to look after their parents, their atti-tudes undergo unbelievable changes. They tend to become defiant. With the sons gone and starvation engulfing them from all around, Ira takes to pros-titution to ward off hunger. This reversal of role matures her into a woman who defies her father. To Nathan's utter dismay she goes out of the house despite his efforts to check her. Hunger has con-verted her into a revolting volcano, the fury of which astounds both Nathan and Rukmani:

"Where do you go at this hour?"

"It is better not to speak."

"I will have an answer."

"I can give you none."

Nathan's brows drew together: she had never before spoken to him in this manner.

Looking at her, it seemed to me that almost overnight she had changed. . . . I think he laid a restraining hand on her for I heard her say, "Let me pass," and there was a rustling sound as she withdrew from his grasp.

"I will not have it said—I will not have you parad-ing at night".

"To night and tomorrow and, every night, so long as there is need. I will not hunger any more."

The bookish norms of propriety and filial obe-dience operate under congenial and placid circum-stances. A hungry man is forced to surrender his values; to act against his cherished convictions. Bhabani Bhattacharya views the theme of hunger in its wider perspective. It makes people helpless and wretched. In *So Many Hungers,* owing to ut-ter helplessness, Kajoli's neighbours give in and "sell" their daughter and Kajoli also at one time gives in, primarily to help her family. In the fierce struggle for survival, all becomes fair. Rukmani and Nathan helplessly bow to Ira: "Well, we let her go. . . . We had for so long accepted her obedience to our will that when it ceased to be given natu-

rally, it came as a considerable shock; yet there was no option but to accept the change, strange and be-wildering as it was for obedience cannot be ex-torted".

However this bewildering change is a transi-tory phase. The bond of love between Ira and her parents remains intact. Nathan remains kindly dis-posed towards her. One day Ira's son asks her about the name of his father. This upsets Ira. Rukmani tries to pacify her agitated mind by suggesting to Ira that she should have declared him dead. The conversation hurts Nathan, who asks Rukmani to discontinue it. As a father he can imagine the com-pound feelings of guilt, hurt, and remorse that are lossing [sic] and tumbling in his daughter's mind:

"Leave it, leave it," said Nathan. "Do not upset the girl any more."

He put out his hand to Ira, but she shied away from him. I saw her leave the hut.

"It is no use going to her," Nathan said sadly.

"Such comfort as there is to be had must come from her own spirit."

Nevertheless, after a little while he did go to her and his gentleness melted her last remnants of control, for she began to weep. I heard her crying for a long time.

Ira's rejection by her husband, her taking re-course to prostitution to save herself as well as oth-ers, and the birth of an albino child have rather too much for her to endure. But a deep understanding and kindness on Nathan's part assuage Ira's emo-tional trauma.

For Erich Fromm, the most important role of a father is parental love and guidance. According to Gandhiji, the best teacher is father and the best school is home. Nathan is an ideal father to his sons. Arjun and Thambi work in the tannery but on hol-idays they help their father on the land. Nathan teaches them various agricultural activities in the field. He values and enjoys their company and his superiority to them in regard to his knowledge makes him feel good:

One day in each week. . . Arjun and Thambi would help their father on the land and this gave Nathan a great pleasure. He liked to see his sons beside him, to teach them the way of the earth, how to sow; to transplant, to reap, to know the wholesome from the rotten, the unwelcome reed from the paddy; and how to irrigate or drain the terraces. In all these matters he had no masters and I think it helped him to know he could impart knowledge to his sons, more skilled though they were in other things, and able to read and write better than any in the town.

Like all other emotional bonds the filial rela-tionship grows and develops through many stages.

A time comes when the parents lose their hold upon the thoughts and acts of their own children. With their first step into adulthood, the children are inclined to judge and evaluate themselves. They tend to march towards autonomy and independence. This happens with Nathan's sons also. Arjun and Thambi hand over their wages to Rukmani, their mother, to spend as she likes. However, a strike in the tannery makes Rukmani and Nathan realise that Arjun and Thambi have grown up, though neither of them has touched twenty. They are aware of their rights and have already started thinking of their posterity. Rukmani vividly describes the conversation that reveals a lot about their grown up sons:

> "What has happened?" We ask with trepidation. They are still our sons but, suddenly they have outgrown us.
>
> "Trouble," they say. "We asked for money and they took from us our eating time."
>
> I bring out some dried fish and rice cakes. They are ravenous. "More money." I say, "What for?" Do they not pay you already? "What for?" one echoes. "Why, to eat our fill and to marry, and for the sons we shall beget." And the other said, "No, it is not enough."

The grown-up children often become strangers to their parents. The phenomenon of generation gap in terms of expectations and attitudes is bound to enter into the parent-child relationship. Nathan, wise as he is, realises that the best course is not to interfere and let them make their choice, their decisions. He advises Rukmani also not to be sentimental at this juncture. "I do not know what reply to make—these men are strangers. Nathan says we do not understand, we must not interfere. He takes my hand and draws me away. To his sons he is gentle."

At times human relationships, howsoever, intimate, do not afford an opportunity to scan other's thoughts and acts. Much remains unseen, unknown even in intimate bonds. Rukmani's sons, though obedient and loyal, keep certain secrets from their parents. They do not want to disturb the calm lake of their parent's lives by tossing the stones of revolutionary thinking. Rukmani narrates:

> Looking back now, I wonder how it came to pass that not until that fateful day did we realise the trouble that had been brewing. No gossip, not a whisper, had come to us of the meetings the men had held at which my sons had been spokesmen; nor of the agitation that followed; nor of the threats by their owners. . . All this we heard only later.

As the bonds are strong, the parents defend their children at all costs though they cannot evaluate objectively the act of their children. Nathan defends his sons when the villagers accuse them of inciting others: "Enough?" he shouted. "More than enough has been said. Our children must act as they choose to, not for our benefit. Is it not enough that they suffer?"

Separation from children is unbearable for parents. Arjun and Thambi cannot remain idle in the face of economic hardships. They leave for Ceylon to work as labourers in a tea plantation. Nathan, as a man, bears the pangs of separation silently, but for Rukmani this is unbearable. She makes desperate efforts to dissuade her sons from going away:

> "If you go away you will never come back," I cried.
>
> "The journey costs hundreds of rupees, you will never have so much."
>
> The tears come hot and bitter, flowing and flowing. . . . They spoke soothingly of how much they would earn, and how one day they would return—as one does to a child. They left at first day light. . . each before he went kissed Nathan's feet, then mine, and we laid our hands on them in blessing. I know we would never see them again.

Nathan is a level headed, practical man, who is fully aware of the fact that the deteriorating economic condition warrants the departure of their sons. As a sole provider for the family of eight people, what moral right has he to force his sons to stay with him? Like Michael in Wordsworth's poem of the same title, Nathan knows full well:

> If here he stays,
> What can be done? Where everyone is poor,
> What can be gained?

They restrain themselves, and as Michael sends Luke away telling him, "but it seems good / that thou should'st go." Rukmani and Nathan bid farewell to their sons. Later they calmly bear even the murder of their third son, Raja. They know that as they have nothing to eat, it is impossible to protest or resort to any legal action. Rukmani assures the tannery people that they would not be claiming anything from them. "You should not care," I said very softly to him alone. "It does not matter." Rukmani now pressed by the rigours [sic] of hunger and deprivation, feels sorry for the ailing Kutti and wishes him release from this wretched, cruel existence: I would go to him with beating heart to see if the fight has ended; but, again and again, he struggled back to consciousness, took up again his tormented living; almost I wished it otherwise." When Kutti dies they become almost insensible to grief or sorrow. Rukmani rather feels relieved: Nathan comes and kneels beside him with harsh sorrowing face and bitter eyes. "I knew too well what he felt. Yet, although I grieved it was not for my son, for in my heart I could not have wished it otherwise. The strife had lasted too long and had been too painful to call him back to continue it."

Rukmani and Nathan are not possessive in their love for their children. Despite adverse circumstances and great suffering they remain kind to their children. They do not force their choice of profession on Selvam, their only son, left now. His love for reading and writing makes him lose all interest in the land. As an assistant to Kenny, he wants to join a hospital. He hesitates to reveal this to his mother. But Rukmani does not want to come in the way of her son's plans or happiness:

> "I have told my father," he said hesitantly. "He is very willing".
>
> I smiled at him, "So am I. I wish you well."
>
> He relaxed, "I am glad. I thought you might be— were—displeased."
>
> "Not displeased. Perhaps disappointed since all our sons have foresaken [sic] the land. But it is the way for you."

The deep understanding between Rukmani and Selvam is of that order where verbal communication is hardly needed. Much remain unsaid about the relationship between Kenny and Rukmani, but he shows great maturity in understanding its true nature. When he decides to work with Kenny, her mother is filled with foreboding, but she does not discourage him:

> "It is the best way," he repeated after me. "It will be a great venture. We have many plans and much hope."
>
> We both relapsed into silence. I watched him covertly, wondering but then I thought resolutely, "I will not take the fire from his resolve or sow suspicion between them," and so I held my peace. But his steady eyes were on me, calm and level.
>
> "I am not unaware," he said quietly. "But is it not sufficient that you have the strength and I have the trust?" "It is indeed," I said with relief. "I wanted only that you should know."
>
> We smiled at each other in perfect understanding.

In human relationships the notion of give and take operates, and giving is often more satisfying than taking Rukmani and Nathan are among the most unselfish parents. They reject Selvam's offer to give up his job at the hospital and rent a piece of land for agriculture. The offer is tempting to Nathan because his roots are there in the land, and without land he cannot survive. Yet resolutely, he turns it down, saying: "No my son, I would not have it so." "There are some things that cannot be

sacrificed. . . besides I would never happy. Certainly your mother would not let me rest, "he added, smiling a little." Even during a time of irredeemable misery the needs and aspirations of their children remain uppermost with them. They are moved by the plight of Ammu, their daughter-in-law, who has been deserted by Murugan, their son, "We will return to our son and daughter." Nathan says, not replying directly. "But what of you, my child? It is we rather than you who should ask. We have had our day, you are still young. . ."

The foregoing discussion brings us to the conclusion that the filial ties, as depicted in *Nectar in a Sieve,* are largely fulfilling and cherishable. The tyranny of circumstances makes them sour at times, but based as they are on mutual understanding, absolute trust and a spirit of self-sacrifice, the bonds do not turn brittle or bitter. The children move away from their parents not because they wish it but because adversity leaves no other option for them. Rukmani and Nathan are proud of their sons who have the courage to find a way out of their misfortunes and confidence to carve a new destiny. They are the wisest of the parents as they encourage their children in their ventures, and let them plan their future.

Source: Usha Pathania, "March to Autonomy," in *Human Bonds and Bondages: The Fiction of Anita Desai and Kamala Markandaya,* Kanishka Publishing House, 1992, pp. 143–54.

Sources

Barr, Donald, "To a Modest Triumph," in *New York Times Book Review,* March 15, 1955, p. 4.

Dunlea, William, "Tale of India," in *Commonwealth,* Vol. LXII, No. 20, August 19, 1955, pp. 500–501.

Glencoe Literature Library, Study Guide for Nectar in a Sieve by Kamala Markandaya, http://www.glencoe.com/sec/literature/litlibrary/pdf/nectar_in_a_sieve.pdf (last accessed July, 2001).

"India," in *Microsoft Encarta CD-ROM,* Microsoft, 1997.

"Kamala (Purnaiya) Taylor," in *Contemporary Authors Online,* The Gale Group, 2001.

Muehl, J. F., Review of *Nectar in a Sieve,* in *Saturday Review,* May 14, 1955.

"Overview: *Nectar in a Sieve,* by Kamala Markandaya," *Literature Resource Center,* The Gale Group, 1999.

South Dakota School of Mines and Technology Study Guide: South Asia Reading Series, Fall 1998, http://www.sdsmt.edu/online-courses/is/hum375/southasia.html (last accessed July, 2001).

Teacher's Guide: Nectar in a Sieve by Kamala Markandaya, http://www.penguinclassics.com/US/resources/teachers_ guides/t_markandaya_nectar.html (last accessed July, 2001).

Walsh, William, "Markandaya, Kamala," in *Contemporary Novelists,* 6th ed., St. James Press, 1996, pp. 653–54.

Further Reading

Bhatnagar, Anil K., *Kamala Markandaya: A Thematic Study,* Sarup & Sons, 1995.
    Bhatnagar's analysis of Markandaya's novels reviews the themes presented by Markandaya throughout the range of settings and characters she creates. Bhatnagar suggests how these themes are drawn from the author's experiences in India and Europe.

Lalita, K., and Susie J. Tharu, eds., *Women Writing in India,* Feminist Press at the City University of New York, 1991.
    This two-volume anthology collects writings of Indian women from 600 B.C. to the 1990s. The editors include critical commentary with this wide-ranging collection of letters, poetry, memoirs, and fiction.

Parameswaran, Uma, *Kamala Markandaya,* Rawat, 2000.
    This overview of the life and career of Markandaya, includes a chapter devoted to each of the author's novels.

Rao, A. V. Krishna, *Kamala Markandaya: A Critical Study of Her Novels, 1954–1982,* B. R. Publishing Corporation, 1997.
    Rao offers a critical look at Markandaya's novels, from *Nectar in a Sieve* through *Pleasure City.*

The Optimist's Daughter

Eudora Welty
1972

The first version of Eudora Welty's best-selling, Pulitzer Prize-winning novel, *The Optimist's Daughter*, appeared as a short story in 1969 in the *New Yorker*. Revised and published as a novel in 1972, it is considered by some to be her sparest novel. In fact, Welty herself thought of the novel as more akin to a short story than a true novel. The book's complexity arises not from its length but from the emotions of the characters.

The Optimist's Daughter is the story of Laurel, a widow who returns to Mississippi when her father is ill and witnesses his death and funeral. From there, she embarks on a deeply personal journey to explore her past and her family in order to make sense of her future.

Welty's novel contains a number of autobiographical elements. Some of the male characters are inspired by Welty's uncles, and the women of the town represent Welty's observations on life in the South. Welty has stated that much of Becky McKelva's background is drawn from her mother's life in West Virginia. In fact, the novel was written not long after her mother's death, a period in which Welty was recalling her mother's life and experiences. In this way, the character of Laurel represents Welty's own desire to inquire into her past and understand how it affects her present and future.

Author Biography

Eudora Alice Welty was born in Jackson, Mississippi, on April 13, 1909, to Chestina and Christian Welty. With her two younger brothers, she was reared in Jackson, although neither of her parents was from the Deep South. Her father came from Ohio, and her mother was from West Virginia. Both were teachers by trade until the family moved to Mississippi, where Christian entered the insurance business.

Welty remembers a very happy childhood in which she was surrounded by books and loved listening to her parents read to each other in the evenings. She also remembers how much she loved listening to the ladies in town trade stories, and her habit of noting their speech patterns and colloquialisms served her well when she began writing about the South.

After completing her public education in Jackson, Welty attended Mississippi State College for Women from 1925 to 1927, finishing a bachelor of arts degree in 1929 at the University of Wisconsin. At the encouragement of her father (who wanted her to have a reliable trade), she studied advertising at Columbia University from 1930 to 1931.

When her father died suddenly, Welty returned home to settle in Jackson. She worked various jobs with newspapers and a radio station before going to work for the Works Progress Administration, a government program established during the Depression that assigned people to work on public projects for much-needed income. Welty also took up photography, snapping pictures of all kinds of people (mostly African Americans) in her native Mississippi.

Her first published story, "Death of a Traveling Salesman," appeared in 1936, after which Welty's stories were accepted by top publications such as *Atlantic* and *Southern Review*. During her early writing career, Welty's work was often narrowly defined as regionalist or feminist. Still, she was admired by other writers, and her first collection of short stories, *A Curtain of Green,* left critics eagerly anticipating Welty's future work. Over the next thirty years, Welty had over fifteen books published, including short fiction, novels, and nonfiction.

In the 1970s and 1980s, there was renewed interest in her work, partially because of the rise in feminist criticism. Although Welty prefers to distance herself from the efforts of feminists, the renewed interest demonstrated to a new generation

Eudora Welty

of readers that her writing was much more than an easily categorized body of work. Readers and critics continue to be drawn to her writing for her subtle, unique style, her handling of daily life, and her depictions of everyday heroism.

Welty's work has been recognized with prestigious awards such as a Guggenheim Fellowship in 1942; the O. Henry Award in 1942, 1943, and 1968; the National Institute of Arts and Letters literary grant in 1944 and Gold Medal for fiction in 1972; and a Pulitzer Prize in 1973 for *The Optimist's Daughter*.

Welty died of pneumonia on July 23, 2001, in Jackson, Mississippi, at the age of 92.

Plot Summary

Part One

As *The Optimist's Daughter* opens, Laurel McKelva Hand leaves Chicago and goes to New Orleans, where her father, Judge McKelva, is seeing an eye specialist to find out why his sight is failing. Laurel meets her father's young, new wife, a selfish, disrespectful woman named Wanda Fay ("Fay"). The doctor tells Judge that he has a detached retina and that it must be operated on at once. After the operation, the eye seems to be recovering normally, but Judge's health is not bearing the rigors of surgery well. He is lethargic and his health declines. Laurel and Fay, along with another woman, watch Judge to assure that he does not move very much, which would jeopardize the recovery of his eye.

Laurel and Fay have adjoining rooms at a nearby hotel, but Laurel fails in her attempts to get to know Fay. Meanwhile, Judge is now sharing a hospital room with a man whose senility makes him speak and behave strangely. The man's loud, colorful family is always in the waiting room.

At one point, Fay decides to try to scare Judge back to vitality by shaking him, but he dies soon after this incident. Welty is never clear about whether or not Fay's action caused the death. The next day, Laurel and Fay board a train to Mount Salus, Mississippi, the McKelvas' hometown.

Part Two

Laurel and Fay arrive in Mount Salus, and Judge's coffin is taken off the train and loaded into a waiting hearse. Many of Laurel's old friends are waiting for her at the station. They go back to the house, where a few people are waiting. The next day, many neighbors and friends stop by the house to view Judge's body, to bring food for the family, and to socialize. Fay's family, the Chisoms, have been invited from Madrid, Texas, and their arrival creates quite a stir among the genteel southerners. The Chisoms are crude and loud and have no sense of decorum. When Fay finally emerges from her room, she screams and wails and throws herself on Judge's body before being dragged away. Next, the mourners go to the church for the funeral, where public turnout is impressive, and then they go to the cemetery for the burial.

When Laurel and Fay return home, there are a few lingering friends. Fay decides to return to Madrid with her family for a few days' visit and is happy to hear that Laurel will be gone in three days. Neither wants to run into the other, as they have found it impossible to get along.

Part Three

The next day, Laurel works in the garden while four elderly neighbor women sit and gossip about Fay. When Laurel goes inside, she walks through her father's library, taking in all the memories inspired by the books, furniture, and general clutter. Later, she meets some friends to reminisce about the days before Laurel moved to Chicago. When

she gets back to the house, Laurel finds that a bird has gotten inside. As she tries to trap it in a single room, she allows herself to think about how much she blames Fay for her father's death, which makes her long to be with her deceased mother.

Laurel goes into the sewing room, which was once her nursery. She finds her mother's small desk, filled with papers, photographs, and letters. A flood of memories washes over her, including the details of her mother's background in West Virginia, their relationship, and her mother's steady decline and death. Her sorrow leads her to remember her husband, Phil, who died in World War II. She imagines that they would have enjoyed the kind of happy marriage her parents had, if only his life had not been cut short.

Part Four

The next morning, with the help of Missouri (an African-American woman who has worked as a cook for the McKelvas since Laurel's childhood), Laurel manages to get the trapped bird out of the house. She packs her suitcase in preparation for her ride to the airport. When she goes into the kitchen, more memories come to her, and she finds her mother's breadboard that Phil had made for her. At the same time, Fay returns home and is irate that Laurel is still there. They argue about the breadboard and then about the importance of the past, and Laurel comes close to striking Fay with the breadboard. She stops herself and decides not to take the breadboard with her because she has come to understand that freedom is more powerful than memories. The knowledge she has gained about herself over the last few days has liberated her from the pain, despair, and sense of obligation she once felt.

Laurel hears her ride honk for her outside, and she hugs Missouri on her way out the door. As she rides out of town on her way to the airport, she waves back at the many people who are waving to her.

Characters

Mrs. Bolt

The minister's wife, Mrs. Bolt is an elderly neighbor woman. She is one of the local ladies who gossips about Fay.

Major Rupert Bullock

Major Bullock is a friend of Judge McKelva. After Judge's death, Major attends the wake and the funeral, making a big show of telling grand stories about his deceased friend. There is an indication that Major may have a drinking problem, although nothing more than a suggestion is made. Major differs from most of the neighbors in that he is sympathetic toward Fay. He embodies southern manners in his attitude toward Fay and when he escorts Laurel safely home in the rain.

Tennyson Bullock

Major Bullock's wife, Tennyson, is a neighbor and close friend of the McKelva family. Despite her husband's commanding presence, she seems to be the dominant one in their marriage. She is typical of the women in her community in that she enjoys sitting with the ladies, gossiping, or playing bridge. Mrs. Bullock is known for her subtle sarcasm.

Tish Bullock

Tish is an old friend of Laurel's. She is the daughter of Major and Tennyson Bullock. Tish was one of Laurel's bridesmaids and their friendship is still warm despite the fact that Laurel now lives in Chicago. Tish married the captain of the high school football team but is now divorced.

Bubba Chisom

Fay's brother, Bubba arrives at the wake inappropriately dressed in a windbreaker, insensitively complaining about how long a drive they took to get there, and grumbling about how they will have to turn around and do the whole drive again.

Grandpa Chisom

Grandpa Chisom is the only member of his family who seems to have any manners. He demonstrates his thoughtfulness by bringing Laurel a candy box full of pecans he has shelled for her. Unlike the rest of his family, he speaks kindly to her and tries to stay out of the way.

Mrs. Chisom

Mrs. Chisom is Fay's mother. She is insensitive and crude. Her only interest is in indulging her daughter, and she gives no thought to expressing any sympathy to anyone else in the house during the wake or the funeral. She is impressed with the money Fay now seems to have as Judge's widow. She suggests that the entire family should move

Media Adaptations

- Random House has produced two audio-book adaptations of *The Optimist's Daughter,* an unabridged version in 1986 and an abridged version in 1999. Both versions are read by Welty herself.

into the house with Fay so she can turn it into a boarding house.

Sis Chisom

Fay's pregnant sister, Sis is no more refined or observant than her mother. She brings her young son to the funeral as a learning experience for him and proceeds to yell at him throughout the events of the day. She allows him to wear a cowboy outfit and say almost anything he pleases.

Adele Courtland

Dr. Courtland's sister, Adele is a nurturing woman who has known the McKelva family for many years and was Laurel's first-grade teacher. She is described as an elegant woman with an authoritative voice. She still wears her hair in the same bun that she wore back when Laurel was a child.

Dr. Nate Courtland

Dr. Courtland is the eye specialist Judge visits about his failing sight. Although Dr. Courtland practices in New Orleans, Judge makes the trip presumably because the two have been friends for so long. Their families know each other, and Judge even helped put his friend through medical school.

Mr. Dalzell

Mr. Dalzell shares a hospital room with Judge McKelva while he recovers from his eye surgery. Dalzell is senile, blind, mostly deaf, and speaks erratically. He is also from Mississippi and is convinced that Judge is his long-lost son, Archie Lee.

Fay

See Wanda Fay (Chisom) McKelva

Laurel McKelva Hand

Laurel is Judge McKelva's only child. Her mother named her after the state flower of West Virginia, her mother's home state. Laurel is in her mid-forties and is tall and slender with dark hair. She is a professional fabric designer in Chicago but flies to New Orleans, where her father is seeing a doctor. She then travels to Mississippi after her father's death, staying for the wake and the funeral. Laurel also spends a few days in her father's house (the house in which she was reared) in order to make peace with her past.

Among the many emotional challenges she faces is the acceptance of Fay, her father's new young wife, whom she blames for her father's death. Laurel and Fay fail to get along from the beginning, and it is heart-wrenching for Laurel to watch Fay take her mother's position in the house that is full of Laurel's childhood memories and cherished objects.

As a result of her personal struggles, Laurel begins evaluating her past and her parents' relationship, including her mother's death. Consequently, she also evaluates her own marriage and the untimely death of her husband, a naval officer named Philip Hand, in World War II. By the time she leaves to return to Chicago, she has made peace with her past and her present and is better equipped for her future.

Laurel is an intelligent and sensitive woman who wants her parents to be remembered as they really were, not as larger-than-life figures. She is perhaps not assertive enough in her dealings with Fay, although there is a sense that Laurel never plans to see her again, anyway. Laurel is welcomed in Mount Salus as a native, having grown up there, but, having been away for so long, she is now able to see the people as they really are. For example, she overhears several neighborhood ladies gossiping about Fay, but refuses to participate. Still, she refrains from passing judgment on anyone in town because she loves them as family friends and past classmates.

Judge Clinton McKelva

Judge McKelva is a retired judge in the small town of Mount Salus, Mississippi. When the book opens, he is seventy-one years old, and is described as tall and heavy. He is a lifelong resident of the town and holds a prominent place in it. At one point, he was the mayor. He is respected by the entire community, from his legal associates to the African Americans in the town.

Judge is described as patient and fair. He enjoyed a long and happy marriage to his first wife, Becky, although he did not handle her declining health well. When she needed strength, he was filled with uncertainty and thus reacted by not reacting at all. Often, he chose denial, reasoning that everything would be all right because he loved her. Eventually, she died. Years later, he married a woman completely different from his first wife. Welty never offers an explanation as to why Judge married Fay, although the neighborhood ladies gossip about it.

Wanda Fay (Chisom) McKelva

Wanda Fay Chisom McKelva ("Fay") is Judge McKelva's second wife. She is small, thin, and blonde with blue eyes. They met at a Southern Bar Association conference, where Fay was a part-time employee in the typing pool. A month later, Judge brought her to his hometown and married her. She is significantly younger than he is (and a little younger than Laurel), and her crude ways prevent her from fitting in with the Mount Salus community.

Fay is selfish, rude, ignorant, and self-indulgent. When her husband is being seen by the eye specialist, she insists that his problem is nothing that nature will not heal on its own. When her husband is recovering from surgery, her attitude is one of being inconvenienced. Thinking she can scare her husband back to vitality, she shakes him and yells at him, shortly after which he dies. During the wake, she bursts from her room in black satin to create a scene. She is never shown expressing any genuine pain or grief.

After the funeral, Fay decides to return to Texas for a visit with her family. She has no understanding of how important the house is to Laurel, nor does she have any interest in sympathizing with her. She seems to entertain her mother's idea of turning the home into a boarding house. This demonstrates how little she understands the community or her husband's standing in it.

Missouri

Missouri is the African-American cook who has worked for the McKelvas since Laurel was a child. She is a matter-of-fact woman who is deeply sympathetic to Laurel's grief. She seems somewhat resentful of Fay.

Topics For Further Study

- Consult psychology textbooks and journals on the subject of grief. From a psychological point of view, how would you evaluate Laurel's ways of handling her grief with reference to her mother, her husband, and her father? How would you evaluate Fay's manner of dealing with grief? Based on your knowledge of the characters' upbringings and backgrounds, why do you think these two women react so differently to the death of Judge McKelva?

- Identify an object (such as a piece of jewelry or furniture, a photo, a letter, or a medal) that makes you feel connected to your past or to someone in your family who has passed away. Take that object and a notebook to a quiet place where you can reflect on your feelings. Write down your feelings about this object and the people or experiences with which you associate it. Write in a stream-of-consciousness style so that you will have an of interior monologue on paper. Later, review what you have written and compare it to Welty's description of how Lau-

rel felt about certain objects in the house in which she was reared.

- Different religions and cultures adopt different traditions and rituals for burying their dead. Learn more about the beliefs about death and the funeral practices in one religion, belief system, or culture which is different from your own (such as Judaism, Hinduism, Buddhism, Muhammadan, African religions, traditional Native-American customs or beliefs, Catholicism, Protestantism, etc.). Compare it to your own. What significant differences are there? What similarities are evident?

- With a partner, stage a debate in which one of you argues that Judge McKelva was right to marry Fay, and the other argues that his marriage to Fay was a mistake. Each of you should support your argument with reasons and examples; point out weaknesses in your opponent's argument; and respond to your opponent's criticisms of your position.

Mrs. Pease

Mrs. Pease is an elderly neighbor woman. She is one of the ladies who gossips about Fay.

Themes

Making Peace with the Past

In *The Optimist's Daughter* Laurel is forced to make peace with her past and her present in order to go on with her future. The event of her father's death is difficult for her because she enjoyed a loving relationship with him, and even more so because his recent marriage to Fay, a selfish, impatient woman, forces Laurel to accept circumstances beyond her control. Having lost her mother, her husband, and now her father—all of whom she loved dearly—Laurel finds herself alone in the

world and faced with the reality of giving up her childhood home to a woman she despises.

Fay returns home with her family for a short visit after the funeral, and Laurel's flight back to Chicago is not for three days. This leaves her with a few days alone in the house. She uses this time to reflect on the past and its joys and trials. Laurel recalls her mother's love of her own home in West Virginia and the difficult period of her extended illness leading to her death. Along with her mother's virtues, she remembers her mother's flaws, just as she does with her father. In the process, she makes peace with the fact that her parents were wonderful people, but only human, and she decides to preserve their memories honestly. Realizing that the truly substantial gifts her parents gave her are not objects in the house that can be willed to someone else, she is able to leave for Chicago in peace.

Laurel confronts another painful chapter of her past as she revisits her memories of her marriage to

Phil Hand, a naval officer killed in World War II. In her heart and mind, those years were blissful and full of promise; while she basks in the memories of their happiness, she must also feel the pain of everything left undone. The way she describes the image of Phil appearing to her suggests that she had kept his memory closed up tightly in a deep part of herself. Once she begins uncovering her past, however, she has no choice but to revisit this part of her past, too. In the end, she is able to finally make peace with the loss of her husband in her youth. By doing so, she leaves Mount Salus with a cleansed spirit, thus allowing her to bid farewell to the comfort of her hometown, because she is now comfortable within herself wherever she goes.

Family Relationships

Welty depicts a wide variety of family relationships over the course of the novel. She shows several marriages in flashback, some healthy and vibrant and others confusing. Laurel and Phil's marriage seems to have been a healthy one that would have lasted, just as Judge and Becky's marriage thrived until Becky's death. Having grown up watching such a healthy relationship, it is little wonder that Laurel would make a similarly good choice for herself. Judge's marriage to Fay confounds everyone who knew and loved him, but it makes perfect sense to Fay's family. This incongruity is merely a matter of perspective; what Judge had to offer a woman was obvious to all, but what Fay had to offer a man was elusive to everybody except her family. Still, even one of the neighborhood gossips has to admit that if Judge was happy, it is nobody's place to judge.

Parent-child relationships are depicted through Laurel's childhood memories. She loved both of her parents and, as an only child, felt a deep sense of responsibility to them. Despite her mother's hurtful ranting after suffering a stroke, Laurel remained steadfast in her commitment to care for her. She excused her mother's behavior because she understood that it was not intentional, but also because her father's inability to deal with the situation left nobody else to be strong in such a difficult situation. When her father dies, Laurel objects when visitors to the house tell stories about him that, while well-meaning, are not true. She feels helpless to control the mayhem of the wake and the funeral, but remains committed to preserving an accurate memory of his life. She doesn't want stories told that make him larger than life or that attribute others' deeds to him. In the end, Laurel is only able to leave her hometown and her childhood home behind because she has examined honest memories of her parents and made peace with the decisions they made and the people they truly were.

Style

Contrast

Perhaps because *The Optimist's Daughter* is a short novel, Welty includes elements of contrast to create a sense of tension in the story. The plot is fairly straightforward, but its drama and depth come from the characters and the tense atmosphere that hangs over the events of the story until the end, when Laurel leaves for Chicago. That the tension lifts when it does signals to the reader that Laurel, the title character and center of the novel, has accomplished what she needed to accomplish on her unexpected trip home. It ensures the reader that resolution has been reached.

Welty's contrasts are both subtle and overt. Her description of the hospital hallway is an example of an overt contrast that hints at underlying tensions: "The whitened floor, the whitened walls and ceiling, were set with narrow bands of black receding into the distance." The title is a more subtle example, as the use of the word "optimist" is ironic. Judge McKelva called himself an optimist in jest, not because he was a pessimist but because he had little choice about circumstances like his detached retina: "He, who had been declared the optimist, had not once expressed hope. Now it was she [Laurel] who was offering it to him." Another example of contrast is when Laurel and Fay leave the hospital after Judge McKelva's death and find themselves in the midst of a Mardi Gras celebration. Welty sets the solemn passing of a genteel man amid one of the largest, most raucous festivals in the United States, thus creating tension and contrast.

Symbolism

Welty's use of symbolism is typical of short story writers. Symbolism is an efficient use of words because it allows the writer to convey multiple messages in a single passage, exchange, or image. For example, Judge McKelva's ailment that takes him to the hospital is an eye condition. This suggests that his ability to see clearly is compromised by his age. This may be one reason why he chose to marry Fay, as Laurel suggests in her observation of Wendell, Sis Chisom's young son: "He was like a young, undriven, unfalsifying, unvindictive Fay. So Fay might have appeared, just at the beginning, to her aging father, with his slipping eyesight."

Laurel goes to close her father's casket so it can be taken to the cemetery for the funeral, but has difficulty with the weight of its lid. She is helped by Mr. Pitts, the undertaker, and her friend Tish, who "helped her to give up bearing the weight of that lid, to let it come down." Closing the lid to the casket is symbolic to Laurel, because it is her conscious choice to accept the end of her relationship with her father. It is literally the last time she will see him.

Perhaps the most dramatic example of symbolism is when Laurel returns to her father's house alone to find that a bird has found its way inside. As she rushes to close interior doors to isolate the bird, she hears it flying against windows and doors, trying to escape. At the same time, she allows herself to form the thoughts that express that she blames Fay for her father's death. Her anger, resentment, and helplessness are struggling, along with the bird, to get out. As Laurel thinks about her case against Fay, Welty writes, "Why, it would stand up in court! Laurel thought, as she heard the bird beating against the door and felt the house itself shake in the rainy wind."

Omniscient Narrator

The narrator in *The Optimist's Daughter* is omniscient ("all-knowing"), meaning that the story is told from a third-person point-of-view. The narrator is not a character in the story, and is able to enter the thoughts of several different characters, but shows an obvious bias toward Laurel and other southern characters. The narrator is typical of an omniscient narrator in the telling of events, such as the wake at Judge McKelva's house, at which the narrator passes from room to room, describing the people and conversations along the way. The narrator also reveals the thoughts and feelings of several different characters, but never reveals those of Fay and her family. There are extended passages of Laurel's interior monologue, such as when she goes through her father's office, taking in the sight of every book, pile of papers, and piece of furniture. As Laurel delves deeper into her heart, so does the narrator, as when Laurel finds her mother's old letters, papers, and photographs. While it is most often Laurel's thoughts that are revealed, the narrator also sees inside the minds of other residents of Mount Salus. For example, when Laurel insists that Major Bullock's story about her father frightening away the "White Caps" (members of the Ku Klux Klan) is not true, the narrator tells the reader that the Major's feelings were hurt.

Historical Context

Life in the South

The small town of Mount Salus represents the gentility and social life of the traditional South. Because of its commitment to tradition and its older population, Mount Salus reflects many of the values and beliefs of the Old South. Despite changes and progress, the people adhere to the chivalric, hierarchical social organization of the South. Family is extremely important, and a person's character is often attributed to his or her bloodline. People treat one another with outward respect and kindness, are quick to help their neighbors, and respect the older residents and natives of the town.

Fay is the subject of mean-spirited gossip, not only because she is an outsider, but also because she is crude and dramatic. In one scene, the older ladies in the neighborhood marvel that she does not know how to separate an egg, can only identify the frying pan in the kitchen, and does not cook Sunday dinner. To these ladies, one of whom is knitting an afghan, domestic skills are a fundamental part of femininity. That Fay's lack of familiarity with the kitchen is the cause of talk all over town is evidence of the narrowly defined roles that traditional southern people expect.

Religion in the South is almost exclusively Protestant, although there are Catholics and Jews. While Baptists are most prominent, other denominations, such as United Methodist and Presbyterian, are also well-represented. Laurel's family, neighbors, and friends are all members of the Presbyterian Church, and they attribute many of Fay's unrefined ways to her being a Baptist.

Some historians believe that the endurance of southern manners and traditions is due to the hardships faced by the South in the past. Rather than tear it apart, they argue, the struggle to survive only made the culture stronger.

Southern Gothic Literature

Some of Welty's writing is associated with the southern gothic style, and there are elements of it in *The Optimist's Daughter*. This style features settings in the American South, fantastic incidents, and characters who are bizarre, grotesque, and outcast. Although the novels do not take place in drafty castles, mazes, and dark woods, the themes derived from such European gothic settings appear in southern gothic writing. These themes include isolation, confusion, and the search for meaning, all of which are reflected in the character of Laurel.

Compare
&
Contrast

- **1970s:** After the death of a loved one, the family has the choice of having the body viewed at home or at the funeral parlor. It is not uncommon to have the viewing at home, in keeping with tradition.

  Today: People still have the option of having the body of a loved one viewed at home on the day of the funeral, although most families choose to have the viewing at the funeral parlor. There is variation according to ethnicity and religion.

- **1970s:** Racial tensions continue to discourage social interaction between African Americans and whites. While the law offers increased opportunities and rights to minorities, the culture is slow in catching up to this progress.

  Today: Racial tensions are still a part of every-

day life, particularly in very large and very small cities. Strides have been impressive, however, and social interaction between races is both common and accepted.

- **1970s:** Traditional male and female roles are the norm. Women are primarily responsible for domestic duties, while men pursue careers to provide for their families. Opportunities exist for women, however, and the women's movement is bringing change.

  Today: Women are free to choose careers or to commit themselves exclusively to caring for their families, if their economic situations permit it. Women are entering the workforce in increasing numbers, and are even making their way into top leadership roles. At the same time, there is little if any stigma in choosing to be a full-time wife and mother.

Other characters in *The Optimist's Daughter* represent the bizarre, including Mr. Dalzell, whose senility causes him to act and speak strangely. Judge McKelva's funeral also offers examples of the bizarre and morbid, as when Miss Tennyson argues with Laurel over the viewing of her father's body. The presence at the funeral of Dot, Judge's secretary, is prompted not by grief but by the desire to take in the spectacle. Fay's erratic and disrespectful behavior is also grotesque.

Other writers associated with southern gothic writing include Tennessee Williams, Flannery O'Connor, Carson McCullers, William Faulkner, Katherine Anne Porter, and Truman Capote.

Critical Overview

Considered by many to be Welty's best novel, *The Optimist's Daughter* has garnered the admiration of readers and critics from the time of its publication to the present. In *U.S. News and World Re-*

port, a critic declares that the publication of this novel secured Welty's position among the great American writers. Scholars find the novel so rich in material that many critical papers have been written about it, considering such ideas as Welty's use of landscape, her place among southern writers, and her portrayal of female characters, which many interpret as feminist in perspective.

Commentators are quick to praise Welty's stylistic choices in *The Optimist's Daughter.* Howard Moss of *New York Times Book Review* is impressed with Welty's skill in creating such a lush story in such a short novel. He describes it as "a miracle of compression, the kind of book, small in scope but profound in its implications, that rewards a lifetime of work." Detailing some of Welty's techniques, Welty scholar Ruth D. Weston writes in *Dictionary of Literary Biography,* "Welty's narrative virtuosity in *The Optimist's Daughter* provides continuing evidence of her modernist experimentation with the interior monologue and other narrative techniques, including character role reversals and split protagonists."

Welty's emphasis on the inner life as it relates to the outer world in this novel have led to comparisons with the acclaimed author Virginia Woolf. Moss notes that Welty's characteristic ability to write regional speech patterns is perfectly balanced with her attention to the truth about her characters. He explains, "Miss Welty is equally adept at redneck lingo, mountain twang and the evasions of middle-class speech, but it is in her inability to falsify feelings that gives the novel its particular sense of truth." Echoing this praise, the well-known literary critic Cleanth Brooks, in "Eudora Welty and the Southern Idiom," finds that this novel is one of Welty's "finest instances of her handling of the speech of the Southern folk."

Critics are often taken with Welty's ability to create unique and colorful characters who are completely realistic. Moss comments:

> there is a danger in *The Optimist's Daughter* of the case being stacked, of Laurel being too much the gentlewoman, and Fay too harshly the brash opportunist. In truth, Fay is a horror but eludes being evil. . . . Laurel is too nice but escapes being a prig.

Moss praises Welty's careful handling of these two opposing characters in such a way that neither is wholly good or wholly bad. Brooks expresses a similar sentiment when he comments,

> Wanda Fay is really awful. . . and Wanda Fay's sister and mother are of the same stripe. But Miss Welty does not allow that even this family is wholly corrupted. Wanda Fay's grandfather, old Mr. Chisom, seems genuine enough, a decent old man.

A *Newsweek* review published at the time of the book's publication likens Welty's handling of her characters to that of Russian writer Anton Chekhov.

Many critics comment on the complex subject matter of the book. In *Twayne's United States Authors Series Online*, Ruth M. Vande Kieft observes:

> Like no other work since a few of Eudora Welty's early stories, *The Optimist's Daughter* comes shrouded in what I have earlier called the dark or "sorrowful" mysteries of life and death, finally impenetrable. The weighting of terrible ambiguities and contraries in the novel has left many readers moved by its depth and beauty as by no other of Eudora Welty's works, and yet strangely baffled and saddened, as if the revelations heaped on Laurel, the understanding won by this intelligent, sensitive, truthful, and loving woman were not the final truth of the novel.

Edward Weeks of *Atlantic Monthly* is particularly drawn to Welty's use of "contrast," as mentioned by Vande Kieft in the above passage. Weeks praises Welty's portrayal of the contrast between the sentimental emotion of the neighbors and the insensitive, rude remarks made by the Chisoms during the funeral scenes. He finds that this contrast provides "shocking comedy" in that the reader is both amused and sympathetic. Commenting on the overt tension between Laurel and Fay, Moss writes, "Two kinds of people, two versions of life, two contending forces in America collide in *The Optimist's Daughter*. Its small dramatic battle sends reverberations in every direction."

That the novel continues to be read and analyzed by critics and scholars of all kinds is a testament to its depth and texture and to its lasting thematic and stylistic strengths.

Criticism

Jennifer Bussey

Bussey holds a master's degree in interdisciplinary studies and a bachelor's degree in English literature. She is an independent writer specializing in literature. In the following essay, she discusses the importance of the concept of home to two women characters in Welty's novel. Bussey briefly relates autobiographical information about Welty to show how the author's own experience is reflected in Laurel's experience.

The saying "home is where the heart is" takes on special meaning in Eudora Welty's *The Optimist's Daughter*. In this novel, the death of Judge McKelva prompts both his daughter, Laurel, and his widow, Fay, to connect with their respective homes. Home is a place that allows for restoration, because it is a comfort zone where people generally feel accepted, regardless of their moods, feelings, or decisions. It is a safe haven where Laurel and Fay can be truthful with themselves among people who know them well enough to know when to challenge them and when to leave them alone. In other words, home is the obvious destination in a time of crisis and change. For Laurel, home is the town of Mount Salus and the house where she grew up. For Fay, home is her hometown of Madrid, where her extended family likely meets the same needs for Fay as the house does for Laurel. In briefly reviewing the events of Eudora Welty's life at the time of writing this novel, it will also become clear that, for Welty, home is both Mississippi and the process of writing.

Laurel is a grown woman, living in Chicago, who returns to her hometown of Mount Salus, Mis-

"In very trying times, charged with emotion and uncertainty, people often long to return to the comfort and security of their childhood homes."

sissippi, when her father dies. While it may seem that Chicago is now her home, the reader soon becomes aware that the house in which she was reared is still very much her home. When Fay decides to stay with her family for a few days after the funeral, Laurel has the opportunity to spend some time alone in the house before Fay takes full possession of it. In this privacy and silence, Laurel begins the grieving process more earnestly than she has during the public funeral. Objects in the house, such as the mantel clock, books, letters, and her father's desk, bring back memories, each intimately attached to one or both of her parents. She is saddened because the clock has stopped, and she knows this is because nobody has wound it since her father last did so. A seemingly minor detail, this stopped clock signifies both her father's absence and the reality that her time with her family and in her home has come to an end. Her grief is projected onto household objects because they represent the life she once cherished. Similarly, the books remind her of her parents' habit of reading to each other, a precious memory that she both savors and grieves over. In one passage, Laurel blends her memories of the books with the overall feeling of family, which, she feels, infuses the house:

> She ran her finger in a loving track across *Eric Brighteyes* and *Jane Eyre, The Last Days of Pompeii* and *Carry On, Jeeves.* Shoulder to shoulder, they had long since made their own family. For every book here she had heard their voices, father's and mother's.

Laurel also feels a connection to the house, and thus to her past, in domestic activities such as gardening. Her mother was an avid gardener, and her father tended the flowers after his wife's passing, so it is fitting that, as part of Laurel's process of connecting with her past, she should take up the task one last time. The activity of gardening helps her to feel comfortable and close to her parents, as she participates in the rhythm of the household as she remembers it. On another level, Laurel is tending her own inner garden and connecting with her own identity. Her mother loved flowers so much that she named her daughter after one, and now that the mother is dead, the daughter is caring for the mother's flowers.

In the house, Laurel finds herself so deeply in touch with her past that she can actually hear the voices of the people she has loved and lost. She hears her mother's voice when she is in the garden: "Laurel went on pulling weeds. Her mother's voice came back with each weed she reached for, and its name with it. 'Ironweed.' 'Just chickweed.' 'Here comes that miserable old vine!'" Later, in a moment of revisiting the pain she felt at losing her husband in World War II, Laurel hears his voice grieving for their lost future together. Welty writes, "'I wanted it!' Phil cried. His voice rose with the wind in the night and went around the house and around the house. It became a roar. 'I wanted it!'" Nowhere else in the world can Laurel experience such personal revelations and be given the opportunity to confront the pain in her past and make peace with it, because her bond with her home is so deep. Only at home is she able to bare her heart and hear what she needs to hear to heal herself. And yet, to truly make peace with her past and her present, she must internalize the significance of the house so she can take it with her wherever she goes. Incredibly, she is able to do so.

Fay is originally from Madrid, Texas, a small, low-income town. Although Welty never takes the reader to Madrid, the comments and personalities of the Chisom family offer some idea of what kind of place it is. It seems to lack all the charm and warmth of Mount Salus, yet for Fay it is home. In Mount Salus, Fay clearly feels out of her element and becomes extremely rude and insecure. The reader can only imagine whether or not she is the same when she is in the comfort zone of her hometown. Nevertheless, in her new community of Mount Salus, she is disrespectful, self-absorbed, and boisterous. She no more appreciates the home and possessions of her late husband than she does his friends and family. In fact, she never makes an effort to understand Laurel's grief or her need to be in the house for a few days. Fay's insistence on returning with her family for a visit after the funeral indicates that Madrid is the only place in which she feels secure. She is frantic to go back with them, insisting that she needs to be among people who "speak her language." In other words, Fay, like Laurel, needs to go where she feels understood either by others or by herself. In Mount Salus, Fay feels uprooted, and her insecurity takes many ugly forms, such as her propensity to disrespect Becky's memory and to deny her own family back in Madrid. Laurel muses, "Very likely, making a scene was, for Fay, like home. Fay had brought scenes to the hospital—and here, to the house. . . . " Laurel understands that Fay's horrible behavior is an outward sign of her need to feel at home. She tries too hard to appear to believe that Judge McKelva's home is truly her own, but she never convinces anyone, including herself.

At the time Welty wrote this story, she was grieving the loss of her mother. In fact, the book is dedicated to C. A. W. (Chestina Andrews Welty), which reveals that this work is closely connected to the author's own personal loss. The autobiographical elements in the novel are numerous, and are especially prominent in the parallels between Becky's background and that of Welty's mother. Other autobiographical features pay homage to Welty's happy childhood and the loving marriage her parents enjoyed. Through Laurel, Welty honors her mother and also works through some of the pain and the issues surrounding the death of a parent. Laurel's personal journey to make peace with her past in order to make sense of her future certainly mirrors Welty's own struggles. Welty differs from Laurel in that Laurel lives far from her hometown, while Welty lived in Mississippi, where she was born, until her death. For Laurel, however, the intensity of her journey comes from the house. In the absence of a house or other single vessel holding all of her childhood memories, Welty wrote this book. She in effect works through some of her grief in her writing, which is as meaningful to her as the house is to Laurel.

Welty comments on Laurel's love of her past: "Firelight and warmth—that was what her memory gave her." Laurel, Fay, and Welty are all working toward such warmth in a difficult time during the course of *The Optimist's Daughter.* In very trying times, charged with emotion and uncertainty, people often long to return to the comfort and security of their childhood homes. Fay and Laurel find the havens they need by going back to their homes, while Welty draws from her hometown and blends it with her most private pain. Laurel is ultimately able to take a piece of that firelight and warmth with her back to Chicago, because she has succeeded in making her heart and her home one.

Source: Jennifer Bussey, Critical Essay on *The Optimist's Daughter,* in *Novels for Students,* The Gale Group, 2002.

What Do I Read Next?

- *Eudora Welty (Modern Critical Views: Contemporary Americans)* (1986), by noted literary scholars Harold Bloom and William Golding, provides biographical and critical overviews to aid the student of Welty's novels and short stories.

- Fellow Mississippian William Faulkner's *As I Lay Dying* (1930) is the story of a poor southern family on a journey to bury their mother. While this book touches on some of the same issues as *The Optimist's Daughter* (such as death, grief, and family relationships), Faulkner's treatment of these themes is dramatically different from Welty's.

- Flannery O'Connor's *The Complete Stories* (1996) provides a comprehensive look at the short stories of another important female writer from the South. O'Connor, like Welty, also wrote novels but is more strongly associated with short fiction.

- Welty's *Collected Stories of Eudora Welty* (1982) includes all forty-one of her published short stories. Welty is recognized primarily for her short fiction, and this collection is an ideal introduction to her body of work.

- Welty's autobiographical *One Writer's Beginnings* (1984) is a rare glimpse into the author's life experiences from her own perspective. Her writing style is the same blend of humor, acute observation, and sensitivity that readers enjoy in her fiction.

Gail L. Mortimer

In the following essay, Mortimer analyzes how Welty "enhances the implications of her images" in The Optimist's Daughter.

One of the striking characteristics of Eudora Welty's fiction—taken as a whole—is the remarkable diversity of styles she summons from story to story. Welty herself has said that when she begins

> " Unlike *The Golden Apples*, in which Welty overtly signals each mythic motif she offers as a way of understanding the patterns of meaning she intends, in this novel she has used—but left submerged—mythic substructures that add coherence and nuance to her depiction of the problematics of understanding."

a new story nothing she has written before is of much help to her, that each new story teaches her how to write itself. Yet when we turn to a novel such as *The Optimist's Daughter* (1972) directly after reading *The Golden Apples* (1949) or *Losing Battles* (1970), for example, the shift in stylistic intensity is nevertheless surprising. The complex allusions and linguistic sensuousness of *The Golden Apples* and the garrulous charm of *Losing Battles* leave us quite unprepared for the spareness and apparent simplicity of the later text.

Two additional factors have contributed to critical readings of *The Optimist's Daughter* that are far different from those we find for works such as *The Golden Apples*. The numerous biographical correspondences between Welty's life and the details of her story and her explicit articulation of her theme at the novel's end—having to do with the fragility of memory and its role in understanding— have led to explications of the novel that nearly always emphasize theme and content. And while the novel's critics have also to varying degrees considered one or more of its pervasive images, no one has yet addressed the nature of the coherence underlying their presence in the text. The narrative strategies that inform *The Optimist's Daughter* deserve, I believe, much closer scrutiny. Toward this end, I want to draw attention to at least three ways in which Welty enhances the implications of her images: through her exploitation of the ambiguity of etymological meanings, her syntactical juxtaposition or pairing of the images themselves, and her

oblique references to various mythic substructures. By creating an explicit structure of relationships *between* images, Welty generates a particularly intricate network of meanings in which no single image stands alone, for each is modified by the simultaneous presence of others. Her strategies for insisting on the interdependence of her images as they affect one another's meanings enable Welty to express more fully the subtlety and complexity of her view of how understanding itself takes place and of how we—ostensible seekers of knowledge—manage so often to evade it.

The story of Laurel McKelva Hand's loss of her father and her struggle to come to terms with her memories of all the loved ones she has lost is on one level an extraordinarily personal meditation. When she wrote it, Welty herself had recently lost both her mother and her brother within a brief interval. Welty has gone well beyond this personal dimension, however, in framing Laurel's story. In particular through the creation of Judge McKelva's young second wife, Wanda Fay, she has transformed the outlines of Laurel's story into a vivid interior drama. In the figure of the exasperating Fay, Laurel recognizes and confronts the forces of disruption and chaos that threaten the ordered perfection of her long-held memories, both of her parents' relationship and of her own brief marriage with Philip Hand. Fay is the first of several characters in the novel who embody a crass oblivion to the needs of anyone beyond themselves: they include the Dalzell family, whom Laurel encounters in the hospital the night her father dies; the audacious handyman, Mr. Cheek; and Fay's own relatives, the Chisoms, who (appropriately) run a wrecking concern back in Texas. It is through her efforts to account for the disturbing presence of Fay and to understand how her father could have chosen to marry such a person that Laurel is led to grapple with the limitations of memories she has long accepted as accurate. For Laurel, Fay becomes an emblem of the terrible disjunctions and violations, the things that don't fit and can never make sense, that enter one's life seemingly at random and destroy peace of mind. Laurel is much like her father, who calls himself an optimist and who has chosen in both of his marriages to avoid any deep acknowledgement of the existence of hurtfulness and pain. When her father refers to Laurel by her childhood name, "Polly", he reminds us of that excessive optimism we associate with a "Pollyanna's" view of the world, but the adult Laurel's epistemological task in the novel is to understand the distortions of her own former thinking, to recognize the failure of mere optimism to do justice to the complexity of experience.

In our reading of Welty's novel, we come to understand her purpose in part through the special cogency of her dominant imagery, that of vision and blindness. On the surface it appears that Welty is simply exploiting the traditional meanings of these images, using them as expressions of the broader symbolism of light and darkness—as emblems of human understanding. But as is true of her use of imagery throughout the novel, she evokes the full range of meanings implicit in each symbol, from the most positive to the most negative. Light connotes illumination, comprehension, and clarity, yet its excess leads to just the opposite. With Emily Dickinson, Welty believes "the Truth must dazzle gradually/Or every man be blind—." Thus, Welty gives an especially appropriate name to the vulgar family Laurel meets at the hospital, who incarnate the ugliness she needs to come to terms with; they are homonymously named the "Dalzells." Similarly, the darkness that normally signifies obscurity, ignorance, or an inability or unwillingness to understand can also imply a restfulness that makes introspection and later "vision" possible. The window *blind* in Judge McKelva's hospital room serves this function, darkening the room and protecting his eyes while they recover; twice it is torn down by disruptive figures in the novel, the blind patient (Mr. Dalzell) in the next bed and later (apparently) by Wanda Fay. On the first occasion, Laurel, the nurse, and the Judge's doctor put it back in place to protect his vulnerable eyes from the light. The second time there is no point in replacing it. The blind falls at the Judge's final crisis, as if signalling his death.

Welty's narrative methods often involve exploring many of the words signifying particular concepts, as she does to pursue the myriad linguistic connections between eyesight and insight. Words like "eye," "see," "watch," and "look" pervade Welty's novel, but so do terms that reflect limitations of vision brought about by factors both internal and external to the perceiving self. The ultimately blinding light mentioned above (conveyed in such terms as "glare," "blaze," "dazzle," and "brightness") is intimated throughout the novel by terms that express the intermittent, ambiguous light of objects themselves ("twinkling," "shimmering," "flickering," and "flashing"), suggesting the indeterminacy and tenuousness of the objects to which we look for understanding. Welty suggests, too, that perceivers allow their own preoccupations to interfere with seeing clearly through

her use of images of "mirrors" or "reflections" that cause them to see themselves instead—a kind of narcissistic blindness. And finally, she shows that vision fails when we look at the wrong object; a major example of this is her use of the word "slipping" which, evoking the idea of an eclipse or a veneer, suggests that an object is hidden by something in front of it that one sees instead. Recurrent references to curtains and screens enhance this motif. Judge McKelva has a "slipped retina," and his larger problem in the novel is that he has mistaken one wife (the young Fay) for his beloved late wife, Becky.

In one of her most fascinating narrative strategies, Welty creates linkages between the sustained motif of blindness and sight and other motifs by using key terms that serve as pivots between them. Thus, she enables the connotations of one set of images to enhance or modify those of a second group. This technique becomes evident as we turn to a second major image pattern in the novel, that of rushing water. With the word "cataract," Welty connects the eye disease leading potentially to blindness with the waterfall to suggest a particular obstacle to clarity of vision. In its destructive aspect, rushing water represents the overwhelming emotions or thoughts that can blind us to what is happening; in its more benign form, it signifies a cleansing of the eyes that frees us to see better, as in the tears that fill Laurel's eyes at the moment of her fullest understanding in the novel.

The Judge, his first wife Becky, and Laurel are all associated with the linkages between vision and rushing water. Before she died, Becky, who lay on her sickbed sightless after a number of eye operations for cataracts, had recaptured a sense of her longed-for childhood world of order and peace by reciting Southey's "The Cataract of Lodore," which in its very rhythms and momentum mimics the experience of rushing water. Years later, when Judge McKelva is recovering from his eye operation, he is told to rest his eyes in the dark and, above all, that there are to be no tears. Laurel sees him just before his death and fights back her own tears, to keep *him* from crying. The Judge dies just after Laurel finds Wanda Fay shaking him to demand that he get up out of bed and take her to the Mardi Gras. Since the novel makes explicit that his eye operation is not the cause of his death, we are urged narratively to recognize that he has "seen" too much—Fay's cruelty and his mistake in believing she is like his first, gentler wife, Becky—and that in his despair at seeing, he has just given up. Welty writes that at the moment just before his death, his "whole, pillowless head went dusky, as if he laid it under the surface of dark, pouring water and held it there." It remains for Laurel to come to terms with what they both have seen.

Images of water are especially significant in connection with Judge McKelva, because his basic emotional failure in the novel is shown to have been his refusal to acknowledge Becky's despair when, in her last days, she experienced a horrible fear that her optimist husband would not face. Welty tells us that in his belief that his love for her would make everything all right, he left her feeling that she was facing the worst crisis of her soul alone. Indeed, her sense of abandonment severely exacerbated her pain as she struggled with her fear of death. In view of his wife's suffering and his inability to acknowledge it, there is both irony and poignancy in the fact that formerly, as Mayor of the town, the Judge had been in charge of flood control for his community. In a letter he wrote to his daughter Laurel shortly before he became engaged to Fay, the Judge's particular blindness that will eventuate in this second marriage is foreshadowed when he is still able to say, "There was never anything wrong with keeping up a little optimism over the Flood." Flood control, in these terms, is precisely what optimism is about. Thus, at the moment of Laurel's fullest epiphany, when she transcends the comfort of optimism, we are told: "A flood of feeling descended on [her]. She. . . put her head down on the open lid of the desk and wept in grief for love and for the dead. . . . Now all she had found had found her. The deepest spring in her heart had uncovered itself, and it began to flow again." The waters here, of course, have become emblems of life itself.

A third image pattern emphasized in the novel involves hands and their functions; how they create, give, manipulate, hold and withhold, touch, restrain, and express. Although there are numerous instances of this pervasive motif (prominent, for example, in the name and the talents of Laurel's lost husband Philip Hand), its *presence* is in some ways less interesting than how Welty incorporates it into her larger concern with the nature of knowledge. She links the hand imagery of this novel to the blindness motif we have looked at through the notion of hands that can see, through *braille*. Although the word itself is not used, this pivotal concept is recurrently enacted, as when Welty writes that the sensitive hands of Dr. Courtland, the eye specialist, "had always looked, to Laurel, as if their mere touch on the crystal of a watch would convey to their skin exactly what time it was", or when Laurel, in exploring her mother's writing desk, discovers the lit-

tle stone boat carved by the Judge when he was courting Becky, "her fingers remembering it before she held it under her eyes." By repeatedly describing the motions of her characters' hands (both sensitive and insensitive ones), Welty pursues nearly every imaginable variation on the image to show us the strategies people use in experiencing and responding to new knowledge by accepting, modifying, denying, or using it. Ineptitude with one's hands is depicted as a type of blindness to the nuances of things, as when Laurel admits late in the novel that—unlike Philip Hand—she, her father, and her mother, Becky "were a family of comparatively helpless people." Moreover, with the word "blunder," used variously at least four times (in association with the Mardi Gras crowds, the men who carry Judge McKelva's coffin, the trapped bird, and the offensive Mr. Cheek), Welty merges hands and blindness once more: to blunder is to stumble or be clumsy as if one cannot see. Thus, Welty connects blundering (a word which at times she italicizes) with the chaotic and disturbing world of darkness and disorder that Laurel and her optimist father have struggled to deny. As for the remembered perfection of her marriage with Philip, Laurel believes "there had not happened a single blunder in their short life together."

A fourth—and for our purposes final—motif in Welty's novel involves her use of birds. They serve several imagistic functions at different points in the novel and ultimately point, even more directly than Welty's other images do, to her explicitly articulated thematic concern with memory. As we shall see, birds not only pull together the issues represented by the other images; they become at crucial moments images of memory itself.

A review of their more traditional uses in the novel helps us to understand the significance of Welty's later amplification of the image and its incorporation into her allusions to mythic stories. At times, for example, birds are used rather straightforwardly to represent nature commenting upon the actions of humans. A mockingbird sings throughout a conversation among four elderly women, Judge McKelva's contemporaries, when, after his funeral and in Laurel's presence, they discuss his two marriages; here birds serve as a kind of chorus to the Greek chorus constituted by the women themselves vis-à-vis Laurel, who is working quietly among the flowers. The flowers themselves reflect her struggle to see: they are irises. The mockingbird, meanwhile, "let fall a *cascade* of song" (emphasis mine).

At other times birds mirror what Laurel fears: the pigeons who feed out of one another's craws, and whose pecking as they ate out of her hands when she was a girl terrified her, seem to represent Laurel's avoidance of the complicating entanglements of human love in the nearly twenty years since Philip died in World War II. She experiences the apparently painful interdependence of these birds ("sticking their beaks down each other's throats, gagging each other") as an entrapment: "They convinced her that they could not escape each other and could not themselves be escaped from." The scene Welty creates is closely reminiscent of the one in D. H. Lawrence's *Lady Chatterley's Lover,* in which Connie Chatterley's fear of life and sexuality is expressed in her timidity in handling baby chickens.

Birds also serve as images of Laurel's own aspiring soul. The chimney swift trapped in her house on her last night there echoes her panic and feelings of entrapment within anachronistic thoughts and feelings that no longer "fit." During the long, stormy night, she and the bird alike struggle toward "light." And in the morning, when she frees it, we feel that she is freeing herself as well. Birds also reflect the souls of Laurel and Philip Hand on a happier occasion. On their train trip to Mount Salus to be married, the young couple had seen a flock of birds "flying in a V of their own, following the same course" south that the lovers were taking, mirroring in fact the convergence of the Ohio and Mississippi rivers beneath them all. This redoubled image of convergence had seemed a reflection to Laurel and Philip of the joy of their coming together.

Finally, as I have suggested, birds are used to suggest a more complex meaning within the novel. Welty enhances her consideration of how memory works and of "the danger of caging memory in" by using birds as images of memory itself. They are present on nearly every occasion when Laurel thinks about the past, at every one of her moments of revelation. When the funeral procession arrives at the cemetery, Welty writes that "as they proceeded there, black wings thudded in sudden unison, and a flock of birds flew up as they might from a ploughed field, still shaped like it, like an old map that still served new territory, and wrinkled away in the air." These birds, and the shape that they retain as they fly upwards, express Welty's vision of how memory continues to pattern our thoughts "like an old map" that may or may not fit new territory. Laurel's memories about her parents and husband, perfect and therefore necessarily dis-

torted, constitute an old map that fails to account for Wanda Fay, fails to accept the reality of the difficult, painful moments in her parents' lives together, and fails as well to acknowledge the implications of Philip's loss of his own life. (In a later vision Laurel sees Philip looking "at her out of eyes wild with the craving for his unlived life" as his voice rises to a "roar" of despair.) Laurel's growth in the novel involves learning to allow her memories to remain vulnerable to the changes in her own understanding. She must, to begin with, stop denying the fact of Fay's existence in her father's life and so come to terms with *his* needs and vulnerabilities. Welty is explicit about the lesson Laurel is to learn, and when she has finally learned it, Welty depicts her as, first, freeing the trapped bird and, then, withstanding waves of emotion in her final confrontation with Fay. In this penultimate scene in the novel, Laurel raises a breadboard Philip had made for her mother "above her head, but for a moment it seemed to be what supported her, a raft in the waters, to keep her from slipping down deep, where the others had gone before her."

It is impossible by merely citing examples to convey a sense of how intricately Welty structures her motifs in this novel. Blindness and sight, hands, birds, and rushing water—as well as a number of analogous motifs, such as fire, time, and bridges—are linked in a variety of ways through individual words that cross etymological paths (as with "cataract" and "iris") and through their juxtaposition in various contexts (as in the mockingbird's "cascade of song"). Welty rarely fails to pursue the thematic suggestiveness of words' synonyms and homonyms. She seems vividly aware of the multiplicity of meanings inherent in single words, and her linguistic playfulness creates echoes throughout our reading as on various levels we grasp the movement among etymological realms. These explorations, in fact, account for a number of otherwise bewildering details in her stories. One decidedly lighthearted example involves her playing with the images associated with braille, a concept I have already mentioned as serving as a link between the motifs of blindness/sight and hands. Welty introduces us to a minor character in the novel, untypically, without her last name: the Judge's former secretary, who "to everyone in town. . . was known simply as Dot." Years ago, we are told, she had bought herself an expensive Mah-Jongg set. The palpable (raised) dots of braille are recalled in Dot's name itself; in the palpable (recessed) dots on the domino-like tiles, the small sticks, and the dice of the Mah-Jongg set (used as graphic signs in themselves or to count points); in expressions like "on the dot" that (like "the blink of an eye") recurrently appear in the text to signify time; and in the fact that Welty herself pauses as narrator of her text to call our attention to the word characterizing the sentimental feelings Dot had for the Judge and the Judge's excessive fondness for his young wife Fay (again, a sign of a type of blindness): "'[H]e doted on her,'" Miss Adele Courtland declares. "'Doted. You've hit on it. That's the word,' said Miss Tennyson." "Mah-Jongg" itself is Chinese for "house sparrow," a bird pictured on one of the tiles and a reminder of the bird who disrupts Laurel's home late in the novel, leaving spots everywhere it touches. Much of this may simply be playfulness, an expression of Welty's exuberant, even sensuous pleasure in the resonances of language. And while I think that we may err in placing very much interpretive importance on such passages, they are consistent with Welty's overall narrative strategies, which so often involve encouraging us, her readers, to let our imaginations roam among the network of meanings implied by her linked motifs.

The linkages I have suggested at the level of language take us repeatedly back to the surface message of her story, a message about how our understanding is jeopardized by our own habits of perception. Welty reinforces our sense of the ironies and complexities of her subject at a deeper level, moreover, through allusions—some straightforward and others more oblique—to mythological stories that themselves have to do with evading and searching for truth. Unlike *The Golden Apples,* in which Welty overtly signals each mythic motif she offers as a way of understanding the patterns of meaning she intends, in this novel she has used—but left submerged—mythic substructures that add coherence and nuance to her depiction of the problematics of understanding. Early in the novel, for example, she mirrors the story of Daphne (whose name is Greek for "laurel"), who eluded Apollo's pursuit of her by being transformed into (or, in another version, replaced by) a laurel tree. Welty shows Laurel as confusing her own image in a window with that of a beech tree as she dozes on the train trip to Mount Salus. When we recognize this brief allusion, it becomes clear that Welty is adumbrating Laurel's problem; Daphne's avoidance of sexual encounter serves as a synecdoche for Laurel's avoidance not only of sexuality but of all entangling human relationships and suggests the nature of her failure to acknowledge fully the complexities of her memory of her parents and her husband.

Similarly, there are suggestions that the mountain in West Virginia where Laurel's grandmother lived is a type of magic mountain, perhaps one of the Venusberg mountains believed in medieval legend to be where the Goddess Venus held court, enticing travelers who then were reluctant to leave. A high priestess served the goddess under the name of Queen Sibyl (recall that Welty calls the river at the foot of the mountain "Queen's Shoals") and, because of her prophecies, the mountain came to be seen as a place of wisdom. The novel places such emphasis on the bliss that Becky experienced when she was there that the mountain seems to be the prototype of the lost paradise Becky thought of when she decided to keep her "diagrams of *Paradise Lost* and Milton's Universe", and so the mountain, like the figure of Daphne, also serves as an image of escape. Becky, remembering that longed-for sanctuary in West Virginia, had expressed scorn for the word "Mount" in Mount Salus' name; and now Becky's daughter, Laurel, in thinking of her experiences on that mountain, undergoes her fullest epiphany, after which she dons her "*Sibyl* Connolly" suit for the flight back to Chicago (emphasis mine). Among the objects sacred to the goddess Venus were the dove/pigeon (recalling Laurel's crucial childhood encounter with pigeons), bread (Becky's breadboard in the final scenes of the novel), and figs—all associated with Laurel's mother. Welty is drawing from the mythological tradition in which mountains represent the Great Mother, a place of nurturance and wisdom.

A more important mythological substructure for the novel, however, consists of the Oedipus/Teiresias story, especially as reflected in Sophocles' *Oedipus Rex.* By alluding to the complex, ironic echoes of Oedipus' story, Welty is able to build upon Sophocles' intricate depiction of the relation between vision/blindness and memory. The paradoxical ways in which memory can both know and yet not know are central to Sophocles' themes, as they are to Welty's, for they explain how our own predilections and motives obscure our ability to see what would otherwise be evident. Oedipus in one sense knew that he had killed a man and married a woman, but his memory failed to grasp the connection with the prophecies about his fate. Laurel, similarly, "knows" of the complex hurtfulness that existed between her parents at the end of Becky's life, but she has needed or preferred to remember only their love and harmony. Judge

McKelva, too, had refused to see his dying wife's pain, preferring to trust in love to make things right. Laurel, the Judge, and Oedipus alike have all been optimists and have blinded themselves to some ugly realities. Fay, in fact, accuses Laurel (as she had the Judge) of "putting your eyes out, too" by reading too much, recalling Oedipus' deliberate blinding of himself. And finally, Laurel, like Oedipus, has failed to know who her parents are, so that her enlightenment at the end of her story, like his, constitutes the overcoming of an otherwise "fatal" flaw.

As is so often true with Welty's stories, she has followed through even to minor details with her mirroring of this mythic source. The incident in which the Judge as a boy cut his foot open and had to be carried home by his friend reminds us of Oedipus' name, which means "swollen foot." Young Clint, on that occasion, would necessarily have walked, as Oedipus does, with a limp. As a legacy of their childhood experience, both have scarred feet. Moreover, the riddle given to Oedipus by the Sphinx—about what being "has sometimes two feet, sometimes three, sometimes four, and is weakest when it has the most?"—itself acted out in Oedipus' story as, blind, he walks with a cane or leaning on others, is also mirrored by various characters in Welty's novel. Tom Farris, the town's "blind man," comes to Judge McKelva's funeral tapping his cane "from side to side in a lordly way"; and Sam, Becky's youngest brother, had attended her funeral some dozen years ago on two canes and was thus, in a sense, four-footed.

The cogency of many such details in Welty's novel consists in their reference to intertextual sources. Euripides' play *Ion,* for example, serves as one minor echo, reinforcing the more prominent Oedipal story. Welty names the place where the Judge and Fay ate Sunday dinner the "Iona Hotel." The Judge's old friends describe their going there as a "saddening exhibition" of the old man's blindness in choosing a wife who could not cook. *Ion* closely resembles *Oedipus Rex* in that both stories chronicle a protagonist's discovery of the true identities of his mother and father. Interestingly, the first scene of the play shows Ion, a servant in the temple of Phoebus Apollo at Delphi, sweeping out the temple with a broom and threatening to use a bow and arrow to shoot the birds who are defiling the temple. This scene mirrors Laurel and her housekeeper Missouri's pursuit (with a broom) of the chimney swift who has entered and left his sooty mark upon so many things in the McKelva home. The bird "shot out of the dining room and

now went arrowing up the stairwell in front of her eyes." When the bird is gone and the curtains have all been pulled down and cleaned, the house resembles the temple of the sun god: "All the windows. . . let in the full volume of spring light. There was nothing she was leaving in the whole shining and quiet house. . ."

Just as significant as the associations with Oedipus are those with Teiresias, the blind old Theban prophet who became a seer by virtue of understanding "the tongue of birds." Just as Sophocles mirrored the ambiguities of blindness and understanding in Oedipus through the parallel blindness and "vision" of Teiresias, so Welty projects the paradox implicit in the figure of a blind seer onto several figures in her novel. A number of her characters, major and minor, are either blind or threatened by blindness; they include the Judge with his slipped retina; Becky, Laurel's mother, who was blind during the last few years of her life; the blind Mr. Dalzell in the Judge's hospital room; and "Mount Salus's blind man," Tom Farris. Moreover, we find scenes of precognition attributed to all three of Welty's central characters. This happens first when, unbeckoned but sensing that something is very wrong, Laurel returns to her father's hospital room the night he dies and discovers Fay abusing him. The Judge foresaw the future twice; although he had only been going to have his eyes examined in New Orleans, he left complete instructions with a friend about how to get in touch with Fay's family should anything happen to him, and years earlier he had made his only trip to Chicago to see Philip during what was to be his "last leave" before dying in the Pacific in World War II. Becky too, Laurel concludes, had "predicted" Fay; part of her anger and sense of betrayal as she lay near death had been her recognition of that aspect of her husband's personality that would make such a choice as Fay possible. As a figure both male and female, who both sees and does not see, Teiresias, then, is embodied in Laurel, Becky, and the Judge alike. Just as Teiresias had been blinded as a result of his poor judgment—in one version of his myth because he had declared that women have more sexual pleasure than men—so too the Judge is blinded for failing to judge a woman rightly. Laurel, a judge's daughter, spends time in the novel introspectively holding a "trial" and marshalling "evidence" to help her reach a "verdict" about Fay; the courtroom language is explicit. Even the mystically potent number seven, associated in a variety of ways with Teiresias, is reflected in the Judge, who at 70 has blindly married the self-absorbed young Fay. Teiresias, moreover, is linked with the Judge in a more subtle way; Robert Graves tells us that he had a daughter named Daphne.

But most central to Welty's purposes is the fact that Teiresias is associated with being able to interpret or "read" the language of birds, a gift he received in compensation for having been blinded. We recall that the Judge's eye troubles began when he saw "flashes" from "bird-frighteners" on the family's fig tree, suggesting perhaps that in the implicit effort to keep birds away, the Judge was leaving himself vulnerable to "blinding" (because unanticipated) flashes of understanding. As I have emphasized, birds are persistently connected with Laurel's moments of understanding, as if the lessons of birds will free her spirit.

In *The Optimist's Daughter* Welty enriches her theme through narrative strategies operating on at least two different levels: the single word or image and the wider mythic substructure. Through the juxtaposition of various pairs of images (i.e., birds and hands, water and eyes) and through exploiting the multiple meanings of single words ("watch," "pupil," "iris," "cataract"), Welty foregrounds different dimensions of meaning to comment upon Laurel's search for understanding. In doing so she manages to recover some of the lost metaphorical dimensions of our everyday language. Through her evocation of mythic tales, moreover, she draws from the wider realms of significance reflected in the stories of such figures as Daphne, Oedipus, and Teiresias. The subtle nature of these linkages enables Welty's readers to experience her story at a variety of depths depending upon our awareness of these linguistic and literary/mythic associations. As happens when we lift a net by any one of its knots, all of the threads and other knots to which it is connected are pulled up along with it; similarly, no single image or pattern can be said to "explain" Welty's text. Since the phenomena I have discussed all have to do in some respect with the theme of understanding—our quest for it, our evasion of it—Welty's strategy has the effect of leaving us with a strong sense of the difficulty and endlessness of the search. The core of Laurel's lesson has been that old patterns of thought cannot do justice to new experience. It is important that Laurel not merely accept Fay or assimilate her into her world view since that would be to fail to recognize Fay's role as an emblem of the fact of disjuncture or chaos in our lives. If Laurel is to eschew the comforts of her old, patterned ways of seeing things, then she must come to tolerate ambiguity, complexity, and even

horror in the world around her. Welty's narrative decisions reinforce this thematic message by refusing to offer clearcut and definitive readings of her story. Each time we glimpse the implications of one image, another modifies what we have seen.

Welty's use of image and myth pulls together the otherwise disparate phenomena from her family's past that she selected for inclusion in her novel. Moreover, the particular ways in which they give subtle structure to her novel are analogous to her concept of how memory itself works. She sees memory much as T. S. Eliot sees literary tradition. In "Tradition and the Individual Talent," Eliot argues that when a genuinely new piece of literary art is created, it causes the pre-existing body of literature to "be, if ever so slightly, altered" as "the relations, proportions, values of each work of art toward the whole are readjusted." Eliot's "historical sense" is quite similar to Welty's idea of memory as something which needs to remain open to new perspectives, "vulnerable to the living moment." Welty is explicit in her novel in saying that the memory is *not* meant to freeze the past into something impervious to new experience. Instead, it repeatedly redefines the patterns of our lives as we reach a fuller understanding; the body of all we know alters slightly with each new addition as memory works its magic. What I want to suggest, then, is that Welty's deliberate evocation of the etymological histories of particular words, the conflation of meanings she creates by juxtaposing key words in various ways, and her use of mythic tales to revive our cultural memories of stories embodying these same concepts are meant to enact in her readers' memories the lessons *about* memory seen in Laurel's story. Just as Laurel is urged to allow her memory to glimpse correspondences and new implications, so we as readers are urged to recognize the connections implicit in Welty's intertextual and etymological allusions. We make "sense" of Welty's novel only to the degree that our cultural memories enable these connections to take place. *The Optimist's Daughter* persuades us of the truth of Welty's statement that memory is her greatest treasure: "during its moment, all that is remembered joins, and lives." In her memory as in her fiction, "the strands are all there: to the memory nothing is ever really lost."

Source: Gail L. Mortimer, "Image and Myth in Eudora Welty's *The Optimist's Daughter,*" in *American Literature,* Vol. 62, No. 4, December 1990, pp. 617–33.

Sources

Bailey, Beth, "Manners and Etiquette," in *Encyclopedia of American Social History,* Charles Scribner's Sons, 1993.

Brooks, Cleanth, "Eudora Welty and the Southern Idiom," in *Eudora Welty: A Form of Thanks,* edited by Louis Dollarhide and Ann J. Abadie, University Press of Mississippi, 1979, pp. 3–24.

Earle, Carville, "Rural Life in the South," in *Encyclopedia of American Social History,* Charles Scribner's Sons, 1993.

Moss, Howard, "Eudora Welty's New Novel about Death and Class," in *New York Times Book Review,* May 21, 1972.

Review of *The Optimist's Daughter,* in *Newsweek,* May 22, 1972.

Review of *The Optimist's Daughter,* in *U.S. News & World Report,* February 15, 1993.

Vande Kieft, Ruth M., "Eudora Welty," in *Concise Dictionary of American Literary Biography: The New Consciousness, 1941–1968,* Gale Research, 1987, pp. 492–505.

——, "Eudora Welty," in *Twayne's United States Authors Series Online,* G. K. Hall & Co., 1999.

Weeks, Edward, Review of *The Optimist's Daughter,* in *Atlantic Monthly,* June 1972.

Weston, Ruth D., "Eudora Welty," in *Dictionary of Literary Biography,* Volume 143: *American Novelists Since World War II,* Gale Research, 1994, pp. 303–20.

Wolff, Sally, "Some Talk about Autobiography: An Interview with Eudora Welty," in *Southern Review,* Vol. 26, No. 1, January, 1990, pp. 81–88.

Further Reading

Bloom, Harold, *Eudora Welty: Comprehensive Research and Study Guide,* Chelsea House, 1999.
   Bloom offers a thorough reference to Welty's short stories, for which she is best known. Ideally suited for the reader new to Welty's work, this book explains themes, techniques, and contexts in Welty's short fiction.

Champion, Laurie, ed., *The Critical Response to Eudora Welty's Fiction,* Greenwood Publishing Group, 1994.
   This volume offers the collected criticism of Welty's writing from the 1940s to the present.

Price, Reynolds, ed., *Eudora Welty Photographs,* University Press of Mississippi, 1993.
   Using Welty's early photographs, Price depicts Welty's personal view of the South. The book includes an introductory interview with Welty, conducted by Price, concerning her photographs.

Weston, Ruth D., *Gothic Traditions and Narrative Techniques in the Fiction of Eudora Welty,* Louisiana State University Press, 1994.
   Weston reviews Welty's work in terms of the gothic tradition to show how she uses gothic themes and narrative techniques within the southern literary framework.

The Remains of the Day

Kazuo Ishiguro

1988

Kazuo Ishiguro's third novel, *The Remains of the Day,* earned the 1989 Booker Prize, England's highest literary honor. The book is, in effect, a character study of Stevens, an aging butler who has spent thirty years in service at Darlington Hall. As he considers his past, he is forced to come to terms with the gravity of the sacrifices he has made in the name of duty.

Ishiguro's first two novels were set in Japan, so *The Remains of the Day* represents a departure in the author's work. Still, it is consistent with his writing style in that the book is told from a first-person point of view by a person who faces past self-deception and regret. Further, the tone is controlled, the language is carefully crafted, and the themes revolve around the position of the individual within a society. While some critics maintain that although Ishiguro's setting is not Japan, the book retains a strong sense of the author's Japanese heritage, Ishiguro is quick to disagree. He responds by saying that most of his life experience has taken place in England and that his fictional influences are Britain's writers. Ishiguro's choice of subject matter in this book—and the realism with which he depicts it—demonstrates the importance of England's past and culture to him.

Author Biography

Kazuo Ishiguro was born in Nagasaki, Japan, on November 8, 1954, to Shizuo (an oceanographer) and Shizuko (a homemaker). When he was six, he and his family moved to England where his father was commissioned by the British government to work on a project. Although the family expected to stay only a few years, his father's work kept them there much longer until England had truly become their home. Although Ishiguro and his two sisters attended English schools and had fairly typical English childhood experiences, at home they spoke Japanese and integrated their Japanese roots into their lives. In fact, Ishiguro has said that his interest in writing started as a way to preserve his fading memories of Japan, a country he would not see again until 1989.

Ishiguro earned a bachelor of arts degree with honors in philosophy and literature in 1978, and then completed his master of arts in creative writing at the University of East Anglia in 1980. He worked as a social worker for a number of years (during and after college) until he was able to make a living as a writer. During his years as a social worker, he met Lorna Anne MacDougall, whom he married in 1986. They have a daughter named Naomi, who was born in 1992. Ishiguro's interests include music and the cinema.

Despite his youth, Ishiguro has already built an impressive literary career. Each of his first three novels won awards—the third, *The Remains of the Day* won the prestigious Booker Prize—and all five of his novels to date have earned critical acclaim. Ishiguro's novels deal with self-deception, regret, and personal reflection. His narratives are carefully wrought first-person accounts with a controlled tone that does not deter from the speaker's deep soul-searching. Ishiguro is credited, alongside such high-profile writers as Salman Rushdie, with breathing new life into contemporary British fiction. In 1995, Ishiguro was named to the Order of the British Empire for his contributions to literature.

Kazuo Ishiguro

Plot Summary

Prologue: July 1956

Readers are introduced to Stevens, an aging butler who has served Darlington Hall for about thirty years. The house has recently come under the ownership of an American man named Mr. Farraday, after belonging to Lord Darlington's family for two centuries. While Lord Darlington was a reserved English gentleman, Mr. Farraday is a carefree man who likes to banter. Because he will be away for a while, he suggests that Stevens take his car and go on a trip. Stevens agrees, reasoning that

he will go see Miss Kenton (the Hall's ex-housekeeper), who has just written a letter to Stevens. Always focused on duty, Stevens hopes to recruit Miss Kenton back to Darlington Hall, where she is needed.

Day One

Stevens begins his trip, feeling uneasy as he leaves Darlington Hall behind him. As he drives, he considers what is to him a very important question: What is a great butler? He recalls lively conversations with past colleagues on the matter. Stevens is humble, however, and never claims to be truly great, only to perform his duties with dignity.

Stevens relates stories about his father, also a butler. These stories reflect the sort of dignity and dedication to duty that Stevens admires. He is proud of his father's accomplishments, yet the reader notices that everything Stevens says about his father is relevant to work.

Day Two

Stevens stays the night at a country inn and wakes early. He provides some background about Miss Kenton, who left Darlington Hall in 1936 to get married. Although she is Mrs. Benn now, her letter to Stevens has indicated that her marriage may be in trouble. Stevens recalls that she was a good housekeeper with a professional demeanor. Stevens also reveals that she came to the Hall at the same time that his father came to serve as under-butler. Stevens's father's employer had recently died, and the old man had nowhere to go, so Stevens brought him to Darlington Hall. Although committed to doing a good job, the elder Stevens was limited by his age.

Reflecting on the past, Stevens provides more detail about Lord Darlington. He was influential and involved in politics, and he entertained frequently. Just after World War I, he was sympathetic toward Germany due to the harsh demands of the Treaty of Versailles. He resolved to do something and organized an unofficial conference in 1923 where important representatives from around the world gathered to make plans for asserting their influence in their respective governments on Germany's behalf. During the conference, Stevens's father became seriously ill and died, but Stevens insisted on continuing with his duties.

Day Three

Stevens is still thinking about what makes a great butler when he has car trouble. Pulling into the driveway of a large house, he speaks with the chauffeur, who fixes the car. The man seems surprised to hear that Stevens worked for *the* Lord Darlington. This is the reader's first sense that Lord Darlington ended his life with a shameful reputation. Stevens explains that he has seen this reaction from people before, and that he has chosen to distance himself from it, not because of shame, but because of his desire to avoid hearing his past employer disparaged.

The next morning, Stevens interacts with the locals and then sits in a cafe enjoying tea. He reflects further about Lord Darlington and the political events and influential Germans that figured prominently in his life. Although Lord Darlington told him to fire two Jewish members of the house staff (which outraged Miss Kenton), Stevens maintains that his employer was not anti-Semitic.

Stevens continues on his drive to see Miss Kenton. He recalls an incident in which she came to his room and found him reading a romance novel. He explains this by saying that he was only reading it to improve his command of the English language. He follows this story by relating that he and Miss Kenton used to meet over cocoa to discuss household matters. Although they got to know

each other better during these meetings, the relationship never became truly personal.

Stevens's thoughts return to Lord Darlington, and he admits that his employer was not the man Stevens thought he was at the time. Lord Darlington became a Nazi sympathizer and was manipulated and used by people in positions of power. Stevens realizes that Lord Darlington was misguided and foolish, but maintains that his own dedication to his employer was not blameworthy or unwise.

Day Four

Stevens's car runs out of gas, and a kind doctor helps him. Once his car is refueled, Stevens reaches his destination, Cornwall. As he prepares to meet with Miss Kenton, he remembers when she told him she was leaving to get married. His memory also takes him back to the time when he found out that Lord Darlington had been used by Hitler to spread propaganda in England.

Day Six

Now in a seaside town, Stevens relates his meeting with Miss Kenton two days previous. They exchanged pleasantries and caught each other up on what they had been doing. Stevens asked Miss Kenton if her husband was treating her well, and she said that he was. She added that she did not love him at first, but came to love him. Now, she said, they are happy and expecting a grandchild. She also confessed that, at times, she wonders what might have been if she and Stevens had shared a life. When her words have sunk in, Stevens is saddened and a little heartbroken at realizing how close he came to having a fuller life.

Stevens shares his regrets with a stranger. He tells the man that he gave so much to Lord Darlington that he has little left for himself or anyone else. While Lord Darlington was not a bad man, he reasons, Stevens regrets not having made his own mistakes. He asks, "Really—one has to ask oneself—what dignity is there in that?" The stranger advises Stevens that it is best simply to look ahead. Stevens resolves to return to Darlington Hall and be the best butler he can be for his new employer, which means learning to banter with him.

Characters

Lord Darlington

Lord Darlington is Stevens's original employer, beginning in the 1920s, and Stevens narrates his recollections of Lord Darlington throughout the novel. At the time of the novel, he has died, and his estate has been sold to an American man. Lord Darlington is proper, reserved, determined, and well-mannered. He is most comfortable keeping his relationship with Stevens as formal as possible, so much so that when he needs to discuss anything with Stevens, he pretends to be engrossed in a reference book while speaking.

Lord Darlington feels strongly that Germany had been mistreated by the restrictive Treaty of Versailles, and he resolves to do something about it. As he becomes enmeshed in international politics, however, he allows himself to be manipulated by the German regime to spread propaganda in England. These actions indicate that he is shortsighted, naïve, and not the best judge of character. As a result, he earns a shameful reputation in England and dies in disgrace.

Mr. Farraday

Mr. Farraday is Stevens's current employer. He is an American businessman who has bought Darlington Hall and wants to keep the staff employed there. Although most of the staff has left, he is happy to have Stevens, a "real old English butler." Mr. Farraday seems less interested in immersing himself in English culture than in enjoying the novelty of the change. He is carefree and often makes jokes to or about Stevens, which makes Stevens very uncomfortable. At the same time, Farraday is considerate and offers to loan Stevens his car for a vacation.

Miss Kenton

Miss Kenton (known as Mrs. Benn after her marriage) is the housekeeper at Darlington Hall until she leaves to get married. She is very professional and detail-oriented in her work and staff management, and she resents the arrogance with which Stevens generally speaks to her when she first arrives at Darlington Hall. She is not intimidated by Stevens and does not hesitate to voice her opinions to him. When he tells her he must let two of the maids go at Lord Darlington's order (because they are Jewish), Miss Kenton is quick to express her outrage. At the same time, she respects Stevens and wants to find out more about the man behind the butler. In fact, she develops a romantic interest in him. She is also realistic, and when she realizes that Stevens will never open up to her, she accepts a marriage proposal and leaves Darlington Hall.

Miss Kenton is not afraid to express her emotions, although she does so in as respectful a way

Media Adaptations

- *The Remains of the Day* was adapted to audio by Random House in 1990 with British actor Michael York as reader.

- In 1993, the novel was adapted to film by Columbia Pictures. Directed by James Ivory, this film starred Anthony Hopkins as Stevens and Emma Thompson as Miss Kenton. It earned numerous prestigious awards and nominations from all over the world, including the American Academy Awards, British Academy Awards, and Golden Globe awards. Hopkins and Thompson won David di Donatello Awards for their performances.

as possible. When she first comes to Darlington Hall, she attempts to demonstrate her thoughtfulness by bringing Stevens a vase of flowers for his room. Not until she reunites with Stevens after twenty years does she admit that she once hoped for romance between them. Although her marriage goes through cycles, she ultimately decides that it is best to stay with her husband.

Mr. Stevens

Stevens is the book's narrator. He is a butler in his sixties and has served Darlington Hall for over thirty years. While taking a short vacation on which he goes to see Miss Kenton, he reflects on his past and on the decisions he has made (and not made) along the way. He realizes that he has put his sense of duty above all, including his family, his emotional needs, and his good judgment. He deeply admired his past employer, Lord Darlington, but he now realizes that this man was not as great a gentleman as Stevens needed to believe he was. Stevens operates on the idea that the best way to serve the world is to serve a great man who does important things. That Lord Darlington was a Nazi sympathizer who was manipulated in the years leading up to World War II creates moral tension within Stevens as he thinks back on those years.

The reader comes to know Stevens through the stories he tells and the way in which he tells them. He is reserved, formal, disciplined, and detail-oriented, all of which is important to his position as a butler. He believes in tradition and does not realize that he has become an anachronism. Through his stories, the reader sees that he was—and is—an ideological chameleon. His beliefs and feelings are dictated by his employer. When Lord Darlington thinks it is best to fire the Jewish maids, Stevens agrees. And when Lord Darlington later says that doing so was a terrible mistake, Stevens agrees.

In his working relationship with Miss Kenton, Stevens avoids intimacy of any kind, including the slightest display of emotion. He seems to have no personality, no self, beyond the qualities necessary for his position. This is because for Stevens, being a butler is not merely a job, it is the core of his identity. At the end of the book, however, he realizes that he has sacrificed his humanity in the name of duty and dignity.

William Stevens

William Stevens is Stevens's father, and also a lifelong butler. At the opening of the novel, he has been dead for over thirty years; his son recalls him in extended flashbacks. Stevens admires his father for his years of service and for the stories he has heard about the dignity with which his father carried out his duties. When the elder Stevens becomes unemployed in later years, the younger Stevens secures him a position as an under-butler in Darlington Hall.

The elder Stevens and his son do not share a warm relationship. They are both focused exclusively on their jobs, and the elder Stevens is abrupt when his son tries to talk to him. He keeps his small room extremely tidy, having few personal items. He is proud and therefore resents his son's limiting his household duties after he trips with a full tray. When he falls ill, he becomes reflective and tries to reach out to his son. He realizes that he was not a good father, but he also seems to realize that it is too late to redress his personal failings.

Themes

Duty

Duty and dedication are at the heart of this novel. Stevens has lived his life in pursuit of perfect dutifulness. He has willingly made every personal sacrifice along the way, and when he realizes what he has given up in life, it is too late. He cannot reconnect with his family members because they are all dead, he cannot choose a different vocation, and he cannot marry and enjoy romantic love. As he made these sacrifices, he did so gladly, because he felt that the best way to be of service in the world was to serve a great gentleman. By convincing himself that Lord Darlington was such a man, Stevens deceived himself into believing he was living honorably. Sadly, he allowed himself to be so blinded by duty that he ignored his own judgment and needs.

Stevens's father provides a role model for his son's extreme devotion to duty. Stevens recalls a story about his father in which a general was coming to visit his employer. This general was responsible for the needless death of the elder Stevens's other son, who was under the general's command at the time. The elder Stevens understandably feels deep loathing for this man, yet when he is called on to act as his valet, he does so with emotionless dedication. The elder Stevens's employer had offered to allow his butler to leave the house for the duration of the general's stay, yet he refused. To him, as to his son, duty came before anything and everything else. It is little wonder, then, that Stevens chose to keep performing his duties without hesitation when his father died. In fact, Stevens comments on that evening when his father died and there was a banquet for the important international guests. He states, "For all its sad associations, whenever I recall that evening today, I find I do so with a large sense of triumph." His triumph is that he orchestrated a well-run banquet and did not waver from his duties even when his father died. In other words, he was the picture of dignity and duty.

Related to the theme of duty is patriotism, because both come from dedication to a larger entity. Stevens is deeply patriotic and loves his native England, although he has seen very little of it. In his mind, he has seen the best of England in the great people who have visited Darlington Hall over the years. When he embarks on his trip, however, he has the opportunity to take in England's expansive landscape. He finds it utterly breathtaking and perfectly beautiful. In a way, he projects himself into the landscape, because he finds it beautiful in its understatement and its confidence in knowing that it is beautiful. He imagines that other countries have stunning features, too, but what he admires about England's landscape is its unwillingness to try too hard to be noticed. On day one in Salisbury, he writes, "It is as though the land knows of its own beauty, of its own greatness, and feels no need to shout it."

Hindsight

As Stevens leaves his microcosm of Darlington Hall, his mind slowly wanders from familiar matters (great butlers, dignity, and the staff plan) to less familiar, more personal, matters. This leads him to reflect on his past and to come to certain realizations in hindsight. As much as he admired Lord Darlington and as deeply dedicated as he was to serving him, he now realizes that Lord Darlington was not the great gentleman Stevens needed to believe he was. Upon reflection, Stevens understands that his employer lacked the wisdom, power, and decency Stevens once believed he possessed. This realization is very troubling to Stevens, who made profound sacrifices to serve his employer. He grapples with this realization, concluding that he is not to blame because, after all, he merely carried out his duties with the dignity appropriate to a butler. At the end of day three, he reflects:

> How can one possibly be held to blame in any sense because, say, the passage of time has shown that Lord Darlington's efforts were misguided, even foolish? Throughout the years I served him, it was he and he alone who weighed up evidence and judged it best to proceed in the way he did, while I simply confined myself, quite properly, to affairs within my own professional realm.

The irony, of course, is that at the time Stevens was not concentrating solely on his professional obligations; his need to serve a "great gentleman" led him to believe that Lord Darlington was something he was not. By the end of his trip, Stevens also realizes that he had the opportunity for love, but he let it go. Now it is too late.

The character of Stevens's father provides foreshadowing. As he approaches death, the elder Stevens shares a rare moment of attempted tenderness with his son. He asks if he has been a good father, and supposes he has not. The elder Stevens seems to realize at the end of his life that he has wasted his years focusing on being a good butler rather than spending them being a good father or a good person. The younger Stevens fails to understand the significance of this exchange and thus loses the opportunity to learn from it. As a result, he too finds himself, late in life, regretting choices he made in the past.

Topics for Further Study

- Imagine that the system of house servants described in *The Remains of the Day* exists today in the United States. Given the cultural differences, consider how the employer/employee relationship would be different and how duties would be defined differently. Prepare an orientation packet for a new butler as if you are an experienced butler.

- Lord Darlington was passionate about the political and economic changes he witnessed after World War I, so he organized an unofficial summit meeting. What wrongs do you feel need to be addressed in the world today? Plan an unofficial summit meeting of your own, complete with guest list, agenda, goals, and social events.

- The story takes place in July 1956, the same month and year as the Suez Crisis. Why do you think Ishiguro chose this particular time for his novel? Write a well-developed essay explaining your interpretation of the importance of the Suez Crisis to the novel.

- The novel portrays the decline of the aristocracy and of the practice of keeping a large staff of house servants on English estates. Research the tradition of the English house staff, along with the factors that brought about its decline. Create a presentation to share your findings with a middle school history class.

Style

First-Person Narration

For the most part, the style of *The Remains of the Day* flows from the voice of Stevens, whose memories provide the novel's text. The entire book is his account of the past and present, which gives the reader a distinct impression of his character. Stevens's style is formal, courteous, and longwinded. He has a tendency to be very precise in his communication, to overthink matters, and to share his every thought. For example, rather than simply explaining that Mr. Farraday's banter makes him uncomfortable, Stevens rambles on with reasons why he is unable to engage with his employer in this way, with what he imagines Mr. Farraday thinks of him, and with his judgment that his inability to banter is a failing of his duties. He returns to this concern repeatedly.

As Stevens relates events of the past, all the while emphasizing the admiration he felt for Lord Darlington, it becomes clear that Stevens is an unreliable narrator. Besides his unwillingness to assess Lord Darlington realistically, there are inconsistencies in his accounts of the past. For example, he credits both Miss Kenton and Lord Darlington with saying about his father, "These errors may be trivial in themselves, Mr. Stevens, but you must yourself realize their larger significance." At a deeper level, Stevens is unreliable because he has an underdeveloped identity and thus has come to experience life through the filters of what he believes is expected of him.

Because the reader has only Stevens's interpretation and recollection of events, there is no way to know what Lord Darlington, Miss Kenton, Stevens's father, or Mr. Farraday experienced. As the reader gets to know Stevens better, the words and actions of others are easier to interpret despite the fact that Stevens is often unable to see them clearly. Still, the reader is limited by the exclusive narration of Stevens. This points to the fact that *The Remains of the Day* is in many ways a character study of Stevens; it is unnecessary to Ishiguro's intentions to include the points of view of other characters.

Tragedy and Comedy

Part of the novel's realism lies in its inclusion of both tragic and comic elements. This makes the novel feel less manufactured and manipulated and more like an honest telling of a man's story. Readers enjoy the comedy that stems from Stevens's stiff demeanor in the face of unusual circumstances. For example, Lord Darlington asks Stevens to tell his godson the "facts of life" in the midst of preparing for a houseful of important international guests. Without the additional pressure of the guests, Stevens would be ill-equipped to have such a candid and heartfelt conversation with a near stranger, but the distractions of preparing for guests add to the comedy. Stevens struggles to get the boy alone and then talks around the subject by extolling the virtues of nature. The young man, of course, has no idea what Stevens is trying to do, and because of ongoing interruptions, Stevens is never successful in telling the boy what he ostensibly needs to

know. Also comic is Stevens's preoccupation with his American employer's love of banter. Despite his intense discomfort with this type of exchange, Stevens makes a pathetic attempt at being witty. The reader is as embarrassed for him as he is for himself.

At the same time, the novel contains tragic incidents, such as when Stevens's father dies and Stevens continues with his domestic duties. This is tragic because Stevens places duty above anything else, and also because there is the suggestion that Stevens does not know how to react to the news of his father's death. He has become so emotionless in his occupation that he is not moved like most people are upon the death of a loved one. That Stevens places himself second to his occupation is in itself tragic. He forgoes developing a sense of self-worth, enjoying personal relationships, and the possibility of love, all in the name of duty. In the end, he comes to regret much of his past, but he is in his sixties and has lost many years.

Historical Context

The 1919 Treaty of Versailles

World War I ended in 1918, and the victorious nations met at the Paris Peace Conference in 1919 to determine the fate of Germany, the loser. Representatives at the Conference included British Prime Minister Lloyd George, Italian Foreign Minister Giorgio Sonnino, French Premier Georges Clemenceau, and American President Woodrow Wilson. Because Germany was blamed for the war, it was forced to pay reparations and to dismantle its military. In addition, Germany was forced to give up its colonies and most of its means of trade (trains, merchant ships, etc.).

The Treaty of Versailles was not sustainable; its punitive terms undermined hopes of lasting peace by discouraging Germany's recovery and return to the European community. Although the leaders of the victorious governments generally supported the treaty, there were individuals and groups who felt that Germany was being treated too harshly. As fascism rose in Europe in the 1920s, many of these people sympathized with its stated goals. Postwar Germany accepted a democratic constitution, but a form of militaristic totalitarianism slowly emerged, promising to fulfill the people's wants more effectively and to protect them from communism. Mussolini rose to power in Italy

Compare & Contrast

- **1920s:** Aristocrats often have extensive family estates in which they live and employ a large staff of house servants, such as butlers, housekeepers, gardeners, cooks, and nannies. Wealth and status are the currencies in the competition to employ the very best servants in England.

  1950s: The tradition of the house staff is waning. Some aristocrats and wealthy foreigners with homes in England keep a modest house staff.

  Today: The tradition of the house staff is a luxury of the past, with the exception of the very wealthy and royalty. People's lifestyles have changed, and they take advantage of modern conveniences that make keeping up a household easier to do with less domestic help. Housecleaners and gardeners are more likely to work for several different employers and to live in their own homes.

- **1920s:** The experience of World War I has made England eager to avoid another war on that scale. As a result, England is a leader in the League of Nations and in disarmament conferences whose mission is to maintain world peace. Still, many English people feel sympathetic toward Germany because of the harsh treatment it received at the 1919 peace conference. As political forces in Europe begin to polarize, many English men and women take Germany's side.

1950s: In the aftermath of World War II, public sentiment is decidedly against Germany. During the war, England fought with the Allies against Germany and the other Axis powers. As the truth about German concentration camps spreads, people are even less sympathetic to the defeated Nazis.

Today: English politics are more centered on domestic affairs than on international issues. Although England participates in international organizations such as the United Nations, the country's government is primarily focused on issues such as taxes, federal spending, health care, crime, and immigration.

- **1920s:** For vacations within Great Britain, people rely primarily on automobiles to take them where they want to go.

  1950s: Many people in Britain take advantage of comfortable passenger trains that take them to vacation destinations. While many people still enjoy a car trip through the country, others prefer to shorten their travel time by taking the trains so that they can enjoy more time at their destinations.

  Today: English men and women continue to use the train system for vacation travel, although many prefer to greatly shorten their travel time by booking an airplane flight. As in the United States, air travel is often an affordable option.

---

in 1922, but not until 1933 did Hitler become Germany's chancellor.

The 1956 Suez Crisis

The Suez Canal is a human-made waterway in northeastern Egypt that acts as a valuable shortcut for trade among Europe, America, Asia, and Africa. In 1854, a French diplomat established the Universal Company of the Maritime Suez Canal. This organization built and maintained the canal, enlisting the help of Egyptian officials. The company was given authority to build the canal and, in re-

turn, ownership of the canal would go to Egypt after ninety-nine years.

Originally, the company was a privately held Egyptian entity, whose stock was owned by Egypt and France. In 1875, however, Great Britain bought Egypt's interests because the canal was crucial to its nautical power and colonization plans. In 1936 an agreement was made that allowed Britain to employ defense forces in the canal area, which meant control of the passageway. As Britain's power over the canal grew, Egyptian nationalists began to demand that Britain evacuate. In 1954, Britain and Egypt signed a seven-year agreement calling for the gradual removal of Britain's military from the area. By June 1956, British troops were gone and Egyptian troops replaced them.

In July, however, the United States and Great Britain withdrew their promises to provide financial help for constructing the Aswan High Dam. Their refusal to assist was based on the fact that Egypt had become friendly with Czechoslovakia and the Soviet Union. In response to this withdrawal of funds, Egyptian officials seized the Suez Canal in order to rechannel its proceeds to the dam project. This loss of income was significant to Britain because it was one of the main causes of the decline of British colonization.

Critical Overview

The Remains of the Day is a critical and commercial success. Reviewers' glowing notices of the novel praise its characterization, language, tone, and thematic content. Lawrence Graver of the *New York Times Book Review* calls the novel "a dream of a book: a beguiling comedy of manners that evolves almost magically into a profound and heart-rending study of personality, class, and culture." In a review for London's *Observer,* noted author Salman Rushdie praises the novel for its ability to simultaneously present surface understatement and tremendous underlying tension. In the *Christian Science Monitor,* critic Merle Rubin declares, "Delicate, devastating, thoroughly ironic, yet never harsh, this is a novel whose technical achievements are matched by its insightfulness." David Gurewich of *New Criterion* deems the novel a "remarkable" book in which "the pitch is perfect." Commenting on the comic tradition of butlers in English literature, Hermione Lee of *New Republic* observes, "Butlers in British fiction are a joke. . . Ishiguro's cunning is to invoke these associations—Stevens, after all, is a comic figure, pompous, funny, antiquated, and obtuse—and turn them to serious ends." Ihab Hassan in *World and I* adds that Ishiguro transcends the tradition, or "more precisely, he perfects and subverts it at the same time. He does so with immaculate craft. . . . "

Not only do critics find Stevens tragic and sympathetic, but they also praise Ishiguro's ability to create a consistent and believable voice for a character so unlike himself. Galen Strawson of the *Times Literary Supplement* writes that the book is

both strong and delicate, adding that Stevens's voice "creates a context which allows Kazuo Ishiguro to put a massive charge of pathos into a single unremarkable phrase." Echoing this idea, Graver remarks that Ishiguro's "command of Stevens' corseted idiom is masterly," adding that the author's "tonal control of Stevens' repressive yet continually reverberating first-person voice is dazzling. So is his ability to present the butler from every point on the compass: with affectionate humor, tart irony, criticism, compassion, and full understanding." In the *New York Times,* Michiko Kakutani also praises Ishiguro's controlled tone and his portrayal of unfolding realization in Stevens's mind. He writes:

> By subtly modulating the flow of Stevens' memories and the nuances of his tone, by revealing to us the increasingly difficult emotional acrobatics that Stevens is forced to perform in order to remain in control, Mr. Ishiguro is able to create a portrait of the man that is uncompromisingly tough, and at the same time elegiac. He shows us the consequences of both emotional repression and misplaced loyalty, the costs of blindly holding onto values formed by another age. The result is an intricate and dazzling novel.

Joseph Coates of the *Chicago Tribune* applauds Ishiguro's use of an unreliable narrator to reveal so much about the character. Gurewich writes that Stevens is "a fully realized character, through whom the author manages the world of his novel as sure-handedly as Stevens himself manages the beloved estate of Darlington Hall." He adds, "There is an almost-perfect harmony of style and substance in the book's relationship between the writer and the narrator. . . . " Rubin is struck by the complexity of Stevens's narrative; he remarks: "Stevens (by his own unwitting admission) has tailored his life to produce a complete façade. What makes his narrative so poignant as well as funny, its pathos and satire evenly matched, is the sincerity with which the façade has been cultivated." Hassan interprets Stevens as an allegorical representation of modern history, suggesting that Ishiguro intends to symbolize modern politics, class, and suffering in the character of an English butler.

Much is made of Ishiguro's Japanese roots, as many critics believe that this heritage deeply influences *The Remains of the Day.* They note that the themes of service, discipline, and duty are Japanese in nature and that the controlled, detached tone is typical of Japanese culture. Hassan, for example, asks, "Is the result a Japanese vision of England or, more slyly, an English version of Japan? Or is it both and neither, a vision simply of our

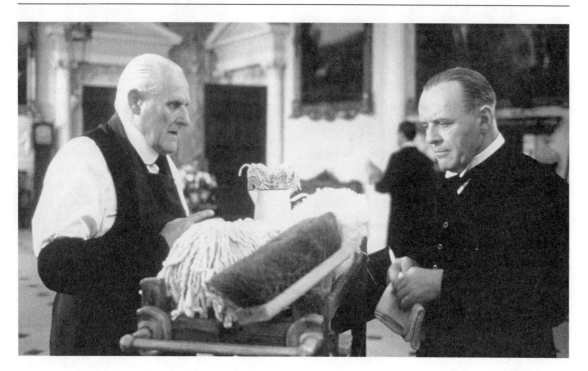

Peter Vaughan (left) as Stevens Sr. and Anthony Hopkins as Stevens in the 1993 film version of the novel

condition, our world?" Gurewich comments on this at length, observing:

> [W]hen Stevens admires the English landscape for "the very *lack* of obvious drama or spectacle that sets the beauty of our land apart," I cannot help thinking how neatly his description fits some of the Japanese criteria for beauty. Stevens' attention to detail is comparable to an origami maker. . . Stevens' insistence on ritual; his stoicism in performing his duties, especially in the face of adversity; his loyalty to his master that conflicts with his humanity—all of these are prominent aspects of the Japanese collective psyche. . . .

Similarly, Gabriele Annan of the *New York Review of Books* finds that Ishiguro's first three novels "are explanations, even indictments, of Japanese-ness," including *The Remains of the Day*, which features no Japanese characters. She explains that Ishiguro "writes about guilt and shame incurred in the service of duty, loyalty, and tradition. Characters who place too high—too Japanese—a price on these values are punished for it."

Although the majority of the reviews are positive, a handful of critics find fault in the book. Geoff Dyer of *New Statesman*, for example, suggests that the notion of narrative irony (in which the reader understands something the speaker says that the speaker does not) is trite. He believes that

Stevens's voice is "coaxed" to achieve this irony and thus lacks integrity. Annan is impressed with Ishiguro's creation of the character of Stevens, but finds the novel's message anti-Japanese and unsatisfying. She explains that the novel "is too much a *roman à these* [a novel written to illustrate a social doctrine], and a judgmental one besides. Compared to his astounding narrative sophistication, Ishiguro's message seems quite banal. Be less Japanese, less bent on dignity, less false to yourself and others, less restrained and controlled."

Criticism

Jennifer Bussey

Bussey holds a master's degree in interdisciplinary studies and a bachelor's degree in English literature. She is an independent writer specializing in literature. In the following essay, she refutes the body of criticism asserting that Ishiguro's novel is largely a Japanese novel.

The author of *The Remains of the Day*, Kazuo Ishiguro, was born in Japan and moved to England with his family when he was six years old. He has lived in England ever since, although he was reared

Readers and critics find
The Remains of the Day realistic
and insightful, and this is
because [Ishiguro] accurately
portrays English aristocratic
culture."

with full awareness and practice of his Japanese heritage. Because of his Japanese background, many critics of the novel hasten to claim that it is Japanese in nature and content. The two novels preceding *The Remains of the Day* featured Japanese settings and characters, and this may be part of the impulse to categorize Ishiguro's third novel as also being Japanese. The idea is that Ishiguro has retained his Japanese worldview and simply filtered an English story through this way of interpreting the world. Critics point to the character of Stevens as evidence of the Japanese undercurrents of the novel. They observe that Stevens expresses himself in a detached tone and that he is driven by his sense of duty, loyalty, and service; that his lifestyle is characterized by propriety, ritual, discipline, and stoicism; and that he grapples with personal guilt and shame. Some critics go so far as to claim that Stevens's unhappy fate and empty feeling when he reaches his sixties is an indictment against being "too Japanese." That Ishiguro is both Japanese and English certainly warrants the assumption that he sees his world in a unique way, but to deem *The Remains of the Day* a Japanese story grossly diminishes his extraordinary accomplishment in the novel.

While every nation has a distinct culture, there are similarities among them. English culture and Japanese culture, although they are subject to the West-East dichotomy, share certain qualities. Yet critics are quick to attribute any overlapping characteristics to Ishiguro's Japanese influence. Both cultures have a history of well-defined, rigid social and political hierarchies. Both have developed a system of manners and accepted means of interacting that are considered "proper," and in both cases proper behavior is reserved, polite, and respectful. While Ishiguro's upbringing may have prompted him to respond to these cultural aspects

in England differently than someone who knew only English culture, Ishiguro is far from unique in recognizing these qualities in England and the English. Readers and critics find *The Remains of the Day* realistic and insightful, and this is because he accurately portrays English aristocratic culture. Further, his portrayal is complex, as it depicts this culture in a time of transition when elitism and dependence on manners are making way for a new social order. The realism—which is so readily recognized by readers—comes from the fact that Ishiguro has drawn from the richness of England's own culture and social history to create his story. Had he included uniquely Japanese elements disguised as English elements, the story would not ring true. For critics to claim that Ishiguro's Japanese sensibility is somehow superimposed onto an English setting and cast of characters only taints the reading of the story.

It is also worth noting that the subject matter of *The Remains of the Day* is distinctly English. The central character is an English butler, a man who, by his own admission, holds a position unparalleled in any other country. Stevens reflects on day one, "It is sometimes said that butlers only truly exist in England. Other countries, whatever title is actually used, have only manservants. I tend to believe this is true." If Ishiguro were trying to make a statement about Japanese culture, he would not put these words in his butler's (the supposed symbol of Japanese restraint) mouth. Besides the tradition of the butler, the novel addresses English aristocracy and its descent in the context of Europe in the years just after World War I. These are all uniquely English concerns and characteristics; they are not universal enough to symbolize anything else.

There are a number of other ways in which Stevens is not a suitable representative for the Japanese. He completely lacks a religious or philosophical foundation, for example, an element of Japanese culture that guides a person's decision-making and way of interpreting life. Stevens comes to realizations about himself not through meditation, reading, or music, but as a side effect of thinking about his career. He does not seek wisdom or honor; the latter is something he does not even want for himself; rather, he is content in deluding himself into believing that he is serving a great man. When he arrives at a personal crossroads, he has no resources on which to draw for insight. He has no religious convictions, philosophical inquiries, or mentor.

This relates to another way in which Stevens is decidedly un-Japanese. He has no sense of family whatsoever. While Japanese society is paternalistic and places a high value on the family unit, Stevens speaks passively about his brother, who died needlessly, and he has a stiff relationship with his father. Stevens and his father are both butlers, and they have transferred whatever energy and attention that would naturally go to family members into their profession. When Stevens's father attempts to make amends on his deathbed, Stevens merely responds that he is busy and has work to do. The years of distance between them cannot be bridged, and the night his father dies, Stevens chooses to continue working. He adds that his father would want him to go on performing his duties with dignity, and he is probably right. In fact, Stevens's father pretended to accept his other son's death rather than seize an opportunity for revenge. Does he do so because of a belief in karma? No, he does so because he values duty absolutely. His son, Stevens, does likewise.

Another aspect of Stevens that makes him an unlikely symbol of Japanese culture is his deep, though long repressed, need to be recognized as an individual. This need is at odds with the Japanese (and, more generally, the Eastern) emphasis on the collective, as opposed to the individual, experience. Once Stevens leaves Darlington Hall, he gradually realizes that he regrets not being more individualistic. He has ignored his potential and his personal needs, and at a level that is almost buried, he realizes that he deserves to be treated as an individual. This need is also revealed when he sees that locals in the town he visits on his way to Cornwall believe he is an important aristocrat, and he enjoys letting them think so. Having never felt important in his own right, he savors the experience. This indicates that his years of putting himself last are not true reflections of his desire or personality. Instead, these are learned behaviors that have become second nature. Yet the truth of Stevens's desires can not be squelched, even after sixty years.

As a writer, Ishiguro is influenced by his dual heritages, but he has stated that his fictional influences are the British greats, such as Joseph Conrad and Ford Madox Ford. If *The Remains of the Day* had been published anonymously, the criticism regarding the possible Japanese connection could be lifted out, and there would still be a Booker Prize and an impressive body of commentary about every aspect of the book. Because of the consistent portrayal of English culture and history, the distinctly English subject matter, and the many ways in which Stevens is not a good representative of Japanese culture, the claims of the novel's Japanese nature

What Do I Read Next?

- *Hope and Glory: Britain 1900–1990* (1997) is the work of P. F. Clarke and Mark Kishlansky, whose contribution to the Penguin History of Britain Series provides an overview of modern British history. Besides providing students with a better understanding of the events leading up to both world wars (and their aftereffects), this book provides commentary on religious, social, and intellectual changes over the past century.

- Ishiguro's *An Artist of the Floating World* (1989) concerns Masuji Ono, an artist who becomes a propagandist during World War II and later witnesses the dramatic changes in his country after the war. This novel complements *The Remains of the Day* because it offers readers an in-depth look at Japan during the postwar era.

- Mike Petry's 1999 *Narratives of Memory and Identity: The Novels of Kazuo Ishiguro* presents detailed analyses and comparisons of Ishiguro's first four novels. Petry also places Ishiguro's novels within the context of contemporary British literature.

- P. G. Wodehouse's *Life with Jeeves: The Inimitable Jeeves, Very Good, Jeeves!, and Right Ho, Jeeves* (1983) contains three novels about the comic fictional character of Jeeves, the butler of Bertie Wooster. Wodehouse's novels about Jeeves, written in the early part of the 1900s, follow Wooster and his butler through various humorous incidents.

- *Kazuo Ishiguro (Writers and Their Work)* (2001) by Cynthia Wong is an authoritative overview of the author's background in Japan and England and his ensuing career as an acclaimed author. Because this is the most recent treatment of Ishiguro's career to-date, it includes updated information.

must be regarded as overstatements. Worse, the overemphasis by many critics on the author's Japanese roots only acts as a distraction to an impressive fictional work.

> The contrast between Eastern and Western attitudes in regard to social roles provides a door into Kazuo Ishiguro's world."

Source: Jennifer Bussey, Critical Essay on *The Remains of the Day,* in *Novels for Students,* The Gale Group, 2002.

John Rothfork

In the following essay, Rothfork asserts that Ishiguro's work "provides a particularly illuminating case study for postcolonial criticism . . . because of the way that his work has been 'translated' for Western audiences."

Although Commonwealth literature (from the Commonwealth of Nations, hence written in English) and postcolonial literature (translated into English) are taught in many English departments, such courses and collections remain problematic for at least two reasons. First, taxonomically the designations never escape their flawed origins. Thus Jayana Clerk and Ruth Siegel, editors of a recent anthology (1995), virtually apologize for their title, *Modern Literatures of the Non-Western World,* saying that they "faced the dilemma of using a negative term that derives from a Western perception". Similarly, the rationale for grouping works and the related supposition for survey courses is a sense of an underlying cultural history (e.g., American literature), which also informs other courses or genres that derive from that history. Lacking any comparable unity, postcolonial literature is presented as a hodgepodge assembly and is often associated with minority studies. By definition, minority views are supplemental; they frequently arise in reaction to majority views, and since they do not voice majority experience, they tend to be regarded as secondary and somewhat exotic.

Yet the views presented by Commonwealth writers are not minority views, though one would hardly know this from the scolding of critics such as Graham Parry who takes the most prominent Indian novelist, R. K. Narayan, to task for "the odd psychology of some of his characters whose emotional responses are often bizarre to a Western reader." Anglo-American readers' cannot understand the actions of Narayan's characters until they know something of the Hindu social psychology that defines normal behavior in Indian society. This, then, is the second problem: to understand something of a profoundly alien society requires a deeper shift in outlook than can be accomplished by an examination of an isolated text or even a collection of works.

Commonwealth writers are native to the regions and cultures they write about: the Caribbean, India, China and parts of Africa. In some measure an Anglo-American audience must appreciate the exotic element of such writing: how different the fictional characters and their situations are from what is ordinary and important in our experience. When this is ignored, critics often bluster, scorning the unfamiliar, or preach, asking for tolerance of the unfamiliar. Evidencing the evangelical approach, Clerk and Siegel hope that their anthology "helps cultivate an awareness that honors different cultural perspectives," as though assuming that it was the professed intent of each author to pitch his or her culture to an audience of North American undergraduates. We do not expect great works from our own tradition to be so transparent and pandering. William Walsh illustrates the bluster approach, concluding that Narayan's Mr Sampath "doesn't quite succeed" because of "an insufficiency of 'composition.'" Exasperated because he cannot explain the accomplished work, Walsh proclaims, "The novel's shape is oddly humpbacked, and repeated readings fail to convince me that I have missed some deeper and more structurally implicit unifying influence." What Walsh could not feel was the Hindu atmosphere, which provides motives for the characters in the novel and themes for readers.

Criticism has recently become sensitive to the presumptive tone of male narrative voices, to racially white voices and to colonial voices. Critical explanations proceeding from such sensitivities, however, tend to remain dialectically two dimensional, assuming that truth can be discovered by stretching the text between two poles: male/female, white/black, majority/minority, America/the world. Moving from one pole to the other is regarded as significant and such movement in a protagonist's understanding and his/her subsequent moral growth provides the model for many Western novels. Nonetheless, the change is measured by distance from the initial pole, which continues to broadcast paradigm assumptions that postcolonial writers do not hear, because they are tuned into the cultural programs which shaped their childhoods. The non-

Western cultures, in which postcolonial and Commonwealth writers typically spend their childhoods, construe identity and motives that often lack Western counterparts. In some cases there is no second pole, either similar to or opposite from the first.

To read postcolonial literature with insight, Anglo-Americans must recognize that cultures are discrete and incommensurable. Indian Hindus are not bizarre British Christians. Readers must accept that there are no Kantian categories of logic or a deep grammar that will explain everything. At the same time, the notion that critical tools should emerge from the culture they seek to explain may be more difficult to put into practice than in principle it might appear. Objections arise on two counts. First, the legacy from Plato through Kant, paralleled by theology, claims a transcendental logic capable of giving the true picture. Although postmodernism opposes this belief by stressing that any specific claim to the truth is necessarily grounded in a concrete language and historic culture, the second problem, as Bishop Berkeley might say, is that we only know what we know. Most readers of postcolonial and Commonwealth literature know only English and its associated culture; even when they do not explicitly assume that Anglo-American culture is normative, such readers are able only partially to escape or suspend the mindset, inevitably smuggling along implicit assumptions. The two problems thus reinforce each other: if one knows only one view, it becomes extremely difficult to imagine exactly where it diverges from the truth or where one culture differs from another.

In the case of postcolonial literature, therefore, the primary thing we need to bear in mind is that there is no neutral or obvious place to begin, a place where truth is bare and universal, which consequently can be used as a standard. This should not forestall critical effort, but should work recurrently to qualify judgments as cultural instead of true. In turn, it could be argued that criticisms of postcolonial literature must have a foot in both the culture of the reader and that of the writer, and must move beyond the confines of strictly literary analysis. Because postcolonial novels offer exotic material, the critical enterprise is closer to anthropology, which studies alien cultures, than sociology, which studies one's own culture. A theoretical basis for such anthropological criticism is provided by the prolific and readable work of McGill philosophy professor, Charles Taylor. Equally, comparative religion and comparative philosophy provide useful critical terms. Pioneered by Huston

Smith, William Cantwell Smith and Joseph Campbell, the discipline of comparative religions opposes the presumption of Christian apologetics to be the true religion. Comparative philosophy is an even younger field. The works of David Hall and Roger Ames on comparing Confucian China to ancient Greece are exemplary, just as Bernard Faure's *The Rhetoric of Immediacy* offers a postmodern reading of Zen Buddhism. Most recently the essays in *Japan in Traditional and Postmodern Perspectives* (Fu & Heine, eds.) offer additional critical tools for readers of Asian postcolonial literature.

With respect to postcolonial/commonwealth writers themselves, one might observe that African-American culture has no doubt aided Western readers to appreciate the fiction of such African writers as Chinua Achebe, Cyprian Ekwensi, Ngugi Wa Thiong'o (James Ngugi) and Nadine Gordimer. The Caribbean worlds of V. S. Naipaul and Sam Selvon are also vaguely familiar, crisscrossing with reggae music and cruise holidays. India has produced many talented novelists who write in English (R. K. Narayan, Nayantara Sahgal, and Ruth Prawer Jhabvala) and of course the Western world has recently become very acquainted with the work and silencing of Salmon Rushdie. Despite the translation efforts of such publishers as Charles Tuttle in Tokyo and the awarding of the Nobel Prize to two Japanese novelists (Yasunari Kawabata and Kenzaburo De), East Asia remains enigmatic to most Western readers.

Among East Asian novelists who write in English, one name stands out, Kazuo Ishiguro. Born in 1954 in Nagasaki, Japan, Ishiguro came to England in 1960. His work provides a particularly illuminating case study for postcolonial criticism not merely because of the cross-cultural issues which his works address but also because of the way that his work has been "translated" for Western audiences. That is, thanks in part to Anthony Hopkins's fame, the movie version of Ishiguro's novel, *The Remains of the Day,* is probably the best known— and probably the most misunderstood—single work by a Commonwealth writer. The work presents the ambivalent reflections of an English butler who recalls highlights from his service to a prominent aristocrat who was involved in formulating national policy toward Nazi Germany. The movie was successful enough to provide a familiar world for a Pepsi Cola television ad in which an ancient butler shuffles through a cavernous English mansion to deliver a tantalizing can of the product sans a straw. Winning the Booker Prize in 1989, *The Remains of the Day* was preceded by two earlier novels, both set in Japan. *A Pale View of Hills* (1982) illustrates the ennui caused by defeat in WWII and the subsequent American occupation. The novel ends with a character recognizing that "It's not a bad thing at all, the old Japanese way," which the war has irrecoverably destroyed. *An Artist of the Floating World* (1986) offers the postwar diary of a prominent painter who produced war propaganda for the government before and during WWII. The "floating world" refers to "the nighttime world of pleasure, entertainment and drink," which Ishiguro uses to symbolize basic tenets of Buddhism.

I will argue that these three novels need to be read as related in order to see that *The Remains of the Day* expresses a Buddhist criticism of Confucian ethics. Although this is a common theme in Japanese culture—which is largely formed by the tensional unity of Buddhism, Confucianism and Shinto, in somewhat the way that Western culture is formed by the tensional unity of Greek and Christian elements—the movie ignores this dimension, and instead renders stock Western formulas of lost love and moral outrage. Somehow the emotionally dead life of Mr. Stevens, the butler whose 1956 diary tells the story, is supposed to explain the blasé British unconcern with anti-Semitism expressed in Neville Chamberlain's appeasement to Hitler. Although these elements, contained in a glossy picture of decrepit aristocracy, are obvious, what is not so easy is explaining how aristocratic haughtiness, and the last glimmer from the dying light of the Raj, serves to kindle Nazism. Western sentiment, if not morality, for example, would seem to dictate that Stevens should be chagrined to have neglected his father on his deathbed to arrange for a physician to treat the blistered feet of a French diplomat. Instead Stevens boasts: "Why should I deny it? For all its sad associations, whenever I recall that evening today, I find I do so with a large sense of triumph." Even more to the point, we expect Stevens to echo Miss Kenton's judgment— "What a terrible mistake I've made with my life"— about both his failed romance with her and his support of Lord Darlington's Nazi sympathies. Instead Stevens talks about trying "to make the best of what remains of my day." This may be no more than denial and evasion in Anthony Hopkins's performance, but there is more at work in the novel.

Mr. Stevens believes that he can sum up his life in the confession, "I gave my best to Lord Darlington." He hopes that his life makes a "small contribution to the creation of a better world." The Japanese term for this is *bushido*:

it required the samurai specifically to serve his lord with the utmost loyalty and in general to put devotion to moral principle (righteousness) ahead of personal gain. The achievement of this high ideal involved a life of austerity, temperance, constant self-discipline. . . qualities long honored in the Japanese feudal tradition. . . [and which were] given a systematic form. . . in terms of Confucian ethical philosophy.

According to Ruth Benedict, whose 1946 book *The Chrysanthemum and the Sword: Patterns of Japanese Culture* remains a classic starting point for the analysis of Japanese culture, "such strength [of character] is the most admired virtue in Japan." The purpose of Confucian ethics is to produce a person who exhibits grace and authority under any social circumstance. Confucian ethics are not eschatological. There is no Last Judgment nor transcendental authority to separate sheep from goats. As Hall and Ames explain: "The model [*chun tcu:* exemplary person] qualifies as model not on the basis of what he can do, but by virtue of the quality of his actions: how he does things."

In contrast to Confucian ethics, Zen Buddhism hopes to liberate a person from all (Confucian) social situations, which are inherently worrisome. In Zen Buddhism, writes T. P. Kasulis, one is enlightened "when one lets go of pre-conceived notions of the self." Such pre-conceptions are not Platonically innate but are derived from memorable performances of behavior evoked by specific social contexts or special occasions, which define tradition. In contrast, "The Zen ideal is to act spontaneously in the situation without first objectifying it in order to define one's role." Against this Japanese Confucian/Buddhist tension, *The Remains of the Day* can be seen as a Buddhist critique of Confucianism. Mr. Stevens's life is stunted by the Confucian *bushido* code that he relies on to render identity and self-worth. The remedy is to develop a Zen Buddhist outlook which is characterized by a unique kind of comedy.

The contrast between Eastern and Western attitudes in regard to social roles provides a door into Kazuo Ishiguro's world. In the Western view, Stevens is pathetic because his obsession with duty has arrested the development of adult autonomy. Westerners believe that something like Erik Erikson's "Eight Stages of Man" specifies objective and universal stages of human, in contrast to cultural, development. Measured by this standard, Stevens fails to grow up; he follows a social role instead of becoming his own person. Exasperated when Stevens fails to drop the role of butler and does not romantically respond to her, Miss Kenton asks,

"Why, Mr Stevens, why, why, why do you always have to pretend?" Stevens's ambitions remain oedipal: to please a father figure. Especially in the movie version, Stevens remains pathetically defensive until he tragically admits, "All those years I served him, I trusted I was doing something worthwhile. I can't even say I made my own mistakes. Really—one has to ask oneself—what dignity is there in that?" Stevens poses this as a rhetorical question because every Westerner knows the answer: that one's deepest obligation is to develop a unique individuality. Christianity demands this. In *Sources of the Self* Charles Taylor illustrates that Romanticism/Modernism simply provided different arguments to insist on the same duty.

Nothing like this analysis can be made from a Confucian outlook. In Japan filial loyalty (*hsiao*)—which is ultimately offered to the person of the Emperor (symbolized in this case by Lord Darlington)—provides the vocabulary for self-worth. Without this loyalty, which derives from a sense of gratitude and obligation (*gimu*: the infinite debt owed to parents for giving life and to the emperor for giving culture; *giri*: the debt owed to teachers, employers and other benefactors), one is no better than a monkey or a sociopath. Benedict explains that "the hero we [Westerners] sympathize with because he is in love or cherishes some personal ambition," the Japanese "condemn as weak because he has allowed these feelings" to erode his moral worth: "Westerners are likely to feel it is a sign of strength to rebel against conventions. . . . But the strong, according to Japanese verdict, are those who disregard personal happiness and fulfill their obligations. Strength of character, they think, is shown in conforming not in rebelling".

Since the time of the pre-Socratics, Western metaphysics has assumed the existence of some single underlying and presocial reality. Asian thought concedes that such a reality exists but has no confidence that reason can mirror it. Its sensitivity to the notion that reality is ultimately indiscernible and ineffable is revealed in self-consciousness about metaphor or the ways in which reality can be traced, in Derrida's sense of the term. For the Japanese, one would be a fool to die for the Truth like Socrates or Jesus. Believing that specific meaning and identity are conferred by social context, Asian concern focuses on adept shifts of identity in response to differing social situations. Hence Joseph Tobin reports that "the most crucial lesson to be learned in the Japanese preschool is not *omote*, not the ability to behave properly in formal situations, but instead *kejime*—the knowledge

needed to shift fluidly back and forth between *omote* and *ura* [literally "rear door," thus informal behavior]." Because Japanese are adept at making such shifts of identity, they generally do not feel compelled to make one choice among Shinto, Confucian and Buddhist outlooks. They unselfconsciously adopt the appropriate identity when social circumstances call for a choice. Using psychological terminology, Takie Sugiyama Lebra identifies four possible Japanese selves: presentational (Confucian), inner (Shinto), empathetic (Mahayana) and boundless (Buddhist).

These shifts between various identities are generally under social and personal control. In contrast, paradigm shifts are occasioned by historical forces, such as the shift from the feudal values of the isolated Tokugawa Shogunate (1603–1867) to the values of the Meiji Restoration of 1868, which committed Japan to modernization. Edwin Reischauer has compared this shift to an earthquake: "The Tokugawa system had been shaken to its foundations by the events since 1853 [caused by an American naval presence and threats of colonization], and the whole antiquated structure began to disintegrate. All policies had become subject to debate by *samurai* from all over Japan." He explains that "the *samurai* in a brief nine year period were deprived of all their special privileges, and Japan was started on a great change which was to transform its society in a mere generation or two from one in which status was primarily determined by heredity to one in which it depended largely on the education and achievements of the individual." Benedict offers a more graphic picture: "The Tokugawas. . . regulated the details of each caste's daily behavior. Every family head had to post on his doorway his class position and the required facts about his hereditary status. The clothes he could wear, the foods he could buy, and the kind of house he could legally live in were regulated according to this inherited rank." In the thirty years that Reischauer mentions, all of this was erased and new scripts were written. Even the emperor had his photo taken in Prussian military regalia.

After less than a century's involvement with the Western outlook, the Japanese world exploded in Hiroshima and Nagasaki. Like many Japanese novel's written after the war—one example is the brooding novel by Jiro Osaragi, *The Journey* (1960)—Ishiguro's first two novels are set in the mushroom shadow of the atomic bomb, which so dramatically ended the outlook provided by state-mandated Shinto. One day it was Emperor Hirohito's portrait in every public building, the next it was Douglas MacArthur's picture in the newspaper. Overnight definitions of honor, dignity and status were redefined. In *A Pale View of Hills,* a retired teacher laments, "I devoted my life to the teaching of the young. And then I watched the Americans tear it all down." The same teacher lectures his son, already converted to the new outlook, "Discipline, loyalty, such things held Japan together once. That may sound fanciful, but it's true. People were bound by a sense of duty. Towards one's family, towards superiors, towards the country." Later the *sensei* (teacher) is lectured by one of his former students who bluntly tells him, "In your day, children in Japan were taught terrible things. They were taught lies of the most damaging kind. Worst of all, they were taught not to see, not to question. And that's why the country was plunged into the most evil disaster in her entire history." How can the teacher respond? Can he meekly admit that his entire world view was wrong, that his life was "spent in a misguided direction"? And what value system should he adopt to assess his putative failings? The contemporary *zeitgeist* of his student, with its "self-evident" democratic values, simply did not exist in the old teacher's world. And who can say how long the current outlook will be fashionable? The teacher is too old to abandon his pre-war outlook; the younger man is too earnest to recognize how arbitrary his own outlook is. Yet millions of people in the 20th century have been caught trying to straddle the conflicting values of two worlds. Ishiguro offers us an example in the second plot of *A Pale View of Hills,* which tells a fragmentary tale of a ghost-like woman and her neglected daughter. The little girl does not attend school and is literally lost at various times in the novel. Her mother is equally lost, chasing an American serviceman in the hope of redemptive immigration to the America that destroyed Japan. Her equivocation and uncertainty are well illustrated by her inability to care for her daughter, who symbolizes the next generation. At one time she says, "I'm a mother, and my daughter's interests come first". At another time she sarcastically asks, "Do you think I imagine for one moment that I'm a good mother to her?"

In addition to the possibilities of exclusively living in the old world or the new world, or equivocating between them, there is a fourth possibility suggested by Zen Buddhism, which recognizes that social roles work like dramatic roles to dictate action and identity, and that the concepts of analytic language simply write more scripts rather than naming pre-existing entities. Kasulis explains that

"We go through life thinking that our words and ideas mirror what we experience, but repeatedly we discover that the distinctions taken to be true are merely mental constructs." Values are a matter of style, a way of seeing things. There is no ultimately true world of essential substances; in positing eternal ideas Plato was simply imagining, functioning as another artist. Human nature does not operate by following a set of formulas. The most we can know is how to act and who we are within concrete social boundaries. Who and what we are beyond these is an enigma, a subject for Zen *koans,* which state paradoxes that are used as a meditative focus for Zen training. "Show me your original face," a Master might demand of a disciple, thereby directing him to reflect on pre-social (nonConfucian) identity. How can this primal state be identified without recourse to an arbitrary social context? Here one must remark that language itself is such a context.

For most of *The Remains of the Day,* Stevens feels that his tragic and wasted life resulted from mistaken loyalty, so that if he had backed a different horse or had played different cards, he would have been a winner instead of a loser. Pondering this issue, Stevens writes: "Naturally, when one looks back to such instances today, they may indeed take the appearance of being crucial, precious moments in one's life; but of course, at the time, this was not the impression one had." Indeed, the very problem is that "There was surely nothing to indicate at the time that such evidently small incidents would render whole dreams forever irredeemable." Zen advises us to cease looking for such definitive and seminal moments because they are not there. These putative moments of choice are characteristic properties of analysis rather than objectively existent or discrete entities waiting to be discovered. The recognition that consciousness is a process like painting, rather than a mirror, can instantly dissolve trust in the analytic process. Suddenly the gestalt shifts from seeing the contents of consciousness to noticing the process itself. One can then develop an esthetic taste for this voyeuristic, detached perspective, which keeps one from too quickly professing another explanation, which promises to explain what was mistaken in the former view. *The Remains of the Day* and *An Artist of the Floating World* are both rendered as diaries in which each diarist searches for (moral) points of judgment in his experience, which he thinks mistakenly committed him to a historically failed vision. The problem is that the diary, or any retrospective analysis, is an interpretation committed to some set of implicit values that the analysis will make explicit. Analysis is a performance which requires "causes" in order to produce "effects." For this reason, as Kasulis explains, "Zen Buddhism criticizes our ordinary, unenlightened existence by refusing to accept a retrospective reconstruction of reality" as uniquely or even especially true or definitive. Any expectation of discovering the "truth" or developing a transcendent identity in such terms is futile. People like Stevens, who cannot escape the deconstruction of beliefs they relied on to make sense of their experience—a world view they thought was objective and universal—have an opportunity for liberation, for not recommitting themselves to an alternative interpretation. In fact the Zen monastic experience is designed to force monks to just such a crisis.

It is Ichiro Ono, the artist in the novel *An Artist of the Floating World,* who, by virtue of a heightened sensitivity to Japanese esthetics—which were largely formulated by Zen Buddhism—is most aware of the possibility of floating rather than diving in hopes of getting to the bottom of things. As Ishiguro depicts him, Ono rose to prominence in the 1930s as a painter. He is enticed to direct his art towards the production of didactic propaganda by earnest men who tell him that as a leader of "the new generation of Japanese artists, you have a great responsibility towards the culture of this nation." They counsel Ono not to "hide away somewhere, perfecting pictures of courtesans", but to paint inspiring pictures of "stern-faced soldiers. . . pointing the way forward" to greatness. Under the American occupation of 1945, Ono admits that he had been "a man of some influence, who used that influence towards a disastrous end." What else could he say? Still, there is a disconcerting tone in Ono's contrition, which makes it sound insincere. He seems to disown too quickly his earlier commitment to the war effort and to equivocate in denouncing it, saying, "Indeed, I would be the first to admit that those same sentiments [expressed in didactic war art] are perhaps worthy of condemnation." Ono's motive is not to defend a choice. He considers any choice to be a consequence of a process. The (moral) problem is unconditional faith in the process: "All I can say is that at the time I acted in good faith. I believed in all sincerity I was achieving good for my fellow countrymen. But as you see, I am not now afraid to admit I was mistaken." People who earlier demanded that Ono support fascist values, now expect the same ardor in condemning those values. As an artist (Buddhist), Ono perceives that the performance is the same.

Art frustrates the wish to get to the bottom of things, to gain a clear and definitive picture of the way things really are. As a young artist, Ono was not ready to sacrifice his vanity, his confidence that as a man of discipline and technical mastery, he would get to the bottom of things. Even when he is middle-aged, basking in the glow of adulation from his students, he considers art a vehicle, something he can use to achieve aims which precede and remain unaffected by the vehicle. When he thinks that he has mastered enough of the instrument, Ono informs his teacher, "I have learnt much in contemplating the world of pleasure, and recognizing its fragile beauty." But he then demonstrates how little he has learned: "I now feel it is time for me to progress" because "artists must learn to value something more tangible than those pleasurable things that disappear with the morning light." The Zen roshi or teacher could tell him that perceiving and thinking are processes like painting a picture. We perceive how light and language connect things, paint things. We fleetingly possess the picture but never the objects.

For the essence of the Buddhist outlook is the recognition that everything, including the values to which we are so earnestly dedicated, is a temporary perceptual amalgam fused by language and emotion. The ground for the existence of things is temporal and as insubstantial as light. Yet, like Ono and Stevens, we become "attached to our characterizations, thinking of them as absolutes, rather than as names convenient for a given purpose." This includes our very identities, which are no more than cultural performances. Identity is a play of light and color, not something static; not a number nor an atom nor a soul. This Buddhist line of thinking gets to the bottom of things in its own way, and in Ishiguro's novel, Ono's teacher, Mori-san, tries to communicate something of this view to his pupil, telling Ono that "the finest, most fragile beauty an artist can hope to capture drifts within those pleasure houses after dark. And on nights like these, Ono, some of that beauty drifts into our own quarters here." The master then refers to some of his own early paintings, saying, "they don't even hint at these transitory, illusory qualities." If Ono were as discerning as the artist he aspires to be—and ironically claims to be—he would recognize this as Japanese politeness, as face-saving admonishment which avoids explicit formulation and consequent direct confrontation. Mori is suggesting that despite whatever technical mastery he achieved in his youth, he could not see with the profundity produced by a life-time of (Buddhist) dedication and practice. The point, he suggests, is for Ono not to think that he has finished the job of development, that he can see to the bottom of things and that consequently he no longer needs to strive for enlightenment. For enlightenment is also a process which needs to be repeatedly performed.

In Christianity, pride is a sin because God is everything and we are merely his creatures. In Buddhism, pride is embarrassing because it so flagrantly ignores elementary principles. In the Buddhist view, one cannot possess anything, including the self that craves possessions; everything dissolves and changes. In a Zen-like tradition of relating how his master enlightened him, Mori-san talks about "a man of no standing" (someone with no conferred authority). Ono complains, saying, "I am puzzled that we artists should be devoting so much of our time enjoying the company of those like Gisaburosan." Mori explains, "The best things, he always used to say, are put together of a night and vanish with the morning." The principle of change (*anicca*) is an axiom of Buddhism. You cannot hold on to nor control experience by retrospective interpretation, which always renders a substitute (sign) for the experience to produce propaganda. Interpretation discovers only what is latent in its own structure. It cannot get to the bottom of experience because interpretation always deals with the substitutes it paints. The artist controls only the illusion of light.

Like a Zen monk, Mori has spent much of his life trying to capture the oblique light of the floating world, which does not spotlight a specific moment or subject, like truth or dignity or even beauty, but rather encompasses all such particulars in a suffusive glow—just as the light of life similarly contains all specific moments, none of which transcends the process. Explaining the eminent Japanese philosopher Nishida Kitaro's idea of satori (enlightenment), Robert Carter writes: "The deep self, which forever eludes our conceptual grasp, is yet somehow known, nevertheless, as that at the background of our experience. It is never known but is ever present as a background 'lining.'" Kasulis defines Zen enlightenment as "the direct recognition of what one most fundamentally is: the purity, unity, and responsiveness of pre-reflective experience." The Trappist monk and student of Buddhism, Thomas Merton, explains that "the chief characteristic of Zen is that it rejects all these systematic elaborations in order to get back, as far as possible, to the pure unarticulated and unexplained ground of direct experience. The direct experience of what? Life itself."

The intent of Buddhism is to achieve an esthetic appreciation rather than to employ analysis in a search for an illusory redemptive moment, a moment of truth, moral choice and justification. In Ishiguro's novel, Mori plays the part of a Zen Master, telling Ono, his disciple:

I was very young when I prepared those prints. I suspect the reason I couldn't celebrate the floating world was that I couldn't bring myself to believe in its worth. Young men are often guilt-ridden about pleasure, and I suppose I was no different. I suppose I thought that to pass away one's time in such places, to spend one's skills celebrating things so intangible and transient, I suppose I thought it all rather wasteful, all rather decadent. It's hard to appreciate the beauty of a world when one doubts its very validity.

Surprisingly this intangible and transient world of perception is the only world we ever experience.

On the last page of the novel, Ono, now an old man, reflects, "when I remember those brightly-lit bars and all those people gathered beneath the lamps, laughing a little more boisterously perhaps than those young men yesterday, but with much the same good-heartedness, I feel a certain nostalgia for the past," but he then goes on to conclude: "one can only wish these young people well" today. Neither Mori nor Ono offer specific advice from theology that would force life to conform to some principle; nor do they offer advice about seizing an opportune or all important moment of decision that once lost results in tragedy. Their advice, which seems so empty to earnest young people, is to encourage them to be esthetically sensitive to the quality of light that illuminates life; to appreciate life itself. In 1949 Ono's son-in-law parrots the same rhetoric Ono heard in the thirties, which was the same rhetoric Ono's grandfather might have heard in the early days of the Meiji restoration: "We needed new leaders with a new approach appropriate to the world of today." The truth is that the light of the lamps and laughter of the people beneath them and the political ardor of Ono's son-in-law are no different now than they ever were; nor will they ever be fundamentally different in the future. There is nothing to find or repudiate in the past; neither is there anything to prove or create in the future. Life is not—except in Christian/Islamic interpretation—moving toward some eschatological moment. A *koan* has it that "When an ordinary man attains knowledge he is a sage; when a sage attains understanding he is an ordinary man."

Mr. Stevens is interested in extraordinary men. As a kind of Victorian *samurai*, his life is dedicated to the great or at least the powerful. A life of devotion requires a worthy object, a fixed point. Thus

Stevens confesses that in his youth "we tended to concern ourselves much more with the moral status of an employer." Sounding like the youthful Ono, Stevens acknowledges that "we were ambitious. . . to serve gentlemen who were, so to speak, furthering the progress of humanity." Stevens speaks not only for himself and the servant class, but for everyone in the empire when he says, "professional prestige lay most significantly in the moral worth of one's employer." Extraordinary people were the measure of empire. No less than the fascist regimes of the 20th century, European aristocracies of early centuries were dedicated to providing an environment for superior people. Thus Lord Darlington's Nazi sympathies are no quirk, and Stevens could have comfortably worn a Nazi uniform.

Stevens is proud to be near the hub of the wheel of empire, where "debates are conducted, and crucial decisions arrived at, in the privacy and calm of the great houses of this country." Initially Stevens is exclusively concerned with *samurai* values. Someone else chooses the game; the butler is content to be a skilled player: "my vocation will not be fulfilled until I have done all I can to see his lordship through the great tasks he has set himself." In 1923 Stevens witnesses a confrontation between his employer and an American Senator, Mr. Lewis, who calls Lord Darlington a fool: "He [Darlington] is an amateur and international affairs today are no longer for gentlemen amateurs. The sooner you here in Europe realize that the better." When Darlington rises with icy civility to correct Lewis— "What you describe as 'amateurism', sir, is what I think most of us here still prefer to call 'honour' "— Stevens heartily approves. Yet Lewis proves to be correct: good intentions are not enough to create a just world. Reginald Cardinal, tragically killed in WWII, represents British hopes for the postempire period. In touch with modern politics, he is less crass than the American senator and might be characterized as a young John Majors. His observation on Darlington is discomfiting: "Over the last few years, his lordship has probably been the single most useful pawn Herr Hitler has had in this country for his propaganda tricks. All the better because he's sincere and honourable and doesn't recognize the true nature of what he's doing." Stevens has himself, if only silently, objected to Darlington's sycophantic behavior towards Hitler's foreign minister, Ribbentrop.

Stevens's loyalty to a single view exhibits a hair-line crack when he is involved in what he would like to dismiss as lower-class political wran-

gling in a village where he is stranded for a night. A garrulous barroom character expresses the opinion that "Dignity isn't just something gentlemen have. Dignity's something every man and woman in this country can strive for and get." Stevens tries to deny this, since it strikes at the foundation of aristocratic, fascist and Confucian claims to possess exclusive authority to set the rules for social games. For example, if each individual could freely decide how to be religious, what authority would the pope retain? Stevens asks, "how can ordinary people truly be expected to have 'strong opinions' on all manner of things?" He has, however, discovered that Darlington and his cronies are as uninformed as the villagers or any other "amateurs" and that their "strong opinions" are nothing more than the gullible fantasies of childhood redefined in Nazi propaganda. Calling someone like Darlington "lord" or the housemaids "Jews" does not denote some inherent property; it simply assigns a position in a social game. Not to have realized this, especially since he was himself such a skilled player—this is Stevens's mistake from a Buddhist perspective.

Although it might appear that the end of the novel leaves Stevens a wreck, regretfully cynical of his misplaced trust, this is not the case. Stevens talks about hoping "to make the best of what remains of my day," in a tone that is not glum. Once again Ono provides instructive insight when in the earlier novel he says, "it is one of the enjoyments of retirement that you are able to drift through the day at your own pace, easy in the knowledge that you have put hard work and achievement behind you." In retirement one is a person of no standing and hence no anxiety. Having no assigned part to play, one has no fear of giving a bad performance. In retiring from the world, as do Buddhist monks, there is an invitation to see life as art, as a performance rather than as a Zoroastrian battle. A Westerner might argue that even Zen Buddhist monks play some social role and that Stevens remains employed. Yet consider what is wanted from Stevens by Mr. Farraday, a rich American who employs him after Darlington's demise: he wants a purely dramatic performance. Farraday is amused by Stevens, until one day when Stevens fails to offer the performance that is expected of him for one of Mr. Farraday's American guests by denying that he was Lord Darlington's butler. At least in part, Stevens's motive is obvious: he did not want to exhibit his part in the pretension and gullibility of drafting policies of appeasement to Hitler. The guest lets Mr. Farraday know that she thinks the house and butler are imitations. Farraday is not amused when he inquires, "I mean to say, Stevens, this is a genuine grand old English house, isn't it? That's what I paid for. And you're a genuine old-fashioned English butler, not just some waiter pretending to be one. You're the real thing, aren't you?". Farraday bought the house because it was a theatrical museum. Stevens is employed as the star actor in this small theme park. What angers Farraday is the quality of performance. Because Stevens's performance failed to entertain the audience, Farraday is disappointed in the way a producer would be disappointed in a stage play flop. The sole concern is esthetic. Death camps and atomic bombs do not threaten.

At the end of *The Remains of the Day,* two features offer opportunities to reconsider the entire novel and to see it as something more than a *tour de force* of style. First, we might note that the final image is almost the same as that in *An Artist of the Floating World.* In the earlier novel the final image is of "all those people gathered beneath the lamps, laughing." In *The Remains of the Day* we find Stevens waiting for pier lights to come on, and when they do he studies "more closely these throngs of people laughing and chatting," discovering that "evidently, they had all paused a moment for the lights coming on." This is a moment of *zazen*, of disengagement from unreflective life preoccupied with details, of noticing the light instead of the objects it illuminates. Consider next how Stevens continues: "As I watch them now, they are laughing together merrily. It is curious how people can build such warmth among themselves so swiftly. It is possible these particular persons are simply united by the anticipation of the evening ahead. But, then, I rather fancy it has more to do with this skill of bantering. Listening to them now, I can hear them exchanging one bantering remark after another." The topic of "bantering" provides the second opportunity to reconsider the novel. At the beginning of the novel, the banter of Mr. Farraday seemed a nuisance to Stevens and seemed perhaps to provide a source of humor to readers. In either case it did not seem especially significant. How astonishing, then, to discover the centrality of bantering in Zen Buddhism and accordingly to recognize that it functions in the novel as a kind of Zen practice which liberates Stevens from his *samurai* role.

There are two schools of Zen Buddhism: Soto and Rinzai. Both rely on *zazen* (seated meditation) to produce enlightenment. Rinzai Masters additionally assign *koan* study to their disciples. Med-

itation temporarily suspends all social roles except that of *zazen,* which Zen Buddhism claims is not really a social role but the natural human condition, our "original face." *Koans* present the student with culturally insoluble problems in order to erode confidence in the assumption that Confucianism has delineated the rules for every game that can be played and in order to question the assumption that analysis can get to the bottom of things. Many Westerners are familiar with the *koan* which asks, "what is the sound of one hand clapping?" Yet what may be misleading in this popular example is that *koans* are not mildly entertaining enigmas. *Koan* study constitutes a formal and intense dialogue (another Confucian game) between a student and his *roshi* (Zen Master). When the Master demands, "Not thinking of good, not thinking of evil, just this moment, what is your original face before your mother and father were born?" he wants an answer. Alan Watts quotes a Zen master's description of *koan* work: the enigma causes a "'feeling of uneasiness and impatience'. After a while this feeling becomes intensified, and the *Koan* seems so overwhelming and impenetrable that the disciple is likened to a mosquito trying to bite a lump of iron." The famous Chinese scholar, Wingtsit Chan, adds: "Literally *koan* means an official document on the desk, connoting a sense of important decisions and the final determination of truth and falsehood." The inability to provide the right answer—like the inability of Stevens to find the key moment on which his life pivots, imagining that he could have turned it in the right direction by giving the correct response—creates great anxiety for a Japanese schooled in Confucian etiquette. To the same effect, Kasulis recounts the story of an exasperated Buddhist monk who tried to turn the tables by asking his master, "What [sort of thing] is this person of no status?" The *roshi* came down from his dais like a thunderstorm. Seizing the student, "Rinzai exclaimed, 'Speak! Speak!'" When the monk hesitated, not knowing how he was expected to respond in this situation, "Rinzai released him," saying of the student, here is "the true person of no status, what a dried-up s—stick he is." He then left the monks to ponder the double entendre hinged between Buddhist and Confucian expectations about how the monk should have acted. Kasulis explains that "while the secular person must have a presupposed status in order to act, the Zen Buddhist is, in Rinzai's words, a person of no status." He has no social situation or stage on which to act, no script to follow, and yet there is an insistent demand to perform. Yes, but which part? The answer is no part, show me your original face: "the Zen ideal is to act spontaneously in the situation without first objectifying it in order to define one's role"; that is, the "message" of Zen is simply to live instead of first studying how to live as specified by Confucian texts.

In a less intense way, the bantering in *The Remains of the Day* produces an effect similar to *koan* study in *zazen*. Bantering will accept neither habitual nor conventional response. In laughing at the proffered response, it forces one to consider how one has acted—from a point of view without rules. On this point Faure says that "There may be a type of sudden awakening that, like humor, totally subverts all. . . categories (and as such is not itself a category)." In this context, we might note that very early in the novel Stevens confesses that "bantering on my new employer's part has characterized much of our relationship over these months." Like a Zen monk challenged to respond to a *koan* assigned to him by his master, Stevens tells us that he "would smile in the correct manner whenever I detected the bantering tone in his voice. Nevertheless, I could never be sure exactly what was required of me on these occasions." Zen monks also compiled lists of *koans*—one might almost call them jokes—and their "answers" in a work called the Mumonkan. Stevens sounds very much like a Zen monk when he puzzles, "how would one know for sure that at any given moment a response of the bantering sort is truly what is expected?" What one needs to appreciate here is Steven's Japanese heritage, wherein a *roshi* requires as much respect as an English lord. Thus Stevens worries, "One need hardly dwell on the catastrophic possibility of uttering a bantering remark only to discover it wholly inappropriate." He experiments with timid and studied witticisms, but admits, "I cannot escape the feeling that Mr Farraday is not satisfied with my responses to his various banterings."

The problem in regard to enlightenment is that the Zen Buddhist monk typically relates to his *roshi* in a manner specified by Confucian ethics, the system that seems coterminous with Japanese culture. In Japanese culture, the whole point of Confucian ethics is security: to provide safety from embarrassment by meticulously following etiquette. Benedict explains that the Japanese tend to "stake everything on ruling their lives like pedants and are deeply fearful of any spontaneous encounter with life". Zen Buddhism provides alterity. It is a crazy "system"—Faure calls it "ritual antiritualism"—dedicated to destroying, or at least suspending, the mediating system of Confucian ethics, which Zen

Buddhism claims alienates one from direct experience. Consequently the *roshi* often employs crazy-wisdom to violate Confucian expectations. The *roshi* may slap the student or denigrate conventional Buddhist piety or do something strange. For example, the Mumonkan tells this shocking story. Some monks are quarreling about a cat when Nansen, their *roshi*, intrudes, saying, "if you can say a word of Zen, I will spare the cat." Not knowing what they are expected to say, the monks are silent and the roshi kills the cat, violating ethical principles about nonviolence and compassion. Imagine the shock among non-Buddhists as well as Buddhists, if the Dalai Lama were filmed today chopping a pet cat in two. The monks must fear that their master had gone crazy. What would they expect when Nansen reports the incident to Joshu, an even greater Zen master? They would expect Joshu to upbraid Nansen, perhaps to expel him from the monastery and proclaim that he is no Buddhist. Instead Joshu "took off his sandal, put it on his head, and walked off"! Nansen then remarked, "If you had been there, I could have saved the cat!". In a formal interview the *roshi* asks his disciple, "what is the meaning of Joshu's putting his shoe on his head?" The Buddhist monk is likely to be as perplexed as Mr. Stevens is by Mr. Farraday's bantering.

The problem with rules and scripts is that they cannot take the measure of life. Even if the code is perfectly, rather than shabbily, enacted, it produces mandarins instead of Buddhas. The perfect Nazi is still a thug. Stevens's father provides an additional illustration. In his seventies, at the end of a life of distinguished service, Stevens's father has always been a paragon of *bushido*, of *samurai* discipline and loyalty. Stevens is shocked when Miss Kenton, at the time a newcomer to the estate, sees in the old man nothing more than an under-butler. Stevens remarks, "I am surprised your powers of observation have not already made it clear to you that he is in reality more than that. A great deal more." Consider Mr. Stevens senior as his son finds him early one morning near the end of his life. Is he a man to be emulated? Stevens offers us the portrait of an old monk living in a "prison cell" garret at the top of the house, as though at the summit of a mountain. Although it is still dark, the old mandarin "was sitting, shaved and in full uniform" waiting for the dawn. Clearly the model of monastic discipline, he admonishes his son, " 'I've been up for the past three hours,' he said, looking me up and down rather coldly." The old man also glanced "disapprovingly at the lamp I had brought to guide me up the rickety staircase." Stevens reports that "the oil lamp beside his bed had been extinguished." We have already become aware of the significance of this symbol from the suffusive lamp-light in *An Artist of the Floating World* and the lights of the pier at the end of *The Remains of the Day*. There is also Gautama Buddha's dying injunction that every Buddhist knows: "be ye lamps unto yourselves." Gautama clarified at least part of his metaphor by ironically admonishing his followers, "Look not for refuge [or light] to any one besides yourselves." Clearly the light has gone out on top of this mountain.

After the death of his father and the death and disgrace of Lord Darlington, Stevens is left with the frail reed of bantering as a discipline. He has no choice in this. Stevens admits that he was part of a "package" deal. He went with the house when the American bought it and Mr. Farraday chooses to confront Stevens with banter. Consequently, Stevens feels forced to devote "some time and effort over recent months to improving my skill in this very area." As though he were talking of *koan* study in *zazen*, Stevens says, "I have devised a simple exercise which I try to perform at least once a day; whenever an odd moment presents itself, I attempt to formulate three witticisms based on my immediate surroundings at that moment." We smile at the oxymoron of such a resolute study of humor, but there is something serious to note in Ishiguro's use of Zen bantering. For if one is to avoid the end of Stevens's father, the sterility of mere discipline—or worse, avoid following Darlington to Auschwitz—one can perhaps only do so by laughing: laughing at the roles others are playing, not because they are badly performing their parts, but for the opposite reason, precisely because in playing their parts so determinedly they strike us as false, as performances which are forced, followed by rote. Above all, such performances are grim and joyless. One believes, not that these people are conscious fakes or interested in manipulating others, but that they are deluded and ignorant of their own identity apart from the scripts they desperately follow. Instead of living they are acting. Then one sees this about one's self. And suddenly the role of *samurai* or butler or even monk is transformed from a matter of humorless and grim discipline into a performance, a dance. The axis shifts from counting the minute details of duty to appreciating an esthetic performance. Life is not confined in a number of Confucian games. As many Japanese descriptions of enlightenment have it, the bottom

of the bucket suddenly falls out and all the water of good karma or dutiful Confucian action is lost.

> In this way and that I tried to save the old pail Since the bamboo strip was weakening and about to break Until at last the bottom fell out. No more water in the pail! No more moon in the water!

One does not need to see the "moon in the water" or one's life rationalized in a diary, if one is in contact with the living moment. Can you see the moon? Do you have a life? The *roshi* laughs at the anxiety that turns life into a diary of moral calculation.

Certainly Stevens is no Buddha at the end of the novel. Yet neither is he like Miss Kenton, now Mrs. Benn, who writes, "I have no idea how I shall usefully fill the remainder of my life," which "stretches out as an emptiness before me." It is true that Stevens is still evasive in regard to realizing how profoundly his code betrayed him: how he could have easily worn a Nazi uniform under slightly different conditions, and consequently how it is reliance on absolute moral systems, which defend the ego, that is the problem in a Buddhist view. Consider that if he had been on the "right" side, Mr. Stevens would not have been a success. He merely would have been a mandarin as smug as his father and Lord Darlington. Reginald Cardinal prompts Stevens to recognize something like this when he asks if Stevens is curious about Darlington's involvement with Ribbentrop: "Tell me, Stevens, don't you care at all? Aren't you curious?" He presses, "You just let all this go on before you and you never think to look at it for what it is." Stevens continues to play his *samurai* part, ironically imagining that his "father might have been proud of" the stance he takes to bar Reginald from barging into Lord Darlington's meeting at the very moment when "his lordship's good name was destroyed for ever." Equally painful, Stevens also stands watch, with "an ever-growing conviction mounting" that "Miss Kenton was at that moment crying," because his script of butler/*samurai* says nothing about how to act in the circumstance of proffered love. Years later he confesses that "at that moment, my heart was breaking."

Regrettable as these incidences are, Stevens cannot redeem them. At best, he can see that such moments of crisis and loss were there in the scripts he was following. The way to avoid such waste and tragedy is not through redoubled dedication and discipline, but paradoxically, less. The *roshi* might ask if, at the time, Stevens truly felt compelled to act as he did in those two crises? If so, then why does he feel guilt-ridden, imagining later that he could have acted otherwise than the script dictated? At this point a Westerner poignantly feels the antagonism between the unique self, dedicated to principles through individual decisions, and a social role, which seems so much more superficial. This is not the case in Japan. Benedict reports that "Unforeseen situations which cannot be handled by rote are frightening" to Japanese precisely because moral principles, as such, are not available in their experience. Benedict turns this around somewhat, explaining "that they have been brought up to trust in a security which depends on others' recognition of the nuances of their observance of a code. When foreigners [or a Zen master] are oblivious of all these proprieties, the Japanese are at a loss. They cast about to find similar meticulous proprieties according to which Westerners live and when they do not find them, some speak. . . of how frightened they are."

Zen would regard the regret that Mr. Stevens feels as a sophisticated way of clinging to the ego. It is a way to inflate the ego into a transcendental state, making it somewhat like the ego of the Christian or Muslim at the Last Judgment when the individual considers all the moments of moral decision, which, being chosen, constituted what the person became. The paradox of imagining alternative lives arises because there is a notion of the self as existing prior to, and in some way remaining unaffected by, the experiences which define the self. The problem comes from an unacknowledged shift or dualism between the self as the product of experience and the self as a transcendental agent that chooses which experiences to have. Buddhism considers this second self to be an illusory product of theology or retrospection. As Stevens discovers, one does not know until one has experienced. There is only one temporal track.

In closing his diary, Stevens feels that "Perhaps it is indeed time I began to look at this whole matter of bantering more enthusiastically. After all, when one thinks about it, it is not such a foolish thing to indulge in particularly if it is the case that in bantering lies the key to human warmth." In teasing and bantering we disallow a conventional response, a reply merely in character. It is something very close to the *roshi* who continually teases, "come on, show me your original face, not your butler's face or some other mask, show me your face." Stevens admits, "I have of course already devoted much time to developing my bantering skills, but it is possible I have never previously approached the task with the commitment I might

have done." We cannot predict that Stevens will become someone different than the Confucian mandarin, that he will become archly sensitive to multiple and detailed disciplines. But we can say that there is a better chance of liberation under the bantering tutelage of Mr. Farraday than under the grim discipline of his father or Lord Darlington. Perhaps Mr. Stevens is further on the way in this regard than we think. In his last sentence, Stevens says that he hopes to "be in a position to pleasantly surprise" his *roshi*, Mr. Farraday. Perhaps he has already surprised us. Is his diary as flat and ironically unselfconscious and morally didactic as we think, or is it in some degree a witticism, which puts the reader in an analogous position to Mr. Stevens *vis-à-vis* Mr. Farraday?

Heinrich Dumoulin illustrates that as an ideology, in contrast to ritual, Zen Buddhism is largely defined by a tradition of crazy-wisdom, paradox and bizarre teaching methods. For example, Hui-neng, who "is regarded, next to Bodhidharma, as the second and actual founder" of the Zen sect of Buddhism, is depicted as an illiterate (possibly retarded) rice-pounder doing menial kitchen work before being elevated to leadership of the entire sect. Finally, we need to remember that Kazuo Ishiguro is the master who has given us the *koan* of Mr. Stevens to study. The reward is insight into the Japanese and Buddhism that supersedes abstract scholarly studies and illuminates a great novel that otherwise may remain closed to most readers. If this explication is convincing in revealing the theme of *The Remains of the Day*, it should also serve to illustrate an appropriate critical technique for the analysis of many Commonwealth and postcolonial novels: using comparative religion and philosophy to provide key terms and concepts to comprehend non-Western identity, motive and values.

Source: John Rothfork, "Zen Comedy in Postcolonial Literature: Kazuo Ishiguro's *The Remains of the Day*," in *Mosaic,* Vol. 29, No. 1, March 1996, pp. 79–102.

Sources

Annan, Gabriele, "On the High Wire," in *New York Review of Books,* Vol. 36, No. 19, December 7, 1989, pp. 3–4.

Coates, Joseph, Review of *The Remains of the Day,* in *Chicago Tribune,* October 1, 1989, p. 5.

Dyer, Geoff, Review of *The Remains of the Day,* in *New Statesman,* May 26, 1989.

Graver, Lawrence, "What the Butler Saw," in *New York Times Book Review,* October 8, 1989, p. 3.

Gurewich, David, "Upstairs, Downstairs," in *New Criterion,* Vol. 8, No. 4, December 1989, pp. 77–80.

Hassan, Ihab, "An Extravagant Reticence," in *World and I,* Vol. 5, No. 2, February 1990, pp. 369–74.

Kakutani, Michiko, "Books of the Times; An Era Revealed in a Perfect Butler's Imperfections," in *New York Times,* September 22, 1989, p. 33.

Lee, Hermione, Review of *The Remains of the Day,* in *New Republic,* Vol. 202, No. 4, January 22, 1990, pp. 36–39.

Mesher, D., "Kazuo Ishiguro," in *Dictionary of Literary Biography,* Volume 194: *British Novelists Since 1960,* The Gale Group, 1998, pp. 145–53.

Rubin, Merle, Review of *The Remains of the Day,* in *Christian Science Monitor,* November 30, 1989, p. 13.

Rushdie, Salman, Review of *The Remains of the Day,* in *Observer,* May 21, 1989, p. 53.

Strawson, Galen, Review of *The Remains of the Day,* in *Times Literary Supplement,* May 19, 1989.

Further Reading

Cannadine, David, *The Decline and Fall of the British Aristocracy,* Vintage Books, 1999.

Cannadine explores the many complex reasons that the British aristocracy went from being an elite group of wealthy landowners to a dwindling class of people who lost their sons in World War I along with their power and status. To give dimension to his explanations, Cannadine includes letters, statistics, and historical accounts in his social history.

Ishiguro, Kazuo, *When We Were Orphans,* Knopf, 2000.

Considered one of Ishiguro's most complex and accomplished novels, this is the story of nine-year-old Christopher, whose parents disappear from their Shanghai home. He is sent to live in England, and when he is older, he returns to his home to uncover his family's mystery.

Shaffer, Brian W., *Understanding Kazuo Ishiguro,* Random House, 1998.

Part of the *Understanding Contemporary British Literature* series, this book explores the life and career of Ishiguro. Shaffer comments on Ishiguro's use of setting, psychology, and first-person narration as he analyzes the profound influence of the author's dual heritage.

Vorda, Allan, and Kim Herzinger, "Stuck on the Margins: An Interview with Kazuo Ishiguro," in *Face to Face: Interviews with Contemporary Novelists,* Rice University Press, 1993, pp. 1–35.

In this interview, Ishiguro discusses Japanese and British cultures and how they have (and have not) influenced his writing. He also addresses how perceptions of him as a British-Japanese writer have affected his career in England.

Snow Falling on Cedars

David Guterson

1994

David Guterson's reputation as a writer began with his first novel, *Snow Falling on Cedars*. It is a blend of courtroom drama and romance that takes place in a small town in Washington. Set in 1954, the novel examines the dynamics of the fictitious community of San Piedro Island after World War II. The past and present stories of many of the citizens of the small community spin off the central murder trial. Critics have embraced this novel for its sensitivity, vivid imagery, well-rounded characters, and thoughtful handling of difficult issues. Guterson admits that Harper Lee's *To Kill a Mockingbird* (which he assigned his high school students to read) was a major influence on his novel. He was inspired by the structure, which brings together separate stories, and the drama created by a racially-motivated trial in a small community.

Snow Falling on Cedars went virtually unnoticed when it was released in hardback. Once it was published in paperback, however, the book's popularity gained momentum from word of mouth, and the book became a paperback bestseller. In fact, Guterson's novel became the fastest-selling book in Vintage Books' (the publisher that picked up the novel's paperback rights) history. Overseas, the novel also enjoyed best-selling status; *Snow Falling on Cedars* has been translated into fifteen languages. The success of the book enabled Guterson to quit his teaching job and focus on writing. In addition, the novel won the Pacific Northwest Booksellers Association Award and the prestigious PEN/Faulkner Award for Fiction in 1995.

Author Biography

David Guterson was born on May 4, 1956, in Seattle, Washington, the middle of five children to Murray (a criminal defense lawyer) and Shirley (a stay-at-home mother) Guterson. He enjoyed a happy childhood and spent lots of time outdoors. Since then, he has grown into an award-winning author, a contributing editor to Harper's magazine, and a vocal advocate of homeschooling.

Guterson first became interested in writing while studying at the University of Washington, from which he earned his bachelor's degree in 1978. The next year, he married Robin Radwick, a high school classmate. The newlyweds moved to Rhode Island, where Guterson attended Brown University's creative writing program for one semester. During the year they spent in Rhode Island, the Gutersons lived in a cabin on a tree farm. Robin worked as a speech therapist while her husband wrote short stories. Upon returning to the Pacific Northwest, Guterson completed a master's degree in writing at the University of Washington in 1982. The couple then moved to Puget Sound where *Snow Falling on Cedars* (1994) takes place.

Guterson continued writing after taking a job as a high school English teacher on Puget Sound, a job he held for ten years. When he accompanied students on a class trip to see an exhibit about Japanese internment camps, Guterson was inspired to write *Cedars*. The novel was so successful that he was able to quit his teaching job in 1994 and concentrate on writing. His teaching days were not over, however, because he and his wife have homeschooled their four children: Taylor, Travis, Henry, and Angelica.

Plot Summary

Chapters One–Eleven

Snow Falling on Cedars opens in 1954 in the small town of Amity Hill. The fictitious island of San Piedro in Washington's Puget Sound is the setting of a trial. Kabuo Miyamoto is charged with the murder of a fellow fisherman, Carl Heine Jr.; Carl's body was discovered in his nets by the sheriff and his deputy. A fracture in Carl's skull cast suspicion on his death. Evidence points to Kabuo.

In addition to fishing, farming (especially strawberries) is a major industry on San Piedro. Many Japanese worked these fields and became members of the community. After the bombing of Pearl Harbor in 1941, however, people of Japanese descent were sent away to internment camps. In 1954, there is still lingering distrust towards the Japanese and the prejudice is an unspoken but important force in Kabuo's trial.

Guterson structures his novel around the trial, the only event told in chronological order. As each witness takes the stand, Guterson allows the reader to enter that character's mind and witness important experiences—related to the trial or not—in his or her life. Guterson also introduces the reader to Ishmael Chambers, the town's newspaper reporter and a veteran of the war.

In his youth, Ishmael had been romantically involved with a beautiful Japanese girl named Hatsue Imada, who is now Kabuo's wife. Ishmael and Hatsue kept their relationship secret, meeting in a large hollow cedar in the woods. Hatsue felt guilty for keeping her romance hidden from her family. Ishmael was a romantic who believed that their love would conquer all obstacles. When Hatsue and her family were forced to go to the internment camp, Manzanar, the romance ended. Hatsue was ready to break off the relationship with Ishmael anyway (because she understood that their love could never survive), so she sent him a letter. Ishmael reacted with profound bitterness and hate.

Chapters Twelve–Twenty-Two

Guterson presents Ishmael's wartime experience, which includes, most notably, the loss of his arm. This experience sharpened Ishmael's feelings of bitterness and resentment. When he returned from the war, he occasionally saw Hatsue with Kabuo (whom she had married at Manzanar) and their children. Rather than move on with his life, Ishmael allowed his bitterness to consume him. At the beginning of Kabuo's trial, Ishmael sees the events as a potential opportunity to get back into Hatsue's life.

As the trial continues, details of a land deal gone wrong are revealed. In 1934, Kabuo's father, Zenhichi, made arrangements to secure seven acres of strawberry fields from Carl Heine Sr. Because foreign-born Japanese were not allowed to become citizens, and because only citizens could own land, Zenhichi and Carl Sr. worked out a lease-to-own arrangement so that the land would be paid for by the time American-born Kabuo would be old enough to own it. Although Carl Sr. was a sympathetic man, his wife, Etta, disapproved of the deal and felt that the Japanese were beneath them. When the Japanese Americans were sent to the internment camps, Carl Sr. assured Zenhichi he was not to worry about the land. Carl Sr. died in 1944, however, and because Zenhichi missed the last two payments on the land, Etta sold it to someone else and returned Zenhichi's money. When Kabuo returned home and discovered what had happened, he was angry and offered to buy the seven acres from the new owner, but the new owner would not sell. Without land, Kabuo opted to support his family as a fisherman. Years later, the new landowner was no longer able to work the land and sold it back to Carl Jr. Kabuo spoke with Carl about the possibility of buying the land from him. Carl agreed to consider it. The facts of this land deal gave Kabuo apparent motive to kill Carl, which only made his case more difficult to defend.

Chapters Twenty-Three–Thirty-Two

As the trial nears its close, Ishmael visits the lighthouse to find weather information for the newspaper. He discovers the watchman's notes from the night of Carl's death, and they contain information that would exonerate Kabuo. A freighter had passed by Carl's boat, throwing off a powerful wall of water that would have knocked a man overboard. Ishmael keeps the notes until he decides whether to reveal his discovery or keep it secret. He hopes that if Kabuo is imprisoned or executed, he will be able to win Hatsue back.

While the jury wrestles with a verdict (eleven members vote "guilty" and one finds reasonable doubt), Ishmael reveals the contents of the notes. The jury is released, Kabuo is freed, and Ishmael is finally able to consider a new life for himself. He makes peace with his painful memories and begins looking to the future.

Characters

Helen Chambers

Helen is Ishmael's mother. The nature of their relationship is revealed toward the end of the book after Ishmael discovers evidence that exonerates Kabuo. Rather than tell her exactly what is bothering him (whether to reveal the evidence), Ishmael talks to his mother about God and about moving on with life after the war. When he asks her what he should do, she thinks he is asking for advice about his life, not about the trial. She encourages him to get married and start a family. This discussion about deeply personal matters shows that their relationship is a close one while the advice she gives Ishmael shows that she still mothers her adult son.

Ishmael Chambers

As the reporter for the island of San Piedro, Ishmael is covering the murder trial. He is a native of the island, thirty-one years old, tall, with a hardened expression. Ishmael's father, Arthur (who is deceased at the time of the trial), started the town's newspaper many years ago, so the boy learned the trade from his father. Arthur was a somewhat controversial figure when he was running the newspaper because of his sympathetic views toward the Japanese. Despite losing subscribers, throughout the war Arthur continued to publish the kind of newspaper of which he could be proud. His dedication and integrity seem to be carried out in the character of Ishmael. Ishmael also studied journalism in college.

Ishmael's interest in the trial is personal, however, because he shared an adolescent romance with the accused's wife, Hatsue. Although Ishmael believed that their love would last despite the social obstacles they faced, Hatsue knew that her future lay elsewhere. When she broke off the relationship, he reacted with bitterness, cynicism, and hate, feelings that were compounded when he lost his left arm in World War II.

At the beginning of the novel, Ishmael harbors feelings for Hatsue and sees the trial as an opportunity to work his way back into her life. In the end, he chooses selflessness over selfishness by revealing evidence exonerating Hatsue's husband. At this point, he makes the important choice to move on with his life and seek a better future.

Nels Gudmundsson

Nels is Kabuo's appointed defense attorney. He is a doddering seventy-nine-year-old man who is plagued by partial blindness, arthritis, and various other ailments. He wears bow ties and often loops his thumbs under his suspenders when he addresses a witness.

Nels has a strong sense of justice, a low tolerance for prejudice, and a keen mind. He is sensitive to the humanity of his client, which the reader sees when he insists on giving Kabuo and Hatsue a few private moments to speak. In court, he is able to draw important facts and observations out of witnesses without being aggressive, and he is forthright in his closing statement when he discourages the jury from allowing the trial to be about race.

Media Adaptations

- *Snow Falling on Cedars* was adapted to audio by Random House in 1998. The abridged version is narrated by B. D. Wong, and the unabridged version is narrated by Peter Marinker.

- In 1999, the novel was adapted to film by Universal Pictures. Directed by Scott Hicks, this well-received film starred Ethan Hawke as Ishmael and Youki Kudoh as Hatsue. In addition to an Oscar nomination for Best Cinematography, the film was nominated for an American Society of Cinematographers Award, and Golden Satellite Awards for Best Cinematography, Best Actress, and Best Picture. The film won a number of awards for Best Cinematography from city and state film critics' groups.

Carl Heine Jr.

As the novel opens, Carl's recent death is the cause of a murder trial. He was a salmon fisherman whose death aboard his boat leads the sheriff to suspect murder. At the time of Carl's death, he had a wife and three children. Carl was a large, quiet man with an imposing stature and a tendency to brood.

The land deal at the center of the trial was made between Kabuo's father, Zenhichi, and Carl's father, both of whom are deceased at the time of the trial. When the land came into Carl's possession ten years after the war, Kabuo approached him about the possibility of buying the seven acres his father had originally tried to purchase. According to Kabuo, Carl agreed to consider it. Because Carl was not a farmer, he probably intended to make money from it by leasing it to other farmers.

Carl Heine Sr.

At the time of the trial, Carl Sr. is deceased. Carl Sr. made the arrangement with Zenhichi that would enable the Japanese man to make payments toward the land he was leasing so that Kabuo could

own it someday (because Kabuo was American-born, he was entitled to own land.) Carl Sr. was an understanding and sympathetic man. Before Zenhichi was sent off to imprisonment, he assured Zenhichi that he need not worry about the land. Unfortunately, Carl Sr. died before Zenhichi returned from the camp.

Etta Heine

Etta is Carl Sr.'s widow, a Bavarian woman described as "stout, faded, and wind worn." Her distaste for the Japanese was evident before the war, and these feelings were only exacerbated by the fact that Japan was America's enemy during the war. She was rude to Zenhichi, and she detested the way her husband interacted with the Japanese and the Native Americans who came to work the strawberry fields. When her husband died, she took advantage of Zenhichi's inability to make the last two payments on his land and sold the land to another buyer. She never shows any sign of regret.

Susan Marie Heine

Susan Marie is Carl Jr.'s widow. She is a twenty-eight-year-old blonde woman who is involved in church activities. She looks fashionable in town, but plain at home. When she hears about her husband's death, she merely responds that she knew it would happen some day.

During her testimony, readers learn that Susan Marie believed that she and her husband were well-matched and that he was a good father. Despite Carl's reticence, Susan Marie feels that she understood her husband. Readers also learn that beneath Susan Marie's tough exterior is a woman who possesses a strong sense of ethics; she admits that what she knows about her husband and Kabuo is only hearsay because she was not present during their interactions. This suggests that she does not seek vengeance.

Alvin Hooks

Alvin is the prosecuting attorney. He presents the facts of the case with convenient omissions to make Kabuo look guilty.

Fujiko Imada

Fujiko is Hatsue's mother. Whether or not Fujiko is still alive at the beginning of the novel is unclear, but a great deal is told of her life before and during the war. Fujiko strove to teach her five daughters good values and self-respect. Having come from Japan under false pretenses (she was led to believe that her husband-to-be was wealthy), she was initially resistant to her new way of life in America. She came to respect her husband, however, and endured many hardships with him until they were able to make a secure life. Knowing what hardship is like, she spoke to her daughters about keeping their dignity in difficult times. This speech reveals to the reader her basic distrust of Americans (especially men).

Hisao Imada

Hisao is Hatsue's father. From him, she learns to respect the unique traditions and qualities of her heritage. He shows her how to behave in a dignified way in the face of disaster, and he demonstrates, through his own marriage, the gender roles appropriate to her culture.

Abel Martinson

Abel is Art's (the sheriff) deputy. He is twenty-four years old, and his family is not from the island. Abel becomes sick when he first sees Carl Jr.'s body, but he still insists on helping and even assists with the autopsy.

Hatsue (Imada) Miyamoto

Hatsue is Kabuo's wife. She watches his trial with intensity and controlled emotion. She is thirty-one, graceful, tall, and thin. When her husband is taken into custody, she becomes terribly lonely. Although she enjoyed a teenage romance with Ishmael, she knew that their relationship would never survive. As a teenager, she was known for her great beauty and was crowned Princess of the Strawberry Festival in 1941. Hatsue's mother taught her to be a proper Japanese young lady and to value tradition and family. Because of her secret romance with Ishmael, Hatsue felt deep shame. She also understood that the cultural differences between them would never support a lasting relationship, so she ended it. She met Kabuo at Manzanar and fell in love with him. When they were married, she finally felt that everything was right.

Hatsue is sensitive, insightful, and humble. Caught between the Japanese culture of her family and the American culture of her home, she struggled in her youth to make sense of her identity. Hatsue is intelligent and aware of the differences between the Eastern and Western cultures. While her husband is on trial, she is devastated, yet she has the ability to advise her husband on how his expressionless manner probably makes him look guilty to the all-white jury.

Kabuo Miyamoto

As the novel opens, Kabuo stands accused of the murder of fellow fisherman Carl Heine Jr. Kabuo is composed, proud, and hard-working. He is physically strong and has angular facial features and short hair. His parents raised him to be a respectable Japanese man, teaching him their trade (strawberry farming) and *kendo*, the method of stick-fighting used by *samurai*. Kabuo's mind is strong, as seen in the description of his time spent in jail. Not only is he an excellent chess player, but he retains control of his surroundings by keeping his light bulb unscrewed so that he does not have to see his cell, allowing him to use his mind to maintain a sense of freedom.

Kabuo is unlike Hatsue in that he has never felt torn between two cultures; he adheres to his Japanese heritage while remaining capable of functioning in American society. As a young man, he admired Hatsue, but it was not until they were at Manzanar that he had the opportunity to pursue her romantically. There, he proved himself to be a reliable, thoughtful, and capable young man, and Hatsue's family was delighted at the union. Against Hatsue's wishes, he enlisted to fight in the war for the Americans as a matter of loyalty. The guilt he continues to feel for having killed three men in Europe haunts him, and his belief in karma leads him to understand his current persecution as a consequence for committing murder during the war. When he returned from the war, he discovered that the land he expected to own on San Piedro had been sold to someone else. He was furious but remained in control of his emotions. He was eventually forced to find another way to support his wife and children, so he learned fishing.

Zenhichi Miyamoto

Zenhichi is Kabuo's father, who is no longer living at the time of the trial. He made an ill-fated land arrangement with Carl Heine Sr. to purchase seven acres of strawberry fields so that when Kabuo was old enough to own land, he would have it. Zenhichi was a hard-working man of honor who sought to treat people fairly and stand by his word. Despite Etta Heine's rudeness, Zenhichi was always polite and respectful to her.

Art Moran

Art is the county sheriff, who is described as "by nature an uneasy person." Despite never having planned on becoming a sheriff, Art believes in the American system of justice. He is thin, over fifty, balding, and chews Juicy Fruit gum con-

stantly. He and his deputy discover the body of Carl
Heine Jr. in his nets, and Art launches a murder in-
vestigation. Art is a longtime resident of the island,
and he takes his job seriously. He is sensitive to
those around him, including his inexperienced
deputy, whom he knows has never seen a dead
body. Although he dreads doing so, he insists on
driving to Heine's house to tell Susan Marie about
the death of her husband. Art is also able to get the
close-knit fishermen to talk to him in a way they
do not normally talk to non-fishermen.

Horace Whaley

Horace is one of three doctors on San Piedro
and the only one willing to act as coroner. He is
almost fifty years old, wears wire-rimmed glasses,
and has bulging eyes and a port wine stain birth-
mark on the left side of his forehead. At the time
of the novel, he has been the coroner for a number
of years and is experienced at the job; he has recently applied this expertise to the case of Carl
Heine Jr.'s death. He is one of many World War II
veterans on the island, and when he saw the skull
fracture on Carl's head, he told the sheriff to look
for a Japanese man with a flat narrow object (like
a gun butt) with blood on it. During the war, Horace was a medical officer for almost two years during which the extreme conditions and sleep deprivation had compromised his ability to care for the
wounded. As a result, he blames himself for the
men who died in his care.

Themes

Interracial Love

The love affair between Ishmael and Hatsue
grew out of innocence and familiarity because they
had known each other since they were very young.
In fact, their first kiss was when they were ten years
old. Romance bloomed when they were teenagers.
They met secretly in a large hollow cedar tree
where they talked and ventured slowly into a physical relationship. Because of the community (and
larger society) in which they lived, they knew they
must keep their relationship secret from everyone
else, including their families. At school, they barely
acknowledged each other. When Hatsue was sent
to Manzanar, Ishmael devised a plan so that they
could write to each other, but it required using false
names and ruses. Because of the limits on their relationship, they never experienced the fullness of
being young and in love.

Both Ishmael and Hatsue felt badly for keeping such a secret from their families, but Hatsue is
bothered by this secret more than is Ishmael. She
feels a deep sense of trust and loyalty to her family, so to hide her romance from them is distress-
ing. Her choice to continue the relationship was
selfish because she was involved in something she
knew her parents would forbid her to see. Ishmael
did not fully understand the cultural influences on
Hatsue or how they affected her emotional un-
availability to him, and so he never really grasped
why she remained somewhat distant. He believed
they could run away together and everything would
be fine, while Hatsue knew that she could never
leave her family responsibilities. Ishmael was a
young dreamer, as the narrator explains in chapter
twelve:

> Sometimes at night he would squeeze his eyes shut
> and imagine how it might be to marry her. It did not
> seem so farfetched to him that they might move to
> some other place in the world where this would be
> possible. He liked to think about being with Hatsue
> in some place like Switzerland or Italy or France. He
> gave his whole soul to love; he allowed himself to
> believe that his feelings for Hatsue had been some-
> how preordained. He had been meant to meet her on
> the beach as a child and then to pass his life with her.

Where Ishmael was a romantic, however, Hatsue was bound to the traditions of her culture. Not
only did Ishmael and Hatsue face external social
barriers to their romance, they also faced fundamental internalized cultural barriers that they were
too young to handle.

Guilt

The theme of guilt runs throughout the novel,
touching individual characters at various levels.
Kabuo is on trial in court, the forum of determining guilt and innocence, although the reader comes
to understand that what Kabuo is ultimately guilty
of in this forum is being Japanese during a time
when prejudice against the Japanese is common.
Guterson shows that guilt is not always what it appears to be and that social institutions can be mis-
used in the name of assigning guilt.

The true guilt in the novel occurs on a personal
level as characters struggle to absolve themselves
of what they see as their own guilt. Although Kabuo
fought in Europe (and therefore did not fight the
Japanese), he feels deep guilt for having killed
other men. In fact, he believes that his current trial
is the result of his having gone unpunished for committing murder during the war, as explained in
chapter eleven: "He was a Buddhist and believed
in the laws of karma, so it made sense to him that

Topics For Further Study

- Read about Japanese internment camps in the United States during World War II. Write a one-week diary from the point of view of a teenager whose family is interned in one of these camps. As you write from this perspective, keep in mind such factors as the life you left behind, how other members of your family are affected, and how this experience may affect your future.

- Guterson uses highly descriptive imagery in portraying the settings of *Snow Falling on Cedars*. Choose three locations that are familiar to you and write about them, using sensory details (sights, sounds, smells, tastes, and feelings) to give a reader a true sense of each place.

- Not surprisingly, some Japanese Americans sought to right the injustices of their internment through the court system. The first case to reach the Supreme Court was as early as 1943 when Gordon Hirabayashi, a student at the University of Washington, disobeyed the curfew and refused to report for evacuation. Study this case and see if you are surprised by the Court's decision. Then pretend you are a member of the Court during this case and write an opinion (an official Court statement explaining a decision) in which you explain why you voted the way you did.

- One of the novel's themes is that of interracial love. This is a theme that has been explored throughout America's history in a variety of media. Look for examples of this theme in film, literature, art, and drama. Try to find examples that portray different types of interracial romance, not only African American and Caucasian. Take what you learn and prepare a presentation for a class on cultural history in the United States. Why is this theme important in American history, and what do you see as the future of this source of controversy?

---

he might pay for his war murders: everything comes back to you, nothing is accidental." He recalls the time he killed a young German man, and muses, "And still there had been more murders after this, three more, less difficult than the first had been but murders nonetheless."

Hatsue feels guilty as an adolescent because she is involved with a *hakujin,* a white person. She knows that her family would disapprove, yet she continues to see him. This act of rebellion disturbs her at a fundamental level and only when she breaks off her relationship with Ishmael and marries Kabuo does she feel that everything is right.

Etta Heine is guilty of prejudice, yet she never acknowledges it to herself. She scoffs at her husband for making the deal with Zenhichi, Kabuo's father, which would allow him to purchase seven acres of strawberry fields. After her husband's death, Etta takes advantage of Zenhichi's absence (while he is at an internment camp) to renege on her husband's agreement. Her language makes it very clear that her motivation is racial; she wants to sell to a white man, not to a Japanese man.

Prejudice

Throughout *Snow Falling on Cedars* the harsh realities of prejudice are portrayed. It is seen not only in the present during the trial, but also in the community's past. The treatment the Japanese received at the hands of both the American government and the white members of their community reflects distrust bred by the war. Because of prejudice, many people did not judge Japanese Americans as individuals; instead, they were all treated as threats to the United States. The stripping of their belongings and rights and their forced internment were outward signs of the prevailing attitude of the time.

On an interpersonal level, prejudice is at work when Zenhichi loses his land and Kabuo is unable to right this wrong. In both cases, the men are at a disadvantage because of prejudice toward Japanese Americans. When Kabuo is charged with the murder of Carl, the community's lingering distrust of the Japanese becomes a heavy burden for Nels, Kabuo's attorney, to bear. He knows that the evidence is only part of what the jury will use to determine Kabuo's innocence or guilt. The legal tradition that a person is innocent until proven guilty is turned upside-down because of prejudice.

In the romantic relationship between Hatsue and Ishmael, prejudice ultimately tears them apart. She knows that her family will never accept a non-Japanese man as her husband, and at a deeper level she knows that their differences are too great to allow a lifelong relationship. Knowing that the rest of the world will not accept them as a couple, Hatsue and Ishmael treat each other as casual acquaintances at school, and when Hatsue is sent to the internment camp, they must communicate by sneaking letters to each other. At every turn, the Japanese-American characters in the novel are forced to deal with prejudice.

Style

Setting

Guterson's descriptive passages about the settings of the novel have drawn a great deal of comment from critics and readers. Having lived in Washington for all but a year of his life, it is no wonder his descriptions of the landscapes are so rich and sensory. In chapter fourteen, Hatsue seeks solitude in the cedar woods:

> In spring great shafts of sun would split the canopy of trees and the litter fall of the forest would come floating down—twigs, seeds, needles, dust bark, all suspended in the hazy air—but now, in February, the woods felt black and the trees looked sodden and smelled pungently of rot. Hatsue went inland to where the cedars gave way to firs hung with lichen and moss. Everything was familiar and known to her here—the dead and dying cedars full of punky heartwood, the fallen, defeated trees as high as a house, the upturned root wads hung with vine maple, the toadstools, the ivy, the salal, the vanilla leaf, the low wet places full of devil's club.

Besides providing lush descriptive passages, Guterson often puts the features of his settings in motion to give them life and realism. In chapter eight, a peaceful scene is interrupted by the arrival of Ishmael and Hatsue:

> Where the path met the beach the madrona trees leaned out over the tidal water. Slender and sinuous, olive green, mahogany red, scarlet, and ash, they were weighted with broad, gleaming leaves and velvet berries and shaded the beach stones and mud flats. Hatsue and Ishmael flushed a roosting blue heron

with feathers the hue of beach mud; it squawked once and, elongated wing tips wide, graceful even in sudden flight, crossed Miller Bay at a soaring angle to perch in the dead top of a far tree.

At times, Guterson gives his settings a history, which gives them a feeling of continuity. Rather than appearing as nice portraits, they seem more permanent, meaningful, and connected to the cycles of life and the town. In chapter one, he writes, "A few wind-whipped and decrepit Victorian mansions, remnants of a lost era of seagoing optimism, loomed out of the snowfall on the town's sporadic hills. Beyond them, cedars wove a steep mat of still green." Describing Carl Heine's house in chapter six, Art thinks,

> It was precisely the sort of home Carl *would* build, he thought—blunt, tidy, gruffly respectable, and offering no affront to the world, though at the same time inviting nobody. . . . He had meant—or so word at church had been—to build an elaborate bungalow of the sort his father had built years before on the family farm at Island Center.

This description of the house not only tells something about the character of Carl, but also gives the house a history because it represents Carl's disappointment of not having built a home like his father's.

Omniscient Narrator

Snow Falling on Cedars provides an excellent example of an omniscient narrator. The narrator moves easily in and out of each character's thoughts, memories, and feelings, and then back to objective reporting of events. Guterson applies his imagination to a great deal of research to write with authority about the experience and expertise of each character. As a result, the narrator talks about fishing, farming, adolescent love, Ishmael's father's publishing ventures, wartime horrors, Japanese culture, the history of Amity Harbor, and autopsies. Within the courtroom alone, the narrator can reveal what the doddering Nels Gudmundsson is feeling in his arthritic bones in the same chapter as he follows a witness' testimony, complete with detailed memories.

An omniscient narrator is not confined to talking about the characters in the third person. In *Snow Falling on Cedars,* the narrator takes the reader into the minds of the characters, and these shifts in perspective are noted by the different voices of the characters. Hatsue's thoughts are expressed differently from Ishmael's, for example, and in these subtle differences the reader gets to know the characters. When Horace Whaley is thinking, he is doing so as a doctor and an experienced coroner, which is a different perspective from that of Nels Gudmundsson, who is an experienced attorney trying to achieve justice against the odds. To provide some separation, the narrator often refers to the characters by their entire names, rather than using familiar first names or nicknames. This subtle technique demonstrates that the narrator is not connected to any of the characters but is merely telling their stories from an objective distance.

When the narrator drifts into one of the character's minds, the story actually goes back in time to the event rather than relating the event as a memory. This allows the reader to know exactly what a character was thinking at a specific moment in the past. For example, in chapter two, Art and Abel are preparing to bring up Carl's nets from his boat. Art knows that Carl's body may be in the net, and he is concerned about his deputy. The narrator comments that Art knew that fishermen sometimes die out on their boats: "It was a part of things, part of the fabric of the place, and as sheriff he knew this well. He knew what bringing up the net really meant, and he knew Abel Martinson didn't."

Historical Context

The Internment of Japanese Americans

On December 7, 1941, the Japanese bombed Pearl Harbor on the island of Oahu in Hawaii. This attack on an American military base sent waves of panic across the country and political pressure led President Franklin Roosevelt to sign Executive Order 9006 on February 19, 1942, forcing citizens of Japanese descent to report to internment camps. On March 31, Japanese Americans along the West Coast were given their instructions to report for registration. The time allowed for preparation ranged from two days to two weeks. During this time, people had to make arrangements for their belongings, which usually meant selling it all at a fraction of its value. Many people took advantage of the Japanese Americans in this situation, including the government. Almost 2,000 internees were told that their cars would be stored safely, but the army soon offered to buy them for less than they were worth. Those who refused to sell were later informed that their cars had been requisitioned for the war effort. A study in 1983 estimated that the total value of lost property and income to the Japanese Americans during this period totaled more than six billion dollars.

In all, there were ten internment camps (sometimes referred to as "concentration camps" although they were not designed for extermination as they were in Germany). The first was southern California's Manzanar. Over the course of the war, the ten camps held approximately 120,000 people. Living conditions were harsh; the camps were surrounded by barbed wire and guarded by armed military personnel, and the internees lived in tiny apartments. Bathrooms and dining rooms were communal. When the internees were released, they were given twenty-five dollars and train fare home.

The cultural ramifications of the Japanese internment camps were significant. The traditional head of the household, the father, was undermined and disempowered. While some American-born Japanese citizens chose to prove their loyalty by enlisting to fight, others renounced their citizenship altogether. The difficult transition from a Japanese identity to a Japanese-American identity was muddied by the American government's treatment of its own citizens.

In 1988, President Ronald Reagan issued a formal apology to the wronged Japanese Americans, offering surviving internees $20,000 as a gesture of recompense.

Life in Puget Sound

The two main occupations in Puget Sound during the time period of the novel were farming and fishing. In both cases, the occupations were lifestyles as well as jobs. Farmers understood each other and fishermen understood each other, but the groups interacted mainly among themselves. As Guterson notes in the novel, fishermen are somewhat solitary men who share a quiet fraternity with each other and are satisfied with only occasional interaction.

During the mid-twentieth century, fishermen in the Pacific Northwest often used gill nets to maximize their daily catches. These nets hung like curtains from the ships and trapped a multitude of fish by their gills. As the industry became more competitive, gill nets became so large that they caught turtles, dolphins, and birds in addition to fish. Environmentalist groups succeeded in getting such nets outlawed, so their use today is limited to those who use them illegally.

The farmers' lifestyle differed from fishermen's in a few important ways. Farmers were more social, occasionally organizing community events, such as the Strawberry Festival. Another difference was that the wives of fishermen had little to do with their husbands' work while farmers' wives often helped with the heavy demands of working the land. The hours worked by men in the two occu-

Compare & Contrast

- **1954:** Wartime experiences figure largely into the lives of veterans who have returned home. Areas in which there is a sizeable Japanese-American population still feel the tension of reintegrating these citizens back into society after they return from internment camps.

  Today: While wartime experiences continue to be important to veterans of World War II, the general population is most aware of them only around Veteran's Day and anniversaries of significant events in the war.

- **1954:** Because of World War II, there is a lingering distrust of the Japanese by many people. As Japanese Americans return from internment camps, they face prejudices that were not present prior to the war.

  Today: While most minority and ethnic groups face a degree of prejudice, the after-effects of World War II are rarely to blame for prejudice against Japanese Americans.

- **1954:** Many Japanese Americans retain a link to their past in their spiritual lives by practicing meditation. This practice enables a person to achieve a heightened state of relaxation and focus, which often results in greater insight and the ability to be calm in difficult situations.

  Today: Many Americans from a wide variety of ethnic and religious backgrounds have discovered meditation and incorporate it into their daily lives. While methods of meditation vary widely, the goals remain the same: relaxation, concentration, insight, and a sense of calm, or inner peace.

---

pations were also very different. Although farmers got up early to begin the long day's duties, fishermen were often finishing around the time the farmers were beginning. Because of the swim patterns of the fish, fishermen had to get out on their boats very early in the morning, finishing around sunrise, while farmers began their day when the animals awoke and daylight made work possible.

Critical Overview

Critical reception of Guterson's *Snow Falling on Cedars* has been overwhelmingly positive. The novel's evocative setting, courtroom drama, tender love story, language, believable characters, and portrayal of fear and prejudice have all earned critical acclaim. *Los Angeles Times* critic Michael Harris notes,

> David Guterson's haunting first novel works on at least two levels. It gives us a puzzle to solve—a whodunit complete with courtroom maneuvering and surprising turns of evidence—and at the same time it offers us a mystery, something altogether richer and deeper.

The unusual structure of the novel could easily be mishandled, but critics often note that Guterson intertwines the past with the present, the personal with the collective, and the various individual stories with control and grace. In a review of Guterson's short story collection and first novel, Philip Graham of the *Chicago Tribune* writes, "Guterson displays a fine eye for the mysteries of the human soul, creating dramatic moments that are often layered with social and historical complexities." Similarly, Susan Kenney of the *New York Times Book Review* praises the novel's "meticulously drawn legal drama" that provides only the outermost layer of this complex narrative. Only a few critics find that the novel lacks a compelling protagonist and loses momentum in all the detail. Malcolm Jones, Jr., of *Newsweek,* for example, writes that Guterson "loads—and sometimes overloads—his novel with lyrical touches, starting with that haiku-y title."

Perhaps because the novel is set in Guterson's native Washington, his ability to describe the setting is frequently praised by critics. Nancy Pate of the *Chicago Tribune* notes that Guterson "is particularly good at evoking a sense of place," noting

One of the War Relocation Centers set up in the Western United States to detain people of Japanese ancestry during WWII

that the details "give his story weight." Kim Hubbard of *People Weekly* comments that "the book's rhapsodic descriptions of the island's beauty came from the heart." In *Publishers Weekly* a critic refers to the book as "luxurious" for its small-town details and presentation of important themes within that context.

That Guterson took five years to complete this novel is not surprising given the level of detail he provides on the many aspects of life portrayed in his complex novel. His time seems to have been well spent because critics frequently comment on how realistic and accurate his descriptions are. These comments refer not only to the novel's setting, but also to fishing, farming, and other important processes and cultural forces present in the book. Kenney remarks on Guterson's ability to expertly balance so many details, warning the reader not to lose sight of what is at stake during the trial. She writes:

> Guterson has done his homework on everything from autopsies to Zen Buddhism, taking on the enormous risk of crossing boundaries not just of time, but of sex and culture as well. The result is a densely packed, multifaceted work that sometimes hovers on the verge of digressiveness, but in Mr. Guterson's skilled hands never succumbs to the fragmentation

that might well have marred such an ambitious undertaking. In fact, so compelling is the narrative that we almost lose sight of the central issue, which is, as the defense attorney Nels Gudmundsson reminds us in his summation, whether Kabuo Miyomoto is on trial for murder–even worse, will be found guilty– simply because he is Japanese.

The book's tone and ability to draw on the reader's emotions are also recognized among its strengths. Hubbard observes that the novel "manages to combine issues of prejudice and personal accountability with a crackling courtroom drama." In *Booklist* Dennis Dodge remarks, "Guterson's first novel is compellingly suspenseful on each of its several levels." Describing the novel as "poetic," the *Publishers Weekly* reviewer writes that it "beautifully captures the painful legacy of war and a community's struggle to deal with that pain."

Criticism

Jennifer Bussey

Bussey holds a master's degree in interdisciplinary studies and a bachelor's degree in English literature. She is an independent writer specializ-

> " Comparing Ishmael and Ishmael Chambers is important because it shows the reader how Ishmael Chambers' life could have been different. If he had been more like Ishmael, he would have seen himself not as a victim of the world, but as a part of it."

ing in literature. In the following essay, she demonstrates how Ishmael Chambers would have experienced a different fate had he been more like Moby Dick's *narrator, Ishmael.*

In many ways, Ishmael Chambers, the World War II veteran and small-town reporter in David Guterson's *Snow Falling on Cedars* is similar to his literary namesake in Herman Melville's classic *Moby Dick*. In fact, the two characters have enough in common to warrant a comparison in an effort to understand Ishmael Chambers better. Fundamentally, however, there are significant differences in the two characters' ways of understanding the world. If Ishmael Chambers had been more like Ishmael at this deeper level, he could have saved himself years of anger, resentment, and cynicism. It is likely that he would have married, had a family, and enjoyed the years he wasted on bitterness.

First, it is important to establish that there are enough substantial similarities between the two characters to justify a meaningful comparison. The first signal to the reader is the name itself. Ishmael is an unusual name, and most American readers immediately think of what is perhaps the most famous opening sentence in American literature: "Call me Ishmael." Briefly, the character of Ishmael in *Moby Dick* is a man who heads for the seas in search of adventure. Along the way, he befriends a cannibal, meets the crazed Captain Ahab (whose sole purpose in life is to kill the whale that took his leg), and survives a disastrous boat wreck. *Moby Dick* is such a cornerstone of American literature and the narrator's name is so memorable, Guterson (an English teacher) was certainly aware that readers would make a connection. Guterson's inclusion of

a passage referring to *Moby Dick*'s Ishmael further assures the reader that the allusion is intentional. Melville's use of the name is a biblical allusion. The name means "God hears," which refers to both characters' eventual triumphs over seemingly insurmountable odds. Ishmael was the only survivor of Captain Ahab's ship that was lost at sea during Ahab's final pursuit of the whale. Ishmael Chambers fought in the South Pacific during World War II, seeing the rest of his group killed. Although he survived, he came close enough to death that he lost his left arm.

Beyond sharing a name and the meaning associated with it, these two characters have other similarities. They are both participants in a passionate pursuit that is not their own. Ishmael finds himself aboard Captain Ahab's ship, and Ahab is single-minded in his pursuit of the whale. Ishmael Chambers fights in World War II, a conflict so passionately pursued by world leaders that it ended with unparalleled atomic devastation. In both cases, the stakes are life and death. They are both then reporters (Ishmael Chambers being formally occupied as one), only witnesses to the events around them.

Both men are essentially alone in the world. Ishmael Chambers has no wife, no co-workers, and no close friends. He is able to talk to his mother, but is guarded even with her. Ishmael is unencumbered enough to set off for adventure, and his only friend is made on the trip—the cannibal Queequeg. While Ishmael and Queequeg are friends, they are too dissimilar to bond at a deep level, and they do not have a history together. Just as Ishmael comes to see the very frightening and strange Queequeg as not so different that they cannot be friends, Ishmael Chambers sees Hatsue as more like him than unlike him. That she is Japanese and he is American is of little consequence to him because he prefers to focus on the person behind the ethnicity.

For all of these similarities, however, they differ dramatically in the ways in which they see the world and themselves in it. Ishmael seeks adventure, which indicates his impulse to be part of the world and to experience what the world has to offer him. He expects to venture into the unknown and be changed by it. In *Moby Dick,* he explains that he sees himself as an eagle that dives down, grasps what is needed, and returns to the sky. He sees himself as part of the pattern of the world and, therefore, as someone who is connected to the universe. Ishmael Chambers, on the other hand, would have been content never to have left the island of

San Piedro. His plans after graduation are not to enlist for service, and the only reason he considers leaving San Piedro is to take Hatsue with him to a place where they can be together. The things that matter to him are in the small community of San Piedro. His adventure (the war) is a decision made for him and forced upon him, not an effort on his part to find adventure. When he returns, his bitterness is heightened by the changes that have taken place in his absence. Hatsue has married and had children, and he feels that everyone stares at him because of his rolled-up sleeve where his left arm once was. Although he never says so, it is clear that he would have been happier if he could have returned to a San Piedro in which nothing had changed since he left it.

Another fundamental difference between the two characters is that Ishmael is open to what the world offers, but Ishmael Chambers keeps himself closed off from the world. Ishmael is willing to see the world in new ways and to learn how other people and cultures think about life. Ishmael Chambers, on the other hand, is unable even to understand the deep cultural divide that keeps Hatsue distant from him. He imagines that the force of their love alone is sufficient to keep them together because he does not open himself up to learning about the culture of the woman he loves. When he goes to war, he is already bitter and cynical, so he avoids learning anything from his experiences or the other men.

Comparing Ishmael and Ishmael Chambers is important because it shows the reader how Ishmael Chambers' life could have been different. If he had been more like Ishmael, he would have seen himself not as a victim of the world but as a part of it. He would have understood that there are highs and lows in life, and that it was sometimes up to him to determine which direction he would take. Rather than stewing in cynicism and hate, he would have had the opportunity to see himself as a man with the power to climb back up to the sky, like the eagle. Instead, his perspective made him feel trapped and powerless. And if he had shared Ishmael's quality of being open to the world, he would have taken the initiative to understand Hatsue's situation better. While it is unlikely that this would have enabled them to stay together, it would have shown him why they were fated to part. His heart would have been broken, but the break may have been mutual and an act of love for each other's best interests. Instead, he perceived the break-up as an act of violence committed against him by Hatsue, and he could not forgive her. Because he felt wronged

What Do I Read Next?

- Guterson's *The Country Ahead of Us, the Country Behind* (1989) is a collection of ten short stories about middle-class suburbia. This collection was Guterson's first published book, and it received accolades from critics.

- Joy Kowaga's award-winning *Obasan* (1994) is based on the author's personal experiences as a Japanese-Canadian girl during World War II. The story is about a young girl named Naomi who is relocated with her family during the war. As an adult, Naomi struggles to make peace with the injustices endured in her past.

- Harper Lee's classic *To Kill a Mockingbird* (1960) is the story of a trial held in a small town in the South. Told from the point of view of a young girl named Scout, this novel explores themes of prejudice, justice, and small-town dynamics.

- E. Annie Proulx's 1994 novel *The Shipping News* is the story of Quoyle, a Newfoundland fisherman who seems unimpressive to others, though not to the reader who witnesses his psychological and spiritual rebirth. Besides being an intriguing character study, this novel gives insight into the lifestyle and culture of fishermen.

- In 1999, John Tateishi compiled the oral histories of thirty Japanese Americans who experienced the indignities of relocation camps during World War II. His book, *And Justice for All: An Oral History of the Japanese American Detention Camps,* preserves the individual accounts of the people who were forced to live in such camps.

by it, he was paralyzed by it. The hate that Ishmael Chambers felt after the war, both because of the break-up and because of the loss of his arm, incapacitated him for almost ten years. He wasted a decade of his youth in resentment rather than enjoying being back home from the war and pursuing a life for himself.

> A former teacher, Guterson conducted extensive research and interviews with the area's Japanese-Americans and so writes with authority about the Miyamotos and the other Japanese-Americans who were herded into internment camps."

The irony of Ishmael Chambers' unnecessarily wasted years is that he was given an opportunity to change his course when he returned from the war. After the war, he attended a university, where he began taking literature classes. He took a course in American literature and read *Moby Dick*. He was even struck by the fact that he and the narrator shared the same name. The reader is told in chapter four:

> The next fall Ishmael took up American literature. Melville, Hawthorne, Twain. He was prepared, in his cynicism, to find *Moby Dick* unreadable—five hundred pages about chasing a whale?—but, as it turned out, it was entertaining. He read the whole thing in ten sittings in his booth at Day's and began pondering the whale's nature at an early juncture. The narrator, he found upon reading the first sentence, bore his own name—Ishmael. Ishmael was all right, but Ahab he could not respect and this ultimately undermined the book for him.

Apparently, Ishmael Chambers could not be taught a better way by his literary namesake, but had to learn his lessons by taking a painful and wasteful road for ten years. He met Ishmael in the pages of *Moby Dick,* and he liked him, but he was too distracted by what he found distasteful to see that an invaluable lesson lurked in the pages. The reader can perhaps find comfort in knowing that Ishmael Chambers did eventually find a better way to live by making peace with his past and taking responsibility for his future. Very often, this is the purpose of great literature, and if Ishmael Chambers missed it in reading *Moby Dick,* maybe modern readers will not miss it by reading *Snow Falling on Cedars.*

Source: Jennifer Bussey, Critical Essay on *Snow Falling on Cedars,* in *Novels for Students,* The Gale Group, 2002.

Ellen Kanner

In the following interview-essay, Guterson discusses influences, inspirations, and sense of place in his works.

David Guterson peers out at Miami's lapis Biscayne Bay as though straining to see something else—an island off Washington's dark Puget Sound, his home and the place of his haunting novel, *Snow Falling on Cedars.* "I'm not an urban person," he confesses in a crowded outdoor restaurant. "And I've been in cities endlessly for the past five or six weeks on this book tour. Cities produce in me melancholy or a tension I don't need."

Guterson, 39, received the 1995 PEN/Faulkner Award for *Snow Falling on Cedars.* "It is such an incredible honor," he says, but what coaxes forth his first smile is the thought of returning home to his wife and four children. "What sustains me is to be with my family and to write."

Amid laughing people in tropical colors, the author wears an olive jacket. It brings out his pale green eyes which still search the water. This quiet passion extant in Guterson shines through in *Cedars.* Set in 1954 on Washington's remote San Piedro Island, the novel begins with the mysterious death of a local fisherman. It rouses the community's postwar distrust of their Japanese-American neighbors, and the island's Kabuo Miyamoto is accused of the fisherman's murder. The incident also awakens feelings within Ishmael Chambers, the town's newspaperman who has long loved Kabuo's wife, Hatsue. What results is a taut, many-angled story, both rich and satisfying.

Guterson looks to Anton Chekhov and Jane Austen as models of style and structure, and though he has set his story in the past, it is not old fashioned. "My book is traditional. It runs counter to the post-modern spirit. A lot of writers are concerned with life in the '90s," he says, "I'm not. Post-modernism is dead because it didn't address human needs. The conventional story endures because it does. I'm interested in themes that endure from generation to generation. Fiction is socially meaningful. Every culture is sustained by certain central myths. At its heart, fiction's role is to see these roles and myths are sustained."

The author has also written the nonfiction book *Family Matters: Why Home-Schooling Makes Sense* and the short story collection *The Country Ahead of Us, The Country Behind,* being released in paper this spring. Guterson wrote the stories before his novel, and now when he looks at them, he feels "removed from them to the degree I feel removed from who I was in my twenties when I wrote them. The stories reflect my concerns at that time. *Snow Falling on Cedars* is the work of someone in his thirties."

It's true. Whereas Guterson's stories possess an emotional edge, his novel has a certain maturity, sweeping the reader away with its lush physical description. "The tide and the wind were pushing in hard now, and the current funneled through the mouth of the harbor; the green boughs and branches of the fallen trees lay scattered across the clean snow. It occurred to Ishmael for the first time in his life that such destruction could be beautiful."

Guterson's gift of evoking a sense of place comes from his love of it. The islands off Puget Sound bear an almost mythic weight for him. "Hemingway said the only way to write about a place is to leave it. There's a certain nostalgia and romance in a place you left. But I don't need to leave to write about it. I don't think anyone but a native could have written this book."

One could argue, then, that with its graceful, restrained images of Japanese-American life, no one but a Nissei could have written it. A former teacher, Guterson conducted extensive research and interviews with the area's Japanese-Americans and so writes with authority about the Miyamotos and the other Japanese-Americans who were herded into internment camps. "It was made real to me. It's part of the history of where I live."

But *Snow Falling on Cedars* goes beyond ethnicity. Guterson explores humanity, penetrating the core of the human heart. "My work comes from inner disturbances, from seeing injustices and accidents and how they affect people's lives in a tragic way."

Guterson agrees one can make almost anything political, including his book, but he hopes it transcends both politics and history. With its evocatively Japanese title and its elegant, restrained prose, *Snow Falling on Cedars* reveals Guterson's affinity for Asian philosophy. "The sense that this world is an illusion, that desire is the root of suffering, the awareness of cause and effect—I have a great respect for all that," he says.

He endows his character Hatsue with this sense of tranquillity. "Hatsue explained her emotional reserve. . . didn't mean her heart was shallow. Her silence, she said, would express something if he would learn to listen to it." The same might be said for the author himself. "I think of myself as a really happy person," says Guterson, allowing him-

Ethan Hawke (left) as Ishmael and Youki Kudoh as Hatsue in the 1999 film version of the novel

self his second fleeting smile of the afternoon. "What some people interpret as brooding melancholy is serenity. I don't feel required to grasp all the time."

What he does feel, what he works toward, is a sort of stillness, the stillness he creates for Hatsue, the stillness he needs to write. Guterson would rise at five a.m. to work on his novel, facing the blank page when it was still dark and the day's intrusions were distant.

While he has enjoyed writing nonfiction and short stories, Guterson is at work on another novel—the medium he feels best suited to in terms of temperament. He will still rise at five o'clock, but otherwise wants this new book to be nothing like his last one. "It must succeed in its own terms," he insists in the fading glow of afternoon. "It has to be just as powerful, though. It must have an impact on people."

It should resonate for readers the way the landscape of his home resonates for the author. "I grew up in Seattle, but I always knew I wanted to leave," says Guterson. "The greenness of the world, the play of light and living things, stretching endlessly and regenerating season after season—to have that

> " David Guterson's well-written first novel is at various moments a courtroom drama, an interracial love story and a war chronicle."

in daily life is so much more satisfying than buildings and people."

Source: Ellen Kanner, "A Wonderful Irony: The Quietest of Books Makes the Splashiest Debut," in *http://www.bookpage.com/9601bp/fiction/snowfallingoncedars.html,* January 25, 2001.

Stan Yogi

In the following review, Yogi praises Guterson for his research but criticizes Snow Falling on Cedars *for its uneven pace and the underdevelopment of its main character.*

David Guterson's well-written first novel is at various moments a courtroom drama, an interracial love story and a war chronicle. Guterson melds these components into a novel that explores how individuals and communities abuse, retreat from or use their histories as motivating forces.

Set in 1954 on the fictional island of San Piedro near the San Juan Islands in Washington, *Snow Falling on Cedars* focuses on the trial of Kabuo Miyomoto, a *Nisei* (second-generation Japanese American) charged with the murder of a fellow fisherman and childhood friend, Carl Heine.

The novel unfolds to reveal complex relationships among the book's main characters: Kabuo; his wife, Hatsue; Carl Heine; and Ishmael Chambers, the local newspaper owner who is covering the trial.

Before the war, Miyomoto's father purchased land from Heine's father, and young Kabuo and Carl were friends. Hatsue and Ishmael were also childhood friends and adolescent sweethearts. The war, however, forever alters these relationships.

Hatsue and Kabuo are interned in Manzanar, where they fall in love and marry. Heine and Chambers see battle in the Pacific, and Kabuo joins the

heroic 442nd all-Japanese American combat team to fight in Europe.

The characters return to San Piedro after the war and try to resume their lives. Kabuo discovers, however, that during the war, Heine's mother, motivated in part by racial prejudice, sold the Miyomotos' land to another farmer. Haunted by this injustice, Kabuo seeks to regain his family's land, creating a strain between him and Carl.

Chambers finds it difficult to readjust to life in San Piedro, in part due to the loss of an arm in the war. He takes over his father's newspaper but finds little meaning in his work. His reintegration is compounded by his lingering love for Hatsue.

The novel is well-researched and, for the most part, emotionally realistic. Guterson has a good eye for telling details and writes vividly about the verdant landscape of San Piedro, the profound distress of combat and the solitariness of fishermen at work.

But because the novel mixes genres, it moves at an uneven pace. Not surprisingly, the courtroom scenes move briskly and suspensefully. Other scenes, especially those focusing on Chambers' existential search for meaning, are more ponderous.

Most of the book is written from the various perspectives of the characters, a tricky and difficult narrative technique that Guterson generally employs with success. But in places it means uneven character development, with some characters more convincingly drawn than others.

The novel's main flaw is the underdevelopment of Kabuo, ostensibly the story's main character. Guterson balances between exploding ethnic stereotypes and reinforcing them.

Kabuo is portrayed as stoic, strong and angry. Although he reveals emotional vulnerability in brief moments, his character could have benefited from more shading.

There are minor points in the novel that seem slightly inconsistent with Japanese American history. It seems unlikely, for example, that so many *Issei* (first-generation Japanese immigrants) would speak English as fluently as they do in the novel. The disintegration of family life in the Manzanar internment camp occurs a bit too quickly. Important distinctions between the *Nisei*-dominated Japanese American Citizens League and *Issei* organizations are not made.

Overall, though, this is an intriguing novel that explores the burdens of history and how random circumstances combined with ethnic stereotypes contribute to resulting troubles and tragedies.

Source: Stan Yogi, "A Friendship Shattered by War," in *San Francisco Chronicle,* January 1, 1995, p. 2.

Sources

"David Guterson," in *Contemporary Authors Online,* The Gale Group, 2000.

"David Guterson," in *Contemporary Literary Criticism,* The Gale Group, 2001.

"David Guterson," in *People Weekly,* Vol. 45, No. 18, May 6, 1996, p. 132.

Dodge, David, "*Snow Falling on Cedars,*" in *Booklist,* Vol. 90, No. 22, August 1994, p. 2022.

Graham, Philip, "In the Country of David Guterson," in *Chicago Tribune,* June 30, 1996.

Harris, Michael, "Sometimes, Even Good People Must Co-exist with Evil," in *Los Angeles Times,* September 19, 1994, p. E4.

Hubbard, Kim, "Out of the Woods: A Surprise Bestseller, *Snow Falling on Cedars,* Puts Novelist David Guterson on the Map," in *People Weekly,* Vol. 45, No. 9, March 4, 1996, pp. 89–90.

"The Internment of Japanese Americans (1940s)," in *American Decades CD-ROM,* Gale Research, 1998.

Jones, Malcom, Jr., "*Snow* on Top, a Literary First Novel Is This Season's Sleeper Success Story," in *Newsweek,* Vol. 126, No. 25, December 18, 1995, p. 72.

Kenney, Susan, "Their Fellow Americans," in *New York Times Book Review,* October 16, 1994, pp. 12–13.

"Manzanar Relocation Center," in *DISCovering Multicultural America,* Gale Research, 1996.

Nathan, Paul, "It Can Still Happen," in *Publishers Weekly,* Vol. 243, No. 50, December 9, 1996, p. 18.

Pate, Nancy, "Murder Unveils an Island's Secrets," in *Chicago Tribune,* January 12, 1995.

"Roosevelt Approves Internment of Japanese Americans, February 19, 1942," in *DISCovering World History,* Gale Research, 1997.

"*Snow Falling on Cedars,*" in *Publishers Weekly,* Vol. 241, No. 31, August 1, 1994, p. 70.

Wasowski, Richard, *Cliffs Notes: "Snow Falling on Cedars,"* Cliffs Notes, Inc., 2000.

Further Reading

Brokaw, Tom, *The Greatest Generation,* Random House, 1998.

Brokaw recounts the firsthand experiences of World War II veterans and the women they left behind. The range of experiences and sentiments captured in this book are educational, moving, and inspiring. Also look for the video documentary featuring Brokaw's interviewees.

Guterson, David, *East of the Mountains,* Harcourt Brace, 2000.

This second novel by Guterson is about a widower in Seattle who discovers that he is dying of cancer. He decides to drive to the Cascades to take his life, but his plans are thwarted, and he begins reflecting on his life.

Houston, Jeanette, *Farewell to Manzanar,* Houghton Mifflin, 1973.

Houston's story of a young girl subjected to life in the internment camp of Manzanar is frequently recommended for its historical accuracy and its sensitive portrayal of one girl's experience. Although it is appropriate for nine- to twelve-year-old readers, this book is also appreciated by older students and adults.

Mantell, Suzanne, "The Rise of *Snow,*" in *Publishers Weekly,* Vol. 242, No. 51, December 18, 1995, pp. 21–22.

Mantell traces the unusual publishing history of *Snow Falling on Cedars,* including information about Guterson's history with his agent and editors' reactions to the novel. The article also explores theories as to why the novel became such a runaway paperback bestseller.

Mathews, Linda, "Amid the Cedars, Serenity and Success," in *New York Times,* February 29, 1996, pp. C1, C4.

Mathews's article includes an overview of the book and its influences and information about the author and his workspace. She also writes about how the success of *Snow Falling on Cedars* has (and has not) affected the author's life.z

Surfacing

Margaret Atwood

1972

Margaret Atwood's second novel, *Surfacing,* earned critical and popular acclaim in Canada and the United States after its publication in 1972. *Surfacing* is structured around the point of view of a young woman who travels with her boyfriend and two married friends to a remote island on a lake in Northern Quebec, where she spent much of her childhood, to search for her missing father. Accompanied by her lover and another young couple, she becomes caught up in her past and in questioning her future. This psychological mystery tale presents a compelling study of a woman who is also searching for herself. Readers praise the novel's style, characterizations, and themes. Critic Patricia F. Goldblatt comments in her essay on Atwood's protagonists that in her construction of the main character in *Surfacing,* Atwood proves

> to her and to us that we all possess the talent and the strength to revitalize our lives and reject society's well-trodden paths that suppress the human spirit. She has shown us that we can be vicariously empowered by our surrogate, who not only now smiles but winks back at us, daring us to reclaim our own female identities.

Author Biography

Margaret Atwood was born November 18, 1939, in Ottawa, Ontario, Canada to Carl Edmund (an entomologist) and Margaret Dorothy (Killam) Atwood. As she was growing up in northern Ontario, Quebec, and Toronto, she spent a great deal of time

Margaret Atwood

in the woods where, like the narrator of *Surfacing,* she developed an enthusiasm for environmental issues. She began writing when she was six years old. By the time she became a teenager, she had written poems, short stories, and cartoons for her high school newspaper, and she had decided that she wanted to devote her life to writing. She earned an undergraduate degree from Victoria College at the University of Toronto in 1961 and her master's degree from Radcliffe College in 1962. After completing her education, she taught at several universities including the University of British Columbia, the Sir George Williams University in Montreal, and York University in Toronto. She and her husband, writer Graeme Gibson, live with their daughter Jess in Toronto.

Atwood has received much acclaim and several awards for her writing, including the Canadian Governor General's Award, Le Chevalier dans l'Ordre des Arts et des Lettres in France, and the National Arts Club Medal of Honor for Literature. She has written more than thirty volumes of poetry, nonfiction and fiction, including children's books and short stories. Her work has been published in more than twenty-five countries. In addition to her best-selling novels and collections of poetry, Atwood gained recognition for *Survival: A Thematic Guide to Canadian Literature,* (1972) a ground-

breaking critical analysis of Canadian literature and a proposal for Canadian writers to focus on native traditions in their works rather than identifying with Great Britain or the United States. Her works also include the best-selling novels *Alias Grace* and *The Robber Bride.*

Plot Summary

Part I

Surfacing opens with the unnamed narrator exclaiming, "I can't believe I'm on this road again." She is traveling with married friends, David and Anna, and her lover, Joe, to a remote island on a lake in Northern Quebec, where she spent much of her childhood, to search for her missing father. As they travel, Joe and David shoot a film that they will call "Random Samples," a compilation of shots "of things they come across." The narrator admits that she doesn't actually want to see her father; she just wants to make sure he is safe. She explains that she has had a strained relationship with him since her parents never forgave her for her hasty marriage, her subsequent divorce, and her abandonment of her child.

Anna confesses to the narrator that her marriage to David is troubled, which prompts the narrator to question her own relationship with Joe. She acknowledges,

> I'm trying to decide whether or not I love him. . . . I sum him up, dividing him into categories. . . . I'm fond of him, I'd rather have him around than not; though it would be nice if he meant something more to me. The fact that he doesn't makes me sad; no one has since my husband. A divorce is like an amputation, you survive but there's less of you.

She notes that she has never told Anna or Joe about her baby, explaining,

> I have to behave as though it doesn't exist, because for me it can't, it was taken away from me, exported, deported. A section of my own life, sliced off from me like a Siamese twin, my own flesh canceled. Lapse, relapse, I have to forget.

Suddenly she becomes furious with her father for vanishing "unresolved, leaving [her] with no answers to give them when they ask."

One day, while looking through the cabin where she lived with her family, she comes across some unintelligible drawings her father made and concludes, "this is the forgotten possibility: he might have gone insane. . . and if insane, perhaps not dead." Later, David catches a fish and when it is killed, the narrator notes, "I feel a little sick, it's because I've killed something, made it dead; but I know that's irrational, killing certain things is all right, food and enemies."

Without consulting the women, David and Joe decide to stay on the island for another week. When the narrator becomes confused about what she remembers of the past, she decides

> I have to be more careful about my memories. I have to be sure they're my own and not the memories of other people telling me what I felt, how I acted, what I said: if the events are wrong the feelings I remember about them will be wrong too, I'll start inventing them and there will be no way of correcting it. . . . To have the past but not the present, that means you're going senile.

She admits her brother did not really drown; her mother saved him at the last minute.

Part II

When Joe tells her, "we should get married," she notes, "I wanted to laugh. . . . He'd got the order wrong, he'd never asked whether I loved him, that was supposed to come first." She tells him, "I've been married before and it didn't work out. I had a baby too. . . . I don't want to go through that again." Disregarding what she said about the baby, Joe responds, "it would be different with us." When she will not agree, Joe turns angrily away from her. She thinks back to the day she and the father of her child got married, but the memory is distorted by the truth. She had never married and on that day, she had an abortion.

Later, she looks through a family scrapbook, explaining, "I searched through it carefully, looking for something I could recognize as myself, where I had come from or gone wrong." She finds her scrapbook filled with pictures of housewives and models, what she had wanted to be when she grew up. She also finds a picture of rabbits and thinks, "perhaps it was a vision of Heaven."

That night Anna admits that David has been frequently unfaithful to her and concludes that he behaves this way to prove "she can't stop him." The next day the narrator finds letters that show her father had not lost his reason, that the disturbing drawings he had made were copies, not originals, of primitive paintings he found on the island. Now she acknowledges, "I had the proof. . . indisputable, of sanity and therefore of death. Relief, grief, I must have felt one or the other. A blank, a disappointment." She determines to find one of the paintings and "verify, match the drawing with reality." As the four of them look for the paintings,

they come across a dead heron that someone has hung upside down and tied to a tree branch. David and Joe film the scene.

That night Joe tells her, "Okay. . . I give up, you win. We'll forget everything I said and do it like you want, back to the way it was before," but she feels that it is too late to reconcile and tells him no. She feels as if she has "already moved out." Joe seems as if he is going to hit her, but he turns away.

On their sixth day on the island, David browbeats Anna into taking her clothes off for the camera. The narrator sets out on her own to look for the painting. After she dives into the water, sure she will see it on a submerged ledge, she sees her father's dead body but confuses it with a vision of her aborted child. Later, David tries to seduce her, but she refuses, telling him she would get pregnant. David tells her Anna is having sex with Joe.

When David tells her they have found her father's body in the lake, she thinks he and Anna are making it up to get back at her for the sexual incident with David. She finds what she considers to be her mother's gift to her, a picture the narrator had drawn of both her mother and of herself as a baby inside her mother's womb. She decides that the pictures she finds are her "guides."

Part III

That night she and Joe make love out of doors, and she hopes he will impregnate her. She decides she will stay on the island alone and so escapes in a canoe when the others come to tell her it is time to leave. After the others leave, she goes back to the cabin and thinks she sees her mother feeding the birds. However, the vision quickly disappears. After she enters the cabin, she smashes everything she can and tears her clothes and linens, determined to live outside of civilization. The next day she sees a vision of her father, but when she gains a closer look, she concludes

> he was not my father. It is what my father saw, the thing you meet when you've stayed here too long alone. . . . I see now that although it isn't my father it is what my father has become. I knew he wasn't dead.

She begins to understand that she is losing touch with reality and acknowledges, "that is the real danger now, the hospital or the zoo, where we are put. . . when we can no longer cope." Yet she determines that she will never be a victim again. Thinking of the welfare of her unborn child, she dresses and decides, "I reenter my own time." Soon

Joe and Paul come to the island, looking for her. She watches from a distance as Joe calls for her, and acknowledges that "he won't wait much longer."

Characters

Anna

Anna is David's wife and the narrator's "best woman friend" for the past two months. Although she appears "always cheerful," Anna

> was desperate, her body her only weapon and she was fighting for her life. . . . She was fighting [David] because if she ever surrendered, the balance of power would be broken and he would go elsewhere. To continue the war.

Her battles with her husband have prompted her feelings of both love and hate toward him. She continually complains to the narrator about his efforts to humiliate her, but when he propositions her friend, she forms a temporary alliance with him. She also shows little regard for her friend when she has sex with Joe to get back at David. The narrator explains another possible motivation for her behavior: she concludes that Anna thinks, "by screwing Joe she's brought us back together. Saving the world, everyone wants to; men think they can do it with guns, women with their bodies."

David

David is Anna's husband. David teaches communications classes in an adult education program with Joe. Although he tries to pass himself off as a "man of the people," the narrator eventually sees through him. He is a misogynist (one who dislikes women) who torments his wife by continually trying to humiliate her. He tells his wife about his various affairs with other women to prove to her that she cannot control him. When the narrator confronts David after he has just propositioned her, he claims that Anna's own infidelities have forced him to be unfaithful to her. He insists that he is "for the equality of women," but then concludes that Anna "just doesn't happen to be equal." David tries to humiliate his wife when he shames her into taking off her clothes for the camera.

David's cruelty and manipulative nature emerge in the strict set of rules he forces Anna to follow. One rule is that Anna must always wear makeup. Anna explains to the narrator, "he wants me to look like a young chick all the time, if I don't

he gets mad." She also admits that if she breaks any of his rules

> he'll get me for it. If I break one of them I get punished, except he keeps changing them so I'm never sure. He's crazy, there's something missing in him. . . . He likes to make me cry because he can't do it himself.

When the narrator exclaims that she cannot believe David would be so demanding about makeup, Anna agrees, concluding, "it's something for him to use. He watches me all the time, he waits for excuses." Anna tells the narrator that sometimes she thinks he wants her to leave. "It used to be good," she notes, "then I started to really love him and he can't stand that, he can't stand having me love him. . . . Sometimes I think he'd like me to die."

Father

The narrator's father is dead at the beginning of the novel, but she strongly feels his influence throughout her time on the island. She admits both of her parents were innocents who had cut themselves off from reality. She notes, "they were from another age, prehistoric, when everyone got married and had a family." As a result, she never told them the truth about her affair with a married man or her abortion.

She describes her father, "islanding his life, protecting both us and himself, in the midst of war and in a poor country, the effort it must have taken to sustain his illusions of reason and benevolent order, and perhaps he didn't." Her father's devotion to logic and reason emerged in his belief that "with the proper guidebooks you could do everything yourself" and in his admiration for "what he called the eighteenth-century rationalists."

Joe

Joe is the narrator's often untalkative lover. She admits that "speech to him was a task, a battle, words mustered behind his beard and issued one at a time, heavy and square like tanks." In his *Introducing Margaret Atwood's Surfacing,* critic George Woodcock characterizes Joe as "the most enigmatic character in the book" and wonders, "is he deep or is he just dumb?" Henry C. Phelps in his article on the novel in the *Explicator* concludes that Joe exhibits "a seeming solicitude toward women that masks a more fundamental antipathy." Phelps notes that Joe's behavior reveals a "blend of overt concern and strained hostility toward women." For example, "relief gleams through his beard" when Joe does not accept the narrator's offer to search for her father. He also appears relieved

Media
Adaptations

- *Surfacing* was made into a film by a Canadian production company in 1981. It starred Joseph Bottoms and Kathleen Beller, was directed by Claude Jutra, produced by Beryl Fox, and adapted from Atwood's novel by Bernard Gordon.

---

when she does not have an emotional response to her inability to find her father: he asks her about her search "in a neutral mumble that signals he'd prefer it if I [the narrator] kept from showing any reaction, no matter what has happened."

He reveals his own lack of emotion when he asks the narrator to marry him. "We should get married," he remarks. "I think we should. . . we might as well." When she refuses, he becomes hostile. Later, when she continues to rebuff his attempts to reconcile, he seems as if he is about to hit her. Phelps notes, though, that Joe is the only one of the group who comes back to the island to find her. Yet, his antipathy again surfaces at this point in the novel as the narrator notes his "annoyed" voice and acknowledges that he will not wait very long for her to appear.

The narrator offers an explanation for his animosity toward women when she describes Joe as having

> the defiant but insane look of a species once dominant, now threatened with extinction. That's how he thinks of himself, too: deposed, unjustly. Secretly he would like them to set up a kind of park for him, like a bird sanctuary.

She concludes, "he didn't love me, it was an idea of himself he loved and he wanted someone to join him." Marriage, to him, would have been a kind of "victory."

Mother

The narrator's mother is also dead when the novel begins. Her influence in her daughter's life becomes evident as the narrator begins her withdrawal from civilization. The narrator's mother was a selfless woman who concealed her cancer pain until it became unbearable. She adapted her exterior and interior life to that of her husband's, as evidenced by the diary that she kept every year, in which she would only record the weather and the work done on that day, "no reflections, no emotion." The narrator concludes, "my father explained everything but my mother never did, which only convinced me that she had the answers but wouldn't tell." Quietly supportive but finally enigmatic, her mother spent her time

> collecting the seasons and the weather and her children's faces, the meticulous records that allowed her to admit the other things, the pain and isolation and whatever it was she was fighting against, something in a vanished history.

Narrator

The narrator is the novel's main character, a young woman returning to the remote island on a lake in Northern Quebec, where she spent much of her childhood, to search for her missing father. The abortion she reluctantly agreed to, coupled with the loss of both of her parents, has caused her to suppress her emotions and shut herself off from her world. At one point in the novel, she admits, "I realized I didn't feel much of anything, I hadn't for a long time. Perhaps I'd been like that all my life, just as some babies are born deaf or without a sense of touch." When she looks at the pictures she had made as a child, searching for some answers to her present condition, she finds

> no hints or facts, I didn't know when it had happened; I must have been all right then; but after that I'd allowed myself to be cut in two. . . . There had been an accident and I came apart. The other half, the one locked away, was the only one that could live; I was the wrong half, detached, terminal. . . numb.

She acknowledges that she "rehearses" emotions, "naming them: joy, peace, guilt, release, love and hate, react, relate, what to feel was like what to wear, you watched the others and memorized it." She suggests, "in a way it was a relief, to be exempt from feeling."

The narrator explains that as a youth, she memorized survival manuals, realizing "that is was possible to lose your way." She has tried to form a relationship with her lover Joe, but only half-heartedly. When he asks her if she loves him, she responds, "I want to. . . . I do in a way," but ultimately, she can not give him what he needs, a confirmation of himself. She concludes

> David is like me. . . . We are the ones that don't know how to love, there is something essential missing in

us. . . atrophy of the heart. Joe and Anna are lucky, they do it badly and suffer because of it,. . . or perhaps we are normal and the ones who can love are freaks.

Toward the end of the novel, she suffers a breakdown and tries to strip off all the trappings of civilization that she blames for her despondency. Yet when she realizes she must care for the unborn child she believes she is carrying, she pulls herself back to reality and finds the strength to insist, "this above all, to refuse to be a victim. . . . I have to recant, give up the old belief that I am powerless and because of it nothing I can do will ever hurt anyone."

Paul

Paul, the narrator's father's friend, is reserved, like her father and "saves everything useful." He is kind to her when she comes to the island looking for her father. Her father trusted him, and admired the fact that he could "build anything and fix anything."

Themes

Appearances and Reality

One the novel's main themes involves the tension between what appears to be and what is. Closely related to that is the theme of deception. The truth about the narrator's past emerges slowly because she has avoided much of the pain she experienced during an abortion she had a few years ago. The pain has been so great that she has deceived herself and others into thinking that she had been married and that she gave birth to a child who she subsequently gave up to her husband. A hint of the truth emerges when she notes that she has never told Anna or Joe about her baby, explaining

> I have to behave as though it doesn't exist, because for me it can't; it was taken away from me, exported, deported. A section of my own life, sliced off from me like a Siamese twin, my own flesh canceled. Lapse, relapse, I have to forget.

The narrator never provides an adequate rationale for giving up her baby, revealing her inability to face reality.

Memory and Reminiscence

As the novel progresses, another theme, memory and reminiscence, emerges in Atwood's characterization of the narrator. After she returns to the island where she grew up, the narrator begins to al-

Topics for Further Study

- Investigate the history of relations between Canada and the United States. Why do you think the narrator has such a strong dislike for Americans?

- Henry C. Phelps, in his article on the novel in the *Explicator,* writes that the novel presents a "remarkably insightful portrait" of the sixties. Research the social changes that took place during this decade and either support or refute Phelps' statement. Write a report or essay supporting your take on his statement and include the facts and details you discovered in your research.

- Write a poem or a short story about a time when you felt victimized. What tone do you think will best help you present this feeling? Consider carefully your tense and point of view.

- Compare and contrast the themes of *Surfacing* with another novel by Atwood. What themes do you find that appear in both novels? Why do you think Atwood seems to explore similar issues in her novels? Provide support for your presentation.

low memories of her past to emerge. She acknowledges, though, that her memory is fuzzy:

> I have to be more careful about my memories. I have to be sure they're my own and not the memories of other people telling me what I felt, how I acted, what I said: if the events are wrong the feelings I remember about them will be wrong to, I'll start inventing them and there will be no way of correcting it.

Her confusion about her past stems from her suppression of her abortion and the painful relationship she had with the man she refers to as her husband.

Apathy and Passivity

For the narrator to successfully suppress her memories, she must maintain a passive state. She has not allowed herself to form any close personal relationships with others. Anna, the narrator insists, is her "best friend," but she admits that she has only known her for a few months, and she continually holds Joe at arm's length. For most of the novel, she refuses to define her feelings about him, and when he tries to get too close by asking her to get married, she rejects him and decides she will move out.

Identity/Search for Self

When her suppressed memories begin to emerge and she struggles with the truth of her past, the narrator embarks on a journey of self-discovery. For most of her adult life, she has blocked important information about her family and herself to avoid the painful realities of her experience. However, when she is confronted with the loss of her father, and Joe pressures her to redefine and strengthen their relationship, she is forced to begin to face her emotionally traumatic past. Her subsequent search for herself will involve questions of sanity and insanity and will eventually lead to change and transformation.

Sanity and Insanity

When the narrator questions the sanity of her father, she foreshadows her own struggle to preserve her mental stability. When she finds strange pictures drawn by her father, she uses the possibility of his descent into insanity as evidence that he might still be alive and so be able to help her with her own search for self. However, when she discovers that the paintings are copies of wall paintings on the island, she realizes that he is dead, which triggers her own mental decline. She decides to stay on the island alone after the others leave to strip off all of the trappings of civilization that she feels have corrupted her. After seeing visions of her dead parents, however, she begins to understand that she is losing touch with reality and acknowledges, "that is the real danger now, the hospital or the zoo, where we are put. . . when we can no longer cope."

Change and Transformation

The narrator's painful process of reminiscence, which requires that she face the traumatic experience of the abortion, helps her to change and ultimately discover some sense of herself. Her conclusion that she has become pregnant with Joe's child and that she must survive for the child to survive, pulls her back into reality and to a reestablishment of her ties with civilization. By the end of the novel, her future with Joe is uncertain, but she has made one significant change: she insists that she will never be a victim again.

Style

Point of View

The novel is related through the narrator's point of view. Atwood never provides her protagonist with a name, which helps readers submerge themselves into her subjective world. Structuring the novel from the narrator's point of view also helps Atwood develop her themes, especially her focus on appearance, reality memory, reminiscence, and a search for self. Since readers understand the development of the plot from the narrator's limited point of view, we see firsthand her struggle to establish an identity as she tries to piece together the reality of the past. As she recalls fragments of the truth about the abortion, readers become engaged in the reconstruction process, which offers a more personal and therefore more complete understanding of her character.

Jerome H. Rosenberg, in *Twayne's World Authors Series Online*, concludes that Atwood's construction of the narrative in the present tense causes problems for the reader who struggles to sift "fact from fabrication." He notes that Atwood's construct compounds the difficulty in its lack of "retrospective contemplation that authenticates what is being said." Atwood allows no omniscient narrator to evaluate the narrator's concept of reality. Rosenberg concludes that, as a result, the narrative becomes "the act of discovery itself—seemingly random, incoherent, and unresolvable—as the narrator engages in a conversation with herself and with the reader."

This narrative style does not allow the reader to get a clear picture of the main character and her experience. The repetition and variation of images of the narrator's marriage/relationship and child/abortion makes it difficult for the reader to privilege any one version. Thus, by the end of the novel, readers are not quite sure what the future will be for the narrator, nor do they have a complete vision of her past. Rosenburg addresses this cognitive problem by insisting the novel has "an irrefutable inner logic." This logic becomes clear by the end of the novel after most of the pieces have been put together. At this point Atwood has provided readers with a compelling portrait of a woman struggling to establish a clear sense of herself.

Compare
&
Contrast

- **1970s:** Canadians, as well as their American neighbors, struggle over the issue of abortion. Although abortion is legal, courts try to find ways to restrict it, as one Canadian judge did when he determined that a woman would not have the right to an abortion without her husband's permission.

  Today: American President Bush has admitted that he is anti-abortion and many pro-choice supporters fear he will try to overturn *Roe v. Wade.* Abortion is also still a controversial topic in Canada.

- **1971:** This year begins a period of rapid decline in the birthrate in Canada, which in 1971 is 3.2 children per family. By the late 1980s, the average will have dropped to 1.7 children per family.

  Today: Many Canadian women, like their American counterparts, are marrying later in life, which has helped keep the birthrate low.

- **1970:** The resurgence of the French-Canadian separatist movement in the sixties reaches a crisis point this year when the Quebec Liberation Front conducts terrorist acts. The terrorism includes the kidnapping of British Trade Commissioner James Cross on October 5 and the kidnapping of Quebec's Minister of Labor, Pierre Laporte, on October 10. The Quebec Liberation Front kills Laporte on October 17, perhaps in response to the institution of the War Measures Act on that day by Canadian Prime Minister Pierre Trudeau, declaring martial law. As a result of the terrorism, the organization is banned.

  Today: Some reforms have been granted to the separatist movement, including the establishment of French as the official language of Quebec in 1974.

Symbols

Tom Marshall, in "Atwood Under and Above Water", in his *Harsh and Lovely Land: The Major Canadian Poets and the Making of a Canadian Tradition,* concludes, "In *Surfacing* the repeated imagery of bottled, trapped and murdered animals builds powerfully to the key scene in which the father's corpse and the aborted foetus are encountered." The heron that has been killed and strung up by hunters becomes the most dominant symbol of death and of the narrator's past. As she walks the island, she keeps inevitably returning to the spot where the dead heron is hung, much the same way she keeps returning to the memory of the abortion. Her feelings of guilt emerge when she kills a fish that David has just caught. She admits, "I feel a little sick, it's because I've killed something, made it dead; but I know that's irrational, killing certain things is all right, food and enemies." Her father's corpse finally symbolizes for her the dead fetus and so sparks the final stage of her search for herself.

Historical Context

A Woman's Place

Women's struggle for equal rights in the Western world gained slow momentum during the middle decades of the twentieth century. During World War II, women were encouraged to enter the workplace where they enjoyed a measure of independence and responsibility. After the war, they were expected (and required) to give up their jobs to the returning male troops. Hundreds of thousands of women were laid off and expected to resume their place in the home.

Training began at an early age to ensure that girls would conform to the feminine ideal—the perfect wife and mother. Women who tried to gain self-fulfillment through a career were criticized and deemed dangerous to the stability of the family. They were pressed to find fulfillment exclusively through their support of a successful husband. Television shows (for example *Ozzie and Harriet, Father Knows Best*), popular magazines (*Good*

Kathleen Beller in the 1980 film version of the novel

Housekeeping), and advertisements all encouraged the image of woman-as-housewife throughout the 1950s. The small number of women who did work outside the home often suffered discrimination and exploitation as they were relegated to low-paying clerical, service, or assembly-line positions. Women would have to wait until the 1960s and 1970s to gain meaningful social and economic advancement.

The Women's Movement

In the 1960s, the Women's Movement reemerged and gained most of its strength in the United States. The National Organization for Women (NOW), formed in 1966, and other groups like the National Women's Political Caucus gained support for abortion reform, federally supported child care centers, equal pay for women, and the removal of educational, political, and social barriers to women. Bella Abzug, Shirley Chisolm, Betty Friedan, Gloria Steinem, and others helped influence Congress to pass the Equal Rights Amendment bill in 1972 that banned sex discrimination at the national level though the bill was never ratified.

Sexuality

Traditional attitudes about sex began to change during this era. Dr. Alfred Kinsey's reports on the sexual behavior of men and women (1948, 1953) helped bring discussions of this subject out in the open. Despite their puritanical ideas about sexuality, Americans could not ignore questions concerning what constituted normal or abnormal sexual behavior. The public was intrigued by movie stars like Marilyn Monroe and Brigitte Bardot, who openly displayed their sexuality, and *Playboy* magazine, begun in 1953, gained a wide audience. Hugh Hefner, publisher of the magazine, claimed that the magazine's pictures of naked women were symbols of "disobedience, a triumph of sexuality, an end of Puritanism." *Playboy* itself promoted a new attitude toward sexuality with its "playboy philosophy" articles and its centerfolds of naked "girls next door." In the 1960s, relaxed moral standards would result in an age of sexual freedom.

In his article on *Surfacing* for the *Explicator,* Henry C. Phelps argues that the novel contains "a remarkably insightful portrait of that legendary decade, the Sixties." He finds a depiction of "the sad aftermath" of the decade's changes in morality, behavior, and social and gender roles. Phelps concludes

> The pervasive sense in the later novel of wasted opportunities, deepening bitterness, isolation, and empty. . . lives casts a consciously dark shadow over the era of so-called freedom and liberation. Atwood's skillful embodiment in a single character of the perniciousness of these changes both displays an unexpected facility for implied social commentary and offers a new perspective for examining her already intriguing narratives.

Critical Overview

When *Surfacing,* was published in 1972, it earned recognition in Canada and in the United States from scholars and from the general public. Most critics applauded the novel's style, characterizations, and themes. Edward Weeks, in a review for *Atlantic,* writes that Atwood's "sense of the place, of the lake in its various moods, or the animal life retreating before the intruder, is beautifully conveyed. . . . [There are] passages of fine writing in this book and scenes of considerable power, such as the diving under the cliff and the discovery of the dead heron." Paul Delany, in the *New York Times Book Review,* determines that

> at a time when many novelists restrict themselves to a single mode of expression, such as documentary realism or unrestrained fantasy, Miss Atwood has undertaken a more serious and complex task. Denying Emerson's maxim that the true art of life is to skate

Lakeside house on a remote island near Quebec, like the one where the novel takes place

well on surfaces, she shows the depths that must be explored if one attempts to live an examined life today.

Barbara Godard, in her piece on Atwood for *Feminist Writers,* asserts that the novel

> exhibits equally complex irony as it explores, through the narrative of a canoe journey into northern Quebec, the convoluted power relations between Anglophobe and Francophone Canadians in an era of intense Quebec separatist activity and between descendants of European immigrants and the culture of the aboriginal inhabitants they have displaced, both complicated by the invasion of American technology.

Praising her characterizations in the novel in her review for *Canadian Forum,* Ellen Godfrey comments that Atwood's "frightened and deadened characters are. . . extremely interesting" and concludes that "[she] reveals them with skill and wit." Henry C. Phelps in his article on the novel for the *Explicator* argues, "Atwood's skillful embodiment" in Joe of the "perniciousness" of the cultural changes that took place in the 1960s "both displays an unexpected facility for implied social commentary and offers a new perspective for examining her already intriguing narratives."

Tom Marshall, in "Atwood Under and Above Water," in *This Harsh and Lovely Land: The Major Canadian Poets and the Making of a Canadian*

Tradition, finds "a certain shallowness of characterization." He adds

> Everything must be filtered through the mind of the Atwood protagonist, who is usually supposed to be both shrewd and confused, a combination that is possible but which tends in certain cases to put some strain on the reader's credulity.

Marshall does, however, commend the author for her "evocative description." He concludes that the problematic characterizations do not interfere "with the powerful flow of the novel as one reads it."

Focusing on the novel's themes, Sherrill Grace, in *Violent Duality: A Study of Margaret Atwood,* praises the novel's complexity, arguing that Atwood is "constantly aware of opposites self/other, subject/object, male/female, nature/man and of the need to accept and work within them." Margaret Wimsatt in an article for *Commonweal* echoes this assessment when she writes, "The novel picks up themes brooded over in the poetry, and knits them together coherently."

Marshall, however, finds fault with Atwood's thematic development in some parts of the novel. He asserts

> the repeated imagery of bottled, trapped and murdered animals builds powerfully to the key scene in which the father's corpse and the aborted foetus are

> What finally brings her back to reality and to a refusal to allow herself to be victimized any longer is her belief that she is pregnant with Joe's child. She considers the possible new pregnancy as a way to absolve herself from the guilt she feels over the abortion."

encountered. . . . It is just that all of this seems too intellectually worked out, too far removed from any very deeply felt or imagined experience of the kind that stood in, so to speak, for any very searching exploration of human character. . . . Though a serious emotional resonance seems quite clearly intended, it is not achieved, mainly because recurrent poetic imagery is finally no substitute for depth of characterization. This is the major limitation of Atwood the novelist. Also, the reader may suspect that Atwood is indulging herself a little in this book, even to the extent of succumbing somewhat to the old-style woman's fiction she parodies.

Weeks criticizes the novel's conclusion, commenting, "I think it a pity that at the end, when she hides and strips herself for a fresh start, the heroine's behavior and her future with Joe are so hard to believe."

Most critics and readers found much to praise in *Surfacing*, which helped cement Atwood's reputation as one of Canada's best writers.

Criticism

Wendy Perkins

Perkins is an associate professor of English at Prince George's Community College in Maryland and has published several articles on British and American authors. In the following essay, she traces the narrator's search for identity in Atwood's novel.

In her most popular and critically acclaimed novel, *The Handmaid's Tale*, Atwood traces her heroine's

efforts to cope, endure, and survive the oppressive totalitarian regime that governs her life. In a similar vein, Atwood places the unnamed narrator in *Surfacing* into a more realistic, contemporary setting that does not threaten her physical safety. Yet, she too must reconstruct herself to preserve a strong sense of self.

The narrator in *Surfacing* has been victimized and disabled by a society that promoted male superiority and domination. She entered into a relationship with a married man who forced her to abort their unborn child. This experience so devastated the narrator that she has suppressed her memory of it and has cut herself off from any real contact with her world. At one point in the novel, she admits

> I realized I didn't feel much of anything, I hadn't for a long time. Perhaps I'd been like that all my life, just as some babies are born deaf or without a sense of touch; but if that was true I wouldn't have noticed the absence. At some point my neck must have closed over, pond freezing on a wound, shutting me into my head.

When she looks at the pictures she had made as a child, searching for some answers to her growing sense of unease, she finds

> no hints or facts, I didn't know when it had happened; I must have been all right then; but after that I'd allowed myself to be cut in two. . . . There had been an accident and I came apart. The other half, the one locked away, was the only one that could live; I was the wrong half, detached, terminal. . . numb.

She acknowledges that she "rehearses" emotions, "naming them: joy, peace, guilt, release, love and hate, react, relate, what to feel was like what to wear, you watched the others and memorized it," and that "in a way it was a relief, to be exempt from feeling."

She has tried to form a relationship with her lover Joe, but only halfheartedly. When he asks her if she loves him, she responds, "I want to. . . . I do in a way," but ultimately, she cannot give him what he needs, a confirmation of himself. She concludes, "David is like me. . . . We are the ones that don't know how to love, there is something essential missing in us. . . atrophy of the heart."

For the first half of the novel, she allows herself to be victimized to a lesser degree by Joe. While she does refuse to marry him, she quietly accepts his bullying. Henry C. Phelps in his article on *Surfacing* for the *Explicator* concludes that Joe exhibits "a seeming solicitude toward women that masks a more fundamental antipathy." Phelps notes that Joe's behavior reveals a "blend of overt concern and strained hostility toward women." For example, "relief gleams through his beard" when Joe does not accept the narrator's offer to search for her father. He reveals his own lack of emotion when he asks the narrator to marry him, couching his proposal in what Phelps considers "tepid, even antagonistic terms": "We should get married," Joe remarks. "I think we should. . . we might as well." When she refuses, he becomes hostile: "Sometimes," he complains, "I get the feeling you don't give a s—-about me." Later, when she continues to rebuff his attempts to reconcile, he seems as if he is about to hit her.

In an effort to suppress the painful memory of the abortion, she creates a fictional past that provides a more comfortable explanation for her inability to commit to a relationship with Joe. She tells him that "I've been married before and it didn't work out. I had a baby too. . . . I don't want to go through that again." She has convinced herself that she had a baby with her "husband" and that for some unnamed reason she gave the baby up. Yet she notes that previously she had never told Anna or Joe about her baby, explaining

> I have to behave as though it doesn't exist, because for me it can't; it was taken away from me, exported, deported. A section of my own life, sliced off from me like a Siamese twin, my own flesh canceled. Lapse, relapse, I have to forget.

Jerome H. Rosenberg, in his article on the novel for *Twayne's World Authors Series Online* comments on the narrator's fictionalization of her past:

> We do not perceive these "facts" as deliberate lies; rather, they are related to us as elements of the narrator's most profound belief regarding her past. If we recognize them as falsehoods at all, we realize that they are the protagonist's psychological defense, her means of avoiding yet one more death, one more sign of mortality—but this one a result of her own actions, her own decision to act, her own assertion of power. It is this secret, what she later calls this "death. . . inside me," that she has layered "over, a cyst, a tumor, black pearl." And it is this repressed guilt that she must bring to the surface, must exorcise, before she can become whole.

Patricia F. Goldblatt notes that "After enduring, accepting, regurgitating, denying, and attempting to please and cope, Atwood's protagonists begin to take action and change their lives." In *Surfacing,* the narrator's search for herself is ironically triggered by her search for her father. As she tries to recall the details of her past while she looks for clues on the island about her father's disappearance, the truth of her own life begins to emerge. When she dives below the surface of the lake, she

What Do I Read Next?

- Margaret Atwood sets *The Handmaid's Tale* (1986) in the futuristic, totalitarian society of the Republic of Gilead, where women are valued only for their ability to breed. This novel also focuses on a woman's struggle to define herself not as a victim but as an individual.

- In *Edible Woman* (1965), Atwood presents another powerful portrait of a woman who suffers under social limitations.

- In the play *A Doll House* (1879), Henrik Ibsen examines a woman's restricted role in the nineteenth century, and the disastrous effects those limitations have on her marriage.

- *The Awakening* (1899) by Kate Chopin chronicles the tragic life of Edna Pontiellier as she tries to discover a true sense of self in America at the beginning of the twentieth century.

symbolically submerges into her own past and allows her emotional response to the abortion to surface. Goldblatt concludes, however, that before the narrator can establish a strong sense of identity, she hits "rock bottom. . . . Fed up with the superficiality of her companions, [she] banishes them and submits to paranoia." Alone on the island, she tries to strip away the trappings of civilization to discover a sense of self:

> Everything I can't break. . . I throw on the floor. . . . I take off my clothes. . . I dip my head beneath the water. . . I leave my dung, droppings on the ground. . . I hollow a lair near the woodpile. . . I scramble on hands and knees. . . I could be anything, a tree, a deer skeleton, a rock.

What finally brings her back to reality and to a refusal to allow herself to be victimized any longer is her belief that she is pregnant with Joe's child. She considers the possible new pregnancy as a way to absolve herself from the guilt she feels over the abortion. After she and Joe have intercourse, she insists, "He trembles and then I can feel my lost child surfacing within me, forgiving me."

She must return to civilization and contact with others because her child "must be born, allowed." This "act of healing" as Rosenberg terms it helps her reconstruct herself by establishing a strong sense of who she is and what she wants. Rosenberg concludes

> To renounce power, to remain a passive victim of others, she sees, is an exercise in futility: if she wishes to survive in the historical, struggle-ridden world into which we are all born, she must "join in the war, or. . . be destroyed." She wishes there were "other choices" but sees there are not. What is morally essential, however, is for her to acknowledge her power, accept her imperfection, take responsibility for her actions, and "give up the old belief that I am powerless and because of it nothing I can do will ever hurt anyone."

By the end of the novel, when she determines to reenter society and perhaps establish a strong relationship with Joe, she accomplishes these goals.

Commenting on Atwood's focus on the "plight of women in society" in her novels, Goldblatt concludes that Atwood:

> has reconstructed this victim, proving to her and to us that we all possess the talent and the strength to revitalize our lives and reject society's well-trodden paths that suppress the human spirit. She has shown us that we can be vicariously empowered by our surrogate, who not only now smiles but winks back at us, daring us to reclaim our own female identities.

In *Surfacing,* Atwood illustrates for her readers, through the transformation of the main character, the indefatigable nature of the human spirit.

Source: Wendy Perkins, Critical Essay on *Surfacing,* in *Novels for Students,* The Gale Group, 2002.

Sources

Delany, Paul, Review in *New York Times Book Review,* March 4, 1973, p. 5.

Godard, Barbara, "Atwood, Margaret," in *Feminist Writers,* edited by Pamela Kester-Shelton, St. James Press, 1996, pp. 29–33.

Godfrey, Ellen, Review, in *Canadian Forum,* Vol. 52, January 1973, p. 24.

Goldblatt, Patricia F., "Reconstructing Margaret Atwood's Protagonists," in *World Literature Today,* Vol. 73, No. 2, Spring 1999, p. 275.

Grace, Sherrill, *Violent Duality: A Study of Margaret Atwood,* Vehicule Press, 1980.

Marshall, Tom, "Atwood Under and Above Water," in *Harsh and Lovely Land: The Major Canadian Poets and the Making of a Canadian Tradition,* University of British Columbia Press, 1978.

Phelps, Henry C., "Atwood's *Edible Woman* and *Surfacing,*" in *Explicator,* Vol. 55, No. 2, Winter 1997, p. 112.

Rosenberg, Jerome H., "Margaret Atwood: Chapter 4," in *Twayne's World Authors Series Online,* G. K. Hall, 1990.

Weeks, Edward, Review, in *Atlantic,* Vol. 231, No. 127, April 1973, p. 127.

Wimsatt, Margaret, Review, in *Commonweal,* July 9, 1973.

Woodcock, George, *Introducing Margaret Atwood's "Surfacing,"* ECW Press, 1990.

Further Reading

Blais, Marie-Clair, "Afterword," in *Surfacing,* Anchor Books, 1972.
  Blais comments on the novel's themes and style.

Buxton, Jackie, "Atwood, Margaret (Eleanor)," in *Contemporary Novelists,* 6th ed., edited by Susan Windisch Brown, St. James Press, 1996, pp. 52–56.
  Buxton offers a study of *Surfacing*'s "powerful mythic dimension."

Gibson, Graeme, "An Interview with Margaret Atwood," in *Eleven Canadian Novelists,* 1973.
  In this interview, Atwood discusses the novel's themes.

The Sweet Hereafter

Russell Banks
1991

Russell Banks's sixth novel, *The Sweet Hereafter* tells the tragic story of a school bus accident, revealing how it impacts the lives of individuals as well as the community as a whole. In *The Reading List, Contemporary Fiction,* Banks is quoted as saying, "I wanted to write a novel in which the community was the hero, rather than a single individual." Although the story is told from the perspectives of four individual narrators, the importance of the community emerges as a strong unifying element.

The Sweet Hereafter has been embraced by critics and readers alike for its unique narrative structure. Banks's intention in writing the novel this way was to avoid what he considers the artifice of omniscient narration and the somewhat preachy tone that often accompanies it. Instead, Banks chose to tell the story four times, each time from a different perspective that is unique, realistic, and limited. The result is a more intimate tone that allows the reader to understand how a single incident can create such different feelings in different individuals. The narration reveals varied threads of guilt, blame, and recovery, and places them in the larger fabric of a community's reaction to a tragedy.

Author Biography

Russell Earl Banks was born March 28, 1940, in Newton, Massachusetts, the eldest of Earl and Flo-

Russell Banks

fiction began to explore racial injustice, class discrimination, poverty, and alcoholism.

Continental Drift (1985) was Banks's first novel to receive widespread acclaim from literary critics. Since its publication, the author's work has been held up as some of the best contemporary American fiction. *The Sweet Hereafter* (1991), Banks's sixth novel, won critical acclaim and was adapted in 1997 as an award-winning film of the same title. His novel *Affliction* (1990) was also adapted to film in a 1998 movie of the same title.

In addition to writing, Banks has taught at various colleges and universities, including Sarah Lawrence and Princeton. He has earned many fellowships and awards, including a Guggenheim Fellowship (1976), two National Endowment for the Arts fellowships (1977, 1983), an American Academy and Institute of Arts and Letters Award (1986), and an O. Henry Memorial Award for his short stories.

Plot Summary

Dolores Driscoll

As *The Sweet Hereafter* opens, a tragic bus accident resulting in the deaths of fourteen children has taken place in the small, rural town of Sam Dent in upstate New York. Each of four characters addresses the reader, describing in turn how the accident affected him or her.

Dolores Driscoll, the first narrator, has been a school bus driver for twenty-two years and was driving the bus at the time of the accident. She lives with her husband, Abbott, who has been wheelchair-bound since suffering a devastating stroke. Dolores recalls the events of the day of the accident, describing many of the children and their families. First, she picks up the Lamston kids, three quiet children who come from a dysfunctional home. Next, she picks up eleven-year-old Bear Otto, the adopted Native-American son of Wanda and Hartley Otto. Dolores explains that the Ottos are "hippies" who are also model citizens. She adds that Bear is "one of those rare children who brings out the best in people instead of the worst."

After picking up several other children, Dolores notices that it is beginning to snow. She is not worried, however, because she is a seasoned driver in this area and is accustomed to its severe weather.

Her next stop is the motel run by Risa and Wendell Walker to get five-year-old Sean. He is a

rence Banks' four children. They were a working-class family who reared their children in Barnstead, New Hampshire. Banks's early life was fraught with difficulty. He endured near-poverty with his family and watched his parents' marriage decline into divorce. Today, Banks is married to his fourth wife and is the father of four daughters.

At the age of eighteen, Banks enrolled at Colgate College but dropped out after only eight weeks. He felt out of place because his fellow students were wealthy. He decided to join Fidel Castro's revolution in Cuba but could only afford to go as far as Florida, where he took odd jobs and lived in a trailer park. At that time, he began writing short fiction. In the mid-1960s, he traveled to the Yucatán and Jamaica; these experiences would later appear in his fiction as would his memories of life in rural New England.

Banks completed an English degree at the University of North Carolina in 1967 and has since written a succession of novels and short stories. His early fiction demonstrates his experimentation with different styles and with blending genres, such as fantasy and realism. From the beginning, his interest has been in communicating the difficulties of life and the relationship between modern people and tradition. In the 1980s, Banks focused his attention more sharply on social hardships, and his sickly boy with a learning disability whose video game prowess earns him the respect of the other children. On this day, he is especially frightened to leave his mother so fourteen-year-old Nichole Burnell asks him to sit with her. The next stop is Billy Ansel's home, where Dolores picks up Billy's nine-year-old twins, Jessica and Mason. Once the twins are on the bus, Billy leaves for work, following the bus into town. In all, Dolores picks up thirty-four children although she does not describe each one.

As the snow gets heavier, Dolores concentrates on the road and sees what looks like a dog running across it. She remembers making a conscious choice to swerve to miss it, as a result of which the bus crashes through a guardrail and plunges into the water-filled sandpit below, which is covered with a thick layer of ice. The last memory she relates is of the children being thrown around the bus as the vehicle tips over.

Billy Ansel

Billy Ansel is a widower whose twins die in the bus accident. A Vietnam veteran, he owns a garage in town. Because Billy followed the bus into town each day, he witnessed the accident. He admits that while he was driving that day, he was thinking about Risa Walker. Risa is the wife of one of Billy's friends, and he is having an affair with her. He talks at length about the affair.

Billy's wife has died of cancer. He remembers good times they had and recalls a frightening incident that happened during a family vacation in Jamaica. Distracted, he and his wife left their daughter at a grocery store and did not realize it until they were almost back to the home they were renting. He remembers how afraid he was that he had lost his daughter forever and how relieved he was to find her safe.

Billy remembers throwing himself into action after the bus accident, helping the rescuers. Although onlookers thought he was being brave, he only wanted to keep busy to delay facing the reality of his personal loss. Later, he starts drinking heavily and keeps to himself.

Billy tells of his first encounter with Mitchell Stevens. He had gone out to look at the bus, which was parked behind his garage. While he was there, Mitchell approached him, asking if he needed legal representation. Billy's response was harsh; he had no interest in a lawsuit that would do nothing to fill the void in his life or in the community.

Mitchell Stephens, Esquire

A lawyer from New York City, Mitchell Stephens arrives in Sam Dent (as do many lawyers) after reading about the bus accident. Mitchell is passionate about this type of case because he has a personal vendetta against the blameworthy. Admitting that Dolores is a bad candidate for blame (because she has no money and is an upstanding member of the community) he sets his sights on the city and possibly the school board.

Mitchell is divorced and has a grown daughter who has adopted a life of sex and drugs. During his stay in Sam Dent, she calls him to say that she has AIDS and speaks to him in her usual adversarial way. Mitchell loves his daughter but does not know how to handle her. He remembers when she was an infant and was bitten by baby black widow spiders. Speeding to the hospital miles away, he held her and kept her calm but was prepared to perform a tracheotomy if necessary, as the doctor had instructed.

Mitchell represents the Walkers, the Ottos, and the Burnells in a lawsuit. He is counting on Nichole's testimony because she can be portrayed as the ultimate victim. He also intends to subpoena Billy to testify that Dolores was not driving over the speed limit although he does not know whether this is true. His strategy seems to be to tell both Dolores and Billy that the other needs confirmation that they were driving fifty-two miles per hour; Mitchell hopes that they will both agree to that story because he needs for them to agree in court although neither is sure how fast they were going.

Nichole Burnell

A survivor of the bus accident, Nichole is a beautiful and intelligent fourteen-year-old girl. Prior to the accident, she was a cheerleader and at the top of her class. Because of the accident, she is now confined to a wheelchair.

Nichole lives with her parents, two brothers, and little sister. Her terrible secret is that her father has been sexually abusing her. Now that she is disabled, he leaves her alone, and she becomes aware of the power she has over him because she holds this secret.

Nichole feels angry and bitter about her condition. She has nothing in common with her friends, and everyone in town pities her. Eventually, she makes peace with being wheelchair-bound, but when she graduates second in her class, she refuses to make a speech. She has been studying at home and has no desire to be put on display.

Nichole disagrees with her parents' decision to try to cash in on her condition with a lawsuit. When she meets Mitchell, she likes him, but comes to believe that the best thing for the community is for the lawyers to leave. She makes a decision to lie on the witness stand to undermine Mitchell's case. She claims that she could see that Dolores was driving well over the speed limit, which means that Mitchell cannot blame the city or the school board for the accident.

Dolores Driscoll

Dolores and Abbott have stayed out of Sam Dent, running their errands at other nearby towns. Dolores has gotten work as a driver for the hotels in Lake Placid but when the county fair begins in Sam Dent, she and Abbott decide to attend the demolition derby. Dolores notices that everyone is snubbing them, but she dismisses it with the assumption that they are still not ready to see her. Billy shows up, drunk and with a woman, and sits with the Driscolls. When Nichole arrives and everyone claps, Billy explains to his date that Nichole saved the town from the lawsuits. This gets Abbott's attention, who demands to know what he means, and Billy is forced to tell them about Nichole's testimony against Dolores. Because the Driscolls had stayed out of Sam Dent, they had not heard about it.

As Dolores absorbs this news, the demolition derby begins, and her old car (which has been bought by a local man) is in the middle. As the other cars smash into it, the crowd cheers its destruction. Oddly, when the driver of her car starts destroying other cars and eventually wins, the crowd cheers for that, too. After the victory, Dolores and Abbott leave, and they are met with a little more respect by the townspeople.

Characters

Billy Ansel

Billy Ansel is a widower and Vietnam veteran whose twins are killed in the bus accident that is the novel's central event. His wife is deceased, and they were his only children, so their deaths leave him alone in the world. Billy owns and manages a garage in Sam Dent where he hires other Vietnam veterans. He is handsome, charming, and well-liked. He says that he likes to be in charge because he is the eldest of five children of an incompetent mother and an absent father. His mother now suf-

fers from Alzheimer's disease and lives in a nursing home. His sisters are all married and have children, and his brother rarely calls. Billy is having an affair with Risa Walker, the wife of a friend. Nobody else in the town knows about the affair and after the accident, they no longer see each other.

Billy always leaves for work after his children board the school bus, and his habit is to follow the bus into town. Because of this, he witnesses the accident. Although he never talks about seeing the accident, he does relate how he helped the rescuers after it happened. He admits that this was his way of delaying facing the reality of his loss. In the following days, Billy begins drinking heavily and staying at home. He attends his children's funeral only to avoid calling attention to himself. As members of the town join various lawsuits, Billy is angry because he hates what the lawsuits are doing to the town he has always loved.

When Billy's children are killed, he finds he has no idea how to handle it. Prior to the accident, he thought he understood death from his experience in Vietnam and from losing his wife, but this loss is more than he can bear. He finds no comfort at all in religion and feels that many of the attempts by churchgoers to comfort the bereft are insulting.

At the end of the novel, Billy is seen drinking and going to the demolition derby with a woman who is not from Sam Dent.

Mrs. Burnell

Mrs. Burnell is Nichole's mother. She is passive, religious, and self-righteous. If she knows anything about her husband's sexual abuse of their daughter, she never indicates this. She generally avoids dealing with difficult issues in a direct manner.

Nichole Burnell

Nichole is a fourteen-year-old girl who is confined to a wheelchair after surviving the bus accident. Prior to the accident, she was a popular cheerleader and was among the school's best students. The people of the town think well of her, and she baby-sits many of the younger children. What nobody knows is that her father has been sexually abusing her, a fact that made her feel ashamed before the accident. Now that she is in a wheelchair and her father will not touch her, she feels powerful because she is safe from further abuse and still holds the secret that her father wants hidden.

Nichole is initially bitter and angry about her wheelchair-bound status, but she gradually comes to accept it. She is an insightful and intelligent girl who is able to see people for what they really are. She is sensitive and loving and looks after the children on the bus.

When Nichole overhears Billy asking her father to drop the lawsuit because of what it will do to the town, she decides to undermine the case her father's lawyer is building. In her testimony, she lies and says that she saw that Dolores was driving seventy-two miles per hour. She knows that her parents were counting on the money from the lawsuit, but she also knows that her father will never say anything to her about it because he is afraid she will reveal the secret of his abuse.

Sam Burnell

Sam Burnell is Nichole's father. He is domineering in his family but friendly to others. He has been sexually abusing Nichole, but nobody else knows about it. After the accident, he is uncomfortable around Nichole so he begins to be kind and respectful toward her. Although he had been counting on the money from the lawsuit, he says nothing to Nichole when she sabotages it.

Abbott Driscoll

Abbott is Dolores's husband. A stroke has left him disabled. He is an intelligent man whose wisdom is a source of guidance and comfort to his wife. His protective nature is revealed in the scene in which Billy mentions Nichole's testimony but is hesitant to tell the Driscolls any more about it. Abbott asks what Billy means by his comment that Nichole saved the town from the lawsuits, and when he senses Billy's unwillingness to elaborate, Abbott stares at him until he tells the rest of the story. Abbott realizes that Billy knows something about Dolores, and when Billy tries to hide it, Abbott forces the truth out of him. This prevents Dolores from having to continue living in ignorance and gives her the opportunity to defend herself if she chooses.

Dolores Driscoll

Dolores Driscoll is the school bus driver who is driving on the day of the accident. She has been driving the bus for twenty-two years and genuinely loves her job. She does all the maintenance on her bus, feeling that she alone will see to every detail. In the summer, she works at the post office. Dolores is a large woman with red hair and a sharp voice. She keeps order on the bus but only insists that the children follow a few rules. She is married to Abbott, who is disabled due to a stroke. Although

Media
Adaptations

- In 1997, an acclaimed film of the same name, directed by Atom Egoyan, was based on *The Sweet Hereafter*. The film earned Academy Award nominations and won awards at the Cannes Film Festival in addition to being a nominee for the festival's highest honor, the Golden Palm. The film adaptation earned numerous other awards and nominations from various film and script societies in the United States and Canada. In an interview with *The Writer,* Banks called the film "brilliant" and "a marvelous piece of work" that is "very imaginative and serious without being somber." The film was produced by Alliance Communications Corporation, Ego Film Arts, and The Harold Greenberg Fund.

nobody else understands him when he speaks, Dolores claims to be able to translate. (Mitchell expresses his doubt of her ability, claiming that she merely hears what she wants or needs to hear, rather than what Abbott is actually saying. The reader is never told conclusively which is the truth.) They have two sons, who are grown and have moved out of Sam Dent.

A lifelong resident of Sam Dent, Dolores is haunted by the loss of the fourteen children who died in the accident. She feels she owes it to all of the children to attend their funerals, but does not want to cause any additional pain by her presence, so she sits in the back and leaves early. As the town heals, she begins spending more time in the neighboring city of Lake Placid. Because of her absence from everyday life in Sam Dent, she is unaware of Nichole's testimony that she was driving seventy-two miles per hour on the day of the accident. When she is told about this, she feels a sense of relief rather than anger. This reaction is confusing to many readers, and Dolores only explains that being singled out for blame lifts an enormous weight from her shoulders. Perhaps she sees the fact that Nichole lied about her speeding as confirmation that, in fact, she was not speeding, something of which she herself is not completely certain. Another possible explanation is that being singled out by the community actually allows her to distance herself from the tragedy; perhaps it is easier to be a villain than a victim. Whatever the explanation, she is unwilling to permanently leave her hometown although many of the townspeople will always resent and blame her.

Hartley Otto

Hartley Otto is Wanda's husband and Bear's father. He wears long hair and sandals and seems to be happy letting his wife be the decision-maker. To many residents of Sam Dent, the Ottos appear to be hippies. Hartley is originally from South Dakota, but he and his wife have become members of the Sam Dent community.

Hartley and his wife adopted Bear, a Native-American orphan, when they believed they would be unable to have children of their own. The lawyer who is preparing the lawsuit over the accident supposes that they were able to adopt Bear because Hartley is part Native American himself.

Wanda Otto

Wanda Otto is Hartley's wife and Bear's mother. Bear, the Ottos' adopted son, is killed in the bus accident, and Wanda is filled with a desire for vengeance. Despite the fact that she is not a native of Sam Dent (she is originally from Long Island), she has become integrated into the community. She and Hartley decided to move to Sam Dent when they were counselors at a nearby summer camp; they borrowed money from Wanda's father to build their house.

Wanda has long, dark hair, and wears turquoise and silver jewelry. She is intelligent, college-educated, and speaks her mind. The lawyer representing the Ottos senses immediately that Wanda is the decision-maker in the family and it is she who ultimately decides to go forward with the lawsuit.

Wanda and her husband live a carefree lifestyle, characterized by loose-fitting clothes, herbal teas, and natural furnishings in their handmade, dome-shaped house. It is rumored in town that they grow marijuana. They adopted Bear (a Native-American orphan) because they believed they would never conceive. At the time of Bear's death, however, Wanda is pregnant.

Mitchell Stephens

Mitchell Stephens is an attorney from New York City who arrives in Sam Dent after hearing about the bus accident. He says that he pursues this type of case because he is on a mission to make sure that the people responsible for such tragedies pay for their negligence. He is passionate about this mission, even though he says that working on such cases is difficult, humiliating, and diminishing.

Mitchell is divorced and his only child, Zoe, is always on the run. She lives a life of sex and drugs and occasionally calls him (from a different city every time) to get money. Even though Mitchell knows she will use it for drugs, he is afraid of how she will get the money if he denies her requests. He loves his daughter deeply, but has run out of ideas as to how to handle her. He has tried every imaginable route, but she is out of control. Readers sense that, because he has lost his child, he is driven to help other people who have lost theirs.

Mitchell is very observant and able to understand what is not being said when he talks to the people of the town. For example, he senses immediately that Risa is having an affair and, based on Risa's body language when Billy's name is spoken, he deduces that Billy is her lover. Mitchell is also an expert manipulator. He makes Billy believe that he is trying to recruit him for his lawsuit when he is actually trying to make sure that Billy will not join any lawyer's lawsuit so that he can be an unbiased witness. Mitchell is likeable and easy to talk to, but he always has an agenda.

Risa Walker

Risa Walker is Wendell's wife and Billy's lover. She and Wendell were high school sweethearts who married and then fell into a disintegrating marriage. They run a motel in Sam Dent although Risa is the one who works hard to try to maintain it. She wears manly clothes and rarely presents herself in a feminine way. She enjoys the fantasy that she and Billy are in love, but she is as aware as Billy that it is not a deeply meaningful relationship. After the accident, she and Billy stop seeing each other and she begins to consider divorcing her husband.

Wendell Walker

Wendell Walker is Risa's husband and a friend of Billy's. He spends most of his time in front of the television and does not seem to have any suspicion that his wife is involved in an affair.

Topics For Further Study

- Look through a recent newspaper to find a story about a tragic incident or other human interest story. Choose four people related to the incident (either by taking names from the story or by imagining related people) and write one page about the incident from each person's point of view. Following Banks's example, keep in mind each person's background, occupation, and personality when writing on his or her behalf. Each account should be written in the first person, and you will need to make up many details about the people.

- Conduct library research on the psychology of parents who have experienced the death of a child, or arrange to interview a therapist and/or a member of the clergy about the sensitive topic of parents who have lost children. Find out if the response to this tragedy follows a typical course or if everyone is different. What consistencies do you find between what your research tells you and Banks's portrayal of the distraught parents? Summarize your findings in a presentation.

- Review the last chapter of *The Sweet Hereafter,* in which Banks tells of the demolition derby and the victory of Boomer. Paying close attention to details and to Dolores's reactions, look for symbolism in this scene. What uses of symbolism

do you notice and how are they presented? Does anything in this scene change your reaction to or thoughts about Dolores?

- Truth is an important concern in the narration of *The Sweet Hereafter.* Different characters conceptualize the truth in different ways. On what basis might you judge the truthfulness of the four narrators of the story? Present evidence from the novel in an argument *supporting* the truthfulness of one of these characters, as if you were a lawyer arguing a case before a judge. Then present evidence from the novel in an argument *against* the truthfulness of that same character.

- What is the role of truth in *The Sweet Hereafter?* Different characters approach it in different ways. Do you find it is easy or difficult to judge the truthfulness of the characters? See what three major philosophers have to say about truth, and apply these principles to one character in the novel. You may choose any philosophers, such as Socrates (the Socratic method for arriving at truth), Plato, Buddha, Soren Kierkegaard, Georg Wilhelm Friedrich Hegel, Henry David Thoreau, or Ralph Waldo Emerson. Present an argument for or against the character's truthfulness as if you were a lawyer arguing a case before a judge.

Themes

Perception

By using four points of view, Banks shows readers how the same events are interpreted differently by different people. He also demonstrates how a person's background influences the way he or she understands and reacts to a situation. For example, Dolores prides herself on taking good care of the bus. From her perspective, she does the best job of maintaining it because she is personally committed to her role as a bus driver. On the other hand, Billy questions her ability to properly oversee the maintenance of the bus. This is not surprising,

given that he is the mechanic who maintains all of the other school buses.

Banks relates the scene in which Billy and Mitchell first meet at the garage from both men's points of view, which enables the reader to experience a single exchange from two very different perspectives. Another example of Banks's presentation of the theme of differing perceptions is in the fact that Wendell is unaware of his wife's infidelity while Mitchell detects it right away. Wendell feels detached from his wife and therefore is not particularly interested in what she does. Mitchell, on the other hand, is an attorney who is accustomed to reading people to interpret what is not being said.

He not only figures out that Risa is having an affair but soon surmises that the affair is with Billy based on Risa's body language when his name is mentioned.

There are numerous subtle ways in which Banks comments on the nature of perception in *The Sweet Hereafter*. For example, Billy states that he believes Dolores is in denial about the whole tragedy, but the reader knows that Dolores is plagued by guilt and self-doubt. She attends the funerals and memorial services because she feels it is the right thing to do, but she sits in the back and leaves before anyone else does. Billy, however, does not attend all of the services, so his perception is limited by his lack of observation of Dolores's actions.

Another contrast in the perceptions of two different characters is that Dolores perceives people who vacation in Sam Dent every year as outsiders while Mitchell thinks that because he spends most of six months there, he is practically a resident. When Mitchell arrives in town, he feels out of place in his suit so he begins wearing casual clothes to blend in with the locals. Nichole comes to believe that the casual attire is his preferred dress, and she is surprised when she sees him in court in his pinstriped suit.

Mitchell and Nichole also have opposing views of the tragedy because Mitchell does not believe in accidents while Nichole states that "the truth was that it was an accident, that's all, and no one was to blame."

Response to Tragedy

At the center of the novel is the terrible tragedy that claims the lives of fourteen children. From this event come a variety of reactions. At the scene of the accident, Dolores reacts by sitting alone and mumbling to herself while Billy reacts by helping the rescuers. He feels that if he keeps moving, he will delay having to face his personal loss. Many people sob and take refuge in the arms of friends while others walk slowly and silently in disbelief. Afterward, some people continue their lives, some are consumed by anger and vengeance, some are in denial, and some move to other towns.

Once he faces the reality of what has happened, Billy descends into drinking and seclusion, emerging only to attend his children's funeral. His decision to go to the funeral has less to do with his desire to go through the mourning ritual than it does with his need to avoid calling attention to himself. He explains how the accident permanently changes

his relationship with Risa. He comments, "She was like a stranger to me then, a stranger whose life had just been made utterly meaningless. I know this because I felt the same way. . . . Our individual pain was so great that we could not recognize any other." Rather than turn to each other for comfort and understanding, Billy and Risa lose the sense of intimacy they shared prior to the tragedy.

Community

The Sweet Hereafter takes place within a single small town. By exploring its reaction to an unthinkable tragedy, Banks shows how an established community can be resilient and self-reliant. The people of Sam Dent never seek help from outside; there is never a call for therapists, arbiters, or state or federal help for the families paying for hospital costs. Although the community becomes divided, it ultimately survives the bus accident tragedy and continues to thrive. In fact, the community seems to be greater than the sum of its parts because some members leave, yet the community of Sam Dent remains intact.

There is something at stake for all the residents of Sam Dent in the aftermath of the bus accident, whether they are seeking support or acceptance from the community. For Billy, Risa, Nichole, and others, the community ultimately provides support and stability. On the other hand, Dolores seeks forgiveness and acceptance back into the community. These characters are not able to permanently remove themselves from the community because the community alone can provide them with what they most need.

Style

Alternating Point-of-View

The Sweet Hereafter is structured by narrators rather than by chapters. There are four narrators, all of whom speak once, with the exception of Dolores, who speaks twice. As the author switches narrators, he presents the characters' points-of-view by taking into consideration their life experiences, backgrounds, occupations, and personal relationships. This allows the reader to peek into the psyches of four distinct people, understanding their motivations for the decisions they make. The reader senses that the speakers are confiding in a trusted confidant: Nichole admits that she lied, and Billy states, "I can only tell you how it felt." Such comments signal to the reader that the speaker is being completely honest in his or her account.

At the same time, Banks is careful to present limited perspectives because none of the narrators are omniscient. By piecing together what each of the four narrators relates, the reader has a fuller and deeper experience of the story. This technique also leaves questions unanswered, such as when Nichole planned her lie and whether she considered beforehand the ramifications to her life and to Dolores's life. The unanswered questions are what draw many readers further into the story because the reader is forced to make assumptions and predictions based not on what the author presents as fact, but on what the narrators present as their perspectives.

Simile

Although Banks presents four distinct narratives, one tendency they all have in common is the use of similes (a figure of speech comparing two unlike things), which serve as a subtle uniting element among the four voices. That four characters as different from one another as Dolores, Billy, Mitchell, and Nichole would all share this characteristic seems unlikely. Thus, this consistency across the four narratives reminds the reader that, as fully-formed as these characters are, they are all the creations of a single writer.

Dolores describes the children as they wait for her to pick them up for school as being "like berries waiting to be plucked." Commenting on their behavior on the bus she says they do "everything we ourselves do, the way puppies and kittens at play mimic grown dogs and cats at work."

Similarly, Billy recalls an incident many years ago when he was driving, and he looked in the back seat to see the twins, expecting "them to be asleep, curled up in each other's arms like litter mates, like puppies or kittens." Remembering the scene of the accident, Billy remarks:

> The bus had not been hauled out—you could see the front end of the vehicle up on the ice-cluttered far bank of the pit, like some huge dying yellow beast caught struggling to clamber out and frozen in the midst of the attempt, with the rest of the thing underwater. The snow and the cold made everyone down there—the rescue workers, the wet-suited divers from Burlington, the state troopers—move slowly, hunched in their bodies as if with fear and permanent resentment, like lifetime prisoners in a Siberian gulag.

Mitchell and Nichole use similes, too. Explaining why he is so passionate about tragic cases,

Mitchell says that, even though in the end he comes out "feeling diminished, like a cinder," he believes fervently that people should be accountable for their negligence in causing such accidents. Commenting on Billy's voice, he describes it as "low but thin, flattened out, like a piece of tin," and describes Wendell's standing posture as "very tough. . . like a fist."

On the first page of her narration, Nichole compares the time before the accident to the time after it happened by saying, "it's like a door between rooms, and there was one room on the far side, and that room I remember fine, and another on the near side, and I remember it too. I'm still in it. But I don't have any memory of passing through." When her father takes her home from the hospital, he wheels her up a new ramp he has built. This only makes Nichole feel "like I was a new piece of furniture." After the accident, Nichole's wheelchair makes her father behave differently toward her. She says, "To Daddy, it was like I was made of spun glass and he was afraid he would break me if he touched me."

Historical Context

Political and Economic Turmoil

In 1991, the year *The Sweet Hereafter* was published, the United States won a military skirmish in the Persian Gulf and suffered an economic recession at home. In 1990, President George Bush had officially brought an end to the Cold War by negotiating with Soviet President Mikhail Gorbachev. He also had sent American troops to defend Kuwait from Iraq in what was called Operation Desert Shield. When it became clear that Saddam Hussein, Iraq's dictator, would not withdraw military forces from Kuwait, Bush sent enough troops to go on the offense. In January 1991, the bombing of Iraq began, and Operation Desert Shield became Operation Desert Storm. By February, Iraq was defeated.

At the same time, America's economy was in the midst of a recession. Since 1983, the economy had been thriving; this growth slowed in 1989 and 1990, and came to a halt in 1991. One result of this downturn was a rise in unemployment in 1992, an election year. These issues were disturbing enough to Americans that President George Bush's overseas victory was not enough to secure his reelection. Although Bush had an impressive 90 percent approval rating in popular polls in 1990, in 1992

Ian Holm (left) as Mitchell Stephens and Sarah Polley as Nichole Burnell in the 1997 film version of the novel

he lost the election (to Bill Clinton), getting only 37 percent of the popular vote.

Life in Rural Upstate New York

Banks depicts life in the fictitious town of Sam Dent, modeled after many of the rural communities in upstate New York. Context clues tell the reader that Sam Dent is near the Adirondack Mountains and Lake Placid. Life in this area can be very difficult because of harsh weather conditions, but the lifestyle is markedly slower than that of a busy city. In fact, people in such towns often perceive city life (especially New York City life) as something completely removed from their reality. Most residents have lived in the same town all their lives; in many cases their families have lived there for generations. The population consists mainly of families, with a limited number of single people. The result is a close-knit community of people who have known one another for years and who know many of one another's secrets. A strong sense of community results, and the members work together to prevent anything from threatening their secure world.

For entertainment, people often get together to go bowling or see a movie. High school sports are popular, and residents support their local athletes in football, baseball, and lacrosse. Many towns have an ongoing rivalry with a nearby town, which heightens the excitement of sports. While the winters are harsh, the summers invite a wide array of outdoor activities. There is generally a town square where people meet socially, and many men are members of organizations like The Rotary Club or The Lion's Club.

Economically, people in the rural towns on which Sam Dent is based are poor or middle-class. For some, their livelihood relies heavily on the thick forests, mountains, and lakes that provide food and materials for shelter. Industry is limited although there are lumber and mining (iron ore and zinc) companies, farms (dairy and corn), and a tourism industry. Most restaurants and stores are family owned.

Critical Overview

From tone to theme to style, critics applaud Banks's accomplishment in this novel.

Many find *The Sweet Hereafter* to be a moving novel about how tragedy affects individuals and a community. Michiko Kakutani of the *New York Times* finds that *The Sweet Hereafter* is "often gripping, consistently engaging, and from time to time genuinely affecting." In *Booklist,* Joanne Wilkinson describes the novel as "haunting" in its portrayal of grief and guilt.

Banks's ability to move in and out of different personae impresses critics, who find this style compelling and artful. They generally agree that this approach to the subject gives a true portrayal of the complicated reactions to tragedy. Kakutani observes that Banks's narrative technique "creates a mosaic-like study of the ways in which a community copes with tragedy."

Reviewers are drawn to Banks's realistic handling of the theme of accidents as unlucky and uncontrollable events that happen in people's lives. A critic for *Economist* commends Banks's ability to communicate "moral ambiguity," adding that by "examining the crash through the sometimes overlapping, sometimes conflicting, accounts of four people whose lives are utterly changed by it, the novel also ponders the wider damage such a disaster does."

Richard Eder of the *Los Angeles Times Book Review* finds Banks's novel to be a "remarkable book" that captures the response of a community in a time of unbelievable tragedy. Eder is impressed with Banks's compassionate portrayal of this community and the stories of its citizens.

Many critics comment on Banks's moving portrayal of a community in crisis. Eder commends Banks's use of "a small town's response to tragedy to write a novel of compelling moral suspense." Kakutani notes that "Banks uses the school bus accident as a catalyst for illuminating the lives of the town's citizens. It's as though he has cast a large stone into a quiet pond, then minutely charted the shape and size of the ripples sent out in successive waves." A reviewer for *Publishers Weekly* writes, "With resonating effect, Banks. . . tackles the provocative subject of a fatal accident involving children, and its effect on a small community." The reviewer adds that Banks handles this "dark theme" with compassion and control.

Most critics rank *The Sweet Hereafter* among Banks's best work, if not the best example to date of his fiction.

Criticism

Jennifer Bussey

Bussey holds a master's degree in interdisciplinary studies and a bachelor's degree in English literature. She is an independent writer specializing in literature. In the following essay, she evaluates Banks's novel, explaining why the small-town setting makes the book's tragedy more devastating to the fictional community—and, by extension, to readers—than it would be if it were set in a big city.

In *The Sweet Hereafter,* Russell Banks demonstrates how devastating the loss of fourteen children is to a small town. The author tells the tragic story of a school bus accident and its aftermath through the voices of four individual characters and portrays clearly the effects of this tragedy on the entire community of Sam Dent. While readers easily understand the grief felt by parents whose children die, the grief felt by the community as a whole may be less understandable. After all, tragic events like the bus accident are not terribly uncommon in modern life, and people who are not directly affected are sympathetic but do not usually feel the deep sense of loss felt by the people of Sam Dent. Clearly, something very important is at stake for the community of Sam Dent that is not at stake in larger American towns and cities. In examining the closeness of the community, the importance of the children as the future of the community, specific comments made by two of the narrators, and the ways in which people react to the tragedy, it becomes clear that the children's deaths actually jeopardize the future of Sam Dent.

Throughout the novel, Banks emphasizes the tight-knit nature of this small rural community. Dolores explains, "Sam Dent was our permanent lifelong community. We belonged to this town, we always had, and they to us; nothing could change that, I thought. It was like a true family." Sam Dent is a town whose residents have lived there all their lives; in many cases, their families have lived there for generations. Everyone knows everyone else; they know one another's families, histories, joys and pains, and status in the town. They accept one another, know what they can expect from one another, and in times of crisis they protect and support one another. As Dolores says, the community is a sort of extended family because everyone has personal feelings about everyone else, and they all go through their trials and tribulations together.

Under the most extreme circumstances, the people of Sam Dent remain protective of one another. Dolores's experience shows how the people respond when one of their own becomes a villain. Prior to Nichole's testimony, people are not sure how to treat Dolores, but they never resort to hate-

> " The children are important, not just to secure the future of their individual families, but to ensure that the small community will go on as it has for generations past."

ful or violent acts. In a larger town where people do not know one another, the residents are quicker to judge and to act on their judgment. Despite questions about Dolores's driving, the people know that she is well-meaning, kind, and loves the children of the town. Mitchell knows immediately that Dolores is not a good candidate to sue, not just because she has no money, but because the people of the town will not support suing her. In addition, he knows that a jury, like the people of Sam Dent, will see her as a victim of the accident rather than as a hardened criminal. After Nichole's testimony (that Dolores was speeding), the town holds Dolores responsible for the accident, yet she is not run out of town. When Nichole gives her damning testimony, she asks her father if anything will happen to Dolores, to which he responds, "Nobody wants to sue Dolores. She's one of us."

Not only is Dolores not sued, she is not even approached by anyone in the town. She only learns about the testimony when she runs into Billy at the demolition derby. The worst that happens to her is that she is socially snubbed. Granted, in this community, being a social outcast is a serious burden to bear, but Dolores has temporarily carried on with her life in Lake Placid while the town heals. The novel ends on a hopeful note for Dolores, who is slowly accepted by a few members of the community and resolves to stay in Sam Dent, regardless. What the reader learns from Dolores's experience is that she is right about the community being like a family. To many, she is responsible for the deaths of innocent children, yet the strength of the community is such that she is still considered an important member.

Within such a close community, the loss of fourteen children is tremendous; virtually every person in Sam Dent feels the grief because the children represent the future of the community itself.

The children are important, not just to secure the future of their individual families, but to ensure that the small community will go on as it has for generations past. In a larger town, people would receive the news as sad and unfair, but to a town like Sam Dent, the loss is personal for everyone. Billy states simply, "A town that loses its children loses its meaning." Certainly, he is also saying that his family has lost its meaning, but his emotional investment in the town enables him to comprehend that everyone in town has suffered a loss. People in the town, including Billy, refer to them as "our" children. Although he struggles to find a way to deal with the loss of his children—the last survivors of his immediate family—he simultaneously mourns the death of the other children. He comments that "when my son and daughter and so many other children of this town were killed in the accident, I could no longer believe in life." Standing before the bus, he says, "I don't know why I was there, staring with strange loathing and awe at this wrecked yellow vehicle, as if it were a beast that had killed our children and then in turn been slain by the villagers." As he looks at the bus, he imagines all the children inside, and remarks, "I wanted to be with them in death, with my children, yes, but with all of them, for they seemed at that moment so much more believable than myself was, so much more alive."

The town's sentiments are expressed by only two of the narrators, Dolores and Billy. Examining why the other two narrators are unable to comment about the loss in the same way lends additional insight into why the loss is so significant to the town. Mitchell never seems to understand the community's loss because he is an outsider. That he comes from a big city like New York, where terrible things happen to people every day, further distances him from being able to grasp the importance of this loss to this town. In New York, he might read about a tragedy in the newspaper and feel badly for the victims, but he is not personally affected by it. His frame of reference is too different from that of his clients to understand the full ramifications of the school bus accident. Nichole has an idea of the importance of the tragedy, but she herself is a child and thus lacks the scope that the adults have. She is a typical teenager who is caught up in her own immediate world of school, friends, and dances. While she loves Sam Dent, she is not yet old enough to appreciate its past and future. She is sympathetic to the families as individuals (for example, she feels deep sorrow for Billy), but she lacks the maturity to sympathize with the town as a whole.

In the last chapter, Dolores brings the loss of the children into sharper focus. She is a lifetime resident of the town and knew the children personally. She also understands the more abstract importance of the children as the future of the community. Clearly, she is haunted by the accident, and her own memories of that day, coupled with her resolve to stay in Sam Dent, outweigh the town's chilly reception of her and her husband. Even after Billy reveals what Nichole claimed in her testimony (that Dolores was driving over the speed limit), Dolores's feelings about the accident are anchored in her experience rather than in the town's misunderstanding of her role in it. She muses on the importance of children to the community:

> The accident had ruined a lot of lives. Or, to be exact, it had busted apart the structures on which those lives had depended—depended, I guess, to a greater degree than we had originally believed. A town needs its children for more than it thinks. . . . A town needs its children, just as much and in the same ways as a family does. It comes undone without them, turns a community into a windblown scattering of isolated individuals.

In the wake of such damage to a community, it is little wonder that some people choose to stay in denial and others choose to move to other towns. Sam Dent will never be the same, and for some residents that reality is unbearable. Billy, despite having lost his entire family, finds a way to stay in Sam Dent. His choice to drink excessively, however, indicates that his life is as permanently damaged as his community is. His choice to stay in a town that holds painful memories supports Dolores's comment that the community is like a family. Now a widower with no children, Billy stays with the only family he has left. Dolores is able to remain committed to the community, even if its future has become less secure. She is flexible enough to continue life in another town, but she does so without really becoming a member of the new community. She works there, eats there, and runs errands there, but she still lives in Sam Dent. She possesses the clarity to understand that her position in the town has changed, but she accepts this. She says:

> All of us—Nichole, I, the children who survived the accident, and the children who did not—it was as if we were the citizens of a wholly different town now, as if we were a town of solitaries living in a sweet hereafter, and no matter how the people of Sam Dent treated us, whether they memorialized us or despised us, whether they cheered for our destruction or ap-

What Do I Read Next?

- Banks's first critically acclaimed novel, *Continental Drift* (1985), is considered by many to be his most approachable novel. It is the story of Bob Dubois, who wants to create a better life for himself. In telling the story, Banks demonstrates how individual lives are deeply affected by unseen forces, such as the drifting of the continents.

- Pete Dexter's National Book Award-winning *Paris Trout* (1988) is the tragic story of the murder of a fourteen-year-old African-American girl in a small southern town. Dexter shows how this horrifying event affects the community and local race relations.

- William Faulkner's acclaimed *As I Lay Dying* (1930) uses the same narrative techniques that Banks uses in *The Sweet Hereafter*. It is the story of a poor southern family on a journey to take their mother's body to be buried.

- Robert Niemi's *Russell Banks* (1997) is an installment in the *Twayne's United States Authors Series,* which offers readers in-depth information about authors' backgrounds, careers, and works. Niemi's study also includes analysis of Banks's writings, including a discussion of his experimental efforts.

plauded our victory over adversity, they did it to meet their needs, not ours. Which, since it could be no other way, was exactly as it should be.

The town has lost fourteen of its children, and some residents have moved to other towns to begin new lives. Still, many residents, like Dolores, Billy, and Nichole, are committed to staying. The future of Sam Dent is uncertain, but there is hope that it will survive because of the residents who suffered from the accident yet are unwilling to give up on the future of their town, just as they would never give up on the future of their families.

Source: Jennifer Bussey, Critical Essay on *The Sweet Hereafter,* in *Novels for Students,* The Gale Group, 2002.

> " It is Russell Banks's last, best word on the subject: that not even art may be able to explain or redeem the unspeakable event that wrecked this town, but it can at least try."

Donna Rifkind

In the following review, Rifkind provides an overview of The Sweet Hereafter *and calls the story's final image "a heart-stopping passage."*

"Gritty", "muscular" and "vigorous" are the words most commonly used to characterize the writing of Russell Banks, whose blue-collar American tragedies have earned him big prizes and teaching positions in leading American universities. Much of the grit in Banks's work comes from autobiographical sources. The heroes of *Continental Drift* (1985) and *Affliction* (1989) hail from the same kind of wintry, disintegrating New Hampshire town in which he himself was brought up. His father, an alcoholic plumber, was surely a model for the abusive father in *Affliction.* And the seedier parts of Florida, where Banks lived for a time, serve as settings for *Continental Drift,* and for some of the short fiction in *Success Stories* (1986).

Banks's latest novel, *The Sweet Hereafter,* has no apparent autobiographical basis. The story, which is based on several real-life news items, begins in a snowstorm with a full school bus descending a hill in the fictional town of Sam Dent, in upstate New York. When the bus swerves, smashing through a guard rail and plunging into a sandpit filled with icy water, fourteen of the thirty-four children in the bus are killed.

Once one knows that this novel is going to be about dead children—and Banks doesn't waste any time making this clear—it is very difficult to keep reading. Yet the author's sympathetic imagining of the events following the accident is so skilful and complex that one is compelled to continue.

His technique is to provide a series of testimonies by the following characters: the bus driver, a woman of sterling character named Dolores Driscoll who sustained no physical injuries; Billy

Ansel, the father of two of the dead children; Mitchell Stephens, a slick New York City lawyer looking for a lawsuit; and one of the survivors, a beautiful fourteen-year-old cheerleader named Nichole Burnell whom the accident has left paralysed and wheelchair-bound.

The point of these testimonies is not to display discrepancies in shifting points of view. In fact, Banks's motive here is just the opposite. Each character takes up the action where the previous one left off, avoiding both corroboration and argument; the result is to make everyone appear more and more alone in their grief. "A town needs its children, just as much and in the same ways a family does", says Dolores Driscoll. "It comes undone without them, turns a community into a windblown scattering of isolated individuals."

This is precisely what happens in the months following the tragedy: marriages break apart, friends turn against each other, respected citizens retreat into perpetual drunkenness. As one of these, the former local hero Billy Ansel, comments: "it was as if we, too, had died when the bus went over the embankment and tumbled down into the frozen water-filled sandpit, and now we were lodged temporarily into a kind of purgatory, waiting to be moved to wherever the other dead ones had gone."

No healing or redemption seems possible here, partly because the town has no one to blame. Dolores, who had been driving the bus safely and responsibly for twenty years, is more or less beyond reproach (though some refuse to see it that way), and her anguish over the event leaves permanent emotional scars. The New York lawyer, after stirring up some initial support for a lawsuit, finally goes away disappointed, for the hard truth is that this catastrophe was villainless: it was a cruelly whimsical event, beyond control.

This fact, and Banks's subtle handling of it, are what lift the novel up out of ordinary gritty realism toward something approaching the sublime. After the bus crash, there are two communities in the town of Sam Dent, as Dolores notes at the novel's end: "All of us—Nichole, I, the children who survived the accident, and the children who did not—it was as if we were the citizens of a wholly different town now, as if we were a town of solitaries living in a sweet hereafter, and no matter how the people of Sam Dent treated us, whether they memorialized us or despised us, whether they cheered for our destruction or applauded our victory over adversity, they did it to meet their needs, not ours."

The book's final image, of a county fair seen from a distance, manages to unite these two sets of citizens in a heart-stopping passage, one that reaches for the same painful beauty as the end of Joyce's "The Dead" or parts of Thornton Wilder's *Our Town.* It is Russell Banks's last, best word on the subject: that not even art may be able to explain or redeem the unspeakable event that wrecked this town, but it can at least try.

Source: Donna Rifkind, "A Town Divided," in *Times Literary Supplement,* April 17, 1992, p. 20.

Chuck Wachtel

In the following review, Wachtel compares elements of The Sweet Hereafter *to Banks's other novels, asserting that Banks "brings his passionate and profoundly exact craft to bear."*

Because *The Sweet Hereafter* is smaller in both scope and page count than *Continental Drift* and *Affliction,* Russell Banks's last two novels, it offers an opportunity to see more easily what is central to the power and importance in his work: the ability to write about ordinary people (most of us) without accepting much apparent guidance or influence from the existing literary manners of doing so, or from the common assumptions of our times.

If not for the effects of the failing national economy, the tentacles of mass media and the upscale vacationers who drive north from the city, the small, upstate New York town of Sam Dent, setting of *The Sweet Hereafter,* would otherwise remain isolated in its own particular late-twentieth-century solitude. On a recent winter morning a schoolbus skids off the road, tumbles down an embankment and into a water-filled sand pit. Fourteen of the town's children are killed. The fabric of order in Sam Dent is suddenly torn apart. The novel does not present this in public acts of mourning or violence; there are few overt acts of vengeance or compensation. Rather, we experience the horror, the uncontainable pain, in the voices of the novel's four narrators, who in the aftermath of the accident present to us not only themselves and the facts as they know them; they also present to us the mysterious and inevitable continuance of their lives.

For the most part, their stories remain inside the perimeters of local, more immediate circumstances. As they tell those stories, increasing our access to their inner lives, the characters do not readily give themselves over to larger, universalizing proportions: We must first experience them in their own terms—their ordinary moments, their revelations—before we respond with the secondary wave of *our* understanding. Lionel Trilling has given us a still very serviceable phrase for what realism in fiction does, or should do: *reveal the human fact in the veil of circumstance.* Central to the power of nearly all of Banks's work is that he is first influenced by his subject matter, the people he writes about. In their context the larger issues become less abstracted, less the possession of idea—more theirs, more ours.

Early in *Continental Drift* (1985), for example, its two main characters, a New Hampshire furnace repairman and a poor, young Haitian woman, escape the lives they were born to and begin separate, haphazard, perilous migrations toward more viable, safer, more comprehendable [sic] lives. Although the narration remains centered in the movements of these two characters, it expands in size to encompass the unnavigated drift that seems to be so much of life at the end of this half-millennium we might remember as Columbian America. *Affliction* (1989), set in New Hampshire, is the story of the events leading up to a murder and the disappearance of the man who commits it. It is also a story about the legacy of male anger—from its untraceable beginnings in a time long before the world that this novel occurs in was ever dreamed of—and its effects on family, community and the culture at large. If it is possible for writers to contain such vast thematic centers in their stories, and if readers are still willing even to attempt to accept delivery of them—in short, if this is to work at all—what is needed is precisely what Banks provides: characters who can be perceived as wholly separate from the conditions their stories make manifest.

As Dolores Driscoll, the bus driver and narrator of the first and last of *The Sweet Hereafter*'s five sections, begins telling her story, the circumstances begin to narrow, to close in around her like a reversal of the circular eddies caused by a stone dropped in water. Dolores has driven the children of Sam Dent to school since 1968, when the bus was her own Dodge station wagon and her own two sons were among the passengers. In the nearly two decades that follow, her husband and companion, Abbott, becomes confined to a wheelchair due to a stroke, making her driver's income the household income; her sons grow up and move on; and the station wagon, which she and the children had named Boomer, is replaced first by a GMC twenty-four seater and, in 1987, "to handle the baby boomers' babies, I'd guess you'd call them, the district had to get me the International fifty-seater."

"

Although things will never be the same, its inhabitants have touched, perhaps only briefly, some source of their collective lives."

The second narrator, Billy Ansel, is already widowed when the accident occurs, taking the lives of his two children. A Vietnam vet, owner of a garage, he is a man possessed of a quiet and isolate integrity. He tells us that people who have lost their children "twist themselves into all kinds of weird shapes in order to deny what has happened. Not because of the pain of losing a person they loved—we lose parents and mates and friends, and no matter how painful, it's not the same—but because what has happened is so wickedly unnatural, so profoundly against the necessary order of things, that we cannot accept it."

Mitchell Stephens, Esq., a lawyer who comes up from New York City hoping to represent the families and survivors, is the book's third narrator. Angry, sophisticated, observant, he provides an outsider's view of the other characters and of Sam Dent. In telling us of his own life, particularly as the father of a hopelessly drug-addicted daughter, he places the novel, the accident itself, in the larger, darker context of our times. He tells us we are all losing our children: "I don't know if it was the Vietnam war, or the sexual colonization of kids by industry, or drugs, or TV, or divorce, or what the hell it was; I don't know what are causes and what are effects; but the children are gone. . . So that trying to protect them is little more than an exercise in denial."

Young Nichole Burnell, a survivor of the accident, has already been forcibly extracted from the fabric of her teenage life by her father, who victimizes her through incest. Outwardly a pretty, popular eighth grader, she lives isolated in an inexpressible silence. The accident, condemning her to a wheelchair for life, completes the process: When we meet her all the connections—to family and friends, to the series of events she had expected to carry her into the future—have already been sev-

ered. Nichole is the book's fourth narrator, both a child and a prophet. Hers is perhaps the deepest, clearest view we get into the inner life of Sam Dent.

As readers, caught up in the life of the novel, we make a leap from our burdened and mysterious real lives to something we perceive in the heart of its characters. We seek, and perhaps find, a kind of communion with something larger. Yet since a character is, after all, simply a construct of crafted language, most of what we find there, as in a dream, has to have been ours in the first place. What we seek is ourselves. Yet the life we live and the lives we read about in so many contemporary novels seem to have less and less in common.

In explaining why the storyteller has become a thing of the past, Walter Benjamin told us, "One reason for this phenomenon is obvious: experience has fallen in value." Since he wrote this, the trend has accelerated. Even the complex technologies of fiction we've been steadily evolving since Chekhov cannot keep apace of this devaluation. I see in much of Banks's work a refusal to find this acceptable. Whether vast or local in scope, the foundation for his fiction is experience in its most familiar and simultaneously mysterious circumstance: as we know it, *be* it, before it is crafted into the larger, rarefied context of fictional narrative. We can find it there.

This realism exemplified by Russell Banks is both old-fashioned and new. New because his characters feel as if he first discovered them outside of fiction, not from pre-existing literary or cultural models. Old-fashioned because his work is dedicated to what Cynthia Ozick has called (in a wonderful brief essay, "A Short Note on 'Chekhovian'") "explicit and definitive portraiture and the muscular trajectory of whole lives."

In the final section of *The Sweet Hereafter,* Dolores Driscoll is watching the demolition derby at the Sam Dent County Fair. The town has shunned her since the accident six months ago. On one side of her, her husband sits in his wheelchair; on the other is Billy Ansel, drunk, the state he has most often been in since the accident. Boomer, now the possession of one of the town's young men, is one of the entries. The crowd cheers each time Boomer is hit. The other drivers, understanding the town's desire to punish the car, to punish Dolores, attack with fury. Even so, the old car prevails. As, one by one, the other cars are eliminated and the process intensifies, the crowd begins chanting "Boomer! Boomer!" The whole town has crossed an invisible border. Although things will never be the same, its inhabitants have touched, perhaps only briefly, some source of their collective lives, one that was there before the accident and, through this time of grief and anger, has somehow remained intact. There is, however, no consolation for Dolores Driscoll, no going back:

> Nichole, I, the children who survived the accident, and the children who did not—it was as if we were the citizens of a wholly different town now, as if we were a town of solitaries living in a sweet hereafter, and no matter how the people of Sam Dent treated us, whether they memorialized us or despised us, whether they cheered for our destruction or applauded our victory over adversity, they did it to meet their needs, not ours. Which, since it could be no other way, was exactly as it should be.

The book's narrative does not go beyond this dark, grim time in the life of its characters, yet it offers us a healing clarity. I think this is because these characters, or the human facts they represent outside of fiction, are the first measure of the story's size and shape. And it seems only after taking that initial measurement that Russell Banks, in *The Sweet Hereafter,* brings his passionate and profoundly exact craft to bear.

Source: Chuck Wachtel, "Character Witness," in *Nation,* Vol. 253, No. 21, December 16, 1991, pp. 786–88.

Sources

Desy, Peter, "Banks, Russell (Earl)" in *Contemporary Novelists,* 6th ed., St. James Press, 1996, pp. 72–73.

Eder, Richard, Review of *The Sweet Hereafter,* in *Los Angeles Times Book Review,* September 1, 1991, p. 3.

Frumkes, Lewis Burke, Interview, in *Writer,* Vol. 111, No. 8, August 1998, p. 18.

Kakutani, Michiko, "Books of the Times: Small-Town Life after a Huge Calamity," in *New York Times,* September 6, 1991.

Review of *The Sweet Hereafter,* in *Economist,* Vol. 321, No. 7729, October 19, 1991, p. 104.

Review of *The Sweet Hereafter,* in *Publishers Weekly,* Vol. 238, No. 26, September 1991, p. 47.

Rubel, David, ed., *The Reading List, Contemporary Fiction: A Critical Guide to the Complete Works of 110 Authors,* Henry Holt and Company, 1998.

Wilkinson, Joanne, Review of *The Sweet Hereafter,* in *Booklist,* June 1, 2000.

Further Reading

Banks, Russell, *Affliction,* Harper, 1990.
> Considered one of Banks's most important novels, *Affliction* tells the story of Wade Whitehouse, a divorced man who lives in a trailer, drinks, and succeeds only in alienating his daughter. By delving into Whitehouse's personal history, Banks shows how the pain in his past destroys his present. *Affliction* was adapted to a film of the same title in 1998.

———, *The Angel on the Roof: The Stories of Russell Banks,* Harper, 2000.
> This volume collects thirty-seven years of short fiction by Russell Banks. Although some characters appear in more than one story, this collection is not meant to be a broad view of a single setting, as in Banks's *Trailerpark.*

———, *Trailerpark,* Houghton, 1981.
> This collection of short fiction introduces the reader to the various members of Granite State Trailerpark. The inhabitants are a colorful cast of characters whose eccentricities, trials, joys, and pains are told by Banks through a series of related short stories.

Meanor, Patrick, ed., *Dictionary of Literary Biography,* Volume 130: *American Short-Story Writers Since World War II,* Gale Research, 1993, pp. 22–27.
> The Banks entry in this volume reviews the author's short-story publications, from his earliest work to his more recent award-winning short fiction. Banks's work is considered in relation to his personal background, as well as other important contextual factors.

Vanity Fair

William Thackeray

1847–1848

Vanity Fair: A Novel without a Hero, the first major work published by William Thackeray under his own name, was published serially in London in 1847 and 1848. Previously, under various comic pseudonyms (such as Michael Angelo Titmarsh and George Savage Fitzboodle) Thackeray made clear, both in his role as the narrator of *Vanity Fair* and in his private correspondence about the book, that he meant it to be not just entertaining, but instructive. Like all satire, *Vanity Fair* has a mission and a moral. The first published installment had an illustration on its cover of a congregation listening to a preacher; both speaker and listeners were shown with donkey ears. In the pages, Thackeray explains the illustration thus:

> my kind reader will please to remember that these histories. . . . have "Vanity Fair" for a title and that Vanity Fair is a very vain, wicked, foolish place, full of all sorts of humbugs and falseness and pretentions. And while the moralist who is holding forth on the cover (an accurate portrait of your humble servant) professes to wear neither gown nor bands, but only the very same long-eared livery in which his congregation is arrayed: yet, look you, one is bound to speak the truth as far as one knows it.

> That Becky is allowed to live, and to live well, is perfectly consistent with Thackeray's view of life and morality. . . . Losing is vanity, and winning is vanity.

By the halfway point in its serial publication, Thackeray's long, rambling tale of relentless and corrupt social climbing, told with biting humor and cynicism, was the talk of London. Readers eagerly

awaited new episodes in the life of Thackeray's deeply immoral, self-serving anti-heroine, Becky Sharp, who has since become one of the most well-known and most argued-about characters in literature. The novel secured Thackeray's place among the literary giants of his time; and the giants of his time, among them Charles Dickens, the Brontë sisters, Thomas Hardy, and Alfred Tennyson, have endured as giants to this day. *Vanity Fair* is considered a classic of English literature and one of the great works of satire in all history.

Author Biography

William Makepeace Thackeray was born in Calcutta, India, on July 18, 1811, the only child of English parents. His father, Richmond, worked for the East India Company until he died four years after William's birth.

At the age of six, William was sent to a boarding school in England while his mother, Anne Becher Thackeray, remained in India. Unsurprisingly, the young child was lonely and unhappy. In 1819, his mother remarried and returned to England where she and her new husband were able to give him the family life for which he longed.

Thackeray attended Charterhouse School and went on to Cambridge University's Trinity College but did not earn a degree. He studied art in Paris and later illustrated many of his written works, including *Vanity Fair.* It was in Paris that Thackeray met and married Isabella Shawe, an Irish woman. They soon moved back to London where Thackeray launched his writing career. He wrote for magazines, including the famous humor magazine *Punch.*

Isabella Thackeray suffered from mental illness after the birth of the couple's third child. After many failed attempts to cure her, Thackeray was forced, in 1842, to send his wife away to be cared for. Unable to rear his young daughters alone, he was separated from them, as well. The loneliness and separation from family that had been so difficult for Thackeray as a child were no less painful for him as a grown man. Because his wife was alive (in fact, she outlived him by many years) and divorce was not an option, Thackeray never remarried.

The first work Thackeray published under his own name was *Vanity Fair,* a long, sprawling satire that was published in four installments in 1847 and

William Makepeace Thackeray

1848. It remains among his most well-known novels, along with *The Luck of Barry Lyndon: A Romance of the Last Century* (later published as *The Memoirs of Barry Lyndon*) and *The Virginians: A Tale of the Last Century,* inspired by Thackeray's travels in the United States in 1852–1853 and 1855–1856.

Thackeray was prolific, writing short fiction and nonfiction as well as novels. By the end of his life, he had achieved both critical and financial success. In addition, he had the joy of having his mother and two of his daughters living with him and of seeing daughter Anne recognized as a successful writer. Thackeray died at his London home on Christmas Eve in 1863.

Plot Summary

Chapters 1–7

As *Vanity Fair* opens, Amelia Sedley, a conventional girl from a well-to-do family, and Becky Sharp, Sedley's orphaned, penniless, and already corrupt friend, are leaving Miss Pinkerton's school where they have met and become friends. They go to the Sedley home where Becky will be a guest until she goes on to the governess position that Miss Pinkerton has arranged for her.

Becky meets Amelia's older brother, Joseph, called Jos, who is on leave from his government post in India. Although Jos is fat, lazy, conceited, and shy with women, he is also financially well off, and Becky schemes to marry him. Through flattery and false modesty, Becky succeeds in making all the Sedleys believe that she truly is enamored of Jos, and Jos is inclined to propose to her. George Osborne, Amelia's fiancé, intervenes, persuading Jos that he has embarrassed himself in Becky's presence. George does not want a governess for a sister-in-law. Defeated, Becky leaves for the Crawley estate where she is to be governess.

Chapters 8–14

The mean-spirited and stingy Sir Pitt Crawley is the patriarch of Queen's Crawley where Becky takes up her post as governess to his two young daughters, Rosalind and Violet. Sir Pitt also has two much older sons by his first wife. The elder, also named Pitt, is pious and proper to an extreme. The younger, Rawdon, is a dandy and a gambler. The two despise each other.

The irreverent and debt-ridden Reverend Bute Crawley, Sir Pitt's brother, and his nosy, overbearing wife come on the scene. Sir Pitt and Bute also hate each other. The family members are united only in their desire to see their wealthy, old Aunt Matilda dead, and they all connive to inherit her fortune.

George is disrespectful of Amelia in the presence of his army comrades, for which his longtime friend William Dobbin berates him. Physically awkward but highly virtuous, Dobbin has loved Amelia since youth but considers himself unworthy of her. George's father, who has long encouraged George to marry Amelia, now suspects that her family has lost its money and wants George to break the engagement. The self-serving George is willing to do so.

Becky has charmed Aunt Matilda and, at the old lady's request, has moved to her home to nurse her. Rawdon is smitten with Becky and spends as much time with her as he can.

Sir Pitt's wife, Lady Crawley, dies, and immediately Sir Pitt asks Becky to marry him. Here, Becky cries the only genuine tears of her life because she must reject the wealthy Sir Pitt, having secretly married Rawdon. Sir Pitt and old Aunt Matilda are both enraged at this news.

Chapters 15–22

Becky and Rawdon go on a honeymoon, and Mrs. Bute Crawley descends on Aunt Matilda, hoping to turn her against Rawdon and secure her fortune for herself and her husband. Then the Sedleys' possessions are sold at an estate sale; the family's financial ruin, due to Mr. Sedley's unwise business speculation, is complete and public. In the meantime, against the wishes of both their fathers, George and Amelia marry. Next, everyone meets in Brighton where Dobbin announces that the men have been ordered to go to Belgium where the First Duke of Wellington, the British general who is commanding a multinational army, plans to launch an attack on Napoleon's army.

Chapters 23–35

The peace-loving, selfless Dobbin tries to get George's father to accept George's marriage to Amelia, but Mr. Osborne instead disinherits George. George blames Dobbin because it was Dobbin who encouraged him to marry Amelia.

Mrs. Bute Crawley is forced to leave Aunt Matilda when the reverend is injured and needs her at home. Becky and Rawdon then try to move in on the old woman, ostensibly to take over her care, but she is wise to their designs on her money.

Everyone goes to Belgium. The men, except Jos, are in military service; Jos and the women accompany them. George and Becky flirt shamelessly, and Amelia is too blind to understand why she is heartsick. George finally passes Becky a mysterious note and then, remorseful, tries to make up with Amelia.

General and Mrs. O'Dowd, the regiment commander and his wife, prepare for the battle. Mrs. O'Dowd, accustomed to sending her husband into battle, mothers the younger women and pursues her goal of finding a husband for the general's sister. Rawdon is distressed at leaving Becky; George is relieved at leaving Amelia.

The battle begins; the women can hear the cannons booming in the distance. Amelia is worried sick for George while Becky fantasizes about her prospects to better herself if Rawdon is killed. In fact, it is George who dies in the Battle of Waterloo.

Back in England, Sir Pitt has taken up with Miss Horrocks, his butler's daughter, scandalizing the family. Young Pitt courts Lady Jane Sheepshanks, and the sweet, kind Lady Jane in turn wins the affection of Aunt Matilda.

Both Becky and Amelia give birth to sons. Dobbin tries to comfort Amelia as she grieves for George.

Chapters 36–42

Becky and Rawdon manage to live well on very little money. Becky is an expert at avoiding paying her bills. Rawdon makes a little money gambling. They lease a house from Mr. Raggles, a former servant of the Crawleys but cannot pay the rent. In turn, Raggles is unable to pay his bills and is sent to debtors' prison.

Aunt Matilda dies, young Sir Pitt inherits her wealth, and Becky and Rawdon try to ingratiate themselves with the heir. Becky ignores her son, little Rawdon, but his father loves him. Dobbin gives Amelia much-needed money, saying it was left to her by George. Jos returns to India.

Sir Pitt becomes ill, lingers for a time, and then dies. Young Sir Pitt takes over Queen's Crawley and sends for Becky and Rawdon in a gesture of family unity.

Chapters 43–50

Dobbin is in India with his regiment when he hears a false rumor that Amelia is going to get married. He requests leave to go to England.

Becky and Rawdon go to Queen's Crawley for Christmas where Becky fawns over everyone who has status or money, especially the young Sir Pitt.

The Sedley family is sinking further into poverty. The Osbornes—George's father and sisters—want George's son Georgy to come live with them and offer Amelia money if she will give him up. After some delay, Amelia agrees to this so that Georgy is not reared in poverty.

Lord Steyne, with whom Becky has a vaguely explained and profitable relationship, arranges for Becky to be presented at court—the successful culmination of all her social climbing. She appears draped in expensive jewels; unbeknownst to Rawdon, these are gifts from Lord Steyne. This begins a period of social triumph for Becky.

Chapters 51–56

Lord Steyne sends little Rawdon away to school, which pleases Becky, who cannot be bothered with him. Rawdon, long ignored by his wife, is jailed for failing to pay a debt. Becky is slow to answer his message asking her to have him released so he contacts Sir Pitt and Lady Jane. Lady Jane arrives without delay to free him. At home, Rawdon finds Becky entertaining Lord Steyne. He at-

tacks Lord Steyne—he hurls a diamond pin at his forehead, leaving Lord Steyne scarred—and goes through Becky's belongings and finds her stash of money and jewelry. Both Rawdon and Lord Steyne abandon Becky, and they plan to duel.

Becky pleads with Sir Pitt to help her reconcile with Rawdon, and he agrees to try. Lord Steyne's man, Wenham, uses diplomacy to prevent the duel. Rawdon takes a post on Coventry Island, a remote place from which he sends money for Becky and his son. Sir Pitt and Lady Jane look after little Rawdon.

Chapters 57–67

Dobbin and Jos return to England from India; Dobbin's return has been delayed by a serious illness. Dobbin goes to see Amelia and is relieved to find that she has not married. Finally, he divulges that he has long loved her, but she continues to think only of George. Dobbin spends time with little Georgy and improves the boy's character while Jos belatedly helps his family financially.

Old Mr. Osborne dies, leaving half his money to Georgy and also leaving some money for Amelia. Jos, Amelia, Georgy, and Dobbin go to Europe. Becky, who has been wandering around Europe since losing Rawdon and Lord Steyne, meets up with them and renews her pursuit of Jos. After warning Jos that Becky is dangerous, Dobbin leaves to rejoin his regiment.

Becky reveals to Amelia the contents of the mysterious note that George gave her on the eve of his death at Waterloo: George urged Becky to run away with him. Amelia finally has some understanding of George's true character. She sends for Dobbin, he returns, and they marry immediately.

Becky continues to ensnare Jos and talks him into taking out a life insurance policy with her as beneficiary. Within months, he dies of poisoning. Becky's role in his death is left unclear. Rawdon then dies on Coventry Island of yellow fever. Sir Pitt dies, and little Rawdon inherits Queen's Crawley. Amelia and Dobbin are happy together and have a daughter.

Becky lives comfortably in Europe on the money from Jos's insurance policy and on an allowance sent to her by her son (who nevertheless refuses to see her). She becomes a churchgoer and gives generously to charity.

Characters

Mrs. Blenkinsop

The Sedleys' housekeeper, Mrs. Blenkinsop is loyal enough to stay with the family when they lose their money. She is also Amelia's trusted confidant.

Miss Briggs

Briggs is at first a maid for Miss Matilda Crawley and later a companion to Becky Sharp. She is good-hearted and naïve enough to loan money to Becky, which Becky, predictably, does not repay. Lord Steyne ends up providing for Miss Briggs.

Frederick Bullock

Frederick, a lawyer, is Maria Osborne's suitor and eventual husband. When Maria's brother George is disinherited, Frederick does not hide his pleasure that Maria is now likely to receive a larger share of the family's money.

Mary Clapp

The daughter of Mr. and Mrs. Clapp, the Sedleys' landlords after they lose their money, Mary becomes Amelia's friend.

Mr. Clapp

Mr. Clapp is the Sedleys' longtime clerk, who takes the family in when they lose their fortune.

Mrs. Clapp

The Sedleys' landlady, Mrs. Clapp, nags Amelia about the rent when the family has fallen on hard times, but she changes her attitude when Amelia comes into money.

Bute Crawley

The brother of Sir Pitt Crawley, Bute is a reverend who is ill-suited to his position. He likes to eat, drink, and gamble (and therefore is in debt) and is happy to let his wife run their household and write his sermons. Like all the Crawleys, he hopes to inherit a substantial amount of money from old Aunt Matilda Crawley.

Mrs. Bute Crawley

The reverend's wife is overbearing, snooty, manipulative, and determined to win Aunt Matilda's fortune. She dislikes Becky Sharp, whom she recognizes as a smart and ambitious competitor. In the end, Mrs. Crawley fails to secure Aunt Matilda's money.

James Crawley

The son of Bute and Mrs. Crawley, James nearly charms Aunt Matilda into leaving him her money. When she discovers that he is a heavy drinker and catches him smoking in her house, he falls from grace and loses his chance at the inheritance.

Miss Matilda Crawley

Miss Crawley, Sir Pitt Crawley's half-sister, is old, unmarried, eccentric, and rich. The entire Crawley clan connives to get their hands on her fortune, and she is well aware of this. She is at first inclined to favor Rawdon, but he loses out when he marries Becky; Miss Crawley disapproves of the union because of Becky's low social standing. Although she dislikes Pitt (mostly for his extreme piety), in the end, Pitt's wife, Lady Jane, wins the old lady's affection through genuine kindness, and Pitt and Lady Jane end up with most of Miss Crawley's fortune.

Pitt Crawley

Pitt is the older son of Sir Pitt Crawley. He is overly pious, proper to a fault, and stingy. It is mostly due to his marriage to the sweet and kind Lady Jane that Pitt ends up with his aunt's fortune. His seat in Parliament is also inherited, and not won by any personal merit. However, Pitt does have some redeeming qualities. He welcomes Rawdon and Becky into the family, and when they split up, Pitt offers his brother kindness and takes care of their son (also named Rawdon).

Sir Pitt Crawley

Sir Pitt is a wealthy nobleman who is nevertheless uneducated, unrefined, unkempt, uncouth, and a penny pincher in the extreme. He has two sons, Pitt and Rawdon, by his deceased first wife, and two young daughters, Rosalind and Violet, by his second wife, Rose. Becky comes to his country estate, Queen's Crawley, to be governess to his girls. When Rose dies, Sir Pitt proposes to Becky (he likes her spunk), who must refuse him because she has secretly married Rawdon. Sir Pitt then turns his affections to his butler's daughter, Miss Horrocks, which horrifies his family. He dies and leaves his fortune, along with his noble title of baronet, to his elder son, Pitt.

Rawdon Crawley

Rawdon is the younger son of Sir Pitt Crawley and, eventually, the husband of Becky Sharp. When he is kicked out of Cambridge University, his aunt, Miss Matilda Crawley, who favors him until he marries Becky, buys him a commission in the Life Guards Green. Although somewhat dull-witted himself, Rawdon is a gambler who takes advantage of less clever men whenever he can and helps support himself and Becky in this way. He truly loves Becky and puts up with her increasing neglect and disregard for him. It is too much for him, however, when he is imprisoned for debt, and it is Lady Jane, not Becky, who comes to free him. Rawdon goes home to find Becky with Lord Steyne and finally leaves her. He takes a position on a far-away tropical island, Coventry Island, from which he sends money for Becky and their son. Eventually, he dies of yellow fever on the island.

Rawdy Crawley

Rawdy is the son of Becky and Rawdon. Although his father loves him, Becky shows no love or affection for him and sends him away to school under the auspices of Lord Steyne. Pitt and Lady Jane take care of him after his parents part ways, and Rawdy inherits Queen's Crawley when Pitt dies. Although he will not see her, he provides for Becky in spite of her ill treatment of him.

Miss Rosalind Crawley

Rosalind is the daughter of Sir Pitt by his second wife and Becky's charge when Becky comes to Queen's Crawley.

Miss Violet Crawley

Violet is the daughter of Sir Pitt by his second wife and Becky's charge when Becky comes to Queen's Crawley.

William Dobbin

Dobbin is the only truly noble character in Vanity Fair. He has few outward virtues—he is awkward and unattractive—and has little money; but he is selfless, loyal, kind, truthful, and generous. He spends his life providing support and service to undeserving and ungrateful friends, among whom the closest are George Osborne and Amelia Sedley. Although Dobbin loves Amelia, he feels that he is not a good enough match for her and so goes out of his way to ensure that George marries her. His dogged devotion to Amelia is finally rewarded when Amelia marries him long after George has died. In the end, however, Dobbin realizes that Amelia was never worthy of him or of the kind of love he has shown her.

Media Adaptations

- Unabridged audio versions of *Vanity Fair* have been published by Audiobook Contractors (1987), Books on Tape, Inc. (1989), and Blackstone Audio Books (1999, in two parts, with Frederick Davidson as the reader). Abridged versions have been published by Highbridge Co. (1997, with Timothy West as the reader), Naxos Audio Books (1997, with Jane Lapotaire as the reader), and HarperCollins (1999, with Miriam Margolyes as the reader).

- Films were made of *Vanity Fair* in 1911, 1915, 1922, 1923, 1932. The 1932 movie was directed by Chester M. Franklin, written by F. Hugh Herbert, and starred Myrna Loy as Becky Sharp. A new film is in production with Janette Day as the producer and scriptwriters Matthew Faulk and Mark Street.

- *Vanity Fair* was made into a television miniseries in 1971, 1987, and 1998. The 1971 version, directed by David Giles III and written by Rex Tucker, is available on videotape. The 1987 version was directed by Diarmuid Lawrence and Michael Owen Morris and written by Alexander Baron. The 1998 version was directed by Marc Munden and written by Andrew Davies, and starred Natasha Little as Becky Sharp. It also is available on videotape.

Horrocks

Horrocks is Sir Pitt's butler.

John

The Sedley's groom, John drives Becky to Sir Pitt's home after her visit with the Sedleys. John is rude to Becky, chiefly because Amelia has given her some clothes that John hoped to have for his girlfriend.

Glorvina Mahoney

Peggy O'Dowd's flirtatious sister, Glorvina pursues William Dobbin, who is too fixated on Amelia to show any interest.

Colonel Michael O'Dowd

The Colonel is George Osborne and William Dobbin's commanding officer, a brave, experienced soldier who becomes a major general. He has an amiable relationship with his wife.

Peggy O'Dowd

The Colonel's wife is Irish, talkative, and genuinely kind. Her primary goal is to make a match for her sister, Glorvina.

George Osborne

George has longstanding relationships with the Sedley family and with Dobbin. He is a good-looking, self-centered, prideful, free-spending, gambler. He has a certain amount of wealth but not nobility, and he courts the favor of all aristocrats who cross his path. It is George who ruins Becky's hopes of marrying Joseph Sedley by convincing Joseph that it would be inappropriate for him to marry a governess. George does this not out of concern for Joseph but because he is engaged to marry Joseph's sister, Amelia, and does not want a governess in the family.

While Amelia loves George, George is incapable of loving anyone as much as he loves himself. He nearly backs out of marrying Amelia (his father is against the union and in fact disinherits George over it), but Dobbin persuades him to go through with it. Then, just before going off to the Battle of Waterloo, George flirts with Becky and passes her a mysterious note. George is killed in the battle, and Amelia grieves deeply. She doesn't find out until many years later that George's note to Becky suggested that the two of them run away together.

Georgy Osborne

Georgy is the son of George and Amelia. His father dies before he is born. Although he is spoiled by his mother and seems destined to grow up to be even more selfish and vain than his father, Dobbin influences him for the better. His grandfather leaves Georgy half the family fortune, in spite of having disinherited his father, George, over George's marriage to Amelia.

Jane Osborne

One of George's sisters, Jane is a lonely, unmarried woman whose life is considerably uplifted when young Georgy comes to live at the Osborne family home.

Old John Osborne

Father of George, John is a mean, calculating, unforgiving man. He has encouraged George to love and marry Amelia throughout his son's youth, but when the Sedley family loses its fortune, John orders George to give Amelia up. When George refuses, John disowns and disinherits him and refuses to have anything to do with Amelia. After George's death, the old man remains hard toward Amelia but wants to rear his grandson, to which Amelia finally agrees. In part because of Dobbin's efforts, John mellows somewhat in his old age. He comes to love Georgy and not only leaves a substantial amount of money to his grandson, but also provides for Amelia.

Maria Osborne

One of John Osborne's three daughters, Maria is rather like her father. She welcomes her brother's disinheritance because it means more of the family fortune for her, and she marries a lawyer who is equally cold and calculating. When her father leaves Georgy and Amelia money, Maria plots to have one of her daughters marry Georgy so that she can control more of the family money.

Miss Barbara Pinkerton

Miss Pinkerton owns the academy where Amelia Sedley and Becky Sharp meet and become friends. Miss Pinkerton dotes on Amelia because her family has money and hates Becky as much for her poverty as for her churlish attitude.

Charles Raggles

Raggles works as a gardener for the Crawleys and saves his money until he is able to buy a green-grocer shop and house of his own. Becky and Rawdon come to be his tenants but do not pay their rent. They cheat him until finally they have ruined him, and Raggles ends up in debtors' prison.

Amelia Sedley

Amelia is the daughter of John Sedley, a businessman who is successful and moneyed as the novel opens. She is sweet, kind, malleable, naïve, and shallow.

Amelia's love for George Osborne is blind love. On the eve of the Battle of Waterloo, as George flirts with Becky, Amelia is deeply distraught at George's imminent departure for the battle. George is handsome, and Amelia doesn't see beneath the surface to the ugliness underneath, any more than she sees the nobility beneath Dobbin's unattractive appearance. Even after George's death, she remains as unaware of his lack of integrity and devotion as she is of William Dobbin's love for her.

Amelia is a loving mother to Georgy, the son born to her after George's death. She finally marries Dobbin but only after Becky awakens her to his virtue.

John Sedley

Father of Amelia and Joseph, John Sedley is, when the novel begins, a well-to-do merchant and a friend of John Osborne. Sedley is amenable to Becky's plot to marry Joseph, as he fears that the alternative will be an Indian woman; Joseph is on leave from his government post in India. Sedley takes unwise business risks in an effort to increase his wealth but instead loses everything. The family is forced to rent a lowly cottage owned by one of their former servants. Sedley then spends his time concocting schemes to regain his wealth, but he dies penniless.

Mrs. John Sedley

John Sedley's wife is sweet-tempered and loyal like her daughter, Amelia, but her good nature gradually is ground down by the family's ongoing poverty. Amelia takes care of her during her last illness.

Joseph Sedley

Joseph is Amelia's older brother. He loves nothing more than food, drink, and sleep. His father tells his mother, "if you and I and his sister were to die tomorrow, he would say, 'Good Gad!' and eat his dinner just as well as usual." He is fat and cowardly, yet conceited and a dandy. At Waterloo, he goes no nearer the battlefield than the women do and still shakes with fear, and yet he later tells such tales of his courage that he is given the nickname "Waterloo Sedley." He believes that Becky is genuinely attracted to him, when her only real interest is in his money, and plans to propose to her until George dissuades him. When his father goes bankrupt, Joseph sends only a little money and is tardy even with that.

Joseph meets Becky in Europe after her husband has left her, and she charms him just as she had years earlier. Joseph and Becky travel together, but Joseph confides to Dobbin that he is frightened of Becky. Joseph soon dies of poisoning, and it is left unclear whether Becky has murdered him for his only remaining asset, an insurance policy whose proceeds are split between Becky and Amelia.

Becky Sharp

See Rebecca Sharp

Rebecca Sharp

Becky Sharp is the central character in *Vanity Fair* and Amelia Sedley's opposite. She is the orphaned daughter of destitute parents, and she learns early on to look after her own interests in all situations. Becky values money and social status above all and is thoroughly corrupt in her pursuit of them. Her most well-known (though often doubted) observation is that for five thousand pounds a year, she could be a good woman. Selfish, unscrupulous, manipulative, and ambitious, she is capable of appearing sweet, mild, and even timid when it furthers her aims to do so. She can blush and cry at will but cries genuinely only once: when she is forced to turn down the wealthy Sir Pitt's marriage proposal because she has already secretly married his son.

Becky is helped in her relentless social climbing both by her wits, which are as keenly honed as her surname implies, and by her physical attributes, which are listed thus: "Green eyes, fair skin, pretty figure, famous frontal development." Nearly all the male characters in the novel are taken in by her, always to their detriment.

As the novel opens, Becky attends Miss Pinkerton's academy where she earns her keep by teaching French (learned from her mother). She becomes Amelia's friend and goes to her home for a long visit when the two leave the academy. There she tries to lure Amelia's brother Joseph into marrying her but is foiled by George Osborne. She then goes to work as a governess for Sir Pitt Crawley and marries his son Rawdon, a marriage that gives her status but not wealth. In a series of attempts to secure money, she sacrifices her marriage and ignores her child. Her vaguely defined relationship with Lord Steyne provides both money and position until Rawdon walks in on them and both men abandon her.

In the end, Becky has attained a measure of middle-class respectability—the place in Vanity Fair that she has so long and so ardently sought. Her status is made possible partly by money inherited from Joseph Sedley, whom she meets again after many years and whose death by poisoning she may have caused.

Becky's corruption does not render her incapable of recognizing or appreciating virtue in others, even though virtue is rare in Vanity Fair. She is able to see the noble character of William Dobbin and, in an unexpected act of caring, helps

Amelia to see it too, so that Amelia will marry Dobbin.

Lord Steyne

Lord Steyne is a wealthy aristocrat and lord of the Powder Closet at Buckingham Palace. He is unattractive in every conceivable way and considerably older than Becky, but she enters into a vague arrangement with him that earns her money, jewelry, and status until her husband walks in on Becky and him and throws a brooch at Lord Steyne, scarring him for life.

The Marchioness of Steyne

Lord Steyne's wife is a good woman, reduced to silence and superstitious religiosity by her husband's degeneracy. She comes to Becky's defense after Rawdon wounds Lord Steyne and both men desert her.

Wenham

Wenham is Lord Steyne's servant. He prevents Lord Steyne from dueling with Rawdon over Becky and turns Sir Pitt against Becky.

Themes

Vanity

There is one clear, overarching theme in *Vanity Fair: A Novel without a Hero,* and Thackeray telegraphs it in his title and subtitle. In the pages of *Vanity Fair,* all is vanity and all are vain. Some are more vain—more obsessed with self and with the ephemeral treasures of social position and money—than others, but none, in the author's estimation, can be called heroic.

The title is borrowed from John Bunyan's *The Pilgrim's Progress,* in which Vanity Fair is a town that exists for the purpose of diverting men and women from the road to heaven. The town's residents are all mean and ignorant, and they all make their living by enticing passersby to spend what they have on worldly vanities—items that offer brief sensual pleasure but have no lasting value. Thackeray transports Vanity Fair to London in the early 1800s and peoples his version with characters, primarily from the middle and upper classes, who live only to obtain higher social status and more money, and who are happy to lie, cheat, steal, manipulate, and betray in the pursuit of these goals. It is worth noting, as well, that Thackeray's Vanity Fair, like Bunyan's, is explicitly a godless place;

Topics for Further Study

- Do some research on Thackeray's life. Write an essay exploring some ways in which the author's life experiences are reflected in the characters and the story of *Vanity Fair.*

- Compare and contrast Becky Sharp and Amelia Sedley. Consider each woman's background, personality, values, strengths and weaknesses, and fate. What, if any, similarities do they share? What elements do you find that point to why they each turned out as they did?

- Imagine that you are Miss Matilda Crawley. Write your last will and testament, telling to whom you are leaving your fortune and why.

- Research the Battle of Waterloo. Give some possible reasons for Thackeray's having included it as a setting in the novel. Why is this battle a fitting background for these characters and their story?

- How is the society in which you live similar to the one depicted in *Vanity Fair,* and how is it different? Present your answer in any form you choose, such as an essay, short story, or poem.

both authors believe that the unrestrained vanity they portray is possible only among people who have no concept of a God who sets, upholds, and enforces moral standards. In an often-quoted letter to a personal correspondent, written in July 1847, before *Vanity Fair* was finished, Thackeray wrote, "What I want is to make a set of people living without God in the world. . . greedy, pompous, mean, perfectly self-satisfied for the most part and at ease about their superior virtue."

Thackeray succeeded so well in doing this that the novel has been faulted, more often than for anything else, for the unrelenting baseness of its characters. The vainest of all is Becky Sharp. Becky is proud of the physical attractiveness and clever wit that allow her to charm men. Her ultimate effect on them is similar to a spider's effect on a fly, which finds itself trapped and consumed. As her first husband, Rawdon Crawley, goes off to the Battle of Waterloo, Becky muses that she will be free to marry a wealthier man if Rawdon is killed. When he is not killed, Becky makes the best of it, using his aristocratic pedigree to win entrance to the social circles she seeks and to help her avoid paying her bills. Meanwhile, she uses other men, especially Lord Steyne, to get what she cannot get from her husband (money), carrying on public relationships that humiliate him, and ignoring him and their son. After Rawdon has finally left her for a faraway island, where he dies of a tropical disease, Joseph Sedley has the bad luck to encounter Becky a second time, and the drama of the spider and the fly again unfolds. Becky seduces Joseph and soon talks him into taking out a life insurance policy with her as beneficiary. Within months, Joseph is dead of poison; whether by Becky's hand or not is left to the reader to decide. There is scant evidence in the novel that murder would be beyond her.

Most of those around Becky are not better than she is, they are simply less clever and less desperate. Joseph is lazy, gluttonous, dull, and uncaring. When his father goes bankrupt and his whole family is on the verge of starvation, he doesn't get around to sending relief until it is nearly too late. George Osborne, Amelia's husband, is unable to love anyone but himself. George's father is mean, calculating, and unforgiving. Old Sir Pitt is a vulgar skinflint. Reverend Bute Crawley is not at all reverent and lets his overbearing gossip of a wife write his sermons. The list goes on and on.

Among the main characters, only Amelia Sedley and William Dobbin approach virtue. Amelia's fault is not so much that she is vain as that she is too blind and too shallow to recognize either vanity or virtue even at point-blank range. She idolizes George, the self-absorbed cad; she fails to see that Dobbin is a better man by far, even after years of his selfless attention to her. And Amelia is not completely above vanity. She is self-centered enough to accept Dobbin's devotion and his generous gifts without thinking of his feelings and without even expressing much gratitude.

Dobbin alone possesses real integrity and moral maturity, but even he is tinged with vanity. He is selfless, loyal, generous, and kind, ever content to give more than he takes. Dobbin's failure, similar to Amelia's, is his lack of discrimination about the characters of those around him. As a result, he gives people much more and much better than they deserve; in other words, he spends his life casting pearls before swine. And Dobbin's vanity lies in his dogged devotion to Amelia, who is,

like the wares hawked at Bunyan's Vanity Fair, glittery but not golden. She is not a heroine, worthy of a hero; she is just a generally decent, conventional, sweet-tempered woman. Though he does finally realize that Amelia has not been worthy of the adoration he has heaped on her, as a character, Dobbin is weakened by the fact that it takes him half a lifetime to develop a realistic view of Amelia.

Style

Victorian Literature

It was during the Victorian period (1837–1901) that the novel became the dominant literary form. *Vanity Fair* is considered one of the classic novels of the era. It was common for novels to be published serially, in magazines or in stand-alone sections. *Vanity Fair* was first published serially, and the early parts were published before the later ones were written. This at least partly explains the novel's many irregularities. A character may be called by different names in different sections (Mrs. Bute Crawley may be Barbara or Martha; Glorvina may be Glorvina Mahoney, the sister of Mrs. O'Dowd, or Glorvina O'Dowd, the sister of the general). One name may also be shared by multiple minor characters, and both the narrative and the passage of time may jump and start in unexpected directions. In one particularly confusing instance, Thackeray relates the details of Joseph's visit to his family and then has Amelia receive a letter from Joseph informing her that his visit will be delayed. To put it simply, Thackeray made it up as he went along, without undue concern for consistency. The novel's generous length and enormous cast of characters are also characteristic of the time.

Thackeray and Charles Dickens were the leading lights in Victorian fiction, constantly compared and always uncomfortable around each other. Dickens was born a year after Thackeray but was well established by the time Thackeray began to attract notice. Thackeray's focus was on the middle and upper classes, while Dickens's was on the poor. Thackeray's works, including *Vanity Fair,* are considered less sentimental and more subtle than Dickens's.

Loose Structure

Vanity Fair is not only long, it is meandering. Thackeray knows where he is taking his readers, but he is in no hurry to get them to their destination. Any slight forward movement of the plot may cause the author to stop, reflect, pontificate, digress. There are many long essays on everything from how to live with no visible means to how women treat one another. Other topics include how people comport themselves at estate sales, what the relationships between servants and employers are like, and what types of wedding and funeral ceremonies are practiced. Thackeray addresses readers directly, sometimes telling them what they can expect in the coming pages, sometimes telling them what to think of a character, and sometimes sharing his own musings and desires (one of which is for a rich, old aunt like Miss Matilda Crawley).

Many characters, including minor ones, also are given space to express their perspectives on other characters, story events, settings, and life in general. The story is told primarily from the point of view of a single narrator, but this narrator is often interrupted by story characters and by the author himself.

Thackeray's wanderings cover more than just philosophical terrain. Readers follow various characters all over England and to Brussels, Paris, Rome, the comically named, fictional German principality of Pumpernickel, and India, as well as to the British royal court and to an infamous debtors' prison.

Satire

Above all else, *Vanity Fair* is a satire. *The Penguin Dictionary of Literary Terms and Literary Theory* cites Thackeray among the principal satirists of the nineteenth century and *Vanity Fair* as a key work. It defines satire by defining its author:

> The satirist is. . . a kind of self-appointed guardian of standards, ideals, and truth; of moral as well as aesthetic values. He is a man (women satirists are very rare) who takes it upon himself to correct, censure, and ridicule the follies and vices of society and thus to bring contempt and derision upon aberrations from a desirable and civilized norm. Thus satire is a kind of protest, a sublimation and refinement of anger and indignation.

As much as *Vanity Fair* meanders in terms of content, it remains steadfastly on point when it comes to tone; it is satirical from start to finish, and all characters, even the few virtuous ones, take their share of darts. The sharpest arrows, though, are aimed at the worst of the lot. When the ignorant, vulgar tightwad Sir Pitt proposes to Becky, he makes a tall tale of a speech that makes him out as a generous gentleman whose only fault might be his advanced age. He tells Becky:

> "I'm an old man, but a good'n. I'm good for twenty years. I'll make you happy, zee if I don't. You shall do what you like; spend what you like; and 'av it all your own way. I'll make you a zettlement. I'll do everything reglar. Look year!" And the old man fell down on his knees and leered at her like a satyr.

The humor is compounded when Becky responds with equal corruption. Although she is distraught only because she is already married to Sir Pitt's much less wealthy son, she does a good job of acting as if she believes Sir Pitt to be the prize of manhood and explaining that that is why she is in tears at having to turn him down.

Virtually every character in the book, starting with Becky Sharp, is satirized every time his or her connotation-laden name is mentioned. But the most obvious and outrageous names are saved for minor characters: the auctioneer is Mr. Hammerdown; the surgeon, Dr. Lance; the hanging judge, Sir Thomas Coffin; the gambler, Deuceace, to give a very few examples. Also on Becky's rain-drenched trip to Queen's Crawley, she passes the towns of Leakington, Mudbury, and Squashmore.

Thackeray's satire often takes the form of irony (figurative speech in which what is meant is the opposite of what is said). People who hate each other address each other as "my love." The degenerate Lord Steyne calls his house a "temple of virtue" and describes his long-suffering and pious wife as being as gay as Lady MacBeth. Of the war-beleaguered Belgians, the author writes, "For a long period of history they have let other people fight there."

Wide-Ranging Allusions

It would take a lifetime study of world literature and history to comprehend every allusion in *Vanity Fair*. References to Greek and Roman classics and the Bible are not unexpected. But Thackeray adds dozens of references much more obscure to modern Western readers. To name just a few: Ahriman, a Zoroastrian evil spirit; the Arabian nights; and a French opera performed in London at the time Thackeray was writing. His several allusions appear as represented in the following passage:

> 'Come, come,' said James, putting his hand to his nose and winking at his cousin with a pair of vinous eyes, 'no jokes, old boy; no trying it on me. You want to trot me out, but it's no go. In vino veritas, old boy. Mars, Bacchus, Apollo virorum, hay? I wish my aunt would send down some of this to the governor; it's a precious good tap.'

James is quoting (not accurately) the *Latin Grammar* he studied at school; the main gist is "truth in wine." "Machiavel" is Thackeray's short form of Machiavelli and the author's nickname for Sir Pitt.

Historical Context

Napoleon and the Battle of Waterloo

The Napoleonic Wars began in the late 1790s, with Napoleon Bonaparte leading the revolutionary government in France. For the next several years, the British suffered military defeats at sea, several attempted invasions by the French, as well as the economic inflation and disruption that often accompany war. The British formed a series of alliances to fight the French, and the Fourth Coalition, comprising Britain, Russia, Prussia, and Austria, succeeded in routing Napoleon and exiling him in 1814. In 1815, Napoleon escaped from exile on the island of Elba and retook the French throne. It is this event that brings the major characters of *Vanity Fair* to Brussels and leads to the famous Battle of Waterloo.

At the news of Napoleon's return, the Fourth Coalition nations quickly committed a force of 150,000 soldiers to gather in Belgium and invade France on July 1, 1815. The British general, Arthur Wellesley, the First Duke of Wellington, was the chief commander of the coalition force. Napoleon responded by planning a secretive, preemptive strike against the assembling troops. He reached the Belgian border on June 14, with nearly 125,000 troops, and crossed it on June 15.

With the advantage of surprise, Napoleon succeeded in splitting the two sections of the coalition force and thus held the strategic upper hand. Four days of fierce fighting and desperate strategizing on both sides followed, culminating at Waterloo on June 18. On that day alone, 40,000 French soldiers and 22,000 coalition soldiers were killed; Waterloo was one of the bloodiest battles of modern times. Here is Thackeray's description:

> All day long, whilst the women were praying ten miles away, the lines of the dauntless English infantry were receiving and repelling the furious charges of French horsemen. Guns which were heard at Brussels were ploughing up their ranks, and comrades falling, and the resolute survivors closing in. Towards evening, the attack slackened in its fury. They. . . were preparing for a final onset. It came at last: the columns of the Imperial Guard marched up the hill of Saint Jean. . . . It seemed almost to crest the em-

inence, when it began to wave and falter. Then it stopped, still facing the shot. Then at last the English troops rushed from the post from which no enemy had been able to dislodge them, and the Guard turned and fled.

> No more firing was heard at Brussels—the pursuit rolled miles away. The darkness came down on the field and city, and Amelia was praying for George, who was lying on his face, dead, with a bullet through his heart.

In the end, strategic errors by Napoleon and his generals and savage, fearless fighting by the coalition troops led to Napoleon's utter and final defeat. He was forced to give up the French throne a second time and was exiled to Saint Helena. King Louis XVIII was restored to the throne.

Vanity Fair is not the only work of literature to feature the Battle of Waterloo. British poet Lord Byron gives it an important place in *Childe Harold's Pilgrimage,* as does Thomas Hardy in *The Dynasts.* Among French writers, Victor Hugo includes the battle in *Les Misérables.*

Victorian England

The Victorian Age began in 1837 when eighteen-year-old Queen Victoria ascended to the British throne, and ended with her death in 1901. Victoria and her husband, Albert, set the tone of English life and culture for most of a century. It was a time of social and moral conservatism; the family values of the time were similar to those touted in late twentieth-century America. Pragmatism was valued above romance, duty above pleasure.

The early Victorian period was a time of social reforms. Laws were passed governing working conditions of women and children (they could not work in underground mines, for example), and attempts were made to improve conditions in prisons and insane asylums. Efforts to broaden access to education (England had no public schools at the time) stalled because of controversy over the Church of England's role in expanded education. Writers such as Thackeray and Charles Dickens took up the cause of reform, using their writing to point out the need for prison reforms and educational programs and to expose the evils of industrialization and the class system.

In the middle of the nineteenth century, England was experiencing unprecedented political, industrial, and economic power, fueled by the Industrial Revolution and by the wealth from the colonies. All forms of transportation boomed; railroad ridership increased sevenfold, and the ship-

Compare
&
Contrast

- **Early to Mid-Nineteenth Century:** People are routinely sent to prison when they are unable to pay their debts. Debtors' prisons are crowded, even during the relatively prosperous Victorian Age, and conditions are deplorable. Those who do not have family members or other benefactors to pay their debts sometimes spend years in prison. Charles Dickens and other authors write movingly of the plight of debtors, and reformers seek to abolish the prisons.

  Today: Debtors' prisons have been replaced by bankruptcy laws, which allow debtors to have most debts forgiven and to make a fresh financial start. Even during the economic boom of the 1990s, millions of individuals and small businesses declare bankruptcy.

- **Early to Mid-Nineteenth Century:** Although the former American colonies have won their independence, the British Empire still spans the globe. India, explored and exploited by the British East India Company, is now completely under British rule and is the "jewel in the crown." Britain also has colonies in Africa, Indonesia, Australia and New Zealand, South America, Canada, and the Caribbean.

  Today: What was once the British Empire is now the British Commonwealth, a collection of former colonies, most of which are independent nations, with formal ties to Britain. Among the Commonwealth nations are India, Canada, Australia, and New Zealand.

building industry grew. Living standards of the working class and middle class were buoyed, and trade unions were formed to promote the interests of skilled workers.

In the late 1850s, after unrest in India, the British government abolished the East India Company and took over direct rule of the subcontinent. Queen Victoria was declared Empress of India in 1876, and the empire continued to expand, especially in Asia and Africa.

Critical Overview

Vanity Fair was published in several installments beginning on January 1, 1847, and reviews soon began appearing in London's magazines. Most writers who reviewed the early segments were not enthusiastic, nor was the public. The primary complaints of both critics and readers were that the novel was progressing slowly and without much action and that all the characters were unlikable.

Reception turned positive, however, after the first four installments. Once the whole of *Vanity*

Fair had been published, it sold well (one 1848 reviewer wrote, "Everybody, it is to be supposed, has read the volume by this time.") and earned many glowing reviews. George Henry Lewes wrote in *The Athenaeum,*

> For some years Mr. Thackeray has been a marked man in letters—but known rather as an amusing sketcher than as a serious artist. Light playful contributions to periodical literature and two amusing books of travel were insufficient to make a reputation; but a reputation he must now be held to have established by his *Vanity Fair*. It is his greatest effort and his greatest success.

In *Quarterly Review,* Elizabeth Rigby wrote,

> We were perfectly aware that Mr. Thackeray had of old assumed the jester's habit, in order the more unrestrainedly to indulge the privilege of speaking the truth. . . but still we were little prepared for the keen observation, the deep wisdom, and the consummate art which he has interwoven in the slight texture and whimsical pattern of *Vanity Fair*.

Charlotte Brontë was such an admirer of *Vanity Fair* that, on its merits, she dedicated the second edition of *Jane Eyre* to Thackeray, writing in her preface:

I think I see in him an intellect profounder and more unique than his contemporaries have yet recognized. . . I think no commentator on his writings has yet found the comparison that suits him, the terms which rightly characterise his talent.

Even an anonymous reviewer for *The London Review,* who felt that the meanness of the characters defeated the novel, acknowledged, "*Vanity Fair* is a remarkable book, brilliant, entertaining," before adding, "but if we plunge beneath the sparkling surface, it is a dreary book. It gives the real, and utterly omits the ideal."

John Forster wrote prophetically in *The Examiner,*

> *Vanity Fair* must be admitted to be one of the most original works of real genius that has of late been given to the world. . . . The very novelty of tone in the book impeded its first success; but it will be daily more justly appreciated; and will take a lasting place in our literature.

In his 1909 book *Studies in Several Literatures,* Harry Thurston Peck assessed the novel after sixty years. "*Vanity Fair* is one of the greatest books in English literature," he wrote, "but it belongs to purely English literature, and not to the great masterpieces which the whole world owns and to which it gives unforced admiration."

History has, to an extent, proven Forster and Peck correct. *Vanity Fair* is still read and admired but not as widely as the best work of Thackeray's contemporary Dickens. It is, however, Thackeray's most lasting work, the one that modern readers most enjoy. Robert A. Colby, in his introduction to a 1989 edition of *Vanity Fair,* wrote,

> We, it seems, are attracted to the very qualities that disturbed Thackeray's contemporaries—impersonality, cynicism, tough-mindedness. Indeed, its coruscating wit, ingenuity, and vivacious style continue to make *Vanity Fair* the most immediately attractive of Thackeray's novels to the general reader.

Criticism

Candyce Norvell

Norvell is an independent educational writer who specializes in literature. She holds degrees in linguistics and journalism. In this essay, she examines the fates of the main characters in Thackeray's novel and considers what lessons he intended readers to take from them.

Thackeray made clear, both in his role as the narrator of *Vanity Fair* and in his private correspon-

"Mrs. Osborne's carriage stopping the way," an illustration from the novel

dence about the book, that he meant it to be not just entertaining but instructive. Like all satire, *Vanity Fair* has a mission and a moral. The first published installment had, on its cover, an illustration of a congregation listening to a preacher; both speaker and listeners were shown with donkey ears. Inside the book, Thackeray explains the illustration thus: "that Becky is allowed to live, and to live well, is perfectly consistent with Thackeray's view of life and morality. . . . Losing is vanity, and winning is vanity."

> My kind reader will please to remember that these histories. . . have "Vanity Fair" for a title and that Vanity Fair is a very vain, wicked, foolish place, full of all sorts of humbugs and falseness and pretensions. And while the moralist who is holding forth on the cover (an accurate portrait of your humble servant) professes to wear neither gown nor bands, but only the very same long-eared livery in which his congregation is arrayed: yet, look you, one is bound to speak the truth as far as one knows it.

Thackeray, then, portrays himself as a preacher. Like his audience and all human beings, he is imperfect, but he has truths to tell that others can benefit by hearing. There is a moral to the story.

The natural place to look for any story's moral is at its end: How do things turn out; and, espe-

> Like his audience and all human beings, he is imperfect, but he has truths to tell that others can benefit by hearing. There is a moral to the story."

cially, how are the various characters rewarded and punished for their deeds? This essay looks at the fates of *Vanity Fair*'s major characters for evidence as to what truths, what morals Thackeray wanted readers to take from his tale.

The first to meet his fate is George, who is shot at the Battle of Waterloo. Structurally, George's death gives Thackeray an emphatic ending to the first part of his story. From a moral standpoint, the lesson of George's short life and violent death is surely about hubris, an ancient Greek word meaning "arrogance," or "excessive pride." Hubris was the downfall of many a classical hero. And while George is certainly no hero, he is thoroughly self-centered and arrogant. He prides himself on his good looks and fancies himself the paragon of manhood. He receives Amelia's adoration not as a precious gift but as if she would be insane to feel otherwise. George is incapable of considering anyone but George, so it is easy to imagine that, as the French bullet sped toward his heart, George was distracted by thoughts of how he looked standing over the battlefield or of how he would speak in light-hearted tones about his bravery in years to come. Arrogance is cut down. George dies young, mourned only by the empty-headed Amelia.

Many years and many episodes pass before Rawdon Crawley meets his fate. It is yellow fever that kills him, but Becky Sharp who destroys him. Thackeray makes clear through allusions to the story of Clytemnestra and Agamemnon what readers are to make of Rawdon's life and death. In Greek mythology, Clytemnestra kills her husband, Agamemnon, when her lover lacks the courage to carry out the deed.

Like nearly every man in the novel, Rawdon is charmed by Becky and entirely smitten with her. He marries her without noticing that she cares not for him, but for his aristocratic pedigree. He then spends years being manipulated, humiliated, impoverished, and ignored by his wife. At last, he dis-

covers both Becky's relationship with the degenerate, wealthy Lord Steyne (which he must have at least suspected before, and can't ignore any longer after walking in on them) and the hoard of money she has kept hidden from him. Rawdon stands up for himself, leaving Becky and planning to duel with Lord Steyne. Yet, there is no victory for him. Becky and Steyne ship his beloved son off to boarding school, and Rawdon is left alone, unloved, and destitute. He exiles himself to a remote island where he has been offered a government post arranged by Steyne. It is on this island that Rawdon dies. The moral is clear: A man who allows himself to be captivated by a bad woman has a miserable life and a pitiful end.

Amelia and Dobbin's fates are settled next—by marriage rather than by death. Not deeply immoral like the others, they are nonetheless morally stunted. Sweet but thick Amelia has spent her life mourning George, whom she continues to see as worthy in spite of bountiful evidence to the contrary. Noble but plodding Dobbin has spent his life idolizing Amelia in spite of her steadfast lack of concern for him. Even when Dobbin finally declares his devotion, Amelia prefers her warped memories of George to Dobbin's genuine, living affection.

Oddly, Thackeray uses Becky to bring these two characters together. Only when Becky reveals to Amelia that George asked her to run away with him just before he died does Amelia finally give up her fantasies about George and marry Dobbin. And so, Amelia and Dobbin, the two characters who come closest to being "good," get their rewards. Amelia gets, finally, a man who is worthy of her love. Dobbin gets what he has wanted all along.

But in *Vanity Fair*, no reward is untainted and no victory is complete or final. By the time Dobbin has Amelia, he has finally realized that she is not worthy of the kind of love he has showered her with. She is not a goddess; she is merely a pleasant, conventional, shallow woman who happens to be a very poor judge of character. Thackeray's description of Dobbin's victory ends with a sting:

> The vessel is in port. He has got the prize he has been trying for all his life. The bird has come in at last. There it is with its head on his shoulder, billing and cooing close up to his heart, with soft outstretched fluttering wings. . . . Grow green again, tender little parasite, round the rugged old oak to which you cling!

The shadow over Dobbin's victory is that having finally gotten what he wanted, he realizes that it is not what he thought it was. The shadow over Amelia's, of course, is that she knows that Dobbin knows. And yet, their coming together is a real reward; they do love each other, even if they are two imperfect human beings who love imperfectly. They have a daughter and are happy.

The moral of Amelia's story might be that providence will find a way to deliver wisdom and salvation to the good-hearted but dumb, even if that way is unexpected. The moral of Dobbin's story may be that perseverance wins the day; or that the meek shall inherit, if not the whole Earth, then a peaceful corner of it in which to retire. It is also worth noting that Dobbin is the one man who is never conned or charmed by Becky and the only one who comes to a happy end.

Joseph's story is a recapitulation of Rawdon's. Having escaped Becky's web in youth with George's unwitting help, he has the bad fortune to encounter her again years later. This time, Joseph ignores Dobbin's warning about the predatory Becky and soon loses his money and his life. Thackeray—the author, the narrator, the preacher—doesn't want this moral missed: A man who falls for a bad woman can come to no good.

And that leaves Becky. She has behaved the worst. How will she end?

She ends living in Europe, financially comfortable and respected. Her son owns the estate at which she arrived as a girl to be a lowly governess. This is not exactly hellfire and brimstone; one wonders what the preacher was thinking. Why does he let Becky off so easy?

One of his reasons is oddly modern: He blames her parents for her badness. "She was of a wild, roving nature, inherited from her father and mother, who were both Bohemians," Thackeray writes.

But that is a minor point. That Becky is allowed to live and to live well is perfectly consistent with Thackeray's view of life and morality. Death is not necessarily a punishment, and life is not necessarily a reward, because it is all vanity—all empty. Losing is vanity, and winning is vanity. At the very end of the book, Thackeray asks, "Which of us is happy in this world? Which of us has his desire? or, having it, is satisfied?"

There's the rub. Even those who get what they want in Vanity Fair are not satisfied and therefore cannot be said to have conquered anything. At the end of *Vanity Fair*, Becky is in comfortable circumstances. That does not mean that she will be comfortable, satisfied, fulfilled, or happy. Becky

famously says that if she had five hundred pounds a year, she could be an honest woman. Most readers have doubted her, as did Thackeray himself in a private letter. When the author leaves Becky, she is well provided for, but she is still depraved Becky, and she still lives in depraved Vanity Fair. Given what is known about them both, readers who want a just outcome needn't worry that Becky has been too richly rewarded. Thackeray assures:

> If quacks prosper as often as they go to the wall—if zanies succeed and knaves arrive at fortune, and, vice versa, sharing ill luck and prosperity for all the world like the ablest and most honest among us—I say, brother, the gifts and pleasures of Vanity Fair cannot be held of any great account.

Source: Candyce Norvell, Critical Essay on *Vanity Fair,* in *Novels for Students,* The Gale Group, 2002.

John Peck

In the following essay, Peck explores "the relentless nature of Thackeray's onslaught on the middle class" in Vanity Fair.

> This revolting reflex of society is literally true enough. But it does not shew us the whole truth. Are there not women, even in *Vanity Fair,* capable of nobler things than are here set down for them? (Robert Bell. *Fraser's Magazine,* 1848)

Everywhere we turn in the early reviews of *Vanity Fair* we encounter this kind of criticism; the reviewers are enthusiastic but appreciation of the brilliance of Thackeray's performance is always qualified by reservations about his view of human nature. Modern critics have, of course, moved beyond the moral quibbling evident in the early reviews. Essentially, criticism of the novel now follows one of three courses: there is appreciation of the complexity of its moral and social vision, or praise for Thackeray's handling of the narrative voice, or, and perhaps most persuasively, a sense of the disturbing darkness of his vision.

Barbara Hardy, identifying Thackeray as a radical social critic, takes the first approach, seeing the novelist as a wise and concerned social commentator. All of Gordon Ray's work on Thackeray, including his biography, was informed by just such a sense of the author's purpose and achievement. The second approach, focusing on the narrative voice, is more concerned with Thackeray's ability to tease and disturb the reader by means of a voice that is so full of twists and turns that it allows us no comfort or security. A. E. Dyson's essay, 'An Irony Against Heroes', sets the standard here, but the same principle underlies structuralist and deconstructive readings of Thackeray; the most so-

The interior court of London's Fleet Prison, a debtor's prison

phisticated example is J. Hillis Miller's brilliant essay on *Henry Esmond.* It is a way of looking at Thackeray in which irony is always a central consideration. The third approach to *Vanity Fair,* seen at its best in an essay by Robert E. Lougy, focuses on the darkness of the novel, the frequent references to death, the sense that we live precarious existences in a world where death is ever-present. This idea also makes itself felt in feminist and psychoanalytic readings: for example, we might consider how Amelia, visiting her mother, looks at 'the little white bed, which had been hers a few days before' and contrasts it with 'the great funereal damask pavilion in the vast and dingy bedroom, which was awaiting her at the grand hotel in Cavendish Square'. The approach of Lougy, and those working along similar lines, differs from the social approach of critics such as Barbara Hardy in that the emphasis is on disturbing currents beneath society rather than on a critique of manners and morals in society.

What links all three approaches, however, is that, directly or indirectly, they declare themselves as moving beyond the moralistic fault-finding that features in the early reviews. It is at this point one hesitates: were the early readers wrong? Were their moral reservations really so simplistic? Or could it

be that, whatever deeper patterns exist in *Vanity Fair,* its *épater les bourgeois* characteristics might be what really matter? Hindsight has benefits, but it could be that we have lost a sense of what was central to *Vanity Fair*'s first readers, a sense of why the novel is so disturbing. Moreover, in distancing ourselves from this sense of shock, we might also have lost an awareness of the social and political relevance of the novel. *Vanity Fair* is obviously a multi-layered work, but I want to suggest that discussions of, say, Thackeray's irony surrender a sense of the impact the novel made in its time, an impact that was dominated by the issue of class.

There is no novel that thrusts us more quickly into a whole set of assumptions about class than *Vanity Fair.* By the end of the first scene we understand most of the niceties and pretensions of social gradation. The world of the school is a middle-class world, where characters are rebuked if their speech is not 'genteel' enough, where a girl must cultivate those 'accomplishments which become her birth and station', where '*industry and obedience*' are prized virtues, but where money is, in the end, everything. Below, we see a world of servants, of tradesmen, and even the mixed-race Miss Swartz, who is only admitted to the school because she pays double. Above is another world, glimpsed through the 'high and mighty Miss Saltire (Lord Dexter's granddaughter)'. It is sometimes assumed that *Vanity Fair* is entirely about middle-class life. It is not: there are clear divisions between the aristocracy, the gentry, the middle class and all those who fall below. But the world of the aristocracy, even of the gentry, is outside and beyond this school where even Miss Saltire is 'rather shabby'; generally, there is something shabby about the school's whole environment of middle-class respectability.

To say that class is central in *Vanity Fair* is to say nothing new. What is less commonly noted, though, is fine relentless nature of Thackeray's onslaught on the middle class. Some critics, indeed, suggest just the opposite; Robert Colby, for example, argues that the narrator positions himself 'as a solid member of the middle class'. What I wish to suggest, however, is that Thackeray, who is indulgent to the aristocracy and gentry, regards the middle class as an almost alien race. Everyone is now familiar with the idea of an 'other' in Victorian thought, whether it be woman, the Irish, people of colour, or the working class, but, in the case of Thackeray, even the middle class is perceived as a strange and threatening 'other'. We begin to see this with the middle-class merchant, Osborne. Described as a 'savage determined man', with a face that is usually 'livid with rage', there seems something animal-like about him, and indeed his fortune has been made importing animal skins from Russia. He is seen in an angry scene with his son:

> Whenever the lad assumed his haughty manner, it always created either great awe or great irritation in the parent. Old Osborne stood in secret terror of his son as a better gentleman than himself. . .

In confrontation, the father is reduced to spluttering incoherence; everything falls apart as he feels he is facing a gentleman. It is a penetrating representation of the drive, but also the limitations, of a middle-class businessman, yet, at the same time, Thackeray's patronising view of someone whom he considers less than civilised.

Initially something rather different seems to be conveyed in the presentation of Mr. Sedley, who, although a businessman, is 'kind to everybody with whom he dealt', but the novel offers some alarming hints about his cruelty. He is described as 'a coarse man, from the Stock Exchange, where they love all sorts of practical jokes', who has bred his daughter to marry George Osborne, and who has 'a feeling very much akin to contempt for his son. He said he was vain, selfish, lazy and effeminate'.

> **There is no novel that thrusts us more quickly into a whole set of assumptions about class than *Vanity Fair*. By the end of the first scene we understand most of the niceties and pretensions of social gradation."**

Jos might well be all these things, but the strain in the relationship comes at precisely those points where the child fails to conform to the father's expectations, where the right kind of manly energy (or, in the case of daughter, the right degree of submissiveness) is not exhibited. Osborne and Sedley represent two faces of tyranny, the tyranny of the strong and the tyranny of the weak, for Sedley, especially when ruined, dominates his family just as much as Osborne. Like all middle-class men, they want their sons to be gentlemen, but are then torn between deference and contempt.

Contempt is, in fact, a central notion in the novel. When the bankrupt Sedley presents a servant with a half-guinea, the man pockets it 'with a mixture of wonder and contempt'. When, rather more noisily, George Osborne apes the manner of a man of standing, demanding an immediate interview with his father's solicitor,

> He did not see the sneer of contempt which passed all round the room, from the first clerk to the articled gents. . . as he sat there lapping his boot with his cane, and thinking what a parcel of miserable poor devils these were.

Such contempt, of one class for another, pervades the novel, including the fact that Thackeray looks down on the middle class with almost unrelieved disdain; for Thackeray, middle-class existence, entirely based around money, lacks culture, character, any kind of substance. Osborne, for example, sings the praises of life

> at our humble mansion in Russell Square. My daughters are plain, disinterested girls, but their hearts are in the right place. . . I'm a plain, simple, humble British merchant—an honest one, as my respected friends Hulker and Bullock will vouch. . .

It is a vain speech, but the only merit claimed is respectability. It would seem that Thackeray can only perceive middle-class life in these terms; his characteristic note is arrogant disdain, a belief that those below him on the social scale have no individuality, no intellectual life, no complexity.

But aren't all Thackeray's judgements just as jaundiced? Isn't he equally quick to condemn the aristocracy and the gentry, indeed everybody at every level of society? The fact is that he isn't, a point which starts to become evident if we consider something basic about our response to *Vanity Fair,* our impression of how Thackeray fills up the pages. Becky, obviously, makes the greatest impact. She wastes very little time on the middle class. She is grateful for a refuge in Amelia's house, having already decided that she aspires higher than the Reverend Mr. Crisp. Her first target is Jos Sedley, who, as an employee of the East India Company, has taken a sideways step out from, and yet up in, British society. She then raises her sights to the gentry, in the person of Rawdon Crawley (although she misses out on the landed gentry, represented by Rawdon's father, Sir Pitt). Finally, with Lord Steyne, she aspires to the aristocracy. What we are most likely to remember from the novel are Becky's forays into the higher levels of society, but this can distort a true picture of what happens page by page; in the first third of the novel, before the characters move to Brussels, there is just one sequence where Becky works for Sir Pitt and one sequence in the home of Miss Crawley. Most of the time, episodes are set in the middle-class homes of the Sedleys and the Osbornes. The same is true of the last third of the novel.

But what we remember are the eccentrics, rather than the dull round of middle-class life. Sir Pitt makes an impression because he is larger than life; we are less likely to take notice of his wife, Rose. An ironmonger's daughter, with 'no sort of character, nor talents, nor opinions, nor occupations, nor amusements', Rose is invisible in the same kind of way that Mrs. Sedley is invisible. She has entered into a business transaction, selling her heart 'to become Sir Pitt Crawley's wife. Mothers and daughters are making the same bargain every day in Vanity Fair'. The hint of sympathy here needs to be set against the underlying assumption that the middle-class wife has no character, no individuality. By contrast, the gentry—the entire Crawley family—may be eccentrics, but another way of putting it is that they are conceived of as individuals with character traits that are all their own. Consequently, Sir Pitt might be disreputable

but eschews middle-class respectability. Similarly, the women of the family, Miss Crawley and Mrs. Bute Crawley, have their ridiculous side but also exhibit strength and resourcefulness that is absent in the middle-class women.

It is this derision of middle-class characters that, more than anything else, created disquiet in the early reviews. The point could be demonstrated across the board, but is most clearly seen in the response of John Forster. His review is sophisticated and enthusiastic: he relishes Thackeray's 'witty malice' and his 'accomplished and subtle' mind, and delights in Becky and Steyne, seeing that it is with 'characters where great natural talents and energy are combined with unredeemed depravity that the author puts forth his full powers'. He then, however, voices his reservation:

> Nor is it so much with respect to these exceptional characters that we feel inclined to complain of the taunting, cynical, sarcastic tone that too much pervades the work, as with respect to a preponderance of unredeemed selfishness in the more common-place as well as the leading characters, such as the Bullocks, Mrs. Clapp, the Miss Dobbinses even, and Amelia's mother. We can relish the shrewd egoism of Miss Crawley; can admire, while we tremble at, the terrible intentness of Mrs. Bute Crawley. . . but we feel that the atmosphere of the work is overloaded with these exhalations of human folly and wickedness.

The sequence of names is revealing: the Bullocks, the middle-class family of the future, are grabbed from insignificance to lead Forster's list. He then picks out other marginal middle-class characters, before altering his tone for the gentry figures. More than anything else, Forster seems to resent criticism of characters who might resemble himself. Most novelists at the time presented their audience with an ultimately flattering reflection of itself; Thackeray does not, and, consequently, irritates and unsettles his critics.

Timing is of importance here; *Vanity Fair* appeared in 1848, when a sense of being middle class was still in a process of formation. Indeed, novels were serving a vital role in creating a sense of middle-class identity and self-worth. Defining middle-classness through fiction had, of course, been going on since the eighteenth century, but *Vanity Fair* appears at a significant juncture in a process of social change. Albeit reluctantly, Thackeray acknowledges a move away from a certain social formation, and searches for a new social dispensation to succeed that based upon property, rank and status. It is a brilliant move to set the novel at the time of Waterloo, for this enables Thackeray both to comment on the developing democratic order of his

What Do I Read Next?

- *W. M. Thackeray Library,* edited by Richard Pearson and published in 1996, presents an array of Thackeray's writing, including short fiction and nonfiction, plus a full-length biography by Lewis Melville.

- *Jane Eyre,* by Charlotte Brontë, was published in 1847, the same year in which the first installments of *Vanity Fair* appeared. Brontë's novel has some similarities to Thackeray's in that the main character is an orphaned English governess who becomes romantically involved with her employer.

- *Wuthering Heights,* by Emily Brontë, also was published in 1847. Like *Vanity Fair,* it is considered one of the classics of Victorian literature. The novel is a story of romance and revenge.

- *Little Dorrit,* by Charles Dickens, was first published serially in 1857. Another Victorian classic, Dickens's book tells the story of Amy Dorrit, born in the debtors' prison where her father lives. Major themes are social class, financial reversals, and romance.

- *Far from the Madding Crowd,* by Thomas Hardy, was published serially in 1874 and also is ranked as a Victorian classic. It is the story of a female farmer and her three suitors. Virginia Woolf commented that this book "must hold its place among the great English novels." It has the distinction of being Hardy's only novel to offer readers a happy ending.

- *Red, Red Rose,* by Marjorie Farrell, was published in 1999. It tells the story of Val Aston, the illegitimate son of an English earl who becomes an officer in the English army during the Napoleonic wars. Aston is noble in character if not by birth, yet his social standing is an obstacle to his marrying the woman he loves.

---

own day and to show the coming into existence of this new social order. Behind the giddiness of Regency life, there is a sense of social change, of society re-drawing itself along new lines.

The point is most interestingly conveyed through the character of the young Pitt Crawley, who reorganises his life along what are, essentially, middle-class lines in order to revive the fortunes of a gentry family that has been in decline. He assumes the orderliness, the earnestness, and also the social ambition, of a middle-class man. As is so often the case in the novel, therefore, Thackeray is astute in his sense of a new order taking shape in society. But the fact that has to be returned to is that Thackeray's judgements are simultaneously suspect, because he cannot see any real depth of value in the middle-class mind. Rather than finding a new moral energy in middle-class experience, Thackeray castigates it as mediocre and selfish. Even in his picture of Dobbin, as we will see, there is an inability to avoid condescension, an inability to take the character seriously. Middle-class characters, and middle-class values, remain for Thackeray alien and vaguely threatening.

Vanity Fair therefore, to a quite extraordinary extent, insults its readers, who for the most part are likely to resemble those 'vulgar intellects' that have always dominated Amelia's life. Middle-class life is seen as dreadful. The Osborne daughters are typical: 'all their habits were pompous and orderly, and all their amusements intolerably dull and decorous'. Maria is engaged, 'but hers was a most respectable attachment'. Jos's much-repeated slight stories provide a kind of parody of the limited number of things that happen in the lives of these characters. Life is so dull that even the most trivial deviation from correctness becomes an anecdote:

"Do you remember when you wrote to him to come on Twelfth Night, Emmy, and spelt twelfth without the f?"

"That was years ago," said Amelia.

"It seems like yesterday, don't it John?" said Mrs. Sedley.

The impression is of pathetically empty lives and nervous deference to correctness. The topic that is always returned to in this world is money, as in a surprisingly eloquent speech from George Osborne:

> "Ours is a ready-money society. We live among bankers and city big-wigs, and be hanged to them, and every man, as he talks to you, is jingling his guineas in his pocket. . . Curse the whole pack of money-grubbing vulgarians!

Perhaps George's eloquence stems from the fact that the sentiments are really Thackeray's own.

Yet as much as Thackeray mocks such lives, he also offers a disquieting sense of claustrophobic containment. We have already seen the reference to Amelia's marriage-bed; the Sedleys' bed is 'a sort of tent, hung round with chintz of a rich and fantastic India pattern, and *double* with calico of a tender-rose colour; in the interior of which species of marquee was a feather-bed, on which were two pillows, on which were two round faces. . . '. The characters are surrounded by material goods, yet also enclosed and trapped by them. In a similar way, they are trapped in their homes, trapped in their families, trapped in their class. When characters, such as George Osborne, attempt to move beyond their circle they simply reveal their crassness. At the same time, there is always a sense of fragility, that middle-class wealth can disappear as quickly as it has appeared, leaving the characters in smaller homes, locked into an even narrower round.

Thackeray provides his most cutting commentary on such existences through his use of two outsiders, Jos Sedley and Mrs. O'Dowd (we could include Becky here, but Becky is a quite exceptional case whereas Jos and Mrs. O'Dowd are representative figures on the margins of British society). With Jos, a lack of social confidence, slavish devotion to material goods, excessive consumption, pomposity and deference are carried to a ridiculous extreme. But behind it all is a sense of an empty life, for 'he was as lonely here as in his jungle as Boggley Wallah'. Jos represents a gross, distorted reflection of middle-class aspirants. Mrs. O'Dowd is used in a similar way, but with the added complication there often is with Thackeray's Irish characters. Initially, with her boasting about her family and connections, we are likely to regard her as just a vulgar Irishwoman, but she really provides an ironic echo of the grovelling and social deference that is so central in the lives of Osborne and his children. In the end, Mrs. O'Dowd is actually superior to the middle-class characters, for she is grand and theatrical, energetic and resourceful, rather than mean and mediocre.

Thackeray's patrician disdain is most obvious in his presentation of middle-class wives who, although a different note is struck at the end of the novel, are seen as insignificant ciphers. There is sympathy for them, as victims of their husbands, but they are primarily seen as empty women who could not play any active role in the middle-class accumulation of wealth. Mrs. Sedley, in particular, is an invisible character, with an 'easy and uninquisitive' nature, whose thoughts cannot extend beyond the home. Thackeray's heroines, especially Becky, are always formidable women, but in the case of his middle-class wives he imagines concubines for domestic tyrants. There is something chilling in Amelia's deference to George:

> crying over George's head, and kissing it humbly, as if he were her supreme chief and master, and as if she were quite a guilty and unworthy person needing every favour and grace from him.

> This prostration and sweet unrepining obedience exquisitely touched and flattered George Osborne. He saw a slave before him in that simple yielding faithful creature, and his soul within him thrilled secretly somehow at the knowledge of his power.

It is an astute passage, especially in its understanding of the victim's sense of her own guilt, but the picture is only achieved by imagining the woman as a nonentity, who tolerates exploitation and abuse. That would be acceptable if all Thackeray's women were like this, but one of Thackeray's distinguishing traits as a novelist is his strong women; in the context of this novel, even leaving aside Becky, we can see the energy of the gentry wife, Mrs. Bute Crawley, who takes action, even if she misjudges her tactics, while her husband fritters away his time. Similarly, Lady Jane, Mr. Pitt Crawley's wife, who seems innocent, even naive, can show the qualities of her class in standing up to and resisting Becky, and resisting her husband: 'you must choose, sir, between her and me'.

What is always apparent, then, is Thackeray's patronising contempt for the middle class. Dobbin is mocked at school because his father is a grocer, but it is Thackeray, throughout the novel, who can never resist telling us that a character's father was a grocer; for example, Miss Grits, who marries the Reverend Binney, bringing with her five thousand pounds. It is as if he can never believe that the children of grocers might be as interesting as the children of the aristocracy or gentry. James Crawley, who ruins his chance of inheriting Miss Crawley's fortune through smoking in her house, is simply laughed at; the middle-class children are always sneered at. Thackeray's contempt invariably becomes most apparent at just those points where he attempts to be most sympathetic. For example, after the dazzle of 'How to Live Well on Nothing a Year'. Thackeray moves to 'A Family in a Small Way', where he offers compassionate reflections on the vagaries of fortune, but then the carping begins: 'Had Mrs. Sedley been a woman of energy, she would have exerted it after her husband's ruin'. She is, however, a small-minded woman, who cannot rise above 'colloquies with the greengrocer about the penn'orth of turnips which Mr. Sedley loved'. Sedley, on the same page, is seen 'pompously' presenting his grandson as the child of Captain Osborne. We are left not with a sense of life's vagaries, but with an impression of the vulgarity and shortcomings of this couple.

Thackeray in *Vanity Fair,* as is true throughout his career, is the awkward outsider in the Victorian novel. Others, for example, Dickens, at this time in *Dombey and Son* and *David Copperfield,* were presenting the middle-class audience with a critical yet, in the end, flattering image of itself. Thackeray does not oblige. *Vanity Fair* is obviously a funny novel, but the source of the amusement is usually someone acting inappropriately for a person of their class. Only Becky has the panache to carry it off, to humiliate others rather than herself. The stance in the novel raises the familiar yet teasing question of Thackeray's politics. The view that is generally held is that Thackeray was a liberal, even a radical, who by the late 1850s had moved steadily to the right. But what seems nearer the truth is that, fairly consistently throughout his career, he displays a familiar form of populism, resenting all those who possess money and power. There is, throughout *Vanity Fair,* the idea of an escape to a rural arcadia, such as the muddy yet happy life Becky's child enjoys in the French countryside when he is placed out at nurse. Informing Thackeray's populism is this longing for a traditional order; it is an impractical politics, lacking constructive ideas, motivated mainly by resentment, by a readiness to condemn those who seem to represent change, who undermine his sense of a more innocent order.

What complicates the picture, however, and complicates *Vanity Fair,* is his awareness that a fundamental change is taking place. He might have felt unhappy about it, but he could not ignore the fact that the initiative, not only economically but also politically and socially, was moving towards the middle class. There is a reluctant realisation that

the middle-class position offers the only hope for the future. This is prepared for by a sense that permeates the novel of aristocratic decline; in addition, there is also a late and unexpected indication of a collapse of gentry power. The future of the aristocracy is conveyed in such details as the impoverished Bareacres family, the appearance of the brass plates of businesses in Gaunt Square, and the strain of madness in the Steyne family: the 'dark mark of fate and doom was on the threshold'. The position of the gentry seems less extreme: young Pitt has, after all, restored the family's fortunes, but then, less than ten pages from the end of the novel, Pitt loses his place in Parliament as a result of the 1832 Reform Act.

It does seem that the future lies with the middle class, and appropriately, the last third of the novel concentrates on Dobbin and Amelia. It is conventional to admire Thackeray's presentation of Amelia, the way in which he has made his sentimental heroine a selfish heroine, but it can be argued that she is simply another of Thackeray's small-minded middle-class women, presented with all his characteristic contempt. He has to bring Amelia to the centre of the novel, but proves incapable of taking a middle-class heroine seriously. Exactly the same problem is evident in the portrayal of Dobbin:

> We all know a hundred whose coats are very well made, and a score who have excellent manners, and one or two happy things who are what they call, in the inner circles, and have shot into the very centre and bull's eye of the fashion; but of gentlemen how many? Let us take a little scrap of paper and each make out his list.
>
> My friend the major I write, without any doubt in mine. He had very long legs, a yellow face, and a slight lisp, which at first was rather ridiculous. But his thoughts were just, his brains were fairly good, his life was honest and pure, and his heart warm and humble.

A patrician voice encounters one of nature's gentlemen: the tone is extraordinarily condescending. The fact is that Thackeray cannot begin to comprehend a character such as Dobbin; he can only be commended on the basis of the way in which he combines upper-class gentlemanliness with a humble sense of his place. The problem with Amelia and Dobbin is that Thackeray requires them to carry the burden of a social and moral role, but is unable to give them the substance required. They remain members of an alien species, seen from a superior perspective, and evaluated in terms of how they compare to, and at times prove better than, their social superiors.

Thackeray's overt effort to point to the future through Amelia and Dobbin is, therefore, rather bungled. Yet the novel, none the less, offers a strong sense of a move towards a new order in society. By the end of *Vanity Fair,* most readers feel they have moved from Waterloo to a post-Reform Act world. This is more than a matter of chronology; a complex case about democratisation, about a shift towards middle-class values, is articulated in the second half of the novel. This sense of a change is not conveyed through subtle characterisation but through a mass of seemingly trivial details. This is entirely appropriate: *Vanity Fair* is, from the outset, a novel crammed full of precise details about the material and social world. In the second half of the novel we are offered an abundance of fresh images that combine to convey a sense of change. It starts when the characters return from the continent: at this point a different kind of detail begins to appear. There is less about what people spend their money on, and rather more about the ordinary, yet distinctively new, characteristics of middle-class life.

To begin with an example which should clarify what I am talking about, we hear a lot in the novel about the dull and pompous round of middle-class entertaining. As early as the aborted trip to Vauxhall, for example, Mr. and Mrs. Sedley have been to dine with Alderman Balls. But we have to wait a long time before we are offered a full guest-list for a middle-class dinner. Eventually, however, we encounter

> a party of dismal friends of Osborne's rank and age. Old Dr Gulp and his lady from Bloomsbury Square: old Mr Frowser the attorney, from Bedford Row, a very great man, and from his business, hand-in-glove with the 'nobs at the West End', old Colonel Livermore, of the Bombay Army, and Mrs Livermore from Upper Bedford Place: old Serjeant Toffy and Mrs Toffy; and sometimes old Sir Thomas Coffin and Lady Coffin, from Bedford Square.

Thackeray conveys the tedium of the occasion. He also reminds us that social aspiration is always a factor, for it is obviously felt to be a coup when a judge can be induced to attend. But, as much as the passage might be designed to operate at the expense of Osborne, other impressions are conveyed as well. The linking of the characters with streets in the Bloomsbury area of London acknowledges the coming into existence of a new middle-class locality, yet also points forward to other middle-class characters, such as the Bullocks, who make the move into more fashionable areas. Osborne's guests seem to be a generation of middle-class char-

acters who have achieved status and respectability, but who, unlike the Bullocks, stop at this point. Yet they are far from insignificant people. All belong to a professional class, a class that would grow and grow in Victorian England. They are middle class but interested in more than money; they have opted for professions that reflect duty and social obligation. Thackeray sneers at such dull people, but at the same time there is a reluctant acknowledgement of a new, solid middle class. The precariousness of Sedley's existence seems a thing of the past; these are middle-class characters who have established secure roots in the social order.

There are other details in the novel that point to the rise of a new professional middle class. At the opening of *Vanity Fair,* the army is the only profession open to young middle-class men who are intent on bettering themselves. But as peace takes over from war, there is a growing sense of a professional class; indeed, young George is taught by a man who prepares his pupils for 'the Universities, the senate, and the learned professions'. We begin to encounter characters such as Wenham, 'the wit and lawyer', who acts on behalf of Steyne. Rawdon has, in the past, fought duels, but now the professional man Wenham negotiates a settlement. It is a shift towards a society where, as in the words of the newspaper report of Rawdon's job, 'We need not only men of acknowledged bravery, but men of administrative talents to superintend the affairs of our colonies'. We might begin to feel that Becky has been overtaken by events, that her kind of spectacular rise is no longer possible in a society where success is most likely for the diligent.

Middle-class confidence, too, is increasing. Even Jos develops 'a more candid and courageous self-assertion of his worth'. This is not entirely surprising, for he is presented at court; the narrator makes a disparaging comment, that Jos had 'worked himself up to believe that he was implicated in the maintenance of the public welfare', yet there is a sense in which this is true, for Jos, as a fairly senior colonial civil servant, is 'implicated'. The developing role of the civil service and the increasing importance of the empire in Victorian England was complemented by a growth in financial services. Banks could still collapse, indeed there was a banking crisis in 1847 and another ten years later, but in the latter stages of *Vanity Fair* we seem to have moved beyond the gambling of the Waterloo era, whether at the card table or on the stock exchange, towards secure banks, such as Hulker, Bullock and Co. and Stumpy and Rowdy's, with substantial reserves. It is middle-class bankers,

such as Fred Bullock, who now seem in the vanguard of society. But financial services extend beyond banks; in the giddy world of *Vanity Fair,* it
represents quite a shift towards sobriety when the
narrator moves to talking about the fact that no Insurance Office will take on Rawdon Crawley as a
client, because of the climate on Coventry Island.
Everywhere the impression is of a more controlled
society. The idea is even conveyed in a description
of Pitt's study:

> with the orderly Blue Books and letters, the neatly
> docketed bills and symmetrical pamphlets; the locked
> account-books, desks and dispatch boxes, the Bible,
> the *Quarterly Review,* and the *Court Guide,* which
> all stood as if on parade awaiting inspection of their
> chief.

The military imagery that is so common in the
novel is called upon again, but is now at the service of a middle-class vision of order.

Nowhere is this sense of a new social formation better conveyed than in the different light in
which middle-class women are seen in the latter
stages of the novel. Thackeray's contempt never
disappears, indeed it becomes more barbed as he is
forced to concede that Maria Bullock and her circle are no longer the wilting middle-class women
that have appeared in the novel up to this point:

> Emmy found herself in the centre of a very genteel
> circle indeed; the members of which could not con-
> ceive that anybody belonging to it was not very lucky.
> There was scarce one of the ladies that hadn't a re-
> lation a peer, though the husband might be a drysalter
> in the City. Some of the ladies were very blue and
> well informed; reading Mrs Somerville, and fre-
> quenting the Royal Institution; others were severe
> and Evangelical, and held by Exeter Hall.

The tone is sarcastic, rather pathetically so, but
behind the sarcasm we can see three remarkable
points: these are self-confident middle-class
women, taking a pride in their own rank and status; part of this pride can be attributed to their success in moving towards the centre of society, making the leap from trade to aristocratic connections;
yet at the same time these are intelligent women,
with a range of intellectual interests. These are
women with minds and a justified sense of their
own importance. No wonder Thackeray's tone is
so unbalanced; he does everything he can to mount
a case against Maria Bullock, dismissing her
'twopenny gentility' and mocking her 'scheming
and managing' to attract accounts to her husband's
bank, but she is likely to strike us as an active
woman playing a role in the family business. The
middle class remain people that Thackeray looks
down on, but now that they are asserting themselves he sinks below contempt and is reduced to
sniping abuse.

Yet it is this unbalanced animosity that gives
the novel so much of its strength, for Thackeray's
perverse and hostile stand represents a unique perspective on the re-drawing of the lines in society.
He sneers, and, as the novel goes on, sneers more
and more, but at the same time reluctantly concedes
the presence and importance of the middle class.
There is, however, one final twist: he might resist
the impulse, but by the end of the novel Thackeray
himself has begun to acquire something of a middle-class outlook. We see it in his revised attitude
to Becky. Dobbin states the case against Becky, trying to persuade Amelia that she is dangerous. He
then makes the same case to Jos: 'Be a man, Jos:
break off this disreputable connection. Come home
to your family'. Manliness, distancing oneself from
anybody disreputable, and the family, are Dobbin's
key points. Jos protests that Becky is innocent, and,
indeed, it would be hard to say what she has done
wrong, but she stands as a vivid illustration of trans-
gression, the kind of social deviant that was required if the middle class was to be convinced of
the soundness of its moral codes. What is more curious is that Thackeray now seems to share this
view of Becky. The point is underlined in his final
selection of a detail to illustrate her villainy: she is
involved in an insurance fraud, making a claim on
Jos's life. It is a strange reversal of Thackeray's
earlier celebration of Becky's vitality when he
starts judging her from the perspective of an insurance company.

Thackeray makes one final protest against
middle-class values: his late hint that Dobbin finds
his marriage a disappointment is a gesture against
the period's increasing reverence for the family.
But it seems only a token gesture against the drift
in the novel towards the family, towards private
life. Yet, perhaps this is not entirely the case.
Thackeray had to finish his novel. He also had to
cater for, and to some extent satisfy, his audience.
The steps towards a middle-class compromise
might be simply steps he could not avoid in concluding *Vanity Fair.* His venom towards Maria Bullock seems closer to his true self. And the subsequent novels also suggest that he could never come
to terms with the middle-class world, that he never
had any time for, or understanding of, middle-class
people. They remain an inferior breed, admirable
in so far as they emulate the manners of their social superiors, but always condemned for attempting to do so.

Source: John Peck, "Middle-Class Life in *Vanity Fair*," in *English: The Journal of the English Association,* Vol. 43, No. 175, Spring 1994, pp. 1–16.

Sources

Brontë, Charlotte, Preface to *Jane Eyre,* Clarendon Press, 1969.

Colby, Robert A., "Historical Introduction," in *Vanity Fair,* Garland, 1989, pp. 632–37.

Cuddon, J. A., *The Penguin Dictionary of Literary Terms and Literary Theory,* Penguin Books, 1992, pp. 827–32.

Forster, John, *Examiner,* No. 2112, July 22, 1848, pp. 468–70.

Karlson, Marilyn Naufftus, "William Makepeace Thackeray," in *Dictionary of Literary Biography,* Volume 55: *Victorian Prose Writers Before 1867,* edited by William B. Thesing, Gale Research, 1987, pp. 303–14.

Lewes, George Henry, *Athenaeum,* No. 1085, August 12, 1848, pp. 794–97.

Peck, Harry Thurston, *Studies in Several Literatures,* Dodd, Mead and Company, 1909, pp. 149–61.

Ray, Gordon N., ed., *The Letters and Private Papers of William Makepeace Thackeray,* Vol. 2, Harvard University Press, 1945–1946, p. 309.

Review of *Vanity Fair,* in *London Review,* Vol. XVI, No. XXXII, July 1861, pp. 291–94.

Rigby, Elizabeth, Review of *Vanity Fair,* in *Quarterly Review,* December 1848, pp. 155–62.

"William Makepeace Thackeray: *Vanity Fair: A Novel without a Hero,*" in *Characters in Nineteenth-Century Literature,* Gale Research, 1993, pp. 490–96.

Further Reading

Mitchell, Sally, *Daily Life in Victorian England,* Greenwood Publishing Group, 1996.
This comprehensive look at both city and country life in Victorian England covers social classes, morals, economics and finance, laws, and more. It includes illustrations and excerpts from primary source documents.

Pascoe, David, ed., *Selected Journalism 1850–1870,* Penguin USA, 1998.
This generous collection of the journalistic writings of Charles Dickens offers minute and gritty details of life in London in the mid-nineteenth century.

Peters, Catherine, *Thackeray: A Writer's Life,* Sutton Publishing, 2000.
This recent biography examines Thackeray's life and how his writing was influenced by his experiences and the world around him.

Thackeray, William Makepeace, *Thackerayana,* Haskell House, 1970.
This is an engaging, self-illustrated collection of anecdotes and observations, many of them humorous, about everything from Thackeray's childhood to his favorite literary characters.

The Wonderful Wizard of Oz

L. Frank Baum

1900

L. Frank Baum never imagined the impact *The Wonderful Wizard of Oz* would have on children's writing or the appeal the book would have to generations of readers. Although he wrote numerous books, *The Wonderful Wizard of Oz* is easily his most enduring. Baum wanted to write a fairy tale that was American, not European, although he introduced elements of traditional European fairy tales (witches, castles, forests) into the story. By presenting a female protagonist, casual language, characters such as the Scarecrow and the Tin Woodman, and settings such as Kansas, Baum created a new approach to children's writing that is distinctly American.

Before *The Wonderful Wizard of Oz*, children's books were stilted morality tales designed to instruct or to frighten readers into behaving properly. Baum, however, presented a thrilling adventure from a child's point of view, showing the child's ability to solve her own problems and return to the security of her home.

The Wonderful Wizard of Oz received praise from critics and readers alike. Critics applauded Baum's simple storytelling, his message, and his imaginative, believable characters. Readers fell in love with the wonders of Oz and demanded more books about this enchanted land. Although the book did not win any awards during Baum's lifetime, it was given the Lewis Carroll Shelf Award in 1968.

L. Frank Baum

Author Biography

Lyman Frank Baum was born on May 15, 1856, in Chittenango, New York, to Cynthia and Benjamin Ward Baum. Benjamin was a wealthy barrel-maker and sawyer who made his fortune during the Pennsylvania oil rush. The Baums' loss of four of their nine children in infancy and Frank's heart condition led the parents to indulge and shelter their young son.

As an adult, Frank Baum had a wildly varied career. Over the years, he was a newspaperman, an actor, a playwright, an axle grease maker, a dime store owner, a salesman, a Hollywood entrepreneur, and a chicken breeder. While touring with an acting troupe performing his play *The Maid of Arran,* Baum met and fell in love with Maud Gage, the youngest daughter of suffragette Matilda Josilyn Gage. Although the elder Gage opposed the union, Maud was determined to marry Baum. They wed in 1882 and built a strong marriage as Maud provided stability for the family while Baum pursued his varied interests. The couple had four sons and moved frequently, eventually settling in Hollywood where medical care was available for Baum's declining health.

Baum's mother-in-law was impressed with the imaginative stories she heard Baum telling the chil-

dren, and she encouraged him to submit them for publication. He did and soon found success as a children's author. *Father Goose: His Book* (1899), a book of children's verse, earned Baum critical acclaim. The following year, *The Wonderful Wizard of Oz* was published. It was so successful that Baum's readers demanded more Oz books. This ongoing demand assured Baum of income, and although he often tired of writing about Oz, he completed a total of fourteen books in the series. After his death, his publisher commissioned other writers to continue the series.

Baum died on May 16, 1919, after complications following gall bladder surgery. His weakened condition, combined with his lifelong heart problems, brought on a twenty-four-hour coma after which the author died in his Hollywood home.

Plot Summary

Chapters One–Six

Dorothy lives on a small farm in Kansas with Aunt Em and Uncle Henry. When a cyclone hits, Dorothy and her dog, Toto, are carried away in the farmhouse. They land in a strange place where a good witch and tiny people called Munchkins greet them. Dorothy's house has landed on (and killed) the Wicked Witch of the East. Dorothy takes the Wicked Witch's charmed silver shoes, and the good witch gives her a protective kiss on her forehead so she can reach Oz safely. Dorothy hopes that the Wizard of Oz will be able to send her back to Kansas, so she sets off on the yellow brick road.

Soon, Dorothy and Toto meet the Scarecrow. He desperately wants a brain, so he accompanies them on their trip. Next, they meet the Tin Woodman, who tells his story of how he was once human and how he longs to have a heart again. Dorothy tells him that the Wizard of Oz can help, so the Tin Woodman joins them. As they make their way through a forest, they encounter the Cowardly Lion. Although he initially tries to frighten them, he admits that he is a coward and wishes he had the courage that the King of the Beasts should have. He joins the travelers, hoping that the Wizard of Oz can help him, too.

Chapters Seven–Twelve

The travelers meet many dangers on the yellow brick road, such as ditches, a river, and terrifying creatures. While crossing a poppy field, Dorothy, Toto, and the Lion are lulled to sleep by the scent. The Scarecrow and the Tin Woodman carry Dorothy and Toto, and then call on thousands of field mice to help them carry the Lion out of the field.

Finally, the travelers arrive at the gates of the Emerald City where they are told that the Wizard of Oz will see them individually. Each traveler tells his or her wish, but the Wizard says that until the Wicked Witch of the West is dead, their wishes will not be granted. Disappointed and afraid, the group sets off to find the Wicked Witch of the West. The Witch has only one eye, but it is as powerful as a telescope so she sees the intruders in her land. She sends crows, bees, and wolves to destroy them, but each fails. When she sends the Winged Monkeys, they tear the Scarecrow apart, ruin the Tin Woodman's metal body, and retrieve the Lion, Dorothy, and Toto for the Witch. She enslaves them and tries to trick Dorothy into taking off the magical silver shoes. Dorothy becomes angry and throws a bucket of water on the Witch, who melts away to nothing.

Chapters Thirteen–Eighteen

Dorothy frees the Lion and the people (the Winkies) enslaved by the Witch. The Winkies help Dorothy restore the Scarecrow and the Tin Woodman, and the group heads back to the Emerald City. Before they leave, however, Dorothy finds a Golden Cap. When she realizes that it enables her to control the Winged Monkeys, she calls them to take the travelers back to the Emerald City.

Dorothy and her friends again visit the Wizard of Oz. Realizing that the Scarecrow, the Tin Woodman, and the Cowardly Lion already possess the qualities they desire, the Wizard gives them false charms that merely help them believe that they have these qualities. Dorothy and the others discover that the Wizard is a fraud; he is a man who has maintained a façade by using trickery. Then the Wizard builds a balloon to carry Dorothy and himself back home, but Dorothy misses the launch and is left behind. Unsure what to do next, Dorothy decides to visit Glinda, the Witch of the South.

Chapters Nineteen–Twenty-Four

On the way to see Glinda, the group encounters fighting trees and a small town made entirely of china. Passing through a forest, the Lion kills a giant spider that has been terrorizing the animals. Unable to get by the Hammer-Heads, Dorothy calls the Winged Monkeys, who transport the travelers safely to Glinda's land.

Dorothy gives Glinda the Golden Cap, and Glinda uses it to send the Scarecrow to rule in Oz, the Lion to be the King of the Beasts in the forest, and the Tin Woodman to rule the Winkies. Glinda explains to Dorothy that the silver shoes have the power to take the wearer anywhere in only three steps. Dorothy bids farewell to her friends, and she and Toto return to Kansas. A new farmhouse has been built, and Aunt Em runs to greet her niece.

Characters

Cowardly Lion

The Cowardly Lion is the third and final creature who joins the Oz-bound group. Dorothy, the Scarecrow, and the Tin Woodman meet him when he jumps out at them as they make their way through a forest. He knocks over the Scarecrow and the Tin Woodman, and when he tries to bite Toto, Dorothy slaps him and calls him a coward. He is ashamed and admits that Dorothy is right. He wants to have the courage that the King of the Beasts should have. Dorothy agrees to allow him to accompany them, reasoning that he needs courage and that he could be helpful in frightening away other creatures.

Despite his belief that he lacks courage, the Lion often demonstrates bravery. He fails to understand that courage is not the absence of fear, but is taking action in the face of fear. Just as in the cases of the Scarecrow and the Tin Woodman, the Wizard soon sees that the Cowardly Lion already possesses the courage he so desires. He gives the Lion a special potion that is supposedly liquid courage. After drinking it, the Cowardly Lion feels empowered instantly. After Dorothy leaves for Kansas, he returns to a forest where he previously killed a giant spider because the animals asked him to return as their leader.

Dorothy

Dorothy is the story's heroine, whose travels to see the Wizard of Oz bring her friendship and adventure. She lives with her aunt and uncle on a small farm in Kansas. Her best friend is her small dog, Toto. When a cyclone whips across Kansas, Dorothy and Toto are carried away in the small farmhouse and eventually are set down in the land of the Munchkins. When Dorothy discovers that her house has landed on (and killed) the Wicked Witch of the East, she is horrified, despite the gratitude and wonder of the Munchkins.

Dorothy only wants to return home, and she is told by the Witch of the North that she must see the Wizard of Oz. Dorothy takes the Wicked Witch of the East's silver shoes, and she and Toto head out on the yellow brick road. Dorothy is a determined child who is single-minded in her goal to get back home. She is brave, smart, compassionate, selfless, and encouraging to the other members of the traveling party. Although Dorothy is honored for killing both of the wicked witches, she never means to hurt anyone. Dorothy is an inadvertent liberator, who improves the lives of everyone (except the wicked witches) with whom she comes in contact. She feels badly about killing anyone, even a wicked witch, but she is glad that doing so will enable her to get home.

Dorothy thinks and speaks for herself. When she and the others discover that the Wizard of Oz is nothing but a "humbug" with no real powers, she expresses her anger openly. Later, when Glinda tells her how to get home, Dorothy is sympathetic to the feelings of her friends who will miss her terribly, but she follows through on her own desire to return to her aunt and uncle in Kansas. Despite the wonders and magic of the new land, she is anxious to get back to the gray setting of Kansas because it is her home, which is most important to her.

Aunt Em

Aunt Em is Dorothy's mother figure. Although she was once a vibrant woman, years on the harsh prairie have taken their toll on her appearance and spirits.

Glinda

Glinda is the Witch of the South. She is a good witch and is youthful and stunningly beautiful. When Dorothy gives her the Golden Cap that allows its owner to call upon the Winged Monkeys three times, she uses it to send the Scarecrow back to the Emerald City, the Lion back to the forest, and the Tin Woodman back to the land of the Winkies (previously ruled by the Wicked Witch of the West). Glinda gives the Golden Cap to the King of the Winged Monkeys so they will no longer be at the bidding of its wearer. She tells Dorothy that she has had the power to return to Kansas all along because of the silver shoes. Glinda explains the secret charm of the shoes, which is that they will take the wearer anywhere she wants to go in three steps.

Uncle Henry

Dorothy's father figure, Uncle Henry is a grim man with a long beard. He is a very hard worker who never laughs.

Scarecrow

The Scarecrow is the first companion who joins Dorothy on her way to see the Wizard of Oz. He is mounted on a pole in the middle of a field where crows are not at all afraid of him. The Scarecrow is humble in appearance, and his single desire is to have a brain. His only fear is fire, and he never needs to eat or sleep. The Scarecrow is very nurturing toward Dorothy, gladly watching over her and Toto as they sleep and often finding fruit and nuts for them to eat. On the other hand, he is a bit clumsy and is not strong like the Lion, so he is not terribly helpful in physical struggles. Because he is not subject to pain, however, he often volunteers to go ahead of the group to test treacherous landscapes, such as jagged rocks.

The Scarecrow fails to realize that he does not need to be given a brain because he is already quite intelligent. He usually comes up with plans that save the travelers, and he is quick to come up with solutions to problems. The Wizard realizes that the Scarecrow is already intelligent, but to make him happy, he creates a "brain" out of bran and pins and needles, which will make him sharp. When he presents the Scarecrow with the brain, the Scarecrow is delighted and feels smart instantly. When the Wizard of Oz builds a balloon to carry him back home, he leaves the Scarecrow in charge of the Emerald City.

Tin Woodman

Dorothy and the Scarecrow discover the Tin Woodman in the woods. He is rusted in position with his axe in the air and has been stuck this way for more than a year. He explains that he was caught in the rain and has been waiting for someone to come by and save him. Once Dorothy retrieves his oil can from his nearby cottage, the Tin Woodman is oiled and able to move freely again.

The Tin Woodman tells his sad story about when he was fully human and planned to marry a Munchkin girl. She lived with an old woman, however, who relied on the girl to care for her so she had the Wicked Witch of the East put a curse on the Tin Woodman's axe. The curse caused him to chop up his own body, little by little. After each "accident," he had a local tinsmith craft a new body part out of tin for him until eventually he was made

Media Adaptations

- The earliest adaptation of *The Wonderful Wizard of Oz* was a 1902 stage musical on which Baum collaborated. It ran very successfully on Broadway, although the play had significant revisions from the original text.

- The most famous adaptation is the 1939 MGM musical film starring Judy Garland as Dorothy. The film won Academy Awards for best original score and best song. In 1989, the film won the National Film Registry Award.

- The following companies and individuals have released film adaptations of Baum's novel: Selig Polyscope Company's (1910; silent); Ray C. Smallwood (1921; silent); Chadwick Pictures (1925; silent); J. R. Booth, Ted Eshbaugh, and Carl W. Stalling (1933; silent); Maud Gage Baum (Baum's widow) and Kenneth McLellan (1938); Teaching Resources Films (1975); Mankato Fine Arts Community Theatre (1976); Films Inc. (1976); Walker Company (1989; animated); Fuji (1991; animated); and American Film Investment Corporation (1991; animated).

- The following companies and individuals have produced television movie adaptations: Burr Tillstrom (1950); Sharon Statz (1964); Gene London & Company (1967); British Broadcasting Corporation (1977; British, musical); Turner Broadcasting Systems (1995; starring Jackson Browne, Roger Daltrey, Natalie Cole, Joel Grey, Nathan Lane, Debra Winger, and Lucy Arnaz); and Unitel Mobile Video (1996; ice skating adaptation starring Oksana Baiul, Bobby McFerrin, and Victor Petrenko).

- Saban Productions (1986; animated), Cinar Films (1987; animated), and Hyperion Entertainment (1993) have released video adaptations.

- Television series adaptations were made by Videocraft Incorporated (1961; animated) and DiC Productions (1990; animated).

- Audio adaptations have been produced by the following: Blackstone Audio Books (1980); Recorded Books (1987); Radio Yesteryear Audio (1988); Books on Tape (1996); Penguin Audiobooks (1997); Monterey Soundworks (1998); and Naxos Audio Books (2001).

---

entirely of tin. He remembers how happy he was to be in love, and so his desire is to have a heart again.

The Tin Woodman is like the Scarecrow in that he already possesses the quality he hopes to be given by the Wizard. He believes that he has no heart, yet he is the most compassionate and emotional member of the group. When he sees the Wizard of Oz, he is fitted with a silk heart that is merely symbolic yet makes him feel different right away. After Dorothy returns to Kansas, he goes back to the Land of the Winkies, who have asked him to be their leader.

Toto

Toto is Dorothy's faithful canine companion. He is her best friend in Kansas and accompanies her on her adventures in Oz. He is playful, wary of strangers, and brave in certain situations.

Wicked Witch of the East

The Wicked Witch of the East is killed when Dorothy's house lands on her after being hurled through the air during a cyclone. She has a pair of silver shoes that have a secret charm. Although Dorothy does not know what the charm is, she takes the shoes.

Wicked Witch of the West

The Wicked Witch of the West is ugly and has only one eye although her one eye is as powerful as a telescope. When Toto bites her, she does not bleed because she is so evil that her blood has dried up in her veins. When she is unable to kill the travelers as they make their way to her castle, she has the Scarecrow dismantled and the Tin Woodman seriously dented. Then she enslaves the Lion and Dorothy. The Lion refuses to submit to the witch, so she decides to starve him, but Dorothy secretly feeds him at night. The witch makes Dorothy a kitchen servant.

The witch wants the silver shoes that Dorothy wears. She trips Dorothy and is able to get one shoe, but Dorothy becomes so angry that she throws a bucket of water on the witch. To Dorothy's surprise, the witch melts before her eyes. Dorothy retrieves her shoe, frees the Lion, and keeps the witch's Golden Cap although she has no idea it allows her to control the Winged Monkeys. The Winkies, who had been enslaved by the witch, are so grateful that they gladly obey Dorothy when she asks them to put the Scarecrow back together and hammer the Tin Woodman back into shape.

Witch of the North

The Witch of the North is the good witch who is a friend of the Munchkins. She is an old woman who believes that Dorothy must also be a witch because her house lands on the Wicked Witch of the East. She tells Dorothy that to return to Kansas, she will have to see the Wizard of Oz. She insists that Dorothy take the Wicked Witch of the East's silver shoes, which possess a secret charm. To protect the girl on her journey, she gives her a kiss on her forehead, which serves as a sign to others not to harm the girl.

Wizard of Oz

The Wizard of Oz is reported to be "great and terrible" and able to appear in any form he pleases. For Dorothy's visit, he is a giant head; for the Scarecrow's visit, he is a beautiful lady; for the Tin Woodman, he appears as a frightening beast; and for the Lion, he appears as a ball of fire. He promises each that he will grant his or her wish once they have all killed the Wicked Witch of the West. After they have done so, however, they discover that he is not really a wizard at all and cannot grant their wishes with magical powers. He admits that he is a "humbug" who should not have deceived the good people of the Emerald City for so long but says that he means no harm. He tells Dorothy that he is not a bad man, just a bad wizard.

The Wizard explains that he originally came from Omaha where he was a circus balloonist. One day, his balloon was caught in a great wind, and he landed in Oz, where his descent from the sky

made everyone believe he was a wizard. He decided to let them believe this, and so he created a persona for himself. He commanded the people to build the great city and made them believe everything was made of emeralds by making everyone wear green glasses. With the help of gadgets and illusions, he was able to pretend to be a great wizard. He feared the witches, however, because he knew they had real powers, which is why he sent the group to kill the Wicked Witch of the West after Dorothy inadvertently killed the Wicked Witch of the East.

The Wizard knows that he can grant the wishes of the Scarecrow, the Tin Woodman, and the Lion with false charms because they already possess the qualities they want. He comes up with a plan to build another balloon to take Dorothy and himself home, but when it is time to go, Dorothy misses the launch by seconds and is left behind. They never hear from the false wizard again.

Themes

Self-Sufficiency

The predominant theme of *The Wonderful Wizard of Oz* is self-sufficiency. The Scarecrow, Tin Woodman, and Cowardly Lion all seek external magic to give them qualities they already possess but fail to recognize. When the travelers come to a wide ditch (chapter seven), the Cowardly Lion volunteers to try jumping over it. If he can make it, he reasons, he can carry each of his friends across safely. Discussing the possibility of falling into the ditch, the Cowardly Lion responds, "'I am terribly afraid of falling, myself. . . but I suppose there is nothing to do but try it.'" The Lion does not realize that courage is acting despite fear, not acting in the absence of fear. In a scene at the end of chapter six, the reader sees both the Tin Woodman and the Scarecrow demonstrating the very qualities they feel they are lacking. The Tin Woodman accidentally steps on a beetle and begins to weep. When his tears rust his jaw shut, no one is able to figure out what his gestures for the oil can mean except for the Scarecrow, who immediately loosens the Tin Woodman's jaws with the oil. This scene shows how emotional the Tin Woodman is and how quick thinking the Scarecrow is. A more mature reader can then recognize that with the Cowardly Lion, the Scarecrow, and the Tin Woodman, Baum is using irony to portray the theme of self-sufficiency.

Topics For Further Study

- Consider why Baum chose a Scarecrow, a Tin Woodman, and a Cowardly Lion as characters desiring a brain, a heart, and courage, respectively. Recast these characters with new creatures or people without changing what each one desires. Draft a character sketch for each of your new characters, complete with background and outcome.

- Watch the film classic (made in 1939, starring Judy Garland) based on this novel. Write a movie review in which you argue that Baum would or would not have approved of this adaptation. Think about the differences between the film and the novel and try to imagine how Baum would react to them. Be as specific as possible in your analysis.

- Look in your library or online for W. W. Denslow's illustrations that originally accompanied *The Wonderful Wizard of Oz*. Why do you think so much is made of these illustrations

among critics? Do you believe they have artistic merit? Do you see why they appealed to children in 1900? Do you think they have the same appeal today? Write a letter to a fictitious publisher in which you make a case for or against including these illustrations in an upcoming edition of the novel.

- *The Wonderful Wizard of Oz* has been subject to a wide variety of interpretations. Scholars with various frames of reference, including politics, feminism, and psychology, have interpreted the novel. Choose a unique point of view from which you can at least partly interpret the events and/or characters of the novel. You might choose a certain discipline (such as economics, technology, or history) or you might choose an ideology or philosophy (such as democracy, a certain religion, or environmentalism). It is not necessary to make every point of the novel fit, but see if you can devise a new way of interpreting certain aspects of the story.

Dorothy's situation is somewhat different because she needs a magical object (the silver shoes) to help her get back home to Kansas. Still, she fails to understand that she has had what she needs all along while continuing to seek it from others. Another important point about the silver shoes is that Dorothy earned them by killing the Wicked Witch of the East. While she did so unintentionally, her actions resulted in the freedom of the Munchkins, which in turn resulted in her being given the magical shoes that will allow her to get home. She was not given a way home simply because she asked for one; she was given a way home because she improved the lives of the Munchkins.

Dorothy's resolve and decisiveness throughout the book also attest to her self-sufficiency. She is independent and determined, and these qualities ultimately enable her to get back home. Rather than resign herself to life in a strange land, she refuses to give up on the idea that there is a way for her to get home.

Good versus Evil

The struggle between good and evil is evident throughout *The Wonderful Wizard of Oz*. There are two good witches and two wicked witches. The wicked witches are unable to protect themselves against Dorothy, who is so good that she feels remorse at killing them. To make the good/evil dichotomy perfectly clear to young readers, Baum places the good witches in the north and the south, and the wicked witches in the east and the west.

In *The Wonderful Wizard of Oz*, good always triumphs over evil, and evil respects the power of good. The Witch of the North gives Dorothy a kiss on the forehead, and this kiss protects her from harm by the Wicked Witch of the West. When the Winged Monkeys are sent to destroy Dorothy and her friends, one of them positions himself to attack her but sees the kiss. He tells the others, "'We dare not harm this little girl. . . for she is protected by the Power of Good, and that is greater than the Power of Evil.'"

Baum also demonstrates that there are cases in which a person is not entirely good or evil, as in the character of the Wizard of Oz. As the Wizard admits to Dorothy, he is not a bad man, just a bad wizard. Although Dorothy deeply disapproves of his willingness to deceive people, she forgives him because she realizes that he is not truly evil. Baum teaches young readers that it is not possible to label real people good or evil because in reality, everybody has a little of both in them.

Style

Description

Baum interjects highly descriptive passages into his text, which bring the fictitious world of Oz alive in the imagination of the reader. Lush descriptions of landscapes are appealing to children, who enjoy getting lost in the fantastic story. In chapter two, Dorothy and her house land among the Munchkins. Baum describes the rich land:

> There were lovely patches of greensward [grassy turf] all about, with stately trees bearing rich and luscious fruits. Banks of gorgeous flowers were on every hand, and birds with rare and brilliant plumage sang and fluttered in the trees and bushes. A little way off was a small brook, rushing and sparkling along between green banks, and murmuring in a voice very grateful to a little girl who had lived so long on the dry, gray prairies.

In describing the poppy field, Baum not only uses visual and auditory images, but he also introduces the very important smell of the poppy field. He writes:

> They walked along listening to the singing of the bright colored birds and looking at the lovely flowers which now became so thick that the ground was carpeted with them. They were big yellow and white and blue and purple blossoms, great clusters of scarlet poppies, which were so brilliant in color they almost dazzled Dorothy's eyes.

> "Aren't they beautiful?" the girl asked, as she breathed in the spicy scent of the flowers.

Some of Baum's descriptions are not only helpful in understanding the story, but also reflect the author's penchant for wordplay. In chapter two, for example, he describes the Scarecrow's voice as "husky," a clear reference to cornhusks.

Foreshadowing

Baum's use of foreshadowing is an indication of a tightly woven story. In some cases, the reader is surprised to find that a piece of information given early in the story becomes relevant later. In chapter one, Baum explains that as the cyclone is carrying Dorothy away in her farmhouse, she "felt as if she were going up in a balloon." Later the Wizard builds a balloon in which to carry Dorothy and himself back home. (Dorothy misses the balloon's launch, however, and must find another way to get home.)

At other times, the reader suspects foreshadowing and waits curiously to see how a bit of information will add to the story. Baum tells the reader that the silver shoes hold an unknown magical power. Although Dorothy does not know that the shoes have the power to take her back home, she keeps them throughout the story, and readers wonder what purpose the shoes will serve. The author similarly makes a special effort to tell the reader that the Wicked Witch of the West fears water more than anything. He writes, "Indeed, the old Witch never touched water, nor ever let water touch her in any way." This information becomes very important later when Dorothy throws a bucket of water on the Witch and she melts.

Historical Context

The Gold Standard Debate

The gold standard is a monetary system in which the value of gold determines the value of money. Each unit of currency represents a certain amount of gold. In the United States, the gold standard was adopted during the 1870s. Although a bimetallic (gold and silver) system had been used before the Civil War, this system changed when the silver dollar was dropped in 1873. Laws allowed for free and unlimited coinage of gold, meaning that people could take their gold and have it made into coins based on its weight and value. The Gold Standard Act of 1900 made the gold standard official.

Not everyone was content with the gold standard. Many groups, such as farmers and other rural workers, believed that the gold standard was a means for maintaining the division between the "haves" and the "have-nots." After the Civil War, farmers struggled as the country focused on industrial advancements such as railroads and telegraphs. From this discontent emerged the Populist Party, a political party that was determined to regain control of the economy by returning to a bimetallic system. They called for free coinage of silver, which

Compare & Contrast

- **1900s:** Children's books are predominantly morality tales that teach heavy-handed lessons. Many of these stories are purposely frightening to intimidate children into behaving properly.

  Today: Many forms and styles of children's books are popular. While many children's books teach lessons, they do so in subtle and appealing ways. Books are generally written to engage children's imaginations so that they will be enjoyable.

- **1900:** Industrial and technological innovations are on the rise. Although the railroad, telephone, and telegraph are changing the face of travel, communication, and trade, domestic life remains simple. The American fascination with technology is seen in *The Wizard of Oz* when the Wizard uses gadgets and special effects to maintain the farce that he is a wizard. He makes his exit in a balloon.

  Today: The technological revolution that began a century ago has radically altered everyday life. The Internet affects business, family life, personal relationships, and education. In science, a map of the human genome (the collective genetic material of the human species) is successfully completed.

would enable them to reclaim the value of their now-worthless silver.

The debate over the gold standard took place directly before and after the publication of *The Wizard of Oz*. Many historians interpret the book as a commentary on the gold standard because of the yellow brick road and the magical silver shoes. These interpretations also maintain that Dorothy's farmhouse killing the Wicked Witch of the East is symbolic of the eventual demise of rich easterners at the hands of rural farmers.

Crossroads of Two Literary Periods

Published in 1900, *The Wizard of Oz* was introduced to the public at a time when one literary period was ending (the Realistic Period, 1865–1900) and another was beginning (the Naturalistic and Symbolistic Period, 1900–1930). The Realistic Period followed the Civil War, an era marked by struggle and opposition. While the North enjoyed an economic boom, the South faced great difficulty in repairing and restoring its land, buildings, and economy. New points of view emerged in the intellectual world, as the works of Darwin, Marx, and others offered scientific arguments that challenged existing religious beliefs. This skepticism is reflected in much of the fiction of the period; the dominant writers were Mark Twain, William Dean Howells, and Henry James. The Realistic Period contrasted with the melodramatic Romantic Period that preceded it as writers began focusing on disillusionment and pragmatism (in which value is based on utility). Although fanciful, *The Wonderful Wizard of Oz* reflects some of the tendencies of the Realistic Period. Dorothy is a realistic child who comes from a humble home, her friends are not grandiose but ordinary, and she is steadfast in her goal to get home despite the wonders of Oz.

Around 1900, however, a new literary movement began to overshadow the Realistic Period. The Naturalistic and Symbolistic Period witnessed a rise in journalistic writing styles, and the realism introduced during the Realistic Period became harsher. Prominent writers were Theodore Dreiser and Jack London. After World War I, the Lost Generation, a group of writers disgruntled by American idealism, emerged. They longed for innovation and admired French symbolists like Marcel Proust. They rejected many aspects of American culture by creating a new, polished style of writing, by writing satire and by recalling simpler times in American history when society was more structured and had a sense of tradition.

Bert Lahr (left) as the Cowardly Lion, Jack Haley as the Tin Woodman, Judy Garland as Dorothy, and Ray Bolger as the Scarecrow in the Academy Award-winning classic 1939 film version of the novel

Because 1900 was a year of change in American literature, it was the perfect time for innovative twists on existing genres. *The Wonderful Wizard of Oz* reflects this openness to change in its new interpretation of the traditional fairy tale.

Critical Overview

When *The Wonderful Wizard of Oz* was published in 1900, it immediately caught the attention of readers and critics. Baum had already enjoyed success with a previous children's book, *Father Goose: His Book,* so the release of Baum's new book was much anticipated. There were a few critics who dismissed the book as lacking style and real substance, and, over the years, the book has come under scrutiny by certain religious groups for its inclusion of witches and magic. Still, the novel continues to be regarded as a classic of children's literature.

What set *The Wonderful Wizard of Oz* apart from other children's books was its imaginative story line, its elaborate illustrations (created by W. W. Denslow), its characterization, and its departure from the typical style of children's writing. In a 1900 review, a critic writes in the *New York Times Saturday Review of Books and Art* that the story's humor and philosophy will surely appeal to children's minds. The critic adds that the "bright and joyous atmosphere" gives the story excitement and

optimism. Leading Oz scholar Michael Patrick Hearn asserts in *Dictionary of Literary Biography: American Writers for Children, 1900–1960,* "Children's books have just not been the same since Dorothy first went to the Emerald City." He adds, "The Scarecrow, the Tin Woodman, and the Cowardly Lion have entered the collective consciousness of childhood."

Critics often credit Baum's characterization for the ongoing success of *The Wonderful Wizard of Oz.* Although the Scarecrow, Tin Woodman, and Lion are not human, Baum makes them seem so with their desires for human qualities. In *Reference Guide to American Literature,* Philip Jose Farmer remarks, "The quest of the Scarecrow for brains, the Woodman for a heart, and the Lion for courage, qualities they already possessed but did not know how to use, is the stuff of which classics are made." On the subject of secondary characters, Hearn writes,

> Like Dickens and Twain, Baum had that rare gift of memorable character invention. While really only a suit stuffed with straw and an odd collection of junk, Baum's Scarecrow and Tin Woodman are among the most beloved personalities in all of juvenile literature.

American author James Thurber remarks in *New Republic* in 1934 that he has been told that Baum wrote the book "to see if he could animate, and make real, creatures never alive before on sea or land." Thurber concludes, "He succeeded, emi-

nently, with the Scarecrow and Tin Woodman."
Commenting on the character of Dorothy, Hearn
comments,

> She is a practical, clear-sighted, modern child; she is
> an American child, full of mother wit and grit. . . .
> She thinks and reacts like a real child. When she lands
> in Oz, she does not go off to seek her fortune; she
> wants to go home.

Many critics note that the book's appeal extends beyond its intended audience of young children. As Farmer observes: "The Oz books have also
been popular with adults, who recognize subtleties
which escaped them as children." A reviewer for
the *New York Times Saturday Review of Books and
Art* in 1900 makes a similar observation:

> In *The Wonderful Wizard of Oz* the fact is clearly rec-
> ognized that the young as well as their elders love
> novelty. They are pleased with dashes of color and
> something new in the place of the old, familiar, and
> winged fairies of Grimm and Andersen.

A contributor to *St. James Guide to Fantasy
Writers* notes that the book should be embraced by
all readers of fantasy because it "is surely the most
famous American fantasy ever written" and "remains one of its most memorable and fully developed fantasy worlds."

Modern critics agree that for all the books
Baum wrote in his prolific career, his reputation is
secured by *The Wonderful Wizard of Oz*. Farmer
calls the novel Baum's masterpiece, noting that it
not only made him famous at the time of its publication but elevated him into the ranks of classic
children's writers. In *U. S. News & World Report*,
Amanda Spake declares, "One hundred years after
its publication, it remains the most significant children's book in American history: No other fantasy
is more beloved, hated, cited, imitated, interpreted,
adapted, or marketed."

Criticism

Jennifer Bussey

*Bussey holds a master's degree in interdisci-
plinary studies and a bachelor's degree in English
literature. She is an independent writer specializing in literature. In the following essay, she considers the elements of Baum's novel that open it up
to so many lines of interpretation.*

Over the years, L. Frank Baum's children's classic,
The Wonderful Wizard of Oz, has been interpreted
from virtually every angle. Feminists, populists,

Marxists, historians, economists, political scientists,
and Freudians and other psychologists have all interpreted the characters and events of the novel in
terms of their particular points of view. The book
has been looked at as a commentary on American
life and as a statement about New World ways replacing Old World ways. Presidential scholars have
considered the possibility that the Wizard of Oz represents Benjamin Harrison, Grover Cleveland,
William McKinley, or a combination of the three.
Still other scholars interpret the novel as a fable
about substitutions: Dorothy lives with substitute
parents; she returns to a substitute farmhouse; a
common man has substituted the identity of the
Wizard for his own; and the Scarecrow, Tin Woodman, and Cowardly Lion are all made happy with
substitute charms. Baum himself never lent cre-
dence to any of these interpretations, and Oz scholars generally dismiss claims that the story is any
kind of social or political commentary. So, what is
it about *The Wonderful Wizard of Oz* that compels
academics to seek out subtexts in the novel?

When *The Wonderful Wizard of Oz* was published in 1900, it was a dramatic departure from
existing children's literature. Other children's
books were morality tales written in lofty language
meant to instruct and guide young minds; Baum's
novel was a flight of fancy for the imagination. It
presented a child protagonist (a female one, which
was particularly unusual) who spoke and acted like
a real child. The story was told from her point of
view, and she turned out to be an independent child
who embodied many of the qualities Americans admire. Add to this innovative protagonist the wildly
imaginative places, fantastic people, and non-
human creatures, and this book was very different
from others in its genre. This brought the book a
lot of attention and scrutiny. While most critics embraced it, others did not; but above all the book
grabbed the reading public's attention. This led to
a wider readership than was originally intended,
and many of those readers began looking to interpret the story as symbolic of some larger reality.

The Wonderful Wizard of Oz contains numerous elements that open it up for interpretation. For
example, the book has a dominant good versus evil
theme, and it is presented in a straightforward manner that is easy for children to understand. From an
adult's point of view, however, the places and characters representing good (a child, the North, the
South) and those representing evil (the East, the
West) can be fitted into ideological categories. Populists' interpretation, for example, viewed the East
as the enemy of the West. They believed that

wealthy eastern politicians were destroying the hard-working farmers of the West; so when Dorothy's house comes from Kansas and kills the Wicked Witch of the East, they viewed this as a symbol of retribution and justice. From a political perspective, the wicked witches are powerful leaders who enslave and oppress people. They rule like tyrants, having no regard for the happiness or well being of the common people. When Dorothy frees them, they choose kinder leaders and different forms of government that allow them to have a say in the way their lands are governed. The Winkies, for example, choose the Tin Woodman as their ruler after Dorothy kills the Wicked Witch of the West. An analogy to real-life rulers and political systems can easily be drawn.

Baum's use of opposites also engenders multiple interpretations of the novel. He has the land of Oz divided into the North, South, East, and West. Dorothy arrives from the dull familiarity of the Kansas plains to the colorful and unfamiliar land of the Munchkins. The beauty of Glinda contrasts sharply with the ugliness of the one-eyed Wicked Witch of the West. Readers can easily associate the colorful and beautiful with whatever people and ideas they favor, and vice versa.

Many readers in 1900 were taken with the silver (the witch's shoes) and the gold (the yellow brick road) in the novel. The gold standard was the subject of much debate at the time, and those who opposed it saw the book as a statement that Dorothy would have to follow the gold to get what she wanted but that ultimately applying silver to gold (walking the road in her silver shoes) would take her home. Opposites are very often a literary clue that the author is using symbolism. Although Baum seems to have intended only to draw clear lines for children to better understand his story, these clear lines can easily be followed to many different conclusions.

Landscapes are often symbolic in literature, and scholars are accustomed to investigating an author's presentations of environments when seeking out the meaning of a novel. In Ernest Hemingway's *A Farewell to Arms,* for example, the author uses mountains to represent safety and plains to represent danger. In *The Wonderful Wizard of Oz,* Dorothy and her new friends encounter forests, rivers, and chasms. Forests are common imagery in fairy tales and symbolize fear, danger, and the unknown. As for rivers, psychologists look for water imagery in dream interpretation, and Freudians, especially, identify water with sexual symbolism.

Rivers in literature often represent the means for a journey, as in *Huckleberry Finn.* Chasms and valleys symbolize seemingly insurmountable difficulties. In addition, Dorothy and the other travelers hear about the great desert that surrounds the entire land of Oz. It is dangerous and mysterious, and it seems to be the only way to get out of Oz and back to Kansas. This can easily be interpreted from a psychological point of view as referring to Dorothy's journey to maturity, as well as to her journey home.

In fact, Dorothy's journey lies at the center of the novel. In *The Wonderful Wizard of Oz,* psychologists see a journey taken by an innocent who wants to restore order in her life. She seeks familiarity and security, and along the way, she grows into a more mature individual. Feminists see the journey of a young girl who, by thinking and acting for herself, is able to achieve her goals and better the lives of those she meets along the way. Because of the rich symbolism associated with travels, there are as many ways to interpret the journey as there are points of view. For this reason, the journey has been symbolic in literature from as far back as classical times and Homer's *The Odyssey.*

Baum's use of anthropomorphism (giving nonhuman characters human characteristics) also opens the book to interpretation. The Scarecrow, the Tin Woodman, the Lion, the Winged Monkeys, the Queen of the Field Mice, and the Stork are all nonhuman characters that possess human qualities. Satirists often use this technique, as do writers wishing to make social commentary (as in George Orwell's *Animal Farm*). Anthropomorphism encourages the reader to broaden his or her view of the character because the character could represent anyone or anything, person or idea, man or woman, famous or not, past or present, individual or collective. The Scarecrow, in other words, could symbolize a certain person, a movement, an event, a piece of legislation, or a phase of personal growth. He can be viewed as an individual or as an extension of Dorothy's experience. To a lesser degree, other characters (such as the china people and the fighting trees) in the novel can be scrutinized in the same manner. These secondary characters are intriguing to scholars looking to find their ideology in Baum's novel.

Although Oz scholars and Baum biographers agree that Baum only intended to write an imaginative story that would engage young children's minds, *The Wonderful Wizard of Oz* continues to be placed under interpretive microscopes. The simple elements that make up the story, the unusual characters and places, and the flow of the story line all give the story the appearance of having a deeper meaning. The book can be made to fit almost any interpretation, and the author's intentions (or lack thereof) do not discourage those who would argue that the book buttresses their point of view. While the book is interesting on its own, the mystique surrounding it as a result of these many interpretations only adds to its popularity among modern readers.

Source: Jennifer Bussey, Critical Essay on *The Wonderful Wizard of Oz,* in *Novels for Students,* The Gale Group, 2002.

Edward Hudlin

In the following essay, Hudlin argues that The Wonderful Wizard of Oz *follows the structure of Joseph Campbell's heroic myth.*

L. Frank Baum's masterpiece, *The Wonderful Wizard of Oz,* has been the subject of psychoanalytical, sociological, political, and even economic analyses. Few critics, however, have attempted to examine it from a truly mythological or philosophical perspective. Lacking such a perspective, some critics have found Baum's writings too episodic, while others have been more concerned with what *Oz* reveals about Baum himself, than with the aesthetic dimensions of the story qua story. While these psycho-social aspects are important, they do not demonstrate how the incidents of the story contribute to its unity, binding it together and driving the plot forward. They do not explain why the book provides such satisfaction to readers of all ages. The value of the interpretation which follows is that it does attempt to satisfy all these concerns.

The thesis of the present essay is that *The Wonderful Wizard of Oz* follows very closely the structure of the heroic myth as defined by Joseph Campbell. The adoption of Campbell's perspective has an immediate heuristic value since, as a result, it becomes possible to demonstrate that *Oz* is not episodic at all, but a highly unified work of art, and, hence, formally satisfying on a purely aesthetic level. Simultaneously, it becomes possible to show that the implicit theme of the work—touching as it does upon eternally recurring problems and values such as love and sacrifice, the conflict of generations, life and death—provides an even deeper satisfaction for the reader on psychic and spiritual levels insofar as these concerns are shared by people of all ages and temperaments. Finally, the use of Campbell's model provides the basis for a more comprehensive, coherent, and sensitive reading of the tale.

Illustration by W. W. Denslow from the novel

Campbell divides mythic stories into three major parts: departure-initiation-return. This pattern is Campbell's abstract of the world-wide nature myths concerning the dying and resurrected savior god: "A hero ventures forth from the world of common day into a region of supernatural wonder; fabulous forces are there encountered and a decisive victory is won; the hero comes back from this mysterious adventure with the power to bestow boons on his fellow man."

Campbell divides each part of the mythic structure into further elements. The subdivisions of the departure have to do with the crossing of the threshold between the two worlds: the ordinary world and the magical world of the adventure. Sometimes the hero or heroine crosses this threshold willingly; sometimes, as in the case with Dorothy, the hero is taken or carried across by an external force. At the threshold, the hero encounters a guardian whom he must either defeat or conciliate. In Dorothy's case it is the Wicked Witch of the East who is defeated when Dorothy's house, carried by a tornado, drops on her. Either before or after the crossing of the first threshold, the hero receives supernatural aid in the form of a magical helper, usually a goddess or an old woman. For Dorothy it is the Good Witch of the North, who acts as her fairy godmother and provides amulets

> The real magic of Oz lies in its "deep" structure and its psychic unity. If critics have sometimes failed to appreciate the story, it is because they have missed the classical allusions and associations embedded in it."

against the forces of darkness Dorothy will encounter. In myth, other helpers, who embody the destiny of the hero, join the quest as well. Dorothy's helpers are the Scarecrow, Tin Man, and Cowardly Lion, whose subplots adumbrate the main plot of Dorothy's adventures.

Beyond the threshold, as part of the initiation, the mythic hero is put to various tests and threatened by various forces. Dorothy must deal with an extraordinary number of natural and supernatural opponents, including fighting trees, killer wolves, deadly bees, hammer-headed creatures who strike out with their heads, poisonous poppy fields, and fierce Kalidahs (tiger-bears).

Next, the hero undergoes a supreme ordeal and wins his reward. The quest is not complete unless the hero returns, with or without the blessing of the powers he has encountered, and brings the boon that restores the world. Dorothy, having redeemed the land of Oz, returns to Kansas and brings to it her life-renewing magic, redeeming both the land and the spiritual lives of Aunt Em and Uncle Henry. In fact, in Baum's sequels (*The Land of Oz, Ozma of Oz, Dorothy and the Wizard in Oz*), Dorothy is enthroned as a princess of Oz and a mistress of both worlds, traveling back and forth at will.

Departure

The mythic hero, as Campbell points out, is a person possessing unusual gifts, which enable him to overcome deficiencies either in himself or in the world. In the beginning of *Oz*, Dorothy's whole world is in a fallen state and cries out for redemption. Dorothy represents its only hope for salvation:

When Dorothy stood in the doorway and looked around, she could see nothing but the great gray

prairie on every side. . . Even the grass was not green for the sun had burned the tops of the long blades until they were the same gray color to be seen everywhere. Once the house had been painted, but the sun blistered the paint, and the rains washed it away, and now the house was as dull and gray as everything else. . .

When Aunt Em came there to live she was a young, pretty wife. The sun and wind had changed her too. They had taken the sparkle from her eyes and left them a somber gray; they had taken the red from her lips and cheeks, and they were gray also. When Dorothy, who was an orphan, first came to her, Aunt Em had been so startled by the child's laughter that she would scream and press her hand upon her heart whenever Dorothy's merry voice reached her ears; and she still looked at the little girl with wonder that she could find anything to laugh at.

Uncle Henry never laughed. He worked hard from morning till night and did not know what joy was. He was gray also, from his long beard to his rough boots, and he looked stern and solemn, and rarely spoke.

It was Toto that made Dorothy laugh, and saved her from growing as gray as her surroundings. . . Toto played all day long, and Dorothy played with him, and loved him dearly.

The fact that Dorothy is an orphan whose parentage and origins are obscure and mysterious is essential to the further development of the story, as it prepares the reader for Dorothy's future apotheosis. The mythic hero or heroine is frequently a person of mystery, and the very puzzlement as to the hero's origins prepares the reader for a later claim of divine or semi-divine parentage. Dorothy is described as an orphan, and no other facts about her past are given except that she came to Aunt Em from somewhere else.

Brian Attebery misses the mythic symbolism of this opening largely because he relies on the fairy tale structure outlined by Vladimir Propp in his *Morphology of the Folk Tale*. According to Propp, the fairy tale always begins with an idyllic situation followed by a profound loss and a subsequent act of rebellion or disobedience. Hence, in *Oz,* Attebery projects an implied beginning in which Dorothy is living happily with her natural parents, loses them, and is then swallowed up by the prairie twister after disobeying the injunction of Aunt Em to stay in the cyclone cellar. However, the text does not support the conjecture that Dorothy ever lived with her natural parents. In the text, Dorothy's origins are totally mysterious, and this mystery is quite appropriate because it prepares the reader for Dorothy's future development. Attebery's mistake is to construe the story purely on the fairy tale level and to ignore its mythic elements. The fairy tale hero(ine) is always an ordinary person, whereas the mythic hero or heroine is someone who stands apart. By attempting to reduce the mystery to something commonplace, Attebery destroys the coherence of the story. The logic of the opening passages in *Oz* is that those who are part and parcel of the ordinary world (Aunt Em and Uncle Henry) cannot transcend it without outside help. If Dorothy can rescue them as Toto has rescued her, it is because she is not wholly of the everyday world. This is consistent with her magic flight to Oz in order to discover her powers as well as the necessity of her return to rejuvenate her foster parents.

In Munchkin Land, Dorothy is immediately recognized as a great sorceress, and this incident prepares the reader for further revelations of a similar kind. Baum also emphasizes that Dorothy came to *her* (Aunt Em), as opposed to saying that Dorothy came to *them*. This emphasis not only focuses the story on the relationship between Dorothy and Aunt Em, but underscores the idea, reinforced later in the tale, that Dorothy comes as a "gift" to Aunt Em from some mysterious source. Ultimately, both Dorothy and Aunt Em experience crises. Dorothy's laughter awakens Aunt Em from the hypnotic spell of Kansas, but the transformation remains incomplete. Meanwhile, Toto saves Dorothy from the danger of falling under the very spell that has transformed Aunt Em from a pretty young wife to a grim reflection of her surroundings. (The name "Toto" is symbolically appropriate, of course, since it implies that he is everything, the catalyst that determines the destinies of all.)

In the Belly of the Cyclone

Dorothy's mythic adventure begins with a magic flight inside a tornado. The psychic need for the life-renewing voyage inside the cyclone can only be understood in reference to the gray, symbolically deficient world of Dorothy's Kansas. Like Jonah in the belly of the whale, Dorothy's transit to Oz is to a world of rebirth symbolized, not only by the whale image, but also by the ambience of the voyage itself. She is carried gently and peacefully—not bludgeoned into unconsciousness as in the movie, but rocked to sleep by the gentle swaying of the house. The journey continues in this way for many hours. At one point, Toto falls through the trap door that used to serve as the entrance to the storm cellar, but Dorothy manages to rescue him by grasping his ears and pulling him back through the door into the safety of her bed. For a

moment Dorothy realizes that Aunt Em and Uncle Henry will think she is dead; but, after a few anxious moments, she is peaceful and serene. Her composure is such that she is even able to rescue Toto, whose passing in and out of the door is yet another image of rebirth. The ultimate sign of this transfiguration is that Dorothy is christened only after the tornado: Her name becomes Dorothy Gale.

The cyclone lands Dorothy, Toto, and the house "very gently—for a cyclone" in the land of Oz. It simultaneously crushes the Wicked Witch of the East, who represents the guardian of the threshold between the two worlds. The crossing of this first magical boundary automatically implies danger, just as the notions of trespass and violation do in ordinary life; therefore, the threshold guardian is a shadowy presence whom Dorothy must defeat or conciliate. In Dorothy's case, the fateful killing of this first guardian by the falling house eliminates any need for conciliation. In classical myth such guardians bound the world in four directions and define as well as confine the hero in his present sphere. So in Oz there are four witches: the Good Witch of the North rules the red land of the Gilligans; the Wicked Witch of the East rules the blue land of the Munchkins; the Good Witch of the South rules the purple land of the Quadlings; and the Wicked Witch of the West rules the yellow land of the Winkies. The navel of this magical realm is the Emerald City itself, ruled by the Great Wizard.

Some critics regard the killing of the Witch of the East as a suggestion that Dorothy commits matricide: the old witch whom Dorothy kills symbolizes her mother. However, mythic symbolism suggests a broader meaning. In Greek myths the guardians of the threshold and the avenging forces of nature are often feminine (for example, the harpies, Medusa). But these forces do not simply represent death; they also represent renewal and rebirth. Mythic symbolism is largely taken from the cycles of nature: the killing of the Winter Witch is necessary for the coming of Spring; the death of the body is necessary for the resurrection of the soul. If we suppose that the meaning of the death of the Witch of the East is that Dorothy killed her mother—and, since Dorothy is only six or seven, that would imply, perhaps, that Dorothy's mother dies in childbirth—then that death must have been necessary for the attainment of a greater object. Given the spiritually impoverished lives of Aunt Em and Uncle Henry, the greater object in Dorothy's world of Kansas would be to redeem them with her love. That is, if the matricidal theme is an acceptable interpretation, the fuller meaning would be that Dorothy is a "gift" from the natural mother to the adoptive parents. However, the opening passages show that Aunt Em and Uncle Henry do not yet understand Dorothy's gift to them. They are too much under the spell of Kansas; hence the need for the magic flight to destroy the witch that has enchanted them. Just as Hansel and Gretel recover their parents by killing the witch in the Gingerbread House, breaking the spell of the stepmother, so Dorothy takes on the forces that have enslaved her step-parents—the wild, destructive forces of nature controlled by the Wicked Witch of the West.

Initiation

After the departure of magic flight, the next stage of the mythic adventure, according to Campbell, is the initiation of the hero: "Once the hero has entered the mythic realm, he encounters strange though intimate forces who may threaten him or offer him supernatural aid. Typically it is an old crone (a fairy godmother) who initiates the hero into the new world, offers him charms and amulets against its dangers, and starts him in his adventures."

The first person that Dorothy encounters in Oz is the Good Witch of the North—an elderly, maternal, kindly protectress. She bears a striking resemblance to Aunt Em: her skin is wrinkled, her hair is nearly white, and she walks stiffly. The Munchkins accompanying the North Witch, Dorothy notices, are "as old as Uncle Henry."

The reference to Uncle Henry reinforces the impression that the Good Witch is the benign alter ego of Aunt Em. Since she appears immediately after the old East Witch has died and resembles the East Witch, it is possible that both witches represent Aunt Em's double aspect: as both nuturing and destroying. Also, the North Witch walks "stiffly," as if the killing of the East Witch has affected her, as if in fact she is dying too. Interestingly, she never appears in the story again or in any of the sequels. If the witches do represent Aunt Em, there may be a hidden Freudian pun in the death of the East Witch: the house(work) is killing Em. Later in the story Dorothy is made to do housework in the castle of the Wicked Witch of the West and to share (temporarily) Aunt Em's dreary existence.

The Wicked Witch of the East was also very old, the North Witch explains; advanced age made her legs dry up quickly, leaving only the silver shoes behind as a legacy. The silver slippers are like Gygel's ring in Plato's *Republic* or the ring of

power and invisibility in Tolkien's *Lord of the Rings*. They are the legacy of evil, yet their proper use (or rather avoidance) can bring ultimate good. Like the hair of the Good Witch and Aunt Em, they are silver, and hence represent projected destinies with which Dorothy must cope. They suggest death and the necessity that Dorothy must be freed from them—as she ultimately is, during her return to Kansas, dropping the slippers into the Deadly Desert which surrounds Oz.

In Oz white is the color of sorcery and witchcraft, hence the color of the magic shoes. Because Dorothy is wearing her blue-and-white checked dress, she is immediately taken for a good witch devoted to the protection of the Munchkins, since blue is the color of the Munchkins and white of the witches. Thus the Munchkins are unafraid of Dorothy and offer her assistance whenever she encounters them. It is clear from the incidents which follow in the story that the Munchkins are right in thinking that Dorothy is a good witch or sorceress; they give the first intimations of her "true" origins: her semi-divine nature or parentage. From this point on, Dorothy will travel through Oz armed with magic, soon to be accompanied by magical attendants.

While some critics, such as Osmond Beckwith, argue that the East and/or North witches are symbolic repesentations of Dorothy's missing, and, hence, mysterious mother, this does not seem a likely interpretation. They are too old; the North Witch is maternal, but more like a fairy godmother than a mother. Moreover, the imputation of a natural mother runs counter to Dorothy's apotheosis as a semi-divine being. Aunt Em seems a more likely model for the East and North witches, though there certainly seems to be an indirect reference to the mother in the cyclone/killing sequence.

Dorothy's quest begins when she expresses the wish to go home to Kansas, thinking that Aunt Em and Uncle Henry must be worrying about her. Getting home will be difficult, the witch explains, since Oz is cut off from the rest of the world by a deadly, impassable desert that surrounds it. The North Witch divines that Dorothy must go to Oz and seek the assistance of the powerful Wizard. It appears she must travel alone, since each witch is confined to her own corner of Oz, but the North Witch gives her a protective magical kiss to safeguard her travels. The kiss becomes a visible halo on Dorothy's forehead and acts as an amulet against all evil.

Before Dorothy's departure the Good Witch of the North explains why witches and sorcerers are so prevalent in Oz; Oz is uncivilized. In civilized places, like Kansas, the sorcerers and witches are long dead; hence, there is no longer any magic there. (Before Dorothy's arrival in Oz, there were four witches: two good and two bad. Once the East Witch has been killed, only one wicked witch remains: the Witch of the West.) The fact that Oz is uncivilized is important, for it prepares the reader for the amoral actions of Oz's inhabitants. It puts aside the moral censorship of conscience in the events to follow: the Wizard's murderous schemes, the cruelty of the Wicked Witch, the attacks of nightmarish creatures, and further killing by Dorothy herself. On this new plane, the meaning of events transcends conventional, civilized understanding. The only assurance is that Dorothy will be protected throughout her adventures by a benign presence symbolized by the magic kiss.

If Dorothy cannot be harmed by the Wicked Witch, what is her encounter with the Witch all about? Mythically, it is the slaying of the forces of darkness as a prelude to transfiguration. The question is not whether the Wicked Witch can slay Dorothy, but whether Dorothy can slay the witch. In the movie the witch is made Dorothy's one and only antagonist; in the book Dorothy must overcome many obstacles, and the witch is only one, although the greatest, opponent. In Baum's story it is not the witch who seeks out Dorothy; rather, Dorothy seeks out the witch, even though the witch has never harmed her. Baum's plot turns on how the killing will be justified, how Dorothy's innocence will be maintained. Mythically, Dorothy's innocence is preserved because her act goes "beyond good and evil." She is dealing with cosmic forces, not individual egos. Moreover, the forces are essentially immortal. What she kills is a symbol, not a human being.

Psychoanalytic interpretations of these opening passages miss much of the nature and magical symbolism of these events. The old Witch of the East dries up in the sun, like the Kansas prairies, with which she is somehow connected to Dorothy's past. The power and status of the East Witch passes to Dorothy with her possession of the silver shoes, which she puts on after the Good Witch of the North has left. She wears them ostensibly to replace her worn-out shoes from Kansas, and in ignorance of their great power. Finally, the last act of the Good Witch of the North is to point out the direction of Oz via the Yellow Brick Road. Yellow is the color of the Winkle country which lies beyond Oz so—though the witch does not mention it—the way to Oz is also the path to the Wicked

What Do I Read Next?

- Lewis Carroll's *Alice's Adventures in Wonderland* (1865) is a classic children's novel. Because of its highly imaginative story, its unusual characters, and its young heroine, it is often compared to *The Wonderful Wizard of Oz*.

- *The Lion, the Witch, and the Wardrobe* (1950) begins C. S. Lewis's series, *The Chronicles of Narnia*. This highly acclaimed series has been loved by children for generations and, like Baum's work, features children protagonists, wondrous settings and characters, a well-paced story, and subtle lessons along the way.

- *Treasure Island* (1883), Robert Louis Stevenson's classic tale of piracy and adventure, presents a young hero facing dangerous and thrilling experiences. This classic is satisfying for readers interested in an exciting and suspenseful story with a young male protagonist.

- Jonathan Swift's *Gulliver's Travels* (1726) relates the curious journey of Gulliver as he passes through a series of strange lands populated with equally strange citizens. This book is symbolic and satirical and has been the subject of much interpretation.

Witch. In the sequels Dorothy becomes the bridge by which one gets to Oz; she becomes the new guardian of the magic threshold.

At the end of the story the last witch Dorothy encounters is Glinda, the Good Witch of the South, who is said to be very old but looks the same age as Dorothy. Glinda seems an amalgam of Dorothy and the North Witch, the old witch rejuvenated by Dorothy's power and with her magic and fertility restored. When Dorothy returns to Kansas, taking her own life-renewing mana, she has already received the powers of two witches and much more.

The Road of Trials

In Campbell's monomyth the trials begin when, "once beyond the threshold, the hero of the mythic cycle encounters not only threatening forces but supernatural helpers overtly or secretly sent by the patron god or goddess." Dorothy receives further supernatural aid and protection from three future kings of Oz: the Scarecrow, the Tin Woodman, and the Cowardly Lion. In addition, their destinies become inexplicably bound up with her own.

Nothing in the Baum books has aroused as much controversy as these non-human and semi-human characterizations. The major controversy is a moral one, namely, whether these characterizations represent healthy role-models for the child reader. Some regard Baum's inventions as sterile, castrated, semi-masculine figures, revealing the author's own psycho-sexual abnormalities. This seems an interesting, but simple view, for even if figures like the Scarecrow, Tin Man, and the other Ozian "automata" reveal something about Baum himself, that does not necessarily imply they carry these meanings in the story itself.

Rather, the subplots concerning these characters develop the major mythic themes of the work. The Scarecrow resembles nothing so much as the dying and resurrected Corn God. Though he was born yesterday (the day Dorothy was reborn in the cyclone), he is immortal. As guardian of the fields he is a symbol of fertility, not infertility. He gains his throne, but not before he is torn to bits by the Winged Monkeys and then resurrected by Dorothy. As Dorothy is a symbol of fertility, he is her symbolic consort—the Osiris to her Isis. Like Dorothy he seeks wisdom to restore the fallen world, symbolized by his inability to guard the grain from his nemesis, the Killer Crows who attack by command of the Wicked Witch of the West. His desire for a brain is, as the Wizard points out later, a desire for experience. He has intelligence, but he wishes to gain wisdom. His destiny is to win the throne of Oz itself, but not before confronting the images of death and destruction symbolized by the crows and the Witch of the West.

The Tin Man is a much more mystical and enigmatic figure than the Scarecrow. Like him, he is immortal; but while the Scarecrow is a thing magically transformed into a person, the Tin Woodman is a person all but transformed into a thing. An ordinary man, working as a woodcutter, he fell in love with a Munchkin girl and desired to marry her; but, under an evil spell cast by the East Witch, he chopped himself to pieces with his own axe. Undaunted, he had the parts of his body replaced by a master tinsmith until, finally, he was all tin; but with the removal of his heart, he lost all

love for the girl, and, hence, had to acknowledge temporary defeat. His rescue by Dorothy and the Scarecrow, however, gives him new hope that his love can be restored. Like the Scarecrow, the Tin Woodman can be associated with death, but in a more positive way than Beckwith suggests when he refers to him as the ineffectual "chopper who chops off your head."

The Tin Man, as a result of his mutilation, is pure spirit. He complains that he has lost his heart, but, in fact, his humanity is all that is left of the original man. He is literally a ghost in a machine, a spirit-power. As a woodcutter, he is a gardener who prunes away all that is dead to make way for new life; hence, he is an image of fertility. As a spiritual being, he has pruned himself, cutting away everything inessential to his own persona. Consumed completely by love and sympathy, he wants, he says, to feel all that is to be felt, whether of joy or sorrow. He weeps when he accidentally steps on a beetle, but he kills when confronted by the hatred of the West Witch. Since Dorothy is a goddess of love, he is her perfect protector against all evil intent. Like the Scarecrow, he is ultimately slain only to reach an even higher plane of being. His destiny is to rule the kingdom of the Wicked Witch herself, and there to remain guardian against the forces of darkness and evil.

The Cowardly Lion is also a symbol of latent and overt power. Unlike the other companions, he is already a king, since his very roar has been enough to frighten all the other animals into submission. Though the symbol of courage, he says he wants to learn real courage: to know real fear and overcome it. That test would provide the occasion for the unleashing of his great strength, which at the moment is quite useless to him, since all creatures bow to him without a fight. Symbolically he must lose his throne in order to regain it, to give meaning to the symbol he represents. More simply put, to test and know his courage, he needs an opponent. At the same time, he is frightened because he does not know what form the challenger will assume, and so he fears everything, even the most insignificant insect. For the moment, he has forsworn any use of force in his own interest; hence, all his power is available to Dorothy. Later, when his challenger appears, a giant spider, he defeats him and regains the throne he deliberately left vacant. He wins the battle because he has found something in his adventures with Dorothy more important than fear itself: love and devotion. When the animals come to him for protection, he can transfer his devotion to them and, on their behalf, find the courage to slay the monster and win his throne.

Beckwith's argument that the companions of Dorothy are impotent and castrated figures ignores their functions in the story. His reaction is largely to the images of mutilation and defeat which the companions suffer, but this is to ignore the themes they represent and how these serve to support Dorothy's quest. The companions' defeats and mutilations are all redeemed before the story ends. Interestingly, Beckwith does not comment on the interpretation of the spider monster—which is a striking lapse, for a Freudian. One immediate conclusion is to see it as a negative female image. But how does it fit into the Lion's own story? The spider seems to be everything the Lion originally wanted to be: fearless, terrifying, capable of destroying every animal (except the lion) in its path. But the spider has no courage because it has no feelings. It is an indifferent power. The Lion cannot meet the spider monster on the field and defeat it in fair combat; his strength is no match for its strength, so he defeats it by cunning. His knightly ambition, to defeat a worthy adversary in open combat, is not realized—at least on one level. He does, however, find his courage in moral ascendancy over his enemy. On a Jungian level, the spider may represent the Lion's repressed alter ego, the repressed violence that is only restrained by his superego.

The three "kingly" companions are presented to Dorothy in forms which Dorothy and Baum's child-readers find nonthreatening, although their hidden aspects represent overwhelming powers—powers summoned perhaps by the silver shoes. The fact that they appear to Dorothy as automata, or toys, does not mitigate their status. Their apparent impotence is merely to reassure and befriend their charge. The toys of children are not just their playthings and playmates, but, like temple gargoyles, their protectors against all the terrors of the external world. Symbolically, the toys are harmless only to the children they protect. Accompanied by these protectors, Dorothy proceeds with confidence to the Emerald city. The trials encountered on the way, such as the attack of the Kalidahs or the deadly Poppy Field, all reveal the character and nature of her companions.

The Emerald City

The Emerald City represents the mythic "World Navel" of Oz: the source of all power and/or illusion, and the dispenser of both good and evil. As Campbell explains, only from the World Navel can the successful hero bring the life-renewing energy, whether an abundant harvest or a manifestation of grace. Hence, Emerald City is green, the color of life and also that of magic. However, since the World Navel is the source of all existence and issues in all the paradoxes of existence, the ruler of the World Navel is sometimes a trickster like the Wizard of Oz—"to God, all things are fair and good and right, while men hold some things wrong and some right." The World Navel is, therefore, as much a seat of illusion as it is of reality: the reality of God appears as an illusion to man; opposites become like to each other. The World Navel, in short, is a fountain of impersonal cosmic forces and energies. For these reasons, the one who is responsible for dispensing the gifts (or curses) that emerge from the fountain may seem to the naive and uninitiated to be a trickster, especially since he does it even-handedly and impersonally. The World Navel, then, represents fate or chance.

All the paradoxes of the World Navel are reflected in the adventures of the Wizard. He is not of Oz, but a carnival illusionist from Omaha. While piloting his balloon during an exhibition, he was blown off course and landed in Oz. Like Dorothy, he was immediately taken to be a sorcerer, and, as a result, was declared ruler of Oz. (Actually, the original ruler of Oz was named "Oz" and the wizard was taken to be his reincarnation.) The Wizard kept the people busy by ordering them to build the Emerald City. In order to reinforce the people's belief that the city is really made of emeralds, he commands them to wear green spectacles whenever they are within its precincts. As it turns out, the Emerald City really is made of emeralds, precious stones being common in Oz, but the people feel no resentment about wearing the glasses because once they become accustomed to them, they prefer to wear them.

The Wizard has made himself a prisoner in the Emerald City, secluded from everyone, including his subjects, to avoid detection by the witches. Although the destruction of the East Witch has left only one potential adversary, when the Wizard hears of Dorothy's arrival in the Emerald City, he is shaken—especially since she comes armed both with magic and guardians. Ultimately he decides to grant her an audience with a view to redirecting her powers against his one potential adversary, the Wicked Witch of the West.

When Dorothy and her companions visit the Wizard to ask for their boons, each is permitted a separate audience with the Wizard and encounters a different image. Altogether there are four, which suggests that they are the threshold guardians of the Navel itself. The Scarecrow sees a winged fairy; the Tin Man sees a gigantic monster resembling a cross between a rhinoceros and elephant, with five arms, eyes, and legs; the Cowardly Lion sees a ball of fire; and Dorothy sees a giant, disembodied head. While the meaning of these images is unclear, they evoke interesting psychological associations.

The beast spied by the Tin Woodman appears as a creature from the id, primitive and sexual. Inasmuch as the Woodman has two bodies (one mortal, one immortal) and an axe, the five-limbed creature he sees may well be a repressed image of himself. He has transcended the flesh and reached an ethereal plane, yet the beast still represents an obstacle to him. Analogously, the five limbs and eyes may represent the five senses, and hence the fleshly experience which he lacks. The beautiful lady of the Scarecrow seems a fairy or sprite (Psyche?), perhaps a symbol of his goal (wisdom, spirituality), while the ball of fire (the sun) represents for the Lion the fiery courage which he wishes to acquire. The giant head which Dorothy sees is awesome, but not fierce. Beckwith contends that it is a father figure, a plausible idea, because it is disembodied and phallic and perhaps prefigures the Wizard's real impotence. However, according to Campbell, it is inevitable that the hero who is about to transform the world should encounter the symbol of authority (in patriarchal myths, the father) of that world. The hero's quest amounts to his supplanting that very authority. As with the threshold guardians, the father must be conciliated or defeated. He may demand that the contender show his worthiness by performing some wondrous or perilous act, or he may simply acknowledge the contender's status and abdicate. The interaction between the hero and the authority figure is complicated by the fact that the father/ruler possesses the power to transform himself, to create endless illusions to confuse the knight-errant.

Dorothy goes to the Wizard because he is identified as the supreme ruler of Oz. When she asks the Wizard to send her back to Kansas, the Wizard demands that she do something for him in return: kill the Wicked Witch of the West. His demand implies that he must abdicate if Dorothy succeeds in the quest, for he has no power to keep his promise; his impotence will be apparent to everyone. But if Dorothy fails, he will maintain his position and authority.

The complications of the sequences concerning the Wizard have to do with Baum's playfulness in exploiting the implications of the "World Navel": what is real appears to be illusion; what is illusory appears to be real. The Wizard thinks that he is tricking Dorothy by sending her to the Wicked Witch; but the killing of the witch, ironically, permits Dorothy's return home. With the uncritical acceptance of a child, Dorothy believes the illusions the Wizard creates, and because she believes in them, she discovers the realities they represent. The self-deceits of the Wizard are a constant source of amusement in the story—for example, when Dorothy returns from her quest, he escapes from the Emerald City at the very moment he is safe.

Some critics deplore what they take to be the immortality of the Wizard. The Wizard, according to Beckwith, is a "horrible" man, a father figure who attempts to immolate his daughter: like the god Baal or Moloch, sacrificing children to placate the elements. However, this interpretation ignores the mythic theme that the Wizard represents impersonal forces. The cosmic hero is the one who ultimately identifies with the World Navel itself and thereby transcends ego-related notions of right and wrong. As with the mystic sage, the hero's self dissolves and becomes one with the cosmic process, a process that contains both good and evil, both Being and Becoming. As a symbol of fertility, Dorothy inevitably must journey to the opposite: the place of death and sterility. The two are, in fact, simply different aspects of the same thing.

The Wicked Witch of the West

In the Land of the Winkies, Dorothy and her friends encounter the threshold guardians of the Wicked Witch's domain and face the first real test of their powers. After Dorothy leaves the Emerald City, she discovers that her clothes, and even Toto's collar, have changed to white: the visit to the Emerald City has increased her magical powers, and the color change foreshadows her success. The land of the Wicked Witch is the only part of Oz that resembles Kansas: the land is treeless, hot, and deserted. There are no roads, because no one in Oz ever wanted to go there. The Witch's power rests on her control of otherwise wild and untamed natural forces: the Winged Monkeys, the Killer Wolves and Crows, and the Deadly Bees. Like the Wizard, she is a usurper of another's throne, but unlike him, she has real power. Her ultimate weapon is the golden cap that controls the Winged Monkeys. Whoever has the golden cap can command the monkeys three times, and only three.

When Dorothy approaches, the witch has already used up two wishes: one to enslave the Winkies and one to drive the Great Oz (not the Wizard, but the ancient ruler of Oz) out of the land of the West. By implication, it is the absence of the Great Oz which has left the land barren and infertile.

The Winged Monkeys themselves are primordial inhabitants of Oz, dating back to the most ancient days of the wonderland. They are amoral, mischievous forces, like Pan and his satyrs. The golden cap studded with diamonds and rubies is the crown of their king. Because of a prank they once pulled in the land of the North, they were enslaved to the cap, which passed from one ruler to another. In time the cap fell into the hands of the Wicked Witch, who used its power to seize the land of the West.

The episode of the Wicked Witch repeats the theme of the World Navel. The ultimate powers are indifferent to human notions of good and evil. The balance of nature requires the release of opposing forces; the Winter Witch is as necessary to the ultimate good as the zephyrs of spring. By implication the enslavement of these forces upsets the balance and brings about the opposite: the apocalypse. The moral passions of the ancient rulers of Oz caused them to enslave the Winged Monkeys to bring about moral harmony. But once the monkeys were enslaved, their powers were no longer truly neutral, since they were bound to do the bidding of their owners. We are not told how the witch got the cap, but her possession of it upset the equilibrium. She overthrew the original rulers and enslaved the people at large.

The West Witch is limited in resources; she has only one wish left from the golden cap, and only the wild things (wolves, crows, and bees) to guard her kingdom. When Dorothy arrives at her border, the situation becomes even more desperate for her: the Tin Woodman decapitates the forty wolves with his axe, while the deadly bees kill themselves attacking his armor; meanwhile the Scarecrow wrings the necks of the forty crows, and the Lion frightens away the Winkie slaves with his terrifying roars. These calamities force the witch to use her final wish of the golden cap. Summoning the monkeys for the last time, she orders them to destroy Dorothy, the Scarecrow, and the Tin Man, but to bring the lion to her so that she can enslave him and make him draw her carriage. With her real powers gone, she desires the symbols of those powers, just as Dorothy's companions seek the symbols of their virtues.

The Winged Monkeys proceed to do as they are told, but, seeing the protective kiss on Dorothy's forehead, they realize they cannot harm her. They take both Dorothy and the lion to the Witch's castle and bid the Witch farewell.

Seeing the silver shoes and magic amulet Dorothy wears, the witch realizes that Dorothy cannot be harmed and becomes frightened for herself. Noticing Dorothy's innocence and her ignorance of the power of the silver shoes, she decides to frighten Dorothy into submission, convincing her that she is helpless. The witch makes Dorothy do housework around the castle, thus reenacting the life of Aunt Em in Kansas—the young, pretty wife who turned gray from over-work. This is the prelude to the killing of the witch: the reminder of the original motivation that brought Dorothy to Oz. Simultaneously there is a Hansel-and-Gretel motif to reinforce the point. The witch puts the lion in a cage in order to starve him into submission; Dorothy plays Gretel by sneaking food out to the Lion. The Hansel-and-Gretel motif again plays on the theme of killing the surrogate parent to recover the original idyllic parent.

The witch's attempts to steal Dorothy's silver shoes are pathetic. She cannot enter Dorothy's room at night because she is afraid of the dark, a fear that prefigures her own death. At another point, when Toto bites the Wicked Witch on the leg, she does not bleed, since her blood had dried up years before (like that of the East Witch). Thus another image of death points to the means of killing the witch: the water (the wet) opposes the dry as the rains transform the parched land of Kansas into a fertile plain. When the witch finally manages to steal one of the shoes by tripping Dorothy and grabbing the shoe that falls off, Dorothy picks up a nearby bucket of water and dissolves her. The witch melts down to a brownish mass. Dorothy then empties the rest of the bucket over the remains of the witch and sweeps it all out the door. The symbolic meaning of this cleansing is obvious. The purification ritual is complete and Dorothy achieves a kind of poetic justice by literally sweeping away the one who condemned her to a life of housework. She then frees the lion and the Winkies, and in gratitude, the Winkies help Dorothy resurrect the Scarecrow and the Tin Man.

The Atonement of the Wizard

When Dorothy returns to the Wizard, bringing the news of the witch's death, she discovers that he is a humbug. To make amends, he promises to take

Dorothy back to Kansas by non-magical means, his balloon. He wants to escape, fearful that the people of Oz will, like Dorothy, discover what a humbug he is and take revenge. As in the cyclone sequence, when Dorothy pursues a runaway Toto and so fails to heed parental injunction, the Wizard floats off alone to parts unknown. The disappearance of the Wizard leaves the throne of Oz vacant and brings about a transition of power and authority. By unmasking the false wizard, Dorothy dethrones the usurper and, symbolically, gains the throne herself. She names the Scarecrow as regent, appropriately, given his relationship to her and the fertility he represents. Symbolically she becomes her own father and assumes the offices of the father-figure. What remains, to complete the mythic tale, is marriage with the goddess and the return home.

The Meeting with the Goddess

The journey to the Good Witch of the South is essentially a triumphal march, a celebration and demonstration of newly discovered powers. The Cowardly Lion defeats his rival, a giant five-legged Spider, and is enthroned as King of the Beasts. The Tin Woodman cuts a path through the fighting trees. Dorothy and her friends tiptoe through the China country where people are made of porcelain. They are frustrated only at the final approach to the Good Witch's territory by the clever defenses of the Hammerheads—Jack-in-the-box creatures—who use their heads as battering rams to force the party back. Since they cannot pass the Hammerhead country, Dorothy uses a wish from the golden cap to summon the Winged Monkeys and have herself and her companions carried through the air over the heads of their adversaries to Glinda, the Good Witch.

Though she is supposed to be very old, Glinda looks like a beautiful young girl about Dorothy's age. She asks Dorothy for the golden cap, uses her three wishes to send Dorothy's companions back to their thrones, restores the cap to the king of the Winged Monkeys, and instructs Dorothy how to use the silver shoes to return home. By her actions Glinda even-handedly frees both the moral and amoral (mischievous) forces. She begins, in fact, the work of restoration of Oz to return it to what it was in the ancient days and sets in motion the next mythic cycle.

In the usual heroic myth, a marriage would be indicated here (a union of the hero with the King's daughter after his victory—Jason, for example.

Baum's unusual twist avoids the romantic theme and keeps the relationship asexual—a "marriage" then is indicated by other means: Glinda is an amalgam of the Good Witch of the North and Dorothy herself, as if the elderly witch were reborn. At the same time, Glinda is Dorothy's alter ego.

Return

In the final part of the myth, the return, the hero may be blessed and returns under the protection of the powers that be, or unfriendly powers may pursue him. During her adventures Dorothy has conquered or conciliated all, and so returns without obstacle. The magic shoes, like Frodo's ring, are lost forever; they fall off in the Deadly Desert. Dorothy finds herself rolling over and over in the Kansas prairies, home at last. Immediately, she sees the transformation that has taken place. A new house replaces the one destroyed by the cyclone; Uncle Henry is milking the cows, Aunt Em is watering the cabbages. When Aunt Em sees Dorothy, she runs over to her, and taking Dorothy in her arms, smothers her with real kisses. The desert of Kansas is beginning to bloom once again.

The real magic of Oz lies in its "deep" structure and its psychic unity. If critics have sometimes failed to appreciate the story, it is because they have missed the classical allusions and associations embedded in it. Baum's genius lay in his playfulness and his ability to juxtapose themes so as to please the adult imagination as well as the child's. What critics sometimes suppose to be lack of unity is really Baum's three-dimensionality: his ability to take us into the world of imagination through the open-endedness and the inexhaustibility of his analogies and metaphors.

Source: Edward Hudlin, "The Mythology of *Oz:* An Interpretation," in *Papers on Language and Literature,* Vol. 25, No. 4, Fall 1989, pp. 443–63.

Sources

Farmer, Philip Jose, "Baum, L(yman) Frank," in *Reference Guide to American Literature,* 3d ed., St. James Press, 1994.

Greene, David L., and Dick Martin, *The Oz Scrapbook,* Random House, 1977.

Hearn, Michael Patrick, "L(yman) Frank Baum," in *Dictionary of Literary Biography,* Vol. 22: *American Writers for Children, 1900–1960,* Gale Research, 1983, pp. 13–36.

McQuade, Molly, "Baumisms," in *Booklist,* Vol. 96, No. 15, April 1, 2000, p. 1464.

"A New Book for Children," in *New York Times Saturday Review of Books and Art,* September 8, 1900, p. 605.

Spake, Amanda, "A Century Later, Still No Place Like Oz," in *U. S. News & World Report,* Vol. 129, No. 18, November 6, 2000, p. 50.

Thurber, James, "The Wizard of Chittenango," in *New Republic,* Vol. 81, No. 1045, December 12, 1934, pp. 141–42.

Westfahl, Gary, "Baum, L(yman) Frank," in *St. James Guide to Fantasy Writers,* St. James Press, 1996, pp. 44–48.

Further Reading

Baum, Frank Joslyn, and Russell P. MacFall, *To Please a Child: A Biography of L. Frank Baum, Royal Historian of Oz,* Reilly & Lee Co., 1961.

> Written by Baum's oldest son and a collaborator, this biography contains their personal memories of the author. It is among the most authoritative sources of biographical information on Baum.

Carpenter, Angelica Shirley, and Jean Shirley, *L. Frank Baum: Royal Historian of Oz,* Lerner Publications, 1991.

> Carpenter and Shirley have compiled biographical information about Baum from a wide variety of sources to create this book. What makes it especially interesting is its inclusion of many photographs and illustrations.

Hearn, Michael Patrick, *The Annotated Wizard of Oz: The Centennial Edition,* Norton, 2000.

> Hearn, the preeminent Oz scholar, updates his 1973 annotated version of Baum's classic novel. This book contains a reproduction of the 1900 edition, complete with Denslow's illustrations, in addition to extensive notes and related materials.

Swartz, Mark Evans, *Oz before the Rainbow: L. Frank Baum's "The Wonderful Wizard of Oz" on Stage and Screen to 1939,* Johns Hopkins Press, 2000.

> Swartz reviews the many stage and film adaptations of Baum's novel, up to the classic 1939 musical produced by MGM. His analysis includes commentary on why and how *The Wonderful Wizard of Oz* has become a part of American culture.

Glossary of Literary Terms

A

Abstract: As an adjective applied to writing or literary works, abstract refers to words or phrases that name things not knowable through the five senses.

Aestheticism: A literary and artistic movement of the nineteenth century. Followers of the movement believed that art should not be mixed with social, political, or moral teaching. The statement "art for art's sake" is a good summary of aestheticism. The movement had its roots in France, but it gained widespread importance in England in the last half of the nineteenth century, where it helped change the Victorian practice of including moral lessons in literature.

Allegory: A narrative technique in which characters representing things or abstract ideas are used to convey a message or teach a lesson. Allegory is typically used to teach moral, ethical, or religious lessons but is sometimes used for satiric or political purposes.

Allusion: A reference to a familiar literary or historical person or event, used to make an idea more easily understood.

Analogy: A comparison of two things made to explain something unfamiliar through its similarities to something familiar, or to prove one point based on the acceptedness of another. Similes and metaphors are types of analogies.

Antagonist: The major character in a narrative or drama who works against the hero or protagonist.

Anthropomorphism: The presentation of animals or objects in human shape or with human characteristics. The term is derived from the Greek word for "human form."

Antihero: A central character in a work of literature who lacks traditional heroic qualities such as courage, physical prowess, and fortitude. Antiheroes typically distrust conventional values and are unable to commit themselves to any ideals. They generally feel helpless in a world over which they have no control. Antiheroes usually accept, and often celebrate, their positions as social outcasts.

Apprenticeship Novel: See *Bildungsroman*

Archetype: The word archetype is commonly used to describe an original pattern or model from which all other things of the same kind are made. This term was introduced to literary criticism from the psychology of Carl Jung. It expresses Jung's theory that behind every person's "unconscious," or repressed memories of the past, lies the "collective unconscious" of the human race: memories of the countless typical experiences of our ancestors. These memories are said to prompt illogical associations that trigger powerful emotions in the reader. Often, the emotional process is primitive, even primordial. Archetypes are the literary images that grow out of the "collective unconscious." They appear in literature as incidents and plots that repeat basic patterns of life. They may also appear as stereotyped characters.

Avant-garde: French term meaning "vanguard." It is used in literary criticism to describe new writing that rejects traditional approaches to literature in favor of innovations in style or content.

B

Beat Movement: A period featuring a group of American poets and novelists of the 1950s and 1960s—including Jack Kerouac, Allen Ginsberg, Gregory Corso, William S. Burroughs, and Lawrence Ferlinghetti—who rejected established social and literary values. Using such techniques as stream of consciousness writing and jazz-influenced free verse and focusing on unusual or abnormal states of mind—generated by religious ecstasy or the use of drugs—the Beat writers aimed to create works that were unconventional in both form and subject matter.

Bildungsroman: A German word meaning "novel of development." The *bildungsroman* is a study of the maturation of a youthful character, typically brought about through a series of social or sexual encounters that lead to self-awareness. *Bildungsroman* is used interchangeably with *erziehungsroman*, a novel of initiation and education. When a *bildungsroman* is concerned with the development of an artist (as in James Joyce's *A Portrait of the Artist as a Young Man*), it is often termed a *kunstlerroman*. Also known as Apprenticeship Novel, Coming of Age Novel, *Erziehungsroman*, or *Kunstlerroman*.

Black Aesthetic Movement: A period of artistic and literary development among African Americans in the 1960s and early 1970s. This was the first major African-American artistic movement since the Harlem Renaissance and was closely paralleled by the civil rights and black power movements. The black aesthetic writers attempted to produce works of art that would be meaningful to the black masses. Key figures in black aesthetics included one of its founders, poet and playwright Amiri Baraka, formerly known as LeRoi Jones; poet and essayist Haki R. Madhubuti, formerly Don L. Lee; poet and playwright Sonia Sanchez; and dramatist Ed Bullins. Also known as Black Arts Movement.

Black Humor: Writing that places grotesque elements side by side with humorous ones in an attempt to shock the reader, forcing him or her to laugh at the horrifying reality of a disordered world. Also known as Black Comedy.

Burlesque: Any literary work that uses exaggeration to make its subject appear ridiculous, either by treating a trivial subject with profound seriousness or by treating a dignified subject frivolously. The word "burlesque" may also be used as an adjective, as in "burlesque show," to mean "striptease act."

C

Character: Broadly speaking, a person in a literary work. The actions of characters are what constitute the plot of a story, novel, or poem. There are numerous types of characters, ranging from simple, stereotypical figures to intricate, multifaceted ones. In the techniques of anthropomorphism and personification, animals—and even places or things—can assume aspects of character. "Characterization" is the process by which an author creates vivid, believable characters in a work of art. This may be done in a variety of ways, including (1) direct description of the character by the narrator; (2) the direct presentation of the speech, thoughts, or actions of the character; and (3) the responses of other characters to the character. The term "character" also refers to a form originated by the ancient Greek writer Theophrastus that later became popular in the seventeenth and eighteenth centuries. It is a short essay or sketch of a person who prominently displays a specific attribute or quality, such as miserliness or ambition.

Climax: The turning point in a narrative, the moment when the conflict is at its most intense. Typically, the structure of stories, novels, and plays is one of rising action, in which tension builds to the climax, followed by falling action, in which tension lessens as the story moves to its conclusion.

Colloquialism: A word, phrase, or form of pronunciation that is acceptable in casual conversation but not in formal, written communication. It is considered more acceptable than slang.

Coming of Age Novel: See *Bildungsroman*

Concrete: Concrete is the opposite of abstract, and refers to a thing that actually exists or a description that allows the reader to experience an object or concept with the senses.

Connotation: The impression that a word gives beyond its defined meaning. Connotations may be universally understood or may be significant only to a certain group.

Convention: Any widely accepted literary device, style, or form.

D

Denotation: The definition of a word, apart from the impressions or feelings it creates (connotations) in the reader.

Denouement: A French word meaning "the unknotting." In literary criticism, it denotes the resolution of conflict in fiction or drama. The *denouement* follows the climax and provides an outcome to the primary plot situation as well as an explanation of secondary plot complications. The *denouement* often involves a character's recognition of his or her state of mind or moral condition. Also known as Falling Action.

Description: Descriptive writing is intended to allow a reader to picture the scene or setting in which the action of a story takes place. The form this description takes often evokes an intended emotional response—a dark, spooky graveyard will evoke fear, and a peaceful, sunny meadow will evoke calmness.

Dialogue: In its widest sense, dialogue is simply conversation between people in a literary work; in its most restricted sense, it refers specifically to the speech of characters in a drama. As a specific literary genre, a "dialogue" is a composition in which characters debate an issue or idea.

Diction: The selection and arrangement of words in a literary work. Either or both may vary depending on the desired effect. There are four general types of diction: "formal," used in scholarly or lofty writing; "informal," used in relaxed but educated conversation; "colloquial," used in everyday speech; and "slang," containing newly coined words and other terms not accepted in formal usage.

Didactic: A term used to describe works of literature that aim to teach some moral, religious, political, or practical lesson. Although didactic elements are often found in artistically pleasing works, the term "didactic" usually refers to literature in which the message is more important than the form. The term may also be used to criticize a work that the critic finds "overly didactic," that is, heavy-handed in its delivery of a lesson.

Doppelganger: A literary technique by which a character is duplicated (usually in the form of an alter ego, though sometimes as a ghostly counterpart) or divided into two distinct, usually opposite personalities. The use of this character device is widespread in nineteenth- and twentieth-century literature, and indicates a growing awareness among authors that the "self" is really a composite of many "selves." Also known as The Double.

Double Entendre: A corruption of a French phrase meaning "double meaning." The term is used to indicate a word or phrase that is deliberately ambiguous, especially when one of the meanings is risqué or improper.

Dramatic Irony: Occurs when the audience of a play or the reader of a work of literature knows something that a character in the work itself does not know. The irony is in the contrast between the intended meaning of the statements or actions of a character and the additional information understood by the audience.

Dystopia: An imaginary place in a work of fiction where the characters lead dehumanized, fearful lives.

E

Edwardian: Describes cultural conventions identified with the period of the reign of Edward VII of England (1901-1910). Writers of the Edwardian Age typically displayed a strong reaction against the propriety and conservatism of the Victorian Age. Their work often exhibits distrust of authority in religion, politics, and art and expresses strong doubts about the soundness of conventional values.

Empathy: A sense of shared experience, including emotional and physical feelings, with someone or something other than oneself. Empathy is often used to describe the response of a reader to a literary character.

Enlightenment, The: An eighteenth-century philosophical movement. It began in France but had a wide impact throughout Europe and America. Thinkers of the Enlightenment valued reason and believed that both the individual and society could achieve a state of perfection. Corresponding to this essentially humanist vision was a resistance to religious authority.

Epigram: A saying that makes the speaker's point quickly and concisely. Often used to preface a novel.

Epilogue: A concluding statement or section of a literary work. In dramas, particularly those of the seventeenth and eighteenth centuries, the epilogue is a closing speech, often in verse, delivered by an actor at the end of a play and spoken directly to the audience.

Epiphany: A sudden revelation of truth inspired by a seemingly trivial incident.

Episode: An incident that forms part of a story and is significantly related to it. Episodes may be either self-contained narratives or events that depend on a larger context for their sense and importance.

Epistolary Novel: A novel in the form of letters. The form was particularly popular in the eighteenth century.

Epithet: A word or phrase, often disparaging or abusive, that expresses a character trait of someone or something.

Existentialism: A predominantly twentieth-century philosophy concerned with the nature and perception of human existence. There are two major strains of existentialist thought: atheistic and Christian. Followers of atheistic existentialism believe that the individual is alone in a godless universe and that the basic human condition is one of suffering and loneliness. Nevertheless, because there are no fixed values, individuals can create their own characters—indeed, they can shape themselves—through the exercise of free will. The atheistic strain culminates in and is popularly associated with the works of Jean-Paul Sartre. The Christian existentialists, on the other hand, believe that only in God may people find freedom from life's anguish. The two strains hold certain beliefs in common: that existence cannot be fully understood or described through empirical effort; that anguish is a universal element of life; that individuals must bear responsibility for their actions; and that there is no common standard of behavior or perception for religious and ethical matters.

Expatriates: See *Expatriatism*

Expatriatism: The practice of leaving one's country to live for an extended period in another country.

Exposition: Writing intended to explain the nature of an idea, thing, or theme. Expository writing is often combined with description, narration, or argument. In dramatic writing, the exposition is the introductory material which presents the characters, setting, and tone of the play.

Expressionism: An indistinct literary term, originally used to describe an early twentieth-century school of German painting. The term applies to almost any mode of unconventional, highly subjective writing that distorts reality in some way.

F

Fable: A prose or verse narrative intended to convey a moral. Animals or inanimate objects with human characteristics often serve as characters in fables.

Falling Action: See *Denouement*

Fantasy: A literary form related to mythology and folklore. Fantasy literature is typically set in non-existent realms and features supernatural beings.

Farce: A type of comedy characterized by broad humor, outlandish incidents, and often vulgar subject matter.

Femme fatale: A French phrase with the literal translation "fatal woman." A *femme fatale* is a sensuous, alluring woman who often leads men into danger or trouble.

Fiction: Any story that is the product of imagination rather than a documentation of fact. Characters and events in such narratives may be based in real life but their ultimate form and configuration is a creation of the author.

Figurative Language: A technique in writing in which the author temporarily interrupts the order, construction, or meaning of the writing for a particular effect. This interruption takes the form of one or more figures of speech such as hyperbole, irony, or simile. Figurative language is the opposite of literal language, in which every word is truthful, accurate, and free of exaggeration or embellishment.

Figures of Speech: Writing that differs from customary conventions for construction, meaning, order, or significance for the purpose of a special meaning or effect. There are two major types of figures of speech: rhetorical figures, which do not make changes in the meaning of the words, and tropes, which do.

Fin de siecle: A French term meaning "end of the century." The term is used to denote the last decade of the nineteenth century, a transition period when writers and other artists abandoned old conventions and looked for new techniques and objectives.

First Person: See *Point of View*

Flashback: A device used in literature to present action that occurred before the beginning of the story. Flashbacks are often introduced as the dreams or recollections of one or more characters.

Foil: A character in a work of literature whose physical or psychological qualities contrast strongly with, and therefore highlight, the corresponding qualities of another character.

Folklore: Traditions and myths preserved in a culture or group of people. Typically, these are passed on by word of mouth in various forms—such as legends, songs, and proverbs—or preserved in customs and ceremonies. This term was first used by W. J. Thoms in 1846.

Folktale: A story originating in oral tradition. Folktales fall into a variety of categories, including legends, ghost stories, fairy tales, fables, and anecdotes based on historical figures and events.

Foreshadowing: A device used in literature to create expectation or to set up an explanation of later developments.

Form: The pattern or construction of a work which identifies its genre and distinguishes it from other genres.

G

Genre: A category of literary work. In critical theory, genre may refer to both the content of a given work—tragedy, comedy, pastoral—and to its form, such as poetry, novel, or drama.

Gilded Age: A period in American history during the 1870s characterized by political corruption and materialism. A number of important novels of social and political criticism were written during this time.

Gothicism: In literary criticism, works characterized by a taste for the medieval or morbidly attractive. A gothic novel prominently features elements of horror, the supernatural, gloom, and violence: clanking chains, terror, charnel houses, ghosts, medieval castles, and mysteriously slamming doors. The term "gothic novel" is also applied to novels that lack elements of the traditional Gothic setting but that create a similar atmosphere of terror or dread.

Grotesque: In literary criticism, the subject matter of a work or a style of expression characterized by exaggeration, deformity, freakishness, and disorder. The grotesque often includes an element of comic absurdity.

H

Harlem Renaissance: The Harlem Renaissance of the 1920s is generally considered the first significant movement of black writers and artists in the United States. During this period, new and established black writers published more fiction and poetry than ever before, the first influential black literary journals were established, and black authors and artists received their first widespread recognition and serious critical appraisal. Among the major writers associated with this period are Claude McKay, Jean Toomer, Countee Cullen, Langston Hughes, Arna Bontemps, Nella Larsen, and Zora Neale Hurston. Also known as Negro Renaissance and New Negro Movement.

Hero/Heroine: The principal sympathetic character (male or female) in a literary work. Heroes and heroines typically exhibit admirable traits: idealism, courage, and integrity, for example.

Holocaust Literature: Literature influenced by or written about the Holocaust of World War II. Such literature includes true stories of survival in concentration camps, escape, and life after the war, as well as fictional works and poetry.

Humanism: A philosophy that places faith in the dignity of humankind and rejects the medieval perception of the individual as a weak, fallen creature. "Humanists" typically believe in the perfectibility of human nature and view reason and education as the means to that end.

Hyperbole: In literary criticism, deliberate exaggeration used to achieve an effect.

I

Idiom: A word construction or verbal expression closely associated with a given language.

Image: A concrete representation of an object or sensory experience. Typically, such a representation helps evoke the feelings associated with the object or experience itself. Images are either "literal" or "figurative." Literal images are especially concrete and involve little or no extension of the obvious meaning of the words used to express them. Figurative images do not follow the literal meaning of the words exactly. Images in literature are usually visual, but the term "image" can also refer to the representation of any sensory experience.

Imagery: The array of images in a literary work. Also, figurative language.

In medias res: A Latin term meaning "in the middle of things." It refers to the technique of beginning a story at its midpoint and then using various flashback devices to reveal previous action.

Interior Monologue: A narrative technique in which characters' thoughts are revealed in a way that appears to be uncontrolled by the author. The interior monologue typically aims to reveal the inner self of a character. It portrays emotional experiences as they occur at both a conscious and unconscious level. Images are often used to represent sensations or emotions.

Irony: In literary criticism, the effect of language in which the intended meaning is the opposite of what is stated.

J

Jargon: Language that is used or understood only by a select group of people. Jargon may refer to terminology used in a certain profession, such as computer jargon, or it may refer to any nonsensical language that is not understood by most people.

L

Leitmotiv: See *Motif*

Literal Language: An author uses literal language when he or she writes without exaggerating or embellishing the subject matter and without any tools of figurative language.

Lost Generation: A term first used by Gertrude Stein to describe the post-World War I generation of American writers: men and women haunted by a sense of betrayal and emptiness brought about by the destructiveness of the war.

M

Mannerism: Exaggerated, artificial adherence to a literary manner or style. Also, a popular style of the visual arts of late sixteenth-century Europe that was marked by elongation of the human form and by intentional spatial distortion. Literary works that are self-consciously high-toned and artistic are often said to be "mannered."

Metaphor: A figure of speech that expresses an idea through the image of another object. Metaphors suggest the essence of the first object by identifying it with certain qualities of the second object.

Modernism: Modern literary practices. Also, the principles of a literary school that lasted from roughly the beginning of the twentieth century until the end of World War II. Modernism is defined by its rejection of the literary conventions of the nineteenth century and by its opposition to conventional morality, taste, traditions, and economic values.

Mood: The prevailing emotions of a work or of the author in his or her creation of the work. The mood of a work is not always what might be expected based on its subject matter.

Motif: A theme, character type, image, metaphor, or other verbal element that recurs throughout a single work of literature or occurs in a number of different works over a period of time. Also known as *Motiv* or *Leitmotiv.*

Myth: An anonymous tale emerging from the traditional beliefs of a culture or social unit. Myths use supernatural explanations for natural phenomena. They may also explain cosmic issues like creation and death. Collections of myths, known as mythologies, are common to all cultures and nations, but the best-known myths belong to the Norse, Roman, and Greek mythologies.

N

Narration: The telling of a series of events, real or invented. A narration may be either a simple narrative, in which the events are recounted chronologically, or a narrative with a plot, in which the account is given in a style reflecting the author's artistic concept of the story. Narration is sometimes used as a synonym for "storyline."

Narrative: A verse or prose accounting of an event or sequence of events, real or invented. The term is also used as an adjective in the sense "method of narration." For example, in literary criticism, the expression "narrative technique" usually refers to the way the author structures and presents his or her story.

Narrator: The teller of a story. The narrator may be the author or a character in the story through whom the author speaks.

Naturalism: A literary movement of the late nineteenth and early twentieth centuries. The movement's major theorist, French novelist Emile Zola, envisioned a type of fiction that would examine human life with the objectivity of scientific inquiry. The Naturalists typically viewed human beings as either the products of "biological determinism," ruled by hereditary instincts and engaged in an endless struggle for survival, or as the products of "socioeconomic determinism," ruled by social and economic forces beyond their control. In their works, the Naturalists generally ignored the highest levels of society and focused on degradation: poverty, alcoholism, prostitution, insanity, and disease.

Noble Savage: The idea that primitive man is noble and good but becomes evil and corrupted as he becomes civilized. The concept of the noble savage originated in the Renaissance period but is more closely identified with such later writers as

Jean-Jacques Rousseau and Aphra Behn. See also Primitivism.

Novel of Ideas: A novel in which the examination of intellectual issues and concepts takes precedence over characterization or a traditional storyline.

Novel of Manners: A novel that examines the customs and mores of a cultural group.

Novel: A long fictional narrative written in prose, which developed from the novella and other early forms of narrative. A novel is usually organized under a plot or theme with a focus on character development and action.

Novella: An Italian term meaning "story." This term has been especially used to describe fourteenth-century Italian tales, but it also refers to modern short novels.

O

Objective Correlative: An outward set of objects, a situation, or a chain of events corresponding to an inward experience and evoking this experience in the reader. The term frequently appears in modern criticism in discussions of authors' intended effects on the emotional responses of readers.

Objectivity: A quality in writing characterized by the absence of the author's opinion or feeling about the subject matter. Objectivity is an important factor in criticism.

Oedipus Complex: A son's amorous obsession with his mother. The phrase is derived from the story of the ancient Theban hero Oedipus, who unknowingly killed his father and married his mother.

Omniscience: See *Point of View*

Onomatopoeia: The use of words whose sounds express or suggest their meaning. In its simplest sense, onomatopoeia may be represented by words that mimic the sounds they denote such as "hiss" or "meow." At a more subtle level, the pattern and rhythm of sounds and rhymes of a line or poem may be onomatopoeic.

Oxymoron: A phrase combining two contradictory terms. Oxymorons may be intentional or unintentional.

P

Parable: A story intended to teach a moral lesson or answer an ethical question.

Paradox: A statement that appears illogical or contradictory at first, but may actually point to an underlying truth.

Parallelism: A method of comparison of two ideas in which each is developed in the same grammatical structure.

Parody: In literary criticism, this term refers to an imitation of a serious literary work or the signature style of a particular author in a ridiculous manner. A typical parody adopts the style of the original and applies it to an inappropriate subject for humorous effect. Parody is a form of satire and could be considered the literary equivalent of a caricature or cartoon.

Pastoral: A term derived from the Latin word "pastor," meaning shepherd. A pastoral is a literary composition on a rural theme. The conventions of the pastoral were originated by the third-century Greek poet Theocritus, who wrote about the experiences, love affairs, and pastimes of Sicilian shepherds. In a pastoral, characters and language of a courtly nature are often placed in a simple setting. The term pastoral is also used to classify dramas, elegies, and lyrics that exhibit the use of country settings and shepherd characters.

Pen Name: See *Pseudonym*

Persona: A Latin term meaning "mask." *Personae* are the characters in a fictional work of literature. The *persona* generally functions as a mask through which the author tells a story in a voice other than his or her own. A *persona* is usually either a character in a story who acts as a narrator or an "implied author," a voice created by the author to act as the narrator for himself or herself.

Personification: A figure of speech that gives human qualities to abstract ideas, animals, and inanimate objects. Also known as *Prosopopoeia*.

Picaresque Novel: Episodic fiction depicting the adventures of a roguish central character ("picaro" is Spanish for "rogue"). The picaresque hero is commonly a low-born but clever individual who wanders into and out of various affairs of love, danger, and farcical intrigue. These involvements may take place at all social levels and typically present a humorous and wide-ranging satire of a given society.

Plagiarism: Claiming another person's written material as one's own. Plagiarism can take the form of direct, word-for-word copying or the theft of the substance or idea of the work.

Plot: In literary criticism, this term refers to the pattern of events in a narrative or drama. In its simplest sense, the plot guides the author in composing the work and helps the reader follow the work. Typically, plots exhibit causality and unity and have a beginning, a middle, and an end. Sometimes, however, a plot may consist of a series of disconnected events, in which case it is known as an "episodic plot."

Poetic Justice: An outcome in a literary work, not necessarily a poem, in which the good are rewarded and the evil are punished, especially in ways that particularly fit their virtues or crimes.

Poetic License: Distortions of fact and literary convention made by a writer—not always a poet—for the sake of the effect gained. Poetic license is closely related to the concept of "artistic freedom."

Poetics: This term has two closely related meanings. It denotes (1) an aesthetic theory in literary criticism about the essence of poetry or (2) rules prescribing the proper methods, content, style, or diction of poetry. The term poetics may also refer to theories about literature in general, not just poetry.

Point of View: The narrative perspective from which a literary work is presented to the reader. There are four traditional points of view. The "third person omniscient" gives the reader a "godlike" perspective, unrestricted by time or place, from which to see actions and look into the minds of characters. This allows the author to comment openly on characters and events in the work. The "third person" point of view presents the events of the story from outside of any single character's perception, much like the omniscient point of view, but the reader must understand the action as it takes place and without any special insight into characters' minds or motivations. The "first person" or "personal" point of view relates events as they are perceived by a single character. The main character "tells" the story and may offer opinions about the action and characters which differ from those of the author. Much less common than omniscient, third person, and first person is the "second person" point of view, wherein the author tells the story as if it is happening to the reader.

Polemic: A work in which the author takes a stand on a controversial subject, such as abortion or religion. Such works are often extremely argumentative or provocative.

Pornography: Writing intended to provoke feelings of lust in the reader. Such works are often condemned by critics and teachers, but those which can be shown to have literary value are viewed less harshly.

Post-Aesthetic Movement: An artistic response made by African Americans to the black aesthetic movement of the 1960s and early '70s. Writers since that time have adopted a somewhat different tone in their work, with less emphasis placed on the disparity between black and white in the United States. In the words of post-aesthetic authors such as Toni Morrison, John Edgar Wideman, and Kristin Hunter, African Americans are portrayed as looking inward for answers to their own questions, rather than always looking to the outside world.

Postmodernism: Writing from the 1960s forward characterized by experimentation and continuing to apply some of the fundamentals of modernism, which included existentialism and alienation. Postmodernists have gone a step further in the rejection of tradition begun with the modernists by also rejecting traditional forms, preferring the anti-novel over the novel and the antihero over the hero.

Primitivism: The belief that primitive peoples were nobler and less flawed than civilized peoples because they had not been subjected to the tainting influence of society. See also Noble Savage.

Prologue: An introductory section of a literary work. It often contains information establishing the situation of the characters or presents information about the setting, time period, or action. In drama, the prologue is spoken by a chorus or by one of the principal characters.

Prose: A literary medium that attempts to mirror the language of everyday speech. It is distinguished from poetry by its use of unmetered, unrhymed language consisting of logically related sentences. Prose is usually grouped into paragraphs that form a cohesive whole such as an essay or a novel.

Prosopopoeia: See *Personification*

Protagonist: The central character of a story who serves as a focus for its themes and incidents and as the principal rationale for its development. The protagonist is sometimes referred to in discussions of modern literature as the hero or antihero.

Protest Fiction: Protest fiction has as its primary purpose the protesting of some social injustice, such as racism or discrimination.

Proverb: A brief, sage saying that expresses a truth about life in a striking manner.

Pseudonym: A name assumed by a writer, most often intended to prevent his or her identification as the author of a work. Two or more authors may work together under one pseudonym, or an author may use a different name for each genre he or she publishes in. Some publishing companies maintain "house pseudonyms," under which any number of authors may write installations in a series. Some authors also choose a pseudonym over their real names the way an actor may use a stage name.

Pun: A play on words that have similar sounds but different meanings.

R

Realism: A nineteenth-century European literary movement that sought to portray familiar characters, situations, and settings in a realistic manner. This was done primarily by using an objective narrative point of view and through the buildup of accurate detail. The standard for success of any realistic work depends on how faithfully it transfers common experience into fictional forms. The realistic method may be altered or extended, as in stream of consciousness writing, to record highly subjective experience.

Repartee: Conversation featuring snappy retorts and witticisms.

Resolution: The portion of a story following the climax, in which the conflict is resolved. See also *Denouement*.

Rhetoric: In literary criticism, this term denotes the art of ethical persuasion. In its strictest sense, rhetoric adheres to various principles developed since classical times for arranging facts and ideas in a clear, persuasive, appealing manner. The term is also used to refer to effective prose in general and theories of or methods for composing effective prose.

Rhetorical Question: A question intended to provoke thought, but not an expressed answer, in the reader. It is most commonly used in oratory and other persuasive genres.

Rising Action: The part of a drama where the plot becomes increasingly complicated. Rising action leads up to the climax, or turning point, of a drama.

Roman a clef: A French phrase meaning "novel with a key." It refers to a narrative in which real persons are portrayed under fictitious names.

Romance: A broad term, usually denoting a narrative with exotic, exaggerated, often idealized characters, scenes, and themes.

Romanticism: This term has two widely accepted meanings. In historical criticism, it refers to a European intellectual and artistic movement of the late eighteenth and early nineteenth centuries that sought greater freedom of personal expression than that allowed by the strict rules of literary form and logic of the eighteenth-century neoclassicists. The Romantics preferred emotional and imaginative expression to rational analysis. They considered the individual to be at the center of all experience and so placed him or her at the center of their art. The Romantics believed that the creative imagination reveals nobler truths—unique feelings and attitudes—than those that could be discovered by logic or by scientific examination. Both the natural world and the state of childhood were important sources for revelations of "eternal truths." "Romanticism" is also used as a general term to refer to a type of sensibility found in all periods of literary history and usually considered to be in opposition to the principles of classicism. In this sense, Romanticism signifies any work or philosophy in which the exotic or dreamlike figure strongly, or that is devoted to individualistic expression, self-analysis, or a pursuit of a higher realm of knowledge than can be discovered by human reason.

Romantics: See *Romanticism*

S

Satire: A work that uses ridicule, humor, and wit to criticize and provoke change in human nature and institutions. There are two major types of satire: "formal" or "direct" satire speaks directly to the reader or to a character in the work; "indirect" satire relies upon the ridiculous behavior of its characters to make its point. Formal satire is further divided into two manners: the "Horatian," which ridicules gently, and the "Juvenalian," which derides its subjects harshly and bitterly.

Science Fiction: A type of narrative about or based upon real or imagined scientific theories and technology. Science fiction is often peopled with alien creatures and set on other planets or in different dimensions.

Second Person: See *Point of View*

Setting: The time, place, and culture in which the action of a narrative takes place. The elements of setting may include geographic location, characters' physical and mental environments, prevailing cultural attitudes, or the historical time in which the action takes place.

Simile: A comparison, usually using "like" or "as", of two essentially dissimilar things, as in "coffee as cold as ice" or "He sounded like a broken record."

Slang: A type of informal verbal communication that is generally unacceptable for formal writing. Slang words and phrases are often colorful exaggerations used to emphasize the speaker's point; they may also be shortened versions of an often-used word or phrase.

Slave Narrative: Autobiographical accounts of American slave life as told by escaped slaves. These works first appeared during the abolition movement of the 1830s through the 1850s.

Socialist Realism: The Socialist Realism school of literary theory was proposed by Maxim Gorky and established as a dogma by the first Soviet Congress of Writers. It demanded adherence to a communist worldview in works of literature. Its doctrines required an objective viewpoint comprehensible to the working classes and themes of social struggle featuring strong proletarian heroes. Also known as Social Realism.

Stereotype: A stereotype was originally the name for a duplication made during the printing process; this led to its modern definition as a person or thing that is (or is assumed to be) the same as all others of its type.

Stream of Consciousness: A narrative technique for rendering the inward experience of a character. This technique is designed to give the impression of an ever-changing series of thoughts, emotions, images, and memories in the spontaneous and seemingly illogical order that they occur in life.

Structure: The form taken by a piece of literature. The structure may be made obvious for ease of understanding, as in nonfiction works, or may be obscured for artistic purposes, as in some poetry or seemingly "unstructured" prose.

***Sturm und Drang*:** A German term meaning "storm and stress." It refers to a German literary movement of the 1770s and 1780s that reacted against the order and rationalism of the enlightenment, focusing instead on the intense experience of extraordinary individuals.

Style: A writer's distinctive manner of arranging words to suit his or her ideas and purpose in writing. The unique imprint of the author's personality upon his or her writing, style is the product of an author's way of arranging ideas and his or her use of diction, different sentence structures, rhythm, figures of speech, rhetorical principles, and other elements of composition.

Subjectivity: Writing that expresses the author's personal feelings about his subject, and which may or may not include factual information about the subject.

Subplot: A secondary story in a narrative. A subplot may serve as a motivating or complicating force for the main plot of the work, or it may provide emphasis for, or relief from, the main plot.

Surrealism: A term introduced to criticism by Guillaume Apollinaire and later adopted by Andre Breton. It refers to a French literary and artistic movement founded in the 1920s. The Surrealists sought to express unconscious thoughts and feelings in their works. The best-known technique used for achieving this aim was automatic writing—transcriptions of spontaneous outpourings from the unconscious. The Surrealists proposed to unify the contrary levels of conscious and unconscious, dream and reality, objectivity and subjectivity into a new level of "super-realism."

Suspense: A literary device in which the author maintains the audience's attention through the buildup of events, the outcome of which will soon be revealed.

Symbol: Something that suggests or stands for something else without losing its original identity. In literature, symbols combine their literal meaning with the suggestion of an abstract concept. Literary symbols are of two types: those that carry complex associations of meaning no matter what their contexts, and those that derive their suggestive meaning from their functions in specific literary works.

Symbolism: This term has two widely accepted meanings. In historical criticism, it denotes an early modernist literary movement initiated in France during the nineteenth century that reacted against the prevailing standards of realism. Writers in this movement aimed to evoke, indirectly and symbolically, an order of being beyond the material world of the five senses. Poetic expression of personal emotion figured strongly in the movement, typically by means of a private set of symbols uniquely identifiable with the individual poet. The principal aim of the Symbolists was to express in words the highly complex feelings that grew out of everyday contact with the world. In a broader sense, the term "symbolism" refers to the use of one object to represent another.

T

Tall Tale: A humorous tale told in a straightforward, credible tone but relating absolutely impossible events or feats of the characters. Such tales were commonly told of frontier adventures during the settlement of the west in the United States.

Theme: The main point of a work of literature. The term is used interchangeably with thesis.

Thesis: A thesis is both an essay and the point argued in the essay. Thesis novels and thesis plays share the quality of containing a thesis which is supported through the action of the story.

Third Person: See *Point of View*

Tone: The author's attitude toward his or her audience may be deduced from the tone of the work. A formal tone may create distance or convey politeness, while an informal tone may encourage a friendly, intimate, or intrusive feeling in the reader. The author's attitude toward his or her subject matter may also be deduced from the tone of the words he or she uses in discussing it.

Transcendentalism: An American philosophical and religious movement, based in New England from around 1835 until the Civil War. Transcendentalism was a form of American romanticism that had its roots abroad in the works of Thomas Carlyle, Samuel Coleridge, and Johann Wolfgang von Goethe. The Transcendentalists stressed the importance of intuition and subjective experience in communication with God. They rejected religious dogma and texts in favor of mysticism and scientific naturalism. They pursued truths that lie beyond the "colorless" realms perceived by reason and the senses and were active social reformers in public education, women's rights, and the abolition of slavery.

U

Urban Realism: A branch of realist writing that attempts to accurately reflect the often harsh facts of modern urban existence.

Utopia: A fictional perfect place, such as "paradise" or "heaven."

V

Verisimilitude: Literally, the appearance of truth. In literary criticism, the term refers to aspects of a work of literature that seem true to the reader.

Victorian: Refers broadly to the reign of Queen Victoria of England (1837-1901) and to anything with qualities typical of that era. For example, the qualities of smug narrowmindedness, bourgeois materialism, faith in social progress, and priggish morality are often considered Victorian. This stereotype is contradicted by such dramatic intellectual developments as the theories of Charles Darwin, Karl Marx, and Sigmund Freud (which stirred strong debates in England) and the critical attitudes of serious Victorian writers like Charles Dickens and George Eliot. In literature, the Victorian Period was the great age of the English novel, and the latter part of the era saw the rise of movements such as decadence and symbolism. Also known as Victorian Age and Victorian Period.

W

Weltanschauung: A German term referring to a person's worldview or philosophy.

Weltschmerz: A German term meaning "world pain." It describes a sense of anguish about the nature of existence, usually associated with a melancholy, pessimistic attitude.

Z

Zeitgeist: A German term meaning "spirit of the time." It refers to the moral and intellectual trends of a given era.

Cumulative Author/Title Index

Numerical

1984 (Orwell): V7

A

Absalom, Absalom! (Faulkner): V13
The Accidental Tourist (Tyler): V7
Achebe, Chinua
  Things Fall Apart: V2
Adams, Douglas
  The Hitchhiker's Guide to the Galaxy: V7
Adams, Richard
  Watership Down: V11
The Adventures of Huckleberry Finn (Twain): V1
The Adventures of Tom Sawyer (Twain): V6
The Age of Innocence (Wharton): V11
Alcott, Louisa May
  Little Women: V12
Alice's Adventures in Wonderland (Carroll): V7
All the King's Men (Warren): V13
Allende, Isabel
  The House of the Spirits: V6
Allison, Dorothy
  Bastard Out of Carolina: V11
All Quiet on the Western Front (Remarque): V4
Alvarez, Julia
  How the García Girls Lost Their Accents: V5
  In the Time of the Butterflies: V9
Always Coming Home (Le Guin): V9
The Ambassadors (James): V12

Anaya, Rudolfo
  Bless Me, Ultima: V12
Anderson, Sherwood
  Winesburg, Ohio: V4
Angelou, Maya
  I Know Why the Caged Bird Sings: V2
Animal Dreams (Kingsolver): V12
Animal Farm (Orwell): V3
Annie John (Kincaid): V3
Appointment in Samarra (O'Hara): V11
As I Lay Dying (Faulkner): V8
Atlas Shrugged (Rand): V10
Atwood, Margaret
  The Handmaid's Tale: V4
  Surfacing: V13
Auel, Jean
  The Clan of the Cave Bear: V11
Austen, Jane
  Pride and Prejudice: V1
The Autobiography of Miss Jane Pittman (Gaines): V5
The Awakening (Chopin): V3

B

Baldwin, James
  Go Tell It on the Mountain: V4
Ballard, J. G.
  Empire of the Sun: V8
Banks, Russell
  The Sweet Hereafter: V13
Bastard Out of Carolina (Allison): V11
Baum, L. Frank
  The Wonderful Wizard of Oz: V13
The Bean Trees (Kingsolver): V5

The Bell Jar (Plath): V1
Bellow, Saul
  Seize the Day: V4
Beloved (Morrison): V6
Betsey Brown (Shange): V11
Billy Budd, Sailor: An Inside Narrative (Melville): V9
Black Boy (Wright): V1
Blair, Eric Arthur
  Animal Farm: V3
Bless Me, Ultima (Anaya): V12
The Bluest Eye (Morrison): V1
Body and Soul (Conroy): V11
Bowen, Elizabeth Dorothea Cole
  The Death of the Heart: V13
Bradbury, Ray
  Fahrenheit 451: V1
Brave New World (Huxley): V6
Breathing Lessons (Tyler): V10
The Bride Price (Emecheta): V12
Brideshead Revisited (Waugh): V13
Brontë, Charlotte
  Jane Eyre: V4
Brontë, Emily
  Wuthering Heights: V2
The Brothers Karamazov (Dostoevsky): V8
Brown, Rita Mae
  Rubyfruit Jungle: V9
Bulgakov, Mikhail
  The Master and Margarita: V8
Butler, Octavia
  Kindred: V8

C

The Caine Mutiny: A Novel of World War II (Wouk): V7

The Call of the Wild (London): V8
Camus, Albert
    The Stranger: V6
Candide (Voltaire): V7
Cane (Toomer): V11
Card, Orson Scott
    Ender's Game: V5
Carroll, Lewis
    Alice's Adventures in
        Wonderland: V7
Catch-22 (Heller): V1
The Catcher in the Rye
    (Salinger): V1
Cather, Willa
    My Ántonia: V2
Ceremony (Marmon Silko): V4
The Chocolate War (Cormier): V2
Chopin, Kate
    The Awakening: V3
The Chosen (Potok): V4
Christie, Agatha
    Ten Little Indians: V8
A Christmas Carol (Dickens): V10
Chronicle of a Death Foretold
    (García Márquez): V10
Cisneros, Sandra
    The House on Mango Street: V2
The Clan of the Cave Bear (Auel):
    V11
Clavell, James du Maresq
    Shogun: *A Novel of Japan:* V10
Clemens, Samuel
    The Adventures of Huckleberry
        Finn: V1
The Adventures of Tom Sawyer: V6
The Color Purple (Walker): V5
Cooper, James Fenimore
    The Last of the Mohicans: V9
Conrad, Joseph
    Heart of Darkness: V2
Conroy, Frank
    Body and Soul: V11
Cormier, Robert
    The Chocolate War: V2
Crane, Stephen
    The Red Badge of Courage: V4
The Crazy Horse Electric Game
    (Crutcher): V11
Crime and Punishment
    (Dostoyevsky): V3
Crutcher, Chris
    The Crazy Horse Electric Game:
        V11
Cry, the Beloved Country
    (Paton): V3

D

The Dead of the House (Green): V10
The Death of the Heart (Bowen): V13
de Cervantes Saavedra, Miguel
    Don Quixote: V8

Defoe, Daniel
    Moll Flanders: V13
    Robinson Crusoe: V9
Deliverance (Dickey): V9
Democracy (Didion): V3
Dick, Philip K.
    Do Androids Dream of Electric
        Sheep?: V5
Dickens, Charles
    A Christmas Carol: V10
    Great Expectations: V4
    A Tale of Two Cities: V5
Dickey, James
    Deliverance: V9
Didion, Joan
    Democracy: V3
Dinesen, Isak
    Out of Africa: V9
Dinner at the Homesick Restaurant
    (Tyler): V2
Do Androids Dream of Electric
    Sheep? (Dick): V5
Doctorow, E. L.
    Ragtime: V6
Don Quixote (de Cervantes
    Saavedra): V8
Dorris, Michael
    A Yellow Raft in Blue Water: V3
Dostoyevsky, Fyodor
    The Brothers Karamazov: V8
    Crime and Punishment: V3
Dr. Jekyll and Mr. Hyde (Stevenson):
    V11
Dreiser, Theodore
    Sister Carrie: V8
du Maurier, Daphne
    Rebecca: V12

E

The Edible Woman (Atwood): V12
Ellen Foster (Gibbons): V3
Ellis, Bret Easton
    Less Than Zero: V11
Ellison, Ralph
    Invisible Man: V2
Emecheta, Buchi
    The Bride Price: V12
Empire of the Sun (Ballard): V8
Ender's Game (Card): V5
Erdrich, Louise
    Love Medicine: V5
Esquivel, Laura
    Like Water for Chocolate: V5
Ethan Frome (Wharton): V5

F

Fahrenheit 451 (Bradbury): V1
A Farewell to Arms
    (Hemingway): V1
Faulkner, William
    Absalom, Absalom!: V13

    As I Lay Dying: V8
    The Sound and the Fury: V4
Fitzgerald, F. Scott
    The Great Gatsby: V2
The Fixer (Malamud): V9
Flagg, Fannie
    Fried Green Tomatoes at the
        Whistle Stop Café: V7
Flowers for Algernon (Keyes): V2
Forster, E. M.
    A Passage to India: V3
    A Room with a View: V11
    Howards End: V10
Fox, Paula
    The Slave Dancer: V12
Frankenstein (Shelley): V1
Fried Green Tomatoes at the Whistle
    Stop Café: (Flagg): V7
Fuentes, Carlos
    The Old Gringo: V8

G

Gaines, Ernest J.
    A Lesson Before Dying: V7
    The Autobiography of Miss Jane
        Pittman: V5
Giants in the Earth (Rölvaag): V5
García Márquez, Gabriel
    Chronicle of a Death Foretold:
        V10
    Love in the Time of Cholera: V1
    One Hundred Years of Solitude:
        V5
Gardner, John
    Grendel: V3
Gibbons, Kaye
    Ellen Foster: V3
The Giver (Lowry): V3
Go Tell It on the Mountain
    (Baldwin): V4
Golding, William
    Lord of the Flies: V2
Gone with the Wind (Mitchell): V9
Gordimer, Nadine
    July's People: V4
The Grapes of Wrath (Steinbeck): V7
The Grass Dancer (Power): V11
Great Expectations (Dickens): V4
The Great Gatsby (Fitzgerald): V2
Green, Hannah
    The Dead of the House: V10
Greene, Bette
    Summer of My German Soldier:
        V10
Grendel (Gardner): V3
Guest, Judith
    Ordinary People: V1
Gulliver's Travels (Swift): V6
Guterson, David
    Snow Falling on Cedars: V13

H

Haley, Alex
  *Roots: The Story of an American
    Family:* V9
The Handmaid's Tale (Atwood): V4
Hardy, Thomas
  The Return of the Native: V11
  Tess of the d'Urbervilles: V3
Hawthorne, Nathaniel
  The Scarlet Letter: V1
The Heart Is a Lonely Hunter
  (McCullers): V6
Heart of Darkness (Conrad): V2
Heller, Joseph
  Catch-22: V1
Hemingway, Ernest
  A Farewell to Arms: V1
  The Old Man and the Sea: V6
  The Sun Also Rises: V5
Hesse, Hermann
  Siddhartha: V6
Hinton, S. E.
  The Outsiders: V5
  Tex: V9
The Hitchhiker's Guide to the Galaxy
  (Adams): V7
The Hobbit (Tolkien): V8
House Made of Dawn (Momaday):
  V10
The House of the Spirits (Allende):
  V6
The House on Mango Street
  (Cisneros): V2
*How the García Girls Lost Their
  Accents* (Alvarez): V5
Howards End (Forster): V10
Hugo, Victor
  Les Misérables: V5
Hurston, Zora Neale
  *Their Eyes Were Watching
    God:* V3
Huxley, Aldous
  Brave New World: V6

I

I Know Why the Caged Bird Sings
  (Angelou): V2
In Country (Mason): V4
In the Time of the Butterflies
  (Alvarez): V9
Invisible Man (Ellison): V2
Irving, John
  The World According to Garp:
    V12
Ishiguro, Kazuo
  The Remains of the Day: V13

J

James, Henry
  The Ambassadors: V12

Jane Eyre (Brontë): V4
The Joy Luck Club (Tan): V1
Joyce, James
  *A Portrait of the Artist as a
    Young Man:* V7
July's People (Gordimer): V4
The Jungle (Sinclair): V6

K

Kafka, Franz
  The Trial: V7
Kerouac, Jack
  On the Road: V8
Kesey, Ken
  *One Flew Over the Cuckoo's
    Nest:* V2
Keyes, Daniel
  Flowers for Algernon: V2
Kincaid, Jamaica
  Annie John: V3
Kindred (Butler): V8
Kingsolver, Barbara
  Animal Dreams: V12
  The Bean Trees: V5
  Pigs in Heaven: V10
Kingston, Maxine Hong
  The Woman Warrior: V6
Kitchen (Yoshimoto): V7
The Kitchen God's Wife (Tan): V13
Knowles, John
  A Separate Peace: V2
Kogawa, Joy
  Obasan: V3
Kosinski, Jerzy
  The Painted Bird: V12

L

The Last of the Mohicans (Cooper):
  V9
Laurence, Margaret
  The Stone Angel: V11
Lee, Harper
  To Kill a Mockingbird: V2
The Left Hand of Darkness (Le
  Guin): V6
Le Guin, Ursula K.
  Always Coming Home: V9
  The Left Hand of Darkness: V6
Les Misérables (Hugo): V5
Less Than Zero (Ellis): V11
A Lesson Before Dying (Gaines): V7
Like Water for Chocolate
  (Esquivel): V5
Little Women (Alcott): V12
Lolita
  (Nabokov): V9
London, Jack
  The Call of the Wild: V8
Lord of the Flies (Golding): V2

Love in the Time of Cholera (García
  Márquez): V1
Love Medicine (Erdrich): V5
Lowry, Lois
  The Giver: V3

M

Machiavelli, Niccolo
  The Prince: V9
Mailer, Norman
  The Naked and the Dead: V10
Malamud, Bernard
  The Fixer: V9
  The Natural: V4
Mama Day (Naylor): V7
Markandaya, Kamala
  Nectar in a Sieve: V13
Marmon Silko, Leslie
  Ceremony: V4
Mason, Bobbie Ann
  In Country: V4
The Master and Margarita
  (Bulgakov): V8
McCullers, Carson
  The Heart Is a Lonely Hunter: V6
  The Member of the Wedding: V13
Melville, Herman
  *Billy Budd, Sailor: An Inside
    Narrative:* V9
  Moby-Dick: V7
The Member of the Wedding
  (McCullers): V13
Méndez, Miguel
  Pilgrims in Aztlán: V12
Mitchell, Margaret
  Gone with the Wind: V9
Moby-Dick (Melville): V7
Moll Flanders (Defoe): V13
Momaday, N. Scott
  House Made of Dawn: V10
Morrison, Toni
  Beloved: V6
  The Bluest Eye: V1
  Song of Solomon: V8
Mrs. Dalloway (Woolf): V12
My Ántonia (Cather): V2

N

Nabokov, Vladimir
  Lolita: V9
The Naked and the Dead (Mailer): V10
Native Son (Wright): V7
The Natural (Malamud): V4
Naylor, Gloria
  Mama Day: V7
  The Women of Brewster Place: V4
Nectar in a Sieve (Markandaya): V13
Night (Wiesel): V4
Norris, Frank
  The Octopus: V12

Cumulative Nationality/Ethnicity Index

African American

Angelou, Maya
  *I Know Why the Caged Bird
    Sings*: V2
Baldwin, James
  Go Tell It on the Mountain: V4
Ellison, Ralph
  Invisible Man: V2
Gaines, Ernest J.
  *The Autobiography of Miss Jane
    Pittman:* V5
Haley, Alex
  *Roots: The Story of an American
    Family:* V9
Hurston, Zora Neale
  *Their Eyes Were Watching
    God:* V3
Kincaid, Jamaica
  Annie John: V3
Morrison, Toni
  Beloved: V6
  The Bluest Eye: V1
  Song of Solomom: V8
Naylor, Gloria
  Mama Day: V7
  The Women of Brewster Place: V4
Shange, Ntozake
  Betsey Brown: V11
Toomer, Jean
  Cane: V11
Walker, Alice
  The Color Purple: V5
Wright, Richard
  Black Boy: V1

Algerian

Camus, Albert
  The Stranger: V6

American

Alcott, Louisa May
  Little Women: V12
Allison, Dorothy
  Bastard Out of Carolina: V11
Alvarez, Julia
  *How the García Girls Lost Their
    Accents:* V5
Anaya, Rudolfo
  Bless Me, Ultima: V12
Anderson, Sherwood
  Winesburg, Ohio: V4
Angelou, Maya
  *I Know Why the Caged Bird
    Sings:* V2
Auel, Jean
  The Clan of the Cave Bear: V11
Banks, Russell
  The Sweet Hereafter: V13
Baum, L. Frank
  The Wonderful Wizard of Oz: V13
Bradbury, Ray
  Fahrenheit 451: V1
Brown, Rita Mae
  Rubyfruit Jungle: V9
Butler, Octavia
  Kindred: V8
Card, Orson Scott
  Ender's Game: V5
Cather, Willa
  My Ántonia: V2
Chopin, Kate
  The Awakening: V3
Cisneros, Sandra
  The House on Mango Street: V2
Clavell, James du Maresq
  Shogun: A Novel of Japan: V10

Clemens, Samuel
  *The Adventures of Huckleberry
    Finn:* V1
  The Adventures of Tom Sawyer: V6
Conroy, Frank
  Body and Soul: V11
Cooper, James Fenimore
  The Last of the Mohicans: V9
Cormier, Robert
  The Chocolate War: V2
Crane, Stephen
  The Red Badge of Courage: V4
Crutcher, Chris
  The Crazy Horse Electric Game:
    V11
Dick, Philip K.
  *Do Androids Dream of Electric
    Sheep?:* V5
Dickey, James
  Deliverance: V9
Didion, Joan
  Democracy: V3
Doctorow, E. L.
  Ragtime: V6
Dorris, Michael
  A Yellow Raft in Blue Water: V3
Dreiser, Theodore
  Sister Carrie: V8
Ellis, Bret Easton
  Less Than Zero: V11
Ellison, Ralph
  Invisible Man: V2
Emecheta, Buchi
  The Bride Price: V12
Erdrich, Louise
  Love Medicine: V5

Faulkner, William
  Absalom, Absalom!: V13
  As I Lay Dying: V8
  The Sound and the Fury: V4
Fitzgerald, F. Scott
  The Great Gatsby: V2
Flagg, Fannie
  *Fried Green Tomatoes at the
    Whistle Stop Café:* V7
Fox, Paula
  The Slave Dancer: V12
Gaines, Ernest J.
  A Lesson Before Dying: V7
  *The Autobiography of Miss Jane
    Pittman:* V5
Gardner, John
  Grendel: V3
Gibbons, Kaye
  Ellen Foster: V3
Green, Hannah
  The Dead of the House: V10
Greene, Bette
  Summer of My German Soldier:
    V10
Guest, Judith
  Ordinary People: V1
Guterson, David
  Snow Falling on Cedars: V13
Hawthorne, Nathaniel
  The Scarlet Letter: V1
Heller, Joseph
  Catch-22: V1
Hemingway, Ernest
  A Farewell to Arms: V1
  The Old Man and the Sea: V6
  The Sun Also Rises: V5
Hinton, S. E.
  Tex: V9
  The Outsiders: V5
Hurston, Zora Neale
  Their Eyes Were Watching God:
    V3
Irving, John
  The World According to Garp:
    V12
James, Henry
  The Ambassadors: V12
Kerouac, Jack
  On the Road: V8
Kesey, Ken
  *One Flew Over the Cuckoo's
    Nest:* V2
Keyes, Daniel
  Flowers for Algernon: V2
Kincaid, Jamaica
  Annie John: V3
Kingsolver, Barbara
  Animal Dreams: V12
  The Bean Trees: V5
  Pigs in Heaven: V10

Kingston, Maxine Hong
  The Woman Warrior: V6
Knowles, John
  A Separate Peace: V2
Le Guin, Ursula K.
  Always Coming Home: V9
  The Left Hand of Darkness: V6
Lee, Harper
  To Kill a Mockingbird: V2
London, Jack
  The Call of the Wild: V8
Lowry, Lois
  The Giver: V3
Mailer, Norman
  The Naked and the Dead: V10
Mason, Bobbie Ann
  In Country: V4
McCullers, Carson
  The Heart Is a Lonely Hunter: V6
  The Member of the Wedding: V13
Melville, Herman
  Billy Budd: V9
  Moby-Dick: V7
Méndez, Miguel
  Pilgrims in Aztlán: V12
Mitchell, Margaret
  Gone with the Wind: V9
Momaday, N. Scott
  House Made of Dawn: V10
Morrison, Toni
  Beloved: V6
  The Bluest Eye: V1
  Song of Solomon: V8
Norris, Frank
  The Octopus: V12
Oates, Joyce Carol
  them: V8
O'Connor, Flannery
  Wise Blood: V3
O'Hara, John
  Appointment in Samarra: V11
Plath, Sylvia
  The Bell Jar: V1
Potok, Chaim
  The Chosen: V4
Power, Susan
  The Grass Dancer: V11
Rand, Ayn
  Atlas Shrugged: V10
Rölvaag, O. E.
  Giants in the Earth: V5
Salinger, J. D.
  The Catcher in the Rye: V1
Sinclair, Upton
  The Jungle: V6
Shange, Ntozake
  Betsey Brown: V11
Steinbeck, John
  The Grapes of Wrath: V7
  Of Mice and Men: V1
  The Pearl: V5
Stowe, Harriet Beecher
  Uncle Tom's Cabin: V6

Tan, Amy
  Joy Luck Club: V1
  The Kitchen God's Wife: V13
Toomer, Jean
  Cane: V11
Twain, Mark
  *The Adventures of Huckleberry
    Finn:* V1
  The Adventures of Tom Sawyer: V6
Tyler, Anne
  The Accidental Tourist: V7
  Breathing Lessons: V10
  *Dinner at the Homesick
    Restaurant:* V2
Updike, John
  Rabbit, Run: V12
Vonnegut, Kurt, Jr.
  Slaughterhouse-Five: V3
Walker, Alice
  The Color Purple: V5
Warren, Robert Penn
  All the King's Men: V13
Welty, Eudora
  The Optimist's Daughter: V13
Wharton, Edith
  The Age of Innocence: V11
  Ethan Frome: V5
Wouk, Herman
  The Caine Mutiny: V7
Wright, Richard
  Black Boy: V1
  Native Son: V7

Asian American

Kingston, Maxine Hong
  The Woman Warrior: V6
Tan, Amy
  The Joy Luck Club: V1
  The Kitchen God's Wife: V13

Asian Canadian

Kogawa, Joy
  Obasan: V3

Australian

Clavell, James du Maresq
  Shogun: A Novel of Japan: V10

British

Adams, Douglas
  *The Hitchhiker's Guide to the
    Galaxy:* V7
Adams, Richard
  Watership Down: V11
Austen, Jane
  Pride and Prejudice: V1
Ballard, J. G.
  Empire of the Sun: V8
Blair, Eric Arthur
  Animal Farm: V3

Russian

Bulgakov, Mikhail
The Master and Margarita: V8
Dostoyevsky, Fyodor
The Brothers Karamazon: V8
Crime and Punishment: V3
Nabokov, Vladimir
Lolita: V9
Rand, Ayn
Atlas Shrugged: V10

Solzhenitsyn, Aleksandr
One Day in the Life of Ivan Denisovich: V6
Tolstoy, Leo
War and Peace: V10

South African

Gordimer, Nadine
July's People: V4

Paton, Alan
Cry, the Beloved Country: V3
Too Late the Phalarope: V12

Spanish

Saavedra, Miguel de Cervantes
Don Quixote: V8

West Indian

Kincaid, Jamaica
Annie John: V3

Subject/Theme Index

Buddhism
    The Remains of the Day: 225–235

C

Change
    Nectar in a Sieve: 174
Change and Transformation
    Surfacing: 260
Charity
    The Member of the Wedding: 140,
        142–143
    Vanity Fair: 287
Childhood
    Brideshead Revisited: 74, 76
    The Death of the Heart: 80, 86,
        91
    The Member of the Wedding:
        122–123, 126–128, 131–137,
        139, 142
Christianity
    The Remains of the Day:
        225–227, 230, 235
Classicism
    The Wonderful Wizard of Oz:
        322–323, 330
Coming-Of-Age
    The Death of the Heart: 87
    All the King's Men: 41–43
Communism
    The Kitchen God's Wife: 99, 102,
        106–108
Community
    The Sweet Hereafter: 274
Conflict
    The Kitchen God's Wife: 106
Confucianism
    The Remains of the Day:
        225–227, 231–235
Courage
    Absalom, Absalom!: 4, 7, 10, 12,
        15–16, 18–20
    The Member of the Wedding: 137,
        140
    Moll Flanders: 154, 157, 160–162
    Nectar in a Sieve: 181, 184
    Vanity Fair: 306
    The Wonderful Wizard of Oz:
        326–328
Cowardice
    The Wonderful Wizard of Oz:
        310–311, 314, 318, 322, 326,
        328, 330
Crime and Criminals
    All the King's Men: 29–31
    Moll Flanders: 145–146, 148,
        151–155, 158–163, 165,
        167–168
Crime and Remorse
    Moll Flanders: 153
Cruelty
    Absalom, Absalom!: 3–4, 7
    All the King's Men: 36, 38, 40

The Kitchen God's Wife: 101,
        106–107, 114–116
    Moll Flanders: 161, 164–167
    Nectar in a Sieve: 181, 184
Curiosity
    Moll Flanders: 160–163, 165–166
Cynicism
    Absalom, Absalom!: 20, 22, 24–25

D

Death
    The Death of the Heart: 88
    Absalom, Absalom!: 3, 8–9,
        19–21, 23–25
    All the King's Men: 29–31,
        36–37, 41–43
    Brideshead Revisited: 57–58,
        62–63, 65–66, 69
    The Death of the Heart: 83,
        87–88, 91
    The Kitchen God's Wife:
        100–102, 105, 107–109, 114,
        116–117
    The Member of the Wedding: 135,
        138–142
    Moll Flanders: 145, 147–148,
        151, 153, 163, 165, 167–168
    The Optimist's Daughter: 192,
        194, 197–201, 204–207,
        209–210
    The Remains of the Day: 214,
        216–218, 226–227, 230–232,
        234
    Snow Falling on Cedars:
        238–239, 243–245
    Surfacing: 255–256, 260–263
    Vanity Fair: 286–287, 293–295,
        298–299
    The Wonderful Wizard of Oz:
        321, 323–326, 328–329
Depression and Melancholy
    Brideshead Revisited: 56, 63–64,
        66, 68–69
    Nectar in a Sieve: 186–187, 190
Despair
    Nectar in a Sieve: 178–180
Disease
    The Kitchen God's Wife:
        101–102, 108
Distrust
    Snow Falling on Cedars: 238,
        242–243, 246
Divorce
    The Kitchen God's Wife:
        101–102, 108, 114, 116–117
Drama
    All the King's Men: 45–46, 48
Dreams and Visions
    The Member of the Wedding:
        137–139, 141–143
    The Optimist's Daughter: 205,
        207–209

Duty
    The Kitchen God's Wife: 104
    The Remains of the Day: 216
Duty and Responsibility
    All the King's Men: 35–36, 41,
        47, 49, 52
    The Kitchen God's Wife:
        104–105, 109
    The Remains of the Day:
        212–213, 216, 218, 220–221,
        226–229, 234

E

Emotions
    Absalom, Absalom!: 10, 12, 15,
        22
    All the King's Men: 36, 48–51
    The Death of the Heart: 80, 88,
        94
    The Kitchen God's Wife: 107, 117
    The Member of the Wedding: 142
    Moll Flanders: 164–166, 168
    Nectar in a Sieve: 184, 188
    The Optimist's Daughter: 192,
        201–203, 205–207
    The Remains of the Day: 216,
        218, 220, 224, 226, 229
    Snow Falling on Cedars: 242,
        247
    Surfacing: 260, 264–265
    The Sweet Hereafter: 278
    The Wonderful Wizard of Oz: 314
Error
    Absalom, Absalom!: 16, 20,
        22–23
    The Optimist's Daughter:
        205–206
    The Remains of the Day:
        225–229, 231
Eternity
    The Sweet Hereafter: 269
Europe
    All the King's Men: 44–45, 51–52
    Brideshead Revisited: 54, 56–58,
        63–67, 69, 72–73, 76
    The Death of the Heart: 80,
        82–83, 86–95, 97
    Moll Flanders: 145–148,
        151–155, 160–161, 165–167
    The Optimist's Daughter:
        201–203
    The Remains of the Day: 212,
        214, 216, 218–222
    Snow Falling on Cedars: 242,
        245
    Vanity Fair: 284, 286–287, 292,
        294–296, 299, 301–302, 306
Evil
    Absalom, Absalom!: 18–20, 22,
        24–25
    All the King's Men: 30, 35, 40,
        44–46, 49, 51